PHILOSTRATUS

II

LCL 17

PHILOSTRATUS

THE LIFE OF
APOLLONIUS OF TYANA

BOOKS V–VIII

EDITED AND TRANSLATED BY

CHRISTOPHER P. JONES

HARVARD UNIVERSITY PRESS
CAMBRIDGE, MASSACHUSETTS
LONDON, ENGLAND
2005

Library of Congress Catalog Card Number 2004060863
CIP data available from the Library of Congress

ISBN 0-674-99614-3

*Composed in ZephGreek and ZephText by
Technologies 'N Typography, Merrimac, Massachusetts.
Printed and bound by Edwards Brothers, Ann Arbor, Michigan
on acid-free paper made by Glatfelter, Spring Grove, Pennsylvania.*

CONTENTS

MAPS   vii

LIFE OF APOLLONIUS

     Book V   2

     Book VI   92

     Book VII   210

     Book VIII   314

INDEX   427

Maps by Patrick Florance. Some locations after R. Talbert, ed., *Barrington Atlas of the Greek and Roman World* (Princeton, 2000), using data courtesy of the Ancient World Mapping Center.

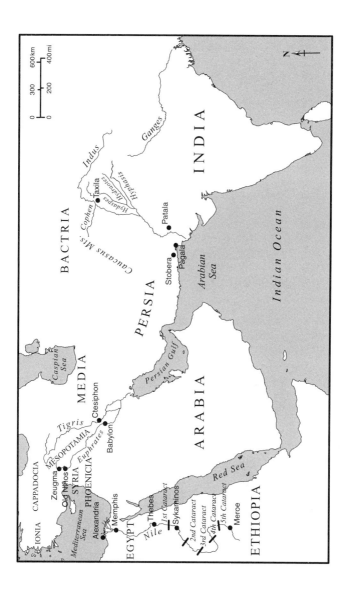

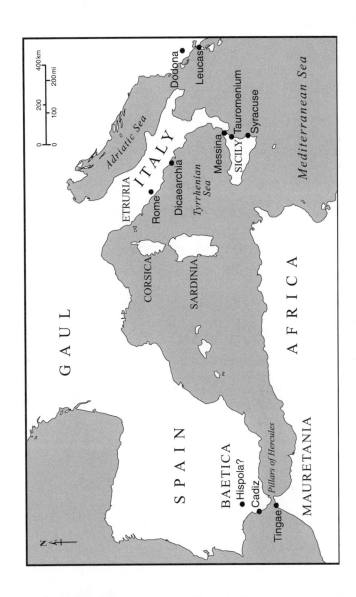

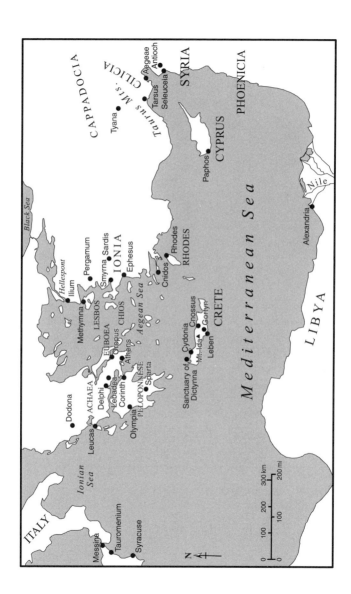

Ε΄

1. Περὶ δὲ τῶν Στηλῶν, ἃς ὅρια τῆς γῆς τὸν Ἡρακλέα φασὶ πήξασθαι, τὰ μὲν μυθώδη ἐῶ, τὰ δ᾽ ἀκοῆς τε καὶ λόγου ἄξια δηλώσω μᾶλλον· Εὐρώπης καὶ Λιβύης ἄκραι σταδίων ἑξήκοντα πορθμὸν ἐπέχουσαι τὸν Ὠκεανὸν ἐς τὰ ἔσω[1] πελάγη φέρουσι, καὶ τὴν μὲν τῆς Λιβύης ἄκραν, ὄνομα δὲ αὐτῇ Ἄβιννα, λέοντες ὑπερνέμονται περὶ τὰς ὀφρῦς τῶν ὀρῶν, ἃ ἔσω ὑπερφαίνεται, ξυνάπτουσαν πρὸς Γαιτούλους καὶ Τίγγας ἄμφω θηριώδη καὶ Λιβυκὰ ἔθνη, παρατείνει δὲ ἐσπλέοντι τὸν Ὠκεανὸν μέχρι μὲν τῶν ἐκβολῶν τοῦ Σάληκος ἐννακόσια στάδια, τὸ δὲ ἐντεῦθεν οὐκ ἂν ξυμβάλοι τις ὁπόσα, μετὰ γὰρ τὸν ποταμὸν τοῦτον ἄβιος ἡ Λιβύη καὶ οὐκέτι ἄνθρωποι. τὸ δὲ τῆς Εὐρώπης ἀκρωτήριον, ὃ καλεῖται Κάλπις, δεξιὰ μὲν ἐπέχει τοῦ ἔσπλου, σταδίων ἑξακοσίων μῆκος, λήγει δὲ ἐς τὰ ἀρχαῖα Γάδειρα.

2. Τὰς δὲ τοῦ Ὠκεανοῦ τροπὰς καὶ αὐτὸς μὲν περὶ Κελτοὺς εἶδον, ὁποῖαι λέγονται, τὴν δὲ αἰτίαν ἐπὶ πολλὰ εἰκάζων, δι᾽ ἣν ἄπειρον οὕτω πέλαγος ἐπιχωρεῖ

[1] ἔσω Rsk.: ἔξω

2

BOOK V

1. About the Pillars which Heracles is said to have set up as boundary markers for the world, I pass over the fanciful stories, preferring to point out those worth hearing and telling.[1] The promontories of Europe and Africa are divided by a strait sixty stades wide, through which they admit the Ocean into the inner waters. On the African promontory, by name the Abinna, lions roam the ridges of the mountains that rise on the horizon. It connects to the Gaetuli and the Tingae, both of which are savage African tribes, and you follow it as you sail into the Ocean for nine hundred stades as far as the mouth of the Salex. You cannot calculate the distance further than that, since beyond that river Africa is deserted and humans are not found. The European promontory, called Calpis, is on the right of the strait, with a length of six hundred stades, ending at Old Gadeira.[2]

2. I myself when I was in the Celtic region[3] saw the tides of the Ocean just as they are described. After many guesses as to why so huge a body of water advances and re-

---

[1] For the geographical references in the first part of this book, see Introduction.   [2] Gadeira (Cádiz) was divided into an "old" and a "new" section.

[3] The Atlantic coast of France, or perhaps of Spain.

τε καὶ ἀνασπᾶται, δοκῶ μοι τὸν Ἀπολλώνιον ἐπεσκέφθαι τὸ ὄν. ἐν μιᾷ γὰρ τῶν πρὸς Ἰνδοὺς ἐπιστολῶν τὸν Ὠκεανόν φησιν ὑφύδροις ἐλαυνόμενον
πνεύμασιν ἐκ πολλῶν χασμάτων, ἃ ὑπ᾽ αὐτῷ τε καὶ
περὶ αὐτὸν ἡ γῆ παρέχεται, χωρεῖν ἐς τὸ ἔξω καὶ
ἀναχωρεῖν πάλιν, ἐπειδὰν ὥσπερ ἆσθμα ὑπονοστήσῃ
τὸ πνεῦμα. πιστοῦται δὲ αὐτὸ κἀκ τῶν νοσούντων περὶ
Γάδειρα· τὸν γὰρ χρόνον, ὃν πλημμυρεῖ τὸ ὕδωρ, οὐκ
ἀπολείπουσιν αἱ ψυχαὶ τοὺς ἀποθνήσκοντας, ὅπερ οὐκ
ἂν ξυμβαίνειν, εἰ μὴ καὶ πνεῦμα τῇ γῇ ἐπεχώρει. ἃ δὲ
περὶ τὴν σελήνην φασὶ φαίνεσθαι τικτομένην τε καὶ
πληρουμένην καὶ φθίνουσαν, ταῦτα περὶ τὸν Ὠκεανὸν
οἶδα, τὰ γὰρ ἐκείνης ἀνισοῖ[2] μέτρα, ξυμμινύθων αὐτῇ
καὶ ξυμπληρούμενος.

3. Ἡμέρα δ᾽ ἐκδέχεται νύκτα καὶ νὺξ τὴν ἡμέραν
περὶ Κελτοὺς μὲν κατ᾽ ὀλίγον ὑπαπιόντος τοῦ σκότους
ἢ τοῦ φωτός, ὥσπερ ἐνταῦθα, περὶ Γάδειρα δὲ καὶ
Στήλας ἀθρόως λέγονται τοῖς ὀφθαλμοῖς ἐμπίπτειν,
ὥσπερ αἱ ἀστραπαί. φασὶ δὲ καὶ τὰς Μακάρων νήσους ὁρίζεσθαι τῷ Λιβυκῷ τέρματι πρὸς τὸ ἀοίκητον
ἀνεχούσας ἀκρωτήριον.

4. Τὰ δὲ Γάδειρα κεῖται μὲν κατὰ τὸ τῆς Εὐρώπης
τέρμα, περιττοὶ δέ εἰσι τὰ θεῖα· γήρως γοῦν[3] βωμὸν
ἵδρυνται καὶ τὸν θάνατον μόνοι ἀνθρώπων παιωνίζον-
ται, βωμοὶ δὲ ἐκεῖ καὶ πενίας καὶ τέχνης καὶ Ἡρακλέους Αἰγυπτίου καὶ ἕτεροι τοῦ Θηβαίου· τὸν μὲν
γὰρ ἐπὶ τὴν ἐγγὺς Ἐρύθειαν ἐλάσαι φασίν, ὅτε δὴ τὸν
Γηρυόνην τε καὶ τὰς βοῦς ἑλεῖν, τὸν δὲ σοφίᾳ δόντα

treats, I conclude that Apollonius perceived the answer. In one of his letters to the Indians, he says that the Ocean is pushed by underwater exhalations coming from the many crevices that are situated both below and around the earth, and goes forwards and retreats again as the breathlike exhalation dies away. This is corroborated by sick persons in the Gadeira region. During the time when the waters are at their height, souls do not leave the dying, something which would not occur unless the exhalation was coming towards land. As for what is said about the moon's appearance when it is new, full, and waning, I know that that affects the Ocean, which follows the moon's phases by sinking and rising in sympathy with it.

3. Day follows night and night day in the Celtic region, with the darkness and the light retreating gradually, as here, though around Gadeira and the Pillars they say the alteration strikes the eyes suddenly, like lightning. They also say that the Islands of the Blessed lie at the extremity of Africa, rising near the deserted promontory.

4. Gadeira lies at the end of Europe, and the inhabitants are very zealous in matters of religion. For they have set up an altar of Old Age, and are the only people to celebrate Death, and there are altars there of Poverty and Art, for the Egyptian Heracles, and others for his Theban counterpart.[4] The former, it is said, penetrated as far as nearby Erytheia,[5] at the time when he captured Geryon and his cattle, but the other Heracles, as a devotee of

4 Cf. II 33.2.
5 Island on which Gadeira stood.

---

2 ἀνισοῖ Rsk.: ἄνεισι   3 γοῦν Jackson: οὖν

γῆν ἀναμετρήσασθαι πᾶσαν ἐς τέρμα. καὶ μὴν καὶ
Ἑλληνικοὺς εἶναί φασι τὰ Γάδειρα, καὶ παιδεύεσθαι
τὸν ἡμεδαπὸν τρόπον· ἀσπάζεσθαι γοῦν Ἀθηναίους
Ἑλλήνων μάλιστα, καὶ Μενεσθεῖ τῷ Ἀθηναίῳ⁴ θύειν
καὶ Θεμιστοκλέα δὲ τὸν ναύμαχον σοφίας τε καὶ
ἀνδρείας ἀγασθέντες χαλκοῦν ἵδρυνται ἔννουν καὶ⁵
ὥσπερ χρησμῷ ἐφιστάντα.⁶

5. Ἰδεῖν καὶ δένδρα φασὶν ἐνταῦθα, οἷα οὐχ ἑτέρωθι τῆς γῆς, καὶ Γηρυόνεια μὲν καλεῖσθαι αὐτά, δύο
δὲ εἶναι, φύεσθαι δὲ τοῦ σήματος, ὃ ἐπὶ τῷ Γηρυόνῃ
ἔστηκε, παραλλάττοντα ἐκ πίτυός τε καὶ πεύκης ἐς
εἶδος ἕτερον, λείβεσθαι δὲ αἵματι, καθάπερ τῷ χρυσῷ
τὴν Ἡλιάδα αἴγειρον. ἡ δὲ νῆσος, ἐν ᾗ τὸ ἱερόν, ἔστι
μὲν ὁπόση ὁ νεώς, πετρῶδες δὲ αὐτῆς οὐδέν, ἀλλὰ
βαλβῖδι ξεστῇ εἴκασται. ἐν δὲ τῷ ἱερῷ τιμᾶσθαι μὲν
ἄμφω τὼ Ἡρακλέε φασίν, ἀγάλματα δὲ αὐτοῖν οὐκ
εἶναι, βωμοὺς δὲ τοῦ μὲν Αἰγυπτίου δύο χαλκοῦς καὶ
ἀσήμους, ἕνα δὲ τοῦ Θηβαίου. τὰς δὲ ὕδρας τε καὶ τὰς
Διομήδους ἵππους, καὶ τὰ δώδεκα Ἡρακλέους ἔργα
ἐκτετυπῶσθαί φασι καὶ ταῦτα, λίθου ὄντα. ἡ Πυγμα-
λίωνος δὲ ἐλαία ἡ χρυσῆ, ἀνάκειται δὲ κἀκείνη ἐς τὸ
Ἡράκλειον, ἀξία μέν, ὥς φασι, καὶ τοῦ θαλλοῦ θαυ-
μάζειν, ὡς εἴκασται, θαυμάζεσθαι δ' ἂν ἐπὶ τῷ καρπῷ
μᾶλλον, βρύειν γὰρ αὐτὸν σμαράγδου λίθου.

2   Καὶ Τεύκρου τοῦ Τελαμωνίου ζωστῆρα χρυσοῦν

---

⁴ Ἀθηναίῳ Rsk.: Ἀθηναίων   ⁵ ἔννουν καὶ Ol.: καὶ
ἔννουν   ⁶ ἐφιστάντα Rsk.: ἐφίστανται

science, surveyed the whole world to its boundary. They say that the Gadeirans are Hellenized, and enjoy our kind of culture. Certainly they welcome Athenians more than anyone, sacrifice to Menestheus the Athenian, and admire Themistocles the naval fighter for his intelligence and courage,[6] so that they have erected a bronze statue of him meditating and as it were pondering an oracle.

5. They claim to have seen trees there of a kind that exists nowhere else on earth, and are called Geryon's. They are two in number, and grow from the grave that holds Geryon. Each combines the natures of a pine and a fir and drips blood, as we are told the Heliad poplar drips gold.[7] The island on which the sanctuary stands is as large as the temple itself, and is in no way like a rock, but resembles a polished platform. Both the Heracles's are said to be honored in the sanctuary, but there are no statues of them. Instead there are two altars of plain bronze for the Egyptian Heracles, and one for the Theban. They say that the hydras, the horses of Diomedes, and the twelve Labors of Heracles were also shown in relief, these too in stone. The golden olive tree of Pygmalion,[8] which is also dedicated in the sanctuary of Heracles, is admirable for the verisimilitude of its branches, they say, but even more admirable for its fruit, since it swarms with emeralds.

They also report that the golden belt of Telamonian   2

[6] Menestheus brought fifty ships to Troy (*Iliad* 2.552–56); the Athenian Themistocles had an oracle near Gadeira.

[7] The daughters of Helios (the Sun) were turned into poplars after the death of their brother Phaethon.

[8] Mythical king of Tyre, and brother of Dido.

APOLLONIUS OF TYANA

φασι δείκνυσθαι, πῶς δὲ ἐς τὸν Ὠκεανὸν πλεύσαντος
ἢ ἐφ' ὅ τι, οὔτε αὐτὸς ὁ Δάμις ξυνιδεῖν φησιν οὔτε
ἐκείνων ἀκοῦσαι. τὰς δὲ ἐν τῷ ἱερῷ στήλας χρυσοῦ
μὲν πεποιῆσθαι καὶ ἀργύρου ξυντετηκότοιν ἐς ἓν χρῶμα, εἶναι δὲ αὐτὰς ὑπὲρ πῆχυν τετραγώνου τέχνης,
ὥσπερ οἱ ἄκμονες, ἐπιγεγράφθαι δὲ τὰς κεφαλὰς οὔτε
Αἰγυπτίοις οὔτε Ἰνδικοῖς γράμμασιν, οὔτε οἵοις ξυμβαλεῖν. ὁ δὲ Ἀπολλώνιος, ὡς οὐδὲν οἱ ἱερεῖς ἔφραζον,
"οὐ ξυγχωρεῖ μοι" ἔφη "ὁ Ἡρακλῆς ὁ Αἰγύπτιος μὴ
οὐ λέγειν, ὁπόσα οἶδα· Γῆς καὶ Ὠκεανοῦ ξύνδεσμοι
αἵδε αἱ στῆλαί εἰσιν, ἐπεγράψατο[7] δὲ αὐτὰς ἐκεῖνος ἐν
Μοιρῶν οἴκῳ, ὡς μήτε νεῖκος τοῖς στοιχείοις ἐγγέ-
νοιτο μήτε ἀτιμάσειαν τὴν φιλότητα, ἣν ἀλλήλων
ἴσχουσιν."

6. Φασὶ δὲ καὶ τὸν ποταμὸν ἀναπλῶσαι τὸν Βαῖτιν,
ὃς δηλοῖ μάλιστα τὴν τοῦ Ὠκεανοῦ φύσιν· ἐπειδὰν
γὰρ πλημμύρῃ τὸ πέλαγος, ἐπὶ τὰς πηγὰς ὁ ποταμὸς
παλίρρους ἵεται πνεύματος δήπου ἀπωθουμένου αὐτὸν
τῆς θαλάττης. τὴν δὲ ἤπειρον τὴν Βαιτικήν, ἧς ὁ
ποταμὸς οὗτος ὁμώνυμος, ἀρίστην ἠπείρων φασί, πό-
λεών τε γὰρ εὖ ἔχειν καὶ νομῶν καὶ διῆχθαι τὸν
ποταμὸν ἐς τὰ ἄστη πάντα, γεωργίας τε ξυμπάσης
μεστὴν εἶναι καὶ ὡρῶν, οἷαι τῆς Ἀττικῆς αἱ μετο-
πώριναί τε καὶ μυστηριώτιδες.

7. Διαλέξεις δὲ τῷ Ἀπολλωνίῳ περὶ τῶν ἐκεῖ παρα-
πεσόντων ὁ Δάμις πλείους μὲν γενέσθαι φησίν, ἀξίας
δὲ τοῦ ἀναγράψαι τάσδε· καθημένων ποτὲ αὐτῶν ἐς τὸ
Ἡράκλειον ἀναγελάσας ὁ Μένιππος, ἀναμέμνητο δὲ

8

Teucer[9] is on display, though how he sailed to the Ocean or for what purpose Damis says that he himself could not see, nor could he learn from the locals. The pillars in the sanctuary are made of gold and silver fused into a single color; they are over a cubit high and square in shape, like anvils, and on the capitals are inscribed letters that are neither Egyptian nor Indian, nor such as could be guessed. When the priests could offer no explanation, Apollonius said, "Egyptian Heracles does not allow me to conceal all that I know. These pillars bind Earth and Ocean together, and he himself inscribed them in the house of the Fates, to ensure that there was no strife between the elements, and that they should not neglect the affection that they feel for each other."

6. They say also that they sailed up the river Baetis, which exactly illustrates the nature of the Ocean, since when the tide is high, the river flows back towards its source, presumably because an exhalation drives it away from the sea. The mainland region of Baetica, which gets its name from the river, they describe as the best of all such regions, being well provided with cities and pastureland, and because the river is distributed among all the towns. It is full of every kind of cereal and seasonal produce, such as those of Attica in the fall at the time of the Mysteries.

7. According to Damis, Apollonius gave many discourses about their experiences there, but these were the ones worth recording. Once as they were sitting in the sanctuary of Heracles, Menippus burst out laughing at the

9 Half-brother of Greater or "Telamonian" Ajax.

---

7 ἐπεγράψατο Kay.: ἐγράψατο

ἄρα τοῦ Νέρωνος "τί" ἔφη "τὸν γενναῖον ἡγώμεθα;[8]
τίνας" ἔφη "ἐστεφανῶσθαι τῶν ἀγώνων; τοὺς δὲ βελ-
τίστους Ἕλληνας οὐ ξὺν ὅλῳ γέλωτι φοιτᾶν ἐς τὰς
πανηγύρεις;" ὁ δὲ Ἀπολλώνιος "ὡς μὲν ἐγὼ" ἔφη
"Τελεσίνου ἤκουον, δέδιεν ὁ χρηστὸς Νέρων τὰς
Ἠλείων μάστιγας· παρακελευομένων γὰρ αὐτῷ τῶν
κολάκων νικᾶν τὰ Ὀλύμπια καὶ ἀνακηρύττειν τὴν
Ῥώμην 'ἤν γε' ἔφη 'μὴ βασκήνωσιν Ἠλεῖοι, λέγονται
γὰρ μαστιγοῦν καὶ φρονεῖν ὑπὲρ ἐμέ,' πολλὰ δὲ καὶ
ἄλλα ἀνοητότερα τούτων προανεφώνησεν.

2   "Ἐγὼ δὲ νικήσειν μὲν Νέρωνα ἐν Ὀλυμπίᾳ φημί,
τίς γὰρ οὕτω θρασύς, ὡς ἐναντίαν θέσθαι; Ὀλύμπια
δὲ οὐ νικήσειν, ἅ γε[9] μηδὲ ἐν ὥρᾳ ἄγουσι· πατρίου μὲν
γὰρ τοῖς Ὀλυμπίοις τοῦ πέρυσιν ἐνιαυτοῦ ὄντος ἐκέλευσε τοὺς Ἠλείους Νέρων ἀναβαλέσθαι αὐτὰ ἐς
τὴν ἑαυτοῦ ἐπιδημίαν, ὡς ἐκείνῳ μᾶλλον ἢ τῷ Διὶ
θύσοντας· τραγῳδίαν δ' ἐπαγγεῖλαι καὶ κιθαρῳδίαν
ἀνδράσιν, οἷς μήτε θέατρόν ἐστι μήτε σκηνὴ πρὸς τὰ
τοιαῦτα, στάδιον δὲ αὐτοφυὲς καὶ γυμνὰ πάντα, τὸν δὲ
νικᾶν, ἃ χρὴ ἐγκαλύπτεσθαι, καὶ τὴν Αὐγούστου τε
καὶ Ἰουλίου σκευὴν ῥίψαντα μεταμφιέννυσθαι νῦν τὴν
Ἀμοιβέως καὶ Τερπνοῦ τί φήσεις; καὶ τὰ μὲν Κρέον-
τός τε καὶ Οἰδίποδος οὕτως ἐξακριβοῦν, ὡς δεδιέναι
μή πῃ λάθῃ ἁμαρτὼν θύρας ἢ στολῆς ἢ σκήπτρου,
ἑαυτοῦ δὲ καὶ Ῥωμαίων οὕτως ἐκπίπτειν, ὡς ἀντὶ τοῦ

8 ἡγώμεθα Kay.: ἡγούμεθα
9 ἅ γε Morel et iterum Rsk.: ἅτε

recollection of Nero, and said, "What should we think about that worthy? Which of the games do you suppose he has won crowns in, and are those excellent Greeks not overcome with laughter as they attend the festivals?" "According to what I heard from Telesinus," replied Apollonius, "the virtuous Nero is afraid of the Eleans' whips. When his flatterers urged him to win the Olympics and proclaim Rome as the winner, he said, 'I will, unless the Eleans are jealous of me. I hear that they use whips, and think me beneath them,' and he made other predictions more idiotic than these.

"As I see it, Nero will win at Olympia, since no one will   2
have the courage to cast a contrary vote, but will not win the Olympics, since they are not even being held at the proper time. Last year was the traditional year for them, but Nero ordered the Eleans to postpone them until his visit, as if they were to sacrifice to him rather than to Zeus. And as for his promising performances in tragedy and on the lyre to men who have neither a theater nor a stage for the purpose, but merely a natural stadium and bare spaces, or of his winning a contest for something which he should have concealed, and casting off the clothing of Augustus and Julius to change now instead into that of Amoebeus and Terpnus,[10] what will you say of this? Or of his having studied the role of Creon and Oedipus so much that he fears he may accidentally get his entrance or his costume or his scepter wrong? While he is so oblivious of himself and Rome that instead of making measures, he is singing

---

[10] Famous lyre-players, the former of the third century BCE, the latter a teacher of Nero.

νομοθετεῖν νόμους ᾄδειν καὶ ἀγείρειν ἔξω θυρῶν, ὧν
ἔσω χρὴ καθῆσθαι τὸν βασιλέα χρηματίζοντα ὑπὲρ
γῆς καὶ θαλάττης; εἰσίν, ὦ Μένιππε, τραγῳδοὶ πλείους, ἐς οὓς Νέρων ἑαυτὸν γράφει· τί οὖν εἴ τις αὐτῶν,
μετὰ τὸν Οἰνόμαον ἢ τὸν Κρεσφόντην ἀπελθὼν τοῦ
θεάτρου, μεστὸς οὕτω τοῦ προσωπείου γένοιτο, ὡς
ἄρχειν μὲν ἑτέρων βούλεσθαι, τύραννον δὲ αὐτὸν
ἡγεῖσθαι, τί καὶ φήσεις τοῦτον;[10] ἆρ᾽ οὐκ ἐλλεβόρου
δεῖσθαι καὶ φαρμακοποσίας, ὁπόση τοὺς νοῦς ἐκκα-
θαίρει;

3   "Εἰ δ᾽ αὐτὸς ὁ τυραννεύων ἐς τραγῳδοὺς καὶ τεχνί-
τας τὰ πράγματα ἑαυτοῦ ἄγοι, λεαίνων τὴν φωνὴν καὶ
δεδιὼς τὸν Ἠλεῖον ἢ τὸν Δελφόν, ἢ μὴ δεδιὼς μέν,
κακῶς δὲ οὕτως ὑποκρινόμενος τὴν ἑαυτοῦ τέχνην,
ὡς μὴ μεμαστιγώσεσθαι[11] νομίζειν πρὸς τούτων, ὧν
αὐτὸς ἄρχειν τέτακται, τί τοὺς κακοδαίμονας ἀνθρώπους ἐρεῖς ὑπὸ τοιούτῳ καθάρματι ζῶντας; τοῖς δὲ
Ἕλλησι τίνα ἡγῇ, ὦ Μένιππε; πότερα Ξέρξην κατα-
πιμπράντα ἢ Νέρωνα ᾄδοντα; εἰ γὰρ ἐνθυμηθείης τὴν
ἀγοράν, ἣν ἐς τὰς ἐκείνου ᾠδὰς ξυμφέρουσι, καὶ ὡς
ἐξωθοῦνται τῶν οἰκιῶν καὶ ὡς οὐκ ἔξεστι σπουδαῖον
οὐδὲν ἢ σκεῦος ἢ ἀνδράποδον αὐτοῖς πεπᾶσθαι, περὶ
γυναίοις τε καὶ παισὶν ὡς δεινὰ πείσονται τὰς ἐπιρ-
ρήτους ἡδονὰς ἐξ ἁπάσης οἰκίας ἐκλέγοντος τοῦ Νέρωνος, δίκαι τε ὡς πολλαὶ ἀναφύσονται, καὶ τὰς μὲν
ἄλλας ἔα, τὰς δὲ ἐπὶ τοῖς θεάτροις καὶ ταῖς ᾠδαῖς· ῾οὐκ
ἦλθες ἀκροασόμενος Νέρωνος᾽ ἢ ῾παρῆσθα μέν, ῥᾳθύμως δὲ ἤκροῶ,᾽ ῾ἐγέλας,᾽ ῾οὐκ ἐκρότησας,᾽ ῾οὐκ ἔθυσας

them, playing the beggar out of doors when a man with the title of king should be sitting indoors, superior to land and sea. There are many tragic actors, Menippus, whose company Nero is joining. Suppose then that one of them left the theatre after playing Oenomaus or Cresphontes,[11] and was so full of his role that he wanted to lord it over others and thought he was a tyrant—what would you think of him? Would you not think he needed hellebore and whatever kind of medicine clears the brain?

"But suppose that the tyrant himself takes his place   3 among actors and artists, trains his voice, fears Eleans or Delphians, or without fearing them so fakes his artistry as to think he will escape being whipped by people whose appointed ruler he is. What do you think of the god-forsaken creatures who live under such scum? How do you think he looks to the Greeks? Is he Xerxes the arsonist or Nero the singer? Think of the supplies that they provide for his performances, how they are evicted from their houses, how they cannot maintain any good furniture or slaves for themselves. Think of the terrible things that will happen to their women and children, with Nero plucking his unspeakable pleasures from every home, of all the trials that will arise. Not to mention the other ones, think of those that concern his audiences and his songs: 'you didn't come to hear Nero,' 'you came but you listened without enthusiasm,' 'you laughed,' 'you didn't clap,' 'you did not sacrifice

---

11 Mythical kings of Messenia and Elis respectively.

---

10 τί οὖν . . . τοῦτον; interpunxit Jackson

11 μεμαστιγώσεσθαι Rsk.: μαστιγώσεσθαι

ὑπὲρ τῆς φωνῆς, ἵνα Πυθῶδε λαμπροτέρα ἔλθοι,ʼ πολλαί σοι δόξουσι κακῶν[12] Ἰλιάδες περὶ τοὺς Ἕλληνας εἶναι.

4   "Τὸ γὰρ τετμήσεσθαι τὸν Ἰσθμὸν ἢ οὐ τετμήσεσθαι, τέμνεται δέ, ὥς φασι, νῦν, πάλαι προὔμαθον θεοῦ φήναντος." ὑπολαβὼν οὖν ὁ Δάμις, "ἀλλ' ἔμοιγε," ἔφη "ὦ Ἀπολλώνιε, τὸ περὶ τὴν τομὴν ἔργον ὑπερφωνεῖν δοκεῖ τὰ Νέρωνος πάντα, ἡ γὰρ διάνοια ὁρᾷς, ὡς μεγάλη." "δοκεῖ μὲν" ἔφη" κἀμοί, ὦ Δάμι, τὸ δὲ ἀτελὲς αὐτῆς διαβαλεῖ[13] αὐτόν, ὡς ἀτελῆ μὲν ᾄδοντα, ἀτελῆ δὲ ὀρύττοντα. τά τοι Ξέρξου ἀναλεγόμενος ἐπαινῶ τὸν ἄνδρα, οὐχ ὅτι τὸν Ἑλλήσποντον ἔζευξεν, ἀλλ' ὅτι διέβη αὐτόν, Νέρωνα δὲ οὔτε πλευσούμενον διὰ τοῦ Ἰσθμοῦ ὁρῶ, οὔτε ἐς τέρμα τῆς ὀρυχῆς ἥξοντα, δοκεῖ δέ μοι καὶ φόβου μεστὸς ἀναχωρῆσαι τῆς Ἑλλάδος, εἰ μὴ ἡ ἀλήθεια ἀπόλωλεν."

8. Ἀφικομένου δέ τινος ἐς Γάδειρα μετὰ ταῦτα τῶν τοὺς ταχεῖς διαθεόντων δρόμους, καὶ κελεύοντος εὐαγγέλια θύειν τρισολυμπιονίκην Νέρωνα ᾄδοντας, τὰ μὲν Γάδειρα ξυνίει τῆς νίκης καὶ ὅτι ἐν Ἀρκαδίᾳ τις εἴη ἀγὼν εὐδόκιμος, ἐπειδή, ὡς εἶπον, ἐς τὰ Ἑλλήνων σπεύδουσιν, αἱ δὲ πόλεις αἱ πρόσοικοι τοῖς Γαδείροις οὔτε ἐγίγνωσκον ὅ τι εἴη τὰ Ὀλύμπια, οὐδ' ὅ τι ἀγωνία ἢ ἀγών, οὐδὲ ἐφ' ὅτῳ θύουσιν, ἀλλ' ἀπήγοντο ἐς γελοίους δόξας, πολέμου νίκην ἡγούμενοι ταῦτα καὶ ὅτι ὁ Νέρων ᾑρήκοι τινὰς ἀνθρώπους Ὀλυμπίους· οὐδὲ γὰρ τραγῳδίας ποτὲ ἢ κιθαρῳδίας θεαταὶ ἐγεγόνεσαν.

on behalf of his voice, so that it would arrive sounding more brilliant at Delphi.' You will see that the Greeks will have many long tales of woe.

"As for whether the Isthmus will be cut or not, an operation which is now being performed, I gather, that is something I learned long ago from a divine revelation."[12] "Apollonius," Damis replied, "I certainly think that this attempt to cut it is the grandest of all Nero's acts, for you see what a lofty plan it is." "I agree, Damis," he replied, "but his failure to accomplish it will give him a bad name for not completing either his recital or his excavation. When I think of Xerxes's accomplishments, I admire that hero not because he bridged the Hellespont but because he crossed it. But I foresee that Nero will not sail through the Isthmus or come to the end of his excavation, but instead I think he will leave Greece in an utter panic, if the truth still exists."

8. Some time later a man traveling by the express postal service arrived in Gadeira, telling them to perform sacrifices for good news and celebrate Nero as a triple Olympic winner. The Gadeirans understood what the victory meant and that there was a celebrated competition in Arcadia, since, as I said, they are eager for Greek culture. But the neighboring cities to Gadeira had no idea what the Olympics were, or even what a competition or a game was, or why they were sacrificing. They formed ridiculous ideas, supposing that this was a victory in war, and that Nero had captured some people called Olympians. In fact they had never seen a tragedy or a lyre concert either.

4

---

12 Cf. IV 24.2.

---

12 κακῶν Jac.: θεατῶν   13 διαβαλεῖ Jon.: διαβάλλει

9. Τοὺς γοῦν οἰκοῦντας τὰ Ἴσπολα, πόλις δὲ κἀκείνη Βαιτική, φησὶν ὁ Δάμις παθεῖν τι πρὸς τραγῳδίας
ὑποκριτήν, οὗ κἀμὲ ἄξιον ἐπιμνησθῆναι· θυουσῶν γὰρ
τῶν πόλεων θαμὰ ἐπὶ ταῖς νίκαις, ἐπειδὴ καὶ αἱ Πυθι-
καὶ ἤδη ἀπηγγέλλοντο, τραγῳδίας ὑποκριτὴς τῶν
οὐκ ἀξιουμένων ἀνταγωνίζεσθαι τῷ Νέρωνι ἐπῄει τὰς
ἑσπερίους πόλεις ἀγείρων, καὶ τῇ τέχνῃ χρώμενος
ηὐδοκίμει παρὰ τοῖς ἧττον βαρβάροις, πρῶτον μὲν δι'
αὐτὸ τὸ ἥκειν παρ' ἀνθρώπους, οἳ μήπω τραγῳδίας
ἤκουσαν, εἶτ' ἐπειδὴ τὰς Νέρωνος μελῳδίας ἀκριβοῦν
ἔφασκε.

2   Παρελθὼν δὲ ἐς τὰ Ἴσπολα φοβερὸς μὲν αὐτοῖς
ἐφαίνετο καὶ ὃν ἐσιώπα χρόνον ἐπὶ τῆς σκηνῆς, καὶ
ὁρῶντες οἱ ἄνθρωποι βαδίζοντα μὲν αὐτὸν μέγα, κε-
χηνότα δὲ τοσοῦτον, ἐφεστῶτα δὲ ὀκρίβασιν οὕτως
ὑψηλοῖς τερατώδη τε τὰ περὶ αὐτὸν ἐσθήματα, οὐκ
ἄφοβοι ἦσαν τοῦ σχήματος, ἐπεὶ δὲ ἐξάρας τὴν φωνὴν γεγωνὸν ἐφθέγξατο, φυγῇ οἱ πλεῖστοι ᾤχοντο,
ὥσπερ ὑπὸ δαίμονος ἐμβοηθέντες. τοιαῦτα μὲν τὰ ἤθη
τῶν ταύτῃ βαρβάρων καὶ οὕτως ἀρχαῖα.

10. Σπουδὴν δὲ ποιουμένου τοῦ τὴν Βαιτικὴν ἐπι-
τροπεύοντος ἐς ξυνουσίαν τῷ Ἀπολλωνίῳ ἐλθεῖν, ὁ
μὲν ἀηδεῖς ἔφη τὰς ξυνουσίας τὰς ἑαυτοῦ φαίνεσθαι
τοῖς μὴ φιλοσοφοῦσιν, ὁ δὲ προσέκειτο αἰτῶν τοῦτο,
ἐπεὶ δὲ χρηστός τε εἶναι ἐλέγετο καὶ διαβεβλημένος
πρὸς τοὺς Νέρωνος μίμους, γράφει πρὸς αὐτὸν ἐπιστολὴν ὁ Ἀπολλώνιος, ἵν' ἐς τὰ Γάδειρα ἔλθοι, ὁ δὲ
ἀφελὼν τὸν τῆς ἀρχῆς ὄγκον ξὺν ὀλίγοις καὶ ἑαυτῷ

9. The natives of Hispola,[13] which is another city in Baetica, were said by Damis to have been affected by a tragic actor in a way that I too must mention. The cities were sacrificing constantly because of Nero's victories, since news of his Pythian ones had started to arrive. A tragic actor who had been thought unworthy to compete with Nero was money-grubbing around the cities of the west. His exhibitions of skill brought him success among the less uncivilized, primarily because of the simple fact that he visited people who had never heard a tragedy, and also because he claimed to be a connoisseur of Nero's songs.

But when he reached Hispola, he seemed terrifying even while he remained silent on the stage, and when the people saw him taking long strides and gaping wide, standing in such high boots, and dressed in outlandish costume, they already felt some fear at his appearance. But when he raised his voice with a booming sound, most of them went running off as if a demon had shouted at them. Such and so quaint are the ways of the barbarians in these parts.

10. When the governor of Baetica professed a desire to meet and converse with him,[14] Apollonius said that those who were not philosophers found his conversation dull. But the man persevered with this request, and since he was said to be virtuous and to take offence at Nero's farces, Apollonius wrote him a letter asking him to come to Gadeira. The man came, leaving aside the dignity of his office,

[13] Possibly the modern Seville.
[14] Unidentified.

ἐπιτηδειοτάτοις ἦλθεν. ἀσπασάμενοι δὲ ἀλλήλους καὶ
μεταστησάμενοι τοὺς παρόντας ὅ τι μὲν διελέχθησαν,
οὐδεὶς οἶδε, τεκμαίρεται δὲ ὁ Δάμις ἐπὶ Νέρωνα ξυμβῆναι σφᾶς. τριῶν γὰρ ἡμερῶν ἰδίᾳ σπουδάσαντες ὁ
μὲν ἀπῄει περιβαλὼν τὸν Ἀπολλώνιον, ὁ δὲ "ἔρρωσο"
ἔφη "καὶ μέμνησο τοῦ Βίνδικος."

2   Τί δὲ τοῦτο ἦν; ἐπὶ Νέρωνα ἐν Ἀχαΐᾳ ᾄδοντα τὰ
ἔθνη τὰ ἑσπέρια λέγεται κινῆσαι Βίνδιξ ἀνὴρ οἶος
ἐκτεμεῖν τὰς νευράς, ἃς Νέρων ἀμαθῶς ἔψαλλε, πρὸς
γὰρ τὰ στρατόπεδα, οἷς ἐπετέτακτο, λόγον κατ' αὐτοῦ
διῆλθεν, οἷον[14] ἐκ πάνυ γενναίας φιλοσοφίας ἐπὶ τύραννον ἄν τις πνεύσειεν· ἔφη γὰρ Νέρωνα εἶναι πάντα
μᾶλλον ἢ κιθαρῳδὸν καὶ κιθαρῳδὸν μᾶλλον ἢ
βασιλέα. προφέρειν δὲ αὐτῷ μανίαν μὲν καὶ φιλοχρη-
ματίαν καὶ ὠμότητα καὶ ἀσέλγειαν πᾶσαν, τὸ δὲ
ὠμότατον τῶν ἐκείνου μὴ προφέρειν αὐτῷ· τὴν γὰρ
μητέρα ἐν δίκῃ ἀπεκτονέναι, ἐπειδὴ τοιοῦτον ἔτεκε.
ταῦτ' οὖν ὡς ἔσται προγιγνώσκων ὁ Ἀπολλώνιος
ξυνέταττε τῷ Βίνδικι ὅμορον ἄρχοντα μόνον οὐχὶ
ὅπλα ὑπὲρ τῆς Ῥώμης τιθέμενος.

11. Φλεγμαινόντων δὲ τῶν περὶ τὴν ἑσπέραν, τρέ-
πονται τὸ ἐντεῦθεν ἐπὶ Λιβύην καὶ Τυρρηνοὺς καὶ τὰ
μὲν πεζῇ βαδίζοντες, τὰ δὲ ἐπὶ πλοίων πορευόμενοι
κατίσχουσιν ἐν Σικελίᾳ, οὗ τὸ Λιλύβαιον. παραπλεύσαντες δὲ ἐπὶ Μεσσήνην τε καὶ πορθμόν, ἔνθα ὁ
Τυρρηνὸς Ἀδρίᾳ ξυμβάλλων χαλεπὴν ἐργάζονται τὴν

---

[14] οἷον Jac.: ὃν

and accompanied by a few very close friends. The two exchanged greetings and asked those present to leave. What they discussed no one knows, though Damis guesses that they conspired against Nero, since after three days of private conversation, the governor on leaving embraced Apollonius, and he replied, "Goodbye, and remember Vindex."

What did this mean? When Nero was singing in 2 Greece, Vindex is said to have raised the western provinces against him.[15] This was a hero worthy to cut those strings Nero played so badly. He gave a speech against him to the armies in his command, and this was of the kind that a very noble love of wisdom might inspire against a tyrant. He said that Nero was anything rather than a lyre-player, and a lyre-player rather than an emperor. He blamed him, he said, for his madness, avarice, savagery, and debauchery of every kind, but not for his most savage deed: he was right to kill his mother for bearing such a son. Seeing in advance how all this would come about, Apollonius tried to unite the neighboring governor[16] with Vindex, virtually taking up arms in the Roman cause.

11. The situation in the west having become inflamed, they set their course from there to Africa and Etruria. After partly going on foot, partly traveling by sea, they put in at Lilybaeum in Sicily. Then they sailed on to Messina and the strait, where the confluence of the Tyrrhenian and the Adriatic seas makes the Charybdis dangerous. There

[15] Julius Vindex, legate of Gallia Lugdunensis and the first governor to rebel against Nero.

[16] Possibly Galba in Tarraconensis (Northern Spain).

χάρυβδιν, ἀκοῦσαί φασιν, ὡς Νέρων μὲν πεφεύγοι, τεθνήκοι δὲ Βίνδιξ, ἅπτοιντο δὲ τῆς ἀρχῆς οἱ μὲν ἐξ αὐτῆς Ῥώμης, οἱ δὲ ὁπόθεν τύχοι τῶν ἐθνῶν. ἐρομένων δὲ αὐτὸν τῶν ἑταίρων, οἳ προβήσοιτο ταῦτα καὶ ὅτου λοιπὸν ἡ ἀρχὴ ἔσοιτο, "πολλῶν" εἶπε "Θηβαίων." τὴν γὰρ ἰσχύν, ᾗ πρὸς ὀλίγον Βιτέλιος τε καὶ Γάλβας καὶ Ὄθων ἐχρήσαντο, Θηβαίοις εἴκασεν, οἳ χρόνον κομιδῇ βραχὺν ἤχθησαν ἐς τὰ τῶν Ἑλλήνων πράγματα.

12. Ὅτι μὲν γὰρ τὰ τοιαῦτα δαιμονίᾳ κινήσει προεγίγνωσκε καὶ ὅτι τοῖς γόητα τὸν ἄνδρα ἡγουμένοις οὐχ ὑγιαίνει ὁ λόγος, δηλοῖ μὲν καὶ τὰ εἰρημένα, σκεψώμεθα δὲ κἀκεῖνα· οἱ γόητες, ἡγοῦμαι δ᾽ αὐτοὺς ἐγὼ κακοδαιμονεστάτους ἀνθρώπων, οἱ μὲν ἐς βασάνους εἰδώλων χωροῦντες, οἱ δ᾽ ἐς θυσίας βαρβάρους, οἱ δὲ ἐς τὸ ἐπᾶσαί τι ἢ ἀλεῖψαι μεταποιεῖν φασι τὰ εἱμαρμένα, καὶ πολλοὶ τούτων κατηγορίαις ὑπαχθέντες τὰ τοιαῦτα ὡμολόγησαν σοφοὶ εἶναι. ὁ δὲ εἵπετο μὲν τοῖς ἐκ Μοιρῶν, προὔλεγε δέ, ὡς ἀνάγκη γενέσθαι αὐτά, προεγίγνωσκε δὲ οὐ γοητεύων, ἀλλ᾽ ἐξ ὧν οἱ θεοὶ ἔφαινον. ἰδὼν δὲ παρὰ τοῖς Ἰνδοῖς τοὺς τρίποδας καὶ τοὺς οἰνοχόους καὶ ὅσα αὐτόματα ἐσφοιτᾶν εἶπον, οὔθ᾽ ὅπως σοφίζοιντο αὐτά, ἤρετο, οὔτ᾽ ἐδεήθη μαθεῖν, ἀλλ᾽ ἐπήνει μέν, ζηλοῦν δ᾽ οὐκ ἠξίου.

13. Ἀφικομένων δὲ αὐτῶν ἐς τὰς Συρακούσας γυνὴ τῶν οὐκ ἀφανῶν τέρας ἀπεκύησεν, οἷον οὔπω ἐμαιεύθη· τρεῖς γὰρ τῷ βρέφει κεφαλαὶ ἦσαν ἐξ οἰκείας ἑκάστη δέρης, τὰ δὲ ἐπ᾽ αὐταῖς ἑνὸς πάντα. οἱ μὲν δὴ παχέως ἐξηγούμενοι τὴν Σικελίαν ἔφασαν, τρινακρία

they claim to have heard that Nero was in exile, Vindex dead, and that people were competing for the power from Rome or from this or that province. His disciples asked him what the result would be, and to whom the throne would finally fall, and he replied, "To many Thebans." The short term of domination which Vitellius, Galba, and Otho enjoyed made him compare them to the Thebans, who gained control of Greek affairs for a very short time.[17]

12. These predictions he made from divine impulse, and those who think him a magician are wrong in their opinion. That emerges from what I have already said, and also from the following. Magicians, who are in my opinion the greatest scoundrels on earth, resort to questioning ghosts or to barbaric sacrifices, or to forms of incantation or unction, and thus profess to alter fate. Many of them have been induced by accusations to admit their skill in such matters. Apollonius, however, followed the warnings of the Fates, and foretold the way they had to be fulfilled, and his clairvoyance was due not to magic but to divine revelation. When he saw the three-legged urns and the servers in India and all the other things which I described moving automatically,[18] he did not ask the locals how they had been constructed, and did not ask to be told, but simply praised without seeing fit to imitate them.

13. When they arrived in Syracuse, a woman of quite high rank had given birth to a freak of a kind never delivered before. The baby had three heads, each on its own neck, but the rest of it was all one body. One ignorant interpretation was that Sicily, which has three headlands, would

---

[17] The Thebans briefly dominated Greece in the mid-fourth century.   [18] III 27.2.

γάρ, ἀπολεῖσθαι, εἰ μὴ ὁμονοήσειέ τε καὶ ξυμπνεύ-
σειεν (ἐστασίαζον δὲ ἄρα πολλαὶ τῶν πόλεων πρὸς
ἑαυτάς[15] τε καὶ πρὸς ἀλλήλας, καὶ τὸ ἐν κόσμῳ ζῆν
ἀπῆν τῆς νήσου)· οἱ δὲ ἔφασαν τὸν Τυφῶ, πολυκέφα-
λον δὲ εἶναι, νεώτερα ἀπειλεῖν τῇ Σικελίᾳ,

2   Ὁ δὲ Ἀπολλώνιος "ἴθι," ἔφη "ὦ Δάμι, καὶ κάτιδε
αὐτό, εἰ οὕτω ξύγκειται." ἐξέκειτο γὰρ δημοσίᾳ τοῖς
τερατολογεῖν εἰδόσιν, ἀπαγγείλαντος δὲ τοῦ Δάμιδος,
ὡς τρικέφαλον εἴη καὶ ἄρρεν, ξυναγαγὼν τοὺς ἑταίρους "τρεῖς" ἔφη "Ῥωμαίων αὐτοκράτορες, οὓς ἐγὼ
πρῴην Θηβαίους ἔφην, τελειώσει δὲ οὐδεὶς τὸ ἄρχειν,
ἀλλ' οἱ μὲν ἐπ' αὐτῆς Ῥώμης, ὁ[16] δὲ περὶ τὰ ὅμορα τῇ
Ῥώμῃ δυνηθέντες ἀπολοῦνται, θᾶττον μεταβαλόντες
τὸ προσωπεῖον ἢ οἱ τῶν τραγῳδῶν τύραννοι." καὶ ὁ
λόγος αὐτίκα ἐς φῶς ἦλθε· Γάλβας μὲν γὰρ ἐπ' αὐτῆς
Ῥώμης ἀπέθανεν ἁψάμενος τῆς ἀρχῆς, ἀπέθανε δὲ καὶ
Βιτέλιος ὀνειροπολήσας τὸ ἄρχειν, Ὄθων δὲ περὶ
τοὺς ἑσπερίους Γαλάτας ἀποθανὼν οὐδὲ τάφου λαμ-
προῦ ἔτυχεν, ἀλλ' ὥσπερ ἰδιώτης κεῖται· διέπτη δὲ ἡ
τύχη ταῦτα ἑνὶ ἔτει.

       14. Πορευθέντες δὲ ἐπὶ Κατάνης, οὗ τὸ ὄρος ἡ
Αἴτνη, Καταναίων μὲν ἀκοῦσαί φασιν ἡγουμένων τὸν
Τυφῶ δεδέσθαι ἐκεῖ καὶ πῦρ ἐξ αὐτοῦ ἀνίστασθαι, ὃ
τύφει τὴν Αἴτνην, αὐτοὶ δ' ἐς πιθανωτέρους ἀφικέσθαι
λόγους καὶ προσήκοντας τοῖς φιλοσοφοῦσιν. ἄρξαι δ'
αὐτῶν τὸν Ἀπολλώνιον ὧδε ἐρόμενον τοὺς ἑταίρους

---

[15] ἑαυτάς Kay.: αὑτάς   [16] ὁ Kay.: οἱ

be ruined if it did not unite and agree, and in fact many of the cities were at variance within themselves and with their neighbors, and orderly existence had vanished from the island. Others said that Typho[19] of the many heads was threatening calamity for Sicily.

Apollonius however said, "Go, Damis, and see if that is the way it is formed," since the child was exposed publicly for those who know how to read portents. When Damis reported that the thing had three heads and was male, Apollonius summoned his disciples and said: "There are three emperors of Rome, whom I called Thebans the other day. None of them will complete his reign, but two will die after holding power in Rome itself, and the other after doing so in the regions near Rome, changing their masks faster than the tyrants of tragedy." The meaning of his words immediately came to light. Galba died after tasting power in Rome itself, Vitellius died after a mere vision of power, and Otho was killed in Gaul of the west, not even getting a fine burial, since he is buried like a private citizen. All these vicissitudes of fate occurred in a single year.

14. Proceeding to Catania, where Mount Etna is, they say they heard the opinion of the Catanians that Typho is imprisoned there, and that the fire which smolders beneath Etna rises from him.[20] They themselves, however, arrived at explanations that were more plausible and more worthy of philosophers. Apollonius took the first step by

---

[19] The gigantic monster believed to lie beneath Etna.

[20] The Greek contains an untranslatable pun on Typho and *typhein*, "consume by fire."

"ἔστι τι μυθολογία;" "νὴ Δί," εἶπεν ὁ Μένιππος "ἥν γε
οἱ ποιηταὶ ἐπαινοῦσι." "τὸν δὲ δὴ Αἴσωπον τί ἡγῇ;"
"μυθολόγον" εἶπε "καὶ λογοποιὸν πάντα." "πότεροι δὲ
σοφοὶ τῶν μύθων;" "οἱ τῶν ποιητῶν," εἶπεν "ἐπειδὴ ὡς
γεγονότες ᾄδονται." "οἱ δὲ δὴ Αἰσώπου τί;" "βάτρα-
χοι" ἔφη "καὶ ὄνοι καὶ λῆροι γραυσὶν οἷοι μασᾶσθαι
καὶ παιδίοις."

2   "Καὶ μὴν" ἔφη "ἐμοὶ" ὁ Ἀπολλώνιος, "ἐπιτηδειότε-
ροι πρὸς σοφίαν οἱ τοῦ Αἰσώπου φαίνονται· οἱ μὲν
γὰρ περὶ τοὺς ἥρωας, ὧν ποιητικὴ πᾶσα ἔχεται, καὶ
διαφθείρουσι τοὺς ἀκροωμένους, ἐπειδὴ ἔρωτάς τε
ἀτόπους οἱ ποιηταὶ ἑρμηνεύουσι καὶ ἀδελφῶν γάμους
καὶ διαβολὰς ἐς θεοὺς καὶ βρώσεις παίδων καὶ παν-
ουργίας ἀνελευθέρους καὶ δίκας <ἀδίκους>,[17] καὶ τὸ ὡς
γεγονὸς αὐτῶν ἄγει καὶ τὸν ἐρῶντα καὶ τὸν ζηλοτυ-
ποῦντα καὶ τὸν ἐπιθυμοῦντα πλουτεῖν ἢ τυραννεύειν
ἐφ' ἅπερ οἱ μῦθοι, Αἴσωπος δὲ ὑπὸ σοφίας πρῶτον
μὲν οὐκ ἐς τὸ κοινὸν τῶν ταῦτα ᾀδόντων ἑαυτὸν κατέστησεν, ἀλλ' ἑαυτοῦ τινα ὁδὸν ἐτράπετο, εἶτα, ὥσπερ
οἱ τοῖς εὐτελεστέροις βρώμασι καλῶς ἑστιῶντες, ἀπὸ
σμικρῶν πραγμάτων διδάσκει μεγάλα, καὶ προθέμε-
νος τὸν λόγον ἐπάγει αὐτῷ τὸ πρᾶττε ἢ μὴ πρᾶττε,

3   "Εἶτα τοῦ φιλαλήθους μᾶλλον ἢ οἱ ποιηταὶ ἥψατο·
οἱ μὲν γὰρ βιάζονται πιθανοὺς φαίνεσθαι τοὺς ἑαυτῶν
λόγους, ὁ δ' ἐπαγγέλλων λόγον, ὃν ὡς ἐστι ψευδὴς
πᾶς οἶδεν, αὐτὸ τὸ μὴ περὶ ἀληθινῶν ἐρεῖν ἀληθεύει.
καὶ ὁ μὲν ποιητὴς εἰπὼν τὸν ἑαυτοῦ λόγον καταλείπει

asking his followers, "Is there such a thing as storytelling?" "Yes, indeed," said Menippus, "at least the kind that the poets favor." "And what do you think Aesop is?" "Nothing but a teller of stories," he replied, "and of fables." "Which kind of story is philosophical?" "The poetic kind," Menippus replied, "since they are recited as if they were fact." "And what about Aesop's kind?" "They are frogs," said Menippus, "donkeys, and nonsense for old women and children to chew on."

"And yet in my opinion," said Apollonius, "Aesop's   2 seem more conducive to philosophy. Stories about heroes, to which all poetry is devoted, corrupt their listeners. The poets relate unnatural loves, marriages between siblings, slander of the gods, children being devoured, base trickery and unjust judgments, and their semblance of fact leads those who feel love, jealousy, or desire of wealth or tyranny, in the direction of the stories. Aesop by contrast had the wisdom first of all not to place himself in the common run of such poets, but traveled a certain path of his own. Moreover, like those who give an excellent dinner with rather modest food, he uses humble subjects to teach great lessons, and after setting out his tale rounds it off with a 'Do this' or a 'Don't do that.'

"He also was more devoted to truth than the poets.   3 They give their own stories a forced appearance of plausibility, while he, by promising a story that everyone knows to be untrue, tells the truth precisely in not undertaking to tell the truth.[21] A poet when he tells his own story leaves it

---

[21] Compare Lucian, *True Histories* I 4.

---

[17] ⟨ἀδίκους⟩ Rsk.

τῷ ὑγιαίνοντι ἀκροατῇ βασανίζειν αὐτόν, εἰ ἐγένετο, ὁ
δὲ εἰπὼν μὲν ψευδῆ λόγον, ἐπαγαγὼν δὲ νουθεσίαν,
ὥσπερ ὁ Αἴσωπος, δείκνυσιν ὡς ἐς τὸ χρήσιμον τῆς
ἀκροάσεως τῷ ψεύδει κέχρηται. χαρίεν δ᾽ αὐτοῦ τὸ καὶ
τὰ ἄλογα ἡδίω ἐργάζεσθαι καὶ σπουδῆς ἄξια τοῖς
ἀνθρώποις, ἐκ παίδων γὰρ τοῖς λόγοις τούτοις ξυγ-
γενόμενοι καὶ ὑπ᾽ αὐτῶν ἐκνηπιωθέντες δόξας ἀνα-
λαμβάνομεν περὶ ἑκάστου τῶν ζῴων, τὰ μὲν ὡς βασι-
λικὰ εἴη, τὰ δὲ ὡς εὐήθη, τὰ δὲ ὡς κομψά, τὰ δὲ ὡς
ἀκέραια, καὶ ὁ μὲν ποιητὴς εἰπὼν ᾽πολλαὶ μορφαὶ τῶν
δαιμονίων᾽ ἢ τοιοῦτό τι ἐπιχορεύσας ἀπῆλθεν, ὁ δὲ
Αἴσωπος ἐπιχρησμῳδήσας τὸν ἑαυτοῦ λόγον κατα-
λύει τὴν ξυνουσίαν ἐς ὃ προὔθετο.

15. Ἐμὲ δέ, ὦ Μένιππε, καὶ μῦθον περὶ τῆς Αἰσώπου σοφίας ἐδιδάξατο ἡ μήτηρ κομιδῇ νήπιον, ὡς εἴη
μέν ποτε ποιμὴν ὁ Αἴσωπος, νέμοι δὲ πρὸς ἱερῷ
Ἑρμοῦ, σοφίας δὲ ἐρῴη καὶ εὔχοιτο αὐτῷ ὑπὲρ τούτου,
πολλοὶ δὲ καὶ ἕτεροι ταὐτὸν αἰτοῦντες ἐπιφοιτῷεν τῷ
Ἑρμῇ ὁ μὲν χρυσόν, ὁ δ᾽ ἄργυρον, ὁ δὲ κηρύκειον
ἐλεφάντινον, ὁ δὲ τῶν οὕτω τι λαμπρῶν ἀνάπτων, ὁ δ᾽
Αἴσωπος ἔχοι μὲν οὕτως, ὡς μηδὲν τῶν τοιούτων
ἔχειν, φείδοιτο δὲ καὶ ὧν εἶχε, γάλακτος δὲ αὐτῷ
σπένδοι, ὅσον ὄις ἀμελχθεῖσα ἐδίδου καὶ κηρίον ἐπὶ
τὸν βωμὸν φέροι, ὅσον τὴν χεῖρα ἐμπλῆσαι, ἑστιᾶν δ᾽
αὐτὸν καὶ μύρτοις ᾤετο καὶ παραθεὶς ἂν τῶν ῥόδων ἢ
τῶν ἴων κομιδῇ ὀλίγα. ᾽τί γὰρ δεῖ, ὦ Ἑρμῆ,᾽ ἔλεγε
᾽στεφάνους πλέκειν καὶ ἀμελεῖν τῶν προβάτων;᾽

2   Ὡς δὲ ἀφίκοντο ἐς ῥητὴν ἡμέραν ἐπὶ τὴν τῆς

to the honest reader to test whether it really happened, but someone who tells an untrue tale while adding instruction, as Aesop does, makes plain that he uses falsehood for the benefit of the listener. It is also a charming trait to make dumb animals nicer and deserving respect from humans. By growing familiar with these stories from childhood, and being raised on them, we form ideas about each of the animals, that some are kingly, some silly, some clever, some innocent. A poet says 'Many the shapes that heaven-sent things assume'[22] or some other tag and off he goes, but Aesop concludes with his own moral, and ends the conversation at the point he intended.

15. "My own mother, Menippus, taught me a tale about Aesop's wisdom, when I was very young. Aesop, so she said, was once a shepherd, and was tending his flock near a sanctuary of Hermes, and being a lover of wisdom, he prayed the god to be given it. Many others visited Hermes with the same request, and dedicated gold, silver, an ivory baton, or something equally dazzling. Aesop, however, was not in a position to possess anything like that, and was thrifty with what he did have. So he used to pour out for the god as much milk as a sheep yields at a milking, and to bring to the altar a honeycomb large enough to fit his hand, and he would think himself to be regaling the god with myrtle when he offered just a few roses or violets. 'Why should I weave crowns, Hermes,' he used to say, 'and neglect my sheep?'

"But when the worshipers came on a day appointed for   2

---

[22] Euripides, *Alcestis* 1159, and also in other plays.

σοφίας διανομήν, ὁ μὲν Ἑρμῆς ἄτε λόγιος καὶ κερδῷος 'σὺ μὲν' ἔφη 'φιλοσοφίαν ἔχε,' τῷ πλεῖστα δήπουθεν ἀναθέντι 'σὺ δὲ ἐς ῥητόρων ἤθη χώρει,' τῷ δεύτερά που χαρισαμένῳ, 'σοὶ δὲ ἀστρονομεῖν χώρα, σοὶ δὲ εἶναι μουσικῷ, σοὶ δὲ ἡρῴου ποιητῇ μέτρου, σοὶ δὲ ἰαμβείου.' ἐπεὶ δὲ καίτοι λογιώτατος ὢν κατανάλωσεν ἄκων ἅπαντα τὰ τῆς φιλοσοφίας μέρη καὶ ἔλαθεν ἑαυτὸν ἐκπεσὼν τοῦ Αἰσώπου, ἐνθυμεῖται τὰς Ὥρας, ὑφ' ὧν αὐτὸς ἐν κορυφαῖς τοῦ Ὀλύμπου ἐτράφη, ὡς ἐν σπαργάνοις ποτὲ αὐτῷ ὄντι μῦθον διελθοῦσαι περὶ τῆς βοός, ὃν διελέχθη τῷ ἀνθρώπῳ ἡ βοῦς ὑπὲρ ἑαυτῆς τε καὶ τῆς γῆς, ἐς ἔρωτα αὐτὸν τῶν τοῦ Ἀπόλλωνος βοῶν κατέστησαν, καὶ δίδωσιν ἐντεῦθεν τὴν μυθολογίαν τῷ Αἰσώπῳ, λοιπὴν ἐν σοφίας οἴκῳ οὖσαν 'ἔχε,' εἰπὼν 'ἃ πρῶτα ἔμαθον.' αἱ μὲν δὴ πολλαὶ μορφαὶ τῆς τέχνης ἐνθένδε ἀφίκοντο τῷ Αἰσώπῳ, καὶ τοιόνδε ἀπέβη τὸ τῆς μυθολογίας πρᾶγμα.

16. "Ἴσως δ' ἀνόητον ἔπαθον· ἐπιστρέψαι γὰρ ὑμᾶς διανοηθεὶς ἐς λόγους φυσικωτέρους τε καὶ ἀληθεστέρους ὧν οἱ πολλοὶ περὶ τῆς Αἴτνης ᾄδουσιν, αὐτὸς ἐς ἔπαινον μύθων ἀπηνέχθην, οὐ μὴν ἄχαρις ἡ ἐκβολὴ τοῦ λόγου γέγονεν· ὁ γὰρ μῦθος, ὃν παραιτούμεθα, οὐ τῶν Αἰσώπου λόγων ἐστίν, ἀλλὰ τῶν δραματικωτέρων καὶ ὧν οἱ ποιηταὶ θρυλοῦσιν· ἐκεῖνοι μὲν γὰρ Τυφῶ τινα ἢ Ἐγκέλαδον δεδέσθαι φασὶν ὑπὸ τῷ ὄρει καὶ δυσθανατοῦντα ἀσθμαίνειν τὸ πῦρ τοῦτο, ἐγὼ δὲ γίγαντας μὲν γεγονέναι φημὶ καὶ πολλαχοῦ τῆς γῆς ἀναδείκνυσθαι τοιαυτὶ σώματα ῥαγέντων τῶν

the distribution of wisdom, Hermes as a lover of erudition and of profit said 'You may have philosophy' to the one whose offering was no doubt the largest. 'You may join the ranks of the orators,' he said to the one next in generosity, 'while *your* place is astronomy, *yours* is music, *yours* is epic poetry, *yours* is iambic poetry.' But despite all his great shrewdness he used up all the branches of wisdom without noticing, and forgot Aesop by mistake. But then he recalled the Seasons who had raised him on the peaks of Olympus, and how, once when he was in his cradle, they had told him about a cow, and how this cow had conversed with a human about itself and the world. In this way they had given him a fancy for Apollo's cows.[23] Accordingly he gave storytelling to Aesop, the last thing left in the house of wisdom, saying 'You may have what I learned first.' And so the 'many shapes' of Aesop's art came to him in this way, and 'thus ended the tale'[24] of storytelling.

16. "But perhaps something silly has happened to me. I meant to lead you towards more scientific and accurate beliefs than most people's cant about Etna, but got carried away myself into praising stories. Still, the digression from our discourse has not proved thankless, since the kind of story we were rejecting is not characteristic of Aesop's tales, but of more dramatic ones, and such as poets repeat. They say that some Typho or Enceladus is imprisoned beneath the mountain, and breathes out this fire in his death agony. While admitting that the giants existed, and that gigantic bodies show up in many parts of the world

[23] The baby Hermes stole the cattle of Apollo.
[24] Euripides, *Alcestis* 1163.

τάφων, οὐ μὴν ἐς ἀγῶνα ἐλθεῖν τοῖς θεοῖς, ἀλλ᾽
ὑβρίσαι μὲν τάχα ἐς τοὺς νεὼς αὐτῶν καὶ τὰ ἕδη,
οὐρανῷ δὲ ἐπιπηδῆσαι καὶ μὴ ξυγχωρεῖν τοῖς θεοῖς
ἐπ᾽ αὐτοῦ εἶναι μανία μὲν λέγειν, μανία δὲ οἴεσθαι.

2   "Καὶ μηδὲ ἐκεῖνος ὁ λόγος, καίτοι δοκῶν εὐφη-
μότερος εἶναι, τιμάσθω, ὡς Ἡφαίστῳ μέλει τοῦ χαλ-
κεύειν ἐν τῇ Αἴτνῃ, καὶ κτυπεῖταί τις ἐνταῦθα ὑπ᾽
αὐτοῦ ἄκμων, πολλὰ γὰρ καὶ ἄλλα ὄρη πολλαχοῦ τῆς
γῆς ἔμπυρα, καὶ οὐκ ἂν φθάνοιμεν ἐπιφημίζοντες
αὐτοῖς γίγαντας καὶ Ἡφαίστους.

17. "Τίς οὖν ἡ τῶν τοιῶνδε ὀρῶν αἰτία; γῆ κρᾶσιν
ἀσφάλτου καὶ θείου παρεχομένη τύφεται μὲν καὶ παρ᾽
ἑαυτῆς φύσει, πῦρ δ᾽ οὔπω ἐκδίδωσιν, εἰ δὲ σηραγ-
γώδης τύχοι καὶ ὑποδράμοι αὐτὴν πνεῦμα, φρυκτὸν
ἤδη αἴρει. πλεονεκτήσασα δὲ ἡ φλόξ, ὥσπερ τὸ ὕδωρ,
ἀπορρεῖ τῶν ὀρῶν καὶ ἐς τὰ πεδία ἐκχεῖται χωρεῖ τε
ἐπὶ θάλατταν πῦρ ἀθρόον ἐκβολὰς ποιούμενον, οἷαι
τῶν ποταμῶν εἰσι. χῶρος δ᾽ Εὐσεβῶν, περὶ οὓς τὸ πῦρ
ἐρρύη, λεγέσθω μὲν κἀνταῦθά τις, ἡγώμεθα δὲ τοῖς
ὅσια πράττουσι γῆν μὲν πᾶσαν ἀσφαλῆ χῶρον εἶναι,
θάλατταν δ᾽ εὔπορον οὐ πλέουσι μόνον, ἀλλὰ καὶ νεῖν
πειρωμένοις." ἀεὶ γὰρ τοὺς λόγους ἀνέπαυεν ἐς τὰ
χρηστὰ τῶν παραγγελμάτων.

18. Ἐμφιλοσοφήσας δὲ τῇ Σικελίᾳ χρόνον, ὃς
ἀποχρῶσαν αὐτῷ σπουδὴν εἶχεν, ἐπὶ τὴν Ἑλλάδα
ἐκομίζετο περὶ ἀρκτούρου ἐπιτολάς. ἀλύπου δὲ τοῦ
πλοῦ γενομένου κατασχὼν ἐς Λευκάδα "ἀποβῶμεν"
ἔφη "τῆς νεὼς ταύτης, οὐ γὰρ λῷον αὐτῇ ἐς Ἀχαίαν

when their graves are broken open, I do not think they tried to compete with the gods. Perhaps they insulted their temples and statues, but it is madness to say and madness to think that they assaulted heaven, and tried to prevent the gods from residing there.

"Let us also not respect another story, though in appearance a less blasphemous one, that Hephaestus works as a blacksmith in Etna, and that some anvil resounds under his blows. There are many other fiery mountains in many parts of the world, and we will soon find ourselves ascribing them to this or that giant or Hephaestus.

17. "What then is the explanation of such mountains? The earth contains a mixture of bitumen and sulfur, and smolders by its own nature, though without producing fire. If however it is hollow, and there is subterranean pressure, then it raises its torch. As the flame overflows, it spills from the mountains like water, and pours into the plains, and a mass of fire advances towards the sea, making outlets as rivers do. Some say that the Homes of the Blessed, who are surrounded by fire, exist here too, but we should believe that every place is safe for those who act righteously, and that the sea is propitious for them not only when they sail, but even when they try to swim." For he always ended his discourses with words of useful advice.

18. After pursuing philosophy in Sicily as long as he had enough material for study, Apollonius set off for Greece about the time of Arcturus's rising.[25] The crossing was uneventful, but on landing at Leucas he said, "Let us leave this ship. It would be better for it not to sail to Achaea."

[25] Mid-September.

APOLLONIUS OF TYANA

πλεῦσαι." προσέχοντος δὲ οὐδενὸς τῷ λόγῳ πλὴν τῶν
γιγνωσκόντων τὸν ἄνδρα, αὐτὸς μὲν ἐπὶ Λευκαδίας
νεὼς ὁμοῦ τοῖς βουλομένοις ξυμπλεῖν ἐς Λέχαιον
κατέσχεν, ἡ δὲ ναῦς ἡ Συρακουσία κατέδυ ἐσπλέουσα
τὸν Κρισαῖον κόλπον.

19. Μυηθεὶς δ' Ἀθήνησιν, ἐμύει δ' αὐτὸν ἱεροφάν-
της, ὃν αὐτὸς τῷ προτέρῳ ἐπεμαντεύσατο, ἐνέτυχε καὶ
Δημητρίῳ τῷ φιλοσόφῳ, μετὰ γὰρ τὸ Νέρωνος βαλα-
νεῖον καὶ ἃ ἐπ' αὐτῷ εἶπε διῃτᾶτο Ἀθήνησιν ὁ Δημήτριος οὕτω γενναίως, ὡς μηδὲ τὸν χρόνον, ὃν Νέρων
περὶ τοὺς ἀγῶνας ὕβριζεν, ἐξελθεῖν τῆς Ἑλλάδος.

2   Ἐκεῖνος καὶ Μουσωνίῳ ἔφασκεν ἐντετυχηκέναι
περὶ τὸν Ἰσθμὸν δεδεμένῳ τε καὶ κεκελευσμένῳ ὀρύτ-
τειν, καὶ αὐτὸς μὲν ἐπευφημῆσαι τὰ εἰκότα, τὸν δὲ
ἔχεσθαι τῆς σμινύης καὶ ἐρρωμένως τῇ γῇ ἐμβάλλειν,
ἀνακύψαντα δὲ "λυπῶ σε," φάναι[18] "ὦ Δημήτριε, τὸν
Ἰσθμὸν ὀρύττων τῇ Ἑλλάδι; εἰ δὲ καὶ κιθαρῳδοῦντά
με εἶδες, ὥσπερ Νέρωνα, τί ἂν ἔπαθες;" καὶ ἐάσθω τὰ
Μουσωνίου πλείω ὄντα καὶ θαυμασιώτερα, ὡς μὴ
δοκοίην θρασύνεσθαι πρὸς τὸν ἀμελῶς αὐτὰ εἰπόντα.

20. Χειμάσας δ' ὁ Ἀπολλώνιος ἐν τοῖς Ἑλληνικοῖς
ἱεροῖς πᾶσιν εἴχετο τῆς ἐπ' Αἰγύπτου ὁδοῦ περὶ ἔαρ,
πολλὰ μὲν ἐπιπλήξας, πολλὰ δὲ συμβουλεύσας ταῖς
πόλεσι, πολλῶν δὲ ἐς ἔπαινον καταστάς, οὐδὲ γὰρ
ἐπαίνου ἀπείχετο, ὁπότε τι ὑγιῶς πράττοιτο, καταβὰς
δὲ ἐς Πειραιᾶ ναῦς μέν τις ὥρμει πρὸς ἱστίοις οὖσα

18 φάναι Kay.: ἂν

32

Nobody paid attention to this remark, except those who knew the Master, so that he sailed in a Leucadian ship with those who wished to accompany him, and landed at Lechaeum, but the Syracusan ship sank as it was entering the Crisaean gulf.

19. He was initiated at Athens, with the ceremony performed by the hierophant whom he had foretold to the man's predecessor.[26] There he met Demetrius the philosopher, who had lived in Athens since the incident of Nero's bath and his speeches about it,[27] so courageously that he did not leave Greece even during the time when Nero was making a mockery of the games.

This man said he had seen Musonius at the Isthmus working in chains and forced to dig.[28] He naturally wished him well, but Musonius clutched his pickaxe and struck the ground vigorously, and then stood up and said, "Does it pain you, Demetrius, if I dig the Isthmus for the sake of Greece? What would you have felt if you had seen me playing the lyre like Nero?" Let me omit Musonius's many admirable remarks, or else I may seem to be doing an injustice to the spontaneous way he said them.

20. After wintering in all the Greek sanctuaries, Apollonius started on the journey to Egypt about springtime. He had issued many reproofs and much advice to the cities, and had been moved to praise many, since he did not withhold praise when something was done rightly. He went down to the Piraeus where a ship was docked, just busy

26 IV 18.
27 IV 42.1.
28 On Musonius, see IV 35. The tradition that he dug the Isthmus as a convict appears to be fictional.

APOLLONIUS OF TYANA

καὶ ἐς Ἰωνίαν ἀφήσουσα, ὁ δ᾽ ἔμπορος οὐ ξυνεχώρει
ἐμβαίνειν, ἰδιόστολον γὰρ αὐτὴν ἄγειν. ἐρομένου δὲ
τοῦ Ἀπολλωνίου "τίς ὁ φόρτος;" "θεῶν" ἔφη "ἀγάλματα ἀπάγω ἐς Ἰωνίαν, τὰ μὲν χρυσοῦ καὶ λίθου, τὰ
δὲ ἐλέφαντος καὶ χρυσοῦ." "ἱδρυσόμενος ἢ τί;" "ἀπο-
δωσόμενος" ἔφη "τοῖς βουλομένοις ἱδρύεσθαι." "δέδιας οὖν, ὦ λῷστε, μὴ συλήσωμεν τὰ ἀγάλματα ἐν τῇ
νηΐ;" "οὐ τοῦτο" ἔφη "δέδια, τὸ δὲ πλείοσι ξυμπλεῖν
αὐτὰ καὶ ὁμιλίας ἀναπίμπλασθαι φαύλου διαίτης τε,
ὁπόση ναυτική, δεινὸν ἡγοῦμαι."

2   "Καὶ μήν, ὦ βέλτιστε," εἶπε "δοκεῖς γάρ μοί τις
Ἀθηναῖος εἶναι, τὰς ναῦς, αἷς ἐπὶ τοὺς βαρβάρους
ἐχρήσασθε, καίτοι ναυτικῆς ἀταξίας ἐμπεπλησμένας
ἐνέβαινον οἱ θεοὶ ξὺν ὑμῖν, καὶ οὐκ ᾤοντο ὑφ᾽ ὑμῶν
χραίνεσθαι, σὺ δὲ ἀμαθῶς οὕτως ἀπωθῇ τῆς νεὼς
φιλοσόφους ἄνδρας, οἷς μάλιστα οἱ θεοὶ χαίρουσι,
καὶ ταῦτα ἐμπορίαν τοὺς θεοὺς πεποιημένος; ἡ δὲ
ἀγαλματοποιία ἡ ἀρχαία οὐ τοῦτο ἔπραττεν, οὐδὲ
περιῄεσαν τὰς πόλεις ἀποδιδόμενοι τοὺς θεούς, ἀλλ᾽
ἀπάγοντες μόνον τὰς αὐτῶν χεῖρας καὶ ὄργανα λι-
θουργὰ καὶ ἐλεφαντουργά, ὕλην τε παρατιθέμενοι
ἀργὸν ἐν αὐτοῖς τοῖς ἱεροῖς, τὰς δημιουργίας ἐποιοῦντο, σὺ δ᾽ ὥσπερ τὰ Ὑρκανικά τε καὶ Σκυθικά,
ἀπείη δὲ εἰπεῖν τινα, οὕτω τοὺς θεοὺς ἐς τοὺς λιμένας
τε καὶ τὰς ἀγορὰς ἄγων οὐδὲν οἴει ἀσεβὲς πράττειν;

3   "Καὶ μὴν καὶ σπερμολογοῦσιν ἔνιοι τῶν ἀνθρώπων, ἐξαψάμενοί τι Δήμητρος ἢ Διονύσου ἄγαλμα καὶ
τρέφεσθαί φασιν ὑπὸ τῶν θεῶν, οὓς φέρουσι, τὸ δ᾽

34

with its sails and about to leave for Ionia. The captain tried to prevent his coming aboard, saying that the ship was on a private run. "What is the cargo?" asked Apollonius. "I am exporting statues of the gods to Ionia," he replied, "some of gold and marble, others of ivory and gold." "In order to dedicate them," asked Apollonius, "or for some other purpose?" "To sell them," was the reply, "to those who wish to dedicate them." "Well then, my friend, are you afraid that we will pilfer the statues on the ship?" "I am not afraid of that," said the other, "but I consider it wrong that they should sail with a large crowd, and be infected by bad company and the way of life on ships."

"And yet, my friend," said Apollonius, "I take you for an   2 Athenian, and the ships which you used against the barbarians were full of disorderly sailors,[29] yet the gods embarked on them in your company without considering themselves polluted by you. Yet are you so foolishly banning philosophers from your ship, men whom the gods approve more than all others, and yet you are trafficking in the gods? The sculptors of old did not do such things, and they did not go round the cities selling the gods. They brought merely their own hands with them, and their tools for working stone and ivory. Taking raw material, they plied their craft in the very sanctuaries. Yet when you treat the gods like wares from Hyrcania or Scythia (I will not say what kind of wares), and transport them to harbors and marketplaces, do you not realize what an impiety you are committing?

"Why, some people hang an image of Demeter or Dio-   3 nysus around their necks, and then prattle that their portable gods are giving them a livelihood. But to live off the

[29] In the battle of Salamis in 480, cf. Herodotus VIII 64–65.

αὐτοὺς σιτεῖσθαι τοὺς θεοὺς καὶ μηδ᾽ ἐμπίπλασθαι
τούτου,[19] δεινῆς ἐμπορίας, εἴποιμι δ᾽ ἂν καὶ ἀνοίας, εἰ
μηδὲν ἐκ τούτου δέδοικας." τοιαῦτα ἐπιπλήξας ἐπὶ
νεὼς ἑτέρας ἔπλει.

21. Καταπλεύσας δὲ ἐς τὴν Χίον, καὶ μηδὲ τὸν
πόδα ἐς τὴν γῆν ἐρείσας, μετεπήδησεν ἐς τὴν ναῦν
τὴν πλησίον (ἐκήρυττε δ᾽ ἡ ναῦς ἐς Ῥόδον). καὶ οἱ
ἑταῖροι δὲ μετεπήδων οὐδὲν εἰπόντες, ἐφιλοσοφεῖτο
γὰρ αὐτοῖς μάλιστα τὸ ἕπεσθαι λέγοντί τε καὶ πράτ-
τοντι. εὐφόρῳ δὲ περαιωθεὶς πνεύματι τάδε ἐσπούδα-
σεν ἐν τῇ Ῥόδῳ· προσιόντα αὐτὸν τῷ τοῦ Κολοσσοῦ
ἀγάλματι ἤρετο ὁ Δάμις, τί ἡγοῖτο ἐκείνου μεῖζον; ὁ
δὲ εἶπεν, "ἄνδρα φιλοσοφοῦντα ὑγιῶς τε καὶ ἀδόλως."

2 Ἐπεχωρίαζε τότε τῇ Ῥόδῳ Κάνος αὐλητής, ὃς
ἄριστα δὴ ἀνθρώπων ἐδόκει αὐλεῖν. καλέσας οὖν
αὐτὸν "τί" ἔφη "ὁ αὐλητὴς ἐργάζεται;" "πᾶν," εἶπεν
"ὅπερ ἂν ὁ ἀκροατὴς βούληται." "καὶ μὴν πολλοὶ"
ἔφη "τῶν ἀκροωμένων πλουτεῖν βούλονται μᾶλλον ἢ
αὐλοῦ ἀκούειν· πλουσίους οὖν ἀποφαίνεις, οὓς ἂν
ἐπιθυμοῦντας τούτου αἴσθῃ;" "οὐδαμῶς," εἶπεν "ὡς
ἐβουλόμην ἄν." "τί δ᾽; εὐειδεῖς ἐργάζῃ τοὺς νέους
τῶν ἀκροατῶν; ἐπειδὴ καλοὶ βούλονται δοκεῖν πάντες,
περὶ οὓς νεότης ἐστίν." "οὐδὲ τοῦτο" ἔφη "καίτοι
πλεῖστον ἀφροδίτης ἔχων ἐν τῷ αὐλῷ."

3 "Τί οὖν ἐστιν," εἶπεν "ὃ τὸν ἀκροατὴν ἡγῇ βούλεσθαι;" "τί δὲ ἄλλο γε," ἦ δ᾽ ὁ Κάνος "ἢ τὸν λυ-

[19] τούτου Rsk.: τούτους

gods themselves, and never to be satisfied—what a horrible trade, or rather what madness, if you do not fear some dreadful consequence!" After issuing this rebuke, he sailed on another vessel.

21. Putting in at Chios, without even setting foot on land he transferred to the ship lying alongside, which gave its destination as Rhodes, and his companions too did the same without a word, since their chief aim in philosophy was to follow whatever he said or did. He crossed with a fair wind, and made the following observations while on Rhodes. As he approached the statue of the Colossus,[30] Damis asked him whether there was anything he thought greater, and he replied, "A true man who pursues wisdom honestly and sincerely."

At the time the piper Canus,[31] thought to be the most 2 skilful piper in the world, was visiting Rhodes. Apollonius summoned him and said, "What is it that the piper does?" "Everything that the listener wishes," was the reply. "Yet many listeners," said Apollonius, "want to be rich rather than hear the pipe; so do you make people rich if you see that that is their desire?" "Of course not," was the answer, "I wish I could," "Well then, do you make your youthful listeners handsome? Since everyone wants to seem attractive, if they have youth." "No, not that either," said Canus, "though my music has great power to inspire love."

"What is it, then," said Apollonius, "that you think your 3 hearer wishes?" "Well," said Canus, "obviously someone in

[30] Colossal statue of the Sun god (Helios), standing in the harbor of Rhodes.

[31] Well known virtuoso on the aulos, an instrument somewhat resembling the modern clarinet.

πούμενον μὲν κοιμίζεσθαι αὐτῷ τὴν λύπην ὑπὸ τοῦ
αὐλοῦ, τὸν δὲ χαίροντα ἱλαρώτερον ἑαυτοῦ γίγνεσθαι,
τὸν δὲ ἐρῶντα θερμότερον, τὸν δὲ φιλοθύτην ἐνθεώ-
τερόν τε καὶ ὑμνῴδη·" "τοῦτο οὖν," ἔφη "ὦ Κάνε,
πότερον αὐτὸς ἐργάζεται ὁ αὐλὸς διὰ τὸ χρυσοῦ τε καὶ
ὀρειχάλκου καὶ ἐλάφων κνήμης ξυγκεῖσθαι, οἱ δὲ καὶ
ὄνων, ἢ ἕτερόν ἐστιν, ὃ ταῦτα δύναται;" "ἕτερον" ἔφη
"ὦ Ἀπολλώνιε, ἡ γὰρ μουσικὴ καὶ οἱ τρόποι καὶ τὸ
ἀναμὶξ καὶ τὸ εὐμετάβολον τῆς αὐλήσεως καὶ τὰ τῶν
ἁρμονιῶν ἤθη, ταῦτα τοὺς ἀκροωμένους ἁρμόττει καὶ
τὰς ψυχὰς ἐργάζεται σφῶν, ὁποίας βούλονται."

4   "Ξυνῆκα" ἔφη "ὦ Κάνε, ὅ τι σοι ἡ τέχνη πράττει·
τὸ γὰρ ποικίλον αὐτῆς καὶ τὸ ἐς πάντας τρόπους,
τοῦτο ἐξασκεῖς τε καὶ παρέχεις τοῖς παρὰ σὲ φοιτῶσιν. ἐμοὶ δὲ πρὸς τοῖς ὑπὸ σοῦ εἰρημένοις καὶ
ἑτέρων δοκεῖ ὁ αὐλὸς δεῖσθαι· τῆς τε εὐπνοίας καὶ τῆς
εὐστομίας καὶ τοῦ εὔχειρα εἶναι τὸν αὐλοῦντα, ἔστι δὲ
εὔπνοια μέν, ἢν τορὸν καὶ λευκὸν ᾖ τὸ πνεῦμα καὶ μὴ
ἐπικτυπῇ ἡ φάρυγξ, τουτὶ γὰρ ἔοικε φθόγγῳ ἀμούσῳ,
εὐστομία δέ, ἢν τὰ χείλη ἐνθέμενα τὴν τοῦ αὐλοῦ
γλῶτταν μὴ πιμπραμένου τοῦ προσώπου αὐλῇ, τὸν δὲ
εὔχειρα αὐλητὴν πολλοῦ ἡγοῦμαι ἄξιον, ἢν μήτε ὁ
καρπὸς ἀπαγορεύῃ ἀνακλώμενος μήτε οἱ δάκτυλοι
βραδεῖς ὦσιν ἐπιπέτεσθαι τοῖς φθόγγοις, καὶ γὰρ τὸ
ταχέως μεταβάλλειν ἐκ τρόπου ἐς τρόπον περὶ τοὺς
εὔχειράς ἐστι μᾶλλον. εἰ δὴ ταῦτα πάντα παρέχεις,
θαρρῶν αὔλει, ὦ Κάνε, μετὰ σοῦ γὰρ ἡ Εὐτέρπη
ἔσται."

grief wishes his grief to be allayed by the pipe, someone happy to become more cheerful still, someone in love to become more passionate, someone devoted to religion to become more inspired and enchanted." "Well then, Canus," said Apollonius, "is this an effect of the pipe itself, that comes from its being made of gold, brass, and the shank bone of either a deer or a donkey, or it is something else that has this power?" "Something else, Apollonius," said Canus; "it is the music, the modes, the variety and versatility of the pipe, the character of the keys, all this is what makes the hearers composed and puts their minds into the state they want them to be."

"I see, Canus," said Apollonius, "what your art does. 4 You cultivate its variety and its multiplicity of modes, and you exhibit them to your audience. But in addition to what you mentioned, I think that the pipe needs other things: breath and lip control, and dexterity on the player's part. Breath control means that the breath is clear and pure, and the windpipe does not squawk, since that is considered an unmusical sound. Lip control is when the reed of the pipe is placed between the lips, and they play without distending the face. I attach great importance to the dexterous piper, whose wrist does not tire from bending, whose fingers are not reluctant to fly over the stops. Modulating quickly from one mode to another requires dexterity above all. If you can exhibit all this, Canus, have no fear about playing, since Euterpe[32] will be with you."

[32] Muse associated with "good pleasure" (*eu terpein*).

22. Ἐτύγχανέ τι καὶ μειράκιον νεόπλουτόν τε καὶ ἀπαίδευτον οἰκοδομούμενον οἰκίαν τινὰ ἐν τῇ Ῥόδῳ, καὶ ξυμφέρον ἐς αὐτὴν γραφάς τε ποικίλας καὶ λίθους ἐξ ἁπάντων ἐθνῶν. ἤρετο οὖν αὐτό, ὁπόσα χρήματα εἴη ἐς διδασκάλους τε καὶ παιδείαν ἀνηλωκός· ὁ δὲ "οὐδὲ δραχμήν" εἶπεν. "ἐς δὲ τὴν οἰκίαν πόσα;" "δώδεκα" ἔφη "τάλαντα, προσαναλώσαιμι δ' ἂν καὶ ἕτερα τοσαῦτα." "τί δ'" εἶπεν "ἡ οἰκία βούλεταί σοι;" "δίαιτα" ἔφη "λαμπρὰ ἔσται τῷ σώματι, καὶ γὰρ δρόμοι ἐν αὐτῇ καὶ ἄλση, καὶ ὀλίγα ἐς ἀγορὰν βαδιοῦμαι καὶ προσεροῦσί με οἱ ἐσιόντες ἥδιον, ὥσπερ ἐς ἱερὸν φοιτῶντες."

2   "Ζηλωτότεροι δὲ" εἶπεν "οἱ ἄνθρωποι πότερον δι' αὐτούς εἰσιν ἢ διὰ τὰ περὶ αὐτοὺς ὄντα;" "διὰ τὸν πλοῦτον," εἶπε, "τὰ γὰρ χρήματα πλεῖστον ἰσχύει." "χρημάτων δ'," ἔφη "ὦ μειράκιον, ἀμείνων φύλαξ πότερον ὁ πεπαιδευμένος ἔσται ἢ ὁ ἀπαίδευτος;" ἐπεὶ δὲ ἐσιώπησε, "δοκεῖς μοι," εἶπε "μειράκιον, οὐ σὺ τὴν οἰκίαν, ἀλλὰ σὲ ἡ οἰκία κεκτῆσθαι. ἐγὼ δὲ ἐς ἱερὸν παρελθὼν πολλῷ ἂν ἥδιον ἐν αὐτῷ μικρῷ ὄντι ἄγαλμα ἐλέφαντός τε καὶ χρυσοῦ ἴδοιμι ἢ ἐν μεγάλῳ κεραμεοῦν τε καὶ φαῦλον."

23. Νεανίαν δὲ ἰδὼν πίονα καὶ φρονοῦντα ἐπὶ τῷ πλεῖστα μὲν ἀνθρώπων ἐσθίειν, πλεῖστον δὲ οἶνον πίνειν "ἀλλ' ἦ σὺ" ἔφη "τυγχάνεις ὢν ὁ γαστριζόμενος;" "καὶ θύω γε" εἶπεν "ὑπὲρ τούτου." "τί οὖν" ἔφη "ἀπολέλαυκας τῆς βορᾶς ταύτης;" "τὸ θαυμάζεσθαί με καὶ ἀποβλέπεσθαι· καὶ γὰρ τὸν Ἡρα-

22. It happened that a young man, who had recently come into wealth but lacked culture, had built a house on Rhodes and was collecting various pictures and marble[33] from every region. When Apollonius asked him how much money he had spent on teachers and education, he replied, "Not a drachma." "And how much on your house?" "Twelve talents," was the reply, "and I may spend the same amount again." "What do you expect from your house?" asked Apollonius. "It will provide an excellent physical setting, since it has avenues and groves. I will only rarely go out into public, and my visitors will be all the more glad to address me, as if they were visiting a sanctuary."

"Are people more envied," asked Apollonius, "on their own account or for their advantages?" "For their wealth," said the man, "since money has very great influence." "And will someone well educated, young man," asked Apollonius, "be a better guardian of his money than someone uneducated?" The other did not reply, and Apollonius said, "In my opinion, young man, you do not own the house, the house owns you. When I go into a sanctuary, I would much prefer to see an image of ivory and gold in a small one, than a cheap idol of clay in a large one."

23. Seeing a fat young man who prided himself on eating more food and drinking more wine than anyone on earth, he said, "Would you be the glutton, by any chance?" "Yes," was the reply, "and I thank the gods that I am." "And what advantage," asked Apollonius, "have you gotten from this ravenousness?" "Admiration and celebrity," was the reply, "for doubtless you have heard of Heracles, and how

[33] Colored marble used as facing in walls and floors.

κλέα ἴσως ἀκούεις, ὡς καὶ τὰ σιτία αὐτοῦ παραπλησίως τοῖς ἄθλοις ᾔδετο." "Ἡρακλέους" ἔφη "ὄντος·
σοῦ δὲ τίς, ὦ κάθαρμα, ἀρετή; τὸ γὰρ περίβλεπτον ἐν
μόνῳ λείπεταί σοι τῷ ῥαγῆναι." τοιάδε μὲν αὐτῷ τὰ ἐν
τῇ Ῥόδῳ,

24. Τὰ δὲ ἐν τῇ Ἀλεξανδρείᾳ, ἐπειδὴ ἐσέπλευσεν· ἡ
Ἀλεξάνδρεια καὶ ἀπόντος μὲν αὐτοῦ ἤρα καὶ ἐπόθουν
τὸν Ἀπολλώνιον, ὡς εἷς ἕνα, καὶ ἡ Αἴγυπτος δὲ ἡ ἄνω
μεστοὶ θεολογίας ὄντες καὶ φοιτῆσαι αὐτὸν ἐς τὰ ἤθη
τὰ αὑτῶν ηὔχοντο, ἅτε γὰρ πολλῶν ἀφικνουμένων μὲν
ἐνθένδε ἐς Αἴγυπτον, πολλῶν δὲ ἐπιμιγνύντων δεῦρο
ἐξ Αἰγύπτου ᾔδετό τε παρ' αὐτοῖς Ἀπολλώνιος καὶ τὰ
ὦτα ἐς αὐτὸν Αἰγυπτίοις ὀρθὰ ἦν· προϊόντα γέ τοι ἀπὸ
τῆς νεὼς ἐς τὸ ἄστυ θεῷ ἴσα ἀπέβλεπον καὶ διεχώ-
ρουν τῶν στενωπῶν, ὥσπερ τοῖς φέρουσι τὰ ἱερά.
παραπεμπομένου δὲ αὐτοῦ μᾶλλον ἢ οἱ τῶν ἐθνῶν
ἡγεμόνες,

2   Ἄνδρες ἤγοντο τὴν ἐπὶ θανάτῳ δώδεκα λῃσταὶ τὴν
αἰτίαν, ὁ δὲ ἐς αὐτοὺς ἰδὼν "οὐ πάντες," εἶπεν "ὁ δεῖνα
γὰρ καταψευσθεὶς ἄπεισι." καὶ πρὸς τοὺς δημίους, ὑφ'
ὧν ἤγοντο, "ὑφεῖναι" ἔφη "κελεύω τοῦ δρόμου καὶ
σχολαιότερον ἥκειν ἐπὶ τὸ ὄρυγμα ὕστατόν τε ἀποκτεῖναι τοῦτον, μετέχει γὰρ οὐδὲν τῆς αἰτιάσεως, ἀλλ'
ὑμεῖς γε ὅσια πράττοιτε φειδόμενοι τούτων βραχὺ
μέρος ἡμέρας, οὓς λῷον ἦν μηδ' ἀποκτείνειν"· καὶ ἅμα
ἐνδιέτριβεν οἷς ἔλεγεν, οὐκ εἰωθὸς ἑαυτῷ ἀποτείνων
μῆκος. τί δ' αὐτῷ ἐνόει τοῦτο, αὐτίκα ἐδείχθη· ὀκτὼ
γὰρ ἤδη ἀποτετμημένων τὰς κεφαλὰς ἱππεὺς ἐλαύνων

his dinners were recorded in song no less than his labors."
"He was Heracles," said Apollonius, "but what good is
there in you, you scum? The only celebrity left for you is to
explode." So much for his doings in Rhodes.

24. This is what he did in Alexandria. The Alexandrians
doted on him even before he arrived, and longed for Apollonius as one human being does another, and the people of
Upper Egypt, who are full of sacred lore, prayed for him to
visit their region too. The reason was that many people
travel from here to Egypt, and many come here as visitors
from Egypt, so that Apollonius was a celebrity there, and
the Egyptians were all ears for him. As he proceeded from
the ship to the city, they looked on him as a god, and parted
before him in the streets as for those carrying the sacred
objects, and he received a greater escort than the governors of the provinces.

Now twelve men were being led to execution on con-   2
viction of robbery, and looking at them Apollonius said,
"Not all, for one of them has been falsely accused and will
go free." To the executioners who were conducting them
he said, "I order you to slacken your pace, to go more
slowly to the pit,[34] and to kill this one last, since he has
nothing to do with the charge. It would be an act of piety if
you spared these men for a small part of the day; it would
be better that you did not kill them at all." At the same time
he lingered over his speech, drawing it out to a length un-
usual for him, and his purpose in doing so quickly became
apparent. When eight of the men had had their heads

[34] Pit at which criminals were executed before their bodies
were thrown in.

ἐπὶ τὸ ὄρυγμα "Φαρίωνος" ἐβόα "φείσασθε," μὴ γὰρ
εἶναι λῃστὴν αὐτόν, ἀλλ' ἑαυτοῦ μὲν κατεψεῦσθαι δέει
τοῦ στρεβλώσεσθαι, βασανισθέντων δὲ ἑτέρων χρηστὸν ὁμολογῆσθαι ἄνδρα. ἐῶ τὸ πήδημα τῆς Αἰγύπτου καὶ ὅσον ἐπὶ τούτῳ ἐκρότησαν καὶ ἄλλως θαυμα-
στικοὶ ὄντες.

25. Ἀνελθόντι δὲ αὐτῷ ἐς τὸ ἱερὸν ὁ μὲν κόσμος ὁ
περὶ αὐτὸ καὶ ὁ ἐφ' ἑκάστῳ λόγος θεῖός τε ἐφαίνετο
καὶ κατὰ σοφίαν ξυντεθείς, τὸ δὲ τῶν ταύρων αἷμα καὶ
οἱ χῆνες καὶ ὁπόσα ἐθύετο, οὐκ ἐπῄνει τὰ τοιάδε, οὐδὲ
ἐς δαῖτας θεῶν ἦγεν· ἐρομένου δ' αὐτὸν τοῦ ἱερέως, τί
μαθὼν οὐχ οὕτω θύοι, "σὺ μὲν οὖν" εἶπεν "ἀπόκριναί
μοι μᾶλλον, τί μαθὼν οὕτω θύεις;" εἰπόντος δὲ τοῦ
ἱερέως "καὶ τίς οὕτω δεινός, ὡς διορθοῦσθαι τὰ Αἰγυπτίων;" "πᾶς" ἔφη "σοφός, ἢν ἀπ' Ἰνδῶν ἥκῃ. καὶ
βοῦν" ἔφη "ἀπανθρακιῶ τήμερον καὶ κοινώνει τοῦ
καπνοῦ ἡμῖν, οὐ γὰρ ἀχθέσῃ περὶ τῆς μοίρας, εἰ
κἀκείνην οἱ θεοὶ δαίσονται."

2   Τηκομένου δὲ τοῦ πλάσματος, "ὅρα" ἔφη "τὰ ἱερά."
"ποῖα;" εἶπεν ὁ Αἰγύπτιος "ὁρῶ γὰρ οὐδὲν ἐνθάδε." ὁ
δὲ Ἀπολλώνιος "οἱ δὲ Ἰαμίδαι" εἶπε "καὶ οἱ Τελλιάδαι[20] καὶ οἱ Κλυτιάδαι καὶ τὸ τῶν Μελαμποδιδῶν
μαντεῖον ἐλήρησαν, ὦ λῷστε, τοσαῦτα μὲν περὶ πυρὸς
εἰπόντες, τοσαύτας δὲ ἀπ' αὐτοῦ ξυλλεξάμενοι φήμας;
ἢ τὸ μὲν ἀπὸ τῆς πεύκης πῦρ καὶ τὸ ἀπὸ τῆς κέδρου

---

[20] Τελλιάδαι P. Leopardus (Kay.): Τελεάδαι

44

cut off, a horsemen rode up to the pit shouting, "Spare Pharion." He was not a bandit, it seemed, but had falsely accused himself from fear of being tortured, and the interrogation of the others had proved him a good man. I pass over the way the Egyptians jumped for joy and cheered this outcome, prone to enthusiasm as they are.

25. When Apollonius had climbed to the sanctuary,[35] its decoration and the lore attached to every part he considered inspired and arranged with wisdom, but he did not approve of the bull's blood, the geese, and all the things offered for sacrifice, nor did he consider them feasts for the gods. The priest asked him on what ground he did not practice this kind of sacrifice, and he replied, "Rather you should answer me on what ground you practice it." The priest replied, "Who is so clever as to correct the customs of Egypt?" "Any wise man," said Apollonius, "if he comes from India. I will roast a bull today," he continued, "and you can join with us in tasting the smoke. You will not complain about your portion, since that is what the gods devour too."[36]

As the figurine melted, Apollonius said, "Behold the rites." "What rites?" said the Egyptian; "I see nothing here." "Were the clan of Iamos," asked Apollonius, "of Tellias, of Clytias, was the oracle of Melampus's clan talking nonsense, my good friend, in all they said about fire, and all the predictions that they derived from it?[37] Or do you think that the fire arising from pinewood and cedar is

2

35 The Serapeum, situated on the hill called Rhacotis.

36 Apollonius sacrifices a bull made of incense: cf. Pythagoras's ox made of pastry, I 1.3.

37 Prophetic families, particularly associated with Olympia.

μαντικὸν ἡγῇ καὶ ἱκανὸν δηλῶσαί τι, τὸ δ' ἀπὸ τοῦ
πιοτάτου τε καὶ καθαρωτάτου δακρύου καόμενον οὐ
πολλῷ αἱρετώτερον; εἰ δ' ἐμπύρου σοφίας ἦσθα εὐ-
ξύνετος, εἶδες ἂν καὶ ἐν τῷ τοῦ ἡλίου κύκλῳ πολλὰ
δηλούμενα, ὁπότε ἀνίσχει." τούτοις ἐπέκοπτε[21] τὸν
Αἰγύπτιον ὡς ἀμαθῆ τῶν θείων.

26. Προσκειμένης δὲ τῆς Ἀλεξανδρείας ἵπποις καὶ
ξυμφοιτώσης μὲν ἐς τὸν ἱππόδρομον ἐπὶ τῇ θέᾳ ταύτῃ,
μιαιφονούντων δὲ ἀλλήλους, ἐπίπληξιν ὑπὲρ τούτων
ἐποιεῖτο, καὶ παρελθὼν ἐς τὸ ἱερὸν "ποῖ" ἔφη "παρα-
τενεῖτε ἀποθνήσκοντες οὐχ ὑπὲρ τέκνων οὐδὲ ἱερῶν,
ἀλλ' ὡς χραίνοιτε μὲν τὰ ἱερά, λύθρου μεστοὶ ἐς ταῦτα
ἥκοντες, φθείροισθε δὲ ἔσω τείχους; καὶ Τροίαν μέν,
ὡς ἔοικεν, ἵππος εἷς διεπόρθησεν, ὃν ἐσοφίσαντο οἱ
Ἀχαιοὶ τότε, ἐφ' ὑμᾶς δὲ ἅρματα ἔζευκται καὶ ἵπποι,
δι' οὓς οὐκ ἔστιν ὑμῖν εὐηνίως ζῆν· ἀπόλλυσθε γοῦν
οὐχ ὑπὸ Ἀτρειδῶν, οὐδ' ὑπὸ Αἰακιδῶν, ἀλλ' ὑπ' ἀλλήλων, ὃ μηδ' οἱ Τρῶες ἐν τῇ μέθῃ.

2   "Κατὰ μὲν οὖν τὴν Ὀλυμπίαν, οὗ πάλης καὶ πυ-
γμῆς καὶ τοῦ παγκρατιάζειν ἆθλα, οὐδεὶς ὑπὲρ ἀθλητῶν ἀπέθανεν, ἴσως καὶ ξυγγνώμης ὑπαρχούσης, εἴ
τις ὑπερσπουδάζοι περὶ τὸ ὁμόφυλον, ὑπὲρ δὲ ἵππων
ἐνταῦθα γυμνὰ μὲν ὑμῖν ἐπ' ἀλλήλους ξίφη, βολαὶ δὲ
ἕτοιμοι λίθων. πῦρ δὲ ἐπὶ τὴν τοιαύτην πόλιν, ἔνθα
οἰμωγή τε καὶ ὕβρις 'ὀλλύντων τε καὶ ὀλλυμένων, ῥέει
δ' αἵματι γαῖα.' αἰδέσθητε τὸν κοινὸν τῆς Αἰγύπτου

---

[21] ἐπέκοπτε Cob.: ἐπέσκωπτε

46

prophetic and able to tell us something, and not that the flame given off by gum of the greatest and richest purity is far preferable? If you understood the wisdom embodied in fire, you would see many things that are revealed in the sun's disk as it rises." With these words he reproved the Egyptian for his ignorance of holy matters.

26. Now the Alexandrians are devoted to horses, and assemble in the hippodrome to watch them. When they started slaughtering one another, Apollonius issued a rebuke to them on the matter. Entering the sanctuary, he said, "How long will you persist in dying not for your children's sake or for your sanctuaries, but in order to pollute the sanctuaries by entering them all covered with gore, and to perish within your own city wall? Troy, they say, was sacked by a single horse, cunningly built by the Achaeans of that time, but chariots and horses have been yoked to destroy you, and they prevent you from reining in your lives. You are being ruined, not by the sons of Atreus or Aeacus, but by one another, as not even the drunken Trojans were.[38]

"Now in Olympia, there are prizes for wrestling, box- 2 ing, and the pancration, but no one has died because of the athletes, though overenthusiasm for a compatriot might perhaps be excused. But here mere horses make you unsheathe swords against one another and prepare to throw stones. Fire awaits such a city, where there is groaning and violence 'of the killers and the killed, and the ground runs red with blood.'[39] Respect the Nile, the joint mixing bowl

[38] The Trojans were celebrating the supposed retreat of the Greeks when they were overcome by the ruse of the wooden horse. [39] *Iliad* 4.451.

κρατῆρα Νεῖλον. ἀλλὰ τί Νείλου μνημονεύω πρὸς
ἀνθρώπους αἵματος ἀναβάσεις διαμετροῦντας μᾶλλον ἢ ὕδατος;" καὶ πλείω ἐς τὴν ἐπίπληξιν ταύτην
διελέχθη ἕτερα, ὡς διδάσκει ὁ Δάμις.

27. Οὐεσπασιανοῦ δὲ τὴν αὐτοκράτορα ἀρχὴν
περινοοῦντος περὶ τὰ ὅμορα τῇ Αἰγύπτῳ ἔθνη, καὶ
προχωροῦντος ἐπὶ τὴν Αἴγυπτον, Δίωνες μὲν καὶ Εὐ-
φρᾶται, περὶ ὧν μικρὸν ὕστερον εἰρήσεται, χαίρειν
παρεκελεύοντο. μετὰ γὰρ τὸν πρῶτον αὐτοκράτορα,
ὑφ' οὗ τὰ Ῥωμαίων διεκοσμήθη, τυραννίδες οὕτω
χαλεπαὶ ἴσχυσαν ἐπὶ πεντήκοντα ἔτη, ὡς μηδὲ Κλαύδιον τὰ μέσα τούτων τρισκαίδεκα ἄρξαντα χρηστὸν
δόξαι· καίτοι πεντηκοντούτης μὲν ἐς τὸ ἄρχειν παρῆλθεν, ὅτε νοῦς μάλιστα ὑγιαίνει ἀνθρώπων, παιδείας δὲ
ξυμπάσης ἐδόκει ἐρᾶν. ἀλλὰ κἀκεῖνος τηλικόσδε ὢν
πολλὰ μειρακιώδη ἔπαθε καὶ μηλόβοτον γυναίοις τὴν
ἀρχὴν ἀνῆκεν, ὑφ' ὧν οὕτω ῥᾳθύμως ἀπέθανεν, ὡς
καίτοι προγιγνώσκων ἃ ἔμελλε[22] πείσεσθαι, μηδ' ἃ
προῄδει φυλάξασθαι.

2   Ἀπολλώνιος δὲ παραπλησίως μὲν Εὐφράτῃ καὶ
Δίωνι περὶ τούτων ἔχαιρε, μελέτην δ' αὐτὰ οὐκ ἐποιεῖτο ἐς πάντας, ῥητορικωτέραν ἡγούμενος τὴν τοιάνδε
ἰδέαν τοῦ λόγου, προσιόντι δὲ τῷ αὐτοκράτορι τὰ μὲν

____

22 ἔμελλε Kay.: μέλλει

____

40 Cities of Egypt used "nilometers," special devices for mea-
suring the level of the Nile.

of Egypt. But why do I mention the Nile to people who measure the rising of blood rather than of water?"[40] He said much more in issuing this rebuke, as we learn from Damis.

27. Vespasian was meditating on the imperial power when he was in the countries bordering Egypt.[41] As he approached it, people like Dio and Euphrates, whom I shall mention shortly, encouraged general rejoicing. After the first emperor who set the affairs of Rome in order,[42] harsh tyrannies had lasted for fifty years, so that even Claudius, who ruled for thirteen years in the middle of this period,[43] did not seem virtuous, even though he rose to power at the age of fifty, when human intelligence is at its highest, and he was considered a devotee of every kind of culture. Even at his age, however, he underwent the vicissitudes of youth, and allowed his power to be nibbled away by mere women. These caused his death, for despite knowing the fate in store for him, he was too careless to guard even against what he foresaw.[44]

Apollonius was no less pleased than Euphrates and Dio 2 about these events, but he did not make them the subject of a declamation, considering that style of discourse to be too rhetorical. When the emperor approached, he was met

[41] Vespasian's rise to power began when he was fighting the Jewish War, but he was first declared emperor by Roman troops in Egypt. In the rest of this book Philostratus calls him "emperor" when in fact Vitellius was still the acknowledged ruler in Rome (cf. 29.3).   [42] Augustus, reigned 31 BCE to 14 CE.

[43] 41–54 CE. Philostratus reckons "fifty years" roughly from Augustus's death to the year 69.

[44] Claudius was poisoned by his wife Agrippina.

ἱερὰ πρὸ πυλῶν ἀπήντα καὶ τὰ τῆς Αἰγύπτου τέλη καὶ οἱ νομοί, καθ' οὓς Αἴγυπτος τέτμηται, φιλόσοφοί τε ὡσαύτως καὶ σοφία πᾶσα, ὁ δὲ Ἀπολλώνιος οὐδὲν ἐπολυπραγμόνει τούτων, ἀλλὰ ἐσπούδαζεν ἐν τῷ ἱερῷ.

3   Διαλεχθεὶς δὲ ὁ αὐτοκράτωρ γενναῖά τε καὶ ἥμερα, καὶ διελθὼν λόγον οὐ μακρόν, "ἐπιδημεῖ" ἔφη "ὁ Τυανεύς;" "ναί," ἔφασαν "βελτίους γε ἡμᾶς ἐργασάμενος." "πῶς ἂν οὖν ξυγγένοιτο ἡμῖν;" ἔφη "σφόδρα γὰρ δέομαι τοῦ ἀνδρός." "ἐντεύξεταί σοι περὶ τὸ ἱερόν," ὁ Δίων εἶπε "πρὸς ἐμὲ γὰρ δεῦρο ἥκοντα ὡμολόγει ταῦτα." "ἴωμεν" ἔφη ὁ βασιλεὺς "προσευξόμενοι μὲν τοῖς θεοῖς, ξυνεσόμενοι δὲ ἀνδρὶ γενναίῳ." ἐντεῦθεν ἀνέφυ λόγος, ὡς ἐνθύμιος μὲν αὐτῷ ἡ ἀρχὴ γένοιτο πολιορκοῦντι τὰ Σόλυμα, μεταπέμποιτο δὲ τὸν Ἀπολλώνιον ὑπὲρ βουλῆς τούτων, ὁ δὲ παραιτοῖτο ἥκειν ἐς γῆν, ἣν ἐμίαναν οἱ ἐν αὐτῇ οἰκοῦντες οἷς τε ἔδρασαν οἷς τε ἔπαθον· ὅθεν αὐτὸς ἐλθεῖν ἐς Αἴγυπτον τὴν μὲν ἀρχὴν κεκτημένος, διαλεξόμενος δὲ τῷ ἀνδρὶ ὁπόσα δηλώσω.

28. Θύσας γάρ, καὶ οὔπω χρηματίσας κατ' ἀξίαν ταῖς πόλεσι, προσεῖπε τὸν Ἀπολλώνιον καὶ ὥσπερ εὐχόμενος αὐτῷ "ποίησόν με" ἔφη "βασιλέα." ὁ δὲ "ἐποίησα," εἶπεν, "ἤδη γὰρ εὐξάμενος βασιλέα δίκαιόν τε καὶ γενναῖον καὶ σώφρονα, καὶ πολιᾷ κεκοσμημένον καὶ πατέρα παίδων γνησίων, σὲ δήπου παρὰ τῶν θεῶν ᾔτουν ἐγώ." ὑπερησθεὶς δὲ τούτοις ὁ βασιλεύς, καὶ γὰρ ἐβόησε τὸ ἐν τῷ ἱερῷ πλῆθος ξυντιθέμενοι τῷ λόγῳ, "τί σοι" ἔφη "Νέρωνος ἀρχὴ ἐφαίνετο;"

before the gates by the priests, the officials of Egypt and the districts into which Egypt is parceled, and by philosophers and every kind of wise man. Apollonius, however, did not meddle in any of this, but stayed conversing in the sanctuary.

The emperor conversed nobly and kindly, and after reciting a short speech said, "Is the man from Tyana here?" "Yes," they answered, "and he has made us better people." "Is there some way he might join us?" the emperor asked, "since I greatly wish to meet the Master." Dio replied, "He will meet you at the temple, for so he agreed with me on my arrival." "Let us go there," said the emperor, "to pray to the gods and meet a virtuous man." That gave rise to a story that Vespasian felt scruples about his power while besieging Jerusalem, and sent for Apollonius to advise him on the matter; but Apollonius refused to enter a country whose inhabitants defiled it by their actions and their misfortunes. It was said therefore that he himself had come to Egypt after achieving power, in order to converse with Apollonius, as I shall describe.

28. After sacrificing, and before he had given proper audience to the cities, he addressed Apollonius, and as if he was praying to him said, "Make me emperor." "I have done so," was the reply, "because I previously prayed for an emperor who was just, noble, and moderate, with becoming white hair, and the father of legitimate children, and it is clear that you are the answer to my prayers." The emperor was delighted by this, since the crowd in the sanctuary also cheered its agreement with Apollonius's speech.

καὶ ὁ Ἀπολλώνιος "Νέρων" εἶπε "κιθάραν μὲν ἴσως
ᾔδει ἁρμόττεσθαι, τὴν δὲ ἀρχὴν ᾔσχυνεν ἀνέσει καὶ
ἐπιτάσει."

2   "Ξύμμετρον οὖν" εἶπε "κελεύεις εἶναι τὸν ἄρχοντα;"
"οὐκ ἐγώ," εἶπε "θεὸς δὲ τὴν ἰσότητα μεσότητα ὁρι-
σάμενος. ἀγαθοὶ δὲ τούτων ξύμβουλοι καὶ οἵδε οἱ
ἄνδρες" τὸν Δίωνα δείξας καὶ τὸν Εὐφράτην μήπω
αὐτῷ ἐς διαφορὰν ἥκοντα. τότε δὴ ἀνασχὼν ὁ βασιλεὺς τὰς χεῖρας "ὦ Ζεῦ" ἔφη "σοφῶν μὲν ἐγὼ ἄρχοιμι,
σοφοὶ δὲ ἐμοῦ." καὶ ἐπιστρέψας ἑαυτὸν ἐς τοὺς Αἰγυπτίους "ἀρύσασθε," εἶπεν "ὡς Νείλου καὶ ἐμοῦ."

29. Ἡ μὲν δὴ Αἴγυπτος ὧδε ἀνέσχεν, ἀπειρηκότες
ἤδη δι᾽ ἃ ἐπιέζοντο. κατιὼν δὲ τοῦ ἱεροῦ ξυνῆψε τῷ
Ἀπολλωνίῳ τὴν χεῖρα, καὶ παραγαγὼν αὐτὸν ἐς τὰ
βασίλεια, "ἴσως" ἔφη "μειρακιώδης ἐνίοις δοκῶ, βασιλείας ἁπτόμενος περὶ ἔτος ἑξηκοστὸν τοῦ βίου·
δώσω οὖν ἀπολογίαν, ὡς ἀπολογοῖο ὑπὲρ ἐμοῦ τοῖς
ἄλλοις.

2   "Ἐγὼ γὰρ πλούτου μὲν ἡττηθεὶς οὐδὲ ἐν μειρακίῳ
ποτὲ οἶδα, τὰς δὲ ἀρχάς τε καὶ λαμπρότητας, ὁπόσαι
τῇ Ῥωμαίων ἀρχῇ προσήκουσιν, οὕτω σωφρόνως καὶ
μετρίως διεθέμην, ὡς μήτε ὑπέρφρων μήτ᾽ αὖ κατ-
επτηχὼς δόξαι, νεώτερα δὲ οὐδ᾽ ἐπὶ Νέρωνα ἐνεθυμήθην, ἀλλ᾽ ἐπειδὴ τὴν ἀρχήν, εἰ καὶ μὴ κατὰ νόμους,
παρ᾽ ἀνδρὸς γοῦν αὐτοκράτορος παραλαβὼν εἶχεν,
ὑφιέμην αὐτῷ διὰ τὸν Κλαύδιον, ὃς ὕπατόν τε ἀπ-
έδειξέ με καὶ ξύμβουλον τῶν ἑαυτοῦ· καὶ νὴ τὴν
Ἀθηνᾶν, ὁπότε Νέρωνα ἴδοιμι ἀσχημονοῦντα, δάκρυά

"What was your opinion of Nero's reign?" he asked. "Perhaps Nero knew how to tune a lyre," replied Apollonius, "but he disgraced his reign by making it too flat and too sharp."

"Is it your advice that a ruler should be well tempered, then?" said the emperor. "Not mine," was the reply, "but God's, who defined equality as moderation. On this subject you have good advisers in these men," pointing to Dio and Euphrates, who was not yet at odds with him. At this the emperor raised his hands and said, "Zeus, may I rule the wise, and may the wise rule me." And turning to the Egyptians he said, "Draw on me as you do on the Nile."

29. Thus Egypt recovered, after oppression had now driven it to despair. Vespasian, however, as he left the sanctuary, took Apollonius by the hand and, after leading him to the palace, said, "Some people perhaps think me like an adolescent for aiming at a throne when I am about sixty. I will therefore defend myself so that you will defend me to others.

"I do not remember that I was ever tempted by wealth even in my youth, and so moderately and reasonably did I manage the offices and honors that the Roman empire confers, that I was never thought either proud or on the contrary cowardly. Nor did I plan rebellion even against Nero, but since he had at least inherited his power from an emperor, even if not lawfully, I submitted to him for the sake of Claudius, who made me consul and his adviser.[45] I swear by Athena, whenever I saw Nero in disgrace, I shed

---

[45] Claudius had advanced Vespasian's career, and appointed him consul in 51.

μοι ἐξέπιπτεν ἐνθυμουμένῳ τὸν Κλαύδιον, ὑφ' οἵου
καθάρματος τὸ μέγιστον τῶν ἑαυτοῦ ἐκληρονομήθη.

3   "Ὁρῶν δὲ μηδ' ὁπότε Νέρων ἐκποδὼν γέγονεν ἐπὶ
τὸ λῷον μεθιστάμενα τὰ τῶν ἀνθρώπων, ἀλλ' οὕτως
ἀτίμως τὴν ἀρχὴν πράττουσαν, ὡς ἐπὶ Βιτελίῳ κεῖσθαι, θαρρῶν ἤδη ἐπ' αὐτὴν εἶμι, πρῶτον μέν, ἐπειδὴ
βούλομαι τοῖς ἀνθρώποις παρασχεῖν ἐμαυτὸν πολλοῦ
ἄξιον, εἶτα, ἐπειδὴ πρὸς ἄνθρωπον ὁ ἀγὼν ἔσται
κραιπαλῶντα· Βιτέλιος γὰρ μύρῳ μὲν λοῦται πλεῖον ἢ
ἐγὼ ὕδατι, δοκεῖ δέ μοι καὶ ξίφει πληγεὶς μύρον
ἐκδώσειν μᾶλλον ἢ αἷμα, οἴνῳ δὲ οἶνον ξυνάπτων
μαίνεται, καὶ κυβεύει μὲν δεδιὼς μή τι αὐτὸν οἱ πεττοὶ
σφήλωσιν, ὑπὲρ δὲ ἀρχῆς ἀναρριπτεῖ παίζων, ἑταί-
ραις δὲ ὑποκείμενος ἐπιθόρνυται ταῖς γεγαμημέναις,
ἡδίω φάσκων τὰ μετὰ κινδύνων ἐρωτικά.

4   "Ἐῶ τὰ ἀσελγέστερα, ὡς μὴ τοιαῦτα ἐπὶ σοῦ
λέγοιμι· μὴ δὴ περιίδοιμι Ῥωμαίους ὑπὸ τοιούτου
ἀρχθέντας, ἀλλ' ἡγεμόνας ποιούμενος τοὺς θεοὺς
ἀνὴρ γιγνοίμην ἐμαυτῷ ὅμοιος. ὅθεν ἐκ σοῦ, Ἀπολλώνιε, πεῖσμα ἐγὼ βάλλομαι, φασὶ γὰρ πλεῖστά σε
τῶν θεῶν αἰσθάνεσθαι, καὶ ξύμβουλον ποιοῦμαί σε
φροντίδων, ἐφ' αἷς ἐστι γῆ καὶ θάλαττα, ἵν' εἰ μὲν
εὐμενῆ τὰ παρὰ τῶν θεῶν φαίνοιτο, πράττοιμι ταῦτα,
εἰ δὲ ἐναντία καὶ μὴ πρὸς ἐμοῦ μηδὲ Ῥωμαίων, μὴ
ἐνοχλοίην τοὺς θεοὺς ἄκοντας."

30. Ἐπιθειάσας δ' ὁ Ἀπολλώνιος τῷ λόγῳ, "Ζεῦ"
ἔφη "Καπιτώλιε, σὲ γὰρ τῶν παρόντων πραγμάτων
βραβευτὴν οἶδα, φύλαττε σεαυτὸν μὲν τούτῳ, σεαυτῷ

tears to think of Claudius and of the good-for-nothing who had inherited his greatest possession.

"Even now that Nero has fallen, I see that humanity is   3
no better off, and the empire has fallen so low as to be in Vitellius's hands, and thus I confidently seek to win it. Firstly, I want to make myself truly valuable to mankind. Secondly, my rival is a drunken wretch. Vitellius has more perfume in his bath than I do water, and if he were struck with a sword I think he would produce perfume rather than blood. He madly adds one drinking bout to another, and dreads a bad roll of the dice when gambling, while he risks the empire for a game. With whores on top of him he copulates with married women, saying that danger makes love affairs more amusing.

"I pass over his more debauched practices, not wanting   4
to mention such things in your presence, but may I never let the Romans be ruled by such a man, and instead may I make the gods my guides and prove a true man constant to myself. That is why, Apollonius, I moor myself to you, because they say that you have a complete understanding of the gods. I make you my adviser for concerns that affect land and sea, so that if the gods show their favor, I may succeed in my aim, but if they do the opposite and are not on my side or the Roman people's, I may not trouble them against their will."

30. Apollonius greeted his speech with a prayer, saying, "Capitoline Zeus, since I know that you are the umpire of the present circumstances, guard yourself for this man and

APOLLONIUS OF TYANA

δὲ τοῦτον· τὸν γὰρ νεών, ὃν χθὲς ἄδικοι χεῖρες ἐνέπρη-
σαν, τόνδε σοὶ τὸν ἄνδρα ἀναστῆσαι πέπρωται." θαυ-
μάσαντος δὲ τοῦ βασιλέως τὸν λόγον, "αὐτὰ" εἶπεν
"αὐτὰ²³ δηλώσει, καὶ μηδὲν ἐμοῦ δέου, πέραινε δέ, ἃ
ὀρθῶς ἐβουλεύσω."

2   Ξυμβεβήκει δὲ ἄρα κατὰ τὴν Ῥώμην Δομετιανὸν
μὲν τὸν Οὐεσπασιανοῦ παῖδα παρατετάχθαι πρὸς τὸν
Βιτέλιον ὑπὲρ τῆς ἀρχῆς τοῦ πατρός, πολιορκίας δ᾽
αὐτὸν περισχούσης ἐν τῷ Καπιτωλίῳ, τὸν μὲν δια-
πεφευγέναι τοὺς πολιορκοῦντας, τὸν νεών δ᾽ ἐμπεπρῆ-
σθαι, καὶ τῷ Ἀπολλωνίῳ φαίνεσθαι πολλῷ θᾶττον ἢ
εἰ κατ᾽ Αἴγυπτον ἐπράττετο. τοσαῦτα σπουδάσαντες,
ὁ μὲν ἀπῆλθε τοῦ βασιλέως, εἰπὼν μὴ ξυγχωρεῖν
αὐτῷ τὰ Ἰνδῶν πάτρια κατὰ μεσημβρίαν ἄλλο τι
‹πράττειν›²⁴ παρ᾽ ἃ ἐκεῖνοι πράττουσι. ὁ δὲ ἀνέλαμπέ
τε ἔτι μᾶλλον, καὶ οὐ ξυνεχώρει τοῖς πράγμασι δια-
φεύγειν ἑαυτόν, ἀλλ᾽ ὡς βεβαίων τε καὶ αὐτῷ καθω-
μολογημένων εἴχετο δι᾽ ἃ ἤκουσεν.

31. Τῇ δ᾽ ὑστεραίᾳ περὶ ὄρθρον ἐπὶ τὰ βασίλεια
ἥκων ὁ Ἀπολλώνιος ἤρετο τοὺς δορυφόρους, ὅ τι
βασιλεὺς πράττοι, οἱ δὲ ἐγρηγορέναι τε αὐτὸν πάλαι
ἔφασαν καὶ πρὸς ἐπιστολαῖς εἶναι. καὶ ἀκούσας τοῦτο
ἀπῆλθεν εἰπὼν πρὸς τὸν Δάμιν "ὁ ἀνὴρ ἄρξει." ἐπ-
ανελθὼν δὲ περὶ ἥλιον ἀνίσχοντα Δίωνα μὲν καὶ
Εὐφράτην ἐπὶ θύραις εὗρε καὶ περὶ τῆς ξυνουσίας
φιλοτίμως ἐρωτῶσι διῆλθε τὴν ἀπολογίαν, ἣν τοῦ
βασιλέως ἤκουσε, τὰς δὲ αὐτοῦ δόξας ἀπεσιώπησεν.
ἐσκληθεὶς δὲ πρῶτος "ὦ βασιλεῦ," εἶπεν "Εὐφράτης

guard him for yourself, for this man is destined to rebuild your temple that wicked hands burned yesterday." The emperor was amazed at these words, and Apollonius said, "These things will become clear of themselves. Ask me nothing, but complete what you have rightly planned."

Now in Rome it happened that Domitian, the son of 2 Vespasian, was battling with Vitellius to secure his father's power, and had been held under siege in the Capitol. He escaped his besiegers, but the temple was burned, as Apollonius perceived much sooner than if this had happened in Egypt. After their conversation he left the emperor, saying that the customs of the Indians forbade him to do anything at noon other than what they did. This fired Vespasian up even more, and from now on he did not let the occasion evade him, but clutched at it as something secure and agreed upon because of what he had heard.

31. Coming to the palace the next day about dawn, Apollonius asked the guards what the emperor was doing. They replied that he had been awake for a long time, and was at work on his correspondence. Hearing this, he went away, saying to Damis, "This man will rule." Returning at sunrise, he found Dio and Euphrates at the door. They questioned him eagerly about his conversation with the emperor, and so he described the defense that he had heard the emperor give, though concealing his own views. Being summoned before the others, he said, "Majesty, your old acquaintances Euphrates and Dio are at the door,

23 αὐτὰ Rsk.: αὐτὰ
24 ⟨πράττειν⟩ Rsk.

καὶ Δίων πάλαι σοι γνώριμοι ὄντες πρὸς θύραις εἰσὶν
οὐκ ἀφρόντιδες τῶν σῶν· κάλει δὴ κἀκείνους ἐς κοινὸν
λόγον, σοφὼ γὰρ τὼ ἄνδρε." "ἀκλείστους" ἔφη "θύρας
παρέχω σοφοῖς ἀνδράσι, σοὶ δὲ καὶ τὰ στέρνα ἀνε-
ῷχθαι δόκει²⁵ τἀμά."

32. Ἐπεὶ δὲ ἐσεκλήθησαν, "ὑπὲρ μὲν τῆς ἐμαυτοῦ
διανοίας," εἶπεν "ὦ ἄνδρες, ἀπολελόγημαι χθὲς Ἀπολλωνίῳ τῷ γενναίῳ." "ἠκούσαμεν" ἦ δ' ὁ Δίων "τῆς
ἀπολογίας, καὶ νοῦν εἶχε." "τήμερον δὲ" εἶπεν "ὦ φίλε
Δίων, ξυμφιλοσοφήσωμεν ὑπὲρ τῶν βεβουλευμένων,
ἵν' ὡς κάλλιστα καὶ κατὰ σωτηρίαν τῶν ἀνθρώπων
πάντα πράττοιμι.

2   "Ἐννοῶν γὰρ πρῶτον μὲν τὸν Τιβέριον, ὡς ἐς τὸ
ἀπάνθρωπόν τε καὶ ὠμὸν τὴν ἀρχὴν μετέστησεν, εἶτα
τὸν ἐπ' ἐκείνῳ Γάιον, ὡς διονυσομανῶν καὶ λυδίζων
τὴν στολήν, καὶ πολέμους νικῶν οὐκ ὄντας, ἐς πάντα
τὰ Ῥωμαίων αἰσχρῶς ἐβάκχευσεν, εἶτα τὸν χρηστὸν
Κλαύδιον, ὡς ὑπὸ γυναίων ἡττηθεὶς ἐπελάθετο τοῦ
ἄρχειν, ἀλλὰ καὶ τοῦ ζῆν, ἀπέθανε γὰρ ὑπ' αὐτῶν, ὥς
φασι· Νέρωνος δὲ τί ἂν καθαπτοίμην, εἰπόντος Ἀπολλωνίου βραχὺν καὶ ἀθρόον λόγον περὶ ἀνέσεώς τε καὶ
ἐπιτάσεως, αἷς Νέρων τὴν ἀρχὴν ᾔσχυνε; τί δ' ἂν
περὶ ὧν Γάλβας ξυνέταττεν εἴποιμι, ὃς ἐπ' ἀγορᾶς
μέσης ἀπέθανεν, ἡταιρημένους ἐσποιῶν ἑαυτῷ παῖδας
τὸν Ὄθωνα καὶ τὸν Πείσωνα; εἰ δὲ καὶ Βιτελίῳ τῷ

²⁵ δόκει Rsk.: δοκεῖ

and since they are not indifferent to your fortunes, call them in too to join our discussion, for they are both wise men." "I keep my doors unlocked to wise men," the emperor replied, "but please consider even my heart open to you."

32. When they had been summoned, the emperor said, "Gentlemen, I gave the noble Apollonius a defense of my intentions yesterday." "We have heard your defense," said Dio, "and it was reasonable." "Today, then, my dear Dio," said the emperor, "let us discuss my plans together, so that I may act in everything with all honor and for the salvation of mankind.

"I think first of Tiberius and how he turned power into 2 something inhuman and cruel; then of his successor Gaius, and the way he acted like one possessed, wore oriental dress, and won nonexistent wars, making a disgusting revel of the whole government of Rome; then of the virtuous Claudius, and how he was undone by mere women and forgot to rule, or even to stay alive, since it is said that they killed him. And why should I attack Nero, when Apollonius has already made a brief and pregnant remark about the 'flats and sharps' with which he disgraced his rule?[46] Why should I mention the arrangements of Galba, who died in the middle of the forum after adopting his ex-lovers, Otho and Piso?[47] And if we were to yield power to

[46] Tiberius ruled 14–37; Gaius, 37–41; Claudius, 41–54; Nero, 54–68. For Apollonius's remark, see 28.1.

[47] Galba adopted Piso just before his death, but did not adopt Otho.

πάντων ἀσελγεστάτῳ τὴν ἀρχὴν παραδοίημεν, ἀνα-
βιῴη Νέρων.

3   "Ὁρῶν οὖν, ὦ ἄνδρες, ὑφ' ὧν εἶπον τυραννίδων
διαβεβλημένον τὸ ἄρχειν ξυμβούλους ὑμᾶς ποιοῦμαι,
πῶς ἂν διαθείμην αὐτὸ προσκεκρουκὸς ἤδη τοῖς ἀνθρώποις." πρὸς ταῦτα ὁ Ἀπολλώνιος "αὐλητὴς" ἔφη
"τῶν πάνυ σοφῶν τοὺς ἑαυτοῦ μαθητὰς παρὰ τοὺς
φαυλοτέρους τῶν αὐλητῶν ἔπεμπε μαθησομένους,
πῶς δεῖ μὴ αὐλεῖν· τὸ μὲν δή, πῶς δεῖ μὴ ἄρχειν,
μεμάθηκας, ὦ βασιλεῦ, παρὰ τούτων, οἳ πονηρῶς
ἦρξαν, τὸ δ', ὅπως δεῖ ἄρχειν, σπουδάσωμεν."

33. Ὁ δ' Εὐφράτης ἀφανῶς μὲν ἤδη ἐβάσκαινε τῷ
Ἀπολλωνίῳ, προσκείμενον αὐτῷ τὸν βασιλέα ὁρῶν
μᾶλλον ἢ τοῖς χρηστηρίοις τοὺς ἐς αὐτὰ ἥκοντας,
ἀνοιδήσας δὲ ὑπὲρ τὸ μέτρον τότε, καὶ τὴν φωνὴν
ἐπάρας παρ' ὃ εἰώθει, "οὐ χρὴ" ἔφη "κολακεύειν τὰς
ὁρμάς, οὐδὲ ἀνοήτως συνεκφέρεσθαι τοῖς παρὰ τὴν
ἡνίαν τι πράττουσι, καταρρυθμίζειν δὲ αὐτούς, εἴπερ
φιλοσοφοῦμεν· ἃ γὰρ εἰ προσήκει πράττειν ἔδει βου-
λευομένους φαίνεσθαι, ταῦθ' ὃν πεπράξεται τρόπον
κελεύεις λέγειν, οὔπω μαθὼν εἰ ὑπὲρ πρακτέων οἱ
λόγοι.

2   "Ἐγὼ δὲ Βιτέλιον μὲν καταλυθῆναι κελεύω, μιαρὸν
γὰρ τὸν ἄνθρωπον οἶδα καὶ μεθύοντα ἀσελγείᾳ πάσῃ,
σὲ δ' ἄνδρα εἰδὼς ἀγαθὸν καὶ γενναιότητι προύχοντα
οὔ φημι χρῆναι τὰ μὲν Βιτελίου διορθοῦσθαι, τὰ
σεαυτοῦ δὲ μήπω εἰδέναι. ὅσα μὲν δὴ αἱ μοναρχίαι
ὑβρίζουσιν, οὐκ ἐμοῦ χρὴ μανθάνειν, ἀλλ' αὐτὸς εἴρη-

Vitellius, the most profligate of them all, Nero would rise again.

"Seeing therefore, gentlemen, that the tyrannies I have 3 mentioned have brought power into disrepute, I ask you to advise me how to wield it, at a time when humanity abhors it." To this Apollonius said, "There was a very expert pipe-player who used to send his pupils to inferior players so that they would learn how not to play.[48] Well, you have learned how not to rule, Majesty, from these men who ruled wickedly, so let us consider how you ought to rule."

33. Euphrates was already secretly jealous of Apollonius, seeing the emperor more devoted to him than pilgrims are to oracles. But now he seethed abnormally, and raising his voice above its usual pitch, he said, "We should not flatter people's impulses, or be carried off like fools when they disobey the reins. Instead we should control them, if we are philosophers. You bid us tell you how to achieve something, when the subject we ought evidently to be discussing is whether its achievement is justified, and when you have not found out if your course is the right one.

"I advise the overthrow of Vitellius, since I know the 2 fellow to be corrupt and drunk with debauchery of every kind. However, I also know that you are a man of virtue and exceptional nobility, and I do not think you should correct Vitellius's misdeeds while ignorant of yourself. The lawless ways of monarchy you do not need to find out from me, having already described them yourself. But you

---

[48] Ismenias of Thebes in the later fourth century.

κας, γιγνώσκοις δ' ἄν, ὡς νεότης μὲν ἐπὶ τυραννίδα
πηδῶσα προσήκοντα ἑαυτῇ που πράττει, τὸ γὰρ τυραννεύειν οὕτως ἔοικε νέοις, ὡς τὸ μεθύειν, ὡς τὸ ἐρᾶν,
καὶ νέος μὲν τυραννεύσας οὔπω κακός, ἢν ⟨μὴ⟩²⁶
μιαιφόνος παρὰ τὴν τυραννίδα καὶ ὠμὸς καὶ ἀσελγὴς
δόξῃ,

3   "Γέροντος δὲ ἐπὶ τυραννίδα ἥκοντος πρώτη αἰτία τὸ
τοιαῦτα βούλεσθαι. καὶ γὰρ ἢν φιλάνθρωπος φαίνηται καὶ κεκοσμημένος, οὐκ ἐκείνου ταῦτα νομίζουσιν,
ἀλλὰ τῆς ἡλικίας καὶ τοῦ κατηρτυκέναι, δόξει δὲ καὶ
πάλαι τούτου καὶ νέος ἔτι ἐπιθυμήσας ἁμαρτεῖν, αἱ δὲ
τοιαῦται ἁμαρτίαι πρόσκεινται μὲν δυστυχίᾳ, πρόσκεινται δὲ δειλίᾳ· δοκεῖ γάρ τις ἢ καταγνοὺς τῆς
ἑαυτοῦ τύχης τὸ ἐν νῷ [τυραννεῦσαι]²⁷ παρεῖναι, ἢ
τυραννευσείοντι²⁸ ἐκστῆναι ἑτέρῳ, δείσας δήπου αὐτὸν ὡς ἄνδρα. τὸ μὲν δὴ τῆς δυστυχίας ἐάσθω, τὸ δὲ
τῆς δειλίας πῶς παραιτήσῃ, καὶ ταῦτα Νέρωνα δοκῶν
δεῖσαι τὸν δειλότατόν τε καὶ ῥᾳθυμότατον;

4   "Ἃ γὰρ ἐνεθυμήθη Βίνδιξ ἐπ' αὐτόν, σέ, νὴ τὸν
Ἡρακλέα, ἐκάλει πρῶτον. καὶ γὰρ στρατιὰν εἶχες καὶ
ἡ δύναμις, ἣν ἐπὶ τοὺς Ἰουδαίους ἦγες, ἐπιτηδειοτέρα
ἦν τιμωρεῖσθαι Νέρωνα· ἐκεῖνοι μὲν γὰρ πάλαι ἀφεστᾶσιν οὐ μόνον Ῥωμαίων, ἀλλὰ καὶ πάντων ἀνθρώ-
πων· οἱ γὰρ βίον ἄμικτον εὑρόντες καὶ οἷς μήτε κοινὴ
πρὸς ἀνθρώπους τράπεζα μήτε σπονδαὶ μήτε εὐχαὶ
μήτε θυσίαι, πλέον ἀφεστᾶσιν ἡμῶν ἢ Σοῦσα καὶ
Βάκτρα καὶ οἱ ὑπὲρ ταῦτα Ἰνδοί· οὐκοῦν οὐδ' εἰκὸς ἦν

ought to know this, that when youth usurps tyranny, it acts like itself, for tyranny is as natural to the young as getting drunk or making love, and a youthful tyrant is not evil unless he proves murderous, cruel, and debauched in his tyranny.

"But if an old man achieves tyranny, the first charge 3 against him is his desire for it. Even if he proves humane and cultivated, people will not take these to be his qualities, but those of his age and maturity. They will think that he desired this position long ago, even as a young man, but failed to achieve it. Such failures are close to misfortune and close to cowardice, since a man is thought either to have despaired of his luck and so put aside his intention, or to have yielded to another's desire for tyranny because he feared him as a true man. Leaving aside the subject of misfortune, how will you defend yourself against the charge of cowardice, especially if people think that you feared Nero, the greatest coward and sloth of them all?

"The plot that Vindex formed against him should have 4 stirred you more than anyone, by Heracles. You had an army, and the forces you were leading against the Jews were more suitable for punishing Nero. The Jews cut themselves off long ago, not only from the Romans, but from all mankind, since people who have devised an unsociable way of life, with no meals, libations, prayers, or sacrifices in common with other men, have moved further away from us than Susa, Bactria, and the Indians beyond

26 ⟨μὴ⟩ Ol.
27 [τυραννεῦσαι] secl. Jon.
28 τυραννευσείοντι Kay.: τυραννεύοντι

APOLLONIUS OF TYANA

τιμωρεῖσθαι τούτους ἀφισταμένους, οὓς βέλτιον ἦν
μηδὲ κτᾶσθαι.

5   "Νέρωνα δὲ τίς οὐκ ἂν ηὔξατο[29] τῇ ἑαυτοῦ χειρὶ
ἀποκτεῖναι, μονονοὺ πίνοντα τὸ τῶν ἀνθρώπων αἷμα
καὶ ἐν μέσοις τοῖς φόνοις ᾄδοντα; καίτοι ἐμοῦ τὰ ὦτα
ὀρθὰ ἦν πρὸς τοὺς ὑπὲρ σοῦ λόγους, καὶ ὁπότε τις
ἐκεῖθεν ἀφίκοιτο, τρισμυρίους Ἰουδαίων ἀπολωλέναι
φάσκων ὑπὸ σοῦ, καὶ πεντακισμυρίους κατὰ τὴν ἐφεξῆς μάχην, ἀπολαμβάνων τὸν ἥκοντα ξυμμέτρως
ἠρώτων, 'τί δ' ὁ ἀνήρ; μὴ μεῖζόν τι τούτων;' ἐπεὶ δὲ τὸν
Βιτέλιον εἴδωλον πεποιημένος τοῦ Νέρωνος ἐπ' αὐτὸν
στρατεύεις, ἃ μὲν βεβούλευσαι, πρᾶττε, καλὰ γὰρ καὶ
ταῦτα, τὰ δὲ ἐπὶ τούτοις ὧδε ἐχέτω· Ῥωμαίοις τὸ
δημοκρατεῖσθαι πολλοῦ ἄξιον καὶ πολλὰ τῶν ὄντων
αὐτοῖς ἐπ' ἐκείνης τῆς πολιτείας ἐκτήθη· παῦε μοναρχίαν, περὶ ἧς τοιαῦτα εἴρηκας, καὶ δίδου Ῥωμαίοις
μὲν τὸ τοῦ δήμου κράτος, σαυτῷ δὲ τὸ ἐλευθερίας
αὐτοῖς ἄρξαι."

34. Τοσαῦτα τοῦ Εὐφράτου εἰπόντος, ὁρῶν ὁ Ἀπολλώνιος τὸν Δίωνα προστιθέμενον τῇ γνώμῃ, τουτὶ γὰρ
καὶ τῷ νεύματι ἐπεδήλου καὶ οἷς ἐπῄνει λέγοντα, "μή
τι," ἔφη "Δίων, τοῖς εἰρημένοις προστίθης;" "νὴ Δί',"
εἶπε "πῇ μὲν ὅμοια, πῇ δὲ ἀνόμοια· τὸ μὲν γὰρ ὡς
πολλῷ βελτίων ἂν ᾖς[30] Νέρωνα καταλύων μᾶλλον ἢ
τὰ τῶν Ἰουδαίων διορθούμενος, ἡγοῦμαι κἀμοὶ πρὸς
σὲ εἰρῆσθαι, σὺ δὲ ἐῴκεις ἀγῶνα ποιουμένῳ μὴ κατα-
λυθῆναί ποτε αὐτόν· ὁ γὰρ τὴν ταραχὴν τῶν ἐκείνου

64

that. There was no point in punishing them as rebels, when they would have been better left unconquered.

"But as for Nero, which of us would not have prayed to 5 kill him with our own hand? He virtually drank human blood, and sang in the midst of his carnage. Certainly my ears were always open for the rumors about you, and whenever somebody came from there, saying that you had destroyed thirty thousand Jews, and fifty thousand in the next battle, I would take the new arrival aside and ask him quietly, 'What of our champion? Is he not too good for such things?' But having made Vitellius the mirror image of Nero, you are going to war against him, so carry out your plans, since they too are honorable, but let the aftermath be as follows. The Romans value democracy highly, and many of their present possessions they got under that form of government. Put an end to monarchy, about which you said such harsh things, and make Rome a vigorous democracy, and yourself the author of its liberty."

34. When Euphrates had said this, Apollonius saw that Dio agreed with his opinion, as appeared from his nodding and the way he praised his speech. So he said, "Dio, might you add something to what we have heard?" "Yes," he replied, "and it is partly similar, and partly not. That you would have been a far better man for deposing Nero than for punishing the Jews is something that I have said to you too, I think. Yet you seemed to be turning all your efforts so that he should never be deposed, for someone who put

---

29 ηὔξατο Kay.: εὔξαιτο
30 ἦς Jon.: ἦν

πραγμάτων εὖ τιθέμενος, ἐρρώννυέ που τὸν ἄνθρωπον
ἐπὶ πάντας, οὓς κακῶς ἔρρωτο.

2   "Τὴν δὲ ἐπὶ τὸν Βιτέλιον ὁρμὴν ἐπαινῶ. τοῦ γὰρ
τυραννίδα καθεστηκυῖαν παῦσαι μεῖζον ἡγοῦμαι τὸ
μηδὲ ἐᾶσαι φῦναι. δημοκρατίαν δὲ ἀσπάζομαι μέν,
καὶ γὰρ εἰ τῆς ἀριστοκρατίας ἥττων ἥδε ἡ πολιτεία,
ἀλλὰ τυραννίδων τε καὶ ὀλιγαρχιῶν αἱρετωτέρα τοῖς
σώφροσι· δέδια δέ, μὴ χειροήθεις ἤδη Ῥωμαίους
αὖται αἱ τυραννίδες πεποιηκυῖαι χαλεπὴν ἐργάσωνται
τὴν μεταβολήν, καὶ μὴ δύνωνται μήτε ἐλευθεριάζειν
μήτε πρὸς δημοκρατίαν ἀναβλέπειν, ὥσπερ οἱ ἐκ
σκότους ἐς ἀθρόον φῶς βλέψαντες.

3   "Ὅθεν φημὶ δεῖν τὸν μὲν Βιτέλιον ἐξωθεῖν τῶν
πραγμάτων, καὶ ὡς τάχιστά γε καὶ ἄριστα τοῦτο
ἔσται, γιγνέσθω, δοκεῖ δέ μοι παρασκευάζεσθαι μὲν
ὡς πολεμήσοντα, πόλεμον δὲ αὐτῷ μὴ προκηρύττειν,
ἀλλὰ τιμωρίαν, εἰ μὴ μεθεῖτο τῆς ἀρχῆς, κἂν ἕλῃς
αὐτόν, τουτὶ δ᾽ ὑπάρξειν ἡγοῦμαί σοι μηδὲ πονήσαντι,
δίδου Ῥωμαίοις αἵρεσιν τῆς αὑτῶν πολιτείας, κἂν μὲν
αἱρῶνται δημοκρατίαν, ξυγχώρει· τουτὶ γάρ σοι πολλῶν μὲν τυραννίδων, πολλῶν δὲ Ὀλυμπιάδων μεῖζον
καὶ πανταχοῦ μὲν γεγράψῃ τῆς πόλεως, πανταχοῦ δὲ
ἐστήξεις χαλκοῦς, ἡμῖν δ᾽ ἀφορμὰς παραδώσεις λόγων, αἷς οὔτε Ἁρμόδιος οὔτε Ἀριστογείτων παραβε-
βλήσεταί τις. εἰ δὲ μοναρχίαν προσδέχοιντο, τίνι
λοιπὸν ἀλλ᾽ ἢ σοὶ ψηφίσασθαι τὴν ἀρχὴν πάντας; ἃ
γὰρ ἔχων ἤδη τῷ κοινῷ παρήσεις, σοὶ δήπου μᾶλλον
ἢ ἑτέρῳ δώσουσιν."

right the confusion in his affairs was empowering the fellow against all those over whom he misused his power.

"But the plan against Vitellius has my approval, since I think it a greater achievement not to let tyranny come about than to end one already established. I think highly of democracy, for even if it is a constitution perhaps inferior to aristocracy, still the wise prefer it to tyranny and oligarchy. I am afraid, however, that these tyrannies, by reducing the Romans to subservience, will make the change difficult, so that they may be unable to be free or to gaze on democracy, like people emerging from darkness to the light of day.

"I therefore think that you should depose Vitellius from power, and may that happen as quickly and as honorably as possible. I advise you to prepare as if for war, without however threatening him with war, but rather with punishment if he refuses to abdicate. If you defeat him, as I think you will succeed in doing without effort, give the Romans the choice of their own constitution. If they choose democracy, grant it to them. That will be a greater act on your part than many tyrannies and many victories at Olympia. Your name will be inscribed everywhere in the city, your statue will everywhere be set up in bronze, and you will give us a subject for speeches which will put Harmodius and Aristogeiton out of contention. But if the Romans accept monarchy, whom are they likely to vote into power if not you? For when you grant the citizens what is already yours, they will doubtless give it to you rather than to someone else."

35. Σιωπὴ μὲν οὖν ἐπὶ τούτοις ἐγένετο, καὶ τὸ
πρόσωπον τοῦ βασιλέως ἀγῶνα ἐπεδήλου τῆς γνώμης, ἐπειδὴ πάνθ' ὥσπερ αὐτοκράτωρ χρηματίζων τε
καὶ πράττων, ἀπάγεσθαι ἐδόκει τῆς βουλῆς ταύτης,
καὶ ὁ Ἀπολλώνιος "δοκεῖτέ μοι" εἶπεν "ἁμαρτάνειν
ἀναλύοντες βασιλέα περὶ πραγμάτων ἤδη βεβουλευμένων, ἐς ἀδολεσχίαν καθιστάμενοι μειρακιώδη καὶ
ἀργοτέραν τοῦ καιροῦ. εἰ μὲν γὰρ ἐμοὶ κεκτημένῳ
δύναμιν, ὁπόσην οὗτος, καὶ βουλευομένῳ, τί δρῴην ἂν
τοὺς ἀνθρώπους ἀγαθόν, ξύμβουλοι τῶν τοιούτων
ἐγίγνεσθε, προὔβαινεν ἂν ὁ λόγος ὑμῖν, αἱ γὰρ φιλό-
σοφοι γνῶμαι τοὺς φιλοσόφους τῶν ἀκροατῶν διορ-
θοῦνται. ἀνδρὶ δὲ ξυμβουλεύοντας ὑπάτῳ καὶ ἄρχειν
εἰθισμένῳ, καὶ ᾧ ἕτοιμον, ἐπειδὰν ἐκπέσῃ τῆς ἀρχῆς,
ἀπολωλέναι, τί δεῖ ἐπιπλήττειν, εἰ μὴ διωθεῖται τὰ
παρὰ τῆς τύχης, ἀλλὰ δέχεται μὲν αὐτὰ ἥκοντα,
βουλεύεται δέ, ὅπως χρήσεται σωφρόνως οἷς ἔχει;

2   "Ὥσπερ οὖν, εἰ ἀθλητὴν ὁρῶντες εὐψυχίᾳ τε κατ-
εσκευασμένον, καὶ μήκει καὶ τὴν ἁρμονίαν τοῦ σώματος ἐπιτήδειον, ἐς Ὀλυμπίαν βαδίζοντα δι' Ἀρκαδίας
ἤδη προσελθόντες ἐπὶ μὲν τοὺς ἀντιπάλους ἐρρώννυ-
μεν, ἐκελεύομεν δὲ αὐτόν, ἐπειδὰν νικήσῃ τὰ Ὀλύμπια, μὴ κηρύττεσθαι τῆς νίκης, μηδὲ ὑπέχειν τὴν
κεφαλὴν τῷ κοτίνῳ, ληρεῖν ἂν ἐδόξαμεν ἢ παίζειν ἐς
τοὺς ἑτέρων πόνους, οὕτως ἐνθυμούμενοι τὸν ἄνδρα,
καὶ ὁπόση μὲν αἰχμὴ περὶ αὐτόν, ὁπόσος δὲ χαλκὸς
ἀστράπτει, πλῆθος δὲ ἵππων ὅσον, αὐτὸς δὲ ὡς
γενναῖός τε καὶ σώφρων καὶ πρέπων κατασχεῖν ἃ

35. There followed a silence in which the emperor's face showed his mental struggle, since after behaving and acting like an emperor, it seemed as if he was diverted from his plan. Apollonius then said, "It seems to me to be wrong of you to change an emperor's mind on a question already decided; you are indulging in nonsense that is puerile and too feeble for the situation. If I had acquired power as great as he has, and was wondering what good I should do to mankind, and you were my advisers on this issue, your words would have been effective, since the opinions of philosophers sway the philosophers among their hearers. But you are advising a consular, a man used to ruling, who is facing ruin if he loses his power. Why should you rebuke him for not refusing the offers of chance, but accepting them when they come, when he is debating how to use his advantage wisely?

"Suppose we saw an athlete endowed with courage and   2 stature, and with a properly proportioned body, who was already on his way through Arcadia to Olympia, and suppose that on approaching him we encouraged him against his competitors, and yet advised him not to accept the victory after winning the Olympics, or to let the olive be put on his head.[49] We would seem to be talking nonsense, or making fun of another's efforts. So also let us remember who our hearer is, all the troops he has with him, all the flashing bronze, and the great number of horses, and how noble and prudent he is, and how well suited to achieve his

---

[49] Wild olive (*kotinos*) was the crown used at the Olympics.

διανοεῖται, πέμπωμεν ἐφ᾽ ἃ ὥρμηκεν αἴσια μὲν φθεγ-
γόμενοι πρὸς αὐτόν, εὐφημότερα δὲ τούτων παρεγ-
γυῶντες.

3   "Οὐδὲ³¹ γὰρ ἐκεῖνο ἐνεθυμήθητε, ὅτι δυοῖν παίδοιν
πατὴρ οὗτος, οἳ στρατοπέδων ἤδη ἄρχουσιν, οἷς εἰ μὴ
παραδώσει τὴν ἀρχήν, ἐχθίστοις χρήσεται, καὶ τί
λοιπόν, ἀλλ᾽ ἢ ἐκπεπολεμῶσθαι³² πρὸς τὸν ἑαυτοῦ
οἶκον; τὴν δὲ ἀρχὴν ὑποδεξάμενος θεραπεύσεται μὲν
ὑπὸ τῶν ἑαυτοῦ παίδων, στηρίξεται δὲ ἐπ᾽ αὐτῶν καὶ
ἐπ᾽ αὐτοῦ οἱ παῖδες, δορυφόροις δὲ αὐτοῦ χρήσεται,
μὰ Δί, οὐ μεμισθωμένοις, οὐδ᾽ ἠναγκασμένοις, οὐδὲ
πλαττομένοις εὔνουν πρόσωπον, ἀλλ᾽ ἐπιτηδειοτάτοις
τε καὶ φιλτάτοις.

4   "Ἐμοὶ πολιτείας μὲν οὐδεμιᾶς μέλει, ζῶ γὰρ ὑπὸ
τοῖς θεοῖς, τὴν δὲ τῶν ἀνθρώπων ἀγέλην οὐκ ἀξιῶ
φθείρεσθαι χήτει βουκόλου δικαίου τε καὶ σώφρονος.
ὥσπερ γὰρ εἷς ἀρετῇ προὔχων μεθίστησι τὴν δημοκρατίαν ἐς τὸ ἑνὸς ἀνδρὸς τοῦ ἀρίστου ἀρχὴν φαίνεσθαι, οὕτως ἡ ἑνὸς ἀρχὴ πάντα ἐς τὸ ξυμφέρον τοῦ
κοινοῦ προορῶσα δῆμός ἐστιν. οὐ κατέλυσας, φησί,
Νέρωνα. σὺ δέ, Εὐφρᾶτα; Δίων δέ; ἐγὼ δέ; ἀλλ᾽ ὅμως
οὐδεὶς ἡμῖν ἐπιπλήττει τοῦτο, οὐδ᾽ ἡγεῖται δειλούς, εἰ
φιλοσόφων ἀνδρῶν μυρίας ἤδη καθελόντων τυραννίδας ἀπελείφθημεν ἡμεῖς τοῦ δόξαι ὑπὲρ ἐλευθερίας τι
πράττειν.

5   "Καίτοι τό γε ἐπ᾽ ἐμοὶ καὶ παρεταττόμην πρὸς
Νέρωνα, πολλὰ μὲν κακοήθως διαλεχθεὶς καὶ τὸν

aims. Let us then send him on his chosen course with words of good omen and with more propitious advice than this.

"You seem also to have forgotten that this man is the father of two sons who already command armies.[50] If he does not hand his power over to them, they will be his bitterest enemies, and he will have no alternative but to make war on his own family. But if he accepts power, he will be served by his own sons, and they will be his support and he theirs. They will serve him as bodyguards, not hired ones of course, or drafted, or ones who assume a friendly expression, but genuinely well disposed and loving.

"To me no constitution matters, since I live as the gods' subject, but I do not think that the human herd should perish for lack of a just and reasonable herdsman. Just as one man of exceptional virtue changes democracy so as to make it so appear the rule of one man better than the rest,[51] so the rule of one man who is always looking out for the common good is a democracy. 'You did not depose Nero,' he says. But did you, Euphrates? Did Dio? Did I? Even so, no one blames us for that, or thinks us cowards, even though true philosophers have overthrown countless tyrannies in the past, and we have failed to be seen doing anything for democracy.

"And yet for my part I did oppose Nero. I was often critical of him in conversation, I censured the monster

50 Titus (ruled 79–81) and Domitian (ruled 81–86).
51 An allusion to Thucydides's judgment on Pericles (2.65.9).

31 οὐδέ Headlam: οὔτε
32 ἐκπεπολεμῶσθαι Kay.: ἐκπεπολεμῆσθαι

APOLLONIUS OF TYANA

ὠμότατον Τιγελλῖνον ἐπικόψας ἀκούοντα, ἃ δὲ περὶ τὰ
ἑσπέρια τῶν χωρίων ὠφέλουν Βίνδικα, Νέρωνι δήπου
ἐπετείχιζον. ἀλλ᾽ οὔτε ἐμαυτὸν διὰ ταῦτα φήσω καθῃ-
ρηκέναι τὸν τύραννον, οὔτε ὑμᾶς, ἐπεὶ μὴ ταῦτ᾽ ἐπράτ-
τετε, μαλακωτέρους ἡγήσομαι τοῦ φιλοσοφίᾳ προσήκοντος.

6   "Ἀνδρὶ μὲν οὖν φιλοσόφῳ τὸ ἐπὶ νοῦν ἐλθὸν εἰρήσεται, ποιήσεται δέ, οἶμαι, λόγον τοῦ μή τι ἀνοήτως
ἢ μανικῶς εἰπεῖν· ὑπάτῳ δ᾽ ἐνθυμουμένῳ καταλῦσαι
τύραννον πρῶτον μὲν δεῖ βουλῆς πλείονος, ἵν᾽ ἐξ ἀφα-
νοῦς προσβαίη τοῖς πράγμασιν, εἶτ᾽ ἐπιτηδείου σχήματος ἐς τὸ μὴ παρορκεῖν δοκεῖν. εἰ γὰρ ἐπ᾽ αὐτόν, ὃς
ἀπέφηνεν αὐτὸν στρατηγὸν καὶ ᾧ τὰ βέλτιστα βου-
λεύσειν τε καὶ πράξειν ὤμοσε, μέλλοι χρήσεσθαι τοῖς
ὅπλοις, ἀπολογεῖσθαι δήπου τοῖς θεοῖς δεῖ πρότερον,
ὡς ξὺν ὁσίᾳ ἐπιορκοῦντα, φίλων τε δεῖ πλειόνων, οὐ
γὰρ ἀχαρακώτους γε, οὐδὲ ἀφράκτους χρὴ τὰ τοιαῦτα
πράττειν, καὶ χρημάτων ὡς πλείστων, ἵν᾽ ὑποποιή-
σαιτο τὰς δυνάμεις καὶ ταῦτα ἐπιτιθέμενος ἀνθρώπῳ
τὰ ἐν πάσῃ τῇ γῇ κεκτημένῳ. τριβὴ δὲ ὅση περὶ
ταῦτα, ὅσοι δὲ χρόνοι.

7   "Καὶ ταῦτα μὲν ἐκδέχεσθε ὅπῃ βούλεσθε, μὴ γὰρ
ἐς ἔλεγχον ἴωμεν ὧν ἐνεθυμήθη μέν, ὡς εἰκός, οὗτος,
ἡ τύχη δὲ οὐδὲ ἀγωνισαμένῳ ξυνέλαβε. πρὸς δὲ ἐκεῖνο
τί ἐρεῖτε; τὸν γὰρ χθὲς ἄρχοντα καὶ στεφανούμενον
μὲν ὑπὸ τῶν πόλεων ἐν τοῖς δεῦρο ἱεροῖς, χρηματίζοντα δὲ λαμπρῶς καὶ ἀφθόνως, τοῦτον κελεύετε δημοσίᾳ κηρύττειν τήμερον, ὡς ἰδιώτης μὲν εἴη λοιπόν,

Tigellinus to his face, and by helping Vindex in the western regions I was no doubt fortifying him against Nero. But that will not make me say that I overthrew the tyrant, nor will I think you more cowardly than philosophers should be because you did not do the same.

"A true philosopher will say what comes into his mind,   6
though taking care in my opinion not to say anything foolish or mad. But a consular who plans to depose a tyrant first of all needs considerable forethought in order to set about his project by stealth, and secondly he needs a suitable pretext so as not to seem to break his oath. He is going to turn his weapons on the very man who made him general, and to whom he swore to dedicate his thoughts and deeds, so that he must first convince the gods that he is breaking his oath without impiety. He needs many friends, since such a step cannot be taken without defense or protection. He needs an abundance of money to win over the armies, especially when attacking a person who owns the whole world. Think how much effort and how much time this requires.

"You can accept this or not, as you please. It is not for us   7
to scrutinize plans that he doubtless would have formed anyway, and fortune would have favored him even without his efforts. But what will you say to this? Just yesterday he was a governor, crowned by the cities in the sanctuaries here, administering honorably and generously, while today do you tell him to proclaim publicly that he will now be a

παρανοῶν δὲ ἐπὶ τὴν ἀρχὴν ἦλθεν; ὥσπερ γὰρ ἐπι-
τελῶν τὰ δεδογμένα προθύμους δορυφόρους, οἷς πιστεύων ταῦτ᾽ ἐνεθυμήθη, παραστήσεται, οὕτως ἐς τὸ
μεθίστασθαι τῶν δοξάντων ἥκων πολεμίῳ τῷ μετὰ
ταῦτα ἀπιστουμένῳ χρήσεται."

36. Ἄσμενος τούτων ἀκούσας ὁ βασιλεὺς "εἰ τὴν
ψυχὴν" ἔφη "τὴν ἐμὴν ᾤκεις, οὐκ ἂν οὕτω σαφῶς, ἃ
ἐνεθυμήθην, ἀπήγγειλας. ἕπομαι δή σοι, θεῖον γὰρ
ἡγοῦμαι τὸ ἐκ σοῦ πᾶν, καὶ ὁπόσα χρὴ τὸν ἀγαθὸν
βασιλέα πράττειν δίδασκε." καὶ ὁ Ἀπολλώνιος "οὐ
διδακτά με" ἔφη "ἐρωτᾷς· βασιλεία γὰρ μέγιστον μὲν
τῶν κατ᾽ ἀνθρώπους, ἀδίδακτον δέ. ὁπόσα δ᾽ οὖν μοι
δοκεῖς πράττων ὑγιῶς ἂν πρᾶξαι, καὶ δὴ φράσω.

2   "Πλοῦτον ἡγοῦ μὴ τὸν ἀπόθετον (τί γὰρ βελτίων
οὗτος τῆς ὁποθενδὴ ξυνενεχθείσης ψάμμου;), μηδὲ τὸν
φοιτῶντα παρ᾽ ἀνθρώπων, οἳ τὰς ἐσφορὰς ὀλοφύρονται, κίβδηλον γὰρ ὁ χρυσὸς καὶ μέλαν, ἢν ἐκ δακρύων
ἥκῃ. πλούτῳ δ᾽ ἂν ἄριστα βασιλέων χρῷο τοῖς μὲν
δεομένοις ἐπαρκῶν, τοῖς δὲ πολλὰ κεκτημένοις παρ-
έχων ἀσφαλῆ τὸν πλοῦτον. τὸ ἐξεῖναί σοι πᾶν ὅ τι
βούλει, δέδιθι, σωφρονέστερον γὰρ αὐτῷ χρήσῃ. μὴ
τέμνε τῶν ἀσταχύων τοὺς ὑψηλούς τε καὶ ὑπεραίρον-
τας, ἄδικος γὰρ ὁ τοῦ Ἀριστοτέλους λόγος, ἀλλὰ τὸ
δύσνουν ἐξαίρει μᾶλλον, ὥσπερ τὰς ἀκάνθας τῶν
ληΐων. καὶ φοβερὸς δόκει τοῖς νεώτερα πράττουσι μὴ
ἐν τῷ τιμωρεῖσθαι, ἀλλ᾽ ἐν τῷ τιμωρήσεσθαι. νόμος, ὦ
βασιλεῦ, καὶ σοῦ ἀρχέτω· σωφρονέστερον γὰρ νομο-
θετήσεις, ἢν μὴ ὑπερορᾷς τῶν νόμων.

private citizen, and was mad to aim at the throne? By carrying out his decisions, he will make willing supporters of those on whom he depended when forming them. But if he starts to abandon his decisions, he will make enemies of those he distrusts hereafter."

36. Hearing this with pleasure, the emperor said, "If you lived in my own soul, you could not have expressed my intentions so clearly. So I will follow you, since I believe everything that comes from you to be inspired, and you must teach me everything a good emperor should do." Apollonius replied, "What you ask cannot be taught, for kingship is the most important of human possessions, and yet impossible to teach. I will certainly tell you what I think you would be wise to do.

"Do not consider what is stored away to be real wealth,   2 since how is that better than sand piled up from anywhere? Nor what comes from people who groan over their taxes, because such gold is counterfeit and black if its source is weeping. You will make better use of gold than any ruler if you help the needy, and make those with large possessions secure in their wealth. Fear your power to do anything you please, for thus you will use it with more restraint. Do not cut down the tallest and most prominent of the stalks, because this advice of Aristotle's is unjust.[52] Instead, uproot ill will like tares from corn, and deter those who attempt rebellion not with actual punishment but with potential punishment. The law, Majesty, must rule you too, since you will be a wiser lawgiver if you do not despise the laws.

[52] *Politics* 1284 a 17.

3   "Θεοὺς θεράπευε μᾶλλον ἢ πρότερον· μεγάλα μὲν
γὰρ παρ᾽ αὐτῶν εἴληφας, ὑπὲρ μεγάλων δὲ εὔχῃ. καὶ
τὰ μὲν τῇ ἀρχῇ προσήκοντα, ὡς βασιλεὺς πρᾶττε, τὰ
δὲ τῷ σώματι, ὡς ἰδιώτης. περὶ δὲ κύβων, καὶ μέθης,
καὶ ἐρώτων, καὶ τοῦ διαβεβλῆσθαι πρὸς τὰ τοιαῦτα, τί
ἄν σοι παραινοίην, ὅν φασι μηδὲ ἐφ᾽ ἡλικίας ταῦτα
ἐπαινέσαι;

4   "Παῖδές εἰσί σοι, βασιλεῦ, δύο καὶ γενναῖοι, ὥς
φασιν. ἄρχε τούτων μάλιστα, τὰ γὰρ ἐκείνοις ἁμαρ-
τηθέντα σὲ δήπου διαβαλεῖ.³³ ἔστω δέ σοι καὶ ἀπειλὴ
πρὸς αὐτούς, ὡς οὐ παραδώσεις τὴν ἀρχήν σφισιν, εἰ
μή που καλοί τε καὶ ἀγαθοὶ μείνωσιν, ἵνα μὴ κληρο-
νομίαν ἡγῶνται τὴν ἀρχήν, ἀλλ᾽ ἀρετῆς ἆθλα. τὰς δὲ
ἐμπολιτευομένας ἡδονὰς τῇ Ῥώμῃ, πολλαὶ δὲ αὗται,
δοκεῖ μοι, ὦ βασιλεῦ, ξυμμέτρως παύειν, χαλεπὸν
γὰρ μεταβαλεῖν δῆμον ἐς τὸ ἀθρόως σῶφρον, ἀλλὰ
δεῖ κατ᾽ ὀλίγον ἐμποιεῖν ῥυθμὸν ταῖς γνώμαις, τὰ μὲν
φανερῶς, τὰ δὲ ἀφανῶς διορθούμενον. ἀπελευθέρων τε
καὶ δούλων, οὓς ἡ ἀρχή σοι δίδωσιν, ἀνέλωμεν τρυ-
φήν, τοσούτῳ ταπεινότερον αὐτοὺς ἐθίσαντες φρονεῖν,
ὅσῳ μείζονος δεσπότου εἰσίν.

5   "Τί λοιπὸν ἀλλ᾽ ἢ περὶ τῶν ἡγεμόνων εἰπεῖν, οἳ ἐς
τὰ ἔθνη φοιτῶσιν, οὐ περὶ ὧν αὐτὸς ἐκπέμψεις, ἀρι-
στίνδην γάρ που τὰς ἀρχὰς δώσεις, ἀλλὰ περὶ τῶν
κληρωσομένων τὸ ἄρχειν· τούτων γὰρ τοὺς μὲν προσ-
φόρους τοῖς ἔθνεσιν, ἃ διέλαχον, φημὶ δεῖν πέμπειν,
ὡς ὁ κλῆρος, ἑλληνίζοντας μὲν Ἑλληνικῶν ἄρχειν,
ῥωμαΐζοντας δὲ ὁμογλώττων καὶ ξυμφώνων. ὅθεν δὲ³⁴

"Worship the gods more than you have in the past, since they have granted you greatness, and greatness is what you ask from them. Act like an emperor in what concerns your power, but like an ordinary citizen in what concerns your person. Gambling, drunkenness, venery, I do not need to warn you against, for they say you did not favor them even as a youth.

"You have two noble sons, Majesty, so I am told. Rule them above all, since their faults will certainly reflect on you. Be ready to threaten that you will not leave them the throne unless they remain honest and good, and then they will think of the throne not as their birthright, but as a reward for virtue. As for the pleasures which are endemic at Rome, Majesty, and many there are, I advise that you be cautious in controlling them. It is difficult to convert a people to sudden temperance, and you must put their minds in order gradually, by both open and unseen correction. Let us end extravagance in the slaves and freedmen that power gives you, but make them used to humbler behavior, as befits a greater master.

"It only remains to mention the governors that go out regularly to the provinces, not the ones you send yourself, since you will surely go by excellence in granting commands, but the ones who receive power by lot.[53] I advise that those you send be appropriate to the provinces they are assigned, so far as the lot allows, so that Greek-speakers rule Greeks, and Latin-speakers rule those who share

---

[53] That is, the proconsuls theoretically selected by lot, in contrast to the legates who ruled at the emperor's pleasure.

---

[33] διαβαλεῖ Cob.: διαβάλλει   [34] δὲ Rsk.: δὴ

τοῦτ᾽ ἐνεθυμήθην, λέξω· κατὰ τοὺς χρόνους, οὓς ἐν
Πελοποννήσῳ διῃτώμην, ἡγεῖτο τῆς Ἑλλάδος ἄνθρωπος οὐκ εἰδὼς τὰ Ἑλλήνων, καὶ οὐδ᾽ οἱ Ἕλληνές τι
ἐκείνου ξυνίεσαν· ἔσφηλεν οὖν καὶ ἐσφάλη τὰ πλεῖστα, οἱ γὰρ ξύνεδροί τε καὶ κοινωνοὶ τῆς ἐν τοῖς
δικαστηρίοις γνώμης ἐκαπήλευον τὰς δίκας, διαλα-
βόντες τὸν ἡγεμόνα ὥσπερ ἀνδράποδον. ταῦτά μοι,
βασιλεῦ, παρέστη τήμερον, εἰ δέ τι καὶ ἕτερον ἐπὶ
νοῦν ἔλθοι, πάλιν ξυνελευσόμεθα. νυνὶ δὲ τὰ προσήκοντα τῇ ἀρχῇ πρᾶττε, μὴ ἀργότερος τοῖς ὑπηκόοις
δόξῃς."

37. Ὁ δὲ Εὐφράτης "τοῖς μὲν δεδογμένοις ξυγχωρῶ," ἔφη "τί γὰρ ἂν πλέον μεταδιδάσκων πράττοιμι; φιλοσοφίαν δέ, ὦ βασιλεῦ, τουτὶ γὰρ λοιπὸν
προσειρήσει,[35] τὴν μὲν κατὰ φύσιν ἐπαίνει καὶ ἀσπά-
ζου, τὴν δὲ θεοκλυτεῖν φάσκουσαν παραιτοῦ, κατα-
ψευδόμενοι γὰρ τοῦ θείου πολλὰ καὶ ἀνόητα ἡμᾶς
ἐπαίρουσιν." ταυτὶ μὲν πρὸς τὸν Ἀπολλώνιον αὐτῷ
ἐλέγετο, ὁ δὲ οὐδὲν ἐπιστραφεὶς ἀπῄει μετὰ τῶν ἑαυτοῦ γνωρίμων, διανύσας τὴν σπουδήν· βουλομένου δὲ
τοῦ Εὐφράτου θρασύτερόν τι περὶ αὐτοῦ λέγειν, ξυν-
ῆκεν ὁ βασιλεὺς καὶ διακρουόμενος αὐτὸν "ἐσκαλεῖτε"
ἔφη "τοὺς δεομένους τῆς ἀρχῆς καὶ ἀπολαβέτω ἡ
βουλὴ τὸ ἑαυτῆς σχῆμα."

2   Οὕτω μὲν δὴ ὁ Εὐφράτης ἔλαθε διαβαλὼν ἑαυτόν,
καὶ γὰρ βάσκανός τε τῷ βασιλεῖ καὶ ὑβριστὴς ἔδοξε,
καὶ τοὺς λόγους τοὺς ὑπὲρ τῆς δημοκρατίας οὐχ ὡς
ἐγίγνωσκεν εἰρηκώς, ἀλλ᾽ ἐς ἀντιλογίαν τοῦ Ἀπολ-

their language and outlook. I will tell you where I got this idea. At the time I was staying in the Peloponnese, Greece was ruled by a man ignorant of Greek customs, and the Greeks for their part did not understand him at all. Thus he made many mistakes by his own fault and by other people's, since those who advised him and joined in his legal decisions auctioned off his verdicts, parceling up the governor like a slave.[54] These are my thoughts for today, Majesty, and if something else comes to mind, we will meet again. Now perform the business that your position involves, so as not to seem rather lazy to your subjects."

37. Euphrates then said, "I concur in your past decisions, for what good could I do by trying to dissuade you? But as for philosophy, Majesty (since that will be your title from now on), favor and embrace the kind that is in accordance with nature, but avoid the kind that claims to be inspired. For by misrepresenting the gods, such people prompt us to many foolish schemes." This was an allusion to Apollonius, but he, without even turning around, left with his pupils, putting an end to the interview. When Euphrates tried to say something rather rash about him, the emperor understood his intention and put him off, saying, "Admit those who need my rule, and let my council resume its usual form."

In this way Euphrates unconsciously injured his reputation, since the emperor took him to be malicious and unprincipled, and to have given his speech about democracy not out of conviction but to contradict Apollonius because

54 Several persons could own shares in a single slave.

35 προσειρήσει Cob.: προσειρήσεται

2

λωνίου δι' ἃ περὶ τῆς ἀρχῆς ἐκείνῳ ἐδόκει. οὐ μὴν
ἀπερρίπτει αὐτόν, οὐδὲ ἐπεδήλου τι ὀργῆς πρὸς ταῦτα.
καὶ τὸν Δίωνα οὐκ ἐπῄνει μὲν ξυναράμενον αὐτῷ τῆς
γνώμης, οὐ μὴν ἐπαύσατο ἀγαπῶν· ἐπίχαρίς τε γὰρ
τὰς διαλέξεις ἐδόκει καὶ τὰς ἔριδας παρῃτεῖτο, ὥραν
τε ἐπέφαινε τοῖς λόγοις, οἷα τοῦ πρὸς τοῖς ἱεροῖς
ἀτμοῦ ἐκπνεῖ, προσῆν δὲ αὐτῷ καὶ τὸ ἀποσχεδιάζειν
ἄριστα ἀνθρώπων.

3   Τὸν δὲ Ἀπολλώνιον ὁ βασιλεὺς οὐκ ἠγάπα μόνον,
ἀλλὰ καὶ ὑπέκειτο αὐτῷ διιόντι μὲν τὰ ἀρχαῖα, διη-
γουμένῳ δὲ τὸν Ἰνδὸν Φραώτην ποταμούς τε ἀναγρά-
φοντι καὶ θηρία, ὑφ' ὧν ἡ Ἰνδικὴ οἰκεῖται, προλέγοντι
δὲ καὶ ὁπόσα οἱ θεοὶ περὶ τῆς ἀρχῆς ἔφαινον. ἐξελαύ-
νων δὲ τῆς Αἰγύπτου ξυνῳκισμένης τε καὶ νεαζούσης,
κοινωνὸν μὲν τῆς ὁδοῦ τὸν Ἀπολλώνιον ἐποιεῖτο, τῷ δὲ
οὐκ ἐδόκει ταῦτα· Αἴγυπτόν τε γάρ, ὁπόση ἐστίν,
οὔπω ἑωρακέναι, τοῖς τε Γυμνοῖς οὔπω ἀφῖχθαι ἐς
λόγον, μάλα ἐσπουδακὼς σοφίᾳ Ἰνδικῇ ἀντικρῖναι
Αἰγυπτίαν. "οὐδὲ Νείλου" ἔφη "ἔπιον, ὅθεν ἄρχεται."
ξυνεὶς οὖν ὁ βασιλεύς, ὅτι ἐπ' Αἰθιοπίαν στέλλεται,
"ἡμῶν δὲ" ἔφη "οὐ μεμνήσῃ;" "νὴ Δί'," εἶπεν "ἢν
βασιλεὺς ἀγαθὸς μένῃς, καὶ σεαυτοῦ μνημονεύῃς."

38. Μετὰ ταῦτα θύσας ὁ βασιλεὺς ἐν τῷ ἱερῷ
δωρεὰς ἐπήγγειλεν αὐτῷ δημοσίᾳ. ὁ δὲ ὥσπερ αἰτή-
σων "τίνας δέ," εἶπεν "ὦ βασιλεῦ, δωρεὰς δώσεις;"
"δέκα" ἔφη "νῦν, ἀφικομένῳ δὲ ἐς τὴν Ῥώμην τἀμὰ
πάντα." καὶ ὁ Ἀπολλώνιος "οὐκοῦν" ἔφη "φείδεσθαί
με χρὴ τῶν σῶν ὡς ἐμῶν, καὶ μὴ σπαθᾶν αὐτὰ νῦν

of what he had advised about the empire. He did not throw him over, however, or show any anger at all this. He was displeased with Dio too for taking Euphrates's side, but did not stop taking pleasure in him. Dio seemed graceful in conversation, was averse to quarrels, and displayed a beauty of language like the perfume of incense in a sanctuary, and had an unrivaled ability to speak extempore.

Apollonius, however, not only had the emperor's affection, but entranced him with his description of ancient customs, his accounts of the Indian Phraotes, his description of the rivers and the animals that inhabit India, and all the predictions about the empire that he received by divine revelation. When Vespasian was about to leave Egypt, now that it was settled and flourishing, he wanted to make Apollonius his companion on the journey, but he declined. He said that he had not yet seen the full extent of Egypt, or conversed with the Naked Ones, though he was extremely eager to compare Egyptian wisdom with Indian. "Nor have I drunk from the Nile at its source," he said. Realizing that his course was for Ethiopia, the emperor said, "You will remember me, will you not?" "Naturally," was the reply, "if you remain a good emperor, and remember yourself."

38. Thereafter having sacrificed in the sanctuary, the emperor promised him gifts at the public expense. As if making a request, Apollonius said, "What gifts will you give, king?" "Ten for the present," said the other, "but all I have when you come to Rome." "Well then," said Apollonius, "I must be as sparing with what is yours as if it were mine, and not squander it now, when it awaits me in abun-

ἀποκεισόμενά μοι ἀθρόα. ἀλλ᾽ ἐπιμελήθητι τούτων, ὦ
βασιλεῦ, μᾶλλον, ἐοίκασι γὰρ δεομένοις." ἐδείκνυε δὲ
ἄρα τοὺς περὶ τὸν Εὐφράτην.

2   Ὁ μὲν δὴ βασιλεὺς ἐκέλευσεν αἰτεῖν θαρροῦντας,
ἐρυθριάσας δὲ ὁ Δίων "διάλλαξόν με, βασιλεῦ," εἶπε
"πρὸς Ἀπολλώνιον τὸν διδάσκαλον ὑπὲρ ὧν ἀντιλέ-
γειν αὐτῷ ἔδοξα μήπω πρότερον ἀντειπὼν τῷ ἀνδρί."
ἐπαινέσας οὖν ὁ βασιλεὺς "χθὲς" ἔφη "τοῦτο ἐγὼ
ᾔτησα, καὶ ὑπάρχει· ἀλλ᾽ αἴτει ὑπὲρ δωρεᾶς." καὶ ὁ
Δίων "Λασθένης" ἔφη "ἐστὶ μὲν ἐξ Ἀπαμείας τῆς ἐν
τῷ Βιθυνῶν ἔθνει, ξυμφιλοσοφῶν δέ μοι χλαμύδος
ἠράσθη καὶ στρατιωτικοῦ[36] βίου· τοῦτον, ἐπειδὴ τρί-
βωνος πάλιν ἐρᾶν φησιν, ἄνες τῆς στρατείας, δεῖται
δὲ αὐτὸς ταῦτα. χαριεῖ δὲ ἐμοὶ μὲν ἀποφῆναι αὐτὸν
ἄνδρα ἀγαθόν, ἐκείνῳ δὲ ζῆν, ὡς βούλεται." "ἀνεί-
σθω," ἔφη "δίδωμι δὲ αὐτῷ καὶ τὰ τῶν ἐστρατευμένων,
ἐπειδὴ σοφίας ἐρᾷ καὶ σοῦ."

3   Καὶ μετὰ τοῦτον ἐς τὸν Εὐφράτην ἐπεστράφη, τῷ
δὲ ἐπιστολὴ ξυνετέτακτο περὶ ὧν ᾔτει. τὴν μὲν δὴ
ἐπιστολὴν ὤρεγεν, ὡς ἀναγνωσομένῳ καθ᾽ ἑαυτόν,
βουληθεὶς δὲ ὁ βασιλεὺς παραδοῦναί τινα κατ᾽ αὐτοῦ
λόγον, ἀνέγνω δημοσίᾳ πᾶσιν· αἰτῶν δὲ ἐφαίνετο τὰ
μὲν ἑαυτῷ, τὰ δὲ ἑτέροις, καὶ τῶν δωρεῶν αἱ μὲν
χρήματα ἦσαν, αἱ δὲ ὑπὲρ χρημάτων. γελάσας οὖν ὁ
Ἀπολλώνιος "εἶτα ὑπὲρ δημοκρατίας" ἔφη "ξυνεβούλευες, τοσαῦτα μέλλων αἰτήσειν βασιλέα;"

---

[36] στρατιωτικοῦ Cob.: στρατιώτου

dance. Look after these men instead, Majesty, since they seem to have a request," pointing at the same time to Euphrates and the others.

When the emperor told them to make their requests 2 confidently, Dio said with a blush, "Reconcile me, Majesty, to my teacher Apollonius for appearing to contradict him, as I have never contradicted the Master before." The emperor said approvingly, "I made that request yesterday, and it is already granted, so ask for a gift." Dio replied, "Lasthenes," said Dio, "is from Apamea in the province of Bithynia,[55] and while studying with me felt an urge for the military cloak and the soldier's life. But since he now claims to desire the philosopher's cloak again, I ask you to release him from armed service, as he too requests. You will grant me the making of a good man, and grant him the life of his choice." "Let him be discharged," said the emperor, "and I will also give him a veteran's privileges, since he desires both wisdom and yourself."

After that he turned to Euphrates, who had already 3 composed a letter containing his requests. He handed the letter to the emperor, expecting him to read it privately, but the emperor wanted to bring out some facts against him, and so read it out openly to everyone. Euphrates turned out to be making some requests for himself, others for other people, and some of the gifts involved money, others the equivalent of money. Apollonius said with a laugh, "So you urged democracy while planning to ask the emperor for all that?"

55 Apameia Myrleia, close to Dio's native Prusa.

39. Τὰ μὲν δὴ τῆς διαφορᾶς, ἣ Ἀπολλωνίῳ τε καὶ
Εὐφράτῃ ἐγένετο, τοιάδε εὗρον, ἐξελάσαντος δὲ τοῦ
βασιλέως καθήπτοντο ἀλλήλων ἐς τὸ φανερόν, ὁ μὲν
Εὐφράτης ξὺν ὀργῇ τε καὶ λοιδορίαις, ὁ δ' αὖ φιλοσόφως καὶ ξὺν ἐλέγχῳ μᾶλλον. ὁπόσα μὲν δὴ Εὐφράτου κατηγόρηκεν, ὡς παρὰ τὸ πρέπον φιλοσοφίᾳ
πράττοντος, ἔξεστιν Ἀπολλωνίου μαθεῖν ἐκ τῶν πρὸς
αὐτὸν ἐπιστολῶν, πλείους γάρ, ἐμοὶ δὲ ἀφεκτέα τοῦ
ἀνδρός, οὐ γὰρ ἐκεῖνον διαβαλεῖν προὐθέμην, ἀλλὰ
παραδοῦναι τὸν Ἀπολλωνίου βίον τοῖς μήπω εἰδόσι.
τὸ μέντοι περὶ τοῦ ξύλου λεγόμενον, λέγεται δὲ ἐπανα-
τείνασθαι μὲν αὐτὸ διαλεγομένῳ τῷ Ἀπολλωνίῳ, μὴ
καθικέσθαι δέ, οἱ μὲν πολλοὶ δεινότητι τοῦ πεπληξο-
μένου προσγράφουσιν, ἐγὼ δὲ λογισμῷ τοῦ πλήξον-
τος, δι' ὃν ἐγένετο κρείττων ὀργῆς νενικηκυίας ἤδη.

40. Ἡ δὲ τοῦ Δίωνος φιλοσοφία ῥητορικωτέρα τῷ
Ἀπολλωνίῳ ἐφαίνετο καὶ ἐς τὸ εὐφραῖνον κατεσκευ-
ασμένη μᾶλλον, ὅθεν διορθούμενος αὐτὸν φησιν "αὐλῷ καὶ λύρᾳ μᾶλλον ἢ λόγῳ θέλγε," καὶ πολλαχοῦ
τῶν πρὸς Δίωνα ἐπιστολῶν ἐπιπλήττει τῇ δημαγωγίᾳ
ταύτῃ.

41. Τὸ δὲ μὴ ἀφικέσθαι αὐτὸν παρὰ τὸν βασιλέα
ἔτι, μηδὲ ξυγγενέσθαι οἱ μετὰ τὴν Αἴγυπτον καίτοι
καλοῦντι καὶ πλεῖστα ὑπὲρ τούτου γράφοντι ὁπόθεν
ξυνέβη, δηλῶσαι βούλομαι· Νέρων ἐλευθέραν ἀφῆκε
τὴν Ἑλλάδα σωφρονέστερόν τι ἑαυτοῦ γνούς, καὶ
ἐπανῆλθον αἱ πόλεις ἐς ἤθη Δωρικὰ καὶ Ἀττικὰ πάντα
τε ἀνήβησε ξὺν ὁμονοίᾳ τῶν πόλεων, ὃ μηδὲ πάλαι ἡ

39. So much for what I have discovered about the quarrel between Apollonius and Euphrates, but after the emperor's departure they attacked each other openly, Euphrates with anger and insult, Apollonius by contrast like a philosopher and with argument. The charges he made against Euphrates, that he did not act in accordance with philosophic propriety, may be learned from Apollonius's letters to him, which are numerous. I however must not criticize the gentleman, since my object is not to slander him, but to recount the life of Apollonius for those who are ignorant of it. As for the story about the stick, for it is said that Euphrates meant to strike Apollonius as he was lecturing, but did not hit him, most authors allege cunning on the part of the intended target, but I allege the assailant's faculty of reason, by which he mastered the anger that had overpowered him.

40. Dio however had a philosophy that Apollonius thought too rhetorical and too directed toward giving pleasure. Hence when he puts him right he says, "Soothe with the pipe and the lyre, not with language." Often in his letters to Dio he criticizes this vulgarity.[56]

41. He never visited the emperor again, or met him after Egypt, even though the emperor invited him and very often wrote to him on the subject, and how this came about I want to reveal. By a decision of uncharacteristic wisdom, Nero had set Greece free, so that the cities went back to their Doric and Attic ways, and there was prosperity everywhere, together with concord in the cities, a situation

[56] See Letter 9.

Ἑλλὰς εἶχεν, Οὐεσπασιανὸς δὲ ἀφικόμενος ἀφείλετο αὐτὴν τοῦτο στάσεις προβαλλόμενος καὶ ἄλλα οὔπω τῆς ἐπὶ τοσόνδε ὀργῆς· ταῦτ᾽ οὖν οὐ μόνον τοῖς παθοῦσιν, ἀλλὰ καὶ τῷ Ἀπολλωνίῳ πικρότερα τοῦ τῆς βασιλείας ἤθους ἔδοξεν, ὅθεν ἐπέστειλε τῷ βασιλεῖ ὧδε·

2   "Ἀπολλώνιος Οὐεσπασιανῷ βασιλεῖ χαίρειν. Ἐδουλώσω τὴν Ἑλλάδα, ὥς φασι, καὶ πλέον μὲν οἴει τι ἔχειν Ξέρξου, λέληθας δὲ ἔλαττον ἔχων Νέρωνος· Νέρων γὰρ ἔχων αὐτὸ παρῃτήσατο. ἔρρωσο."

3   "Τῷ αὐτῷ. Διαβεβλημένος οὕτω πρὸς Ἕλληνας, ὡς δουλοῦσθαι αὐτοὺς ἐλευθέρους ὄντας τί ἐμοῦ ξυνόντος δέῃ; ἔρρωσο."

4   "Τῷ αὐτῷ. Νέρων τοὺς Ἕλληνας παίζων ἠλευθέρωσε, σὺ δὲ αὐτοὺς σπουδάζων ἐδουλώσω. ἔρρωσο."

5   Τὰ μὲν δὴ διαβάλλοντα Οὐεσπασιανὸν Ἀπολλωνίῳ τοιάδε ἐγένετο, ἀκούων δ᾽ αὐτὸν εὖ διατιθέμενον τὴν μετὰ ταῦτα ἀρχὴν πᾶσαν, οὐκ ἀφανὴς ἦν χαίρων καὶ ἡγούμενος ἑαυτῷ ἀγαθὸν πράττεσθαι.

42. Θαυμάσιον Ἀπολλωνίου κἀκεῖνο ἐν Αἰγύπτῳ ἔδοξε. λέοντα ἥμερον ἀπὸ ῥυτῆρος ἦγέ τις, ὥσπερ κύνα, ὁ δὲ οὐ μόνον τὸν ἄγοντα ἦκαλλεν, ἀλλὰ καὶ ὅστις προσέλθοι, καὶ ἤγειρε μὲν πολλαχοῦ τῶν πόλεων, παρῄει δὲ καὶ ἐς τὰ ἱερὰ ὑπὸ τοῦ καθαρὸς εἶναι· οὐδὲ γὰρ τὸ τῶν θυομένων αἷμα ἀνελιχμᾶτο, οὐδ᾽ ἐπὶ τὰ δερόμενά τε καὶ ῥαχιζόμενα τῶν ἱερείων ᾔτνεν, ἀλλὰ μελιττούταις διήγετο καὶ ἄρτοις καὶ τραγήμασι καὶ κρεῶν τοῖς ἑφθοῖς, ἐντυχεῖν δὲ ἦν αὐτῷ καὶ οἶνον

not enjoyed even by ancient Greece. On his arrival there, however, Vespasian deprived the Greeks of this gift, giving as his reason their quarrels and other charges which did not justify such anger. All this seemed to the victims, as also to Apollonius, harsher than a ruler should be, and so he wrote the emperor as follows.[57]

"Apollonius greets the emperor Vespasian. You have 2 enslaved Greece, I am told. You think you possess more than Xerxes did, but without realizing it you possess less than Nero did. Nero both had it and refused it. Goodbye."

"Apollonius to the same. If you think so ill of the Greeks 3 as to make them slaves when they are free, why do you need my presence? Goodbye."

"Apollonius to the same. Nero freed the Greeks in play, 4 but you have enslaved them in earnest. Goodbye."

This then was what offended Apollonius about Vespa- 5 sian. But hearing how well he conducted his reign thereafter, he did not conceal his pleasure and his belief that he had gained a good thing for himself.

42. Something else that Apollonius did in Egypt was considered a miracle. A man was leading a tame lion on a leash like a dog, and the creature fawned not only on its master but on all comers. It went begging from city to city, and was even admitted to sanctuaries because of its purity, since it never licked up sacrificial blood or pounced on the victims when they were being flayed and cut up. It lived on honey cakes, bread, dried fruits, and cooked meat, and it

---

[57] These three letters also survive separately, see Letters 42f–h.

πίνοντι μὴ μεθισταμένῳ τοῦ ἤθους. προσελθὼν δὲ τῷ
Ἀπολλωνίῳ καθημένῳ ἐς τὸ ἱερὸν τοῖς τε γόνασιν
αὐτοῦ προσεκνυζᾶτο καὶ ἐλιπάρει παρὰ πάντας ἀνθρώπους, ὡς μὲν οἱ πολλοὶ ᾤοντο, μισθοῦ ἕνεκα, ὁ δὲ
Ἀπολλώνιος "δεῖταί μου" ἔφη "ὁ λέων ἀναδιδάξαι
ὑμᾶς, ὅτου ἀνθρώπου ψυχὴν ἔχει· ἔστι τοίνυν Ἄμασις
οὗτος, ὁ βασιλεὺς Αἰγύπτου <τῆς>³⁷ περὶ τὸν Σαΐτην
νομόν."

2   Ἐπεὶ δ' ἤκουσεν ὁ λέων ταῦτα, ἀνεβρυχήσατο
ἐλεεινὸν καὶ θρηνῶδες καὶ ὠλοφύρατο ξυνοκλάσας,
δάκρυα ἱεὶς αὐτά. καταψῶν οὖν αὐτὸν ὁ Ἀπολλώνιος
"δοκεῖ" ἔφη "πέμπειν τὸν λέοντα ἐς Λεοντόπολιν ἀνα-
κεισόμενον τῷ ἱερῷ, βασιλέα γὰρ ἐς τὸ βασιλικώ-
τατον τῶν θηρίων μεταβαλόντα οὐκ ἀξιῶ ἀγείρειν,
καθάπερ τοὺς πτωχοὺς τῶν ἀνθρώπων." ἐντεῦθεν οἱ
ἱερεῖς ξυνελθόντες ἔθυσαν τῷ Ἀμάσιδι καὶ κοσμή-
σαντες τὸ θηρίον στρεπτῷ καὶ ταινίαις παρέπεμπον ἐς
τὴν Αἴγυπτον αὐλοῦντες καὶ ὑμνοῦντες καὶ ἐπ' αὐτῷ
ᾄδοντες.

43. Ἱκανῶς δὲ ἔχων τῶν περὶ τὴν Ἀλεξάνδρειαν
ἐστέλλετο ἐς Αἴγυπτόν τε καὶ ἐς Αἰθιοπίαν ἐς ξυνουσίαν τῶν Γυμνῶν. τὸν μὲν δὴ Μένιππον, ἐπειδὴ τῶν
διαλεγομένων ἤδη ἐτύγχανε καὶ παρρησίᾳ χρῆσθαι
δεινὸς ἦν, κατέλιπεν αὐτόθι ἔφεδρον τῷ Εὐφράτῃ, καὶ
τὸν Διοσκορίδην ἰδὼν οὐκ ἐρρωμένως πρὸς τὴν ἀποδημίαν διακείμενον παρῃτήσατο τῆς ὁδοῦ, τοὺς δὲ
λοιποὺς ξυναγαγών, μετὰ γὰρ τοὺς ἀπολιπόντας αὐ-

could also be found drinking wine without its behavior being affected. It came up to Apollonius when he was sitting in the sanctuary, nuzzled his knees, and particularly begged from him. Most people thought it wanted something in return, but Apollonius said, "The lion is begging me to tell you whose human soul it has. Well, this is Amasis, the king of Egypt in the Saite district."[58]

When the lion heard this, it gave a pathetic, mournful 2 roar, and collapsed in sobs, shedding actual tears. Apollonius stroked it and said, "I advise you to send the lion to Leontopolis[59] to be dedicated in the sanctuary, for I do not think a king who has turned into the king of beasts should have to scrounge like a human beggar." So the assembled priests sacrificed to Amasis, and after adorning the creature with a collar and ribbons escorted it up country, piping and singing hymns and odes in its honor.

43. Having now had enough of Alexandria, Apollonius prepared to leave for Egypt and Ethiopia to meet the Naked Ones. Menippus was now a qualified disputant and clever at using frankness, so Apollonius left him behind to take over the struggle with Euphrates. However, he saw Dioscorides was not eager for the journey, so he excused him from the voyage. Then he assembled the rest, because many others had joined him after those that had deserted

58 Amasis, king of Egypt in the sixth century, who originated from the Saite nome (Herodotus 1.172).

59 Literally "Lion City." Philostratus seems to mean the more northerly of the two cities of Egypt with this name, the capital of the Leontopolite nome.

---

37 ⟨τῆς⟩ Rsk.

APOLLONIUS OF TYANA

τὸν περὶ τὴν Ἀρικίαν προσεγένοντο πλείους ἔτεροι,
διῄει πρὸς αὐτοὺς περὶ τῆς ἀποδημίας ἐνθένδε ἀρ-
ξάμενος·

2   "Ὀλυμπικῆς προρρήσεως" ἔφη "δέομαι πρὸς ὑμᾶς,
ὦ ἄνδρες· Ὀλυμπικὴ δὲ πρόρρησις ἡ τοιάδε εἴη
ἄν· Ἠλεῖοι τοὺς ἀθλητάς, ἐπειδὰν ἥκῃ Ὀλύμπια,
γυμνάζουσιν ἡμερῶν τριάκοντα ἐν αὐτῇ τῇ Ἤλιδι, καὶ
ξυναγαγόντες αὐτοὺς ὁ μὲν Δελφός, ὅτε Πύθια, ὁ δὲ
Κορίνθιος, ὅτε Ἴσθμια, "ἴτε" φασὶν "ἐς τὸ στάδιον,
καὶ γίγνεσθε ἄνδρες οἷοι νικᾶν," Ἠλεῖοι δέ, ἐπειδὰν
ἴωσιν ἐς Ὀλυμπίαν, διαλέγονται πρὸς τοὺς ἀθλητὰς
ὧδε· "εἰ πεπόνηται ὑμῖν ἐπαξίως τοῦ ἐς Ὀλυμπίαν
ἐλθεῖν καὶ μηδὲν ῥάθυμον μηδὲ ἀγεννὲς εἴργασται,
ἴτε θαρροῦντες, οἷς δὲ μὴ ὧδε ἤσκηται, χωρεῖτε οἷ
βούλεσθε."

3   Ξυνῆκαν οἱ ὁμιληταὶ τοῦ λόγου, καὶ κατέμειναν
ἀμφὶ τοὺς εἴκοσι παρὰ τῷ Μενίππῳ, οἱ δὲ λοιποὶ δέκα,
οἶμαι, ὄντες εὐξάμενοι τοῖς θεοῖς, καὶ οἷον ἐμβατήρια
πλοῦ θύσαντες, ἐχώρουν εὐθὺ πυραμίδων ἐπὶ καμήλων ὀχούμενοι, δεξιὸν θέμενοι τὸν Νεῖλον. πολλαχοῦ
δὲ διεπλεῖτο αὐτοῖς ὁ ποταμὸς ὑπὲρ ἱστορίας τῶν ἐν
αὐτῷ πάντων, οὔτε γὰρ πόλιν οὔτε ἱερὸν οὔθ᾽ ὁπόσα
τεμένη κατ᾽ Αἴγυπτον, οὐδὲν τούτων ἄφωνοι παρῆλ-
θον, ἀλλ᾽ ἱερούς τινας ἀεὶ λόγους διδασκόμενοί τε καὶ
διδάσκοντες, καὶ ἡ ναῦς, ἢν ἐμβαίη Ἀπολλώνιος,
ἐῴκει θεωρίδι.

at Aricia,[60] and gave them a lecture about the voyage, beginning in this way:

"I have to make an Olympic announcement to you, my 2 friends, and an Olympic announcement goes rather like this. When the Olympics come round, the Eleans train the athletes for thirty days in Elis itself. While the Delphians assemble them at the time of Pythian games, and the Corinthians at that of the Isthmian, and say 'Proceed to the stadium, and show yourselves to be true men qualified for victory,' the Eleans address the athletes as follows on their arrival at Olympia: 'If you have trained in a way worthy of your coming to Olympia, and have done nothing lazy or dishonorable, proceed with confidence. But those of you who have not so trained in this way may go wherever you please.'"

His disciples understood his speech, and about twenty 3 of them stayed behind with Menippus. But others, ten of them, I believe, after praying to the gods and sacrificing as if about to start on a sea voyage, set out straight for the pyramids on camelback, keeping the Nile on their right. They also crossed the river at many points in order to learn about everything on its banks, and there was no city, sanctuary, or any sacred place in Egypt that they passed in silence, but were constantly hearing or giving a kind of sacred discourse, and any vessel that carried Apollonius resembled a pilgrim ship.

[60] See IV 36–37.

1. Αἰθιοπία δὲ τῆς μὲν ὑπὸ ἡλίῳ πάσης ἐπέχει τὸ ἑσπέριον κέρας, ὥσπερ Ἰνδοὶ τὸ πρὸς ἔω, κατὰ Μερόην δ' Αἰγύπτῳ ξυνάπτουσα, καί τι τῆς ἀμαρτύρου Λιβύης ἐπελθοῦσα, τελευτᾷ ἐς θάλατταν, ἣν Ὠκεανὸν οἱ ποιηταὶ καλοῦσι, τὸ περὶ γῆν ἅπαν ὧδε ἐπονομάζοντες. ποταμὸν δὲ Νεῖλον Αἰγύπτῳ δίδωσιν, ὃς ἐκ Καταδούπων ἀρχόμενος, ἣν ἐπικλύζει πᾶσαν Αἴγυπτον ἀπ' Αἰθιόπων ἄγει. μέγεθος μὲν οὖν οὐκ ἀξία παραβεβλῆσθαι πρὸς Ἰνδοὺς ἥδε ἡ χώρα, ὅτι μηδ' ἄλλη μηδεμία, ὁπόσαι κατ' ἀνθρώπους ὀνομασταὶ ἤπειροι, εἰ δὲ καὶ πᾶσαν Αἴγυπτον Αἰθιοπίᾳ ξυμβάλοιμεν, τουτὶ δὲ ἡγώμεθα καὶ τὸν ποταμὸν πράττειν, οὔπω ξύμμετροι πρὸς τὴν Ἰνδῶν ἄμφω, τοσαύτη ξυντεθεῖσα, ποταμοὶ δὲ ἀμφοῖν ὅμοιοι λογισαμένῳ τὰ Ἰνδοῦ τε καὶ Νεῖλον· ἐπιρραίνουσί τε γὰρ τὰς ἠπείρους ἐν ὥρᾳ ἔτους, ὁπότε ἡ γῆ ἐρᾷ τούτου, ποταμῶν τε παρέχονται μόνοι τὸν κροκόδειλον καὶ τὸν ἵππον, λόγοι τε ὀργίων ἐπ' αὐτοῖς ἴσοι, πολλὰ γὰρ τῶν Ἰνδῶν καὶ Νείλῳ ἐπιθειάζεται.

2   Τὴν δὲ ὁμοιότητα τῶν ἠπείρων πιστούσθων μὲν καὶ τὰ ἐν αὐταῖς ἀρώματα, πιστούσθων δὲ καὶ οἱ λέοντες

BOOK VI

1. Ethiopia occupies the western extension of the whole world beneath the sun, as India does of the eastern. It adjoins Egypt at Meroe, includes a part of unexplored Africa, and ends at the sea which the poets call the Ocean, that being their name for the whole element surrounding the earth.[1] Ethiopia supplies Egypt with the river Nile, which beginning at the Falls[2] brings from Ethiopia all the soil with which it floods Egypt. In extent this region cannot be compared with India, as indeed none of the other continents that are famous among men can. Even if we were to join all of Egypt with Ethiopia, as we must consider the river does, the two of them are still not comparable to India in extent when set against so large a country. But the rivers of the two continents are alike when one considers the natures of the Indus and the Nile. They irrigate their continents in the summer season, when the soil desires it, and they are the only rivers to produce the crocodile and the hippopotamus.

Both rivers are equally famous for their sacred rites,   2
since many of the Indians' sacred beliefs also apply to the

[1] For Philostratus's very confused geography in this book, see Introduction.   [2] Philostratus seems to consider the "Falls" (*katadoupoi*) a mountain range (cf. ch. 23), separate from the various cataracts of the Nile.

καὶ ὁ ἐλέφας ἐν ἑκατέρᾳ ἁλισκόμενός τε καὶ δουλεύων. βόσκουσι δὲ καὶ θηρία, οἷα οὐχ ἑτέρωθι, καὶ ἀνθρώπους μέλανας, ὃ μὴ ἄλλαι ἤπειροι, Πυγμαίων τε ἐν αὐταῖς ἔθνη καὶ ὑλακτούντων ἄλλο ἄλλῃ καὶ ὧδε θαυμαστά. γρῦπες δὲ Ἰνδῶν καὶ μύρμηκες Αἰθιόπων εἰ καὶ ἀνόμοιοι τὴν ἰδέαν εἰσίν, ἀλλ᾽ ὅμοιά γε, ὥς φασι, βούλονται, χρυσοῦ γὰρ φύλακες ἐν ἑκατέρᾳ ᾄδονται τὸ χρυσόγεων τῶν ἠπείρων ἀσπαζόμενοι. ἀλλὰ μὴ πλείω ὑπὲρ τούτων, ὁ δὲ λόγος ἐς τὸ ἑαυτοῦ ἴτω καὶ ἐχώμεθα τοῦ ἀνδρός.

2. Ἀφικόμενος γὰρ ἐπὶ τὰ Αἰθιόπων τε καὶ Αἰγυπτίων ὅρια, Συκάμινον δὲ αὐτὰ ὀνομάζουσι, χρυσῷ τε ἀσήμῳ ἐνέτυχε, καὶ λίνῳ, καὶ ἐλέφαντι, καὶ ῥίζαις, καὶ μύρῳ, καὶ ἀρώμασιν, ἔκειτο δὲ πάντα ἀφύλακτα ἐν ὁδῷ σχιστῇ· καὶ ὅ τι βούλεται ταῦτα, ἐγὼ δηλώσω, νομίζεται γὰρ καὶ ἐς ἡμᾶς ἔτι. ἀγορὰν Αἰθίοπες ἀπάγουσιν, ὧν Αἰθιοπία δίδωσιν, οἱ δ᾽ ἀνελόμενοι πᾶσαν ξυμφέρουσιν ἐς τὸν αὐτὸν χῶρον ἀγορὰν Αἰγυπτίαν ἴσου ἀξίαν ὠνούμενοι τῶν αὐτοῖς ὄντων τὰ οὐκ ὄντα. οἱ δὲ τὰ ὅρια τῶν ἠπείρων οἰκοῦντες οὔπω μέλανες, ἀλλὰ ὁμόφυλοι τὸ χρῶμα, μελαίνονται γὰρ οἱ μὲν ἧττον Αἰθιόπων, οἱ δὲ μᾶλλον Αἰγυπτίων.

2   Ξυνεὶς οὖν ὁ Ἀπολλώνιος τοῦ τῆς ἀγορᾶς ἤθους, "οἱ δὲ χρηστοὶ" ἔφη "Ἕλληνες, ἢν μὴ ὀβολὸς ὀβολὸν τέκῃ καὶ τὰ ὤνια αὐτοῖς ἐπιτιμήσωσι καπηλεύοντες ἢ καθειργνύντες, οὔ φασι ζῆν ὁ μὲν θυγατέρα σκηπτόμενος ἐν ὥρᾳ γάμων, ὁ δ᾽ υἱὸν ἤδη τελοῦντα ἐς ἄνδρας, ὁ δ᾽ ἐράνου πλήρωσιν, ὁ δ᾽, ὡς οἰκοδομοῖτο

Nile. The similarity of the two continents may also be corroborated by the spices they produce, and by the fact that lions and elephants are caught and made to work in both. They also produce beasts seen nowhere else, and black people, as no other continents do, and they contain tribes of Pygmies and of humans that bark in various ways, and similar wonders. Indian griffins and Ethiopian ants may be of different shape, but they are said to have the same pursuits, because both are celebrated on the two continents for guarding gold and for favoring the gold-producing regions. But let us have no more on these topics, as my story must return to its subject and we must follow the Master.

2. He arrived at the crossing point between Ethiopia and Egypt, which is called Kaminos. There he came across uncoined gold, linen, ivory, herbs, perfume, and spices, all lying unguarded at a road junction. I will explain the meaning of this, since the custom is observed to this day. The Ethiopians market the products of Ethiopia, and the Egyptians carry it all away, while they bring Egyptian goods of equal value to the same place, using what they have to buy what they lack. Those who live at the border of the two countries are not quite black but of the same color as each other, for the Egyptians are less black than the Ethiopians and the Ethiopians more so than the Egyptians.

Understanding the custom of the exchange, Apollonius 2 said, "Yet the honorable Greeks think they have no life unless an obol breeds an obol, and they can sell their goods at high prices to one another by huckstering and hoarding. One man claims to have a daughter of marriageable age, another a son entering manhood, another payment of club

οἰκίαν, ὁ δέ, ὡς αἰσχύνοιτο χρηματιστὴς ἥττων τοῦ
πατρὸς δόξαι. καλῶς δ' ἄρ' εἶχεν, ἵνα ὁ πλοῦτος
ἀτίμως ἔπραττεν ἰσότης τε ἤνθει, 'μέλας δ' ἀπέκειτο
σίδηρος,' ὁμονοούντων τῶν ἀνθρώπων, καὶ ἡ γῆ πᾶσα
ἐδόκει μία."

3. Τοιαῦτα διαλεγόμενος καὶ ξυμβούλους τῶν διαλέξεων, ὥσπερ εἰώθει, ποιούμενος τοὺς καιροὺς ἐχώρει
ἐπὶ Μέμνονος, ἡγεῖτο δ' αὐτοῖς μειράκιον Αἰγύπτιον,
ὑπὲρ οὗ τάδε ἀναγράφει Δάμις· Τιμασίων μὲν τῷ
μειρακίῳ τούτῳ ὄνομα ἦν, ἐφήβου δὲ ἄρτι ὑπαπήει καὶ
τὴν ὥραν ἔτι ἔρρωτο. σωφρονοῦντι δὲ αὐτῷ μητρυιὰ
ἐρῶσα ἐνέκειτο καὶ χαλεπὸν τὸν πατέρα ἐποίει, ξυν-
τιθεῖσα μὲν οὐδὲν ὧνπερ ἡ Φαίδρα, διαβάλλουσα δ'
αὐτὸν ὡς θῆλυν καὶ ἐρασταῖς μᾶλλον ἢ γυναίοις
χαίροντα. ὁ δ' ἐκλιπὼν Ναύκρατιν, ἐκεῖ γὰρ ταῦτα
ἐγίγνετο, περὶ Μέμφιν διῃτᾶτο, καὶ ναῦν δὲ ἤδη ἄκατον[1] ἐκέκτητο καὶ ἐναυκλήρει ἐν τῷ Νείλῳ.

2   Ἰδὼν οὖν ἀναπλέοντα τὸν Ἀπολλώνιον καταπλέων
αὐτὸς ξυνῆκέ τε, ὡς ἀνδρῶν σοφῶν εἴη τὸ πλήρωμα
ξυμβαλλόμενος τοῖς τρίβωσι καὶ τοῖς βιβλίοις, οἷς
προσεσπούδαζον, καὶ ἱκέτευε προσδοῦναί οἱ τῆς τοῦ
πλοῦ κοινωνίας ἐρῶντι σοφίας, ὁ δ' Ἀπολλώνιος "σώφρων" ἔφη "ὁ νεανίσκος, ὦ ἄνδρες, καὶ ἀξιούσθω ὧν
δεῖται," καὶ διῆλθε τὸν περὶ τῆς μητρυιᾶς λόγον πρὸς
τοὺς ἐγγὺς τῶν ἑταίρων ὑφειμένῳ τῷ τόνῳ προσ-
πλέοντος τοῦ μειρακίου ἔτι. ὡς δὲ ξυνῄεσαν[2] αἱ νῆες,

---

[1] ἄκατον Bentl.: ἄτοπον   [2] ξυνῄεσαν Kay.: ξυνῆσαν

dues, another a house he is building, another that he would be ashamed to make less money than his father. It was indeed a good time when wealth was in dishonor, equality flourished, 'dark iron was hidden away'[3] because mankind was united, and the whole world was considered one."

3. This was the way he conversed, characteristically taking circumstances as his prompters for each discourse. He proceeded towards Memnon, guided by an Egyptian youth of whom Damis gives the following account. This youth's name was Timasion. He was just passing out of his teens and was still in the prime of youthful beauty. Though chaste himself, his stepmother persecuted him out of passion, and made his father harsh by concocting stories quite different from Phaedra's,[4] and slandering him as effeminate and fonder of male lovers than of female. Leaving Naucratis, the scene of these events, he was living near Memphis, where he had now bought a light boat and was plying it on the Nile.

He saw Apollonius sailing up river when he was sailing down, and realized that the passengers were wise men by inference from their philosophers' cloaks and the attention they gave to their books. He begged them therefore to let him share their journey, because he loved wisdom, whereupon Apollonius said, "This young man is chaste, my friends, and let him be granted what he asks." He then related the story about the stepmother to those of his companions nearby, speaking in a low voice while the youth was still sailing towards them. When the boats met, 2

[3] Hesiod, *Works and Days* 151 (slightly altered).

[4] In Euripides's *Hippolytus* Phaedra falsely accuses her stepson Hippolytus of making sexual advances to her.

μεταβὰς ὁ Τιμασίων καὶ πρὸς τὸν ἑαυτοῦ κυβερνήτην
εἰπών τι ὑπὲρ τοῦ φόρτου προσεῖπε τοὺς ἄνδρας.
κελεύσας οὖν αὐτὸν ὁ Ἀπολλώνιος κατ᾽ ὀφθαλμοὺς
αὑτοῦ ἱζῆσαι "μειράκιον" ἔφη "Αἰγύπτιον, ἔοικας γὰρ
τῶν ἐπιχωρίων εἶναί τις, τί σοι φαῦλον ἢ τί χρηστὸν
εἴργασται, λέξον, ὡς τῶν μὲν λύσις παρ᾽ ἐμοῦ γένοιτό
σοι δι᾽ ἡλικίαν, τῶν δ᾽ αὖ ἐπαινεθεὶς ἐμοί τε ξυμφιλο-
σοφοίης καὶ τοῖσδε."

3   Ὁρῶν δὲ τὸν Τιμασίωνα ἐρυθριῶντα καὶ μετα-
βάλλοντα τὴν ὁρμὴν τοῦ στόματος ἐς τὸ λέξαι τι ἢ
μή, θαμὰ ἤρειδε τὴν ἐρώτησιν, ὥσπερ οὐδεμιᾷ προ-
γνώσει ἐς αὐτὸν κεχρημένος, ἀναθαρσήσας δὲ ὁ Τιμασίων "ὦ θεοί," ἔφη "τίνα ἐμαυτὸν εἴπω; κακὸς μὲν
γὰρ οὐκ εἰμί, ἀγαθὸν δὲ εἰ χρὴ νομίζεσθαί με, οὐκ
οἶδα, τὸ γὰρ μὴ ἀδικεῖν οὔπω ἔπαινος." καὶ ὁ Ἀπολλώνιος "βαβαί," ἔφη "μειράκιον, ὡς ἀπὸ Ἰνδῶν μοι
διαλέγῃ, ταυτὶ γὰρ καὶ Ἰάρχᾳ δοκεῖ τῷ θείῳ. ἀλλὰ
πῶς³ ταῦτα δοξάζεις, κἀξ ὅτου; φυλαξαμένῳ γάρ τι
ἁμαρτεῖν ἔοικας."

4   Ἐπεὶ δὲ ἀρξαμένου λέγειν, ὡς ἡ μητρυιὰ μὲν ἐπ᾽
αὐτὸν φέροιτο, αὐτὸς δ᾽ ἐρώσῃ ἐκσταίη, βοὴ ἐγένετο,
ὡς δαιμονίως αὐτὰ τοῦ Ἀπολλωνίου προειπόντος, ὑπολαβὼν ὁ Τιμασίων "ὦ λῷστοι," ἔφη "τί πεπόνθατε;
τοσοῦτον γὰρ ἀπέχει τὰ εἰρημένα θαύματος, ὅσον,
οἶμαι, γέλωτος." καὶ ὁ Δάμις "ἕτερόν τι" ἔφη "ἐθαυ-
μάσαμεν, ὃ μήπω γιγνώσκεις. καὶ σὲ δέ, μειράκιον,

³ ἀλλὰ πῶς West.: ἀλλ᾽ ὅπως

Timasion came across, and after giving some instruction to his own steersman about the cargo addressed the gentlemen. Apollonius asked him to sit where he could observe him, and said, "Egyptian youth (since you look like one of the natives), tell me what bad or good you have done, so that you may get my absolution for the bad on account of your age, and being praised for the good may become a philosopher like myself and these people here."

Seeing that Timasion blushed and changed the position of his lips, uncertain whether to speak or not, Apollonius kept pressing his question as if he had no foreknowledge about him, until Timasion plucked up courage and said, "Gods, what shall I call myself? I am not wicked, but I do not know that I can be thought good, because avoiding wrong is no praise in itself." "Bless me, young man," said Apollonius, "you answer me as if you were from India, since the inspired Iarchas is of your very opinion.[5] But how did you come to have this belief, and since when? For you seem to have been shunning some error." 3

When the youth began to tell how his stepmother had made advances to him, and he had avoided her passion, there was a shout, so miraculously had Apollonius predicted all this. But Timasion reacted by saying, "Good people, what is wrong with you? What I have said has as little to do with amazement as with laughter, I think." But Damis replied, "We were surprised by something else that you do not know of. And yet we also praise you, 4

[5] Cf. III 25.1.

ἐπαινοῦμεν, ὅτι μηδὲν οἴει λαμπρὸν εἰργάσθαι."

5 "Ἀφροδίτῃ δὲ θύεις, ὦ μειράκιον;" ἤρετο ὁ Ἀπολλώνιος, καὶ ὁ Τιμασίων, "νὴ Δί'," εἶπεν, "ὁσημέραι γε,
πολλὴν γὰρ ἡγοῦμαι τὴν θεὸν ⟨ἐν⟩⁴ ἀνθρωπείοις τε
καὶ θείοις πράγμασιν." ὑπερησθεὶς οὖν ὁ Ἀπολλώνιος, "ψηφισώμεθα," ἔφη "ὦ ἄνδρες, ἐστεφανῶσθαι
αὐτὸν ἐπὶ σωφροσύνῃ καὶ πρὸ Ἱππολύτου τοῦ Θησέως, ὁ μὲν γὰρ ἐς τὴν Ἀφροδίτην ὕβρισε καὶ διὰ
τουτὶ ἴσως οὐδὲ ἀφροδισίων ἥττητο, οὐδὲ ἔρως ἐπ'
αὐτὸν οὐδεὶς ἐκώμαζεν, ἀλλ' ἦν τῆς ἀγροικοτέρας τε
καὶ ἀτέγκτου μοίρας, οὑτοσὶ δὲ ἡττᾶσθαι τῆς θεοῦ
φάσκων οὐδὲν πρὸς τὴν ἐρῶσαν ἔπαθεν, ἀλλ' ἀπῆλθεν
αὐτὴν δείσας τὴν θεόν, εἰ τὸ κακῶς ἐρᾶσθαι μὴ
φυλάξοιτο,⁵ καὶ αὐτὸ δὲ τὸ διαβεβλῆσθαι πρὸς ὁντι-
ναδὴ τῶν θεῶν, ὥσπερ πρὸς τὴν Ἀφροδίτην ὁ Ἱππό-
λυτος, οὐκ ἀξιῶ σωφροσύνης, σωφρονέστερον γὰρ τὸ
περὶ πάντων θεῶν εὖ λέγειν καὶ ταῦτα Ἀθήνησιν, οὗ
καὶ ἀγνώστων δαιμόνων βωμοὶ ἵδρυνται." τοσαῦτα ἐς
τὸν Τιμασίωνα αὐτῷ ἐσπουδάσθη. πλὴν ἀλλὰ Ἱππό-
λυτόν γε ἐκάλει αὐτὸν διὰ τοὺς ὀφθαλμούς, οἷς τὴν
μητρυιὰν εἶδεν. ἐδόκει δὲ καὶ τοῦ σώματος ἐπιμεληθῆναι καὶ γυμναστικῆς ἐπαφροδίτως ἅψασθαι.

4. Ὑπὸ τούτῳ ἡγεμόνι παρελθεῖν φασιν ἐς τὸ
τέμενος τοῦ Μέμνονος. περὶ δὲ τοῦ Μέμνονος τάδε
ἀναγράφει Δάμις· Ἠοῦς μὲν παῖδα γενέσθαι αὐτόν,
ἀποθανεῖν δὲ οὐκ ἐν Τροίᾳ, ὅτι μηδὲ ἀφικέσθαι ἐς
Τροίαν, ἀλλ' ἐν Αἰθιοπίᾳ τελευτῆσαι βασιλεύσαντα
Αἰθιόπων γενεὰς πέντε. οἱ δ', ἐπειδὴ μακροβιώτατοι

young man, for not thinking you have done anything extra-ordinary."

"Do you sacrifice to Aphrodite, my boy?" asked Apollo-nius. "Certainly," said the boy, "every day. She is a goddess who I think has great power in the affairs of humans and gods." Overjoyed, Apollonius said, "Gentlemen, let us vote him a crown for chastity above even Hippolytus, the son of Theseus. *He* insulted Aphrodite, and hence perhaps he did not fall victim to sexual passion, or feel the waywardness of love, but was a rather boorish and heartless sort. But this youth admits that while obedient to the goddess he was un-moved by the woman's passion, and left, fearing the god-dess herself if he did not escape being the object of an evil passion. Indeed, I do not think it a sign of modesty to be on bad terms with any of the gods, as Hippolytus was with Aphrodite. It is more modest to speak well of every god, especially at Athens where there are altars set up to un-known divinities."[6] That was his discourse about Timasion, though he did call him "Hippolytus" because of the way he had eyed his stepmother, and he also seemed to have cultivated his physique and increased his attractiveness by exercise.

4. With this man as guide, they say they reached the sanctuary of Memnon, and about Memnon Damis gives this account. He was the son of Dawn, and did not fall at Troy, in fact he did not even get to Troy, but died in Ethio-pia, after ruling the Ethiopians for five generations. As the longest-lived people on earth, the Ethiopians mourn for

[6] Cf. Acts of the Apostles 17.23.

---

4 ⟨ἐν⟩ Kay.   5 φυλάξοιτο Suda: φυλάξαιτο

ἀνθρώπων εἰσίν, ὀλοφύρονται τὸν Μέμνονα ὡς κομιδῇ
νέον καὶ ὅσα ἐπὶ ἀώρῳ κλαίουσι, τὸ δὲ χωρίον, ἐν ᾧ
ἵδρυται, φασὶ μὲν προσεοικέναι ἀγορᾷ ἀρχαίᾳ, οἷαι
τῶν ἀγορῶν ἐν πόλεσί ποτε οἰκηθείσαις λείπονται
στηλῶν παρεχόμεναι τρύφη, καὶ τειχῶν ἴχνη, καὶ
θάκους, καὶ φλιάς, ἑρμῶν τε ἀγάλματα, τὰ μὲν ὑπὸ
χειρῶν διεφθορότα, τὰ δὲ ὑπὸ χρόνου.

2   Τὸ δὲ ἄγαλμα τετράφθαι πρὸς ἀκτῖνα μήπω γε-
νειάσκον, λίθου δὲ εἶναι μέλανος, ξυμβεβηκέναι δὲ τὼ
πόδε ἄμφω κατὰ τὴν ἀγαλματοποιίαν τὴν ἐπὶ Δαι-
δάλου καὶ τὰς χεῖρας ἀπερείδειν ὀρθὰς ἐς τὸν θᾶκον,
καθῆσθαι γὰρ ἐν ὁρμῇ τοῦ ὑπανίστασθαι. τὸ δὲ
σχῆμα τοῦτο καὶ τὸν τῶν ὀφθαλμῶν νοῦν καὶ ὁπόσα
τοῦ στόματος ὡς φθεγξομένου ᾄδουσι, τὸν μὲν ἄλλον
χρόνον ἧττον θαυμάσαι φασίν, οὔπω γὰρ ἐνεργὰ
φαίνεσθαι, προσβαλούσης δὲ τὸ ἄγαλμα τῆς ἀκτῖνος,
τουτὶ δὲ γίγνεσθαι περὶ ἡλίου ἐπιτολάς, μὴ κατασχεῖν
τὸ θαῦμα.

3   Φθέγξασθαι μὲν γὰρ παραχρῆμα τῆς ἀκτῖνος ἐλ-
θούσης αὐτῷ ἐπὶ στόμα, φαιδροὺς δὲ ἱστάναι τοὺς
ὀφθαλμοὺς δόξαι πρὸς τὸ φῶς, οἷα τῶν ἀνθρώπων
οἱ εὐήλιοι. τότε ξυννεῖναι λέγουσιν, ὅτι τῷ Ἡλίῳ δοκεῖ
ὑπανίστασθαι, καθάπερ οἱ τὸ κρεῖττον ὀρθοὶ θερα-
πεύοντες. θύσαντες οὖν Ἡλίῳ τε Αἰθίοπι καὶ Ἠῴῳ
Μέμνονι, τουτὶ γὰρ ἔφραζον οἱ ἱερεῖς, τὸν μὲν ἀπὸ
τοῦ αἴθειν τε καὶ θάλπειν, τὸν δὲ ἀπὸ τῆς μητρὸς
ἐπονομάζοντες, ἐπορεύοντο ἐπὶ καμήλων ἐς τὰ τῶν
Γυμνῶν ἤθη.

Memnon as one who died very young, and they bewail him as they do the prematurely dead. The place containing his statue they say resembles an ancient marketplace, like the deserted marketplaces in cities inhabited long ago, which have broken-off tablets, traces of walls, seats, doorposts, and sacred herms that have been destroyed either by human hands or by time.

The statue itself faces the sun, and is still beardless. It is 2 of dark stone, with both its feet together like the style of Daedalus's time, and presses its arms straight down on its throne, in the position of a sitter just getting up. This position, the expression of its eyes, and the celebrated look of its lips, as if it was about to speak, did not seem particularly wonderful to them at first, they say, because none of it seemed lifelike. But when the sun's ray struck the statue, as it did at sunrise, they could not withhold their amazement.

It immediately spoke as the ray touched its lips, and 3 fixed its eyes cheerfully on the light, as sunbathers do. It was then, they say, that they realized that it seemed to be rising in honor of the Sun, like those who stand to worship powers above. So they sacrificed to the Ethiopian Sun and Memnon of the Dawn, as the priests instructed them (they give these titles to the sun because he "heats" and "glows," to Memnon because of his mother).[7] The party then traveled on camels to the region of the Naked Ones.

[7] The Greek plays on the proper name *Aithiopia* and the verbs *aithein* (to burn or blaze) and *thalpein* (to warm).

5. Ἀνδρὶ δὲ ἐντυχόντες ἐσταλμένῳ τρόπον, ὅνπερ
οἱ Μεμφῖται καὶ ἀλύοντι μᾶλλον ἢ ξυντείνοντι ἤροντο
οἱ περὶ τὸν Δάμιν, ὅστις εἴη καὶ ὅ τι πλανῷτο, καὶ ὁ
Τιμασίων "ἐμοῦ" ἔφη "πυνθάνεσθε, ἀλλὰ μὴ τούτου,
οὗτος μὲν γὰρ οὐκ ἂν εἴποι πρὸς ὑμᾶς τὸ ἑαυτοῦ
πάθος αἰδοῖ τῆς ξυμφορᾶς, ᾗ κέχρηται, ἐγὼ δέ,
γιγνώσκω γὰρ τὸν ἄνδρα καὶ ἐλεῶ, λέξω τὰ περὶ
αὐτὸν πάντα· ἀπέκτεινε γὰρ Μεμφίτην τινὰ ἄκων,
κελεύουσι δ᾽ οἱ κατὰ Μέμφιν νόμοι τὸν φεύγοντα ἐπ᾽
ἀκουσίῳ, δεῖ[6] δὲ φεύγειν, ἐπὶ τοῖς Γυμνοῖς εἶναι, κἂν
ἐκνίψηται τοῦ φόνου, χωρεῖν ἐς ἤθη καθαρὸν ἤδη,
βαδίσαντα πρότερον ἐπὶ τὸ τοῦ πεφονευμένου σῆμα
καὶ σφάξαντά τι ἐκεῖ οὐ μέγα. τὸν δὲ χρόνον, ὃν οὔπω
τοῖς Γυμνοῖς ἐνέτυχεν, ἀλᾶσθαι χρὴ περὶ ταυτὶ τὰ
ὅρια, ἔστ᾽ ἂν αἰδέσωνται αὐτόν ὥσπερ ἱκέτην."

2   Ἤρετο οὖν τὸν Τιμασίωνα ὁ Ἀπολλώνιος, πῶς οἱ
Γυμνοὶ περὶ τοῦ φεύγοντος ἐκείνου φρονοῦσιν, ὁ δὲ
"οὐκ οἶδα," εἶπε "μῆνα γὰρ τουτονὶ ἕβδομον ἱκετεύει
δεῦρο καὶ οὔπω λύσις." "οὐ σοφοὺς λέγεις ἄνδρας,"
ἔφη "εἰ μὴ καθαίρουσιν αὐτόν, μηδὲ γιγνώσκουσιν,
ὅτι Φιλίσκος, ὃν ἀπέκτεινεν οὗτος, ἀνέφερεν ἐς Θαμοῦν τὸν Αἰγύπτιον, ὃς ἐδῄωσέ ποτε τὴν τῶν Γυμνῶν
χώραν." θαυμάσας οὖν ὁ Τιμασίων "πῶς" ἔφη "λέγεις;" "ὥς γε" εἶπεν, "ὦ μειράκιον, διαπέπρακται·[7]
Θαμοῦν γάρ ποτε νεώτερα ἐπὶ Μεμφίτας πράττοντα
ἤλεγξαν οἱ Γυμνοὶ καὶ ἔσχον, ὁ δὲ ὁρμῆς ἁμαρτὼν

6 δεῖ Kay.: δεῖν

5. They met a man dressed like a Memphite, who was wandering rather than traveling, so that Damis and the others asked him his name and the reason for his wandering. At this Timasion said, "Ask me, not him, since he will not tell you his condition in shame for his misfortune. But as I know and I pity the man, I will tell you his whole story. He killed a Memphite by accident, and the laws of Memphis order a man who is exiled for an involuntary crime (as exiled he must be) to appeal to the Naked Ones. If he is absolved of the bloodshed, he can at last return to society purified, though first he has to visit the slaughtered man's tomb and make some small blood offering there. But during the time before his meeting with the Naked Ones, he must wander about in this border area, until they take compassion on him as a suppliant."

When Apollonius asked Timasion what opinion the Naked Ones had about this exile, he replied, "I do not know, for he has been a suppliant here for six months without yet being purified." "The gentlemen you mention are not wise," said Apollonius, "if they do not absolve him, or realize that Philiscus, whom this man killed, was descended from Thamus the Egyptian[8] who once ravaged the Naked Ones' land." "What do you mean?" asked Timasion in amazement. "The actual facts, young man," said Apollonius. "Thamus once plotted revolution in Memphis, but the Naked Ones exposed and stopped him. Disappointed in his plan, he began to pillage all the land that they cul-

---

[8] Legendary king of Egyptian Thebes.

---

[7] "ὥς γε" εἶπεν, "ὦ μειράκιον, διαπέπρακται" West.: ὥς γε εἶπε τὸ μειράκιόν τι πέπρακται

ἔκειρε πᾶσαν, ἣν οὗτοι νέμονται, ληστρικῶς γὰρ περὶ
Μέμφιν ἔρρωτο· τούτου Φιλίσκον, ὃν οὗτος ἀπέκτεινεν, ὁρῶ ἔκγονον τρίτον ἀπὸ δεκάτου, κατάρατον δη-
λαδὴ τούτοις, ὧν ὁ Θαμοῦς τότε διεπόρθει τὴν χώραν·
καὶ ποῦ σοφόν, ὃν στεφανοῦν ἐχρῆν, εἰ καὶ προνοή-
σας ἀπέκτεινε, τοῦτον ἀκουσίου μὲν φόνου,[8] ὑπὲρ
αὐτῶν δ᾽ εἰργασμένου μὴ καθῆραι;"

3   Ἐκπλαγὲν οὖν τὸ μειράκιον "ξένε," εἶπε "τίς εἶ;"
καὶ ὁ Ἀπολλώνιος "ὃν ἂν" ἔφη "παρὰ τοῖς Γυμνοῖς
εὕροις.[9] ἐπεὶ δὲ οὔπω μοι ὅσιον προσφθέγξασθαι τὸν
ἐν τῷ αἵματι, κέλευσον αὐτόν, ὦ μειράκιον, θαρρεῖν,
ὡς αὐτίκα δὴ καθαρεύσοντα, εἰ βαδίσειεν οὗ κατα-
λύω." ἀφικομένῳ δὲ ἐπιδράσας ὅσα Ἐμπεδοκλῆς τε
καὶ Πυθαγόρας ὑπὲρ καθαρσίων νομίζουσιν, ἐκέλευσεν ἐς ἤθη ἀποστείχειν[10] ὡς καθαρὸν ἤδη τῆς αἰτίας.

6. Ἐντεῦθεν ἐξελάσαντες ἡλίου ἀνίσχοντος, ἀφίκοντο πρὸ μεσημβρίας ἐς τὸ τῶν Γυμνῶν φροντιστή-
ριον. τοὺς δὲ Γυμνοὺς τούτους οἰκεῖν μὲν ἐπί τινος
λόφου φασὶ ξυμμέτρου μικρὸν ἀπὸ τῆς ὄχθης τοῦ
Νείλου, σοφίᾳ δὲ Ἰνδῶν λείπεσθαι πλέον ἢ προὔχειν
Αἰγυπτίων, γυμνοὺς δὲ ἐστάλθαι κατὰ ταὐτὰ τοῖς
εἰληθεροῦσιν Ἀθήνησι. δένδρα δὲ ἐν τῷ νομῷ ὀλίγα
καί τι ἄλσος οὐ μέγα, ἐς ὃ ξυνίασιν ὑπὲρ τῶν κοινῶν,

2   Ἱερὰ δὲ οὐκ ἐς ταὐτόν, ὥσπερ τὰ Ἰνδῶν, ἄλλο δὲ
ἄλλῃ τοῦ γηλόφου ἵδρυται σπουδῆς ἀξιούμενα, ὡς
Αἰγυπτίων λόγοι. θεραπεύουσι δὲ Νεῖλον μάλιστα,

[8] μὲν φόνου Headlam: φόνου μὲν

tivate, since he had become a powerful brigand around Memphis. Philiscus, whom this man killed, I see was his descendant in the thirteenth generation, and so was obviously a sworn enemy of these people, whose land Thamus ravaged at that time. They should have crowned him even for premeditated murder. How was it wise not to absolve him of unintentional bloodshed from which they profited?"

Overcome with amazement, the youth said, "Stranger, 3 who are you?" Apollonius replied, "You will learn my name among the Naked Ones. But since it is forbidden for me to address a man with bloodguilt, tell him to be cheerful, young man. He will receive immediate absolution if he comes to where I am staying." When he came, Apollonius performed all the rites of purification prescribed by Empedocles and Pythagoras, and then told the man to depart, being now free from fault.

6. Setting out from there at sunrise, before noon they reached the Naked Ones' ashram. They say that these Naked Ones live on a hill of moderate height a short distance from the bank of the Nile. In wisdom they are more inferior to the Indians than they are superior to the Egyptians. They wear as little clothing as do sunbathers at Athens. There are a few trees in their region, and a rather small grove where they gather to discuss community affairs.

Their sanctuaries are not built in one place, like the 2 Indians', but in different places on the hill, and are highly regarded, according to the accounts of the Egyptians. They worship the Nile above all, considering it to be earth

---

τὸν γὰρ ποταμὸν τοῦτον ἡγοῦνται γῆν καὶ ὕδωρ.
καλύβης μὲν οὖν ἢ οἰκίας οὐδὲν αὐτοὶ δέονται, ζῶντες
ὑπαίθριοι καὶ ὑπὸ τῷ οὐρανῷ αὐτῷ, καταγωγὴν δὲ
ἀποχρῶσαν τοῖς ξένοις ἐδείμαντο στοὰν οὐ μεγάλην,
ἰσομήκη ταῖς Ἠλείων, ὑφ' αἷς ὁ ἀθλητὴς περιμένει τὸ
μεσημβρινὸν κήρυγμα.

7. Ἐνταῦθά τι ἀναγράφει Δάμις Εὐφράτου ἔργον,
ἡγώμεθα δὲ αὐτὸ μὴ μειρακιῶδες, ἀλλ' ἀφιλοτιμό-
τερον τοῦ φιλοσοφίᾳ προσήκοντος· ἐπεὶ γὰρ τοῦ
Ἀπολλωνίου θαμὰ ἤκουε βουλομένου σοφίαν Ἰνδικὴν
ἀντικρῖναι Αἰγυπτίᾳ, πέμπει παρὰ τοὺς Γυμνοὺς Θρασύβουλον τὸν ἐκ Ναυκράτιδος ὑπὲρ διαβολῆς τοῦ
ἀνδρός, ὁ δὲ ἥκειν μὲν ὑπὲρ ξυνουσίας ἔφη τῆς πρὸς
αὐτούς, ἀφίξεσθαι δὲ καὶ τὸν Τυανέα, τουτὶ δὲ ἐκείνοις
ἀγῶνα ἔχειν οὐ σμικρόν, φρονεῖν τε γὰρ αὐτὸν ὑπὲρ
τοὺς Ἰνδῶν σοφούς, οὓς ἐν λόγῳ παντὶ αἴρει, μυρίας
δὲ ἐλέγξεις ἐπ' αὐτοὺς συνεσκευάσθαι, ξυγχωρεῖν τε
οὔτε ἡλίῳ οὐδὲν οὔτε οὐρανῷ καὶ γῇ, κινεῖν γὰρ καὶ
ὀχεῖν αὐτὸς ταῦτα καὶ μετατάττειν οἷ βούλεται.

8. Τοιαῦτα ὁ Ναυκρατίτης ξυνθεὶς ἀπῆλθεν, οἱ δ'
ἀληθῆ ταῦτα ἡγούμενοι τὴν μὲν ξυνουσίαν οὐ παρη-
τοῦντο ἥκοντος, ὑπὲρ μεγάλων δὲ σπουδάζειν ἐπλάτ-
τοντο καὶ πρὸς ἐκείνοις εἶναι, ἀφίξεσθαι δὲ κἀκείνῳ ἐς
λόγους, ἢν σχολὴν ἄγωσι μάθωσί τε, ὅ τι βούλεται
καὶ ὅτου ἐρῶν ἥκεν. ἐκέλευε δὲ ὁ παρ' αὐτῶν ἥκων καὶ
καταλύειν αὐτοὺς ἐν τῇ στοᾷ, ὁ δὲ Ἀπολλώνιος "ὑπὲρ
μὲν στέγης" ἔφη "μηδὲν διαλέγου, ξυγχωρεῖ γὰρ
πᾶσιν ὁ οὐρανὸς ὁ ἐνταῦθα γυμνοῖς ζῆν," διαβάλλων

and water. For themselves they do not need huts or houses, and live outside under the open sky. As a hostel large enough for their visitors, however, they have constructed a fairly small colonnade, about the length of the ones at Elis in which the athletes wait for the noon announcement.

7. At this point Damis recounts an act of Euphrates which we should regard not merely as juvenile, but disgraceful by the standards of philosophy. Having heard Apollonius many times express a wish to compare Indian and Egyptian wisdom, he sent Thrasybulus of Naucratis to the Naked Ones in order to slander the Master. This man said that he had come to converse with them, as also had the man from Tyana, and this promised no small competition for them, since Apollonius was prouder even than the sages of India, whom he extolled in every conversation. He had devised endless tests for the Naked Ones, and did not even yield to the sun, sky, or earth, but moved and carried these elements himself and transported them to wherever he pleased.

8. After concocting all this, the man from Naucratis left. The Naked Ones, entirely convinced, did not refuse Apollonius an interview on his arrival, but pretended to be attending to important affairs and to be occupied with them. They would, they said, come to converse with him too, if they had leisure, and if he could inform them of the motive and the object of his coming. Their messenger also invited the party to stay in the colonnade, to which Apollonius replied, "You do not need to mention shelter, because the climate here allows anybody to live naked" (this was a hint

αὐτοὺς ὡς οὐ καρτερίᾳ γυμνούς, ἀλλ' ἀνάγκη, "ὅ τι δὲ
βούλομαι καὶ ὑπὲρ ὅτου ἥκω τοὺς μὲν οὐ θαυμάζω
οὔπω γιγνώσκοντας, Ἰνδοὶ δέ με οὐκ ἤροντο ταῦτα."

9. Ὁ μὲν δὴ Ἀπολλώνιος ἑνὶ τῶν δένδρων ὑπο-
κλιθεὶς ξυνῆν τοῖς ἑταίροις ὁπόσα ἠρώτων, ἀπολαβὼν
δὲ τὸν Τιμασίωνα ὁ Δάμις ἤρετο ἰδίᾳ· οἱ Γυμνοὶ
οὗτοι, βέλτιστε, ξυγγέγονας γὰρ αὐτοῖς, ὡς τὸ εἰκός,
τί σοφοί εἰσι;" "πολλὰ" ἔφη "καὶ μεγάλα." "καὶ μὴν οὐ
σοφὰ" εἶπεν "αὐτῶν, ὦ γενναῖε, τὰ πρὸς ἡμᾶς ταῦτα,
τὸ γὰρ μὴ ξυμβῆναι τοιῷδε ἀνδρὶ ὑπὲρ σοφίας, ὄγκῳ
δ' ἐπ' αὐτὸν χρήσασθαι τί φῶ οὐκ οἶδα ἢ τῦφον," ἔφη
"ὦ ἑταῖρε." "τῦφον," εἶπεν,¹¹ "οὔπω πρότερον περὶ
αὐτοὺς εἶδον, δὶς ἤδη ἀφικόμενος, ἀεὶ γὰρ μέτριοί τε
καὶ χρηστοὶ πρὸς τοὺς ἐπιμιγνύντας ἦσαν· πρώην
γοῦν, πεντήκοντα δὲ τοῦτ' ἴσως ἡμέραι, Θρασύβουλος
μὲν ἐπεχωρίαζεν ἐνταῦθα λαμπρὸν οὐδὲν ἐν φιλοσοφίᾳ πράττων, οἱ δ' ἄσμενοι αὐτὸν ἀπεδέξαντο, ἐπειδὴ
προσέγραψεν ἑαυτὸν τῷ Εὐφράτῃ."

2   Καὶ ὁ Δάμις "τί λέγεις, ὦ μειράκιον; ἑώρακας σὺ
Θρασύβουλον τὸν Ναυκρατίτην ἐν τῷ φροντιστηρίῳ
τούτῳ;" "καὶ πρός γε" εἶπε "διήγαγον αὐτὸν τῇ ἐμαυτοῦ νηὶ κατιόντα ἐνθένδε." "τὸ πᾶν ἔχω, νὴ τὴν Ἀθηνᾶν," ἔφη ὁ Δάμις ἀναβοήσας τε καὶ σχετλιάσας
"ἔοικε γὰρ πεπανουργῆσθαί τι." ὑπολαβὼν οὖν ὁ
Τιμασίων "ὁ μὲν ἀνήρ," ἔφη "ὡς ἠρόμην αὐτὸν χθές,
ὅστις εἴη, οὔπω με ἠξίου τοῦ ἀπορρήτου, σὺ δ', εἰ μὴ
μυστήρια ταῦτα, λέγε ὅστις οὗτος, ἴσως γὰρ ἂν κἀγώ
τι ξυμβαλοίμην τῇ τοῦ ζητουμένου θήρᾳ."

that they went naked not out of endurance but necessity). "That they should not know my motive, however, and the object of my coming does not surprise me, though the Indians did not ask me about them."

9. Apollonius reclined under one of the trees, and conversed with his disciples about problems they put to him, while Damis taking Timasion aside asked him privately, "You have met these Naked Ones, I suppose, my friend, so in what way are they wise?" "In many important ways," he replied. "Still, it is not wise of them, sir," said Damis, "to act like this with us. Refusing to converse with such a Master about philosophy, and putting on airs with him, I can only describe as insolence, my friend." "Insolence," said Timasion, "is something I have never seen in them on my two previous visits. They have always been modest and kind with visitors. Why, not long ago, fifty days perhaps, there was a Thrasybulus staying here, a man without any distinction in philosophy, and yet they welcomed him warmly, because he claimed to follow Euphrates."

"What did you say, young man?" asked Damis. "Did you see Thrasybulus of Naucratis in the ashram here?" "Not only that," said the youth, "but I carried him in my own boat when he was going down from here." "I see it all, by Athena," said Damis, with a shout of indignation; "this looks like a piece of trickery." Timasion replied, "When I asked the Master's name yesterday, he did not think me worthy of the secret. Tell me who he is, if this is not for initiates only, and I might be able to help you hunt down your quarry."

2

---

11 εἶπεν West.: ἂν

3 Ἐπεὶ δὲ ἤκουσε τοῦ Δάμιδος καὶ ὅτι ὁ Τυανεὺς εἴη, "ξυνείληφας" ἔφη "τὸ πρᾶγμα. Θρασύβουλος γὰρ καταπλέων μετ᾽ ἐμοῦ τὸν Νεῖλον ἐρομένῳ μοι ἐφ᾽ ὅ τι ἀναβαίη ἐνταῦθα, σοφίαν οὐ χρηστὴν ἑαυτοῦ διηγεῖτο, τοὺς Γυμνοὺς τούτους ὑποψίας ἐμπεπληκέναι φάσκων πρὸς τὸν Ἀπολλώνιον, ὡς ὑπεροφθείη, ὁπότε ἔλθοι. κἀξ ὅτου μὲν διαφέρεται πρὸς αὐτὸν οὐκ οἶδα, τὸ δὲ ἐς διαβολὰς καθίστασθαι γυναικεῖόν τε ἡγοῦμαι καὶ ἀπαίδευτον. ἐγὼ δ᾽ ἄν, ὡς διάκεινται, μάθοιμι προσειπὼν τοὺς ἄνδρας, φίλοι γάρ." καὶ ἐπανῆλθε περὶ δείλην ὁ Τιμασίων πρὸς μὲν τὸν Ἀπολλώνιον οὐδὲν φράζων πλὴν τοῦ προσειρηκέναι σφᾶς, ἰδίᾳ δ᾽ ἀπαγγέλλων πρὸς τὸν Δάμιν, ὡς ἀφίξοιντο αὔριον μεστοὶ ὧν τοῦ Θρασυβούλου ἤκουσαν.

10. Τὴν μὲν δὴ ἑσπέραν ἐκείνην μέτριά τε καὶ οὐκ ἄξια τοῦ ἀναγράψαι σπουδάσαντες, ἐκοιμήθησαν οὗ ἐδείπνησαν, ἅμα δὲ τῇ ἡμέρᾳ ὁ μὲν Ἀπολλώνιος, ὥσπερ εἰώθει, θεραπεύσας τὸν Ἥλιον ἐφειστήκει τινὶ γνώμῃ, προσδραμὼν δὲ αὐτῷ Νεῖλος, ὅσπερ ἦν νεώτατος τῶν Γυμνῶν "ἡμεῖς" ἔφη "παρὰ σὲ ἥκομεν." "εἰκότως," εἶπεν ὁ Ἀπολλώνιος "καὶ γὰρ ἐγὼ πρὸς ὑμᾶς ὁδὸν τὴν ἀπὸ θαλάττης ἐνταῦθα." καὶ εἰπὼν ταῦτα εἵπετο τῷ Νείλῳ. προσειπὼν οὖν καὶ προσρηθείς, ξυνέτυχον δὲ ἀλλήλοις περὶ τὴν στοάν, "ποῖ," ἔφη "ξυνεσόμεθα;" "ἐνταῦθα" ἔφη ὁ Θεσπεσίων δείξας τὸ ἄλσος. ὁ δὲ Θεσπεσίων πρεσβύτατος ἦν τῶν Γυμνῶν, καὶ ἡγεῖτο μὲν αὐτὸς πᾶσιν, οἱ δέ, ὥσπερ Ἑλλανοδίκαι τῷ πρεσβυτάτῳ, εἵποντο κοσμίῳ ἅμα

Hearing from Damis that it was actually the man from   3
Tyana, "You have grasped the situation," he said. "When
Thrasybulus was sailing down the Nile with me, and I
asked him his reason for coming up here, he described a
rather malicious trick of his. He said he had filled these
Naked Ones with suspicion of Apollonius, so that he would
meet with neglect when he arrived. How long he has been
his enemy I do not know, but resorting to slander I consider womanish and uncivilized. I could find out their
Eminences' attitude by talking to them, as they are my
friends." Timasion came back towards evening, and while
saying nothing to Apollonius, except that he had spoken to
them, he reported to Damis privately that they would be
coming the next day, filled with Thrasybulus's stories.

10. That evening they had an ordinary discussion not
worth recording, and lay down to sleep where they had
dined. At dawn the next day Apollonius, after worshiping
the sun in his usual way, was absorbed in some idea when
Nilus, the youngest of the Naked Ones, ran up to him
and said, "We are coming to you." "Fair enough," said
Apollonius, "since I came to you here all the way from the
sea," and with these words he followed Nilus. After greeting them and being greeted in return, he asked, "Where
shall we talk?" "Here," said Thespesion, pointing to the
grove. This Thespesion was the oldest of the Naked Ones,
and walked at their head while they followed him at a
composed and leisurely pace, like Judges of the Hellenes

καὶ σχολαίῳ βαδίσματι. ἐπεὶ δ᾽ ἐκάθισαν ὡς ἔτυχε,
τουτὶ γὰρ οὐκέτι ἐν κόσμῳ ἔδρων, ἐς τὸν Θεσπεσίωνα
εἶδον πάντες οἷον ἑστιάτορα τοῦ λόγου, ὁ δὲ ἤρξατο
ἐνθένδε·

2 "Τὴν Πυθὼ καὶ τὴν Ὀλυμπίαν ἐπεσκέφθαι σέ
φασιν, Ἀπολλώνιε, τουτὶ γὰρ ἀπήγγειλεν ἐνταῦθα καὶ
Στρατοκλῆς ὁ Φάριος ἐντετυχηκέναι σοι φάσκων ἐκεῖ,
καὶ τὴν μὲν Πυθὼ τοὺς ἐς αὐτὴν ἥκοντας αὐλῷ τε
παραπέμπειν καὶ ᾠδαῖς καὶ ψάλσει, κωμῳδίας τε καὶ
τραγῳδίας ἀξιοῦν, εἶτα τὴν ἀγωνίαν παρέχειν τὴν
γυμνὴν ὀψὲ τούτων, τὴν δὲ Ὀλυμπίαν τὰ μὲν τοιαῦτα
ἐξελεῖν ὡς ἀνάρμοστα καὶ οὐ χρηστὰ ἐκεῖ, παρέχεσθαι δὲ τοῖς ἐς αὐτὴν ἰοῦσιν ἀθλητὰς γυμνούς, Ἡρακλέους ταῦτα ξυνθέντος. τοῦτο ἡγοῦ παρὰ τὴν Ἰνδῶν
σοφίαν τὰ ἐνταῦθα· οἱ μὲν γάρ, ὥσπερ ἐς τὴν Πυθὼ
καλοῦντες, ποικίλαις δημαγωγοῦσιν ἴυγξιν, ἡμεῖς δέ,
ὥσπερ ἐν Ὀλυμπίᾳ, γυμνοί. οὐχ ὑποστρώννυσιν ἡ γῆ
οὐδὲν ἐνταῦθα, οὐδὲ γάλα ὥσπερ βάκχαις ἢ οἶνον
δίδωσιν, οὐδὲ μετεώρους ἡμᾶς ὁ ἀὴρ φέρει, ἀλλ᾽
αὐτὴν ὑπεστορεσμένοι τὴν γῆν ζῶμεν μετέχοντες αὐτῆς τὰ κατὰ φύσιν, ὡς χαίρουσα διδοίη αὐτὰ καὶ μὴ
βασανίζοιτο ἄκουσα.

3 "Ὅτι δ᾽ οὐκ ἀδυνατοῦμεν σοφίζεσθαι, τὸ δεῖνα"
ἔφη "δένδρον," πτελέα δὲ ἦν, τρίτον ἀπ᾽ ἐκείνου, ὑφ᾽ ᾧ
διελέγοντο, "πρόσειπε τὸν σοφὸν Ἀπολλώνιον," καὶ
προσεῖπε μὲν αὐτόν, ὡς ἐκελεύσθη, τὸ δένδρον, ἡ
φωνὴ δὲ ἦν ἔναρθρός τε καὶ θῆλυς. ἀπεσήμαινε δὲ
πρὸς τοὺς Ἰνδοὺς ταῦτα μεταστήσειν ἡγούμενος τὸν

behind the chief Judge. After they had sat down anywhere, doing so in no particular order, they all looked
at Thespesion as the chairman of the discussion, and he
began thus:

"I am told that you have inspected Delphi and Olympia, 2
Apollonius, since Stratocles of Pharos[9] reported as much
to us, saying he had met you there. They say too that
Delphi greets its visitors with pipes, songs, and lyre music,
and treats them to comedy and tragedy, and only after all
this presents the athletes competing naked. Olympia, however, avoids such preliminaries as unbecoming and im-
proper there, and presents its visitors merely with naked
athletes, following the arrangements of Heracles. You may
consider our life like that, as compared with the philosophy of the Indians. They, as if inviting you to Delphi, be-
guile you with various enchantments, but we are naked, as
if we were at Olympia. Here the earth does not provide any
bedding, or produce milk or wine as it does to followers of
Bacchus, and the air does not hold us suspended. We make
the earth itself our bed, and live off its natural products, expecting it to supply them gladly and not be forced against
its will.

"However, to show that we do not lack the power to 3
work miracles, you tree there," he said to an elm which was
third along from the one under which they were conversing, "Speak to the wise Apollonius." The tree spoke to him
as it was told, and its voice was articulate and feminine.
He made these allusions to the Indians thinking that he

9 Island off Alexandria in Egypt.

Ἀπολλώνιον τῆς ὑπὲρ αὐτῶν δόξης, ἐπειδὴ διῄει ἐς
πάντας λόγους τε Ἰνδῶν καὶ ἔργα. προσετίθει δὲ
κἀκεῖνα, ὡς ἀπόχρη τῷ σοφῷ βρώσεώς τε καθαρῷ
εἶναι, ὁπόση ἔμπνους, ἱμέρου τε, ὃς φοιτᾷ δι᾽ ὀμμάτων, φθόνου τε, ὃς διδάσκαλος ἀδίκων ἐπὶ χεῖρα
καὶ γνώμην ἥκει, θαυμασιουργίας τε καὶ βιαίου
τέχνης μὴ δεῖσθαι ἀλήθειαν.

4   "Σκέψαι γὰρ τὸν Ἀπόλλω" εἶπε "τὸν Δελφικόν, ὃς
τὰ μέσα τῆς Ἑλλάδος ἐπὶ προρρήσει λογίων ἔχει·
ἐνταῦθα τοίνυν, ὥς που καὶ αὐτὸς γιγνώσκεις, ὁ μὲν
τῆς ὀμφῆς δεόμενος ἐρωτᾷ βραχὺ ἐρώτημα, ὁ δὲ
Ἀπόλλων οὐδὲν τερατευσάμενος λέγει, ὁπόσα οἶδε.
καίτοι ῥᾴδιόν γε ἦν αὐτῷ σεῖσαι μὲν τὸν Παρνασὸν
πάντα, τὴν Κασταλίαν δὲ οἰνοχοῆσαι μεταβαλόντι
τὰς πηγάς, Κηφισῷ δὲ μὴ ξυγχωρῆσαι ποταμῷ εἶναι,
ὁ δὲ οὐδὲν τούτων ἐπικομπάσας ἀναφαίνει τἀληθὲς
αὐτό. ἡγώμεθα δὲ μηδὲ τὸν χρυσὸν ἢ τὰ δοκοῦντα
λαμπρὰ τῶν ἀναθημάτων ἑκόντι αὐτῷ φοιτᾶν, μηδὲ τῷ
νεῷ τὸν Ἀπόλλω χαίρειν, εἰ καὶ διπλάσιος ἀποφαν-
θείη τοῦ νῦν ὄντος· ᾤκησε γάρ ποτε καὶ λιτὴν στέγην
ὁ θεὸς οὗτος, καὶ καλύβη αὐτῷ ξυνεπλάσθη μικρά, ἐς
ἣν ξυμβαλέσθαι λέγονται μέλιτται μὲν κηρόν, πτερὰ
δὲ ὄρνιθες. εὐτέλεια γὰρ διδάσκαλος μὲν σοφίας,
διδάσκαλος δὲ ἀληθείας, ἣν ἐπαινῶν σοφὸς ἀτεχνῶς
δόξεις ἐκλαθόμενος τῶν παρ᾽ Ἰνδοῖς μύθων. τὸ γὰρ
πρᾶττε ἢ μὴ πρᾶττε, ἢ οἶδα ἢ οὐκ οἶδα, ἢ τὸ δεῖνα,
ἀλλὰ μὴ τὸ δεῖνα, τί δεῖται κτύπου; τί δὲ τοῦ βροντᾶν,
μᾶλλον δὲ τοῦ ἐμβεβροντῆσθαι;

would cause Apollonius, who spoke of the Indians' words and deeds to everybody, to change his opinion of them. Thespesion added that it was enough for a wise man to keep himself undefiled by the flesh of living things, by the desire that enters through the eyes, and by jealousy that comes as a teacher of evil to hands and hearts, and that truth did not need miracles and magic compulsion.

"Look at Apollo of Delphi," he said. "He inhabits the 4 middle of Greece to proclaim oracles. There, as you too must know, anybody needing the sacred utterance puts a brief question, and Apollo tells all he knows without any miracles. Though it would be easy for him to shake all of Parnassus, to make Castalia flow with wine by transforming its sources, or to forbid the Cephisus from being a river, he reveals the simple truth without any such pomp. We may suppose that he is reluctant even to receive the gold or the splendid-seeming dedications, and that Apollo takes no pleasure in his temple, nor would he even if it were doubled in size. For this god once lived in a humble cottage, and a little hut was made for him to which the bees, we are told, contributed wax and the birds their feathers.[10] Simplicity is the teacher of wisdom, and the teacher of truth, and if you admire that, and forget the tales told by the Indians, you will have an unqualified reputation for wisdom. 'Act' or 'Do not act,' 'I know' or 'I do not know,' 'This but not that'—what fanfare do they need? Or what roaring, not to say raving?

[10] For this tradition see Pausanias, *Description of Greece* 10.5.9.

APOLLONIUS OF TYANA

5   "Εἶδες ἐν ζωγραφίας λόγοις καὶ τὸν τοῦ Προδίκου
Ἡρακλέα, ὡς ἔφηβος μὲν ὁ Ἡρακλῆς, οὔπω δὲ ἐν
αἱρέσει τοῦ βίου, Κακία δ᾽ αὐτὸν καὶ Ἀρετὴ δια-
λαβοῦσαι παρὰ σφᾶς ἄγουσιν, ἡ μὲν χρυσῷ τε κατ-
εσκευασμένη καὶ ὅρμοις, ἐσθῆτί τε ἁλιπορφύρῳ, καὶ
παρειᾶς ἄνθει, καὶ χαίτης ἀναπλοκαῖς, καὶ γραφαῖς
ὀμμάτων, ἔστι δ᾽ αὐτῇ καὶ χρυσοῦν πέδιλον, γέγραπται γὰρ καὶ τούτῳ ἐνσοβοῦσα, ἡ δ᾽ αὖ πεπονη-
κυίᾳ μὲν προσφερής, τραχὺ δὲ ὁρῶσα, τὸν δὲ αὐχμὸν
πεποιημένη κόσμημα, καὶ ἀνυπόδετος ἡ Ἀρετὴ καὶ
λιτὴ τὴν ἐσθῆτα, καὶ γυμνὴ δ᾽ ἂν ἐφαίνετο, εἰ μὴ
ἐγίγνωσκε τὸ ἐν θηλείαις εὔσχημον.

6   "Ἡγοῦ δὴ καὶ σεαυτόν, Ἀπολλώνιε, μέσον τῆς
Ἰνδικῆς τε καὶ τῆς ἡμεδαπῆς σοφίας ἑστάναι, καὶ τῆς
μὲν ἀκούειν λεγούσης, ὡς ὑποστορέσει σοι ἄνθη καθεύδοντι, καί, νὴ Δί᾽, ὡς ποτιεῖ γάλακτι καὶ ὡς κηρίοις
θρέψει, καὶ ὡς νέκταρ σοί τι παρ᾽ αὐτῆς ἔσται καὶ
πτερά ὁπότε βούλοιο, τρίποδάς τε ἐσκυκλήσει πίνοντι
καὶ χρυσοῦς θρόνους, καὶ πονήσεις οὐδέν, ἀλλ᾽ αὐτό-
ματά σοι βαδιεῖται πάντα, τῆς δέ γε ἑτέρας, ὡς
χαμευνεῖν μὲν ἐν αὐχμῷ προσήκει, γυμνὸν δέ, ὥσπερ
ἡμεῖς, μοχθοῦντα φαίνεσθαι, ὃ δὲ μὴ πονήσαντί σοι
ἀφίκετο, μήτε φίλον ἡγεῖσθαι μήτε ἡδύ, μηδὲ ἀλα-
ζόνα εἶναι μηδὲ τύφου θηρατήν, ἀπέχεσθαι δὲ καὶ
ὀνειράτων ὄψεις, ὁπόσαι ἀπὸ τῆς γῆς αἴρουσιν. εἰ μὲν
δὴ κατὰ τὸν Ἡρακλέα αἱροῖο καὶ δόξῃ ἀδαμαντίνῃ
χρῷο, μὴ ἀτιμάζων ἀλήθειαν,[12] μηδὲ τὴν κατὰ φύσιν
εὐτέλειαν παραιτούμενος, πολλοὺς μὲν ᾑρηκέναι φή-

118

"In descriptions of pictures you have seen the Heracles   5
of Prodicus.[11] Heracles is a youth who has not yet chosen a
way of life, and Vice and Virtue each take hold of him and
pull him to her side. The former is adorned with gold, or-
naments, purple robes, rouged cheeks, curled hair, mas-
cara, and she has golden shoes, since she is shown prancing
in these too. The latter, by contrast, looks like a woman
exhausted by work, with a fierce expression, who has grime
for make-up. Virtue goes barefoot and humbly dressed,
and indeed would show herself naked except that she
knows womanly proprieties.

"Well, Apollonius, think of yourself standing between   6
the Wisdom of India and that of our land. You can hear the
one saying that it will strew flowers for you when you go to
sleep, give you milk to drink, by Zeus, and honeycombs to
eat; you will have a bit of nectar and wings whenever you
like; it will wheel in three-legged tables[12] and golden arm-
chairs for you when you drink, and you will have no work,
but everything will come to you spontaneously. But from
our Wisdom you will hear that it is right to sleep on the
bare ground, to be seen toiling in nakedness, as we do, to
think nothing welcome or pleasant that has come to you
without toil, not to be boastful or a seeker of vanity, and
also to avoid dream visions that lift you from the earth. If
you make the Choice of Heracles and show an iron will, not
dishonoring the truth or avoiding the simplicity of nature,

[11] Xenophon, *Memorabilia* 2.1.21–34.
[12] On these tables see III 27.

---

[12] ἀλήθειαν Kay.: εὐτέλειαν

σεις λέοντας, πολλὰς δὲ ὕδρας ἐκτετμῆσθαί σοι, Γη-
ρυόνας τε καὶ Νέσσους καὶ ὁπόσοι ἐκείνου ἆθλοι, εἰ δὲ
τὸ τῶν ἀγειρόντων ἀσπάσῃ, κολακεύσεις ὀφθαλμοὺς
τε καὶ ὦτα, καὶ οὔτε σοφώτερος ἑτέρου δόξεις, γενήσῃ
τε ἆθλος ἀνδρὸς Αἰγυπτίου Γυμνοῦ."

11. Ταῦτα εἰπόντος, ἐστράφησαν ἐς τὸν Ἀπολλώνιον πάντες, οἱ μὲν ἀμφ' αὐτόν, ὡς ἀντιλέξοι, γι-
γνώσκοντες, οἱ δὲ ἀμφὶ τὸν Θεσπεσίωνα θαυμάζοντες,
ὅ τι ἀντερεῖ. ὁ δὲ ἐπαινέσας αὐτὸν τῆς εὐροίας καὶ τοῦ
τόνου, "μή τι" ἔφη "προστίθης;" "μὰ Δί'," εἶπεν "εἴρηκα γάρ." τοῦ δ' αὖ ἐρομένου "μὴ τῶν ἄλλων τις
Αἰγυπτίων;" "πάντων" ἔφη "δι' ἐμοῦ ἤκουσας."

2 Ἐπισχὼν οὖν ὀλίγον, καὶ τοὺς ὀφθαλμοὺς ἐρείσας
ἐς τὰ εἰρημένα, οὑτωσὶ ἔλεξεν· "ἡ μὲν Ἡρακλέους
αἵρεσις, ἥν φησι Πρόδικος ἐν ἐφήβῳ ἑλέσθαι αὐτόν,
ὑγιῶς τε ὑμῖν λέλεκται καὶ κατὰ τὸν φιλοσοφίας νοῦν,
ὦ σοφοὶ Αἰγυπτίων, προσήκει δέ μοι οὐδέν. οὔτε γὰρ
ξυμβούλους ὑμᾶς βίου ποιησόμενος ἥκω, πάλαι γε
ᾑρημένος τὸν ἐμαυτῷ δόξαντα, πρεσβύτατός τε ὑμῶν
πλὴν Θεσπεσίωνος ἀφιγμένος, αὐτὸς ἂν μᾶλλον εἰκότως ξυνεβούλευον ὑμῖν σοφίας αἵρεσιν, εἰ μήπω ᾑρη-
μένοις ἐνέτυχον.

3 "Ὧν δ' ὅμως τηλικόσδε καὶ σοφίας ἐπὶ τοσόνδε
ἀφιγμένος, οὐκ ὀκνήσω λογισταῖς ὑμῖν τῆς ἐμαυτοῦ
βουλῆς χρήσασθαι, διδάσκων ὡς ὀρθῶς εἱλόμην
ταῦτα, ὧν μήπω βελτίω ἐπὶ νοῦν ἦλθέ μοι. κατιδὼν
γάρ τι ἐν Πυθαγόρου μέγα καὶ ὡς ὑπὸ σοφίας ἀρρήτου μὴ μόνον γιγνώσκοι ἑαυτόν, ὅστις εἴη, ἀλλὰ καὶ

you can say that you have caught many lions, exterminated many a Hydra, a Geryon, and a Nessus, and all of Heracles's conquests. But if you choose the life of a wandering huckster, you will flatter people's eyes and ears, and seem no better than anyone else, but become the conquest of a Naked Master from Egypt."

11. When he had spoken, all turned towards Apollonius. Whereas his followers knew that he would answer, Thespesion's party wondered what he could say. Apollonius praised Thespesion for his fluency and power, and said, "Do you have anything to add?" "Of course not," he said, "I have spoken." "Does any of the other Egyptians?" asked Apollonius. "You heard them all," replied Thespesion, "when you heard me."

Apollonius then was silent for a little while, with his inward gaze fixed on what had been said, and then he began, "The Choice of Heracles, which according to Prodicus he made as a young man, you have narrated truly and in the spirit of philosophy, Wise Ones of Egypt, but it is no concern of mine. I have not come here to take your advice about a way of life, since I long ago chose the one that seemed right to me. I am also older than all of you except Thespesion, so that I, your visitor, would have been better suited to advise you about choosing a philosophy, if I had not found that you had already chosen one.

"However, old as I am, and far advanced in wisdom, I will not hesitate to make you judges of my choice, and will show you how right I was to choose my path, since none better has ever come to my attention. I saw a sign of greatness in Pythagoras. His ineffable wisdom enabled him to know not only his own true self but also his past identity.

121

ὅστις γένοιτο, βωμῶν τε ὡς καθαρὸς ἅψαιτο καὶ ὡς
ἀχράντῳ μὲν ἐμψύχου βρώσεως γαστρὶ χρήσαιτο,
καθαρῷ δὲ σώματι πάντων ἐσθημάτων, ὁπόσα θνησειδίων ξύγκειται, γλῶττάν τε ὡς πρῶτος ἀνθρώπων
ξυνέσχε βοῦν ἐπ᾽ αὐτῇ σιωπῆς εὑρὼν δόγμα, καὶ τὴν
ἄλλην φιλοσοφίαν ὡς χρησμώδη καὶ ἀληθῆ κατ-
εστήσατο, ἔδραμον ἐπὶ τὰς ἐκείνου δόξας,

4   "Οὐ μίαν σοφίαν ἐκ δυοῖν ἑλόμενος, ὡς σύ, βέλτιστε Θεσπεσίων, ξυμβουλεύεις. παραστήσασα γάρ
μοι φιλοσοφία τὰς ἑαυτῆς δόξας, ὁπόσαι εἰσί, περι-
βαλοῦσά τε αὐταῖς κόσμον, ὃς ἑκάστῃ οἰκεῖος, ἐκέλευσεν ἐς αὐτὰς βλέπειν καὶ ὑγιῶς αἱρεῖσθαι· ὥρα μὲν
οὖν σεμνή τε ἁπασῶν ἦν καὶ θεία, καὶ κατέμυσεν ἄν
τις πρὸς ἐνίας αὐτῶν ὑπ᾽ ἐκπλήξεως, ἐμοὶ δὲ εἱστήκει
τὸ ὄμμα ἐς πάσας, καὶ γάρ με καὶ παρεθάρρυνον
αὐταὶ προσαγόμεναί τε καὶ προκηρύττουσαι, ὁπόσα
δώσουσιν, ἐπεὶ δ᾽ ἡ μέν τις αὐτῶν οὐδὲν μοχθήσαντι
πολὺν ἐπαντλήσειν ἔφασκεν ἡδονῶν ἑσμόν, ἡ δ᾽ αὖ
μοχθήσαντα ἀναπαύσειν, ἡ δ᾽ ἐγκαταμίξειν εὐφρο-
σύνας τῷ μόχθῳ, πανταχοῦ δὲ ἡδοναὶ διεφαίνοντο
καὶ ἄνετοι μὲν ἡνίαι γαστρός, ἑτοίμη δὲ χεὶρ ἐς
πλοῦτον, χαλινὸς δὲ οὐδεὶς ὀμμάτων, ἀλλ᾽ ἔρωτές τε
καὶ ἵμεροι καὶ τὰ τοιαῦτα πάθη ξυνεχωρεῖτο, μία δὲ
αὐτῶν ἴσχειν μὲν τῶν τοιούτων ἐκόμπαζε, θρασεῖα δὲ
ἦν καὶ φιλολοίδορος καὶ ἀπηγκωνισμένη πάντα,

5   "Εἶδον σοφίας εἶδος ἄρρητον, οὗ καὶ Πυθαγόρας
ποτὲ ἡττήθη, καὶ εἱστήκει δὲ ἄρα οὐκ ἐν ταῖς πολλαῖς,
ἀλλ᾽ ἀπετέτακτο αὐτῶν καὶ ἐσιώπα, ξυνεῖσα δέ, ὡς

He approached altars in purity, he kept his stomach undefiled by the flesh of living things, and his body uncontaminated by all clothes made from dead creatures. He was the first man to hold his tongue by inventing 'the ox on the tongue' as a rule of silence,[13] and he kept his general philosophy oracular and true.

"And so I ran to embrace his doctrines and did not   4 choose one philosophy out of two, as you advise, excellent Thespesion. Philosophy set the whole range of her doctrines before me, adorning each with its own special charms, and then told me to look at them and choose wisely. All of them had a venerable, divine beauty, and some were such as to make one dazzled with amazement. I, however, looked steadily at them all, while they themselves encouraged me, by trying to win me over and by advertising their gifts. One said that without any toil I would exhaust a great swarm of pleasures, another, that I would toil before resting, another, that she would mix delights with toil, and on every side I could see pleasures, all restraints on gluttony abandoned, hands grasping for wealth, the eyes unblinkered, and love, desire, and all such experiences were permitted. Another philosophy boasted that she would keep me from such things, and she was rude, quarrelsome, and utterly unabashed.[14]

"But I saw an ineffable kind of philosophy, which once   5 won the devotion of Pythagoras. She was not standing in the crowd, but apart from them and in silence. Seeing that

[13] Proverbial expression, cf. Aeschylus, *Agamemnon* 36.
[14] Which four philosophies are meant is not clear, but the first is perhaps hedonism, founded by Aristippus of Cyrene, the last Cynicism founded by Antisthenes.

ταῖς μὲν ἄλλαις οὐ ξυντίθεμαι, τὰ δὲ ἐκείνης οὔπω
οἶδα, 'μειράκιον,' εἶπεν, 'ἀηδὴς ἐγὼ καὶ μεστὴ πόνων·
εἰ γὰρ ἀφίκοιτό τις ἐς ἤθη τὰ ἐμά, τράπεζαν μέν,
ὁπόση ἐμψύχων, ἀνῃρῆσθαι πᾶσαν ἕλοιτο, οἴνου δὲ
ἐκλελῆσθαι καὶ τὸν σοφίας μὴ ἐπιθολοῦν κρατῆρα, ὃς
ἐν ταῖς ἀοίνοις ψυχαῖς ἔστηκεν, οὐδὲ χλαῖνα θάλψει
αὐτόν, οὐδὲ ἔριον, ὃ ἀπ' ἐμψύχου ἐπέχθη, ὑπόδημα δὲ
αὐτοῖς βύβλου δίδωμι καὶ καθεύδειν ὡς ἔτυχε, κἂν
ἀφροδισίων ἡττηθέντας αἴσθωμαι, βάραθρά ἐστί μοι,
καθ' ὧν Σοφίας ὀπαδός, Δίκη, φέρει τε αὐτοὺς καὶ
ὠθεῖ, χαλεπὴ δ' οὕτως ἐγὼ τοῖς τἀμὰ αἱρουμένοις, ὡς
καὶ δεσμὰ γλώττης ἐπ' αὐτοὺς ἔχειν.

6   "Ἃ δ' ἐστί σοι καρτερήσαντι ταῦτα, ἐμοῦ μάθε·
σωφροσύνη μὲν καὶ δικαιοσύνη αὐτόθεν, ζηλωτὸν δὲ
ἡγεῖσθαι μηδένα τυράννοις τε φοβερὸν εἶναι μᾶλλον
ἢ ὑπ' αὐτοῖς κεῖσθαι, θεοῖς τε ἡδίω φαίνεσθαι μικρὰ
θύσαντα ἢ οἱ προχέοντες αὐτοῖς τὸ τῶν ταύρων αἷμα,
καθαρῷ δὲ ὄντι σοι καὶ προγιγνώσκειν δώσω καὶ τοὺς
ὀφθαλμοὺς οὕτω τι ἐμπλήσω ἀκτῖνος, ὡς διαγιγνώ-
σκειν μὲν θεόν, γιγνώσκειν δὲ ἥρωα, σκιοειδῆ δ'
ἐλέγχειν φαντάσματα, ὅτε ψεύδοιντο εἴδη ἀνθρώπων.'

7   "Ἥδε μοι βίου αἵρεσις, ὦ σοφοὶ Αἰγυπτίων, ἣν
ὑγιῶς τε καὶ κατὰ τὸν Πυθαγόραν ἑλόμενος οὔτε
ἐψευσάμην οὔτε ἐψεύσθην, ἐγενόμην μὲν γὰρ ἃ χρὴ
τὸν φιλοσοφήσαντα, φιλοσοφοῦντι δὲ ὁπόσα δώσειν
ἔφη, πάντ' ἔχω. ἐφιλοσόφησα γὰρ ὑπὲρ γενέσεως τῆς
τέχνης καὶ ὁπόθεν αὐτῆς αἱ ἀρχαί, καί μοι ἔδοξεν
ἀνδρῶν εἶναι περιττῶν τὰ θεῖα ψυχήν τε ἄριστα ἠσκη-

I resisted the others, but did not yet know her own gifts, she said, 'Young man, I am joyless, and full of pains. A man who joins my society must choose to put aside all food that consists of living flesh. He must forget wine, and not cloud the vessel of wisdom that stands in the hearts of those that shun wine. No cloak or wool shorn from a living creature shall warm him, and I give him shoes of bark and any chance spot to sleep on. If I see him yield to love, I have abysses to which Justice, the servant of Wisdom, takes him and pushes him down. So harsh am I to those that choose my way that I have curbs for their tongues.

"'But let me tell you what you will gain by enduring all this. You will of course be self-controlled and just. You will think no one worth envying. You will terrify tyrants rather than being in their power. You will give greater pleasure to the gods with humble sacrifices than those who spill the blood of bulls for them. Being pure, you will receive from me the gift of foreknowledge, and I will so fill your eyes with radiance that you will recognize gods, know heroes, and unmask insubstantial ghosts when they disguise themselves in human form.'

"This is the way of life I have chosen, wise men of Egypt. I chose it honestly and by Pythagoras's example, and I neither deceived myself nor was deceived, because I have become what a philosopher should become, and I have received all that I was promised when I became a philosopher. I have enquired into the origin of the doctrine and into its sources, and I have observed that it belongs to true men who are expert in divine science, and have the best spiritual discipline. For it is the soul, having neither

6

7

μένων,[13] ἧς τὸ ἀθάνατόν τε καὶ ἀγέννητον πηγαὶ
γενέσεως.

8   "Ἀθηναίοις μὲν οὖν οὐ πάνυ προσήκων ἐφαίνετό
μοι ὅδε ὁ λόγος, τὸν γὰρ Πλάτωνος λόγον, ὃν θεσπε-
σίως ἐκεῖ καὶ πανσόφως ὑπὲρ ψυχῆς ἀνεφθέγξατο,
αὐτοὶ διέβαλλον ἐναντίας ταύτῃ καὶ οὐκ ἀληθεῖς
δόξας ὑπὲρ ψυχῆς προσέμενοι, ἔδει δὲ σκοπεῖν, τίς
μὲν εἴη πόλις, ποῖον δὲ ἀνδρῶν ἔθνος, παρ' οἷς οὐχ ὁ
μέν τὸ ὁ δὲ τό,[14] πᾶσα δὲ ἡλικία ταὐτὸν ὑπὲρ ψυχῆς
φθέγγοιτο· κἀγὼ μὲν νεότητός τε οὕτως ἀγούσης καὶ
τοῦ μήπω ξυνιέναι πρὸς ὑμᾶς ἔβλεψα, ἐπειδὴ πλεῖστα
ἐλέγεσθε ὑπερφυῶς εἰδέναι,

9   "Καὶ πρὸς τὸν διδάσκαλον τὸν ἐμαυτοῦ διῄειν
ταῦτα, ὁ δὲ ἐφιστάς με 'εἰ τῶν ἐρώντων' εἶπεν 'ἐτύγχα-
νες ὢν ἢ τὴν ἡλικίαν ἐχόντων τοῦ ἐρᾶν, εἶτα μειρακίῳ
καλῷ ἐντυχὼν καὶ ἀγασθεὶς αὐτὸ τῆς ὥρας σὺ δὲ καὶ
ὅτου εἴη παῖς ἐξήτεις, ἦν δὲ ὁ μὲν ἱπποτρόφου καὶ
στρατηγοῦ πατρὸς καὶ χορηγοὶ οἱ πάπποι, σὺ δ'
αὐτὸν τριηράρχου τινὸς ἢ φυλάρχου ἐκάλεις, ἆρά γ'
ἂν οἴει προσάγεσθαι τὰ παιδικὰ τούτοις, ἢ κἂν ἀηδὴς
δόξαι μὴ πατρόθεν ὀνομάζων τὸ μειράκιον, ἀλλ' ἀπ'
ἐκφύλου σπορᾶς καὶ νόθου; σοφίας οὖν ἐρῶν, ἣν
Ἰνδοὶ εὗρον, οὐκ ἀπὸ τῶν φύσει πατέρων ὀνομάζεις
αὐτήν, ἀλλ' ἀπὸ τῶν θέσει; καὶ δίδως τι μεῖζον Αἰ-

---

13 ἠσκημένων Cob.: ἐσκεμμένων
14 ὁ μέν τὸ ὁ δὲ τό Cob.: ὁ μέν τις, ὁ δὲ οὔ

death nor birth, that is the source of creation.

"I did not think this doctrine very suitable for the Athe- 8
nians, since they criticized the doctrine of the soul that
Plato expounded with inspiration and true wisdom, because they professed views directly contrary to this, and
false ones, about the soul.[15] I needed to ask what kind of
city, and what kind of race of men, there could be in which
there was no division of opinion, but all ages professed the
same view of the soul. Thus I myself, led by my youth and
my lack of understanding, looked to you, who were said to
have extraordinary knowledge of many things.

"But when I began to explain this to my teacher, he 9
stopped me, saying: 'Suppose you were in love, or of an age
to fall in love, and you had met a handsome youth, and out
of admiration for his beauty you made inquiries about his
father. Suppose he had a father who was a horsebreeder or
a general, and a grandfather who financed choruses, and
yet you called him the son of some ship's captain or ser-
geant-major, do you think you would attract your lover
with such expressions? Would you not seem tactless not
naming the youth as his father's son, but as someone of
foreign and illegitimate parentage? Well, if you love the
wisdom invented by the Indians, do you not name it not by
its natural fathers but by its adoptive ones? And do you not
give the Egyptians greater credit than if they were to make

[15] *On the Soul* was an alternative title of Plato's *Phaedo*. It is
said that when he read this work in public at Athens, everyone but
Aristotle left (Diogenes Laertius, *Lives of the Philosophers* 3.37).

γυπτίοις, ἢ εἰ πάλιν αὐτοῖς, ὡς αὐτοὶ ᾄδουσι, μέλιτι
ξυγκεκραμένος ἀναβαίη ὁ Νεῖλος·

10   "Ταῦτά με πρὸ ὑμῶν ἐπ᾽ Ἰνδοὺς ἔτρεψεν ἐνθυμηθέντα περὶ αὐτῶν, ὡς λεπτότεροι μὲν τὴν ξύνεσιν οἱ
τοιοίδε ἄνθρωποι καθαρωτέραις ὁμιλοῦντες ἀκτῖσιν,
ἀληθέστεροι δὲ τὰς περὶ φύσεώς τε καὶ θεῶν δόξας,
ἅτε ἀγχίθεοι καὶ πρὸς ἀρχαῖς τῆς ζῳογόνου καὶ θερμῆς οὐσίας οἰκοῦντες· ἐντυχών τε αὐτοῖς ἔπαθόν τι
πρὸς τὴν ἐπαγγελίαν τῶν ἀνδρῶν, ὁποῖον λέγονται
πρὸς τὴν Αἰσχύλου σοφίαν παθεῖν Ἀθηναῖοι. ποιητὴς
μὲν γὰρ οὗτος τραγῳδίας ἐγένετο, τὴν τέχνην δὲ ὁρῶν
ἀκατάσκευόν τε καὶ μήπω κεκοσμημένην, εἰ μὲν ξυν-
έστειλε τοὺς χοροὺς ἀποτάδην ὄντας, ἢ τὰς τῶν ὑπο-
κριτῶν ἀντιλέξεις εὗρε παραιτησάμενος τὸ τῶν μονῳ-
διῶν μῆκος, ἢ τὸ ὑπὸ σκηνῆς ἀποθνήσκειν ἐπενόησεν,
ὡς μὴ ἐν φανερῷ σφάττοι, σοφίας μὲν μηδὲ ταῦτα
ἀπηλλάχθω, δοκείτω δὲ κἂν ἑτέρῳ παρασχεῖν ἔννοιαν
ἧττον δεξιῷ τὴν ποίησιν.

11   "Ὁ δ᾽ ἐνθυμηθεὶς μὲν ἑαυτόν, ὡς ἐπάξιον τοῦ τραγῳδίαν ποιεῖν [φθέγγοιτο],¹⁵ ἐνθυμηθεὶς δὲ καὶ τὴν
τέχνην, ὡς προσφυᾶ τῷ μεγαλείῳ μᾶλλον ἢ τῷ κατα-
βεβλημένῳ τε καὶ ὑπὸ πόδα, σκευοποιίας μὲν ἥψατο
εἰκασμένης τοῖς τῶν ἡρώων εἴδεσιν, ὀκρίβαντος δὲ
τοὺς ὑποκριτὰς ἐνεβίβασεν, ὡς ἴσα ἐκείνοις βαίνοιεν,
ἐσθήμασί τε πρῶτος ἐκόσμησεν, ἃ πρόσφορον ἥρωσί
τε καὶ ἡρωίσιν ἠσθῆσθαι, ὅθεν Ἀθηναῖοι πατέρα
μὲν αὐτὸν τῆς τραγῳδίας ἡγοῦντο, ἐκάλουν δὲ καὶ

the Nile at its height once again to flow with honey, as they
proclaim?'

"Here is what turned me to the Indians rather than to   10
you, for I concluded that people of their kind have more
refined perceptions, since they live in purer sunlight, and
have truer views of nature and of the gods, being close to
the gods and living near the sources of warm, life-giving
nature. When I met them, I was struck by their Eminences' message, as the Athenians are said to have been
struck by the artistry of Aeschylus. He was a tragic poet,
and saw the art to be crude and as yet unsophisticated. If
he had merely shortened the choruses from the existing
length, or invented dialogue between the actors, rejecting
long solos, or devised offstage deaths, so that murder did
not occur openly, that might seem something not devoid of
talent, but still such as could have given ideas to another
less skilled as a poet.

"Believing himself to be someone worthy to write trag-   11
edy, however, and conceiving his art as more appropriate
to the sublime style than to the humble and pedestrian
one, he invented sets that corresponded to the appearance
of heroes, and put his actors into high boots, so that they
might walk as the heroes did, and was the first to dress
actors in clothing that it was appropriate for heroes and
heroines to wear. Hence the Athenians called him the Father of Tragedy, and even after his death they summoned

---

15 [φθέγγοιτο] secl. Jon.

τεθνεῶτα ἐς Διονύσια, τὰ γὰρ τοῦ Αἰσχύλου ψηφισα-
μένων ἀνεδιδάσκετο καὶ ἐνίκα ἐκ καινῆς.

12   "Καίτοι τραγῳδίας μὲν εὖ κεκοσμημένης ὀλίγη
χάρις, εὐφραίνει γὰρ ἐν σμικρῷ τῆς ἡμέρας, ὥσπερ ἡ
τῶν Διονυσίων ὥρα, φιλοσοφίας δὲ ξυγκειμένης μέν,
ὡς Πυθαγόρας ἐδικαίωσεν, ὑποθειαζούσης δέ, ὡς πρὸ
Πυθαγόρου Ἰνδοί, οὐκ ἐς βραχὺν χρόνον ἡ χάρις,
ἀλλ' ἐς ἄπειρόν τε καὶ ἀριθμοῦ πλείω. οὐ δὴ ἀπεικός τι
παθεῖν μοι δοκῶ φιλοσοφίας ἡττηθεὶς εὖ κεκοσμημένης, ἣν ἐς τὸ πρόσφορον Ἰνδοὶ στείλαντες ἐφ' ὑψηλῆς
τε καὶ θείας μηχανῆς ἐκκυκλοῦσιν.

13   "Ὡς δὲ ἐν δίκῃ μὲν ἠγάσθην αὐτούς, ἐν δίκῃ δὲ
ἡγοῦμαι σοφούς τε καὶ μακαρίους, ὥρα μανθάνειν·
εἶδον ἄνδρας οἰκοῦντας ἐπὶ τῆς γῆς καὶ οὐκ ἐπ' αὐτῆς,
καὶ ἀτειχίστως τετειχισμένους, καὶ οὐδὲν κεκτημένους
ἢ τὰ πάντων. εἰ δ' αἰνιγμάτων ἅπτομαι, σοφία Πυθαγόρου ξυγχωρεῖ ταῦτα, παρέδωκε γὰρ καὶ τὸ αἰνίττειν
διδάσκαλον εὑρὼν σιωπῆς λόγον. σοφίας δὲ ταύτης
ἐγένεσθε μὲν καὶ αὐτοὶ Πυθαγόρᾳ ξύμβουλοι χρόνον,
ὃν τὰ Ἰνδῶν ἐπῃνεῖτε, Ἰνδοὶ τὸ ἀρχαῖον [πάλαι][16]
ὄντες· ἐπεὶ δ' αἰδοῖ τοῦ λόγου, δι' ὃν ἐκ μηνιμάτων τῆς
γῆς ἀφίκεσθε δεῦρο, ἕτεροι μᾶλλον ἐβούλεσθε δοκεῖν
ἢ Αἰθίοπες οἱ ἀπὸ Ἰνδῶν ἥκοντες, πάντα ὑμῖν ἐς τοῦτο
ἐδρᾶτο. ὅθεν ἐγυμνώθητε μὲν σκευῆς, ὁπόση ἐκεῖθεν,
ὥσπερ ξυναποδυόμενοι τὸ Αἰθίοπες εἶναι, θεοὺς δὲ
θεραπεύειν ἐψηφίσασθε τὸν Αἰγύπτιον μᾶλλον ἢ τὸν

16 [πάλαι] secl. Cob.

him to the Dionysia, since Aeschylus's plays were revived
by public vote, and he won all over again.

"Yet a well produced tragedy gets little gratitude, since   12
it pleases only for a small part of a day, like the season of the
Dionysia. But when philosophy is constituted in the way
Pythagoras ordained, and is divinely inspired in the way
the Indians ordained before Pythagoras, then the gratitude lasts not for a short time, but for a time beyond number and infinite. I do not therefore think that the effect on
me was at all an unreasonable one, when I was enthralled
by a well produced philosophy that the Indians have sup-
plied with the appropriate decor, and bring on with lofty,
inspired stage machinery.[16]

"To prove that I justly admired them, and justly believe   13
their wisdom and bliss, you should know this. I saw men on
the earth and not on it, walled without walls and owning
nothing except everything.[17] If I am venturing on riddles,
the wisdom of Pythagoras permits me, since he made rid-
dling a precept when he invented speech as the teacher of
silence. You yourselves supported Pythagoras in this wisdom so long as you spoke well of the Indians, since you too
were originally Indians. But when you were shamed by the
report that the displeasure of the Earth caused you to
come here, and you preferred to be anything rather than
Ethiopians arrived from India, then all your actions were
directed to that. You stripped yourselves of your original
clothing, as if simultaneously casting off your Ethiopian
identity, you determined to worship the gods in the Egyp-

---

[16] Literally, "wheel out on a lofty, inspired mechanism," referring to the wheeled platform (*ekkuklēma*) used by Aeschylus and
other Attic dramatists.   [17] Cf. III 15.1.

APOLLONIUS OF TYANA

ὑμέτερον τρόπον, ἐς λόγους τε οὐκ ἐπιτηδείους ὑπὲρ
Ἰνδῶν κατέστητε, ὥσπερ οὐκ αὐτοὶ διαβεβλημένοι τῷ
ἀφ' οἵων διαβεβλῆσθαι ἥκειν,

14   "Καὶ οὐδὲ μετερρύθμισθέ πώ γε τοῦτο, οἳ καὶ τήμερον ἐπίδειξιν αὐτοῦ πεποίησθε φιλολοίδορόν τε καὶ
ἰαμβώδη, χρηστὸν οὐδὲν ἐπιτηδεύειν Ἰνδοὺς φάσκοντες, ἀλλ' ἢ ἐκπλήξεις καὶ ἀγωγάς, τὰς μὲν ὀφθαλμῶν,
τὰς δὲ ὤτων, σοφίαν δὲ οὔπω ἐμὴν εἰδότες ἀναίσθητοι
φαίνεσθε τῆς ἐπ' αὐτῇ δόξης. ἐγὼ δ' ὑπὲρ ἐμαυτοῦ μὲν
λέξω οὐδέν, εἴην γάρ, ὅ με Ἰνδοὶ ἡγοῦνται, Ἰνδῶν δὲ
οὐ ξυγχωρῶ ἅπτεσθαι. ἀλλ' εἰ μέν τις ὑγιῶς καὶ ὑμᾶς
ἔχει σοφία Ἱμεραίου ἀνδρός. ὃς ᾄδων ἐς τὴν Ἑλένην
ἐναντίον τῷ προτέρῳ λόγῳ παλινῳδίαν αὐτὸν ἐκάλε-
σεν, 'οὐκ ἔστιν ἔτυμος ὁ λόγος οὗτος' ἤδη καὶ αὐτοὺς
ὥρα λέγειν, ἀμείνω τῆς νῦν παρεστηκυίας μεταλα-
βόντας περὶ αὐτῶν δόξαν. εἰ δὲ καὶ ἄμουσοι πρὸς
παλινῳδίαν ὑμεῖς, ἀλλὰ φείδεσθαί γε χρὴ ἀνδρῶν,
οὓς ἀξιοῦντες θεοὶ τῶν αὐτοῖς ὄντων οὐδὲ ἑαυτοὺς
ἀπαξιοῦσιν ὧν ἐκεῖνοι πέπανται.

15   "Διῆλθές τινα, Θεσπεσίων, καὶ περὶ τῆς Πυθοῦς
λόγον ὡς ἁπλῶς τε καὶ ἀκατασκεύως χρώσης, καὶ
παράδειγμα ἐγένετό σοι τοῦ λόγου νεὼς κηροῦ καὶ
πτερῶν ξυντεθείς· ἐμοὶ δὲ ἀκατάσκευα μὲν δοκεῖ οὐδὲ
ταῦτα, τὸ γὰρ 'ξυμφέρετε πτερά τ' οἰωνοί, κηρόν τε
μέλιτται,' κατασκευαζομένου ἦν οἶκον καὶ οἴκου σχῆ-

132

tian way rather than your own, and you began to tell un-
seemly stories about the Indians, as if you yourselves were
not discredited by having come from discreditable people.

"Even now you have not abolished this habit, since you   14
gave an abusive, satirical display of it today, saying that the
Indians had no decent practices, but only miracles and
spells, some for the eyes, others for the ears. And your
ignorance of my own philosophy shows you to be ignorant
of the reputation it enjoys. I will say nothing about myself,
since I hope I am what the Indians believe me to be, but I
will not permit you to criticize the Indians. If you are
blessed with some of the wisdom of the man of Himera,
who composed a poem on Helen to cancel his previous account, and called it a palinode, it is now time for you too to
say 'This story is not true,'[18] and to adopt a better opinion
about them than the one you hold at present. Even if
you lack inspiration for a palinode, at least you should
spare Eminences whom the gods think worthy of their own
prerogatives, and whose privileges they themselves do not
disdain.

"You also gave a discourse, Thespesion, about Delphi,   15
to the effect that it gave its oracles in a simple and unadorned fashion, and your discourse used the example of
the temple constructed out of wax and feathers. To me,
however, even that does not seem 'unadorned,' since the
line, 'Bring feathers, ye birds, and wax, ye bees,'[19] suggests
someone constructing a house and the outline of a house.

[18] The opening of Stesichorus's "palinode" on Helen of Troy,
written to correct his previous poem about her.

[19] Line from an unknown poet, also cited by Plutarch, *On the
Oracles of the Pythia* 402 D.

μα, ὁ δ', οἶμαι, μικρὰ ταῦτα ἡγούμενος καὶ τῆς ἑαυτοῦ
σοφίας ἥττω, καὶ ἄλλου ἐδεήθη νεὼ καὶ ἄλλου, καὶ
μεγάλων ἤδη καὶ ἑκατομπέδων, ἑνὸς δὲ αὐτῶν καὶ
χρυσᾶς ἴυγγας ἀνάψαι λέγεται Σειρήνων τινὰ ἐπεχού-
σας πειθώ, ξυνελέξατό τε τὰ εὐδοκιμώτατα τῶν ἀναθημάτων ἐς τὴν Πυθὼ κόσμου ἕνεκα, καὶ οὔτ' ἀγαλματοποιίαν ἀπήλασεν ἀπάγουσαν αὐτῷ κολοσσοὺς ἐς
τὸ ἱερὸν τοὺς μὲν θεῶν, τοὺς δὲ ἀνθρώπων, τοὺς δὲ
ἵππων τε καὶ ταύρων καὶ ἑτέρων ζῴων, οὔτε Γλαῦκον
μετὰ τοῦ ὑποκρατηριδίου ἥκοντα, οὔτε τὴν ἁλισκο-
μένην Ἰλίου ἀκρόπολιν, ἣν Πολύγνωτος ἐκεῖ γράφει.
οὐ γὰρ δὴ τὸν χρυσόν γε τὸν Λύδιον καλλώπισμα τῆς
Πυθοῦς ἡγεῖτο, ἀλλ' ἐκεῖνον μὲν ὑπὲρ τῶν Ἑλλήνων
ἐσήγετο ἐνδεικνύμενος, οἶμαι, αὐτοῖς τὸν τῶν βαρβάρων πλοῦτον, ἵνα γλίχοιντο ἐκείνου μᾶλλον ἢ τοῦ
διαπορθεῖν τὰ ἀλλήλων, τὸν δὲ δὴ Ἑλληνά τε καὶ
προσφυᾶ τῇ ἑαυτοῦ σοφίᾳ τρόπον κατεσκευάζετο καὶ
ἠγλάιζε τούτῳ τὴν Πυθώ.

16   "Ἡγοῦμαι δὲ αὐτὸν κόσμου ἕνεκα καὶ ἐς μέτρα
ἐμβιβάζειν τοὺς χρησμούς. εἰ γὰρ μὴ τοῦτο ἐπ-
εδείκνυτο, τοιάσδε ἂν τὰς ἀποκρίσεις ἐποιεῖτο· δρᾶ τὸ
δεῖνα ἢ μὴ δρᾶ, καὶ ἴθι ἢ μὴ ἴθι, καὶ ποιοῦ ξυμμάχους
ἢ μὴ ποιοῦ, βραχέα γάρ που ταῦτα, ἤ, ὥς φατε ὑμεῖς,
γυμνά, ὁ δ' ἵνα μεγαλορρήμων τε φαίνοιτο καὶ ἡδίων

---

[20] For this tradition, see Pausanias, *Description of Greece*
10.5.9–13.

[21] For the stand made by Glaucus of Chios, see Herodotus

Moreover, thinking all this too humble and unworthy of his wisdom, I suppose, the god called first for one temple and then for another, and at last for great ones a hundred feet long. From one of these, they say, he suspended golden fetishes containing a Siren-like persuasiveness, and collected the most precious of offerings at Delphi for its adornment.[20] Nor did he reject the sculptor's art when it brought colossal statues to his sanctuary, some of gods, some of men, some of horses, bulls, and other animals. Nor did he reject Glaucus coming with his stand for a mixing bowl, or *The Capture of the Citadel of Ilion*, which Polygnotus painted there.[21] However, he did not consider the Lydian gold to be an ornament of Delphi, [22] but welcomed it for the Greeks' sake, so as to show them the wealth of the barbarians, I imagine, and awaken a desire for that in them rather than for plundering one another's possessions. But the Greek style, which matched his own wisdom, he used for his adornment, and with it he made Delphi radiant.

"It is for ornament too, I think, that he gave his oracles a metrical basis. If he had not prided himself on this, he would have issued answers such as these, 'Do this,' or 'Do not do that,' 'Go,' 'Do not go,' 'Make such-and-such your allies,' or 'Do not make them,' since these statements are brief or 'bare,' to use your own word. In order to seem grandiloquent and more pleasing to his consultants, he

16

1.25.2. Polygnotus, the celebrated Thasian artist of the fifth century, painted a series of frescoes at Delphi, which included the taking of Troy.

[22] For these gifts of Croesus, king of Lydia, see Herodotus 1.50–51.

τοῖς ἐρωτῶσι, ποιητικὴν ἡρμόσατο, καὶ οὐκ ἀξιοῖ
εἶναι, ὅ τι μὴ οἶδεν, ἀλλὰ καὶ τὴν ψάμμον εἰδέναι
φησίν ὁπόση, ἀριθμήσας[17] αὐτήν, καὶ τὰ τῆς θαλάττης μέτρα ξυνειληφέναι πάντα. ἢ καὶ ταῦτα τερατο-
λογίᾳ προσγράφεις, ἐπειδὴ σοβαρῶς αὐτὰ ὁ Ἀπόλλων καὶ ξὺν φρονήματι ὀρθῷ φράζει;

17   "Εἰ δὲ μὴ ἀχθέσῃ, Θεσπεσίων, τῷ λόγῳ, γρᾶες
ἀνημμέναι κόσκινα φοιτῶσιν ἐπὶ ποιμένας, ὅτε δὲ καὶ
βουκόλους, ἰώμεναι τὰ νοσοῦντα τῶν θρεμμάτων μαντικῇ, ὥς φασιν, ἀξιοῦσι δὲ σοφαὶ ὀνομάζεσθαι καὶ
σοφώτεραι ἢ οἱ ἀτεχνῶς μάντεις. τοῦτό μοι καὶ ὑμεῖς
παρὰ τὴν Ἰνδῶν σοφίαν φαίνεσθε, οἱ μὲν γὰρ θεῖοί τέ
εἰσι καὶ κεκόσμηνται κατὰ τὴν Πυθίαν, ὑμεῖς δέ—
ἀλλ' οὐδὲν εἰρήσεται περαιτέρω, εὐφημία γὰρ φίλη
μὲν ἐμοί, φίλη δὲ Ἰνδοῖς, ἣν ἀσπαζοίμην ὡς ὀπαδὸν
ἅμα καὶ ἡγεμόνα τῆς γλώττης, τὰ μὲν ἐμαυτῷ δυνατὰ
θηρεύων ξὺν ἐπαίνῳ τε αὐτῶν καὶ ἔρωτι, ὅ τι δὲ μὴ
ἐφικτὸν εἴη μοι, καταλείπων αὐτὸ ἄχραντον ψόγου.

18   "Σὺ δὲ Ὁμήρου μὲν ἐν Κυκλωπίᾳ ἀκούων, ὡς ἡ γῆ
τοὺς ἀγριωτάτους καὶ ἀνομωτάτους ἄσπορος καὶ ἀνή-
ροτος ἑστιᾷ, χαίρεις τῷ λόγῳ, κἂν Ἠδωνοί τινες ἢ
Λυδοὶ βακχεύωσιν, οὐκ ἀπιστεῖς, ὡς γάλακτος αὐτοῖς
καὶ οἴνου πηγὰς δώσει καὶ ποτιεῖ τούτους, τοὺς δὲ
σοφίας ἁπάσης βάκχους ἀφαιρήσῃ δῶρα αὐτόματα
παρὰ τῆς γῆς ἥκοντα; τρίποδες δὲ αὐτόματοι καὶ ἐς τὰ
ξυμπόσια τῶν θεῶν φοιτῶσι, καὶ ὁ Ἄρης ἀμαθής περ

_____
[17] ἀριθμήσας Rsk.: ἀριθμῆσαι

composed poetry, and holds that nothing should exist of which he does not know, and claims to know the number of the sands, having measured it, and to have surveyed all the distances of the sea.[23] Or do you ascribe this too to exaggeration, just because Apollo pronounces them grandly and with a just pride?

"If my saying so will not annoy you, Thespesion, old   17
women with sieves hanging from them go around among shepherds, or sometimes cowherds, curing their sick animals by divination, so they claim, and they expect to be called 'wise ones,' wiser than real diviners. That is what you seem to me compared to the wisdom of the Indians. They are both inspired and decked out like the Pythia, while you—but I will say no more, since moderation of language is dear to me, and dear to the Indians, and I welcome it both to escort and to guide my tongue. Such things as are possible for me I seek with praise and love, but what is beyond my grasp I leave undefiled by censure.

"You, by contrast, having heard how Homer in his de-   18
scription of the Cyclops says that the earth feeds that most rustic and uncivilized race without their sowing or reaping,[24] take pleasure in his story. If Edonians or Lydians are possessed by Bacchus, you are ready to believe that the earth will give them streams of milk and wine, and quench their thirst.[25] Will you then not allow those who are totally possessed by philosophy to have the gifts that the earth yields to them spontaneously? Three-legged tables travel spontaneously around the banquets of the gods, and Ares

[23] For this oracle, Herodotus 1.47.3.
[24] *Odyssey* 9.106–111.
[25] Euripides, *Bacchae* 704–711.

ὧν καὶ ἐχθρὸς οὔπω τὸν Ἥφαιστον ἐπ' αὐτοῖς γέγραπται, οὐδ' ἔστιν, ὡς ἤκουσάν ποτε οἱ θεοὶ τοιαύτης
γραφῆς· 'ἀδικεῖς, Ἥφαιστε, κοσμῶν τὸ ξυμπόσιον
τῶν θεῶν καὶ περιστὰς αὐτῷ θαύματα,' οὐδὲ ἐπὶ ταῖς
δμωαῖς αἰτίαν ποτὲ ἔσχε ταῖς χρυσαῖς ὡς παραφθεί-
ρων τὰς ὕλας, ἐπειδὴ τὸν χρυσὸν ἔμπνουν ἐποίει,

19   "Κόσμου γὰρ ἐπιμελήσεται τέχνη πᾶσα, ὅτι καὶ
αὐτὸ τὸ εἶναι τέχνας ὑπὲρ κόσμου εὕρηται. ἀνυπο-
δησία δὲ καὶ τρίβων καὶ πήραν ἀνῆφθαι κόσμου
εὕρημα· καὶ γὰρ τὸ γυμνοῦσθαι, καθάπερ ὑμεῖς, ἔοικε
μὲν ἀκατασκεύῳ τε καὶ λιτῷ σχήματι, ἐπιτετήδευται
δὲ ὑπὲρ κόσμου καὶ οὐδὲ ἄπεστιν αὐτοῦ τὸ 'ἑτέρῳ'
φασὶ 'τύφῳ.'

20   "Τὰ δὲ Ἡλίου τε καὶ Ἰνδῶν πάτρια, καὶ ὅπη χαίρει
θεραπευόμενος, ἐχέτω τὸν αὐτῶν νόμον, θεοὶ μὲν γὰρ
χθόνιοι βόθρους ἀσπάζονται καὶ τὰ ἐν κοίλῃ τῇ γῇ
δρώμενα, Ἡλίου δὲ ἀὴρ ὄχημα, καὶ δεῖ τοὺς προσ-
φόρως ἀσομένους αὐτὸν ἀπὸ γῆς αἴρεσθαι καὶ ξυμ-
μετεωροπολεῖν τῷ θεῷ· τοῦτο δὲ βούλονται μὲν πάντες, δύνανται δὲ Ἰνδοὶ μόνοι."

12. Ἀναπνεῦσαι ὁ Δάμις ἑαυτόν φησιν, ἐπειδὴ
ταῦτα ἤκουσεν· ὑπὸ γὰρ τῶν τοῦ Ἀπολλωνίου λόγων
οὕτω διατεθῆναι τοὺς Αἰγυπτίους, ὡς τὸν Θεσπεσίωνα
μὲν καίτοι μέλανα ὄντα κατάδηλον εἶναι, ὅτι ἐρυ-

for all his ignorance and malice never indicted Hephaestus
on their account, nor would the gods conceivably have
admitted an indictment such as this: 'You are accused,
Hephaestus, of decorating the banquet of the gods, and
furnishing it with marvels.' Nor did his golden serving
women ever cause him to be sued on the ground that he
corrupted the elements, just because he made gold come
to life.[26]

"All art will concern itself with decoration, since the   19
very existence of the arts came about for the purpose
of decoration. Going barefoot, wearing the philosophers'
cloak, and carrying a satchel, were all devised for adornment's sake. Why, going naked as you do may look like
dressing in a naïve and simple style, but it is an affectation
for the sake of ornament, and not exempt from the proverbial 'different kind of pride.'[27]

"As for the customs of the Sun god and the Indians, and   20
the way he pleases to be worshiped, let that be subject to
its own law, for the gods of earth welcome ditches and rites
performed in a hollow of the earth, while the air is the
Sun's vehicle, and those who would please him properly
must rise above the earth and join the god on his celestial
journey. Everybody desires that, but only the Indians can
achieve it."

12. When he heard this, says Damis, he breathed again,
since Apollonius's words had such an effect on the Egyptians that Thespesion could be clearly seen blushing, black
though he was. The others too showed a certain astonish-

---

[26] Alluding to the Athenians' charge against Socrates of "corrupting the young men" (Plato, *Apology* 24 B).

[27] See I 34.2.

θριῴη, φαίνεσθαι δέ τινα καὶ περὶ τοὺς λοιποὺς ἔκ-
πληξιν ἐφ' οἷς ἐρρωμένως τε καὶ ξὺν εὐροίᾳ διαλεγο-
μένου ἤκουσαν, τὸν νεώτατον δὲ τῶν Αἰγυπτίων, ᾧ
ὄνομα ἦν Νεῖλος, καὶ ἀναπηδῆσαί φησιν ὑπὸ θαύματος, μεταστάντα τε πρὸς τὸν Ἀπολλώνιον ξυμβαλεῖν
τε αὐτῷ τὴν χεῖρα καὶ δεῖσθαι αὐτοῦ τὰς ξυνουσίας,
αἳ ἐγένοντο αὐτῷ πρὸς τοὺς Ἰνδούς, φράζειν. τὸν δὲ
Ἀπολλώνιον "σοὶ μὲν οὐδενὸς ἂν" φάναι, "βασκή-
ναιμι ἐγὼ λόγου φιληκόῳ τε, ὡς ὁρῶ, τυγχάνοντι καὶ
σοφίαν ἀσπαζομένῳ πᾶσαν. Θεσπεσίωνι δὲ καὶ εἴ τις
ἕτερος λῆρον τὰ Ἰνδῶν ἡγεῖται, μὴ ἂν ἐπαντλήσαιμι[18]
τοὺς ἐκεῖθεν λόγους."

2   Ὅθεν ὁ Θεσπεσίων "εἰ δὲ ἔμπορος" εἶπεν "ἢ ναύ-
κληρος ἦσθα καί τινα ἡμῖν ἀπῆγες ἐκεῖθεν φόρτον,
ἆρα ἂν ἠξίους, ἐπειδὴ ἀπ' Ἰνδῶν οὗτος, ἀδοκίμαστον
αὐτὸν διατίθεσθαι καὶ μήτε γεῦμα παρέχειν αὐτοῦ
μήτε δεῖγμα;" ὑπολαβὼν δὲ ὁ Ἀπολλώνιος "παρειχό-
μην ἂν" εἶπε "τοῖς γε χρήζουσιν, εἰ δ' ἥκων τις ἐπὶ τὴν
θάλατταν καταπεπλευκυίας ἄρτι τῆς νεὼς ἐλοιδορεῖτο
τῷ φόρτῳ, καὶ διέβαλλε μὲν αὐτὸν ὡς ἥκοντα ἐκ γῆς,
ἢ μηδὲν ὑγιὲς φέρει, ἐμοὶ δὲ ἐπέπληττεν ὡς οὐχ ὑπὲρ
σπουδαίων ἀγωγίμων πλεύσαντι, τούς τε ἄλλους ἔπει-
θεν οὕτω φρονεῖν, ἆρ' ἄν σοι δοκεῖ τις καταπλεύσας ἐς
τοιόνδε λιμένα βαλέσθαι τινὰ ἄγκυραν ἢ πεῖσμα,
ἀλλ' οὐχὶ μᾶλλον ἀνασείσας τὰ ἱστία μετεωρίσαι ἂν
τὴν ναῦν ἐς τὸ πέλαγος, ἀνέμοις ἐπιτρέψας τὰ ἑαυτοῦ
ἥδιόν γε ἢ ἀκρίτοις τε καὶ ἀξένοις ἤθεσιν;" "ἀλλ' ἐγὼ"
ἔφη ὁ Νεῖλος "λαμβάνομαι τῶν πεισμάτων καὶ ἀντι-

ment on hearing Apollonius converse so boldly and elo-
quently, and the youngest of the Egyptians, whose name
was Nilus, jumped up in admiration, and going over to
Apollonius and putting his hand in his, asked him to describe his conversations with the Indians. "I would not be-
grudge any subject to you," Apollonius replied, "because
you are attentive, I can see, and welcoming to philosophy
of every kind. But as for Thespesion or anybody else who
considers Indian wisdom to be nonsense, I would not flood
them with doctrines from there."

This made Thespesion say, "Suppose you were a mer- 2
chant or a captain importing some cargo to us from there.
Would you expect to dispose of it unexamined, just because it was from India, and not give out a taste or a sam-
ple?" "To those who wanted one," replied Apollonius, "I
would provide it. But suppose somebody came down to the
sea when my ship had just put in, and denounced my cargo,
maliciously claiming that it came from a land that had no
decent products; and suppose he attacked me for sailing
with a worthless cargo, and persuaded everyone else to believe him. Do you imagine that someone who had sailed
into such a harbor would let out his anchor or cable at all?
Would he not rather hoist his sails and put out again to the
open sea, trusting his goods to the winds rather than to un-
discerning and unfriendly peoples?" "Well, I," said Nilus,
"grasp the cables and beg you, captain, to give me some of

---

18 ἐπαντλήσαιμι Bentl.: ἐπαντλῆσαι

βολῶ σε, ναύκληρε, κοινωνῆσαί μοι τῆς ἐμπορίας, ἣν
ἄγεις, καὶ ξυνεμβαίην ἄν σοι τὴν ναῦν περίνεώς τε καὶ
μνήμων τοῦ σοῦ φόρτου."

13. Διαπαύσας δὲ ὁ Θεσπεσίων τὰ τοιαῦτα "χαίρω"
ἔφη "Ἀπολλώνιε, ὅτι ἄχθῃ ὑπὲρ ὧν ἤκουσας· καὶ γὰρ
ἂν καὶ ἡμῖν ξυγγιγνώσκοις ἀχθομένοις ὑπὲρ ὧν δι-
έβαλες τὴν δεῦρο σοφίαν, οὐδὲ ἐς πεῖράν πω αὐτῆς
ἀφιγμένος." ὁ δ' ἐκπλαγεὶς μὲν ὑπὸ τοῦ λόγου πρὸς
βραχὺ τῷ μηδ' ἀκηκοέναι πω τὰ περὶ τὸν Θρασύ-
βουλόν τε καὶ τὸν Εὐφράτην, ξυμβαλὼν δ', ὥσπερ
εἰώθει, τὸ γεγονός, "Ἰνδοὶ δέ," εἶπεν "ὦ Θεσπεσίων,
οὐκ ἂν τοῦτο ἔπαθον, οὐδ' ἂν προσέσχον Εὐφράτῃ
καθιέντι ταῦτα, σοφοὶ γὰρ προγιγνώσκειν. ἐγὼ δὲ
ἴδιον μὲν ἐμαυτοῦ πρὸς Εὐφράτην διηνέχθην οὐδέν,
χρημάτων δὲ ἀπάγων αὐτὸν καὶ τοῦ μὴ ἐπαινεῖν τὸ ἐξ
ἅπαντος κέρδος, οὔτ' ἐπιτήδεια ξυμβουλεύειν ἔδοξα
οὔτε ἐκείνῳ δυνατά, καὶ ἔλεγχον δὲ ἡγεῖται ταῦτα καὶ
οὐκ ἀνίησιν ἀεί τι κατ' ἐμοῦ ξυντιθείς.

2   "Ἐπεὶ δὲ πιθανὸς ὑμῖν ἔδοξε τοὐμὸν διαβάλλειν
ἦθος, ἐνθυμεῖσθε, ὡς προτέρους ὑμᾶς ἐμοῦ διέβαλεν·
ἐμοὶ γὰρ κίνδυνοι μὲν καὶ περὶ τὸν διαβεβλησόμενον
οὐ σμικροὶ φαίνονται, μισήσεται γάρ που ἀδικῶν
οὐδέν, ἐλεύθεροι δὲ κινδύνων οὐδ' οἱ τῶν διαβολῶν
ἀκροασόμενοι δοκοῦσιν, εἰ πρῶτον μὲν ἁλώσονται
ψευδολογίαν τιμῶντες καὶ ἀξιοῦντες αὐτὴν ὧνπερ τὴν
ἀλήθειαν, εἶτα κουφότητα καὶ εὐαγωγίαν (ἡττᾶσθαι
δὲ τούτων καὶ μειρακίῳ αἰσχρόν). φθονεροί τε δόξουσι, διδάσκαλον ἀκοῆς ἀδίκου ποιούμενοι τὸν φθό-

the merchandise you are bringing. I would be willing to embark with you as a deck hand and guardian of your cargo."

13. Interrupting talk of this kind, Thespesion said, "I am glad, Apollonius, that what you have heard annoys you, since you will now pardon us for our annoyance at the way you criticized our philosophy before you had even come to examine it." Apollonius was briefly taken aback by these words, not yet having heard the story about Thrasybulus and Euphrates, but then, inferring what had happened as he usually did, he said, "The Indians, Thespesion, would not have reacted like that, and would not have listened to Euphrates putting this story about, since they are experienced in prediction. I had no personal quarrel with Euphrates, but I tried to divert him from money and from being satisfied with profit from every source, but he thought that my advice was unsuitable and beyond his power. He thinks this was all a rebuke, and never stops inventing some new story against me.

"But as you thought him plausible when he slandered 2 my character, you must realize that he slandered you rather than me. It seems to me that a victim of slander incurs no slight danger, being hated when he has done no harm, but those who listen to slander will not be thought free from danger either. First, they will be convicted of honoring falsehood, and valuing it as highly as truth; second, they will be convicted of frivolity and naïveté, in which it is disgraceful even for the young to be caught; and they will be considered jealous, because they allow jealousy to teach them harmful information. They will also

143

νον, αὐτοί τε μᾶλλον ἔνοχοι ταῖς διαβολαῖς, ἃς ἐφ᾽
ἑτέρων ἀληθεῖς ἡγοῦνται, αἱ γὰρ τῶν ἀνθρώπων φύσεις ἑτοιμότεραι δρᾶν, ἃ μὴ ἀπιστοῦσι.

3   "Μὴ τυραννεύσειεν ἀνὴρ ἕτοιμος ταῦτα, μηδὲ
προσταίη δήμου, τυραννὶς γὰρ καὶ ἡ δημοκρατία ὑπ᾽
αὐτοῦ ἔσται, μηδὲ δικάσειεν, ὑπὲρ μηδενὸς γὰρ γνώ-
σεται, μηδὲ ναυκληρήσειεν, ἡ γὰρ ναῦς στασιάσει,
μηδὲ ἄρξειε στρατοῦ, τὸ γὰρ ἀντίξοον εὖ πράξει, μηδὲ
φιλοσοφήσειεν οὕτως ἔχων, οὐ γὰρ πρὸς τἀληθὲς
δοξάσει. ὑμᾶς δὲ Εὐφράτης ἀφήρηται καὶ τὸ σοφοὺς
εἶναι, οὓς γὰρ ψεύδει ὑπηγάγετο, πῶς ἂν οὗτοι σοφίας
αὑτοὺς ἀξιώσειαν, ἧς ἀπέστησαν τῷ τὰ μὴ πιθανὰ
πείσαντι;"

4   Διαπραΰνων δ᾽ αὐτὸν ὁ Θεσπεσίων "ἅλις Εὐφράτου" ἔφη "καὶ μικροψύχων λόγων, καὶ γὰρ ἂν καὶ
διαλλακταὶ γενοίμεθά σοι τε κἀκείνῳ, σοφὸν ἡγούμενοι καὶ τὸ διαιτᾶν σοφοῖς. πρὸς δὲ ὑμᾶς," εἶπε "τίς
διαλλάξει με; χρὴ γάρ που καταψευσθέντα ἐκπεπολεμῶσθαι." "ὑπὲρ τοῦ ψεύδους ἐχέτω οὕτως," ἦ δ᾽ ὁ
Ἀπολλώνιος "καὶ σπουδῆς ἁπτώμεθα, τουτὶ γὰρ ἡμᾶς
διαλλάξει μᾶλλον."

14. Ἐρῶν δὲ ὁ Νεῖλος τῆς ἀκροάσεως τοῦ ἀνδρὸς
"καὶ μὴν σὲ" ἔφη "προσήκει ἄρξαι τοῦ σπουδάσαι,
διελθόντα ἡμῖν τήν τε ἀποδημίαν τὴν γενομένην σοι
ἐς τὸ Ἰνδῶν ἔθνος τάς τε ἐκεῖ σπουδάς, ἃς ὑπὲρ
λαμπρῶν δήπου ἐποιεῖσθε." "ἐγὼ δὲ" ἔφη ὁ Θεσπεσίων "καὶ περὶ τῆς Φραώτου σοφίας ἀκοῦσαι ποθῶ,
λέγεσθε γὰρ καὶ τῶν ἐκείνου λόγων ἀγάλματα ἀπὸ

seem more guilty themselves of the slanders which others persuade them to believe true, for human nature is all the more prone to do what it is unwilling to disbelieve.

"May a man of such tendency never be a tyrant, or a 3 popular leader either, because even democracy will become tyranny in his hands. May he not be a judge, because he will judge in favor of neither side, nor a ship's captain, because the crew will quarrel, or lead an army, because the enemy will profit. And may someone so disposed not be a philosopher, because he will not decide in accordance with truth. Euphrates has deprived you of your claim to be wise men, for how can people that he has misled by falsehood think themselves worthy of wisdom? They deserted it for someone who made them believe the unbelievable."

To mollify him, Thespesion said, "Enough of Euphra- 4 tes and narrow-minded topics. We would be glad to reconcile you, because we think it a wise act to arbitrate between wise men. But who will reconcile me," he continued, "with you? For having been slandered I should be your enemy." "As for the slander, let that be," said Apollonius, "and let us turn to serious things. That will reconcile us sooner."

14. But Nilus, passionately eager to hear the Master, said, "No, it is you that should begin the conversation by narrating for us your journey to the country of the Indians and your conversations there, which must have been on exalted subjects." "I too," said Thespesion, "desire to hear about the wisdom of Phraotes, since I am told you have brought from India precious reproductions of his dis-

Ἰνδῶν ἄγειν." ὁ μὲν δὴ Ἀπολλώνιος ἀρχὴν τοῦ λόγου
τὰ ἐν Βαβυλῶνι ποιησάμενος διῄει πάντα, οἱ δὲ ἄσμενοι ἠκροῶντο ὑποκείμενοι τῷ λόγῳ. μεσημβρία δ' ὡς
ἐγένετο, διέλυσαν τὴν σπουδήν, τὸν γὰρ καιρὸν τοῦτον καὶ οἱ Γυμνοὶ πρὸς ἱεροῖς γίγνονται.

15. Δειπνοῦντι δὲ τῷ Ἀπολλωνίῳ καὶ τοῖς ἀμφ'
αὐτὸν ὁ Νεῖλος ἐφίσταται λαχάνοις ἅμα καὶ ἄρτοις
καὶ τραγήμασι, τὰ μὲν αὐτὸς φέρων, τὰ δὲ ἕτεροι, καὶ
μάλα ἀστείως "οἱ σοφοὶ" ἔφη "ξένια πέμπουσιν ὑμῖν
τε κἀμοὶ ταῦτα, κἀγὼ γὰρ ξυσσιτήσω ὑμῖν οὐκ ἄκλη-
τος, ὡς φασιν, ἀλλ' ἐμαυτὸν καλῶν." "ἡδὺ" εἶπεν ὁ
Ἀπολλώνιος "ἀπάγεις, ὦ νεανία, ξένιον, σεαυτόν τε
καὶ τὸ σεαυτοῦ ἦθος, ὃς ἀδόλως μὲν φιλοσοφοῦντι
ἔοικας, ἀσπαζομένῳ δὲ τὰ Ἰνδῶν τε καὶ Πυθαγόρου.
κατακλίνου δὴ ἐνταῦθα καὶ ξυσσίτει." "κατάκειμαι,"
ἔφη "σιτία δὲ οὐκ ἔσται σοι τοσαῦτα, ὡς ἐμπλῆσαί
με." "ἔοικας" εἶπεν "εὔσιτος εἶναι καὶ δεινὸς φαγεῖν."
"δεινότατος μὲν οὖν," ἔφη "ὃς γὰρ τοσαύτην καὶ οὕτω
λαμπρὰν δαῖτά σου παραθέντος οὔπω ἐμπέπλησμαι,
διαλιπὼν δὲ ὀλίγον πάλιν ἐπισιτιούμενος ἥκω, τί
φήσεις ἀλλ' ἢ ἀκόρεστόν τε εἶναί με καὶ δεινῶς
γάστριν;" "ἐμπίπλασο," εἶπεν "ἀφορμαὶ δ', ὁπόσαι
λόγων, τὰς μὲν αὐτὸς παραδίδου, τὰς δὲ ἐγὼ δώσω."

16. Ἐπεὶ δ' ἐδείπνησαν, "ἐγὼ" ἦ δ' ὁ Νεῖλος "τὸν
μὲν ἄλλον χρόνον ἐστρατευόμην ὁμοῦ τοῖς Γυμνοῖς,
οἷον ψιλοῖς τισιν ἢ σφενδονήταις ἐκείνοις ἐμαυτὸν
ξυντάττων, νυνὶ δὲ ὁπλιτεύσω καὶ κοσμήσει με ἡ
ἀσπὶς ἡ σή." "ἀλλ' οἶμαί σε," εἶπεν "Αἰγύπτιε, παρὰ

courses." Apollonius therefore began with their experiences in Babylon, and described their whole story, while the Egyptians were delighted to listen, hanging on his words. When noon came, they ended their conversation, since at this hour the Naked Ones too attend to their rites.

15. Apollonius and his company were at dinner when Nilus came up, bringing vegetables, bread, and dried fruits, some of which he himself carried while others carried the rest. With great friendliness he said, "The wise men send these as gifts to you and me. I am going to dine with you, not uninvited, as the phrase is,[28] but inviting myself." "It is a delightful gift you bring," said Apollonius, "in yourself and your nature, young man, as you seem to be a sincere lover of wisdom, and well disposed to the doctrines of the Indians and of Pythagoras. Sit down here, then, and dine with us." "I will sit down," he said, "but you do not have enough food to satisfy me." "You seem to have a good appetite and to be a huge eater," said Apollonius. "Yes, very huge," was the reply. "Despite the great, sparkling feast you offered, I am still not full, and after a short interval I have come to feed again. What then can you call me if not insatiable and hugely gluttonous?" "Eat your fill," said Apollonius, "but some of the food for discussion you must provide, and I will provide the rest."

16. After their dinner, Nilus said, "Up to now I myself have campaigned with the Naked Ones, and joined their ranks as if they used light armor or slings; but now I carry heavy arms and your shield will be my glory." "I am afraid, my Egyptian friend," said Apollonius, "that you will get

[28] Cf. Plato, *Symposium* 174 C.

Θεσπεσίωνί τε καὶ τοῖς ἄλλοις ἕξειν αἰτίαν, ἐφ᾽ οἷς
οὐδὲ ἐς ἔλεγχον ἡμῶν καταστὰς πλείω, σὺ δ᾽ ἑτοιμό-
τερον ἢ ξυγχωρεῖ βίου αἵρεσις ἐς τὰ ἡμέτερα ἤθη
ἀφήσεις." "οἶμαι," ἔφη "εἰ δ᾽ ᾿αἰτία ἑλομένου᾽ ἔσται
τις, τάχα καὶ μὴ ἑλομένου αἰτία, καὶ ἁλώσονται μᾶλλον ἅπερ ἐγὼ <μὴ>[19] ἑλόμενοι· τὸ γὰρ πρεσβυτέρους
ὁμοῦ καὶ σοφωτέρους ὄντας μὴ πάλαι ᾑρῆσθαι, ἅπερ
ἐγὼ νῦν, δικαίαν αἰτίαν κατ᾽ ἐκείνων ἔχοι ἂν μᾶλλον
οὕτω πλεονεκτοῦντας μὴ ἐς τὸ βέλτιον ἑλέσθαι, ὅ τι
χρήσονται."

2   "Οὐκ ἀγεννῆ μέν, ὦ νεανίσκε, λόγον εἴρηκας· ὅρα
δέ, μὴ αὐτῷ τῷ οὕτω μὲν σοφίας, οὕτω δὲ ἡλικίας
ἔχειν ἐκεῖνά γε ὀρθῶς ᾑρημένοι φαίνωνται, ταῦτά τε
ξὺν εἰκότι λόγῳ παραιτούμενοι, σύ τε θρασυτέρου
λόγου δοκῇς ἅπτεσθαι, καθιστὰς μᾶλλον αὐτὸς ἢ[20]
ἐκείνοις ἑπόμενος." ὑποστρέψας δὲ ὁ Αἰγύπτιος παρὰ
τὴν τοῦ Ἀπολλωνίου δόξαν, "ἃ μὲν εἰκὸς ἦν" ἔφη
"πρεσβυτέροις ὁμαρτεῖν νέον, οὐ παρεῖταί μοι, σοφίαν γὰρ ὁπότ᾽ ᾤμην εἶναι περὶ τοὺς ἄνδρας, ἣν οὐκ
ἄλλοις τισὶν ἀνθρώπων ὑπάρχειν, προσεποίησα ἐμαυτὸν τούτοις.

3   "Πρόφασις δέ μοι τῆς ὁρμῆς ἥδε ἐγένετο· ἔπλευσέ
ποτε ὁ πατὴρ ἐς τὴν Ἐρυθρὰν ἑκών, ἦρχε δὲ ἄρα τῆς
νεώς, ἣν Αἰγύπτιοι στέλλουσιν ἐς τὸ Ἰνδῶν ἔθνος,
ἐπιμίξας δὲ τοῖς ἐπὶ θαλάττῃ Ἰνδοῖς, διεκόμισε λόγους περὶ τῶν ἐκείνη σοφῶν ἀγχοῦ τούτων, οὓς πρὸς
ἡμᾶς διῆλθες. ἀκούων δὲ αὐτοῦ καὶ τοιουτονί τινα
λόγον, ὡς σοφώτατοι μὲν ἀνθρώπων Ἰνδοί, ἄποικοι δὲ

blame from Thespesion and the others because you have not put us to any further test, but have joined our society more readily than choosing a way of life usually permits." "Perhaps so," said Nilus, "but if 'the fault lies with the chooser,'[29] so perhaps it lies with failure to choose, so that they will be more to blame for not choosing as I have. For since they did not choose long ago as I have now, despite being older and wiser, they might deserve an even juster blame for not making the better choice of action, considering their advantage."

"That is quite a fine speech you have made, young man. 2 Yet simply because those philosophers have reached such a stage in wisdom and in years, they may in fact prove to have chosen their way rightly, and to have rejected ours for good reason. You may then prove to have spoken too rashly in taking your own stand, rather than following them." The Egyptian, however, turning Apollonius's argument back on him, said, "I have not failed to do anything in which a young man might properly follow his elders, and when I thought their Eminences had wisdom such as no other men possessed, I subjected myself to them.

"Here is the reason for my decision. My father once 3 sailed to the Red Sea of his own free will, since he commanded the ship that the Egyptians send to the land of India.[30] He conversed with the Indians of the shore, and brought back accounts of the wise men there similar to those that you recounted to us. I also heard from him some such story as this, that the Indians were the wisest people

---

[29] Plato, *Republic* 617 E.   [30] On this see III 35.

---

[19] ⟨μὴ⟩ cod. Vratislav.   [20] αὐτὸς ἢ Kay.: ἢ αὐτὸς

Ἰνδῶν Αἰθίοπες, πατρῴζουσι δὲ οὗτοι τὴν σοφίαν καὶ
πρὸς τὰ οἴκοι βλέπουσι, μειράκιον γενόμενος τὰ μὲν
πατρῷα τοῖς βουλομένοις ἀφῆκα, γυμνὸς δὲ Γυμνοῖς
ἐπεφοίτησα τούτοις, ὡς μαθησόμενος τὰ Ἰνδῶν ἢ
ἀδελφά γε ἐκείνων, καί μοι ἐφαίνοντο σοφοὶ μέν, οὐ
μὴν ἐκεῖνα. ἐμοῦ δ' αὐτοὺς ἐρομένου, τοῦ χάριν οὐ
τὰ Ἰνδῶν φιλοσοφοῦσιν, ἐκείνων μὲν ἐς διαβολὰς
κατέστησαν παραπλησίως ταῖς πρὸς σὲ εἰρημέναις
τήμερον.

4 "Ἐμὲ δὲ νέον ἔτι, ὡς ὁρᾷς, ὄντα κατέλεξαν ἐς
τὸ αὐτῶν κοινόν, δείσαντες, οἶμαι, μὴ ἀποπηδήσας
αὐτῶν πλεύσαιμι ἐς τὴν Ἐρυθράν, ὥσπερ ποτὲ ὁ
πατήρ. ὃ μὰ τοὺς θεοὺς οὐκ ἂν παρῆκα· προῆλθον γὰρ
ἂν καὶ μέχρι τοῦ ὄχθου τῶν σοφῶν, εἰ μή σέ τις
ἐνταῦθα θεῶν ἔστειλεν ἐμοὶ ἀρωγόν, ὡς μήτε τὴν
Ἐρυθρὰν πλεύσας μήτε πρὸς τοὺς Κολπίτας παρα-
βαλόμενος σοφίας Ἰνδικῆς γευσαίμην, οὐ τήμερον
βίου ποιησόμενος αἵρεσιν, ἀλλὰ πάλαι μὲν ᾑρημένος,
ἃ δὲ ᾤμην ἕξειν, οὐκ ἔχων.

5 "Τί γὰρ δεινόν, εἰ ὁτουδὴ ἁμαρτών τις ἐπάνεισιν
ἐφ' ὃ ἐθήρευεν; εἰ δὲ κἀκείνους ἐς τουτὶ μεταβιβάζοιμι
καὶ γιγνοίμην αὐτοῖς ξύμβουλος ὢν ἐμαυτὸν πέπεικα,
τί ἄν, εἰπέ μοι, θρασὺ πράττοιμι; οὔτε γὰρ ἡ νεότης
ἀπελατέα τοῦ τι[21] καὶ αὐτὴ βέλτιον ἐνθυμηθῆναι ἂν
τοῦ γήρως, σοφίας τε ὅστις ἑτέρῳ γίγνεται ξύμβουλος, ἣν αὐτὸς ᾕρηται, διαφεύγει δήπου τὸ μὴ οὐχ ἃ
πέπεισται πείθειν, τοῖς τε ἥκουσιν ἀγαθοῖς παρὰ τῆς
τύχης ὅστις ἀπολαβὼν αὐτὰ χρῆται μόνος, ἀδικεῖ

in the world, and that the Ethiopians were migrants from
India who maintained their ancestral wisdom and respected their origins. So on entering manhood I gave my
inheritance to anyone wanting it, and joined these Naked
Ones as naked as they were, expecting to learn Indian wisdom or something close to it. The Naked Ones seemed
wise to me, but not in the Indian way, and when I asked
them why their philosophy was not that of the Indians,
they started to slander them, similarly to what they said to
you today.

"They enrolled me in their community when I was still   4
young, as you see, doubtless fearing that I would desert
them and sail off to the Red Sea, as my father once did.
That I swear I would have done, indeed I would have gone
as far as the Wise Men's hill if some god had not sent you
here to be my helper, in order that I could get a taste of Indian philosophy without sailing to the Red Sea or putting
in among the Gulf Dwellers. I was not destined to choose a
way of life only today, but chose long ago, though without
obtaining what I thought I had obtained.

"What is so surprising if someone misses his aim, and   5
then goes back after his former quarry? If I tried to bring
even them over to this path and to urge on them what I believe myself, tell me, would I be doing anything rash?
Youth must not be discouraged from having some better
ideas than old age has. Someone who advises another to
adopt the philosophy he has chosen for himself can certainly not be charged with not giving advice in which he
believes. When fortune brings gifts, the one who monopo-
lizes them for his own enjoyment does wrong to the gifts,

---

²¹ τοῦ τι Rsk.: τουτὶ

APOLLONIUS OF TYANA

τἀγαθά, ἀφαιρεῖται γὰρ αὐτῶν τὸ πλείοσιν ἡδίω φαίνεσθαι."

17. Τοιαῦτα εἴραντος τοῦ Νείλου καὶ οὕτω νεανικά, ὑπολαβὼν ὁ Ἀπολλώνιος "ὑπὲρ μισθοῦ δὲ" εἶπεν "οὐ διαλέξῃ μοι πρότερον, σοφίας γε ἐρῶν τῆς ἐμῆς;" "διαλεγώμεθα" ἦ δ' ὁ Νεῖλος "καὶ ὅ τι βούλει, αἴτει." "αἰτῶ σε," εἶπεν "ἃ μὲν αὐτὸς εἵλου, ᾑρῆσθαι, τοὺς δὲ Γυμνοὺς μὴ ἐνοχλεῖν ξυμβουλεύοντα ἃ μὴ πείσεις." "πείσομαι" ἔφη "καὶ ὁμολογείσθω ὁ μισθός." ταῦτα μὲν δὴ οὕτως ἐσπούδασαν, ἐρομένου δ' αὐτὸν μετὰ ταῦτα τοῦ Νείλου, πόσου χρόνου διατρίψοι περὶ τοὺς Γυμνούς, "ὁπόσου" ἔφη "χρόνου ἀξία ἡ τῶνδε σοφία τῷ ξυνεσομένῳ σφίσιν, εἶτα ἐπὶ Καταδούπων τὴν ὁδὸν ποιησόμεθα τῶν πηγῶν ἔνεκα, χαρίεν γὰρ τὸ μὴ μόνον ἰδεῖν τὰς τοῦ Νείλου ἀρχάς, ἀλλὰ καὶ κελαδοῦντος αὐτοῦ ἀκοῦσαι." ὧδε διαλεχθέντες καί τινων Ἰνδικῶν μνημονεύσαντες, ἐκάθευδον ἐν τῇ πόᾳ.

18. Ἅμα δὲ τῇ ἡμέρᾳ προσευξάμενοι τὰ εἰωθότα, εἴποντο τῷ Νείλῳ παρὰ τὸν Θεσπεσίωνα αὐτοὺς ἄγοντι. προσειπόντες οὖν[22] ἀλλήλους καὶ ξυνιζήσαντες ἐν τῷ ἄλσει, διαλέξεως ἥπτοντο, ἦρχε δ' αὐτῆς ὁ Ἀπολλώνιος. "ὡς μὲν γὰρ πολλοῦ" ἔφη "ἄξιον τὸ μὴ κρύπτειν σοφίαν, δηλοῦσιν οἱ χθὲς λόγοι. διδαξαμένων γάρ με Ἰνδῶν, ὁπόσα τῆς ἐκείνων σοφίας ᾤμην προσήκειν ἐμοί, μέμνημαί τε τῶν ἐμαυτοῦ διδασκάλων καὶ περίειμι[23] διδάσκων, ἃ ἐκείνων ἤκουσα. καὶ ὑμῖν δ' ἂν ἐν κέρδει γενοίμην, εἴ με καὶ τὴν ὑμετέραν σοφίαν

152

and denies them the chance of giving pleasure to other people."

17. When Nilus had poured out these youthful ideas, Apollonius replied, "Well, are you not going to discuss your fee with me first, if you are enamored of my philosophy?" "Let us discuss it," said Nilus, "and ask for whatever you want." "I ask," said Apollonius, "that you persevere in the choice you have made, and not bother the Naked Ones by giving advice that they will not take." "I will obey," said Nilus, "and let this be the agreed fee." This ended their discussion, but when Nilus asked Apollonius later how long he would stay with the Naked Ones, he replied, "As long as their wisdom repays someone for their company. Then we will travel to the Falls to see the sources of the Nile, since it would be gratifying not only to see its head-waters, but to hear it thundering." After this conversation, and discussion of certain Indian matters, they went to sleep on the grass.

18. At dawn, they made their usual prayers and then followed Nilus as he led them to Thespesion. After greeting each other and sitting down in the grove, they began a discussion, which Apollonius started by saying, "Our talk yesterday showed how important it is not to conceal wisdom. Now that the Indians have taught me as much of their wisdom as I considered relevant to myself, I both remember my teachers, and go around teaching what I heard from them. I could do you a favor as well if you sent me off with some knowledge of your wisdom, since I would con-

εἰδότα πέμποιτε, οὐ γὰρ ἂν παυσαίμην Ἕλλησί τε διιὼν τὰ ὑμέτερα καὶ Ἰνδοῖς γράφων."

19. "Ἔρωτα," ἔφασαν "ἕπεται γάρ που ἐρωτήσει λόγος." καὶ ὁ Ἀπολλώνιος "περὶ θεῶν" εἶπεν "ὑμᾶς ἐρήσομαι πρῶτον, τί μαθόντες ἄτοπα καὶ γελοῖα θεῶν εἴδη παραδεδώκατε τοῖς δεῦρο ἀνθρώποις πλὴν ὀλίγων· ὀλίγων γάρ; πάνυ μέντοι ὀλίγων, ἃ σοφῶς καὶ θεοειδῶς ἵδρυται, τὰ λοιπὰ δ' ὑμῶν ἱερὰ ζῴων ἀλόγων καὶ ἀδόξων τιμαὶ μᾶλλον ἢ θεῶν φαίνονται." δυσχεράνας δὲ ὁ Θεσπεσίων "τὰ δὲ παρ' ὑμῖν" εἶπεν "ἀγάλματα πῶς ἱδρῦσθαι φήσεις;" "ὥς γε" ἔφη "κάλλιστόν τε καὶ θεοφιλέστατον δημιουργεῖν θεούς." "τὸν Δία που λέγεις" εἶπε "τὸν ἐν τῇ Ὀλυμπίᾳ, καὶ τὸ τῆς Ἀθηνᾶς ἕδος, καὶ τὸ τῆς Κνιδίας τε καὶ τὸ τῆς Ἀργείας, καὶ ὁπόσα ὧδε καλὰ καὶ μεστὰ ὥρας."

2 "Οὐ μόνον" ἔφη "ταῦτα, ἀλλὰ καὶ καθάπαξ τὴν μὲν παρὰ τοῖς ἄλλοις ἀγαλματοποιίαν ἅπτεσθαί φημι τοῦ προσήκοντος, ὑμᾶς δὲ καταγελᾶν τοῦ θείου μᾶλλον ἢ νομίζειν αὐτό." "οἱ Φειδίαι δὲ" εἶπε "καὶ οἱ Πραξιτέλεις μῶν ἀνελθόντες ἐς οὐρανόν, καὶ ἀπομαξάμενοι τὰ τῶν θεῶν εἴδη, τέχνην αὐτὰ ἐποιοῦντο, ἢ ἕτερόν τι ἦν, ὃ ἐφίστη αὐτοὺς τῷ πλάττειν;" "ἕτερον" ἔφη "καὶ μεστόν γε σοφίας πρᾶγμα." "ποῖον;" εἶπεν "οὐ γὰρ ἂν τι παρὰ τὴν μίμησιν εἴποις." "φαντασία" ἔφη "ταῦτα εἰργάσατο σοφωτέρα μιμήσεως δημιουργός· μίμησις μὲν γὰρ δημιουργήσει, ὃ εἶδεν, φαντασία δὲ καὶ ὃ μὴ εἶδεν, ὑποθήσεται γὰρ αὐτὸ πρὸς τὴν ἀναφορὰν τοῦ ὄντος, καὶ μίμησιν μὲν πολλάκις ἐκκρούει ἔκπληξις,

stantly describe your ways to the Greeks and write about them to the Indians."

19. "Ask," they replied, "since questions of course lead to explanations." So Apollonius said, "I will ask you first about the gods. What induced you to give people here strange and ridiculous shapes for the gods, except for a few of them? Why do I say few? Very few, which are represented as knowledgeable and in godlike form, while your other holy places appear to honor dumb, worthless animals rather than gods." Annoyed, Thespesion said, "How will you describe the way your cult statues are represented?" "In the most honorable and pious way for representing gods," said Apollonius. "You must mean the Zeus at Olympia," said the other, "the image of Athena, of the Cnidian goddess and the Argive one, all the images that are as beautiful as those and as full of charm."

"Not those merely," said Apollonius, "but in general I hold that the sculpture of other peoples aims at propriety, but you mock divinity rather than worshiping it." "Your Phidias," said Thespesion, "your Praxiteles, they did not go up to heaven and make a cast of the gods' forms before turning them into art, did they? Was it not something else that set them to work as sculptors?" "It was," said Apollonius, "and something supremely philosophical." "What is that?" asked Thespesion; "for you cannot mean anything but Imitation." "Imagination created these objects," replied Apollonius, "a more skilful artist than Imitation. Imitation will create what it knows, but Imagination will also create what it does not know, conceiving it with reference to the real. Shock often frustrates Imitation, but nothing

φαντασίαν δὲ οὐδέν, χωρεῖ γὰρ ἀνέκπληκτος πρὸς ὃ
αὐτὴ ὑπέθετο.

3   "Δεῖ δέ που Διὸς μὲν ἐνθυμηθέντα εἶδος ὁρᾶν αὐτὸν
ξὺν οὐρανῷ καὶ ὥραις καὶ ἄστροις, ὥσπερ ὁ Φειδίας
τότε ὥρμησεν, Ἀθηνᾶν δὲ δημιουργήσειν μέλλοντα
στρατόπεδα ἐννοεῖν καὶ μῆτιν καὶ τέχνας καὶ ὡς Διὸς
αὐτοῦ ἀνέθορεν. εἰ δὲ ἱέρακα ἢ γλαῦκα ἢ λύκον ἢ κύνα
ἐργασάμενος ἐς τὰ ἱερὰ φέροις ἀντὶ Ἑρμοῦ τε καὶ
Ἀθηνᾶς καὶ Ἀπόλλωνος, τὰ μὲν θηρία καὶ τὰ ὄρνεα
ζηλωτὰ δόξει τῶν εἰκόνων, οἱ δὲ θεοὶ παραπολὺ τῆς
αὑτῶν δόξης ἑστήξουσιν." "ἔοικας" εἶπεν "ἀβασα-
νίστως ἐξετάζειν τὰ ἡμέτερα· σοφὸν γάρ, εἴπερ τι
Αἰγυπτίων, καὶ τὸ μὴ θρασύνεσθαι ἐς τὰ τῶν θεῶν
εἴδη, ξυμβολικὰ δὲ αὐτὰ ποιεῖσθαι καὶ ὑπονοούμενα,
καὶ γὰρ ἂν καὶ σεμνότερα οὕτω φαίνοιτο."

4   Γελάσας οὖν ὁ Ἀπολλώνιος "ὦ ἄνθρωποι," ἔφη
"μεγάλα ὑμῖν ἀπολέλαυται τῆς Αἰγυπτίων τε καὶ Αἰθιόπων σοφίας, εἰ σεμνότερον ὑμῶν καὶ θεοειδέστερον
κύων δόξει καὶ ἶβις καὶ τράγος, ταῦτα γὰρ Θεσπεσίωνος ἀκούω τοῦ σοφοῦ. σεμνὸν δὲ δὴ ἢ ἔμφοβον τί
ἐν τούτοις; τοὺς γὰρ ἐπιόρκους καὶ τοὺς ἱεροσύλους
καὶ τὰ βωμολόχα ἔθνη καταφρονεῖν τῶν τοιούτων
ἱερῶν εἰκὸς μᾶλλον ἢ δεδιέναι αὐτά, εἰ δὲ σεμνότερα
ταῦτα ὑπονοούμενα, πολλῷ σεμνότερον ἂν ἔπραττον
οἱ θεοὶ κατ' Αἴγυπτον, εἰ μὴ ἵδρυτό τι αὐτῶν ἄγαλμα,
ἀλλ' ἕτερον τρόπον σοφώτερόν τε καὶ ἀπορρητότερον
τῇ θεολογίᾳ ἐχρῆσθε· ἦν γάρ που νεὼς μὲν αὐτοῖς
ἐξοικοδομῆσαι καὶ βωμούς, καὶ ὁρίζειν²⁴ ἃ χρὴ θύειν

will frustrate Imagination, as it goes imperturbably towards its own appointed purpose.

"Doubtless if you envisage the shape of Zeus, you must 3 see him together with the heaven, the seasons, and the planets, as Phidias ventured to do in his day. If you are planning to portray Athena, you must think of armies, intelligence, the arts, and how she sprang from Zeus himself. But if you create a hawk, an owl, a wolf, or a dog, and bring it into your holy places instead of Hermes, Athena, or Apollo, people will think animals and birds worth envying for their images, but the gods will fall far short of their own glory." "You appear," said Thespesion, "to be examining our practices without due scrutiny. If there is one respect in which the Egyptians are wise, it is that they are not presumptuous about the forms taken by the gods. They make these forms symbolic and suggestive, since in that way they seem more venerable."

Apollonius replied with a laugh, "Gentlemen, you have 4 made great use of the wisdom of Egypt and Ethiopia if a dog, an ibis, or a goat seems more venerable and godlike than yourselves, or so I hear from the wise Thespesion. What is venerable or formidable about these things? Perjurers, temple robbers, and sacrilegious gangs are more likely to despise such sacred objects than to fear them. If these things gain venerability by being 'suggestive,' the gods would be much more venerable in Egypt if no cult statue were set up to them at all, and you applied your divine lore in some other way, more profound and more mysterious. You could build temples and altars to them,

---

24 καὶ ὁρίζειν Rsk.: ὁρίζειν καὶ

καὶ ἃ μὴ χρή, καὶ ὁπηνίκα, καὶ ἐφ᾽ ὅσον, καὶ ὅ τι
λέγοντας ἢ δρῶντας, ἄγαλμα δὲ μὴ ἐσφέρειν, ἀλλὰ τὰ
εἴδη τῶν θεῶν καταλείπειν τοῖς τὰ ἱερὰ ἐσφοιτῶσιν.
ἀναγράφει γάρ τι ἡ γνώμη καὶ ἀνατυποῦται δημιουργίας κρεῖττον, ὑμεῖς δὲ ἀφῄρησθε τοὺς θεοὺς καὶ τὸ
ὁρᾶσθαι καλοὺς²⁵ καὶ τὸ ὑπονοεῖσθαι."

5   Πρὸς ταῦτα ὁ Θεσπεσίων, "ἐγένετό τις" ἔφη "Σωκράτης Ἀθηναῖος ἀνόητος, ὥσπερ ἡμεῖς, γέρων, ὃς
τὸν κύνα καὶ τὸν χῆνα καὶ τὴν πλάτανον θεούς τε
ἡγεῖτο καὶ ὤμνυ." "οὐκ ἀνόητος," εἶπεν "ἀλλὰ θεῖος
καὶ ἀτεχνῶς σοφός, ὤμνυ γὰρ ταῦτα οὐχ ὡς θεούς,
ἀλλ᾽ ἵνα μὴ θεοὺς ὀμνύοι."

20. Μετὰ ταῦτα ὁ Θεσπεσίων, ὥσπερ μεθιστάμενος
τουτουὶ τοῦ λόγου, ἤρετο τὸν Ἀπολλώνιον περὶ τῆς
Λακωνικῆς μάστιγος, καὶ εἰ δημοσίᾳ οἱ Λακεδαιμόνιοι παίονται. "τὰς ἐξ ἀνθρώπων γε," εἶπεν "ὦ
Θεσπεσίων, αὐτοὶ μάλιστα οἱ ἐλευθέριοι²⁶ τε καὶ εὐ-
δόκιμοι." "τοὺς δὲ οἰκέτας ἀδικοῦντας τί" ἔφη "ἐργάζονται;" "οὐκέτ᾽ ἀποκτείνουσιν," εἶπεν "ὡς ξυνεχώρει ποτὲ ὁ Λυκοῦργος, ἀλλ᾽ ἡ αὐτὴ καὶ ἐπ᾽ ἐκείνους
μάστιξ." "ἡ δὲ Ἑλλὰς πῶς" ἔφη "περὶ αὐτῶν γιγνώσκει;" "ξυνίασιν," εἶπεν "ὥσπερ ἐς τὰ Ὑακίνθια
καὶ τὰς Γυμνοπαιδιάς, θεασόμενοι ξὺν ἡδονῇ τε καὶ
ὁρμῇ πάσῃ."

2   "Εἶτ᾽ οὐκ αἰσχύνονται" ἔφη "οἱ χρηστοὶ Ἕλληνες

²⁵ καλοὺς Cob.: καλῶς
²⁶ ἐλευθέριοι Kay.: ἐλεύθεροι

and prescribe how to sacrifice and how not, when and for how long, what to say or do, and rather than introducing a statue, you could leave the shapes of the gods to those visiting your holy places. The mind portrays and imagines an object better than creation does, yet you have prevented the gods both from seeming and being imagined as beautiful."

To this Thespesion replied: "There once was a certain 5 Socrates of Athens, an old fool like us, who considered the dog, the goose, and the plane tree gods, and swore by them." "No fool," said Apollonius, "but inspired and fully wise, since he did not swear by these things as if they were gods, but to avoid swearing by the gods."

20. After this, as if trying to change the subject, Thespesion asked Apollonius about Laconian flogging, and whether the Spartans were beaten in public. "Floggings by humans, Thespesion," said Apollonius, "are particularly given to those of high birth and reputation." "What do they do with law-breaking slaves?" asked the other. "They no longer put them to death," said Apollonius, "as Lycurgus[31] formerly permitted, but the same whipping is for them too." "And what do the Greeks think about them?" asked Thespesion. "They assemble," said Apollonius, "as for the Hyacinthia and the Naked Games,[32] expecting to watch with pleasure and unalloyed enthusiasm."

"So those fine Greeks," said the other, "are not ashamed 2

[31] Semi-mythical lawgiver of early Sparta.
[32] Two festivals of Sparta, the second of which was a musical contest in which the competitors went naked in public.

[ἢ]²⁷ τοὺς αὑτῶν ποτε ἄρξαντας ὁρῶντες μαστιγου-
μένους ἐς τὸ κοινόν, ἢ ἀρχθέντες ὑπ' ἀνθρώπων, οἳ
μαστιγοῦνται δημοσίᾳ; σὺ δὲ πῶς οὐ διορθώσω ταῦτα; φασὶ γάρ σε καὶ Λακεδαιμονίων ἐπιμεληθῆναι."
"ἅ γε" εἶπε "δυνατὸν διορθοῦσθαι, ξυνεβούλευον μὲν
ἐγώ, προθύμως δ' ἐκεῖνοι ἔπραττον, ἐλευθεριώτατοι
μὲν γὰρ τῶν Ἑλλήνων εἰσί, μόνοι δ' ὑπήκοοι τοῦ εὖ
ξυμβουλεύοντος, τὸ δὲ τῶν μαστίγων ἔθος τῇ Ἀρτέμιδι τῇ ἀπὸ Σκυθῶν δρᾶται χρησμῶν, φασιν, ἐξηγου-
μένων ταῦτα· θεοῖς δ' ἀντινομοθετεῖν²⁸ μανία, οἶμαι."

3   "Οὐ σοφούς, Ἀπολλώνιε," ἔφη "τοὺς τῶν Ἑλλήνων
θεοὺς εἴρηκας, εἰ μαστίγων ἐγίγνοντο ξύμβουλοι τοῖς
τὴν ἐλευθερίαν ἀσκοῦσιν." "οὐ μαστίγων," εἶπεν "ἀλλὰ τοῦ αἵματι ἀνθρώπων τὸν βωμὸν ῥαίνειν, ἐπειδὴ
καὶ παρὰ Σκύθαις τούτων ἠξιοῦτο, σοφισάμενοι δὲ οἱ
Λακεδαιμόνιοι τὸ ἀπαραίτητον τῆς θυσίας ἐπὶ τὸν τῆς
καρτερίας ἀγῶνα ἥκουσιν, ἀφ' ἧς ἐστι μήτε ἀποθνήσκειν καὶ ἀπάρχεσθαι τῇ θεῷ τοῦ σφῶν αἵματος."
"διὰ τί οὖν" ἔφη "τοὺς ξένους οὐ καταθύουσι τῇ
Ἀρτέμιδι, καθάπερ ἐδικαίουν ποτὲ οἱ Σκύθαι;" "ὅτι"
εἶπεν "οὐδενὶ Ἑλλήνων πρὸς τρόπου βάρβαρα ἐξ-
ασκεῖν ἤθη." "καὶ μὴν καὶ φιλανθρωπότεροι ἐδόκουν
ἂν ἕνα που καὶ δύο θύοντες, ἢ ξενηλασίᾳ χρώμενοι ἐς
πάντας." "μὴ καθαπτώμεθα," εἶπεν "ὦ Θεσπεσίων, τοῦ
Λυκούργου, χρὴ γὰρ ξυνιέναι τοῦ ἀνδρός, καὶ ὅτι τὸ
μὴ ἐνδιατρίβειν ἐᾶν τοὺς ξένους οὐκ ἀμιξίας αὐτῷ

²⁷ secl. Jac.   ²⁸ ἀντινομοθετεῖν Ol.: ἀντινομεῖν

to see their former masters getting a collective flogging, or that they were once ruled by people who get flogged in public? How is it that you did not put that right? Since we hear that you reformed Sparta too." "What admitted of reform," said Apollonius, "I advised them to do, and had their enthusiastic obedience, since they are the freest of all the Greeks, and uniquely submissive to good advice. But the custom of flogging is performed in honor of Artemis of Scythia. They say oracles prescribed these acts, and it is madness to countermand the gods, in my opinion."

"You do not make the Greek gods sound wise, Apollonius," said Thespesion, "if they advised devotees of freedom to practice flogging." "They did not advise flogging," said Apollonius, "but rather that the altar should be sprinkled with human blood, since the Scythians too honored it in that way. But the Spartans refined the indispensable part of the sacrifice, and have evolved the endurance contest. By this they can avoid death, and yet give the gods a ritual taste of their own blood." "Why then," said Thespesion, "do they not sacrifice their visitors to Artemis, as the Scythians once thought they should do?" "Because it is not the way of any Greek to practice barbarian customs," was the reply. "And yet the Spartans would have appeared less antisocial if they sacrificed one or maybe two people than when they applied their expulsion of strangers indiscriminately."[33] "Let us not attack Lycurgus," said Apollonius, "but we must understand the hero. His rule forbidding strangers to overstay their visit was not intended as

[33] Spartans of the classical era occasionally expelled all aliens from their territory.

νοῦν εἶχεν, ἀλλὰ τοῦ ὑγιαίνειν τὰς ἐπιτηδεύσεις, μὴ
ἐνομιλούντων τῇ Σπάρτῃ τῶν ἔξωθεν."

4   "Ἐγὼ δὲ ἄνδρας" ἔφη "Σπαρτιάτας ἡγούμην ἄν,
οἷοι δοκεῖν ἀξιοῦσιν, εἰ συνδιαιτώμενοι τοῖς ξένοις μὴ
μεθίσταντο τῶν οἴκοι, οὐ γὰρ τῷ ἀπόντων, ἀλλὰ καὶ
τῷ παρόντων ὁμοίους ὁρᾶσθαι ἔδει, οἶμαι, τὰς ἀρετὰς
κτᾶσθαι. οἱ δὲ καίτοι ξενηλασίαις χρώμενοι διε-
φθάρησαν τὰς ἐπιτηδεύσεις καὶ οἷς μάλιστα τῶν
Ἑλλήνων ἀπήχθοντο, τούτοις ὅμοια πράττειν ἔδοξαν.
τὰ γοῦν περὶ τὴν θάλατταν καὶ αἱ μετὰ ταῦτα ἐπι-
τάξεις τῶν φόρων ἀττικώτερον αὐτοῖς ἐβουλεύθη, καὶ
ὑπὲρ ὧν πολεμητέα πρὸς Ἀθηναίους ᾤοντο αὐτοῖς
εἶναι, ταῦτ᾽ ἐς τὸ καὶ αὐτοὶ δρᾶν κατέστησαν, τὰ μὲν
πολέμια τοὺς Ἀθηναίους νικῶντες, ὧν δὲ ἐκείνοις ἐπιτηδεύειν ἔδοξεν ἡττώμενοι.

5   "Καὶ αὐτὸ δὲ τὸ τὴν ἐκ Ταύρων τε καὶ Σκυθῶν
ἐσάγεσθαι δαίμονα ξένα ἦν νομιζόντων. εἰ δὲ χρησμῶν ταῦτα, τί ἔδει μάστιγος; τί δὲ καρτερίαν ἀνδρα-
ποδώδη πλάττεσθαι; λακωνικώτερον πρὸς θανάτου
ῥώμην ἐκεῖνο ἦν, οἶμαι, Σπαρτιάτην ἔφηβον ἑκόντα
ἐπὶ τοῦ βωμοῦ θύεσθαι. τουτὶ γὰρ τὴν μὲν Σπάρτην
εὐψυχοτέρους ἐδείκνυε, τὴν δὲ Ἑλλάδα ἀπῆγε τοῦ μὴ
ἐς ἀντίπαλα αὐτοῖς ἀντικαθίστασθαι. εἰ δὲ ἐς τὰ
πολέμια φείδεσθαι τῶν νέων εἰκὸς ἦν, ἀλλ᾽ ὅ γε νόμος
ὁ παρὰ Σκύθαις ἐπὶ τοῖς ἑξηκοντούταις κείμενος οἰ-
κειότερος ἦν Λακεδαιμονίοις ἐπιτηδεύειν ἢ Σκύθαις, εἰ
τὸν θάνατον ἀτεχνῶς, ἀλλὰ μὴ κόμπου ἕνεκα ἐπαινοῦσι.

xenophobia, but as a way of keeping Sparta's customs pure by lack of contact with outsiders."

"And yet I myself," said Thespesion, "would think the 4 Spartans the heroes they consider themselves to be if they had mingled with outsiders without abandoning their local customs. It was not by appearing to resemble those who were in their midst, but rather those who were elsewhere, that they should have sought virtue. As it is, though they practiced the expulsion of strangers, their manners were corrupted, and they appeared to act like their worst enemies among the Greeks. Their actions at sea and their subsequent levying of tribute were more like Athenian policies, and the very things that they had considered as grounds for war against Athens they ended up doing themselves. They defeated the Athenians in war, but fell victim to the practices that the other side had chosen to adopt.

"Why, merely to import the divinity from the Taurians 5 and the Scythians was to observe foreign rites. If oracles authorized that, what need was there of the whip? Or to devise a servile kind of endurance? It would have been a more Spartan way of fortifying them against death, I think, to sacrifice a young Spartiate on the altar with his consent. That would have showed the Spartans to be more courageous, and deterred the Greeks from forming a coalition against them. Even if it was reasonable to preserve their youth for war, still the law which the Scythians enacted for sixty-year olds would have been a more fitting one for Spartans to follow than Scythians, if they value death sincerely and not only for ostentation.

6 "Ταῦτα οὐ πρὸς Λακεδαιμονίους εἴρηταί μοι, πρὸς δὲ σέ, Ἀπολλώνιε· εἰ γὰρ τὰ παλαιὰ νόμιμα καὶ πολιώτερα ἢ γιγνώσκειν αὐτὰ πικρῶς ἐξετάζοιμεν. ἐς ἔλεγχον καθιστάμενοι τοῦ θείου, διότι αὐτοῖς χαίρουσι, πολλοὶ καὶ ἄτοποι λόγοι τῆς τοιᾶσδε φιλοσοφίας ἀναφύσονται. καὶ γὰρ ἂν καὶ τῆς Ἐλευσῖνι τελετῆς ἐπιλαβοίμεθα, δι᾽ ὅτι τό, ἀλλὰ μὴ τό, καὶ ὧν Σαμόθρᾳκες τελοῦσιν, ἐπεὶ μὴ τὸ δεῖνα, τὸ δεῖνα δὲ αὐτοῖς δρᾶται, καὶ Διονυσίων καὶ φαλλοῦ καὶ τοῦ ἐν Κυλλήνῃ εἴδους· καὶ οὐκ ἂν φθάνοιμεν συκοφαντοῦντες πάντα. ἴωμεν οὖν ἐφ᾽ ὅ τι βούλει ἕτερον, τιμῶντες καὶ τὸν Πυθαγόρου λόγον ἡμεδαπὸν ὄντα· καλὸν γάρ, εἰ καὶ μὴ περὶ πάντων, ἀλλ᾽ ὑπέρ γε τῶν τοιούτων σιωπᾶν."

7 Ὑπολαβὼν δ᾽ ὁ Ἀπολλώνιος "εἰ σπουδάσαι," εἶπεν "ὦ Θεσπεσίων, ἐβούλου τὸν λόγον, πολλὰ ἄν σοι καὶ γενναῖα ἔδοξεν ἡ Λακεδαίμων λέγειν ὑπὲρ ὧν ὑγιῶς τε καὶ παρὰ πάντας ἐπιτηδεύει τοὺς Ἕλληνας, ἐπεὶ δὲ οὕτως ἀποσπουδάζεις αὐτόν, ὡς μηδὲ ὅσιον ἡγεῖσθαι τὸ ὑπὲρ τοιούτων λέγειν, ἴωμεν ἐφ᾽ ἕτερον λόγον πολλοῦ ἄξιον, ὡς ἐμαυτὸν πείθω· περὶ δικαιοσύνης γάρ τι ἐρήσομαι."

21. "Ἁπτώμεθα" ὁ Θεσπεσίων ἔφη "τοῦ λόγου, προσήκων γὰρ σοφοῖς τε καὶ μὴ σοφοῖς. ἀλλ᾽ ἵνα μὴ τὰς Ἰνδῶν δόξας ἐνείροντες ξυγχέωμεν αὐτὸν καὶ ἀπέλθωμεν ἄπρακτοι τοῦ λόγου, πρῶτον εἰπὲ τὰ περὶ δικαιοσύνης Ἰνδοῖς δόξαντα (εἰκὸς γὰρ βεβασανίσθαι σοι ἐκεῖ ταῦτα), κἂν μὲν ἡ δόξα ὀρθῶς ἔχῃ,

"These remarks of mine are not aimed at the Spartans,   6
Apollonius, but at you. If we subject ancient customs, too
antique to be well understood, to severe examination, and
reproach the gods for taking pleasure in them, then many
bizarre conclusions will spring from this kind of specula-
tion. We might attack the Eleusinian mysteries because
they involve this act and not that, or the Samothracian rites
because they involve that and not this, the Dionysia, the
phallus, the image at Cyllene,[34] and we would soon start
criticizing everything. So let us move to any subject you
like, in honor of the doctrine that Pythagoras borrowed
from us: it is right to be silent, not perhaps about everything, but at least about things like this."

"If a serious discussion," said Apollonius in reply, "was   7
what you wanted, Thespesion, Sparta could have given you
a long and dignified reply about her customs, which are
sound and superior to anything in Greece. But as you are
so reluctant to pursue the discussion that you consider it
impious even to mention such matters, let us move to another topic, which I like to believe is important, for I want
to ask something about justice."

21. "Let us take up that topic," said Thespesion, "suitable as it is both for the wise and for the ignorant. But since
we should not muddle it by introducing the views of the Indians, and leave our discussion inconclusively, tell me first
the Indians' views about justice, since you surely must
have investigated such things there. If their opinion seems

[34] The cults at Eleusis and Samothrace were mystery cults,
and phalloi were carried in festivals of Dionysus. The image of the
Hermes at Cyllene in Arcadia was shaped like a phallus.

ξυνθησόμεθα, εἰ δ' αὐτοί τι σοφώτερον εἴποιμεν, ξυντίθεσθε, δικαιοσύνης γὰρ καὶ τοῦτο." "ἄριστα," εἶπεν
"ὦ Θεσπεσίων, καὶ ὡς ἐμοὶ ἥδιστα εἴρηκας· ἄκουε δὴ
τῶν ἐκεῖ σπουδασθέντων.

2   "Διήειν πρὸς αὐτοὺς ἐγώ, κυβερνήτης ὡς γενοίμην
μεγάλης νεώς, ὁπόθ' ἡ ψυχὴ σώματος ἑτέρου ἐπεμέ-
λετο, καὶ δικαιότατον ἡγούμην ἐμαυτόν, ἐπειδὴ λῃσταὶ
μὲν ἐμισθοῦντό με προδοῦναι τὴν ναῦν καθορμισάμε-
νον οἷ λοχήσειν αὐτὴν ἔμελλον, δι' ἃ ἦγεν, ἐγὼ δὲ
ἐπαγγειλαίμην μὲν ταῦτα, ὡς μὴ ἐπίθοιντο ἡμῖν,
παραπλεύσαιμι δ' αὐτοὺς καὶ ὑπεράραιμι τοῦ χω-
ρίου." "ξυνέθεντο δ'" ἦ δ' ὁ Θεσπεσίων "δικαιοσύνην
εἶναι Ἰνδοὶ ταῦτα;" "κατεγέλασαν μὲν οὖν," εἶπε "μὴ
γὰρ εἶναι δικαιοσύνην τὸ μὴ ἀδικεῖν." "ὑγιῶς" ἔφη
"ἀπέδοξε τοῖς Ἰνδοῖς, οὔτε γὰρ φρόνησις τὸ μὴ
ἀνοήτως τι ἐνθυμεῖσθαι, οὔτε ἀνδρεία τὸ μὴ λείπειν
τὴν τάξιν, οὔτε σωφροσύνη τὸ μὴ ἐς τὰ τῶν μοιχῶν
ἐκπίπτειν, οὔτε ἄξιον ἐπαίνου τὸ μὴ κακὸν φαίνεσθαι·
πᾶν γάρ, ὃ τιμῆς τε καὶ τιμωρίας ἴσον ἀφέστηκεν,
οὔπω ἀρετή."

3   "Πῶς οὖν, ὦ Θεσπεσίων," εἶπε "στεφανώσομεν τὸν
δίκαιον, ἢ τί πράττοντα;" "ἀνελλιπέστερον"[29] ἔφη "καὶ
προσφορώτερον ἂν ὑπὲρ δικαιοσύνης ἐσπουδάσατε, ἢ
ὁπότε βασιλεὺς τοσῆσδέ τε καὶ οὕτως εὐδαίμονος
χώρας ἄρχων ἐπέστη φιλοσοφοῦσιν ὑμῖν ὑπὲρ τοῦ
βασιλεύειν, δικαιοτάτου κτήματος;" "εἰ ὁ Φραώτης"
εἶπεν "ὁ ἀφικόμενος ἦν, ὀρθῶς ἂν ἐμέμφου τὸ μὴ ὑπὲρ

166

sound, let us agree on it, but if we have something wiser to say, you must agree with us, since that too is a part of justice." "That is excellently said, Thespesion," replied Apollonius, "and most agreeable to me, so let me tell you of our conversations there.

"I told them the following. I had been the pilot of 2 a large ship when my soul was guiding another body. I thought myself very just, because pirates bribed me to betray the ship by mooring at a place where they were going to ambush it for its cargo. I promised all this in order to prevent their attacking us, but then sailed past them and got clear of the place." "And did the Indians agree that was justice?" asked Thespesion. "No, they laughed at me," said Apollonius, "saying that avoidance of injustice was not justice." "A sound verdict of the Indians," said Thespesion, "since it is not prudence to plan something foolish, or courage not to desert the ranks, or self-control not to fall into adulterous habits, or praiseworthy not to appear wicked. Whatever is equidistant from honor and dishonor is not virtue."

"How then are we to crown the just man, Thespesion," 3 said Apollonius, "and what must he do?" "Could you have had," said the other, "a more thorough, more pertinent discussion of justice than when the king of so large and prosperous a realm had joined your speculations about kingship, that most just of possessions?" "If the new arrival had been Phraotes," said Apollonius, "you would be right to blame me for not discussing justice in his presence. But

29 ἀνελλιπέστερον Kay.: ἐλλιπέστερον

δικαιοσύνης ἐπ' αὐτοῦ σπουδάσαι, ἐπεὶ δὲ εἶδες τὸν
ἄνθρωπον ἐν οἷς χθὲς ὑπὲρ αὐτοῦ διῄειν μεθύοντα καὶ
ἀχθόμενον φιλοσοφίᾳ πάσῃ, τί ἔδει παρέχειν ὄχλον;
τί δ' αὐτοὺς ἔχειν φιλοτιμουμένους ἐπ' ἀνθρώπου
σύβαριν ἡγουμένου πάντα; ἀλλ' ἐπεὶ σοφοῖς ἀνδράσιν, ὥσπερ ἡμῖν, ἰχνευτέα ἡ δικαιοσύνη μᾶλλον ἢ
βασιλεῦσί τε καὶ στρατηγοῖς, ἴωμεν ἐπὶ τὸν ἀτεχνῶς
δίκαιον. ὁ γὰρ ἐμαυτόν τε ἡγούμην, ὁπότε ἡ ναῦς,
ἑτέρους τε, οἳ μὴ ἀδίκων ἅπτονται, οὔπω δικαίους
φατέ, οὐδ' ἀξίους τιμᾶσθαι."

4   "Καὶ εἰκότως" εἶπεν "οὐδὲ γὰρ ἂν Ἀθηναίοις ποτὲ ἢ
Λακεδαιμονίοις ἐγράφη γνώμη τὸν δεῖνα στεφανοῦν,
ἐπεὶ μὴ τῶν ἡταιρηκότων ἐστίν, ἢ τὸν δεῖνα ποιεῖσθαι
πολίτην, ἐπεὶ μὴ τὰ ἱερὰ ὑπ' αὐτοῦ συλᾶται. τίς οὖν ὁ
δίκαιος καὶ ὁ τί[30] πράττων; οὐδὲ γὰρ ἐπὶ δικαιοσύνῃ
τινὰ στεφανωθέντα οἶδα, οὐδὲ γνώμην ἐπ' ἀνδρὶ δι-
καίῳ γραφεῖσαν, ὡς τὸν δεῖνα χρὴ στεφανοῦν, ἐπειδὴ
τὸ δεῖνα πράττων δίκαιος φαίνεται, τὰ μὲν γὰρ Παλα-
μήδους ἐνθυμηθέντι τὰ ἐν Τροίᾳ καὶ τὰ Σωκράτους τὰ
Ἀθήνησιν οὐδ' εὐτυχεῖν ἡ δικαιοσύνη δόξει παρὰ τοῖς
ἀνθρώποις, ἀδικώτατα γὰρ δὴ οἶδε ἔπαθον δικαιό-
τατοι ὄντες. πλὴν ἀλλ' οὗτοι μὲν ἐπὶ δόξῃ ἀδικημάτων
ἀπώλοντο ψήφου παρὰ τὸ εὐθὺ ἐνεχθείσης, Ἀριστείδην δὲ τὸν Λυσιμάχου καὶ αὐτή ποτε ἡ δικαιοσύνη
ἀπώλλυ καὶ ἀνὴρ τοιόσδε ἐπὶ τοιᾷδε ἀρετῇ φεύγων
ᾤχετο. καὶ ὡς μὲν γελοία ἡ δικαιοσύνη δόξει, γι-

30 ὁ τί Kay.: ὅτι

168

you saw from my description of him yesterday[35] that this fellow was a drunkard and averse to any kind of philosophy, so why should I give him trouble? Why should we trouble ourselves with lofty aspirations before a man whose only thought was luxury? Justice is more for wise men like you and me to investigate than for kings and generals, so let us take up the man who is perfectly just, since you do not count as just or worthy of honor the kind of man I thought myself to be in the matter of the ship, or others who refrain from injustice."

"And rightly too," said Thespesion. "The Athenians and 4 the Spartans would never have passed a decree to crown someone for not having prostituted himself, or to make someone a citizen because he had not burgled their holy places. So what is the just man, and what does he do? I have never heard of someone receiving a crown for justice, or of any proposal made to honor a man, to the effect that he deserved a crown because a particular act showed him to be just. In fact, when one recalls the story of Palamedes at Troy and of Socrates at Athens, he might suppose that justice does not even prosper on this earth, since they were highly just and yet suffered the greatest injustice. You might argue that they were killed for apparent crimes, when the vote was perverted, and yet Aristides the son of Lysimachus was once brought down precisely by his justice, and went into exile, though he was such a hero and of such virtue.[36] I know well that Justice will be thought ridic-

[35] I.e., the boorish and unnamed king of III 26–33. Apollonius presumably described him in the narrative mentioned in ch. 14.

[36] The Athenian statesman, exiled in 483/82 despite his reputation for justice and fair-dealing with the Athenians' allies.

γνώσκω, τεταγμένη γὰρ ὑπὸ Διός τε καὶ Μοιρῶν ἐς τὸ
μὴ ἀδικεῖσθαι τοὺς ἀνθρώπους οὐδαμοῦ ἑαυτὴν ἐς τὸ
μὴ αὐτὴ ἀδικεῖσθαι τάττει.

5   "Ἐμοὶ δὲ ἀπόχρη τὰ τοῦ Ἀριστείδου ἐς τὸ δηλῶσαι
τίς μὲν ὁ μὴ ἄδικος, τίς δὲ ὁ δίκαιος. εἰπὲ γάρ μοι, οὐχ
οὗτος Ἀριστείδης ἐκεῖνος, ὃν φατε ὑμεῖς οἱ ἀφ᾽ Ἑλλήνων ἥκοντες πλεύσαντα ἐς τὰς νήσους ὑπὲρ τῶν
φόρων ξυμμέτρους τε αὐτοὺς τάξαι, καὶ ξὺν τῷ αὐτῷ
ἐπανελθεῖν τρίβωνι;" "οὗτος," εἶπε "δι᾽ ὃν καὶ πενίας
ἔρως ποτὲ ἤνθησεν." "εἰ οὖν," ἔφη "δύο Ἀθήνησι
δημαγωγοὶ γενοίσθην ἐπαινοῦντες τὸν Ἀριστείδην
ἄρτι ἐκ τῆς ξυμμαχίδος ἥκοντα, καὶ ὁ μὲν γράφοι
στεφανοῦν αὐτόν, ἐπειδὴ μὴ πλουτῶν ἀφίκται μηδὲ
βίον ἑαυτῷ ξυνειλοχὼς μηδένα, ἀλλὰ πενέστατος μὲν
Ἀθηναίων, πενέστερος δὲ ἑαυτοῦ, ὁ δ᾽ αὖ τοιουτονί τι
γράφοι ψήφισμα· ἐπειδὴ Ἀριστείδης οὐχ ὑπὲρ τὸ
δυνατὸν τῶν ξυμμάχων τάξας τοὺς φόρους, ἀλλ᾽ ὡς
ἕκαστοι γῆς ἔχουσι, τῆς τε ὁμονοίας αὐτῶν ἐπεμελήθη τῆς πρὸς Ἀθηναίους καὶ τοῦ μὴ ἀχθομένους
δοκεῖν φέρειν ταῦτα, δεδόχθω στεφανοῦν αὐτὸν ἐπὶ
δικαιοσύνῃ,᾽ ἆρ᾽ οὐκ ἄν σοι δοκεῖ τῇ μὲν προτέρᾳ
γνώμῃ κἂν ἀντειπεῖν αὐτός, ὡς οὐκ ἀξίᾳ τῶν ἑαυτῷ
βεβιωμένων, εἰ ἐφ᾽ οἷς οὐκ ἀδικεῖ τιμῷτο, τὴν δ᾽ ἴσως
ἂν καὶ αὐτὸς ἐπαινέσαι, στοχαζομένην ὧν διενοήθη;
βλέψας γάρ που ἐς τὸ Ἀθηναίων τε καὶ τῶν ὑπηκόων
ξυμφέρον ἐπεμελήθη τῆς ξυμμετρίας τῶν φόρων.

6   "Καὶ τοῦτο μετὰ τὸν Ἀριστείδην ἐδείχθη μᾶλλον·
ἐπειδὴ γὰρ παραβάντες Ἀθηναῖοι τοὺς ἐκείνῳ δόξαν-

ulous because it was placed by Zeus and the Fates to prevent injustice among mankind, and yet it never places itself so as to prevent others from injuring it.

"For me, Aristides's fate shows with sufficient clarity 5 who is unjust and who is not. For tell me, was it not he, the famous Aristides, who you visitors from Greece say sailed to the islands in connection with the taxes, assessed them equitably, and returned still wearing the same poor cloak?" "Yes," said Apollonius, "that is the one, who in his day caused a love of poverty to flourish." "Suppose, then," said Thespesion, "that there were two politicians at Athens who praised Aristides just after his return from the allied territory. One of them proposed a crown for him for returning not as a rich man, or indeed having amassed any fortune for himself, but as the poorest man in Athens, indeed poorer than he had ever been. The other proposed some such motion as this: 'Whereas Aristides has set the taxes within the means of the allies, and in proportion to the land that each possesses; and whereas he has fostered their concord with the Athenians, so that they do not seem to chafe under their burdens: be it hereby resolved to crown him for his justice.' Do you not think that Aristides himself might have opposed the first motion, as unworthy of his past career, because it honored him for avoiding injustice, while he might have given his personal approval to the second one as a general description of his policy? For doubtless it was his understanding of what was to the advantage of the Athenians and their subjects that made him provide for equitable taxation.

"That became all the more clear after Aristides, since 6 once the Athenians had exceeded the rates that he had

τας βαρυτέρους ἐπέγραψαν ταῖς νήσοις, διεσπάσθη
μὲν αὐτοῖς ἡ ναυτικὴ δύναμις, ᾗ μάλιστα φοβεροὶ
ἦσαν, παρῆλθε δὲ ἡ Λακεδαιμονίων ἐς τὴν θάλατταν,
ξυνέμεινε δὲ τῆς δυνάμεως οὐδέν, ἀλλ' ἅπαν τὸ ὑπ-
ήκοον ἐς νεώτερα ὥρμησε καὶ ἀποστροφῆς ἥψατο.
δίκαιος οὖν, ὦ Ἀπολλώνιε, κατὰ τὸν εὐθὺν λόγον οὐχ
ὁ μὴ ἄδικος, ἀλλ' ὁ δίκαια μὲν αὐτὸς πράττων, καθιστὰς δὲ καὶ ἑτέρους ἐς τὸ μὴ ἀδικεῖν, καὶ φύσονται
τῆς τοιαύτης δικαιοσύνης καὶ ἄλλαι μὲν ἀρεταί, μάλιστα δὲ ἡ δικαστική τε καὶ ἡ νομοθετική. δικάσει μὲν
γὰρ τοιόσδε πολλῷ δικαιότερον ἢ οἱ κατὰ τῶν τομίων
ὀμνύντες, νομοθετήσει δέ, ὥσπερ οἱ Σόλωνές τε καὶ οἱ
Λυκοῦργοι, καὶ γὰρ δὴ κἀκείνοις τοῦ γράψαι νόμους
δικαιοσύνη ἦρξεν."

22. Τοσαῦτα ὁ Δάμις διαλεχθῆναί φησιν αὐτοὺς
ὑπὲρ ἀνδρὸς δικαίου, καὶ τὸν Ἀπολλώνιον ξυμφῆσαι
τῷ λόγῳ, τοῖς γὰρ ὑγιῶς λεγομένοις ξυμβαίνειν.
φιλοσοφήσαντες δὲ καὶ περὶ ψυχῆς, ὡς ἀθάνατος εἴη,
καὶ περὶ φύσεως παραπλήσια ταῖς Πλάτωνος [ἐν
Τιμαίῳ][31] δόξαις, περί τε τῶν παρ' Ἕλλησι νόμων
πλείω διαλεχθέντες, "ἐμοὶ" εἶπεν ὁ Ἀπολλώνιος "ἡ
δεῦρο ὁδὸς ὑμῶν τε ἕνεκα καὶ τῶν τοῦ Νείλου πηγῶν
ἐγένετο, ἃς μέχρι μὲν Αἰγύπτου προελθόντι ξυγγνώμη
ἀγνοῆσαι, προχωρήσαντι δὲ ἐπ' Αἰθιοπίαν, ὃν ἐγὼ
τρόπον, κἂν ὄνειδος φέροι τὸ παρελθεῖν αὐτάς, καὶ μὴ
ἀρύσασθαί τινας αὐτῶν λόγους."

2   "Ἴθι χαίρων" ἔφη "καὶ ὅ τι σοι φίλον, εὔχου ταῖς
πηγαῖς, θεῖαι γάρ. ἡγεμόνα δὲ οἶμαι ποιήσῃ τὸν

fixed, and imposed heavier ones on the islands, that
wrecked their chief deterrent, their naval power. Sparta
took to the sea, and not a trace of their power was left, all
their subjects yearned for change, and began rebellion.
The just man, therefore, Apollonius, on a correct estimate
is not the one who avoids injustice, but the one who acts
justly himself and induces others not to commit injustice.
From justice of that kind spring other virtues, above all
those connected with judicial and legislative justice. A man
of that kind will judge more justly than those who swear
oaths over the sacrificial victims, and he will legislate as
your Solon or your Lycurgus did, for in their case too justice guided their legislation."

22. This is how Damis describes their conversation
about the just man, saying that Apollonius assented to
Thespesion's speech, since he agreed with statements that
were correct. In addition, they discussed the immortality
of the soul and nature in terms similar to Plato. When they
had also spoken at length about the laws of the Greeks,
Apollonius said, "My own purpose in coming here was to
visit you and the sources of the Nile. It would be pardon-
able to miss these in one who got only as far as Egypt, but
for one who has advanced into Ethiopia, as I have, it would
be a disgrace to pass them by, and not draw some learning
from them."

"Go your way cheerfully," said Thespesion, "and make 2
any prayer to the sources that you please, since they are
divine. I believe you will take as your guide someone who

---

31 [ἐν Τιμαίῳ] secl. Kay.

πάλαι Ναυκρατίτην, νῦν δὲ Μεμφίτην, Τιμασίωνα,
τῶν τε γὰρ πηγῶν ἐθὰς οὗτος καὶ οὕτω τι καθαρός, ὡς
μὴ δεῖσθαι τοῦ ῥαίνεσθαι. σοὶ δέ, ὦ Νεῖλε, βουλόμεθα
ἐφ' ἑαυτῶν διαλεχθῆναί τι." ὁ μὲν δὴ νοῦς τῶν λόγων
οὐκ ἀφανὴς ἦν τῷ Ἀπολλωνίῳ, ξυνίει γὰρ αὐτῶν
δυσχερῶς διακειμένων, ἐπειδὴ ἤρα αὐτοῦ ὁ Νεῖλος,
ἐξιστάμενος δὲ αὐτοῖς τῆς διαλέξεως ἀπήει συσκευασόμενος,[32] ὡς ἐξελῶν ἅμα τῇ ἕῳ, μετ' οὐ πολὺ δὲ
ἧκων ὁ Νεῖλος, ἀπήγγειλε μὲν οὐδὲν ὧν ἤκουσεν, ἐφ'
ἑαυτοῦ δὲ θαμὰ ἐγέλα· ἠρώτα δ' οὐδεὶς ὑπὲρ τοῦ
γέλωτος, ἀλλ' ἐφείδοντο τοῦ ἀπορρήτου.

23. Τότε μὲν δὴ δειπνήσαντες, καὶ διαλεχθέντες
οὐχ ὑπὲρ μεγάλων, αὐτοῦ ἐκοιμήθησαν. ἅμα δὲ τῇ
ἡμέρᾳ τοὺς Γυμνοὺς προσειπόντες, ἐπορεύοντο τὴν ἐς
τὰ ὄρη τείνουσαν ἀριστεροὶ τοῦ Νείλου, τάδε ὁρῶντες
λόγου ἄξια· οἱ Κατάδουποι γεώδη ὄρη καὶ παραπλήσια τῷ Λυδῶν Τμώλῳ, κατάρρους δὲ ἀπ' αὐτῶν φέρε-
ται Νεῖλος, ἣν ἐπισπᾶται γῆν ποιῶν Αἴγυπτον. ἡ δὲ
ἠχὼ τοῦ ῥεύματος καταρρηγνυμένου τῶν ὁρῶν καὶ
ψόφῳ ἅμα ἐς τὸν Νεῖλον ἐκπίπτοντος χαλεπὴ δοκεῖ
καὶ οὐκ ἀνεκτὴ ἀκοῦσαι, καὶ πολλοὶ τῶν πρόσω τοῦ
μετρίου προσελθόντων[33] ἀνέζευξαν ἀποβαλόντες τὸ
ἀκούειν.

24. Προϊόντι δὲ τῷ Ἀπολλωνίῳ καὶ τοῖς ἀμφ' αὐτὸν
μαστοὶ ὁρῶν ἐφαίνοντο παρεχόμενοι δένδρα, ὧν Αἰθίοπες τὰ φύλλα καὶ τὸν φλοιὸν καὶ τὸ δάκρυον
καρπὸν ἡγοῦνται, ἑώρων δὲ καὶ λέοντας ἀγχοῦ τῆς
ὁδοῦ καὶ παρδάλεις καὶ τοιαῦτα θηρία ἕτερα, καὶ

was previously from Naucratis but now from Memphis, Timasion. He is familiar with the sources, and so pure that he needs no ablution. As for you, Nilus, we would like a private word with you." Apollonius was not deceived about the subject of this talk, knowing that they were ill disposed because of Nilus's affection for him, and he therefore left them to their conversation, and went off to pack, intending to leave at dawn. Not long afterwards, however, Nilus came to them, not divulging anything he had been told, but repeatedly laughing to himself. No one asked the reason for his laughter, but they respected his secret.

23. They then had dinner and after no very serious conversation went to sleep on the spot. At dawn the next day, they said goodbye to the Naked Ones and started on the road that leads to the mountains, with the Nile on their right, and here they saw the following notable sights. The Falls consist of mountains with deep soil about the height of the Tmolus in Lydia. The Nile flows steeply down them, making Egypt from the soil it carries. The noise of the stream as it bursts from the mountains and falls with a crash into the Nile is apparently harsh and intolerable to the ears, so that many people have come too close and lost their hearing on their return.

24. As Apollonius and his party advanced, they could see mountain peaks on which there grew trees whose leaves, bark, and gum are considered valuable by the Egyptians. Near the road, they also saw lions, leopards, and other such animals, none of which approached them,

---

32 συσκευασόμενος Rsk.: συσκευαζόμενος

33 προσελθόντων Jon.: προελθόντες (προσελθόντες Phot.)

APOLLONIUS OF TYANA

ἐπήει οὐδὲν αὐτοῖς, ἀλλ' ἀπεπήδα σφῶν, ὥσπερ ἐκπε-
πληγμένα τοὺς ἀνθρώπους, ἔλαφοι δὲ καὶ δορκάδες
καὶ στρουθοὶ καὶ ὄνοι πολλὰ μὲν καὶ ταῦτα ἑωρᾶτο,
πλεῖστα δὲ οἱ βόαγροί τε καὶ οἱ βούτραγοι· ξύγκειται
δὲ τὰ θηρία ταῦτα τὸ μὲν ἐλάφου τε καὶ ταύρου, τὸ δὲ
ἀφ' ὧνπερ τὴν ἐπωνυμίαν εὕρηκε.³⁴ καὶ ὀστοῖς δὲ
τούτων ἐνετύγχανον καὶ ἡμιβρώτοις σώμασιν, οἱ γὰρ
λέοντες, ἐπειδὰν θερμῆς τῆς θήρας ἐμφορηθῶσιν, ἀτι-
μάζουσιν αὐτῆς τὰ περιττά, πιστεύοντες, οἶμαι, τῷ
καὶ³⁵ αὖθις θηράσειν.

25. Ἐνταῦθα νομάδες οἰκοῦσιν Αἰθίοπες ἐφ' ἁμαξῶν πεπολισμένοι, καὶ πλησίον τούτων οἱ τοὺς ἐλέ-
φαντας θηρῶντες, κατακόπτοντες δὲ αὐτοὺς ποιοῦνται
βοράν,³⁶ ὅθεν ἐπώνυμοί εἰσι τῆς τῶν ἐλεφάντων βρώσεως. Νασαμῶνες δὲ καὶ Ἀνδροφάγοι, καὶ Πυγμαῖοι,
καὶ Σκιάποδες ἔθνη μὲν Αἰθιόπων καὶ οἶδε, καθήκουσι
δὲ ἐς τὸν Αἰθίοπα Ὠκεανόν, ὃν μόνον ἐσπλέουσιν οἱ
ἀπενεχθέντες ἄκοντες.

26. Διαλεγομένους δὲ ὑπὲρ τῶν θηρίων τοὺς ἄνδρας καὶ φιλοσοφοῦντας ὑπὲρ τῆς φύσεως ἄλλο ἄλλως βοσκούσης, ἠχὼ προσέβαλεν οἷον βροντῆς οὔπω
σκληρᾶς, ἀλλὰ κοίλης ἔτι καὶ ἐν τῷ νέφει. καὶ ὁ
Τιμασίων "ἐγγὺς" ἔφη "ὁ καταρράκτης, ὦ ἄνδρες, ὁ
κατιόντων μὲν ὕστατος, ἀνιόντων δὲ πρῶτος." καὶ
στάδια δέκα ἴσως προελθόντες ἰδεῖν φασι ποταμὸν
ἐκδιδόμενον τοῦ ὄρους μείω οὐδὲν ἢ ἐν πρώταις ξυμ-
βολαῖς ὁ Μαρσύας καὶ ὁ Μαίανδρος, προσευξάμενοι
δὲ τῷ Νείλῳ χωρεῖν πρόσω καὶ θηρία μὲν οὐκέτι ὁρᾶν,

but all fled as if terrified of human beings. They also observed deer, gazelles, ostriches, and asses, all of them in large numbers, but even larger numbers of wild bulls and goat-oxen, creatures that are respectively a cross between a deer and a bull and between the two animals after which they are named. Of these they also saw bones and half-eaten carcasses, because after lions have satisfied their hunger on their prey when fresh, they neglect the leftovers, no doubt being confident of catching more.

25. In that region also live the nomad Ethiopians in caravan communities, and next to them, the Elephant Hunters. These cut up their quarry and devour it, and so get their name from eating elephants. Nasamones, Cannibals, Pygmies, and Shadow Feet are other Ethiopian tribes, and reach as far as the Ethiopian Ocean,[37] into which people sail only when carried off course unwillingly.

26. The company was conversing about these animals and speculating about nature, and the different way it feeds different creatures, when they heard a noise like that of thunder that is not yet loud but still rumbling in the clouds. "The Cataract is near, gentlemen," said Timasion, "the last as you go down river but the first as you go up." After proceeding about ten stades, they say they saw a river breaking from the mountains no smaller than the Marsyas and Maeander where they first join. After a prayer to the Nile they went on, but no longer saw animals, because

---

[37] The Indian Ocean off east Africa.

---

[34] εὕρηκε Phot.: ἥρηκε
[35] τῷ καὶ Rsk.: τὸ καὶ
[36] βορὰν Cob.: ἀγορὰν

ψοφοδεᾶ γὰρ φύσει ὄντα προσοικεῖν τοῖς γαληνοῖς
μᾶλλον ἢ τοῖς ῥαγδαίοις τε καὶ ἐνήχοις, ἑτέρου δὲ
καταρράκτου ἀκοῦσαι μετὰ πεντεκαίδεκά που στάδια
χαλεποῦ ἤδη καὶ οὐκ ἀνεκτοῦ αἰσθέσθαι, διπλασίω
μὲν γὰρ εἶναι αὐτὸν τοῦ προτέρου, ὁρῶν δὲ ὑψηλο-
τέρων ἐκπίπτειν.

2   Ἑαυτοῦ μὲν οὖν καί τινος τῶν ἑταίρων οὕτω τι
κτυπηθῆναι τὰ ὦτα ὁ Δάμις φησίν, ὡς αὐτός τε[37]
ἀναζεῦξαι τοῦ τε Ἀπολλωνίου δεῖσθαι μὴ χωρεῖν
πρόσω, τὸν δὲ ἐρρωμένως ξύν τε τῷ Τιμασίωνι καὶ τῷ
Νείλῳ τοῦ τρίτου καταρράκτου ἔχεσθαι, περὶ οὗ τάδε
ἀπαγγεῖλαι ἥκοντα· ἐπικρέμασθαι μὲν τῷ Νείλῳ κο-
ρυφὰς ἐκεῖ σταδίων μάλιστα ὀκτὼ ὕψος, τὴν δὲ ὄχθην
τὴν ἀντικειμένην τοῖς ὄρεσιν ὀφρὺν εἶναι λιθοτομίας
ἀρρήτου, τὰς δὲ πηγὰς ἀποκρεμαννυμένας τῶν ὁρῶν
ὑπερπίπτειν ἐς τὴν πετρώδη ὄχθην, ἀναχεῖσθαι δὲ
ἐκεῖθεν ἐς τὸν Νεῖλον κυμαινούσας τε καὶ λευκάς. τὰ
δὲ πάθη τὰ περὶ αὐτὰς ξυμβαίνοντα πολλαπλασίας ἢ
αἱ πρότεραι οὖσας, καὶ τὴν πηδῶσαν ἐκ τούτων ἠχὼ
ἐς τὰ ὄρη δυσήκοον ἐργάζεσθαι τὴν ἱστορίαν τοῦ
ῥεύματος. τὴν δὲ πρόσω ὁδὸν τὴν ἐπὶ τὰς πρώτας
πηγὰς ἄγουσαν ἄπορον μὲν ἐλθεῖν φασιν, ἄπορον δὲ
ἐνθυμηθῆναι, πολλὰ γὰρ καὶ περὶ δαιμόνων ᾄδουσιν,
οἷα καὶ Πινδάρῳ κατὰ σοφίαν ὕμνηται περὶ τοῦ δαίμονος, ὃν ταῖς πηγαῖς ταύταις ἐφίστησιν ὑπὲρ ξυμμετρίας τοῦ Νείλου.

27. Καταλύσαντες δὲ μετὰ τοὺς καταρράκτας ἐν
κώμῃ τῆς Αἰθιοπίας οὐ μεγάλῃ, ἐδείπνουν μὲν περὶ

these, having an innate dislike of noise, prefer silent haunts to noisy, echoing ones. After about fifteen stades, they heard another cataract, this time fierce and intolerably loud, since it was twice the volume of the previous one and fell from higher mountains.

According to Damis, he and another member of the 2 company found their ears so deafened that he himself turned back and begged Apollonius not to go on. He, however, went on confidently with Timasion and Nilus to the third cataract, and reported the following on his return. Crags about eight stades high overhang the Nile there, and the bank opposite the mountains is a ledge of stone mysteriously cut away. The water as it falls from the mountains hits the bank of stone, and from there pours into the Nile frothy and white. The effects caused by these sources, which are much larger than the previous ones, and by the noise that echoes from them to the mountains, made investigation of the stream dangerous to the hearing. The road leading on to the headwaters was impossible to take and impossible to imagine, because there are many poetic stories of divinities there. For example Pindar has a learned poem on the divinity which he represents as guarding this source, to make the Nile flow evenly.[38]

27. After the Cataracts, they stopped in a rather small Ethiopian village, and were having their evening dinner,

[38] Fragment 282 Snell.

---

[37] τε Cob.: γε

ἑσπέραν ἐγκαταμιγνύντες σπουδὴν παιδιᾷ, βοῆς δὲ
ἀθρόας τῶν ἐν τῇ κώμῃ γυναικῶν ἤκουσαν ἐπικελευ-
ομένων ἀλλήλαις ἑλεῖν καὶ διῶξαι, παρεκάλουν δὲ καὶ
τοὺς αὐτῶν ἄνδρας ἐς κοινωνίαν τοῦ ἔργου, οἱ δ᾽
ἁρπασάμενοι ξύλα καὶ λίθους καὶ ὅ τι ἐς χεῖρας
ἑκάστῳ ἔλθοι, ξυνεκάλουν ὥσπερ ἀδικούμενοι τοὺς
γάμους. ἐπεφοίτα δὲ ἄρα τῇ κώμῃ δέκατον ἤδη μῆνα
σατύρου φάσμα λυττῶν ἐπὶ τὰ γύναια, καὶ δύο ἀπεκτονέναι σφῶν ἐλέγετο, ὧν μάλιστα ἐδόκει ἐρᾶν.

2   Ἐκπλαγέντων οὖν τῶν ἑταίρων, "μὴ δέδιτε," εἶπεν
ὁ Ἀπολλώνιος "ὑβρίζει γάρ τις ἐνταῦθα σάτυρος." "νὴ
Δί᾽," ἔφη ὁ Νεῖλος "ὅν γε ἡμεῖς οἱ Γυμνοὶ χρόνῳ[38] ἤδη
ὑβρίζοντα μήπω μετεστήσαμεν τοῦ σκιρτᾶν." "ἀλλ᾽
ἔστιν" εἶπεν "ἐπὶ τοὺς ὑβριστὰς τούτους φάρμακον, ᾧ
λέγεται Μίδας ποτὲ χρήσασθαι. μετεῖχε μὲν γὰρ τοῦ
τῶν σατύρων γένους ὁ Μίδας οὗτος, ὡς ἐδήλου τὰ
ὦτα, σάτυρος δὲ ἐπ᾽ αὐτὸν εἷς κατὰ τὸ ξυγγενὲς
ἐκώμαζε τὰ τοῦ Μίδου διαβάλλων ὦτα, καὶ οὐ μόνον
ᾄδων, ἀλλὰ καὶ αὐλῶν τούτῳ, ὁ δ᾽, οἶμαι, τῆς μητρὸς
ἀκηκοώς, ὅτι σάτυρος οἴνῳ θηρευθείς, ἐπειδὰν ἐς
ὕπνον καταπέσῃ, σωφρονεῖ καὶ διαλλάττεται, κρήνην
τὴν οὖσαν αὐτῷ περὶ τὰ βασίλεια κεράσας οἴνῳ
ἐπαφῆκεν αὐτῇ τὸν σάτυρον, ὁ δὲ ἔπιέ τε καὶ ἥλω. καὶ
ὅτι μὴ ψεύδεται ὁ λόγος, ἴωμεν παρὰ τὸν κωμάρχην,
καὶ ἢν ἔχωσιν οἱ κωμῆται οἶνον, κεράσωμεν αὐτὸν τῷ
σατύρῳ, καὶ ταὐτὰ τῷ Μίδου πείσεται."

[38] χρόνῳ Kay.: χρόνον

mixing light and serious topics. They heard a loud shout
from the village women urging each other on to "catch it"
and "drive it away," and also calling on their husbands to
help them with the task. The men grabbed sticks, stones,
and whatever came to hand, and were shouting for their
friends as if the sanctity of their marriages was at stake. In
fact, for nine months a spirit in the form of a satyr had been
haunting the village, lusting for the womenfolk, and it was
already said to have killed two that it seemed most in love
with.

Apollonius's disciples were terrified, but he said, "Do   2
not be afraid, there is a satyr on the rampage here." "Yes,
by Zeus," said Nilus, "it has been rampaging for some time
now, but we Naked Ones have never yet deterred it from
its frolics." "There is a remedy for these lawbreakers," said
Apollonius, "which they say Midas once used.[39] He himself
was related to the satyr family, as his ears showed, and a
satyr exploited the relationship by mounting a skit about
him, making fun of Midas's ears not only in song but also on
his pipe. Now Midas had doubtless heard from his mother
that a satyr, if snared with wine, falls asleep and then be-
haves and settles down. So he mixed wine into the fountain
near the palace and gave the satyr access to it, so that the
creature drank and was caught. To prove that the story is
not made up, let us go to the village headman, and if the
villagers have wine, let us mix some for the satyr, and it will
have the same effect on it as it did on Midas's one."

[39] Legendary king of Phrygia.

3   Ἔδοξε ταῦτα, καὶ ἀμφορέας Αἰγυπτίους τέτταρας
οἰνοχοήσας ἐς ληνόν, ἀφ᾽ ἧς ἔπινε τὰ ἐν τῇ κώμῃ
πρόβατα, ἐκάλει τὸν σάτυρον ἀφανῶς τι ἐπιπλήττων,
ὁ δὲ οὔπω μὲν ἑωρᾶτο, ὑπεδίδου δὲ ὁ οἶνος, ὥσπερ
πινόμενος· ἐπεὶ δὲ ἐξεπόθη "σπεισώμεθα" ἔφη "τῷ
σατύρῳ, καθεύδει γάρ." καὶ εἰπὼν ταῦτα ἡγεῖτο τοῖς
κωμήταις ἐς Νυμφῶν ἄντρον, πλέθρον οὔπω ἀπέχον
τῆς κώμης, ἐν ᾧ καθεύδοντα δείξας αὐτὸν ἀπέχεσθαι
εἶπε τοῦ παίειν ἢ λοιδορεῖσθαί οἱ, "πέπαυται γὰρ τῶν
ἀνοήτων."

4   Τοῦτο μὲν δὴ τοιοῦτον Ἀπολλωνίου, μὰ Δί᾽, οὐχὶ
ὁδοῦ πάρεργον, ἀλλὰ παρόδου ἔργον, κἂν ἐντύχῃ τις
ἐπιστολῇ τοῦ ἀνδρός, ἣν πρὸς μειράκιον ὑβρίζον
γράφων καὶ σάτυρον δαίμονα σωφρονίσαι φησὶν ἐν
Αἰθιοπίᾳ, μεμνῆσθαι χρὴ τοῦ λόγου τούτου. σατύρους
δὲ εἶναί τε καὶ ἐρωτικῶν ἅπτεσθαι μὴ ἀπιστῶμεν·
οἶδα γὰρ κατὰ τὴν Λῆμνον τῶν ἐμαυτοῦ τινα ἰσηλί-
κων, οὗ τῇ μητρὶ ἐλέγετό τις ἐπιφοιτᾶν σάτυρος, ὡς
εἰκὸς ἦν τῇ ἱστορίᾳ ταύτῃ, νεβρίδα γὰρ ξυμφυᾶ ἐῴκει
ἐνημμένῳ κατὰ τὸν νῶτον, ἧς οἱ ποδεῶνες οἱ πρῶτοι
ξυνειληφότες τὴν δέρην περὶ τὸ στέρνον αὐτῷ[39] ἀφ-
ήπτοντο. ἀλλὰ μὴ πλείω ὑπὲρ τούτων, οὔτε γὰρ ἡ
πεῖρα ἀπιστητέα οὔτε ἐγώ.

28. Καταβάντι δὲ αὐτῷ ἐξ Αἰθιοπίας ἡ μὲν πρὸς
τὸν Εὐφράτην διαφορὰ τότε μάλιστα ἐπέδωκε ἐκ τῶν
ὁσημέραι διαλέξεων, ἐπέτρεπε δὲ αὐτὰς Μενίππῳ τε

----

[39] αὐτῷ Kay.: αὐτὸ

All agreed, and so Apollonius poured four Egyptian jars   3
of wine into a trough from which the village cattle drank,
and then summoned the satyr by means of some mysterious rebuke. Without the creature becoming visible, the
wine began to go down as if being drunk, and when it had
been drained Apollonius said, "Let us make a truce with
the satyr, now that he is asleep." So saying, he led the
villagers to a cave of the Nymphs, less than a furlong from
the village, and showed them the satyr sleeping there,
ordering them not to hit or insult it, since it had stopped its
silly tricks.

So much for the deed of Apollonius, certainly not a   4
sideshow on his trip but a show on his side trip. If one reads
a letter of the Master written to a young hooligan, in which
he claims to have sobered up a demon-satyr in Ethiopia,[40]
he should keep this story in mind. That satyrs exist and
have erotic tendencies is not to be disbelieved. I know of a
contemporary of mine in Lemnos whose mother was said
to be haunted by a satyr, or so the present story suggests.[41]
He appeared to wear a close-fitting fawnskin down his
back, with the forefeet drawn around his neck and tied
over his chest. No more of all this, however, because neither experience nor I myself should meet with disbelief.

28. When Apollonius had returned from Ethiopia, his
disagreement with Euphrates became extremely sharp because of their daily lectures, but Apollonius left these to

[40] This letter is not preserved.
[41] Philostratus was born on Lemnos in the northern Aegean.

καὶ Νείλῳ, σμικρὰ ἐπιτιμῶν αὐτὸς τῷ Εὐφράτῃ, τοῦ
δὲ Νείλου σφόδρα ἐπεμελεῖτο.

29. Ἐπεὶ δὲ Τίτος ᾑρήκει τὰ Σόλυμα, καὶ νεκρῶν
πλέα ἦν πάντα, τὰ ὅμορά τε ἔθνη ἐστεφάνουν αὐτόν, ὁ
δὲ οὐκ ἠξίου ἑαυτὸν τούτου, μὴ γὰρ αὐτὸς ταῦτα
εἰργάσθαι, θεῷ δὲ ὀργὴν φήναντι ἐπιδεδωκέναι τὰς
ἑαυτοῦ χεῖρας, ἐπῄνει ὁ Ἀπολλώνιος ταῦτα, γνώμῃ τε
γὰρ περὶ τὸν ἄνδρα ἐφαίνετο καὶ ξύνεσις ἀνθρωπείων
τε καὶ θείων, καὶ σωφροσύνης μεστὸν τὸ μὴ στεφανοῦσθαι ἐφ᾽ αἵματι. ξυντάττει δὴ πρὸς αὐτὸν ἐπιστο-
λήν, ἧς διάκονον ποιεῖται τὸν Δάμιν, καὶ ἐπιστέλλει
ὧδε·

2   "Ἀπολλώνιος Τίτῳ στρατηγῷ Ῥωμαίων χαίρειν.
Μὴ βουληθέντι σοι ἐπ᾽ αἰχμῇ κηρύττεσθαι μηδ᾽ ἐπὶ
δηΐῳ αἵματι, δίδωμι ἐγὼ τὸν σωφροσύνης στέφανον,
ἐπειδὴ ἐφ᾽ οἷς δεῖ στεφανοῦσθαι γιγνώσκεις. ἔρρωσο." ὑπερησθεὶς δὲ ὁ Τίτος τῇ ἐπιστολῇ "καὶ ὑπὲρ
ἐμαυτοῦ" ἔφη "χάριν οἶδά σοι καὶ ὑπὲρ τοῦ πατρός,
καὶ μεμνήσομαι τούτων, ἐγὼ μὲν γὰρ Σόλυμα ᾕρηκα,
σὺ δὲ ἐμέ."

30. Ἀναρρηθεὶς δὲ αὐτοκράτωρ ἐν τῇ Ῥώμῃ καὶ
ἀριστείων ἀξιωθεὶς τούτων, ἀπῄει μὲν ἰσομοιρήσων
τῆς ἀρχῆς τῷ πατρί, τὸν δὲ Ἀπολλώνιον ἐνθυμηθείς,
ὡς πολλοῦ ἄξιος αὐτῷ ἔσται κἂν πρὸς βραχὺ ξυγ-
γενόμενος, ἐδεῖτο αὐτοῦ ἐς Ταρσοὺς[40] ἥκειν, καὶ περιβαλὼν ἐλθόντα "πάντα μοι ὁ πατὴρ" ἔφη "ἐπέστειλεν,
ὧν ξύμβουλον ἐποιεῖτό σε, καὶ ἰδοὺ ἡ ἐπιστολή, ὡς
εὐεργέτης τε αὐτοῦ ἐν αὐτῇ γέγραψαι καὶ πᾶν ὅ τι

Menippus and Nilus, addressing only slight rebukes of his own to Euphrates, while he took close care of Nilus.

29. Titus had now taken Jerusalem, and there were corpses everywhere. Though the neighboring provinces sent him crowns, he thought himself unworthy of them, believing that he had not accomplished all this personally, but had only lent his aid when heaven displayed its wrath. This won Apollonius's approval, since he could see that the hero had intelligence and an understanding of divine and human affairs, and it showed the highest restraint not to want a crown for bloodshed. He therefore wrote a letter to him, making Damis the carrier, and wrote as follows:

"Apollonius greets Titus, the general of the Romans. 2 Since you did not want to be proclaimed for military prowess or for enemy blood, I give you the crown for modesty, because you know what deeds merit crowning. Goodbye."[42] Delighted with this letter, Titus replied, "I thank you on my own behalf and on my father's, and I will remember this. I have captured Jerusalem, and you have captured me."

30. When Titus had been declared emperor in Rome and had been judged worthy of this prize, he set out to divide the power with his father. With the reflection, however, that Apollonius would be of great value to him even from a short meeting, he begged him to come to Tarsus. Embracing him on his arrival, he said, "My father has written to me about all the matters on which he consulted you. Look at his letter, and how he writes of you in it as someone

---

[42] Also preserved as Letter 77 d.

---

[40] ἐς Ταρσοὺς Cob.: ἐπ᾽ Ἄργους

APOLLONIUS OF TYANA

ἐσμέν, ἐγὼ δὲ ἔτη μὲν τριάκοντα ταυτὶ γέγονα, ἀξιού-
μενος δὲ ὧν ὁ πατὴρ ἑξηκοντούτης ὢν καὶ καλούμενος
ἐς τὸ ἄρχειν πρὶν οὐκ οἶδ' εἰ ἀρχθῆναι εἰδέναι, δέδια
μὴ μειζόνων, ἢ ἐμὲ χρή, ἅπτωμαι."

2   Ἐπιψηλαφήσας δὲ αὐτοῦ τὸν αὐχένα ὁ Ἀπολλώνιος, καὶ γὰρ δὴ ἔρρωτο αὐτὸν ἴσα τοῖς ἀσκοῦσι τὸ
σῶμα, "καὶ τίς" εἶπε "βιάσεται ταῦρον αὐχένα οὕτω
κρατερὸν ὑποσχεῖν ζυγῷ;" "ὁ ἐκ νέου" ἔφη, "μοσχεύ-
σας με," τὸν πατέρα τὸν ἑαυτοῦ λέγων ὁ Τίτος καὶ τὸ
ὑπ' ἐκείνου ἂν μόνου ἀρχθῆναι, ὃς ἐκ παιδὸς αὐτὸν τῇ
ἑαυτοῦ ἀκροάσει ξυνείθιζε. "χαίρω" εἶπεν ὁ Ἀπολλώνιος "πρῶτον μὲν παρεσκευασμένον σε ὁρῶν ἕπεσθαι
τῷ πατρί, ὑφ' οὗ χαίρουσιν ἀρχόμενοι καὶ οἱ μὴ φύσει
παῖδες, θεραπεύσοντά τε τὰς ἐκείνου θύρας, ᾧ ξυν-
θεραπευθήσῃ. νεότητος δὲ γήρᾳ ἅμα ἐς τὸ ἄρχειν
ἰούσης τίς μὲν λύρα, τίς δὲ αὐλὸς ἡδεῖαν ὧδε ἁρμονίαν καὶ ξυγκεκραμένην ᾄσεται; πρεσβύτερα γὰρ
ξυμβήσεται νέοις, ἐξ ὧν καὶ γῆρας ἰσχύσει καὶ νεότης
οὐκ ἀτακτήσει."

31. "Ἐμοὶ δέ," εἶπεν, "ὦ Τυανεῦ, περὶ ἀρχῆς καὶ
βασιλείας τί ὑποθήσῃ;" "ἅ γε" ἔφη "σεαυτὸν πέπει-
κας, ὑποκείμενος γὰρ τῷ πατρὶ δῆλά που, ὡς ὁμοιώσῃ
αὐτῷ. καὶ τὸν Ἀρχύτου δ' ἂν εἴποιμι νυνὶ λόγον,
γενναῖος γὰρ καὶ μαθεῖν ἄξιος. ἐγένετο ὁ Ἀρχύτας
ἀνὴρ Ταραντῖνος τὰ Πυθαγόρου σοφός· οὗτος ὑπὲρ
παίδων ἀγωγῆς γράφων 'ἔστω' φησὶν 'ὁ πατὴρ
παράδειγμα ἀρετῆς τοῖς παισίν, ὡς καὶ τῶν πατέρων

he counts among his benefactors, and as responsible for everything we are. But I am only thirty years old, and yet I have been accorded the status which my father has at sixty. Being called to rule before I perhaps know how to be ruled, I am afraid of accepting a position higher than I ought."

Apollonius stroked Titus's neck, which was as strong as that of a bodybuilder, and said, "Who will force a bull to put such a strong neck beneath the yoke?" "The man who yoked me as a youth," said Titus, meaning his father, and that he could only be governed by the person who had accustomed him to obedience from his boyhood. "It pleases me," said Apollonius, "above all to see you prepared to follow your father, whose rule pleases even those who are not his bodily sons, and to see you courting his doors, when you are going to be courted with him. When youth joins with age in government, what lyre or what pipe will produce such sweet and melodious harmony? The ways of old and young will unite, and thus age will be strong and youth will be disciplined."

31. "What advice," asked Titus, "do you have for me about ruling and kingship, man of Tyana?" "Advice of which you are already convinced," said Apollonius, "because as your father's subject you will obviously come to resemble him. I would also at this point mention the saying of Archytas,[43] excellent as it is and worth remembering. Archytas was a man of Tarentum, wise in the lore of Pythagoras, and writing about the education of children he says, 'Let the father be a lesson in virtue to his children.

[43] Pythagorean philosopher, contemporary and friend of Plato.

ξυντονώτερον βαδιουμένων ἐπὶ τὰς ἀρετάς, ἢν ὁμοι-
ῶνταί σφισιν οἱ παῖδες.· ἐγὼ δέ σοι καὶ Δημήτριον
ξυστήσω τὸν ἐμαυτοῦ ἑταῖρον, ὃς ξυνέσται σοι ὁπόσα
βούλει, διδάσκων τί δεῖ πράττειν τὸν ἀγαθὸν."

2   "Τίς δέ," ἔφη "Ἀπολλώνιε, ἡ σοφία τοῦ ἀνδρὸς
τούτου;" "παρρησία" εἶπε "καὶ τὸ ἀληθεύειν ἐκπλήτ-
τεσθαί τε ὑπὸ μηδενός, ἐστὶ γὰρ τοῦ Κυνικοῦ κρά-
τους." δυσχερῶς δὲ τοῦ Τίτου τὸν κύνα ἀκούσαντος
"Ὁμήρῳ μέντοι" ἔφη "νέος ὢν ὁ Τηλέμαχος καὶ δυοῖν
ἐδόκει κυνῶν δεῖσθαι, καὶ ξυμπέμπει[41] αὐτοὺς ὀπαδοὺς
τῷ μειρακίῳ ἐς τὴν τῶν Ἰθακησίων ἀγορὰν καίτοι
ἀλόγους ὄντας, σοὶ δὲ ξυνέσται κύων, ὃς ὑπὲρ σοῦ τε
πρὸς ἑτέρους καὶ πρὸς αὐτόν σε, εἴ τι ἁμαρτάνοις,
σοφῶς ἅμα καὶ οὐδὲ ἀλόγως ὑλακτήσει." "δίδου" εἶπε
"τὸν ὀπαδὸν κύνα, ξυγχωρῶ δὲ αὐτῷ καὶ δακεῖν, εἴ τι
με ἀδικοῦντα αἴσθοιτο." "γεγράψεται"[42] ἔφη "πρὸς
αὐτὸν ἐπιστολή, φιλοσοφεῖ δὲ ἐπὶ τῆς Ῥώμης." "γε-
γράφθω," εἶπεν "ἐβουλόμην δ᾽ ἂν καὶ πρὸς σὲ ὑπὲρ
ἐμοῦ τινα γράφειν, ὡς ἅμα τῆς ἐς τὴν Ῥώμην ὁδοῦ
κοινωνὸς ἡμῖν γένοιο." "ἀφίξομαι," ἔφη "ὁπότε ἀμφοῖν λῷον."

32. Μεταστησάμενος δὲ ὁ Τίτος τοὺς παρόντας
"αὐτοί," εἶπεν "ὦ Τυανεῦ, γεγόναμεν, ξυγχωρεῖς γάρ
που ἐρωτᾶν ὑπὲρ τῶν ἐμοὶ σπουδαιοτάτων;" "ἐρώτα,"
ἔφη "καὶ τοσούτῳ προθυμότερον, ὅσῳ ὑπὲρ μειζόνων."
"περὶ ψυχῆς" εἶπε "τῆς ἐμαυτοῦ, καὶ οὓς μάλιστα

---

[41] ξυμπέμπει Bentl.: ξυμπέμπειν

Fathers will be all the keener to attain the virtues if their own sons come to resemble them.' I will also introduce my friend Demetrius to you, and he will join you whenever you please, teaching how a good man should behave."

"What kind of philosophy," asked Titus, "does this Master practice, Apollonius?" "Frankness," he replied, "truth, and refusal to be cowed by anyone, since he has the determination of a Cynic." As Titus was displeased to hear the word "Cynic,"[44] Apollonius said, "Yet Homer thought that as a young man Telemachus needed two dogs, and he sends them to accompany the youth to the marketplace of Ithaca, irrational animals though they be.[45] You will have a dog that will bark on your behalf at other people, and at you too if you do any wrong, and it will do so wisely, and not irrationally." "Give me that dog to accompany me," said Titus, "and I even allow it to bite me, if it sees me doing any wrong." "I will write him a letter," said Apollonius, "since he practices in Rome." "Please write," Titus replied, "and I only wish someone would write to you on my behalf, so that you would be my partner on the journey to Rome." "I will come," said Apollonius, "when it is best for both of us."

32. Then, after dismissing the bystanders, Titus said, "We are alone, man of Tyana, so you will surely allow me to question you on subjects of the highest importance to me?" "Do so," said Apollonius, "and with all the more readiness, the more important they are." "My question," said Titus, "will concern my own life, and those whom I

2

[44] Literally "dog" (kuōn), a term often applied to the Cynics.
[45] *Odyssey* 2.11.

[42] γεγράψεται Rsk.: γέγραπται

φυλαττοίμην ἄν, ἔσται μοι ἡ ἐρώτησις, εἰ μὴ δόξω
δειλὸς δεδιὼς ἤδη ταῦτα." "ἀσφαλὴς μὲν οὖν" ἔφη
"καὶ ἐφεστηκώς, προορᾶν γὰρ τούτου χρὴ μάλιστα."
καὶ ἐς τὸν ἥλιον ἀναβλέψας ὤμνυ αὐτόν, ἦ μὴν αὐτὸς
μέλλειν ὑπὲρ τούτων πρὸς αὐτὸν λέξειν μηδὲ ἐρω-
τῶντα, τοὺς γὰρ θεοὺς φῆναί οἱ προειπεῖν αὐτῷ ζῶν-
τος μὲν τοῦ πατρὸς δεδιέναι τοὺς ἐκείνῳ πολεμιωτάτους, ἀποθανόντος δὲ τοὺς ἑαυτῷ οἰκειοτάτους.

2   "Ἀποθανοῦμαι δὲ" εἶπε "τίνα τρόπον;" "ὅν γε" ἔφη
"Ὀδυσσεὺς λέγεται, φασὶ γὰρ κἀκείνῳ τὸν θάνατον
ἐκ θαλάττης ἐλθεῖν." ταῦτα ὁ Δάμις ὧδε ἑρμηνεύει·
φυλάττεσθαι μὲν αὐτὸν τὴν αἰχμὴν τῆς τρυγόνος, ᾗ
τὸν Ὀδυσσέα βεβλῆσθαί φασι, δυοῖν δὲ ἐτοῖν μετὰ
τὸν πατέρα τὴν ἀρχὴν κατασχόντα ὑπὸ τοῦ θαλαττίου
λαγὼ ἀποθανεῖν, τὸν δὲ ἰχθὺν τοῦτον παρέχεσθαι
χυμοὺς ἀπορρήτους ὑπὲρ πάντα τὰ ἐν τῇ θαλάττῃ καὶ
γῇ ἀνδροφόνα, καὶ Νέρωνα μὲν ἐσποιῆσαι τοῖς ἑαυτοῦ
ὄψοις τὸν λαγὼν τοῦτον ἐπὶ τοὺς πολεμιωτάτους, Δομετιανὸν δὲ ἐπὶ τὸν ἀδελφὸν Τίτον, οὐ τὸ ξὺν ἀδελφῷ
ἄρχειν δεινὸν ἡγούμενον, ἀλλὰ τὸ ξὺν πράῳ τε καὶ
χρηστῷ. τοιαῦτα διαλεχθέντες ἰδίᾳ περιέβαλον ἀλλήλους ἐν φανερῷ, ἀπιόντα δὲ προσειπὼν "νίκα, ὦ βασιλεῦ," ἔφη "τοὺς μὲν πολεμίους ὅπλοις, τὸν δὲ πατέρα
ἀρεταῖς."

33. Ἡ δὲ πρὸς τὸν Δημήτριον ἐπιστολὴ ὧδε εἶχεν·
"Ἀπολλώνιος φιλόσοφος Δημητρίῳ κυνὶ χαίρειν. Δί-
δωμί σε βασιλεῖ Τίτῳ διδάσκαλον τοῦ τῆς βασιλείας
ἤθους, σὺ δ' ἀληθεῦσαί τέ μοι πρὸς αὐτὸν δίδου καὶ

should guard against most, unless you think me cowardly for having such fears already." "No," replied Apollonius, "I think you cautious and vigilant, because this is a matter requiring the greatest forethought." Looking up at the sun, he swore by it that he himself had intended to speak to him on these matters without even being asked. The gods had revealed to him that he must warn Titus to fear his worst enemies while his father lived, and after his death those closest to himself.

"And how shall I die?" asked Titus. "The way they say 2 Odysseus did," said Apollonius, "since for him too, they say, death came from the sea."[46] This remark Damis expounds as follows. Titus took precautions against the sting of the stingray, with which Odysseus is supposed to have been struck, but when he had held power for two years after his father he died from a seahare, a fish that produces mysterious secretions, which are the most deadly thing on land or sea. Nero used to mix this seahare into his dishes to kill his greatest enemies, but Domitian did so to kill his brother Titus, not because he objected to sharing power with a brother, but rather with someone gentle and good. After this private conversation, they embraced publicly, and as Titus left, Apollonius said, "Surpass your enemies in arms, Majesty, and your father in virtues."

33. His letter to Demetrius, however, ran as follows:[47] "Apollonius the philosopher greets Demetrius the Cynic. I give you to the emperor Titus so that he may learn the ways of kingship. Do me the favor of speaking truth to him, and

[46] *Odyssey* 11.134.
[47] A version of this letter survives as no. 77 e.

γίγνου αὐτῷ, πλὴν ὀργῆς, πάντα. ἔρρωσο."

34. Οἱ δὲ τοὺς Ταρσοὺς οἰκοῦντες τὸν μὲν ἄλλον χρόνον ἤχθοντο τῷ Ἀπολλωνίῳ διά τε τὰς ἐπιπλήξεις, ἐπειδὴ ξυντόνους αὐτὰς ἐποιεῖτο, διά τε τὸ ἀνειμένοι καὶ τρυφῶντες μηδὲ τὴν τοῦ λόγου ἀνέχεσθαι ῥώμην, τότε δ᾽ οὕτω τι ἡττήθησαν τοῦ ἀνδρός, ὡς οἰκιστήν τε αὐτὸν ἡγεῖσθαι καὶ στήριγμα τοῦ ἄστεος. ἔθυε μὲν γὰρ δημοσίᾳ ὁ βασιλεύς, ξυνελθοῦσα δὲ ἡ πόλις ἱκέτευεν ὑπὲρ τῶν μεγίστων, ὁ δὲ μεμνήσεσθαι[43] τού- των πρὸς τὸν πατέρα ἔφη, καὶ πρεσβεύσειν αὐτὸς ὑπὲρ ὧν δέονται.

2   Παρελθὼν δὲ ὁ Ἀπολλώνιος "εἰ δὲ ἐνίους" ἔφη "τούτων ἐλέγξαιμι σοὶ μὲν καὶ πατρὶ τῷ σῷ πολεμίους, πεπρεσβευμένους δὲ ὑπὲρ νεωτέρων ἐς τὰ Σόλυ- μα, ξυμμάχους δ᾽ ἀφανεῖς τῶν σοι φανερωτάτων ἐχθρῶν, τί πείσονται;" "τί δὲ ἄλλο γε," εἶπεν "ἢ ἀπολοῦνται;" "εἶτα οὐκ αἰσχρὸν" ἔφη "τὰς μὲν τιμω- ρίας αὐτίκα ἀπαιτεῖν, τὰς δὲ εὐεργεσίας ὀψὲ διδόναι, καὶ τὰς μὲν καθ᾽ ἑαυτὸν ποιεῖσθαι, τὰς δὲ ἐς κοινωνίαν γνώμης ἀνατίθεσθαι;" ὑπερησθεὶς δὲ ὁ βασιλεὺς "δί- δωμι τὰς δωρεάς," εἶπεν "οὐ γάρ μοι ἀχθέσεται ὁ πατὴρ ἀληθείας ἡττωμένῳ καὶ σοῦ."

35. Τοσαῦτα ἔθνη φασὶν ἐπελθεῖν τὸν Ἀπολλώνιον σπουδάζοντά τε καὶ σπουδαζόμενον. αἱ δὲ ἐφεξῆς ἀποδημίαι πολλαὶ μὲν ἐγένοντο τῷ ἀνδρί, οὐ μὴν τοσαῦταί γε ἔτι, οὐδὲ ἐς ἕτερα ἔθνη πλὴν ἃ ἔγνω, περί τε γὰρ τὴν ἐπὶ θαλάττῃ Αἴγυπτον καταβάντι αὐτῷ ἐξ Αἰθιοπίας διατριβὴ πλείων ἐγένετο, περί τε Φοίνικας

be all in all to him except for your anger. Goodbye."

34. The inhabitants of Tarsus had previously been vexed with Apollonius because of the rebukes that he administered so severely,[48] and because in their laxity and extravagance they could not stand even strong language, but now they were so won over by the Master as to consider him the founder and the mainstay of the city. For the emperor was making a public sacrifice when the assembled citizens began to make a very urgent petition to him, and he replied that he would mention it to his father and represent their request personally.

Apollonius came forward and said, "Suppose I show 2 that some of these people are hostile to you and your father, that they have negotiated with Jerusalem about revolt, and have been secret allies of your most declared enemy. What will happen to them?" "They will perish, of course," said Titus. "Well then," replied Apollonius, "is it not disgraceful to seek revenge immediately, but to grant favors slowly? To make yourself responsible for the first, and to refer the second to a shared decision?" Delighted, the emperor said, "I grant the gifts, since my father will not be angry with me for yielding to truth and to you."

35. These are the countries that they say Apollonius visited as a student and the subject of study. Though the Master made many journeys thereafter, they were no longer so frequent, and did not involve countries other than those he knew. He made a long stay in the coastal region of Egypt on his return from Ethiopia, and similarly in

48 Cf. I 7.1.

---

43 μεμνήσεσθαι Valck.: μνήσεσθαι

APOLLONIUS OF TYANA

καὶ Κίλικας, Ἴωνάς τε καὶ Ἀχαιοὺς, καὶ Ἰταλοὺς
πάλιν, οὐδαμοῦ ἐλλείποντι τὸ μὴ οὐχ ὁμοίῳ φαίνεσθαι. χαλεποῦ γὰρ τοῦ γνῶναι ἑαυτὸν δοκοῦντος,
χαλεπώτερον ἔγωγε ἡγοῦμαι τὸ μεῖναι τὸν σοφὸν
ἑαυτῷ ὅμοιον· οὐδὲ γὰρ τοὺς πονηρῶς φύντας ἐς τὸ
λῷον μεταστήσει μὴ πρότερον ἐξασκήσας τὸ μὴ αὐτὸς μεθίστασθαι.

2   Ὑπὲρ μὲν δὴ τούτων ἐν ἑτέροις λόγοις ἱκανῶς
εἴρηκα, διδάσκων τοὺς μὴ μαλακῶς αὐτοῖς ὁμιλοῦν-
τας, ὅτι τὸν ἀτεχνῶς ἄνδρα μήτε μεταστήσει τι μήτε
δουλώσεται. ὡς δὲ μήτε ἐς λόγων ἴοιμεν μῆκος ἀκριβῶς ἀναδιδάσκοντες τὰ παρ᾽ ἑκάστοις αὐτῷ φιλο-
σοφηθέντα, μήτ᾽ αὖ διαπηδῶντες φαινοίμεθα λόγον,
ὃν οὐκ ἀπόνως παραδίδομεν τοῖς ἀπείροις τοῦ ἀνδρός,
δοκεῖ μοι τὰ σπουδαιότερα ἐπελθεῖν τούτων, καὶ ὁπόσα μνήμης ἀξιώτερα.[44] ἡγώμεθα δὲ αὐτὰ παραπλήσια
ταῖς τῶν Ἀσκληπιαδῶν ἐπιδημίαις.

36. Μειράκιον ἑαυτοῦ μὲν ἀπαιδεύτως εἶχε, τοὺς δὲ
ὄρνις ἐπαίδευε καὶ ξυνοίκους ἐπὶ σοφίᾳ ἐποιεῖτο·
ἐδίδασκε δὲ αὐτοὺς λαλεῖν τε ὅσα οἱ ἄνθρωποι καὶ
τερετίζειν ὅσα αὐλοί. τούτῳ περιτυχὼν "τί" ἔφη "ἐπι-
τηδεύεις;" ἐπεὶ δὲ τάς τε ἀηδόνας αὐτῷ διῄει καὶ τοὺς
κοψίχους καὶ ὁπόσα εὐγλωττίζοι τοὺς χαραδρίους,
τὴν φωνὴν δὲ ἀπαίδευτον ἐφαίνετο "δοκεῖς μοι" ἔφη
"διαφθείρειν τοὺς ὄρνις, πρῶτον μὲν τῷ μὴ ξυγχωρεῖν
αὐτοῖς τὸ ἑαυτῶν φθέγμα οὕτως ἡδὺ ὄν, ὡς μηδ᾽ ἂν τὰ

[44] ἀξιώτερα Cob.: ἀξιώσεται

194

Phoenicia, Cilicia, Ionia, Achaea, and Italy once more, never failing anywhere to seem unaltered. They say that the command "Know yourself" is difficult, but more difficult, it seems to me, is for a wise man to remain unaltered, since he cannot change evil natures for the better unless he has first trained himself not to change.

On this subject I have spoken at length in other pas- 2 sages, showing those who read them in a manly spirit that a true Master will neither change nor be servile.[49] But I do not wish to prolong my account by relating in detail Apollonius's discourses in every place, and yet I do not wish my history to seem superficial, when I have taken some trouble to transmit it to those ignorant of the Master. I think it best, then, to report the more important discourses and every item especially worth recording, for we should think of them as equivalent to visits from the followers of Asclepius.

36. There was a young man who neglected his own education and yet educated birds, which he kept at home for their improvement. He was training them to talk as humans do, and to warble as pipes do. When they met, Apollonius said to him, "What do you study?" The young man described his nightingales and blackbirds, and all the words he was teaching his plovers, though his own language was obviously uneducated. Apollonius said to him, "You seem to me to be spoiling your birds, first by not permitting them their natural voices, which are so sweet that

---

[49] This may be a lost work, but may simply refer to those parts of the *Life* that show Apollonius's fearlessness, e.g. IV 44.

μουσικὰ τῶν ὀργάνων ἐς μίμησιν αὐτοῦ καταστῆναι,
εἶτα καὶ τῷ κάκιστα Ἑλλήνων αὐτὸς διαλεγόμενος
μαθητὰς αὐτοὺς ποιεῖσθαι ἀφωνίας.

2   "Ἐπιτρίβεις δ', ὦ μειράκιον, καὶ τὸν σεαυτοῦ οἶκον. βλέψαντι γὰρ ἐς τοὺς ἀκολούθους καὶ ὡς κατ-
εσκεύασαι, τῶν ἁβρῶν ἔμοιγε καὶ οὐκ ἀπλούτων φαίνῃ, τοὺς δὲ τοιούτους ὑποβλίττουσιν οἱ συκοφάνται
κέντρα ἐπ' αὐτοὺς ἠρμένοι τὴν γλῶτταν. καὶ τί χρήσῃ
τῇ φιλορνιθίᾳ τότε; οὐδὲ γὰρ τὰ πασῶν ἀηδόνων μέλη
ξυμφέρων ἀποσοβήσεις αὐτοὺς ἐγκειμένους τε καὶ
ἐρείδοντας, ἀλλ' ἐπαντλεῖν χρὴ τῶν ὄντων καὶ προ-
βάλλειν αὐτοῖς τὸ χρυσίον, ὥσπερ τὰ μειλίγματα τοῖς
κυσί, κἂν ὑλακτῶσιν, αὖθις διδόναι καὶ αὖθις, εἶτα
αὐτὸν πεινῆν ὕστερον καὶ ἀπορεῖν.

3   "Δεῖ δέ σοι ἐκτροπῆς λαμπρᾶς καὶ μεταβολῆς ἤδη
τινὸς τῶν τρόπων, ὡς μὴ λάθῃς πτερορρυήσας τὸν
πλοῦτον καὶ ἀξίως πράττων τοῦ θρηνεῖσθαι μᾶλλον
ὑπ' ὀρνίθων ἢ ᾄδεσθαι. τὸ δὲ φάρμακον τῆς μεταβολῆς οὐ μέγα, ἐστὶ γάρ τι ἐν ἁπάσαις πόλεσιν ἔθνος
ἀνθρώπων, ὃ σὺ οὔπω μὲν γιγνώσκεις, καλοῦσι δὲ
αὐτὸ διδασκάλους· τούτοις ἀπὸ τῆς οὐσίας μικρὰ δοὺς
ἀσφαλῶς κεκτήσῃ τὰ πλείω, ῥητορικὴν γάρ σε παι-
δεύσουσι τὴν τῶν ἀγοραίων, ῥᾳδία δ' ἡ τέχνη. εἰ μὲν
γὰρ παῖδά σε ἑώρων ἔτι, ξυνεβούλευον ἂν φοιτᾶν ἐπὶ
φιλοσόφων τε καὶ σοφιστῶν θύρας καὶ σοφίᾳ πάσῃ
τὴν οἰκίαν τὴν σεαυτοῦ φράττειν. ἐπεὶ δὲ ἔξωρος
τούτων τυγχάνεις ὤν, τὸ γοῦν ὑπὲρ σεαυτοῦ λέγειν
ἔκμαθε, νομίσας, εἰ μὲν τὰ τελεώτερα ἔμαθες, κἂν

not even musical instruments can manage to imitate them; and second, since you talk the worst possible Greek yourself, by giving them lessons in incomprehensibility.

"Moreover, young man, you are wasting your fortune. 2 When I look at your servants and your appearance, you strike me as a refined and quite wealthy type, and people like you get cleaned out by scroungers, who are armed with stings in their tongues. What use will your bird-fancying be then? Even with your whole collection of nightingales' songs, you will not be able to ward these men off as they harry and press you. You will have to drain your property dry, throw gold to them like cakes to dogs, and if they bark, to give them more and more, and then you yourself will go hungry and poor for ever after.

"You need some honorable escape and some immedi- 3 ate reform in your ways, or else you will find that you have unwittingly shed all your wealth, and will deserve to be mourned by birds rather than serenaded. The medicine that will reform you is not at all uncommon, since in every city there is a class of men, unknown to you as yet, whom they call teachers. Give them a few of your possessions, and you will have safe enjoyment of the rest, because they will teach you oratory of the forensic kind, a skill easily acquired. If I had seen you when still a boy, I would have advised you to attend the schools of philosophers and sophists, and fortify your own house with every kind of wisdom. However, you are too old for that now, so at least learn to speak in your own defense. Realize that if your education had been more thorough, you would seem like a

APOLLONIUS OF TYANA

ὅμοιος ἀνδρὶ ὁπλιτεύοντί τε καὶ φοβερῷ δόξαι, ταυτὶ
δ᾽ ἐκμαθὼν τὴν τῶν ψιλῶν τε καὶ σφενδονητῶν σκευὴν
ἕξειν.⁴⁵ βάλλοις γὰρ ἂν τοὺς συκοφάντας, ὥσπερ τοὺς
κύνας." ξυνῆκε τὸ μειράκιον τούτων, καὶ τὰς τῶν
ὀρνίθων διατριβὰς ἐκλιπὸν, ἐς διδασκάλων ἐβάδισεν,
ὑφ᾽ ὧν καὶ ἡ γνώμη αὐτῷ καὶ ἡ γλῶττα ἴσχυσεν.

37. Δυοῖν δὲ λόγοιν ἐν Σάρδεσι λεγομένοιν, τοῦ
μέν, ὡς ὁ Πακτωλός ποτε τῷ Κροίσῳ ψῆγμα χρυσοῦ
ἄγοι, τοῦ δέ, ὡς πρεσβύτερα τῆς γῆς εἴη τὰ δένδρα,
τὸν μὲν πιθανῶς ἔφη πεπιστεῦσθαι, χρυσία γὰρ εἶναί
ποτε τῷ Τμώλῳ ψαμμώδη καὶ τοὺς ὄμβρους αὐτὰ
φέρειν ἐς τὸν Πακτωλὸν κατασύροντας, χρόνῳ δέ,
ὅπερ φιλεῖ τὰ τοιαῦτα, ἐπιλιπεῖν αὐτὰ ἀποκλυσθέντα,
τοῦ δ᾽ ἑτέρου λόγου καταγελάσας "ὑμεῖς μὲν" ἔφη
"προγενέστερα τῆς γῆς φατε εἶναι τὰ δένδρα, ἐγὼ δὲ
πολὺν οὕτω χρόνον φιλοσοφήσας οὔπω ἔγνων οὐρα-
νοῦ προγενεστέρους ἀστέρας," διδάσκων ὅτι μηδ᾽ ἂν
γένοιτό τι τοῦ ἐν ᾧ φύεται μὴ ὄντος.

38. Στασιάζοντος δὲ τὴν Ἀντιόχειαν τοῦ τῆς Συ-
ρίας ἄρχοντος καὶ καθιέντος ἐς αὐτοὺς ὑποψίας, ὑφ᾽
ὧν διειστήκεσαν, ἠκκλησίαζε μὲν ἡ⁴⁶ πόλις, σεισμοῦ
δὲ γενναίου προσπεσόντος, ἔπτηξαν καὶ ὅπερ ἐν διο-
σημίαις εἴωθεν, ὑπὲρ ἀλλήλων ηὔξαντο. παρελθὼν
οὖν ὁ Ἀπολλώνιος "ὁ μὲν θεὸς" ἔφη "διαλλακτὴς ὑμῶν
σαφὴς γέγονεν, ὑμεῖς δὲ οὐδ᾽ ἂν αὖθις στασιάσαιτε,
τὰ αὐτὰ φοβούμενοι." καὶ κατέστησεν αὐτοὺς ἐς ἔννοιαν ὧν πείσονται, καὶ <ὡς>⁴⁷ ταὐτὸ τοῖς ἑτέροις
φοβήσονται.

man heavily armed and formidable, but if you learn what I have mentioned, you will have the equipment of a skirmisher and a slinger, and you will hit scroungers as if they were dogs." The young man took this to heart, gave up his bird-fancying, and attended teachers, who strengthened both his mind and his tongue.

37. Two stories were current in Sardis. One was that the Pactolus once brought gold grains to Croesus, and the other that trees were older than the earth. The first Apollonius said was rightly believed, since the Tmolus had once contained gold flakes which the rains had swept down into the Pactolus, but in time, as often happened, they had been washed away and been exhausted. But the other story made him laugh, and he said, "You claim that trees existed before the earth, and yet I have been a philosopher for all this long time, and never heard that the stars were older than the sky." By this he conveyed that nothing could ever come about if the element containing it did not exist.

38. The governor of Syria was throwing Antioch into turmoil by sowing suspicion that had divided the citizens. The city was holding an assembly, when a major earthquake occurred that caused them to cower and, as usually happens in divine visitations, to pray for one another. Apollonius came forward and said, "God has clearly shown himself your mediator, and you should never be at variance again for fear of the same result." He thus made them realize what would happen, and that the same danger threatened both sides.

---

45 ἕξειν Rsk.: ἕξεις
46 ἠκκλησίαζε μὲν ἡ Rsk.: ἐκκλησιαζομένη
47 ⟨ὡς⟩ Kay.

39. Ἄξιον δὲ καὶ τούτου ἐπιμνησθῆναι· ἔθνέ τις ὑπὲρ θησαυροῦ τῇ Γῇ καὶ οὐδὲ τῷ Ἀπολλωνίῳ προσεύχεσθαι ὑπὲρ τούτου ὤκνει, ὁ δὲ ἐνθυμηθείς, οἵων ἐρᾷ, "δεινόν γε," ἔφη "χρηματιστὴν ὁρῶ." "κακοδαίμονα μὲν οὖν," εἶπεν "ᾧ γέ ἐστιν οὐδὲν πλὴν ὀλίγων, ἃ μὴ ἀπόχρη βόσκειν τὸν οἶκον." "ἔοικας" ἔφη "πολλοὺς τρέφειν καὶ ἀργοὺς οἰκέτας, οὐδὲ γὰρ αὐτός γε τῶν ἀσόφων φαίνῃ." ὁ δὲ ἠρέμα ἐπιδακρύσας "θυγάτριά μοι" εἶπεν "ἐστὶ τέτταρα καὶ φερνῶν δεῖ τεττάρων, ἐμοὶ δέ εἰσι δισμύριαί που δραχμαὶ νῦν, ἐπειδὰν δὲ ταῖς θυγατράσι κατανεμηθῶσιν, ἐκεῖναί τε σμικρὰ εἰληφέναι δόξουσιν ἐγώ τε ἀπολοῦμαι ἔχων οὐδέν."

2 Παθὼν οὖν τι πρὸς αὐτὸν ὁ Ἀπολλώνιος "ἐπιμελησόμεθά σου" ἔφη "κἀγὼ καὶ ἡ Γῆ, φασὶ γάρ σε θύειν αὐτῇ." καὶ εἰπὼν ταῦτα προῄει <ἐς>[48] τὰ προάστεια, ὥσπερ οἱ τοὺς καρποὺς ὠνούμενοι, ἰδὼν δέ τι χωρίον ἐλαῶν πλῆρες καὶ ἡσθεὶς τοῖς δένδρεσιν, ὡς εὐφυᾶ τε ἦν καὶ μεγάλα καί τινος κηπίου ἐν αὐτῷ ὄντος, ἐν ᾧ σμήνη τε καὶ ἄνθη ἑωρᾶτο, παρῆλθεν ἐς τὸ κηπίον ὥς τι ἐπισκεψόμενος μεῖζον καὶ προσευξάμενος τῇ Πανδώρᾳ ἐχώρει ἐς τὸ ἄστυ. βαδίσας δὲ παρὰ τὸν τοῦ ἀγροῦ δεσπότην, ᾧ πλοῦτος ἐκ τῶν παρανομωτάτων πεπόριστο τὰς Φοινίκων οὐσίας ἐνδεικνύντι "χωρίον" ἔφη "τὸ δεῖνα πόσου ἐπρίω καὶ τί πεπόνηταί σοι ἐς αὐτό;" τοῦ δὲ πέρυσι μὲν ἐωνῆσθαι τὸν ἀγρὸν πεντακισχιλίων καὶ μυρίων φήσαντος, οὔ-

39. The following is also worth mention. A man was sacrificing to Earth in hope of a treasure, and did not blush even to pray to Apollonius for the purpose. Understanding his desire, Apollonius said, "A good businessman, I see." "No, an unlucky one," was the reply, "as I have nothing except a little money, which is insufficient to feed my family." "You seem to maintain many idle slaves," said Apollonius, "and you yourself look not unintelligent." With tears in his eyes, the man said, "I have four daughters and need four dowries, but while I have twenty thousand drachmas for now, when my daughters each get a share, they will seem to have got only a little, while I will be ruined and destitute."

Rather moved by the man, Apollonius said, "We will look after you, both I and Earth, for they say you sacrifice to it." So saying he made for the suburbs, like someone intending to buy fresh produce. Seeing a plot full of olives, he admired the trees, which were well grown and tall. It also contained a little garden in which beehives and flowers could be seen. After entering the plot as if in search of something more important, and praying to Pandora,[50] he returned to the city. He then went to the owner of the land, who had got his wealth in the most disreputable way, by informing on the estates of Phoenicians,[51] and said, "How much did you pay for such-and-such property, and what improvements have you made on it?" The other replied that he had bought it recently for fifteen thousand drach-

2

[50] Epithet of Mother Earth as "giver of all."
[51] These Phoenicians presumably lacked the right to own property, and the man had made money by informing on them.

---

[48] ⟨ἐς⟩ Ol.

πω δ' ἐκπεπονηκέναι τι, πείθει τὸν ἄνθρωπον ἀποδόσθαι οἱ δισμυρίων αὐτόν, εὕρημα ποιησάμενον τὰς
πεντακισχιλίας.

3   Ὁ μὲν δὴ τοῦ θησαυροῦ ἐρῶν οὔπω ξυνίει τοῦ
δώρου, ἀλλ' οὐδ' ᾤετο ἴσα ἔχειν, τοσούτῳ δὲ ἐλάττω,
ὅσῳ τὰς μὲν δισμυρίας ἐν ταῖν χεροῖν οὔσας ἐφ'
ἑαυτῷ εἶναι ἄν, τὸν δ' ἀντ' αὐτῶν ἀγρὸν ἐπὶ πάχναις
κείσεσθαι καὶ χαλάζαις καὶ τοῖς ἄλλοις, ἃ τοὺς καρποὺς φθείρει· ἐπεὶ δὲ ἀμφορέα μὲν τρισχιλίων δαρει-
κῶν αὐτίκα εὗρε περὶ αὐτὸ μάλιστα τὸ ἐν τῷ κηπίῳ
σμῆνος, εὐφόρου δὲ τοῦ τῆς ἐλαίας καρποῦ ἔτυχεν οὐκ
εὐφορούσης τότε τῆς ἄλλης γῆς, ὕμνοι αὐτῷ ἐς τὸν
ἄνδρα ᾔδοντο καὶ μνηστήρων θεραπευόντων αὐτὸν
πλέα ἦν πάντα.

40. Κἀκεῖνα ἀξιομνημόνευτα εὗρον τοῦ ἀνδρός.
ἐρᾶν τις ἐδόκει τοῦ τῆς Ἀφροδίτης ἕδους, ὃ ἐν Κνίδῳ
γυμνὸν ἵδρυται, καὶ τὰ μὲν ἀνετίθει, τὰ δ' ἀναθήσειν
ἔφασκεν ὑπὲρ τοῦ γάμου, Ἀπολλωνίῳ δὲ καὶ ἄλλως
μὲν ἄτοπα ἐδόκει ταῦτα, ἐπεὶ δὲ μὴ παρῃτεῖτο ἡ
Κνίδος, ἀλλ' ἐναργεστέραν ἔφασαν τὴν θεὸν δόξειν, εἰ
ἐρῷτο, ἔδοξε τῷ ἀνδρὶ καθῆραι τὸ ἱερὸν τῆς ἀνοίας
ταύτης, καὶ ἐρομένων τῶν Κνιδίων αὐτόν, εἴ τι βού-
λοιτο τῶν θυτικῶν ἢ εὐκτικῶν διορθοῦσθαι "ὀφθαλμοὺς" ἔφη "διορθώσομαι, τὰ δὲ τοῦ ἱεροῦ πάτρια
ἐχέτω, ὡς ἔχει."

2   Καλέσας οὖν τὸν θρυπτόμενον ἤρετο αὐτόν, εἰ
θεοὺς νενόμικε, τοῦ δ' οὕτω νομίζειν θεοὺς φήσαντος,

mas, but had not yet made improvements. So he persuaded the man to sell it to the other for twenty thousand, and to consider the five a windfall.

The treasure-seeker, however, did not understand that 3 this was a gift, but thought he had made an unequal bargain, in fact all the less equal in that the twenty thousand in hand would have been his to use, but the land he had got for them was subject to frost, hail, and all the other things damaging to crops. But he immediately found a jar with three thousand darics[52] just near the beehive in the plot, and got a good crop from his olive grove, though the general region was not productive at the time. So he praised the Master to the skies, and his household was full of eager suitors.

40. This too I have found worth mentioning about the Master. A man thought he was in love with the statue of Aphrodite that is set up naked in Cnidos. He had already made some dedications and promised others in return for marriage with it.[53] Apollonius thought all this was generally bizarre, but when the Cnidians raised no objections, saying that the goddess would be more celebrated if she had a lover, the Master decided to purify the sanctuary of this folly. When the Cnidians asked him if he wished to correct any of their ways of praying or sacrificing, he replied: "I will correct your eyesight, but the customs of the sanctuary may remain as they are."

Summoning the lovesick man, he asked him if he re- 2 vered the gods. The other replied that he revered them

52 Gold coin first minted by Darius I of Persia.

53 Praxiteles's statue of Aphrodite at Cnidos was famously lifelike.

ὡς καὶ ἐρᾶν αὐτῶν, καὶ τῶν γάμων μνημονεύσαντος,
οὓς θύσειν ἡγεῖτο, "σὲ μὲν ποιηταὶ" ἔφη "ἐπαίρουσι
τοὺς Ἀγχίσας τε καὶ τοὺς Πηλέας θεαῖς ξυζυγῆναι
εἰπόντες, ἐγὼ δὲ περὶ τοῦ ἐρᾶν καὶ ἐρᾶσθαι τόδε
γιγνώσκω· θεοὶ θεῶν, ἄνθρωποι ἀνθρώπων, θηρία θηρίων, καὶ καθάπαξ ὅμοια ὁμοίων ἐρᾷ, ἐπὶ τῷ ἔτυμα καὶ
ξυγγενῆ τίκτειν, τὸ δὲ ἑτερογενὲς τῷ μὴ ὁμοίῳ ξυν-
ελθὸν οὔτε ζυγὸς οὔτε ἔρως. εἰ δὲ ἐνεθυμοῦ τὰ Ἰξίονος,
οὐδ' ἂν ἐς ἔννοιαν καθίστασο τοῦ μὴ ὁμοίων ἐρᾶν.
ἀλλ' ἐκεῖνος μὲν <ἐν>[49] τροχῷ ἠκασμένος[50] δι' οὐρα-
νοῦ κνάμπτεται, σὺ δ', εἰ μὴ ἄπει τοῦ ἱεροῦ, ἀπολεῖ ἐν
ἁπάσῃ τῇ γῇ οὐδ' ἀντειπεῖν ἔχων τὸ μὴ οὐ δίκαια τοὺς
θεοὺς ἐπὶ σοὶ γνῶναι." ὧδε ἡ παροινία ἐσβέσθη καὶ
ἀπῆλθεν ὁ φάσκων ἐρᾶν ὑπὲρ ξυγγνώμης θύσας.

41. Σεισμῶν δὲ κατασχόντων ποτὲ τὰς ἐν τῷ ἀρι-
στερῷ Ἑλλησπόντῳ πόλεις, Αἰγύπτιοι μὲν καὶ Χαλ-
δαῖοι περὶ αὐτὰς ἠγείροντο ὑπὲρ ξυλλογῆς χρημάτων,
ὡς δεκαταλάντους θυσίας Γῇ καὶ Ποσειδῶνι θύσον-
τες, ξυνέφερον δ' αἱ πόλεις τὰ μὲν ἀπὸ τοῦ κοινοῦ, τὰ
δὲ ἀπὸ τῶν οἴκων ὑποκείμενοι τῷ φόβῳ, οἱ δέ, εἰ μὴ
ἐπὶ τραπεζῶν ἐκτεθείη τὸ ἀργύριον, οὐκ ἂν ἔφασαν
ὑπὲρ αὐτῶν θῦσαι· δοκεῖ δὴ τῷ ἀνδρὶ μὴ περιιδεῖν
τοὺς Ἑλλησποντίους, καὶ παρελθὼν ἐς τὰς πόλεις
τοὺς μὲν ἀπήλασεν ὡς θησαυρὸν πεποιημένους τὰ
ἑτέρων κακά, τὰς δὲ αἰτίας τῶν μηνιμάτων ξυλλαβὼν

[49] <ἐν> Cob.
[50] ἠκασμένος Bentl.: εἰκασμένος

so much as to fall in love with them, and mentioned the wedding which he was planning to celebrate. "You are excited," said Apollonius, "by poets who tell you that men like Anchises and Peleus were joined with goddesses, but I know this about giving and receiving love. Gods love gods, humans love humans, animals love animals, and in short like loves like for the purpose of producing genuine offspring of its own kind. But when something alien unites with something unlike itself, there is neither union nor love. If you had thought about Ixion, it would not even have occurred to you to love something unlike yourself. He is racked in the sky by being tortured on a wheel, and you, if you do not leave the sanctuary, will perish throughout the world. You will not even be able to say that the gods' verdict on you was other than just." That extinguished the man's frenzy, and the self-proclaimed lover left after begging forgiveness with a sacrifice.

41. Earthquakes were once shaking the cities on the left side of the Hellespont, and Egyptians and Chaldeans went scrounging around them, promising to make sacrifices worth ten talents to Earth and Poseidon.[54] The cities had begun to contribute both from their common funds and from households, being overcome by fear, but the scroungers refused to sacrifice for them unless the money was deposited in the banks. Deciding not to neglect the Hellespontines, the Master visited the cities and drove out the strangers for making a fortune from the misfortunes of others. Inferring the reasons for the gods' wrath, he made

[54] Poseidon had the power both to cause and to end earthquakes.

καὶ ὡς ἑκάστῃ πρόσφορον θύσας ἀπεύξατο τὴν προσ-
βολὴν δαπάνῃ σμικρᾷ, καὶ ἡ γῆ ἔστη.

42. Δομετιανοῦ δὲ βασιλέως ὑπὸ τὸν αὐτὸν χρόνον
εὐνούχους τε μὴ ποιεῖν νομοθετήσαντος ἀμπέλους τε
μὴ φυτεύειν, ἔτι καὶ τὰς πεφυτευμένας δὲ αὐτῶν ἐκ-
κόπτειν, παρελθὼν ἐς τοὺς Ἴωνας ὁ Ἀπολλώνιος "τὰ
μὲν προστάγματα οὐ πρὸς ἐμέ" ἔφη "ταῦτα, μόνος
γὰρ ἴσως ἀνθρώπων οὔτε αἰδοίων δέομαι οὔτε οἴνου,
λέληθε δὲ ὁ θαυμασιώτατος τῶν μὲν ἀνθρώπων φειδό-
μενος, τὴν δὲ γῆν εὐνουχίζων." ὅθεν ἐς θάρσος ἡ
Ἰωνία ἦλθε πρεσβεύσασθαι πρὸς τὸν βασιλέα ὑπὲρ
ἀμπέλων καὶ παραιτήσασθαι νόμον, ὃς ἐκέλευε καὶ
δῃοῦσθαι τὴν γῆν καὶ μὴ φυτεύεσθαι.

43. Κἀκεῖνα ἐν Ταρσοῖς τοῦ ἀνδρὸς ᾄδουσι· κύων
ἐνεπεπτώκει ἐφήβῳ λυττῶν καὶ ἀπῆγε τὸν ἔφηβον τὸ
δῆγμα ἐς τὰ τῶν κυνῶν πάντα, ὑλάκτει τε γὰρ καὶ
ὠρύετο καὶ τετράπους ἔθει τὼ χεῖρε ὑπέχων τῷ δρόμῳ.
νοσοῦντι δ' αὐτῷ τριακοστὴν ἡμέραν ἐφίσταται μὲν ὁ
Ἀπολλώνιος ἄρτι ἐς τοὺς Ταρσοὺς ἥκων, κελεύει δὲ
ἀνιχνευθῆναί οἱ τὸν κύνα, ὃς ταῦτα εἰργάσατο, οἱ δ'
οὔτε ἐντετυχηκέναι τῷ κυνὶ ἔφασαν, ἔξω γὰρ τείχους
εἰλῆφθαι αὐτὸν τοῦ ἐφήβου πρὸς ἀκοντίοις ὄντος, οὔτ'
ἂν τοῦ νοσοῦντος μαθεῖν, ἥτις ἡ ἰδέα τοῦ κυνός, ἐπεὶ
μηδὲ αὐτὸν ἔτι οἶδεν. ἐπισχὼν οὖν "ὦ Δάμι," ἔφη
"λευκὸς ὁ κύων λάσιος προβατευτικός, Ἀμφιλοχικῷ
ἴσος, προσέστηκε δὲ τῇ δεῖνι κρήνῃ τρέμων, τὸ γὰρ

the sacrifice appropriate to each city, and averted the disaster at a small cost, so that the earth stopped shaking.

42. The emperor Domitian made two laws about the same time, against castrating men and planting vines, and for cutting down the vines that had been planted.[55] Apollonius came before the Ionians and said, "These edicts do not concern me, because I am perhaps the only human who needs neither genitals nor wine. But this fine fellow does not realize that he is sparing humans and castrating the earth." That gave the Ionians the courage to send an embassy to the emperor about vines, and to request the repeal of a law that required the earth both to be ravaged and not to be planted.

43. There is another celebrated deed of Apollonius in Tarsus. A mad dog had attacked a youth, and the bite had caused the youth to act just like a dog, so that he barked, howled, and ran about on all fours with his hands to support him. He had been ill for thirty days when Apollonius, who had just arrived in Tarsus, met him, and ordered that the dog responsible for all this should be tracked down. They said that they had never seen the creature, since it had attacked the youth outside the wall during javelin practice, and they could not find out from the patient what the dog looked like, since he no longer even recognized himself. After a pause, Apollonius said, "Damis, it is a white, shaggy sheepdog, the size of one from Amphilochia,[56] and it is standing by such-and-such a fountain,

[55] In fact, Domitian's law against castration appears to date from 82, and his edict on the growing of vines to 92.

[56] Amphilochia in northwestern Greece was famous for its fierce dogs.

ὕδωρ καὶ ποθεῖ καὶ δέδοικεν. ἄγε μοι τοῦτον ἐπὶ τὴν
τοῦ ποταμοῦ ὄχθην, ἐφ᾿ ἧς αἱ παλαῖστραι, μόνον
εἰπών, ὅτι ὑπ᾿ ἐμοῦ καλοῖτο."

2   Ἑλχθεὶς δ᾿ ὁ κύων ὑπὸ τοῦ Δάμιδος ὑπεκλίθη τοῖς
τοῦ Ἀπολλωνίου ποσίν, ὥσπερ οἱ βώμιοι τῶν ἱκετῶν
κλαίων, ὁ δ᾿ ἥμερού τε αὐτὸν ἔτι μᾶλλον καὶ τῇ χειρὶ
ἐπράυνε. τὸν ἔφηβόν τε ἵστη ἐγγὺς ξυνέχων αὐτός, ὡς
δὲ μὴ λάθοι τοὺς πολλοὺς μέγα ἀπόρρητον, "μεθ-
έστηκε μὲν" ἔφη "ἐς τὸν παῖδα τοῦτον ἡ Τηλέφου
ψυχὴ τοῦ Μυσοῦ, Μοῖραι δ᾿ ἐπ᾿ αὐτῷ ταῦτα[51] βουλεύονται,"[52] καὶ εἰπὼν ταῦτα ἐκέλευσε τὸν κύνα περι-
λιχμήσασθαι τὸ δῆγμα, ὡς ἰατρὸς αὐτῷ πάλιν ὁ
τρώσας γένοιτο. ἐπεστράφη τὸ ἐντεῦθεν ἐς τὸν πατέρα
ὁ παῖς καὶ ξυνῆκε τῆς μητρὸς προσεῖπέ τε τοὺς
ἥλικας καὶ ἔπιε τοῦ Κύδνου, περιώφθη δὲ οὐδὲ ὁ κύων,
ἀλλὰ κἀκεῖνον εὐξάμενος τῷ ποταμῷ δι᾿ αὐτοῦ ἧκεν. ὁ
δ᾿ ἐπεὶ διέβη τὸν Κύδνον, ἐπιστὰς τῇ ὄχθῃ φωνήν τε
ἀφῆκεν, ὅπερ ἥκιστα περὶ τοὺς λυττῶντας τῶν κυνῶν
ξυμβαίνει, καὶ τὰ ὦτα ἀνακλάσας ἔσεισε τὴν οὐράν,
ξυνιεὶς τοῦ ἐρρῶσθαι. φαρμακοποσία γὰρ λύττης
ὕδωρ, ἣν θαρσήσῃ αὐτὸ ὁ λυττῶν.

3   Τοιαῦτα τοῦ ἀνδρὸς τὰ ὑπὲρ ἱερῶν τε καὶ πόλεων,
καὶ τὰ πρὸς δήμους καὶ ὑπὲρ δήμων, καὶ τὰ ὑπὲρ
τεθνεώτων ἢ νοσούντων, καὶ τὰ πρὸς σοφούς τε καὶ μὴ
σοφούς, καὶ τὰ πρὸς βασιλέας, οἳ ξύμβουλον αὐτὸν
ἀρετῆς ἐποιοῦντο.

[51] ταὐτὰ Jac.: ταῦτα

trembling because it both desires and fears water. Bring it to me by the riverbank where the wrestling grounds are. Just say I sent for it."

When Damis had dragged the dog along, it lay at Apollonius's feet, weeping like a suppliant at an altar. After making it even tamer and stroking it with his hand, he made the youth stand beside him, while he himself held him. Then, so that the crowd should not miss a great miracle, he said, "The soul of Telephus the Mysian has migrated into this boy, and the Fates are planning the same treatment for him."[57] So saying, he told the dog to lick the bite, so that the boy's wounder should also be his healer. Immediately the boy turned to greet his father, recognized his mother, spoke to his friends, and took a drink from the Cydnus. Apollonius did not neglect the dog either, but after praying to the river told it to swim across. When it had crossed the Cydnus, it stood on the bank and let out a bark, which does not happen at all when dogs are rabid, and it bent back its ears and wagged its tail, realizing that it had been cured, since water is the remedy for rabies if the victim has the courage to drink it.

These are the Master's deeds on behalf of sanctuaries and cities, with regard to populaces and on their behalf, and on behalf of the dead and the sick, and with regard to the wise, the ignorant, and those emperors who made him their adviser on the subject of virtue.

2

3

---

[57] King of Mysia during the Trojan War. Wounded in combat with Achilles, he was promised by an oracle that "the wounder will heal," and was cured by the touch of Achilles's spear.

---

[52] βουλεύονται Headlam: βούλονται

Z´

1. Οἶδα καὶ τὰς τυραννίδας, ὡς ἔστιν ἀρίστη
βάσανος ἀνδρῶν φιλοσοφούντων, καὶ ξυγχωρῶ σκοπεῖν, ὅ τι ἕκαστος ἑτέρου ἧττον ἢ μᾶλλον ἀνὴρ ἔδοξεν, ὁ λόγος δέ μοι ξυντείνει ἐς τόδε· κατὰ τοὺς
χρόνους, οὓς Δομετιανὸς ἐτυράννευσε, περιέστησαν
τὸν ἄνδρα κατηγορίαι καὶ γραφαί, ὅπως μὲν ἀρ-
ξάμεναι καὶ ὁπόθεν καὶ ὅ τι ἑκάστῃ ὄνομα, δηλώσω
αὐτίκα, ἐπεὶ δὲ ἀνάγκη λέξαι, τί μὲν εἰπών, τίς δὲ εἶναι
δόξας ἀπῆλθε τῆς κρίσεως ἑλὼν μᾶλλον τὸν τύραννον
ἢ ἁλοὺς αὐτός, δοκεῖ μοι διελθεῖν πρὸ τούτων, ὁπόσα
εὗρον ἀφηγήσεως ἄξια σοφῶν ἀνδρῶν πρὸς τυράννους ἔργα, παραδεικνύειν τε αὐτὰ τοῖς Ἀπολλωνίου·
χρὴ γάρ που τἀληθὲς οὕτω μαστεύειν.

2. Ζήνων μὲν τοίνυν ὁ Ἐλεάτης, διαλεκτικῆς δὲ
οὗτος δοκεῖ ἄρξαι, τὴν Νεάρχου τοῦ Μυσοῦ καταλύων
τυραννίδα ἥλω, καὶ στρεβλωθεὶς τοὺς μὲν ἑαυτοῦ
ξυνωμότας ἀπεσιώπησεν, οἳ δ᾽ ἦσαν τῷ τυράννῳ βέ-
βαιοι, διαβαλὼν τούτους ὡς οὐ βεβαίους, οἱ μὲν ὡς
ἐπ᾽ ἀληθέσι ταῖς αἰτίαις ἀπέθανον, ὁ δ᾽ ἐλεύθερα

210

BOOK VII

1. I know that tyranny is the surest test of true philosophers, and I am prepared to ask in what respect any one philosopher has proved more or less heroic than another. The point of my remark is this. At the time of Domitian's tyranny, the Master was beset by accusations and indictments, and I will discuss later how they began, from what quarter, and their terms. But I am bound to record the words he spoke and the impression that he made, which brought it about that he left the court after condemning the tyrant rather than being condemned. I think, therefore, that before all this I must recount such noteworthy deeds as I have been able to find performed by truly wise men against tyrants, and compare them with those of Apollonius, because this is surely how we must arrive at the truth.

2. Zeno of Elea, who is the reputed founder of dialectic, was caught trying to overthrow the tyranny of Nearchus the Mysian,[1] and under torture withheld the names of his fellow conspirators, but accused the tyrant's loyal supporters of being disloyal. These were therefore put to death as if the charges were true, while Zeno led Mysia into free-

---

[1] Philosopher of the early fifth century, originator of the famous paradoxes. Mysia is the region around Pergamum in Asia.

τὰ Μυσῶν ἤγαγε τὴν τυραννίδα περὶ ἑαυτῇ σφήλας. Πλάτων δὲ ὑπὲρ τῆς Σικελιωτῶν ἐλευθερίας ἀγω-
νά φησιν ἄρασθαι, συλλαβὼν τῆς διανοίας ταύτης
Δίωνι.

2   Φύτων δὲ Ῥηγίου ἐκπεσὼν κατέφυγε μὲν ἐπὶ Διονύσιον τὸν Σικελίας τύραννον, μειζόνων δὲ ἀξιωθεὶς ἢ
τὸν φεύγοντα[1] εἰκὸς ξυνῆκε μὲν τοῦ τυράννου καὶ ὅτι
τοῦ Ῥηγίου ἐρῴη, Ῥηγίνοις δ᾽ ἐπιστέλλων ταῦτα ἥλω,
καὶ ὁ μὲν τύραννος ἑνὸς τῶν μηχανημάτων ἀνάψας
αὐτὸν ζῶντα προσήγαγε τοῖς τείχεσιν, ὡς μὴ βάλοιεν
οἱ Ῥηγῖνοι τὸ μηχάνημα φειδοῖ τοῦ Φύτωνος, ὁ δὲ
ἐβόα βάλλειν, σκοπὸς γὰρ αὐτοῖς ἐλευθερίας εἶναι.
Ἡρακλείδης δὲ καὶ Πύθων οἱ Κότυν ἀποκτείναντες
τὸν Θρᾷκα Αἰνίῳ[2] μὲν ἤστην ἄμφω, τὰς δὲ Ἀκαδη-
μίους διατριβὰς ἐπαινοῦντες σοφώ τε ἐγενέσθην καὶ
οὕτως ἐλευθέρω. τὰ δὲ Καλλισθένους τοῦ Ὀλυνθίου
τίς οὐκ οἶδεν; ὃς ἐπὶ τῆς αὐτῆς ἡμέρας ἐπαινέσας τε
καὶ διαβαλὼν Μακεδόνας, ὅτε μέγιστοι δυνάμει ἦσαν,
ἀπέθανεν ἀηδὴς δόξας.

3   Διογένης δὲ ὁ Σινωπεὺς καὶ Κράτης ὁ Θηβαῖος ὁ
μὲν εὐθὺ Χαιρωνείας ἥκων ἐπέπληξεν ὑπὲρ Ἀθηναίων
Φιλίππῳ περὶ ὧν Ἡρακλείδης εἶναι φάσκων ἀπώλλυ
ὅπλοις τοὺς ὑπὲρ ἐκείνων ὅπλα ἠρμένους, ὁ δ᾽ ἀνοικι-
εῖν Θήβας Ἀλεξάνδρου δι᾽ αὐτὸν φήσαντος οὐκ ἂν

[1] φεύγοντα Cob.: φυγόντα
[2] Αἰνίῳ Paris. 1696 (ut coni. Valck.): ἀνίω

dom by making the tyranny stumble over itself. As for Plato, he claims to have undertaken the struggle to free Sicily by taking Dion as his partner in the plan.[2]

Phyton was expelled from Rhegium, but fled to Diony- 2 sius the tyrant of Sicily.[3] Receiving higher consideration than might be expected for an exile, he grasped the king's motive, his desire for Rhegium, and was convicted for writing to the Rhegians about it. The tyrant had him tied still alive to one of the siege engines and brought it up to the walls, expecting that the Rhegians would not fire at the machine in order to spare Phyton. He, however, shouted to them to fire, saying that he was the target of their freedom. Heraclides and Python, who killed Cotys the Thracian, were from Aenos, but admired the teachings of the Academy and thus became first wise and then free.[4] Who does not know the story of Callisthenes of Olynthus?[5] In one and the same day he both praised and rebuked the Macedonians when they were at the height of their power, and his tactless behavior caused his death.

As for Diogenes of Sinope and Crates of Thebes, Diog- 3 enes went straight to Chaeronea and reproached Philip on the Athenians' behalf, saying that Philip claimed to be descended from Heracles, and yet his arms were destroying the people who took up arms to defend the children of Heracles. Crates, when Alexander promised to rebuild

[2] Plato encouraged his pupil Dion, the brother-in-law of Dionysius II of Syracuse, in a futile attempt to reform the kingdom.
[3] Rhegium is the modern Reggio Calabria, taken by Dionysius I of Sicily in 387.   [4] Pupils of Plato who assassinated the king of the Odrysian Thracians in 360/59.   [5] Nephew of Aristotle, executed by Alexander of Macedon in 327.

APOLLONIUS OF TYANA

ἔφη δεηθῆναι πατρίδος, ἣν κατασκάψει τις ὅπλοις
ἰσχύσας. καὶ λέγοιτο μὲν πολλὰ τοιαῦτα, ὁ λόγος δὲ
οὐ ξυγχωρεῖ μῆκος τῷ γε ἀνάγκην ἔχοντι καὶ πρὸς
ταῦτα ἀντειπεῖν οὐχ ὡς οὐ καλὰ ἢ οὐκ ἐν λόγῳ πᾶσιν,
ἀλλ' ὡς ἥττω τῶν Ἀπολλωνίου, κἂν ἄριστα ἑτέρων
φαίνηται.

3. Τὸ μὲν τοίνυν τοῦ Ἐλεάτου ἔργον καὶ οἱ τὸν
Κότυν ἀπεκτονότες οὔπω ἀξιόλογα, Θρᾷκας γὰρ καὶ
Γέτας δουλοῦσθαι μὲν ῥᾴδιον, ἐλευθεροῦν δὲ εὔηθες,
οὐδὲ γὰρ τῇ ἐλευθερίᾳ χαίρουσιν, ἅτε, οἶμαι, οὐκ
αἰσχρὸν ἡγούμενοι τὸ δουλεύειν. Πλάτων δὲ ὡς μὲν οὐ
σοφόν τι ἔπαθε τὰ ἐν Σικελίᾳ διορθούμενος μᾶλλον ἢ
τὰ Ἀθήνησιν, ἢ ὡς εἰκότως ἐπράθη σφαλείς τε καὶ
σφήλας, οὐ λέγω διὰ τοὺς δυσχερῶς ἀκροωμένους. τὰ
δὲ τοῦ Ῥηγίνου πρὸς Διονύσιον μὲν ἐτολμᾶτο τυραν-
νεύοντα οὐ βεβαίως Σικελίας, ὁ δ' ὑπ' ἐκείνου πάντως
ἀποθανὼν ἄν, εἰ καὶ μὴ ὑπὸ Ῥηγίνων ἐβλήθη, θαυμαστόν, οἶμαι, οὐδὲν ἔπραττε τὸν ὑπὲρ τῆς ἑτέρων ἐλευθερίας θάνατον μᾶλλον ἢ τὸν ὑπὲρ τῆς αὑτοῦ δουλείας
αἱρούμενος.

2   Καλλισθένης δὲ τὸ δόξαι κακὸς οὐδ' ἂν νῦν διαφύγοι, τοὺς γὰρ αὐτοὺς ἐπαινέσας καὶ διαβαλὼν ἢ
διέβαλεν, οὓς ἐνόμισεν ἐπαίνων ἀξίους, ἢ ἐπήνεσεν,
οὓς ἐχρῆν διαβάλλοντα φαίνεσθαι, καὶ ἄλλως ὁ μὲν
καθιστάμενος ἐς τὸ λοιδορεῖσθαι τοῖς ἀγαθοῖς ἀνδράσιν οὐκ ἔχει ἀποδρᾶναι τὸ μὴ οὐ δόξαι βάσκανος,

Thebes for his sake, said that he did not need a city that could be razed by force of arms.[6] Indeed many such instances could be given, but my work does not allow me to run on when I am obliged to refute even these ones. Not that they are not honorable or generally famous, but they fall short of Apollonius's deeds, even if they surpass those of everyone else.

3. The deed of the man from Elea and the murder of Cotys are not particularly noteworthy, since it is easy to enslave the Thracians and Goths, and pointless to free them. They do not enjoy liberty, I suppose from not considering servitude a disgrace. If Plato showed something less than wisdom in trying to correct affairs in Sicily rather than at Athens, or if he deserved to be sold because he had both caused and suffered a downfall, I will not say so because of the annoyance that would cause to some readers. The man from Rhegium only dared act when Dionysius's tyranny over Sicily was no longer secure. Moreover, since he would in any case have died at Dionysius's hands if he had not been a target for the citizens of Rhegium, he did not do anything very wonderful, in my opinion, in choosing death to make other men free rather than death to make himself a slave.

Callisthenes cannot escape the imputation of coward-   2 ice even now, since by both praising and criticizing the same people he either criticized those he thought worthy of praise, or praised those he should have openly blamed. Besides, someone who sets about abusing those who are truly virtuous cannot escape the imputation of malice,

[6] Diogenes and Crates: early Cynics. Philip of Macedon defeated the Greeks at Chaeronea in 338, and Alexander destroyed Thebes in 335.

ὁ δὲ τοὺς πονηροὺς κολακεύων ἐπαίνοις αὐτὸς ἀποίσεται τὴν αἰτίαν τῶν ἁμαρτηθέντων σφίσιν, οἱ γὰρ κακοὶ κακίους ἐπαινούμενοι. Διογένης δὲ πρὸ Χαιρωνείας μὲν εἰπὼν ταῦτα πρὸς τὸν Φίλιππον κἂν ἐφύλαξε τὸν ἄνδρα καθαρὸν τῶν ἐπ' Ἀθηναίους ὅπλων, εἰργασμένοις δ' ἐπιστὰς ὠνείδιζε μέν, οὐ μὴν διωρθοῦτο. Κράτης δὲ καὶ αἰτίαν ἂν λάβοι πρὸς ἀνδρὸς φιλοπόλιδος μὴ ξυναράμενος Ἀλεξάνδρῳ τῆς βουλῆς, ᾗ ἐς τὸ ἀνοικίσαι τὰς Θήβας ἐχρῆτο.

3   Ἀπολλώνιος δὲ οὔθ' ὑπὲρ πατρίδος κινδυνευούσης δείσας, οὔτε τοῦ σώματος ἀπογνούς, οὔτ' ἐς ἀνοήτους ὑπαχθεὶς λόγους, οὔθ' ὑπὲρ Μυσῶν ἢ Γετῶν, οὔτε πρὸς ἄνδρα ὃς ἦρχε νήσου μιᾶς ἢ χώρας οὐ μεγάλης, ἀλλ' ὑφ' ᾧ θάλαττά τε ἦν καὶ γῆ πᾶσα, πρὸς τοῦτον, ἐπειδὴ πικρῶς ἐτυράννευε, παρέταττεν ἑαυτὸν ὑπὲρ τοῦ τῶν ἀρχομένων κέρδους, χρησάμενος μὲν τῇ διανοίᾳ ταύτῃ καὶ πρὸς Νέρωνα,

4. Ἡγείσθω δ' οὖν τις ἀκροβολισμοὺς ἐκεῖνα, ἐπεὶ μὴ ὁμόσε χωρῶν, ἀλλὰ τὸν Βίνδικα ἐπιρρωννὺς καὶ τὸν Τιγελλῖνον ἐκπλήττων σαθροτέραν τὴν τυραννίδα ἐποίει, καί τις ἀναφύεται λόγος ἀλαζὼν ἐνταῦθα, ὡς οὐδὲν γενναῖον ἐπιθέσθαι Νέρωνι ψαλτρίας τινὸς ἢ αὐλητρίδος βίον ζῶντι. ἀλλὰ περί γε Δομετιανοῦ τί φήσουσιν; ὃς τὸ μὲν σῶμα ἔρρωτο, ἡδονὰς δὲ τὰς μὲν ἐξ ὀργάνων τε καὶ κτύπων τὰς τὸ θυμοειδὲς ἀπομαραινούσας παρῃτεῖτο, τὰ δὲ ἑτέρων ἄχη καὶ ὅ τι ὀλοφύραιτό τις, ἐς τὸ εὐφραῖνον εἷλκε, τὴν δ' ἀπιστίαν δήμων μὲν ἐκάλει πρὸς τοὺς τυράννους φυλακτήριον,

and someone who flatters the wicked with praise shares the responsibility for their crimes, since praise makes bad people worse. If Diogenes had said what he did to Philip before Chaeronea, he might have kept that hero guiltless of taking up arms against Athens, but by arriving only after the event he merely insulted him without any salutary effect. Crates could even be blamed by a patriot for not encouraging Alexander in the plan he was entertaining for the reconstruction of Thebes.

Apollonius, however, did not tremble because of danger to his native city, nor despair of his life, nor resort to foolish speeches. It was not for the sake of Mysians or Goths, or against the ruler of one island or a small country, but against the lord of the whole earth and sea, when the tyranny had become harsh, that he took his stand for the benefit of its victims, having shown the same intention against Nero too. 3

4. That indeed one might think a mere skirmish, since it was not in close combat, but by encouragement. In this connection, the impudent idea has grown up that attacking Nero required no courage, because he lived the life of a woman harp- or pipe-player. But what will people say about Domitian? He was physically strong. He despised the pleasures which undermine the active mind by musical instruments and percussion, and made the pains of others and people's groans into a source of pleasure. He called mistrust the safeguard of cities against tyrants and of ty-

τυράννων δὲ πρὸς πάντας, τὴν δὲ νύκτα πάντων μὲν
ἔργων ἠξίου παύειν βασιλέα, φόνων δὲ ἄρχειν.

2   Ὅθεν ἠκρωτηριάσθη μὲν ἡ βουλὴ τοὺς εὐδοκιμω-
τάτους, φιλοσοφία δὲ οὕτω τι ἔπτηξεν, ὡς ἀποβαλόντες τὸ σχῆμα οἱ μὲν ἀποδρᾶναι σφῶν ἐς τὴν Κελτῶν
ἑσπέραν, οἱ δὲ ἐς τὰ ἔρημα Λιβύης τε καὶ Σκυθίας,
ἔνιοι δ' ἐς λόγους ἀπενεχθῆναι ξυμβούλους τῶν ἁμαρ-
τημάτων. ὁ δ', ὥσπερ τῷ Σοφοκλεῖ πεποίηται πρὸς τὸν
Οἰδίπουν ὁ Τειρεσίας ὑπὲρ ἑαυτοῦ λέγων "οὐ γάρ τι
σοὶ ζῶ δοῦλος, ἀλλὰ Λοξίᾳ," οὕτω τὴν σοφίαν δέσποι-
ναν πεποιημένος ἐλεύθερος ἦν τῆς Δομετιανοῦ φορᾶς,
τὰ Τειρεσίου τε καὶ Σοφοκλέους ἑαυτῷ ἐπιθεσπίσας,
καὶ δεδιὼς μὲν οὐδὲν ἴδιον, ἃ δὲ ἑτέρους ἀπώλλυ
ἐλεῶν.

3   Ὅθεν ξυνίστη ἐπ' αὐτὸν νεότητά τε, ὁπόσην ἡ
βουλὴ εἶχε, καὶ ξύνεσιν, ὁπόση περὶ ἐνίους αὐτῶν
ἑωρᾶτο, φοιτῶν ἐς τὰ ἔθνη καὶ φιλοσοφῶν πρὸς τοὺς
ἡγεμόνας, ὡς οὔτε ἀθάνατος ἡ τῶν τυράννων ἰσχὺς
αὐτῷ τε τῷ φοβεροὶ δοκεῖν ἁλίσκονται μᾶλλον. διῄει
δὲ αὐτοῖς καὶ τὰ Παναθήναια τὰ Ἀττικά, ἐφ' οἷς
Ἁρμόδιός τε καὶ Ἀριστογείτων ᾄδονται, καὶ τὸ ἀπὸ
Φυλῆς ἔργον, ὃ καὶ τριάκοντα ὁμοῦ τυράννους εἷλε,
καὶ τὰ Ῥωμαίων δὲ αὐτῶν διῄει πάτρια, ὡς κἀκεῖνοι
δῆμος τὸ ἀρχαῖον ὄντες τὰς τυραννίδας ἐώθουν ὅπλοις.

5. Τραγῳδίας δὲ ὑποκριτοῦ παρελθόντος ἐς τὴν

rants against everybody. He considered that night should make a ruler end all his work and start all his murder.

The senate was thus shorn of its most eminent mem- 2 bers, philosophy was so cowed that its followers forgot their dignities and fled either to the Celts of the west or to the deserts of Libya and Scythia, while a few were induced to give speeches in support of the emperor's crimes.[7] But just as Sophocles represents Tiresias defending himself before Oedipus with the words, "I live not in your service, but Apollo's,"[8] so also Apollonius, who had put himself in the service of wisdom, was safe from Domitian's fury. He took the words of Tiresias and Sophocles as a motto for himself, so that he had no fear on his own behalf, but could pity the ruin of others.

Thus he turned against Domitian such younger men as 3 the senate contained, and such intelligence as he observed in certain of its members. He visited the provinces and demonstrated to the governors that the power of tyrants was not everlasting, and that they were overthrown precisely because they seemed to be terrifying. He recounted to them also how the Attic Panathenaea made celebrities of Harmodius and Aristogeiton, and how the expedition from Phyle overthrew thirty tyrants all at once,[9] and moreover recounted the ancient history of the Romans, and how they were originally a democracy after expelling their tyrannies by force of arms.

5. A tragic actor visited Ephesus to appear in the play

[7] Apparently referring to Domitians's "reign of terror" from 93 to 96.   [8] Sophocles, *Oedipus the King* 410.

[9] Harmodius and Aristogeiton: see V 34.3. Phyle: base from which democrats overthrew the pro-Spartan "Thirty" in 403.

Ἔφεσον ἐπὶ τῇ Ἰνοῖ τῷ δράματι καὶ ἀκροωμένου
τοῦ τῆς Ἀσίας ἄρχοντος, ὃς καίτοι νέος ὢν φανερὸς
ἐν ὑπάτοις ἀτολμότερον ὑπὲρ τούτων διενοεῖτο, ὁ
μὲν ὑποκριτὴς ἐπέραινεν ἤδη τὰ ἰαμβεῖα, ἐν οἷς ὁ
Εὐριπίδης διὰ μακρῶν αὐξηθέντας τοὺς τυράννους
ἁλίσκεσθαί φησιν ὑπὸ μικρῶν, ἀναπηδήσας δὲ ὁ
Ἀπολλώνιος "ἀλλ' ὁ δειλὸς" ἔφη "οὗτος οὔτε Εὐριπίδου ξυνίησιν οὔτε ἐμοῦ."

6. Καὶ μὴν καὶ λόγου ἀφικομένου, ὡς λαμπρὰν
κάθαρσιν εἴη Δομετιανὸς πεποιημένος τῆς Ῥωμαίων
Ἑστίας, ἐπειδὴ τρεῖς τῶν Ἑστιάδων ἀπέκτεινεν ἐπ'
αἰτίᾳ τῆς ζώνης καὶ τῷ μὴ καθαρεῦσαι γάμων, ἃς
ἁγνῶς τὴν Ἰλιάδα Ἀθηνᾶν καὶ τὸ ἐκεῖ πῦρ θεραπεύειν
ἔδει, "εἰ γὰρ καὶ σὺ" ἔφη "καθαρθείης, Ἥλιε, τῶν
ἀδίκων φόνων, ὧν πᾶσα ἡ οἰκουμένη μεστὴ νῦν." καὶ
οὐδὲ ἰδίᾳ ταῦτα, ὥσπερ οἱ δειλοί, ἀλλ' ἐν τῷ ὁμίλῳ καὶ
ἐς πάντας ἐκήρυττέ τε καὶ ηὔχετο.

7. Ἐπεὶ δὲ Σαβῖνον ἀπεκτονὼς ἕνα τῶν ἑαυτοῦ
ξυγγενῶν Ἰουλίαν ἤγετο (ἡ δὲ Ἰουλία γυνὴ μὲν ἦν τοῦ
πεφονευμένου, Δομετιανοῦ δὲ ἀδελφιδῆ, μία τῶν Τίτου
θυγατέρων), ἔθυε μὲν ἡ Ἔφεσος τοὺς γάμους, ἐπιστὰς
δὲ τοῖς ἱεροῖς ὁ Ἀπολλώνιος "ὦ νύξ" ἔφη "τῶν πάλαι
Δαναΐδων, ὡς μία ἦσθα."

8. Καὶ μὴν καὶ τὰ ἐν τῇ Ῥώμῃ ὧδε αὐτῷ ἐπράττετο.
ἀρχῇ πρέπειν ἐδόκει Νερούας, ἧς μετὰ Δομετιανὸν
σωφρόνως ἥψατο, ἦν δὲ καὶ περὶ Ὀρφιτόν τε καὶ
Ῥοῦφον ἡ αὐτὴ δόξα. τούτους Δομετιανὸς ἐπιβουλεύ-

Ino, and the governor of Asia was in the audience. Though young and a distinguished consular, he had rather a timid view of these subjects. The actor was just finishing the iambic lines in which Euripides says that tyrants whose power lasts long are overthrown by trifles,[10] when Apollonius jumped up and said, "But this coward understands neither Euripides nor me."

6. News came that Domitian had made a fine purification of the Roman Vesta. He killed three of the Vestal Virgins on a charge of unchastity and failure to refrain from sexual relations, when they were bound to be pure in serving Trojan Athena and her fire there.[11] "If only you too," said Apollonius, "could be purified, Sun, of the unjust murders with which the earth is now teeming." These things too he did not say privately as cowards do, but proclaimed and prayed for them in the crowd and before all.

7. Domitian had killed one of his kinsmen, Sabinus, and was planning to marry Julia, the wife of the murdered man and the niece of the emperor, being one of Titus's daughters. The Ephesians were sacrificing to celebrate the marriage when Apollonius appeared at the rites and said, "Night of the ancient Danaids, how unique you were."[12]

8. Furthermore, this is how he influenced events in Rome. Nerva was thought suitable for power, which he held with wisdom after Domitian, and the same belief prevailed about Orfitus and Rufus. Claiming that all three

---

10 Euripides, fr. 420 Nauck.

11 Cf. Suetonius, *Domitian* 8.4: the date is uncertain.

12 Flavius Sabinus, Domitian's cousin, was consul in 82. Domitian allegedly committed incest with Sabinus's wife Julia (Titus's only child), but they never married. All but one of Danaus's fifty daughters killed their husbands in a single night.

ειν ἑαυτῷ φήσας οἱ μὲν ἐς νήσους καθείρχθησαν,
Νερούᾳ δὲ προσέταξεν οἰκεῖν Τάραντα. ὧν δὲ ἐπιτήδειος αὐτοῖς ὁ Ἀπολλώνιος τὸν μὲν χρόνον, ὃν Τίτος
ὁμοῦ τῷ πατρὶ καὶ μετὰ τὸν πατέρα ἦρχεν, ἀεί τι
ὑπὲρ σωφροσύνης ἐπέστελλε τοῖς ἀνδράσι προσ-
ποιῶν αὐτοὺς τοῖς βασιλεῦσιν ὡς χρηστοῖς, Δομετιανοῦ δέ, ἐπεὶ χαλεπὸς ἦν, ἀφίστη τοὺς ἄνδρας καὶ ὑπὲρ
τῆς ἁπάντων ἐλευθερίας ἐρρώννυ.

2   Τὰς μὲν δὴ ἐπιστολιμαίους ξυμβουλίας οὐκ ἀσφα-
λεῖς αὐτοῖς ᾤετο, πολλοὺς γὰρ τῶν ἐν δυνάμει καὶ
δοῦλοι προύδοσαν καὶ φίλοι καὶ γυναῖκες καὶ οὐδὲν
ἀπόρρητον ἐχώρησε τότε οἰκία, τῶν δὲ αὐτοῦ ἑταίρων
τοὺς σωφρονεστάτους ἄλλοτε ἄλλον ἀπολαμβάνων
"διάκονον" εἶπεν ἂν "ποιοῦμαί σε ἀπορρήτου λαμ-
προῦ· βαδίσαι δὲ χρὴ ἐς τὴν Ῥώμην παρὰ τὸν δεῖνα
καὶ διαλεχθῆναί οἱ καὶ γενέσθαι πρὸς τὴν πειθὼ τοῦ
ἀνδρὸς πᾶν ὅ τι ἐγώ." ἐπεὶ δὲ ἤκουσεν, ὅτι φεύγοιεν
ὁρμῆς μὲν ἐνδειξάμενοί τι ἐπὶ τὸν τύραννον, ὅκνῳ δ᾽
ἐκπεσόντες ὧν διενοήθησαν, διελέγετο μὲν ὑπὲρ Μοιρῶν καὶ ἀνάγκης περὶ τὸ νέμος τῆς Σμύρνης, ἐν ᾧ ὁ
Μέλης,

       9. Εἰδὼς δὲ τὸν Νερούαν ὡς αὐτίκα δὴ ἄρξοι, διῄει
τὸν λόγον καὶ ὅτι μηδ᾽ οἱ τύραννοι τὰ ἐκ Μοιρῶν οἷοι
βιάζεσθαι, χαλκῆς τε εἰκόνος ἱδρυμένης Δομετιανοῦ
πρὸς τῷ Μέλητι, ἐπιστρέψας ἐς αὐτὴν τοὺς παρόντας
"ἀνόητε," εἶπεν "ὡς πολὺ διαμαρτάνεις Μοιρῶν καὶ

were plotting against him, Domitian had the last two confined to islands, while he ordered Nerva to live in Tarentum.[13] Apollonius had been their friend during the time when Titus ruled with his father and after him, and was in constant communication with them about moderation, ensuring their loyalty to those virtuous emperors. Domitian by contrast was harsh, so that Apollonius began to make these men disaffected, and to urge them on for the sake of the general freedom.

Advice sent by letter would not be safe for them, he thought, because many man of high station had been betrayed by their slaves, friends, and wives, and just then no house could keep a secret. So on different occasions, taking aside certain of his most temperate followers, he would say, "I am making you the bearer of a glorious secret. You must go to so-and-so in Rome, speak with him, and have as much influence to persuade him as I do." But when he heard that the three were in exile for showing some kind of energy against the tyrant, but had abandoned their plan out of timidity, he gave a discourse about the Fates and Necessity near the grove in Smyrna that is traversed by the Meles.[14]

9. Knowing that Nerva would be ruler very soon, in the course of his speech he was saying that not even tyrants can compel the decisions of the Fates. A bronze statue of Domitian had been erected by the Meles, and calling his listeners' attention to it, Apollonius said, "You fool, how

[13] Domitian is not known to have exiled Nerva (ruled 98–98), but he did exile and then execute (Salvidienus) Orfitus (Suetonius, *Domitian* 10. 2). If "Rufus" is the elder statesman Verginius Rufus, he survived until 97, but he too is not known to have been exiled.   [14] River of Smyrna.

Ἀνάγκης· ᾧ γὰρ μετὰ σὲ τυραννεῦσαι πέπρωται, τοῦτον κἂν ἀποκτείνῃς, ἀναβιώσεται."

2   Ταῦτα ἐς Δομετιανὸν ἀφίκετο ἐκ διαβολῶν Εὐφράτου, καὶ ὑπὲρ ὅτου μὲν τῶν ἀνδρῶν ἐχρησμῴδει
αὐτά, οὐδεὶς ξυνίει, τιθέμενος δὲ ὁ τύραννος εὖ τὸν
ἑαυτοῦ φόβον ὥρμησεν ἀποκτεῖναι τοὺς ἄνδρας. ὡς δὲ
μὴ ἔξω λόγου πράττων αὐτὸ φαίνοιτο, ἐκάλει τὸν
Ἀπολλώνιον ἀπολογησόμενον ὑπὲρ τῶν πρὸς αὐτοὺς
ἀπορρήτων· ἢ γὰρ ἀφικομένου καταψηφισάμενος οὐδὲ
ἀκρίτους ἀπεκτονέναι δόξειν, ἀλλ᾽ ἐν ἐκείνῳ ἑαλωκό-
τας, ἢ εἰ σοφίᾳ τινὶ τοῦ φανεροῦ ὑπεξέλθοι, μᾶλλον
ἤδη ἀπολεῖσθαι σφᾶς ὡς κατεψηφισμένους καὶ ὑπὸ
τοῦ κοινωνοῦ τῆς αἰτίας.

10. Διανοουμένου δὲ αὐτοῦ ταῦτα, καὶ γράφοντος
ἤδη πρὸς τὸν τῆς Ἀσίας ἄρχοντα, ὡς ξυλληφθείη τε
καὶ ἀναχθείη, προεῖδε μὲν ὁ Τυανεὺς πάντα δαιμονίως
τε καὶ ὥσπερ εἰώθει. πρὸς δὲ τοὺς ἑταίρους εἰπὼν
δεῖσθαι ἀποδημίας ἀπορρήτου, τοὺς μὲν ἐσῆλθεν
Ἀβάριδος τοῦ ἀρχαίου δόξα, καὶ ὅτι ἐς τοιόνδε τι
ὡρμήκοι,[3] ὁ δὲ οὐδὲ τῷ Δάμιδι τὸν ἑαυτοῦ νοῦν ἐκφή-
νας ἐς Ἀχαιοὺς ξὺν αὐτῷ ἔπλει, Κορίνθου δὲ ἐπιβὰς
καὶ τῷ Ἡλίῳ περὶ μεσημβρίαν ὁπόσα εἰώθει δράσας,
ἀφῆκεν ἐς τὸ Σικελῶν καὶ Ἰταλῶν ἔθνος ἅμα ἑσπέρᾳ.
τυχὼν δὲ οὐρίου πνεύματος καί τινος εὐροίας ὑπο-
δραμούσης τὸ πέλαγος ἀφίκετο ἐς Δικαιαρχίαν πεμ-
πταῖος.

3 ὡρμήκοι Kay.: ὡρμήκει

wrong you are about the Fates and Necessity, for even if you kill the man destined to rule after you, he will live again."

These words came to the ears of Domitian through the slanders of Euphrates, and though no one could tell which of the three heroes Apollonius was predicting, the tyrant tried to calm his own fears by having them killed. So that he would not appear to have no excuse for doing so, he summoned Apollonius to explain his secret communication with them. Either he would condemn Apollonius on his arrival, and so not seem to have executed them all without trial, since he and they would be found guilty by proxy; or if Apollonius by some craft avoided appearing in public, they would perish all the more certainly, having been convicted by their partner in crime.

10. While Domitian was planning this, and was writing a letter to the governor of Asia for the arrest and the summons of Apollonius, the man of Tyana anticipated it all with his usual miraculous foresight. He told his disciples that he needed to make a secret journey, which put them in mind of the reputation of the ancient Abaris,[15] as if Apollonius had a similar plan. Without even revealing his own intention to Damis, he sailed with him to Achaea, and disembarked at Corinth. After performing his usual rites in honor of the sun, he set sail for Sicily and Italy about evening. Blessed by a following wind and a kind of favoring current beneath the sea, he reached Dicaearchia in four days.

[15] A legendary figure who was believed to ride though the air on an arrow.

2   Δημητρίῳ δὲ ἐντυχών, ὃς ἐδόκει θαρσαλεώτατος
τῶν φιλοσόφων, ἐπεὶ μὴ πολὺ ἀπὸ τῆς Ῥώμης διῃτᾶτο, ξυνίει μὲν αὐτοῦ ἐξεστηκότος τῷ τυράννῳ, δια-
τριβῆς δὲ ἕνεκα "εἴληφά σε" εἶπε "τρυφῶντα καὶ τῆς
εὐδαίμονος Ἰταλίας, εἰ δὴ εὐδαίμων, τὸ μακαριώτατον
οἰκοῦντα, ἐν ᾧ λέγεται καὶ Ὀδυσσεὺς Καλυψοῖ ξυνὼν
ἐκλαθέσθαι καπνοῦ Ἰθακησίου καὶ οἴκου." περιβαλὼν
δ᾽ αὐτὸν ὁ Δημήτριος καί τι καὶ ἐπευφημήσας, "ὦ
θεοί," ἔφη "τί πείσεται φιλοσοφία κινδυνεύουσα περὶ
ἀνδρὶ τοιούτῳ;" "κινδυνεύει δὲ" εἶπε "τί;" "ἅ γε," ἔφη
"προειδὼς ἥκεις· εἰ γὰρ τὸν σὸν ἀγνοῶ νοῦν, οὐδὲ τὸν
ἐμαυτοῦ οἶδα. διαλεγώμεθα δὲ μὴ ἐνταῦθα, ἀλλ᾽ ἴωμεν
οὗ μόνων ἡμῶν ἡ ξυνουσία ἔσται, παρατυγχανέτω δὲ
καὶ ὁ Δάμις, ὃν ἐγώ, νὴ τὸν Ἡρακλέα, Ἰόλεων ἡγοῦμαι τῶν σῶν ἄθλων."

11. Ἄγει δὲ αὐτοὺς εἰπὼν ταῦτα ἐς τὸ Κικέρωνος
τοῦ παλαιοῦ χωρίον, ἔστι δὲ τοῦτο πρὸς τῷ ἄστει.
ἱζησάντων δὲ ὑπὸ πλατάνῳ οἱ μὲν τέττιγες ὑποψαλ-
λούσης αὐτοὺς τῆς αὔρας[4] ἐν ᾠδαῖς ἦσαν, ἀναβλέψας
δὲ ἐς αὐτοὺς ὁ Δημήτριος "ὦ μακάριοι" ἔφη "καὶ
ἀτεχνῶς σοφοί, ὡς ἐδίδαξάν τε ὑμᾶς ᾠδὴν ἄρα Μοῦ-
σαι μήπω ἐς δίκας ἢ διαβολὰς ὑπαχθεῖσαν, γαστρός
τε κρείττους ἐποίησαν καὶ ἀνῴκισαν τοῦ ἀνθρωπείου
φθόνου ἐς ταυτὶ τὰ δένδρα, ἐφ᾽ ὧν ὄλβιοι τὴν ἐφ᾽ ὑμῶν
τε καὶ Μουσῶν εὐδαιμονίαν ᾄδετε."

---

[4] αὔρας Valck.: ὥρας

He met Demetrius, who was thought to be the boldest   2
of the philosophers, and was staying not far from Rome.
He knew that he had retreated before the tyrant, but for
the sake of conversation he said, "I have found you living
luxuriously and inhabiting the richest region of rich Italy, if
it is blessed. Here they say Odysseus lived with Calypso,[16]
and forgot the smoke of Ithaca and his home." Embracing
him, and calling a kind of blessing on him, "O Gods," said
Demetrius, "what will happen to Philosophy when she is in
danger because of such a man as this?" "And what danger is
that?" asked Apollonius. "What you anticipated in coming
here," said Demetrius, "since I know your intention as
well as my own. Let us not converse here, however, but
find a place where our conversation will be all ours, though
Damis too may join us, since, by Heracles, I consider him
the Iolaos of your labors."[17]

11. So saying he led them to the estate belonging to
the Cicero of long ago, which is situated near the town.[18]
As they sat under a plane tree, the cicadas were singing
away, softly accompanied by the breeze, and looking up
at them Demetrius said, "You blessed, truly wise creatures, it seems the Muses taught you a song not subject to
lawsuits or accusations. They made you superior to greed,
and settled you far away from human envy in these trees
here, where you blissfully sing of your happiness and the
Muses'."

---

[16] Calypso's isle was sometimes placed off the coast of Cam-
pania.   [17] Iolaos assisted Heracles in his twelve Labors.

[18] Inherited by Cicero in 45 from a rich client, and later owned
by the emperor Hadrian, who was buried there (*Historia Augusta*
25.7).

APOLLONIUS OF TYANA

2   Ὁ δὲ Ἀπολλώνιος ξυνίει μέν, οἷ τείνει ταῦτα, διαβαλὼν δ' αὐτὰ ὡς ἀργότερα τῆς ἐπαγγελίας, "εἶτα"
εἶπε "τεττίγων βουληθεὶς διελθεῖν ἔπαινον οὐκ ἐς τὸ
φανερὸν διήεις αὐτόν, ἀλλ' ἐνταῦθα πτήξας, ὥσπερ
δημοσίᾳ κειμένου νόμου μηδένα ἐπαινεῖν τέττιγας;"
"οὐχ ὑπὲρ ἐπαίνου" ἔφη "ταῦτα εἶπον, ἀλλ' ἐνδεικνύμενος, ὅτι τούτοις μὲν ἀνεῖται τὰ αὐτῶν μουσεῖα, ἡμῖν
δὲ οὐδὲ γρύξαι συγγνώμη, ἀλλ' ἔγκλημα ἡ σοφία
εὕρηται, καὶ ἡ μὲν Ἀνύτου καὶ Μελήτου γραφὴ 'Σωκράτης' φησὶν 'ἀδικεῖ διαφθείρων τοὺς νέους καὶ δαιμόνια καινὰ ἐπεσάγων,' ἡμᾶς δὲ οὑτωσὶ γράφονται·
'ἀδικεῖ ὁ δεῖνα σοφὸς ὢν καὶ δίκαιος, καὶ ξυνιεὶς μὲν
θεῶν, ξυνιεὶς δὲ ἀνθρώπων, νόμων τε πέρι πολλὰ
εἰδώς.' σὺ δ', ὅσῳπερ ἡμῶν σοφώτατος, τοσούτῳ σοφωτέρα κατηγορία ἐπὶ σὲ εὕρηται· βούλεται γάρ σε
Δομετιανὸς μετέχειν τῶν ἐγκλημάτων, ἐφ' οἷς Νερούας τε καὶ οἱ ξὺν αὐτῷ φεύγουσι."

3   "Φεύγουσι δ'" ἦ δ' ὃς "ἐπὶ τῷ;" "ἐπὶ τῇ μεγίστῃ γε"
ἔφη "τῶν νῦν αἰτιῶν, ὡς δοκεῖ τῷ διώκοντι· φησὶ γὰρ
αὐτοὺς ἐπὶ τὴν ἀρχὴν τὴν αὐτοῦ πηδῶντας ἡρηκέναι,
σὲ δὲ ἐξορμῆσαι τοὺς ἄνδρας ἐς ταῦτα παῖδα, οἶμαι,
τεμόντα." "μῶν" ἔφη "ὡς ὑπ' εὐνούχου ἡ ἀρχὴ κατα-
λυθείη;" "οὐ τοῦτο" ἔφη "συκοφαντούμεθα, φασὶ δ',
ὡς παῖδα θύσαις ὑπὲρ μαντικῆς, ἣν τὰ νεαρὰ τῶν
σπλάγχνων φαίνει, πρόσκειται δὲ τῇ γραφῇ καὶ περὶ
ἀμπεχόνης καὶ διαίτης, καὶ τὸ ἔστιν ὑφ' ὧν προσκυνεῖσθαί σε. ταυτὶ γὰρ Τελεσίνου ἤκουον ἀνδρὸς
ἐμοί τε καὶ σοὶ ἐπιτηδείου."

228

Though realizing where this was tending, Apollonius 2
disapproved of it as more timid than the promise had suggested, and said, "So you wanted to recite an encomium of
crickets, but did not recite it openly, but do so cowering
here, as if there was a public law forbidding encomia of
crickets?" "I did not mean this as an encomium," said
Demetrius, "but as an illustration of the fact that these
are permitted their own concert halls, but we are not
allowed to make a sound, since wisdom has been turned
into an offense. The indictment of Anytos and Meletos
says, 'Socrates is guilty of corrupting the young and importing new divinities,' but the indictments against us are
these: 'So-and-so is guilty of being wise and just, understanding gods and understanding men, and knowing much
about the laws.' As you are the most clever of us, accordingly a cleverer accusation has been devised against you,
and Domitian wants to associate you in the charges that
have caused Nerva and his associates to be exiled."

"What are they exiled for?" asked Apollonius. "For the 3
most serious accusation that there now is," was the reply,
"or so your prosecutor thinks. He says he has found them
plotting against his rule, and (so I hear) that you incited
those men to this act by butchering a boy." "Surely not so
that his rule should be overthrown by a eunuch?" said
Apollonius. "We are not accused of that," said Demetrius,
"but they say that you sacrificed a boy for the insight that
young entrails reveal, and another charge concerns your
clothing and diet, and your receiving obeisance from
certain people. So much I heard from Telesinus, a man
friendly both to you and to me."

4   "Ἕρμαιον," εἶπεν "εἰ Τελεσίνῳ ἐντευξόμεθα, λέγεις
γάρ που τὸν φιλόσοφον, ὃς ἐπὶ Νέρωνος ἐν ὑπάτοις
ἦρξεν;" "ἐκεῖνον μὲν οὖν" ἔφη "λέγω, ξυγγένοιο δ᾽ ἂν
αὐτῷ τίνα τρόπον; αἱ γὰρ τυραννίδες ὑποπτότεραι
πρὸς τοὺς ἐν ἀξίᾳ πάντας, ἢν ἐς κοινὸν ἴωσι λόγον
τοῖς ἐν οἵᾳ σὺ νῦν αἰτίᾳ, Τελεσῖνος δὲ καὶ τῷ κη-
ρύγματι ὑπεξῆλθεν, ὃ κεκήρυκται νῦν ἐς φιλοσοφίαν
πᾶσαν, ἀσπασάμενος μᾶλλον τὸ φεύγειν ὡς φιλόσοφος ἢ τὸ ὡς ὕπατος μένειν." "μὴ κινδυνευέτω" εἶπεν
"ὁ ἀνὴρ ἐμοῦγε ἕνεκα, ἱκανῶς γὰρ ὑπὲρ φιλοσοφίας
κινδυνεύει.

12. "Ἀλλ᾽ ἐκεῖνό μοι εἰπέ, Δημήτριε, τί δοκῶ σοι
λέγων ἢ τί πράττων εὖ θήσεσθαι τὸν ἐμαυτοῦ φόβον;"
"μὴ παίζων," ἔφη "μηδέ, ἃ <μὴ>[5] δέδιας, φοβεῖσθαι
λέγων, εἰ γὰρ φοβερὰ ἡγοῦ ταῦτα, κἂν ᾤχου ἀποδρὰς
τὸν ὑπὲρ αὐτῶν λόγον." "σὺ δ᾽ ἂν ἀπέδρας," εἶπεν "εἰ
περὶ ὧν ἐγὼ ἐκινδύνευες;" "οὐκ ἄν," ἔφη "μὰ τὴν
Ἀθηνᾶν, εἴ τις ἐδίκαζε, τὸ δ᾽ ἄνευ δίκης καὶ ὃ μηδ᾽,
εἰ ἀπολογοίμην, ἀκροασόμενος ἢ ἀκροασόμενος μέν,
ἀποκτενῶν δὲ καὶ μὴ ἀδικοῦντα. οὐκ ἂν ἔμοιγ᾽ οὖν
ξυνεχώρησας ἑλέσθαι ποτὲ ψυχρὸν οὕτω καὶ ἀνδρα-
ποδώδη θάνατον ἀντὶ τοῦ φιλοσοφίᾳ προσήκοντος.
φιλοσοφίᾳ δέ, οἶμαι, προσήκει ἢ πόλιν ἐλευθεροῦντα
ἀποθανεῖν, ἢ γονεῦσι τοῖς ἑαυτοῦ καὶ παισὶ καὶ ἀδελφοῖς καὶ τῇ ἄλλῃ ξυγγενείᾳ ἀμύνοντα, ἢ ὑπὲρ φίλων
ἀγωνιζόμενον, οἳ ξυγγενείας αἱρετώτεροι σοφοῖς ἀνδράσιν ἢ οἱ ἡμπολημένοι ἐξ ἔρωτος,

"We will be in luck," said Apollonius, "if we meet Tele-   4
sinus, since you must mean the philosopher who had the
office of consul in Nero's time."[19] "Yes, I mean him," said
the other, "but how might you meet him? Tyrants tend to
be suspicious of all those of high repute, if they enter into
conversation with people charged as you are now. And
Telesinus has yielded to the edict that has just been issued
against all philosophy, preferring to embrace exile as a
philosopher than to remain as a consular." "Let the man
run no risks for me," said Apollonius, "since he is risking
enough for philosophy."

12. "But tell me this, Demetrius: what do you think I
can say or do to calm my own fear?" "You should not make
fun," was the reply, "or say that you fear what you do not
fear, since if you did think the situation terrifying, you
would have run away, and shunned giving a speech in your
own defense." "And would you have run away," said Apollonius, "if you were in the danger that I am?" "Certainly
not, by Athena," said the other, "if there were a judge, but
here there is no justice, but someone who will not listen
even if I defend myself, or will listen but kill me even when
innocent.[20] You would not have permitted me to choose
such a pointless, servile death instead of a death befitting
a philosopher; and what befits a philosopher, in my opinion, is to die while liberating a city, defending your parents, children, brothers, and other kin, or fighting for your
friends, who are more precious to truly wise men than
their kin, or those they have acquired by the act of love.

---

[19] See IV 40.   [20] The Greek is uncertain.

---

[5] ‹μὴ› Ol.

APOLLONIUS OF TYANA

2   "Τὸ δὲ μὴ ἐπ' ἀληθέσι, κεκομψευμένοις δ' ἀποθανεῖν, καὶ παρασχεῖν τῷ τυράννῳ σοφῷ δόξαι, πολλῷ
βαρύτερον ἢ εἴ τις, ὥσπερ φασὶ τὸν Ἰξίονα, μετέωρος
ἐπὶ τροχοῦ κνάμπτοιτο. σοὶ δὲ ἀγῶνος οἶμαι ἄρξειν
αὐτὸ τὸ ἥκειν ἐνταῦθα, σὺ μὲν γὰρ τῷ τῆς γνώμης
ὑγιαίνοντι προστίθης τοῦτο, καὶ τῷ μὴ ἂν θαρρῆσαι
τὴν δεῦρο ὁδόν, εἴ τι ἠδίκεις, Δομετιανῷ δὲ οὐ δόξεις,
ἀλλ' ἀπόρρητόν τινα ἰσχὺν ἔχων θρασέως ἐρρῶσθαι.
τὸ γὰρ καλοῦντος μέν (οὔπω δ' ἡμέραι δέκα, ὥς φασι),
σὲ δ' ἀφῖχθαι πρὸς τὴν κρίσιν οὐδ' ἀκηκοότα πω, ὡς
κριθήσῃ, νοῦν τῇ κατηγορίᾳ δώσει, προγιγνώσκων
γὰρ ἂν φαίνοιο καὶ ὁ λόγος ὁ περὶ τοῦ παιδὸς ἰσχύσει. καὶ ὅρα, μὴ τὰ περὶ Μοιρῶν καὶ Ἀνάγκης, ὑπὲρ
ὧν ἐν Ἰωνίᾳ διειλέχθαι σέ φασιν, ἐπὶ σὲ ἥκῃ. καὶ
βουλομένης τι τῆς Εἱμαρμένης ἄτοπον, σὺ δ' ἠναγ-
κασμένος χωρῇς ἐπ' αὐτὸ οὐκ εἰδώς, ὡς σοφώτερον
ἀεὶ τὸ φυλάττεσθαι.

3   "Εἰ δὲ μὴ ἐκλέλησαι τῶν ἐπὶ Νέρωνος, οἶσθά που
τοὐμὸν καὶ ὅτι μὴ ἀνελεύθερος ἐγὼ πρὸς θάνατον.
ἀλλ' εἶχέ τι ῥᾳστώνης ἐκεῖνα· Νέρωνα γὰρ ἡ κιθάρα
τοῦ μὲν προσφόρου βασιλείᾳ σχήματος ἐδόκει ἐκ-
κρούειν, τὰ δὲ ἄλλα οὐκ ἀηδῶς ἥρμοττεν, ἦγε γάρ
τινας πολλάκις δι' αὐτὴν ἐκεχειρίας, καὶ ἀπείχετο τῶν
φόνων· ἐμὲ γοῦν οὐκ ἀπέκτεινε καίτοι τὸ ξίφος ἐπ'
ἐμαυτὸν ἕλκοντα διὰ τοὺς σούς τε κἀμοῦ λόγους, οὓς
ἐπὶ τῷ βαλανείῳ διῆλθον, αἴτιον δ' ἦν τοῦ μὴ ἀποκτεῖ-

"But to die not on true charges but trumped up ones,   2
and to allow a tyrant to appear prudent, is a much more
grievous fate than if one were to be racked on a wheel in
the sky, as they say Ixion is.[21] In your case, I think your very
arrival will begin your ordeal, since you ascribe it to your
purity of purpose, and to the fact that you would not have
ventured to come if you were at all guilty, but that is not
how you will seem to Domitian. He will think that some
mysterious power that you possess makes you rash and
strong. He summoned you less than ten days ago, so they
say, and yet you have come to trial even before having
heard how you will be tried, and all this will give color to
the accusation. You will appear to know the future, and the
rumor about the boy will prevail. And it may also happen
that the lectures which they say you gave in Ionia about the
Fates and Necessity may come to haunt you, and that Fate
has some dreadful plan, into which you are walking under
compulsion, ignoring the fact that caution is always the
more prudent course.

"If you have not forgotten what happened in Nero's   3
time, you must know my story, and that I am no coward
in the face of death. But in those days there was some relief. The lyre seemed to put Nero out of harmony with the
majesty befitting a king, but in other ways it kept him
pleasantly tuned, since it often led him to declare certain
truces on its account and to refrain from murder. Certainly
he did not kill me, though I had attracted his sword because of your doctrines and mine, which I expounded in
the matter of his bathhouse.[22] His reason for not killing me

[21] Cf. VI 40.2.
[22] Cf. IV 42.

ναι τὸ τὴν εὐφωνίαν αὐτῷ ἐπιδοῦναι τότε καὶ τό, ὡς
ᾤετο, μελῳδίας λαμπρᾶς ἅψασθαι.

4   "Νυνὶ δὲ τίνι μὲν εὐφωνίᾳ, τίνι δὲ κιθάρᾳ θύσομεν;
ἄμουσα γὰρ καὶ μεστὰ χολῆς πάντα, καὶ οὔτ᾽ ἂν ὑφ᾽
ἑαυτοῦ ὅδε οὔτ᾽ ἂν ὑφ᾽ ἑτέρων θελχθείη. καίτοι Πίν-
δαρος ἐπαινῶν τὴν λύραν φησίν, ὡς καὶ τὸν τοῦ
Ἄρεος θυμὸν θέλγει καὶ τῶν πολεμικῶν ἴσχει αὐτόν,
οὑτοσὶ δὲ καίτοι μουσικὴν ἀγωνίαν καταστησάμενος
ἐνταῦθα καὶ στεφανῶν δημοσίᾳ τοὺς νικῶντας ἔστιν
οὓς καὶ ἀπέκτεινεν αὐτῶν, ὕστατά φασι μουσικὴν
ἀγωνίαν αὐλήσαντάς τε καὶ ᾄσαντας. βουλευτέα δέ
σοι καὶ ὑπὲρ τῶν ἀνδρῶν, προσαπολεῖς γὰρ κἀκείνους
ἢ θρασὺς δόξας ἢ εἰπών, ἃ μὴ πείσεις.

5   "Ἡ σωτηρία δέ σοι παρὰ πόδα· τῶν γὰρ νεῶν
τούτων, πολλαὶ δ᾽, ὡς ὁρᾷς, εἰσίν, αἱ μὲν ἐς Λιβύην
ἀφήσουσιν, αἱ δ᾽ ἐς Αἴγυπτον, αἱ δ᾽ ἐς Φοινίκην καὶ
Κύπρον, αἱ δ᾽ εὐθὺ Σαρδοῦς, αἱ δ᾽ ὑπὲρ Σαρδώ. μιᾶς
ἐπιβάντι σοι κομίζεσθαι κράτιστον ἐς ὁτιδὴ τῶν
ἐθνῶν τούτων, αἱ γὰρ τυραννίδες ἧττον χαλεπαὶ τοῖς
φανεροῖς τῶν ἀνδρῶν, ἢν ἐπαινοῦντας αἴσθωνται τὸ
μὴ ἐν φανερῷ ζῆν."

13. Ἡττηθεὶς δ᾽ ὁ Δάμις τῶν τοῦ Δημητρίου λόγων,
"ἀλλὰ σύ γε" ἔφη "φίλος ἀνδρὶ παρὼν γένοιο ἂν
ἀγαθόν τι τούτῳ μέγα, ἐμοῦ γὰρ σμικρὸς λόγος, εἰ
ξυμβουλεύοιμι αὐτῷ μὴ κυβιστᾶν ἐς ὀρθὰ ξίφη, μηδ᾽
ἀναρριπτεῖν πρὸς τυραννίδα, ἧς οὐ χαλεπωτέρα ἐνομίσθη. τῆς γοῦν ὁδοῦ τῆς ἐνταῦθα, εἰ μή σοι ξυνέτυ-

was that his *bel canto* had recently improved, and he was about to be brilliantly melodious, so he thought.

"But now what *bel canto*, what lyre shall we sacrifice to? 4 Everything is unmusical and full of malice, and the present ruler can be soothed neither by himself nor by others, though Pindar praises the lyre by saying that it soothes even Ares's wrath, and restrains him from acts of war.[23] This ruler, by contrast, though he has instituted a musical contest here and publicly crowns the winners,[24] has nonetheless killed some of them, so that people say they played or sang their farewell concert. You must also think about those heroes,[25] since you will destroy them too by seeming rash, or by saying what will not be believed.

"Escape is at hand, since you see how many ships there 5 are here, some setting off for Africa, others for Egypt, or for Phoenicia and Cyprus, or straight for Sardinia, or beyond Sardinia. It is best for you to embark on one of them, and travel to any of those regions, for tyrants are less harsh on conspicuous men if they see them embracing life spent in obscurity."[26]

13. Overcome by Demetrius's arguments, Damis said, "Well, if you stand beside the Master as a friend, you will do him a great service, since I would be of little account if I were to advise him not to dance among bare swords, or to gamble against a tyranny that is considered the harshest of all time. As for his purpose in coming here, I would not have learned of it had I not met you. Though I follow him

[23] Pindar, *Pythian* 1.10–13.

[24] In 86, Domitian founded a contest called the Capitolia, over which he himself presided.   [25] See 8.1.

[26] "Live unobserved" was a precept of Epicurus.

χον, οὐδὲ τὸν νοῦν ἐγίγνωσκον, ἕπομαι μὲν γὰρ αὐτῷ
θᾶττον ἢ ἑαυτῷ τις, εἰ δὲ ἔροιό με, ποῖ πλέω ἢ ἐφ' ὅ τι,
καταγέλαστος ἐγὼ τοῦ πλοῦ Σικελικὰ μὲν πελάγη καὶ
Τυρρηνοὺς κόλπους ἀναμετρῶν, οὐκ εἰδὼς δέ, ὑπὲρ
ὅτου. καὶ εἰ μὲν ἐκ προρρήσεως ἐκινδύνευον, εἶχον ἂν
πρὸς τοὺς ἐρωτῶντας λέγειν, ὡς Ἀπολλώνιος μὲν
θανάτου ἐρᾷ, ἐγὼ δ' ἀντεραστὴς ξυμπλέω,

2   "Ἐπεὶ δ' οὐδὲν οἶδα, ἐμὸν ἤδη λέγειν, ὑπὲρ ὧν
οἶδα, λέξω δὲ αὐτὸ ὑπὲρ τοῦ ἀνδρός· εἰ μὲν γὰρ ἐγὼ
ἀποθάνοιμι, οὔπω δεινὰ φιλοσοφία πείσεται, σκευο-
φόρῳ γὰρ εἴκασμαι στρατιώτου γενναίου λόγου ἀξι-
ούμενος, ὅτι τοιῷδε ἕπομαι, εἰ δὲ ἔσται τις, ὃς ἀποκτενεῖ τοῦτον, εὔποροι δ' αἱ τυραννίδες τὰ μὲν ξυνθεῖναι,
τὰ δὲ ἐξᾶραι, τρόπαιον μὲν οἶμαι κατὰ φιλοσοφίας
ἑστήξει, σφαλείσης περὶ τῷ ἄριστα ἀνθρώπων φιλο-
σοφήσαντι. πολλοὶ δὲ Ἄνυτοι καθ' ἡμῶν καὶ Μέλητοι,
γραφαὶ δ' αἱ μὲν ἔνθεν, αἱ δὲ ἐκεῖθεν ἐπὶ τοὺς Ἀπολλωνίῳ ξυγγενομένους, ὡς ὁ μέν τις ἐγέλασε καθαπτο-
μένου τῆς τυραννίδος, ὁ δ' ἐπέρρωσε λέγοντα, ὁ δ'
ἐνέδωκε λέξαι τι, ὁ δ' ἀπῆλθε ξὺν ἐπαίνῳ ὧν ἤκουσεν.
ἐγὼ δ' ἀποθνήσκειν μὲν ὑπὲρ φιλοσοφίας οὕτω φημὶ
δεῖν, ὡς ὑπὲρ ἱερῶν καὶ τειχῶν καὶ τάφων, ὑπὲρ
σωτηρίας γὰρ τῶν τοιῶνδε πολλοὶ καὶ ὀνομαστοὶ
ἄνδρες ἀποθανεῖν ἠσπάζοντο, ὡς δὲ ἀπολέσθαι φιλοσοφίαν μήτε ἐγὼ ἀποθάνοιμι μήτε ὅστις ἐκείνης τε
καὶ Ἀπολλωνίου ἐρᾷ."

14. Πρὸς ταῦτα ὁ Ἀπολλώνιος "Δάμιδι μὲν ὑπὲρ
τῶν παρόντων εὐλαβῶς διειλεγμένῳ ξυγγνώμην" ἔφη

more closely than a man follows himself, still if you ask me where I am sailing or why, I will look ridiculous for sailing in this way, crossing Sicilian waters and Tyrrhenian Gulfs without knowing the purpose. If I were running the risk deliberately, I could tell those who asked me that Apollonius is in love with death, and that I accompany him as a jealous lover.

"But not knowing anything, my only course is to say   2
what I do know, and I will say it for the benefit of the Master. If I die, Philosophy will suffer nothing very grave, since I am like the batman of a fine soldier, valued only because I follow a man like him. But if someone is planning to kill him (and tyrants have many ways of inventing some charges and exaggerating others), then in my opinion a victory monument will be raised over Philosophy, and people will think that she fell in the person of the best of all philosophers. There is many an Anytos, many a Meletos waiting for us, and there are indictments on this side and on that against Apollonius's acquaintances, 'This one laughed when Apollonius attacked tyranny,' 'That one egged him on to speak,' 'Another one suggested this or that subject,' 'Another went away full of praise for what he had heard.' For myself, I think one is as much bound to die for Philosophy as for temples, walls, and tombs, for many noble men have gladly died for such causes as that, but may I never die for the ruin of Philosophy, nor may anyone who loves her and Apollonius."

14. On hearing this Apollonius said, "We must be forgiving of Damis for speaking timidly about our situation,

"προσήκει ἔχειν, Ἀσσύριος γὰρ ὢν καὶ Μήδοις προσ-
οικήσας, οὗ τὰς τυραννίδας προσκυνοῦσιν, οὐδὲν
ὑπὲρ ἐλευθερίας ἐνθυμεῖται μέγα, σὺ δ' οὐκ οἶδ' ὅ τι
πρὸς φιλοσοφίαν ἀπολογήσῃ, φόβους ὑποτιθεὶς ὧν,
εἴ τι καὶ ἀληθὲς ἐφαίνετο, ἀπάγειν ἐχρῆν μᾶλλον ἢ
ἔσω καθιστάναι τοῦ φοβεῖσθαι τὸν μηδ' ἃ παθεῖν
εἰκὸς ἦν δεδιότα. σοφὸς δ' ἀνὴρ ἀποθνησκέτω μὲν
ὑπὲρ ὧν εἶπας, ἀποθάνοι δ' ἄν τις ὑπὲρ τούτων καὶ μὴ
σοφός, τὸ μὲν γὰρ ὑπὲρ ἐλευθερίας ἀποθνήσκειν νόμῳ
προστέτακται, τὸ δ' ὑπὲρ ξυγγενείας ἢ φίλων ἢ παιδικῶν φύσις ὥρισε, δουλοῦται δὲ ἅπαντας ἀνθρώπους
φύσις καὶ νόμος, φύσις μὲν καὶ ἑκόντας, νόμος δὲ
ἄκοντας.

2   "Σοφοῖς δὲ οἰκειότερον τελευτᾶν ὑπὲρ ὧν ἐπετήδευ-
σαν· ἃ γὰρ μὴ νόμου ἐπιτάξαντος, μηδὲ φύσεως
ξυντεκούσης αὐτοὶ ὑπὸ ῥώμης τε καὶ θράσους ἐμελέ-
τησαν, ὑπὲρ τούτων, εἰ καταλύοι τις αὐτά, ἴτω μὲν πῦρ
ἐπὶ τὸν σοφόν, ἴτω δὲ πέλεκυς, ὡς νικήσει αὐτὸν οὐδὲν
τούτων, οὐδὲ ἐς ὁτιοῦν περιελᾷ ψεῦδος, καθέξει δέ,
ὁπόσα οἶδε, μεῖον οὐδὲν ἢ ἃ ἐμυήθη. ἐγὼ δὲ γιγνώσκω
μὲν πλεῖστα ἀνθρώπων, ἅτε εἰδὼς πάντα, οἶδα δὲ ὧν
οἶδα τὰ μὲν σπουδαίοις, τὰ δὲ σοφοῖς, τὰ δὲ ἐμαυτῷ,
τὰ δὲ θεοῖς, τυράννοις δὲ οὐδέν.

3   "Ὡς δὲ οὐχ ὑπὲρ ἀνοήτων ἥκω, σκοπεῖν ἔξεστιν·
ἐγὼ γὰρ περὶ μὲν τῷ ἐμαυτοῦ σώματι κινδυνεύω οὐδέν, οὐδ' ἀποθάνοιμι ὑπὸ τῆς τυραννίδος, οὐδ' εἰ αὐτὸς
βουλοίμην, ξυνίημι δὲ κινδυνεύων περὶ τοῖς ἀνδράσιν,
ὧν εἴτε ἀρχὴν εἴτε προσθήκην ποιεῖταί με ὁ τύραννος,

for he is an Assyrian and has lived on the borders of Media, where they kowtow to tyrants, and he has no lofty ideas of freedom. But I cannot imagine what answer *you* will make to Philosophy for suggesting such terrors. Even if they appeared to have any truth, you should make a man forget them, rather than putting someone in a state of fear who has no fear even of what he is likely to suffer. Let a wise man die for the causes you spoke of, and let even an unwise one do so too, since dying for freedom's sake is a duty prescribed by law, whereas doing so for family, friends, or lovers is determined by nature. Everyone is subject to nature and law, to nature by choice, but to law by compulsion.

"But for the wise it is more proper to die on behalf of 2 their beliefs. If someone attacks practices that they have followed not from legal ordinance or natural affinity, but out of their own strength and courage, then let fire, let the axe, assail the wise man, but none of these will overcome him, or induce him to say anything untrue. He will keep his knowledge not less secure than what he learned on initiation into the mysteries. I perceive more than any one does because I know everything, but some of my knowledge benefits the virtuous, some the wise, some myself, some the gods, but none of it benefits tyrants.

"You may infer from this that I have not come on a fool's 3 errand. I myself am in no danger to my own person, nor will I be killed by the tyrant, even were I to wish it. I realize that I am running a risk for those brave men, and if the tyrant considers me their leader or their follower, I am what

εἰμὶ πᾶν ὅ τι βούλεται. εἰ δὲ προυδίδουν σφᾶς ἢ
βραδύνων ἢ βλακεύων πρὸς τὴν αἰτίαν, τίς ἂν τοῖς
σπουδαίοις ἔδοξα; τίς δ᾽ οὐκ ἂν ἀπέκτεινέ με εἰκότως,
ὡς παίζοντα ἐς ἄνδρας, οἷς, ἃ παρὰ τῶν θεῶν ἤτουν,
ἀνετέθη;

4   "Ὅτι δ᾽ οὐκ ἦν μοι διαφυγεῖν τὸ μὴ οὐ προδότης
δόξαι, δηλῶσαι βούλομαι· τυραννίδων ἤθη διττά, αἱ
μὲν γὰρ ἀκρίτους ἀποκτείνουσιν, αἱ δὲ ὑπαχθέντας
δικαστηρίοις, ἐοίκασι δ᾽ αἱ μὲν τοῖς θερμοῖς τε καὶ
ἑτοίμοις τῶν θηρίων, αἱ δὲ τοῖς μαλακωτέροις τε
καὶ ληθάργοις. ὡς μὲν δὴ χαλεπαὶ ἄμφω, δῆλον
πᾶσι παράδειγμα ποιουμένοις τῆς μὲν ὁρμώσης καὶ
ἀκρίτου Νέρωνα, τῆς δὲ ὑποκαθημένης Τιβέριον, ἀπ-
ώλλυσαν γὰρ ὁ μὲν οὐδ᾽ οἰηθέντας, ὁ δ᾽ ἐκ πολλοῦ
δείσαντας. ἐγὼ δ᾽ ἡγοῦμαι χαλεπωτέρας τὰς δικάζειν
προσποιουμένας καὶ ψηφίζεσθαί τι ὡς ἐκ τῶν νόμων,
πράττουσι μὲν γὰρ κατ᾽ αὐτοὺς οὐδέν, ψηφίζονται δ᾽,
ἅπερ οἱ μηδὲν κρίναντες, ὄνομα τῷ διατρίβοντι τῆς
ὀργῆς θέμενοι νόμον.

5   "Τὸ δ᾽ ἀποθνήσκειν κατεψηφισμένους ἀφαιρεῖται
τοὺς ἀθλίους καὶ τὸν παρὰ τῶν πολλῶν ἔλεον, ὃν
ὥσπερ ἐντάφιον χρὴ ἐπιφέρειν τοῖς ἀδίκως ἀπελ-
θοῦσι. δικαστικὸν μὲν δὴ τὸ τῆς τυραννίδος ταύτης
ὁρῶ σχῆμα, τελευτᾶν δέ μοι δοκεῖ ἐς ἄκριτον, ὧν γὰρ
πρὶν ἢ δικάσαι κατεψηφίσατο, τούτους ὡς μήπω δε-
δικασμένους ὑπάγει τῇ κρίσει, καὶ ὁ μὲν ψήφῳ ἁλοὺς
ἐν αὐτῇ δῆλον ὡς ὑπὸ τοῦ μὴ κατὰ νόμους κρίναντος

he wishes me to be. But if I had betrayed them by showing reluctance or timidity under indictment, what would good people have thought of me? Would they not have killed me justifiably, for toying with the lives of men who have been entrusted with the thing I prayed the gods to give them?

"I could not have escaped the charge of treachery, as 4 I will prove to you. Tyrants are of two kinds. Some kill people unheard, others after putting them on trial. The first resemble fiery, crafty animals, the second torpid, sleepy ones. Both are dangerous, as anyone can see by taking Nero as the example of the aggressive, indiscriminate kind, and Tiberius of the insidious. The former killed people before they were aware, the latter when they had long been afraid. I consider more dangerous those men who pretend to judge and to decide in accordance with the laws, when in fact they do nothing legally, but decide in the same way as those who do without trials, and give the name of law to the slowness of their anger.

"To die under sentence robs the poor victims even of 5 the general pity, which should be placed like a shroud on those who have left us unjustly. This present tyranny is legal in appearance, I can see, but in my opinion it amounts to injustice, since it condemns people before trial, and then submits them to trial as if they were not already condemned. Someone condemned by verdict in court will of course claim to have fallen victim to one who did not judge

ἀπολωλέναι φησίν, ὁ δ' ἐκλιπὼν τὸ δικάσασθαι πῶς
ἂν διαφύγοι τὸ μὴ οὐκ ἐφ' ἑαυτὸν ἐψηφίσθαι;

6   "Τὸ δὲ καὶ τοιῶνδε ἀνδρῶν κειμένων ἐπ' ἐμοὶ νῦν
ἀποδρᾶναι τὸν ἐμαυτοῦ τε κἀκείνων ἀγῶνα ποῖ με τῆς
γῆς ἐάσει καθαρὸν δόξαι; ἔστω γὰρ σὲ μὲν εἰρηκέναι
ταῦτα, ἐμὲ δὲ ὀρθῶς εἰρημένοις πείθεσθαι, τοὺς δὲ
ἀπεσφάχθαι, τίς μὲν ὑπὲρ εὐπλοίας εὐχὴ τῷ τοιῷδε;
ποῖ δὲ ὁρμιεῖται; πορεύσεται δὲ παρὰ τίνα; ἐξαλλάτ-
τειν γὰρ χρὴ οἶμαι πάσης, ὁπόσης Ῥωμαῖοι ἄρχουσι,
παρ' ἄνδρας δὲ ἥκειν ἐπιτηδείους τε καὶ μὴ ἐν φανερῷ
οἰκοῦντας, τουτὶ δ' ἂν Φραώτης τε εἴη καὶ ὁ Βαβυ-
λώνιος καὶ Ἰάρχας ὁ θεῖος καὶ Θεσπεσίων ὁ γενναῖος.

7   "Εἰ μὲν δὴ ἐπ' Αἰθιόπων στελλοίμην, τί ἄν, ὦ
λῷστε, πρὸς Θεσπεσίωνα εἴποιμι; εἴτε γὰρ κρύπτοιμι
ταῦτα, ψευδολογίας ἐραστὴς δόξω, μᾶλλον δὲ δοῦλος,
εἴτε ἐς ἀπαγγελίαν αὐτῶν ἴοιμι, τοιῶνδέ που δεήσει
λόγων· ἐμέ, ὦ Θεσπεσίων, Εὐφράτης πρὸς ὑμᾶς διέβαλεν, ἃ μὴ ἐμαυτῷ ξύνοιδα· ὁ μὲν γὰρ κομπαστὴν
ἔφη καὶ τερατώδη με εἶναι καὶ ὑβριστὴν σοφίας,
ὁπόσῃ <μὴ>[6] Ἰνδῶν, ἐγὼ δὲ ταυτὶ μὲν οὐκ εἰμί, προδότης δὲ τῶν ἐμαυτοῦ φίλων καὶ σφαγεὺς καὶ οὐδὲν
πιστὸν καὶ τὰ τοιαῦτά εἰμι, στέφανόν τε ἀρετῆς, εἴ τις,
στεφανωσόμενος ἥκω τοῦτον, ἐπειδὴ τοὺς μεγίστους
τῶν κατὰ τὴν Ῥώμην οἴκων οὕτως ἀνεῖλον, ὡς μηδὲ
οἰκήσεσθαι αὐτοὺς ἔτι.'

8   "Ἐρυθριᾷς, Δημήτριε, τούτων ἀκούων, ὁρῶ γάρ. τί
οὖν, εἰ καὶ Φραώτην ἐνθυμηθείης κἀμὲ παρὰ τὸν

according to law, but one who avoids trial must always appear to be condemned by himself.

"When heroes such as these depend on me, if I ran 6 away from the ordeal facing both myself and them, where in the world could I be thought innocent? Suppose that you had spoken as you did, and I had assented to it as rightly spoken, and then they had been slaughtered—what prayer for a favorable voyage could such a man make? Where will he put in? To whom will he travel? I think he would have to avoid the whole Roman empire, and to go to people who are sympathetic and live somewhere obscure, such as Phraotes, the Babylonian,[27] the divine Iarchas, or the noble Thespesion.

"If then I were to make my way to Ethiopia, my dear 7 friend, whatever could I say to Thespesion? If I were to conceal these actions, I would seem to be a lover of falsehood, or rather its slave, but if I began to describe them, I would need words such as these: 'Thespesion, Euphrates falsely charged me to you with actions for which I cannot reproach myself, saying I was a boaster, an exaggerator, a mocker of all philosophy that is not Indian, when I am none of these things. But I am a traitor and an executioner of my own friends, a creature not to be trusted, and so on. If there is any crown of virtue, I have come to crown myself with it, since I have so completely destroyed the greatest houses in Rome that they will no longer have inhabitants.'

"You blush to hear this, Demetrius, I see. Suppose then 8 that you could imagine Phraotes and my taking refuge with

[27] I.e. Vardanes, king of the "Medes" in Book I; cf. I 27 ff.

---

6 ⟨μὴ⟩ Jac.

ἄνδρα τοῦτον ἐς Ἰνδοὺς φεύγοντα, πῶς μὲν ἂν ἐς
αὐτὸν βλέψαιμι; τί δ' ἂν εἴποιμι ὑπὲρ ὧν φεύγω; μῶν
ὡς ἀφικόμην μὲν καλὸς κἀγαθὸς πρότερον καὶ τὸν
θάνατον τὸν ὑπὲρ φίλων οὐκ ἄθυμος, ἐπεὶ δὲ ξυνεγε-
νόμην αὐτῷ, τὸ θειότατον τουτὶ τῶν κατὰ ἀνθρώπους
ἄτιμον ἔρριψά σοι; ὁ δὲ Ἰάρχας οὐδὲ ἐρήσεται οὐδὲν
ἥκοντα, ἀλλ' ὥσπερ ὁ Αἰολός ποτε τὸν Ὀδυσσέα
κακῶς χρησάμενον τῷ τῆς εὐπλοίας δώρῳ ἄτιμον
ἐκέλευσε χωρεῖν τῆς νήσου, κἀμὲ δήπου ἀπελᾷ τοῦ
ὄχθου, κακὸν εἰπὼν ἐς τὸ Ταντάλειον γεγονέναι πῶμα,
βούλονται γὰρ τὸν ἐς αὐτὸ κύψαντα καὶ κινδύνων
κοινωνεῖν τοῖς φίλοις.

9   "Οἶδα ὡς δεινὸς εἶ, Δημήτριε, λόγους ξυντεμεῖν
πάντας, ὅθεν μοι δοκεῖς καὶ τοιοῦτό τι ἐρεῖν πρός με·
'ἀλλὰ μὴ παρὰ τούτους ἴθι, παρ' ἄνδρας δέ, οἷς μήπω
ἐπέμιξας, καὶ εὖ κείσεταί σοι τὸ ἀποδρᾶναι, ῥᾷον γὰρ
ἐν οὐκ εἰδόσι λήσῃ.' βασανιζέσθω δὲ καὶ ὅδε ὁ λόγος,
ὅπῃ τοῦ πιθανοῦ ἔχει· δοκεῖ γάρ μοι περὶ αὐτοῦ τάδε.
ἐγὼ ἡγοῦμαι τὸν σοφὸν μηδὲν ἰδίᾳ μηδ' ἐφ' ἑαυτοῦ
πράττειν, μηδ' ἂν ἐνθυμηθῆναί τι οὕτως ἀμάρτυρον,
ὡς μὴ αὐτὸν γοῦν ἑαυτῷ παρεῖναι, καὶ εἴτε Ἀπόλλωνος αὐτοῦ τὸ Πυθοῖ γράμμα, εἴτε ἀνδρὸς ὑγιῶς
ἑαυτὸν γνόντος καὶ διὰ τοῦτο γνώμην αὐτὸ ποιουμένου
ἐς πάντας, δοκεῖ μοι ὁ σοφὸς ἑαυτὸν γιγνώσκων, καὶ
παραστάτην ἔχων τὸν ἑαυτοῦ νοῦν, μήτ' ἂν πτῆξαί τι
ὧν οἱ πολλοί, μήτ' ἂν θαρσῆσαί τι ὧν ἕτεροι μὴ ξὺν
αἰσχύνῃ ἅπτονται· δοῦλοι γὰρ τῶν τυραννίδων ὄντες
καὶ προδοῦναι αὐταῖς ποτε τοὺς φιλτάτους ὥρμησαν,

that noble man in India: how could I look him in the face? What reason could I give for my exile? Could I say that previously I came as a man of honor, not unready to die for my friends, but after meeting with him I had thrown away this most heaven-sent of all human gifts, dishonoring it because of you? Iarchas will not even question me when I arrive, but just as Aeolus once told Odysseus to leave his island in shame after misusing the gift of a safe voyage, so no doubt he will drive me from his riverbank, saying that I have disgraced the draught of Tantalus.[28] They expect the man who has drunk deep from this to share the dangers of his friends.

"I know that you are skilled at refuting any argument, Demetrius, and I think you will say something like this to me: 'Well then, do not go to them, but to people whom you have never met, and then your running away will be no problem, since you will more easily hide among strangers.' But let us test this argument too for its plausibility, since this is my opinion of it. As I believe, the wise man will do nothing privately or by himself, and could never even conceive an act so obscure that he was not at least in his own presence. Whether the inscription at Delphi[29] is from Apollo himself, or whether it is from someone who truly knew himself and thereafter made it into a maxim for everybody, the wise man who knows himself, and has his own intellect as his companion, can never quail before the same things as most men do, nor bring himself to do what others can venture on only with shame. As slaves of tyranny, they have undertaken to betray their closest friends to it, fear-

9

---

[28] Aeolus: *Odyssey* 10.72–75. Tantalus: III 32.2.
[29] "Know thyself," the best known of the Delphic maxims.

τὰ μὲν μὴ φοβερὰ δείσαντες, ἃ δὲ χρὴ δεῖσαι μὴ φοβηθέντες.

10   "Σοφία δὲ οὐ ξυγχωρεῖ ταῦτα· πρὸς γὰρ τῷ Πυθικῷ ἐπιγράμματι καὶ τὸ τοῦ Εὐριπίδου ἐπαινεῖ ξύνεσιν ἡγουμένου περὶ τοὺς ἀνθρώπους εἶναι τὴν ἀπολλῦσαν αὐτούς, ἐπειδὰν ἐνθυμηθῶσιν, ὡς κακὰ εἰργασμένοι εἰσίν. ἥδε γάρ που καὶ τῷ Ὀρέστῃ τὰ τῶν Εὐμενίδων εἴδη ἀνέγραφεν, ὅτε δὴ ἐμαίνετο ἐπὶ τῇ μητρί, νοῦς μὲν γὰρ τῶν πρακτέων κύριος, σύνεσις δὲ τῶν ἐκείνῳ δοξάντων. ἢν μὲν δὴ χρηστὰ ἔληται ὁ νοῦς, πέμπει ἤδη τὸν ἄνδρα ἡ ξύνεσις ἐς πάντα μὲν ἱερά, πάσας δὲ ἀγυιάς, πάντα δὲ τεμένη, πάντα δὲ ἀνθρώπων ἤθη κροτοῦσά τε καὶ ᾄδουσα, ἐφυμνήσει δὲ αὐτῷ καὶ καθεύδοντι, παριστᾶσα χορὸν εὔφημον ἐκ τοῦ τῶν ὀνείρων δήμου,

11   "Ἢν δ' ἐς φαῦλα ὀλίσθῃ⁷ ἡ τοῦ νοῦ στάσις, οὐκ ἐᾷ τοῦτον ἡ ξύνεσις οὔτε ὄμμα ὀρθὸν ἐς ἀνθρώπων τινὰ ἀφεῖναι οὔτε τὸ ἀπ' ἐλευθέρας γλώττης φθέγμα, ἱερῶν τε ἀπελαύνει καὶ τοῦ εὔχεσθαι, οὐδὲ γὰρ χεῖρα αἴρειν ξυγχωρεῖ ἐς τὰ ἀγάλματα, ἀλλ' ἐπικόπτει αἴροντας, ὥσπερ τοὺς ἐπανατεινομένους οἱ νόμοι, ἐξίστησι δὲ αὐτοὺς καὶ ὁμίλου παντὸς καὶ δειματοῖ καθεύδοντας, καὶ ἃ μὲν ὁρῶσι μεθ' ἡμέραν καὶ εἰ δή τινα ἀκούειν ἢ λέγειν οἴονται, ὀνειρώδη καὶ ἀνεμαῖα ποιεῖ τούτοις, τὰς δὲ ἀμυδρὰς καὶ φαντασιώδεις πτοίας ἀληθεῖς ἤδη καὶ πιθανὰς τῷ φόβῳ. ὡς μὲν δὴ ἐλέγξει με ἡ σύνεσις ἐς εἰδότας τε καὶ μὴ εἰδότας ἥκοντα, προδότης εἰ γενοίμην τῶν ἀνδρῶν, δεδεῖχθαί μοι σαφῶς οἶμαι καὶ

ing what holds no terrors, and not fearing what should deter them.

"Wisdom forbids such things, and it approves not only 10 of the inscription at Delphi, but of Euripides's words, when he holds that men's conscience is what destroys them when they realize that they have done evil. Conscience conjured up the vision of the Eumenides for Orestes, when he went mad after killing his mother, since his intellect determined his actions, but conscience determined his visions.[30] If the intellect makes good choices, Conscience will escort a true man into every sanctuary, every street, every sacred enclosure, and every haunt of men, applauding him and singing his praises. It will sing to him even while he sleeps, surrounding him with propitious choirs from the commonwealth of dreams.

"But if mental conflict makes him fall into evil ways, 11 Conscience will not allow him to look another in the eye, or speak with a free tongue. It drives him from sanctuaries and from prayer, not allowing him to raise his hands to any image, but restraining him when he does so, as the laws restrain those who contravene them. It drives him from all company, and terrifies him as he sleeps. Whatever he sees in the daytime, or whatever he seems to hear or say, all these things it makes phantasmal and evanescent for him, but vague and imaginary alarms it makes real and productive of fear. Conscience will condemn me whether the people I visit know me or not, once I become a traitor to those heroes, as I think I have shown convincingly in accordance

[30] *Orestes* 395–96.

---

7 ὀλίσθη Cob.: ὀλίσθησῃ

APOLLONIUS OF TYANA

ὡς φαίνει ἀλήθεια, προδώσω δὲ οὐδὲ ἐμαυτόν, ἀλλ᾿
ἀγωνιοῦμαι πρὸς τὸν τύραννον, τὸ τοῦ γενναίου Ὁμήρου ἐπειπών· ξυνὸς Ἐννάλιος.᾿᾿᾿

15. Ὑπὸ τούτων ὁ Δάμις τῶν λόγων αὐτὸς μὲν οὕτω
διατεθῆναί φησιν, ὡς ὁρμήν τε ἀναλαβεῖν καὶ θάρσος, τὸν Δημήτριον δὲ μὴ ἀπογνῶναι τοῦ ἀνδρός,
ἀλλ᾿ ἐπαινέσαντα, καὶ ξυνθέμενον οἷς εἶπεν, ἐπιθει-
άσαι οἱ ὑπὲρ οὗ κινδυνεύει καὶ φιλοσοφίᾳ αὐτῇ, ὑπὲρ
ἧς καρτερεῖ ταῦτα, ἡγεῖσθαί τε αὐτοῖς οὗ καταλύων
ἐτύγχανε, τὸν δὲ Ἀπολλώνιον παραιτούμενον τοῦτο
“δείλη ἤδη” φάναι “καὶ χρὴ περὶ λύχνων ἀφὰς ἐς τὸν
Ῥωμαίων λιμένα ἀφεῖναι, τουτὶ γὰρ ταῖς ναυσὶ ταύταις νόμιμον, ξυσσιτήσομεν δέ, ἐπειδὰν εὖ τἀμὰ ἔχῃ,
νυνὶ γὰρ ἂν καὶ κατασκευασθείη τις αἰτία ἐπὶ σὲ ὡς
ξυσσιτήσαντα τῷ τοῦ βασιλέως ἐχθρῷ, καὶ μηδὲ τὴν
ἐπὶ τοῦ λιμένος μεθ᾿ ἡμῶν ἴθι, μὴ καὶ τὸ λόγου κε-
κοινωνηκέναι μοι διαβάλῃ σε ἐς ἀπορρήτους βουλάς.”

2   Ξυνεχώρησε μὲν δὴ ὁ Δημήτριος, καὶ περιβαλὼν
αὐτοὺς ἀπήει μεταστρεφόμενός τε καὶ τὰ δάκρυα
ἀποψῶν, ὁ δὲ Ἀπολλώνιος ἰδὼν ἐς τὸν Δάμιν “εἰ μὲν
ἔρρωσαι” ἔφη “καὶ θαρσεῖς ἅπερ ἐγώ, βαδίσωμεν
ἄμφω ἐπὶ τὴν ναῦν, εἰ δὲ ἀθύμως ἔχεις, ὥρα σοι
καταμένειν ἐνταῦθα, Δημητρίῳ γὰρ ξυνέσῃ τὸν χρόνον τοῦτον ἀνδρὶ σοί τε κἀμοὶ ἐπιτηδείῳ.” ὑπολαβὼν
δὲ ὁ Δάμις “καὶ τίνα” ἔφη “νομιῶ ἐμαυτόν, εἰ τοιαῦτά
σου διειλεγμένου σήμερον ὑπὲρ φίλων καὶ κοινωνίας
κινδύνων, οἳ ἐπ᾿ αὐτοὺς ἥκουσιν, ἐγὼ δ᾿ ἀνήκοος τοῦ
λόγου φεύγοιμί σε καὶ ἀποκινδυνεύοιμί σου, μήπω

248

with the revelation of truth. I will not betray myself either, but struggle against the tyrant, echoing the words of great Homer, 'Impartial is the War god.'"[31]

15. The speech so moved Damis, he says, that he recovered energy and courage, and it so moved Demetrius that he did not give up hope for the Master. Instead he praised what he had said and assented to it, blessed him for the risk he was running, and blessed Philosophy too for whom Apollonius showed such endurance. He wanted to take them to his lodging, but Apollonius declined, saying, "It is already evening, and I must be off to the port of Rome at dusk, the usual departure time of these ships. We will dine together when my affairs are in order, but for the moment some charge might be fabricated against you because you have dined with the emperor's enemy. Do not come to the harbor with us either, or else your conversing with me may make you suspected of secret plots."

Demetrius agreed and embraced them, but as he went away he looked back and dabbed away his tears. Looking at Damis, Apollonius said, "If you are as bold and as confident as I am, let us both go to the ship. But if you are despondent, then you must remain here and spend the interim with Demetrius, a man well disposed both to you and to me." Damis however replied, "But what would I think of myself, after you have spoken as you have today about friends and sharing the dangers that befall them, and I then ignored your words, deserted you, and aban-

2

---

[31] *Iliad* 18.309.

πρότερον κακὸς ὑπὲρ σοῦ δόξας·"

3   "Ὀρθῶς" ἔφη "λέγεις καὶ ἴωμεν, ἐγὼ μέν, ὡς ἔχω,
σὲ δὲ χρὴ μετασκευάζειν σαυτὸν ἐς τὸ δημοτικώτερον
καὶ μήτε κομᾶν, ὡς γοῦν ἔχεις, τρίβωνά τε ἀνταλλάτ-
τεσθαι τουτουὶ τοῦ λίνου, καὶ τὸ ὑπόδημα παραιτεῖ-
σθαι τοῦτο. τί δὲ βούλεταί μοι ταῦτα, χρὴ διαλεχθῆ-
ναι. λῷον γὰρ καὶ πλείω καρτερῆσαι πρὸ τῆς δίκης·
οὐ δὴ βούλομαι κοινωνῆσαί ‹σέ›[8] μοι τούτων ξυλληφθέντα, ξυλληφθείης γὰρ ἂν διαβεβλημένου τοῦ
σχήματος, ἀλλ᾽ ὡς μὴ φιλοσοφοῦντα μέν, ἐπιτήδειον
δὲ ἄλλως ὄντα μοι ξυνέπεσθαί τε καὶ παρατυγχάνειν
οἷς πράττω." αἰτία μὲν ἥδε τοῦ μεταβαλεῖν τὸν Δάμιν
τὸ τῶν Πυθαγορείων σχῆμα, οὐ γὰρ ὡς κακίων γε
αὐτὸ μεθεῖναί φησιν, οὐδὲ μεταγνούς, τέχνην δὲ ἐπαινέσας, ἣν ὑπῆλθεν ἐς τὸ ξυμφέρον τοῦ καιροῦ.

16. Ἀποπλεύσαντες δὲ τῆς Δικαιαρχίας τριταῖοι
κατῆραν ἐς τὰς ἐκβολὰς τοῦ Θύμβριδος, ἀφ᾽ ὧν ξύμ-
μετρος ἐς τὴν Ῥώμην ἀνάπλους. τὸ μὲν δὴ βασίλειον
ξίφος ἦν ἐπ᾽ Αἰλιανῷ τότε, ὁ δ᾽ ἀνὴρ οὗτος πάλαι τοῦ
Ἀπολλωνίου ἤρα, ξυγγεγονώς ποτε αὐτῷ κατ᾽ Αἴγυπτον, καὶ φανερὸν μὲν οὐδὲν ὑπὲρ αὐτοῦ πρὸς τὸν
Δομετιανὸν ἔλεγεν, οὐ γὰρ ξυνεχώρει ἡ ἀρχή, τὸν γὰρ
δοκοῦντα τῷ βασιλεῖ ἀπηχθῆσθαι πῶς μὲν ἂν πρὸς
αὐτὸν ἐπήνεσε, πῶς δ᾽ ἂν ὡς ἐπιτήδειον ἑαυτῷ παρη-
τήσατο; τέχναι μὴν ὁπόσαι εἰσὶν ἀφανῶς ἀμύνουσαι,
πάσαις ὑπὲρ αὐτοῦ ἐχρῆτο.

---

[8] ‹σέ› Rsk.

doned you in danger? I have never shown myself a coward
in your cause before."

"You are right," said Apollonius, "so let us go, I as I am   3
now, while you must dress more like a commoner, and not
wear your hair long, at any rate as it is now, you must assume a coarse cloak instead of this linen one, and renounce
those shoes. I must explain to you what I mean by all this,
since it would be better to put up with even worse than that
before the trial begins. I do not want you to share my fate
by getting arrested as you might be if your appearance
caused suspicion. I wish rather for you to follow me and
witness my actions as if you were not a philosopher, but a
mere acquaintance." This was the reason why Damis put
off his Pythagorean dress, not giving it up because he had
grown more cowardly or changed his mind, he says, but
because he approved of the ruse, and entered into it as the
crisis demanded.

16. Two days after setting sail from Dicaearchia, they
put in at the mouth of the Tiber, from which it is a moderate distance by water to Rome. The person then in charge
of the emperor's sword was Aelianus, a man who had long
admired Apollonius from the time when he met him in
Egypt.[32] He did not speak openly on his behalf before
Domitian, since his office did not allow it. How could he
have praised to the emperor a man supposed to be his
enemy, or interceded for him as a friend of his own? Yet he
used every possible means to help Apollonius secretly.

[32] Casperius Aelianus was prefect of the Praetorian Guard late
in the reign of Domitian and again under Nerva.

2 Ὅς γε καὶ τὸν χρόνον, ὅν, πρὶν ἥκειν, διεβάλλετο "ὦ βασιλεῦ," ἔφη "κουφολόγον οἱ σοφισταὶ χρῆμα καὶ ἀλαζὼν ἡ τέχνη, καὶ ἐπεὶ μηδὲν χρηστὸν τοῦ εἶναι ἀπολαύουσι, θανάτου γλίχονται, καὶ οὐ περιμένουσιν αὐτοῦ τὸ αὐτόματον, ἀλλ' ἐπισπῶνται τὸν θάνατον ἐκκαλούμενοι τοὺς ἔχοντας ξίφη. ταῦθ' ἡγοῦμαι καὶ Νέρωνα ἐνθυμηθέντα μὴ ὑπαχθῆναι ὑπὸ Δημητρίου ἀποκτεῖναι αὐτόν. ἐπεὶ γὰρ θανατῶντα ᾔσθετο, οὐ κατὰ ξυγγνώμην ἐπανῆκεν αὐτῷ τὸν θάνατον, ἀλλὰ καθ' ὑπεροψίαν τοῦ κτεῖναι. καὶ μὴν καὶ Μουσώνιον τὸν Τυρρηνὸν πολλὰ τῇ ἀρχῇ ἐναντιωθέντα τῇ νήσῳ ξυνέσχεν, ᾗ ὄνομα Γύαρα, καὶ οὕτω τι τῶν σοφιστῶν τούτων ἥττους Ἕλληνες, ὡς τότε μὲν κατὰ ξυνουσίαν αὐτοῦ ἐσπλεῖν πάντας, νυνὶ δὲ κατὰ ἱστορίαν τῆς κρήνης· ἐν γὰρ τῇ νήσῳ ἀνύδρῳ οὔσῃ πρότερον εὕρημα Μουσωνίου κρήνη ἐγένετο, ἣν ᾄδουσιν Ἕλληνες, ὅσα Ἑλικῶνι τὴν τοῦ ἵππου."

17. Τούτοις μὲν δὴ διῆγεν ὁ Αἰλιανὸς τὸν βασιλέα πρὶν ἥκειν Ἀπολλώνιον, ἀφικομένου δὲ σοφωτέρων ἥπτετο, κελεύει μὲν γὰρ ξυλληφθέντα αὐτὸν ἀναχθῆναί οἱ, λοιδορουμένου δ' αὐτῷ τοῦ τὴν κατηγορίαν ξυνθέντος ὡς γόητι καὶ ἱκανῷ τὴν τέχνην, ὁ μὲν Αἰλιανὸς "τῷ βασιλείῳ δικαστηρίῳ" ἔφη "σαυτόν τε καὶ τὰ τούτου φύλαττε," ὁ δ' Ἀπολλώνιος "εἰ μὲν γόης" ἔφη "ἐγώ, πῶς κρίνομαι; εἰ δὲ κρίνομαι, πῶς γόης εἰμί; εἰ μὴ ἄρα τὸ συκοφαντεῖν ἰσχυρὸν οὕτως

Even during the interval when Apollonius was under 2
attack but had not yet arrived, he said: "Majesty, sophists[33]
are irresponsible babblers, and their profession makes
great claims. Because they get no real pleasure out of life
they long for death, and do not wait for it to come in due
course, but court death by provoking those armed with
swords. That was what Nero thought, I imagine, when he
refused to be provoked by Demetrius into killing him.
Seeing him eager to die, he remitted his death sentence,
not out of mercy, but out of contempt for the act of killing
him. Musonius the Etruscan, too, often opposed his rule,
but he confined him on the island called Gyara.[34] The
Greeks are such fans of these sophists that at the time they
all sailed to visit him, and now do so to see the spring. The
island had been waterless before, but Musonius discovered a spring, which the Greeks celebrate as highly as the
horse's one on Helicon."[35]

17. With these words, Aelianus tried to distract the emperor before Apollonius's arrival, but after it he tried a
cleverer ruse. He ordered him to be arrested and summoned to his presence, and when the man bringing the
fabricated charge attacked Apollonius as a magician skilful
in the art, Aelianus said, "Save yourself and this man's record for the emperor's court." Apollonius, however, said,
"If I am a magician, how can I be brought to court? And if
brought to court, how can I be a magician? Unless perhaps

[33] This word here means "sham philosophers," by contrast
with VI 36.3.   [34] A small island in the northern Cyclades,
often used to hold political exiles.   [35] Hippocrene ("Horse's
Spring") on Mount Helicon in Boeotia, named from the winged
horse Pegasus and closely associated with the Muses.

εἶναί φησιν, ὡς μηδὲ τῶν γοητευόντων ἡττᾶσθαι αὐτό."

2   Βουλομένου δὲ τοῦ κατηγόρου λέγειν τι ἀμαθέστερον, ἐκκρούων αὐτὸν ὁ Αἰλιανὸς "ἐμοὶ" εἶπεν "ἄφες τὸν καιρὸν τὸν πρὸ τῆς δίκης, ἔλεγχον γὰρ ποιήσομαι τῆς τοῦ σοφιστοῦ γνώμης ἰδίᾳ καὶ οὐκ ἐν ὑμῖν, κἂν μὲν ὁμολογῇ ἀδικεῖν, ξυντετμήσονταί οἱ ἐν τῷ δικαστηρίῳ λόγοι καὶ σὺ ἄπει εἰρηνικῶς, εἰ δὲ ἀντιλέγει, δικάσει ὁ βασιλεύς." παρελθὼν οὖν ἐς τὸ ἀπόρρητον δικαστήριον, ἐν ᾧ τὰ μεγάλα καὶ ἐλέγχεται καὶ σιωπᾶται, "χωρεῖτε" ἔφη "ἐνθένδε καὶ μηδεὶς ἐπακροάσθω, δοκεῖ γὰρ τῷ βασιλεῖ τοῦτο."

18. Ὡς δὲ ἐγένοντο αὐτοί, "ἐγώ," ἔφη "ὦ Ἀπολλώνιε, μειράκιον ἦν κατὰ τοὺς χρόνους, οὓς ὁ πατὴρ τοῦ βασιλέως ἐπ' Αἴγυπτον ἦλθε τοῖς μὲν θεοῖς θύσων, χρησόμενος δ' ὑπὲρ τῶν ἑαυτοῦ σοί, καὶ χιλίαρχον μὲν ὁ βασιλεὺς ἦγεν ἤδη τῶν πολεμικῶν εἰδότα, σὺ δ' οὕτω τι μοι ἐπιτηδείως εἶχες, ὡς χρηματίζοντος τοῦ βασιλέως ταῖς πόλεσιν ἀπολαβών με ἰδίᾳ ποδαπός τε εἴην λέγειν, καὶ ὅ τι μοι τὸ ὄνομα, καὶ ὡς ἔχω τοῦ πατρός, προὔλεγες δέ μοι καὶ τὴν ἀρχὴν ταύτην, ἣ τοῖς μὲν πολλοῖς μεγίστη δοκεῖ καὶ μείζων ἢ πάντα ὁμοῦ τὰ ἀνθρώπων, ἐμοὶ δὲ ὄχλος καὶ κακοδαιμονία φαίνεται, τυραννίδος γὰρ φύλαξ χαλεπῆς εἰμι, κἂν μὲν σφήλω αὐτήν, δέδοικα τὰ ἐκ τῶν θεῶν,

2   "Σοὶ δ' ὅπως εὔνους εἰμί, δεδήλωκα, ὁ γὰρ εἰπὼν ἀφ' ὧν εἴρηκά που τὸ μηδ' ἂν παύσασθαί σε ἀγαπῶν, ἔστ' ἂν ᾖ τὸ ἐκείνων μεμνῆσθαι. τὸ δὲ ἰδίᾳ ἐθελῆσαι

254

he thinks that slander is so powerful as not to yield even to magicians."

The accuser wanted to say something even more stu-   2
pid, but Aelianus stopped him by saying, "You must allow
me the hours before the trial, as I want to test the sophist's
opinions privately and out of your presence. If he con-
fesses his crime, that will shorten the speeches in court
and you will leave in peace, but if he denies the charge, the
emperor will be the judge." So Aelianus proceeded to the
secret court in which important matters are both examined
and concealed, and said, "Leave, everybody, and let there
be no listening, in accordance with the emperor's wish."

18. When they were alone, Aelianus said, "Apollonius, I
was a youth at the time when the emperor's father came to
Egypt to sacrifice to the gods, and to get your prediction
about his affairs. I was in the retinue of the emperor as a
tribune, already having some experience of war, and you
were so friendly to me as to take me aside privately when
the emperor was giving audience to the cities. You told me
my origin, my name, and my father's name, and you also
predicted to me that I would hold this office. Most people
think it is very great, greater than anything on the whole
earth, but I find it a burden and a curse. I am appointed to
guard a harsh tyranny, and if I cause its fall I fear divine
punishment.

"Towards you, however, I have shown my goodwill. For   2
when I mentioned what caused it, surely I conveyed that I
will cherish you as long as I have those memories. When I

ἐρέσθαι σε, ὑπὲρ ὧν ὁ κατήγορος ξυντέθεικε, σό-
φισμα οὐ φαῦλον ὑπὲρ ξυνουσίας ἐμοὶ τῆς πρὸς σὲ
γέγονεν, ὅπως θαρροίης μὲν τὰ ἐπ' ἐμοὶ ὄντα, προ-
γνοίης δὲ τὰ ἐπὶ τῷ βασιλεῖ· ὅ τι μὲν γὰρ ψηφιεῖται
ἐπὶ σοί, οὐκ οἶδα, διάκειται δέ, ὥσπερ οἱ καταψηφίσα-
σθαι μὲν ἐπιθυμοῦντες, αἰσχυνόμενοι δὲ τὸ μὴ ἐπ'
ἀληθέσι, καὶ πρόφασιν ἀπωλείας ἀνδρῶν ὑπάτων ποιεῖταί σε, βούλεται μὲν γάρ, ἃ μὴ δεῖ, πράττει δ' αὐτὰ
καταρρυθμίζων ἐς τὴν τοῦ δικαίου δόξαν. δεῖ δὴ κἀμοὶ
πλάσματος καὶ ὁρμῆς ἐπὶ σέ, εἰ γὰρ ὑπόψεταί με ὡς
ἀνιέντα, οὐκ οἶδ' ὁπότερος ἡμῶν ἀπολεῖται θᾶττον."

19. Πρὸς ταῦτα ὁ Ἀπολλώνιος "ἐπεὶ ὑγιῶς" ἔφη
"διαλεγόμεθα καὶ ὁπόσα καρδία ἴσχει σύ τε εἴρηκας
ἐμοί τε εἰπεῖν δίκαιον, φιλοσοφεῖς τε ὑπὲρ τῶν σεαυτοῦ πραγμάτων, ὡς οἱ σφόδρα μοι ξυνδιατρίψαντες,
καί, νὴ Δία, οὕτω φιλανθρώπως πρὸς ἡμᾶς ἔχεις, ὡς
ξυγκινδυνεύειν αἱρεῖσθαί[9] μοι, λέξω τὸν ἐμαυτοῦ νοῦν.
ἐμοὶ γὰρ ἀποδρᾶναι μὲν ἦν ὑμᾶς ἐς πολλὰ μέρη τῆς
γῆς, ἃ μὴ ὑμῶν ἀκροᾶται, παρ' ἄνδρας τε ἀφικέσθαι
σοφοὺς καὶ σοφωτέρους ἢ ἐγώ, θεούς τε θεραπεύειν
ξὺν ὀρθῷ λόγῳ βαδίσαντι ἐς ἤθη ἀνθρώπων θεοφιλε-
στέρων ἢ οἱ ἐνταῦθα, παρ' οἷς οὔτε ἔνδειξις οὔτε
γραφὴ οὐδεμία, δι' αὐτὸ γὰρ τὸ μήτε ἀδικεῖν μήτε
ἀδικεῖσθαι δικαστηρίων οὐ δέονται. δείσας δὲ προ-
δότου λαβεῖν αἰτίαν, εἰ φύγοιμι[10] μὲν αὐτὸς τὴν ἀπολογίαν, ἀπόλοιντο δὲ οἱ δι' ἐμοῦ κινδυνεύοντες, ἥκω
ἀπολογησόμενος. ὑπὲρ δὲ ὧν ἀπολογεῖσθαί με δεῖ,
φράζε."

said that I wished to question you privately about your accuser's fabrications, that was quite a clever ruse so that I could talk with you, and you could feel confidence in me and be forewarned about the emperor. What his verdict on you will be I do not know, but his attitude is that of one who wants to condemn, but is embarrassed to do so on false grounds. He is making you his excuse to execute men of consular rank, because he wants something that he ought not, and brings it about by affecting a show of legality. I too must pretend to be hostile to you, since if he suspects me of aiming at your acquittal I do not know which of us will die first."

19. To this Apollonius replied, "We are speaking honestly, and you have told me everything in your heart, and I ought to do the same. You are as philosophical about your own position as my keenest followers are, and indeed you are so generous to us as to choose to share my danger. I will tell you my thoughts, therefore. I could have escaped from all of you into many parts of the world that are not subject to you, visited truly wise men, wiser than myself, and served the gods on correct principles. I could have gone to the lands of people more blessed than those here, among whom there are no indictments or accusations, since by the very fact of neither committing nor suffering injustice they need no courts of justice. But I was afraid to be accused as a traitor if I failed to appear in my own defense, while those who risked themselves because of me perished. So I have come to make my defense, but you must tell me against what charges I must make it."

---

9 αἱρεῖσθαι Radermacher: ἡγεῖσθαι
10 φύγοιμι Kay.: φύγω

20. "Αἱ μὲν ἰδέαι τῆς γραφῆς ποικίλαι τε" ἔφη "καὶ πλείους, καὶ γὰρ τὴν ἐσθῆτα διαβάλλουσι καὶ τὴν ἄλλην δίαιταν, καὶ τό ἐστιν ὑφ' ὧν προσκυνεῖσθαί σε, καὶ τὸ ἐν Ἐφέσῳ ποτὲ ὑπὲρ λοιμοῦ χρῆσαι, διειλέχθαι δὲ καὶ κατὰ τοῦ βασιλέως τὰ μὲν ἀφανῶς, τὰ δ' ἐκφάνδην, τὰ δ' ὡς θεῶν ἀκούσαντα, τὸ δὲ ἐμοὶ μὲν ἀπιθανώτατον (γιγνώσκω γάρ, ὅτι μηδὲ τὸ τῶν ἱερείων αἷμα ἀνέχῃ), τῷ δὲ βασιλεῖ πιθανώτατον διαβάλλεται· φασὶν ἐς ἀγρὸν βαδίσαντά σε παρὰ Νερούαν τεμεῖν αὐτῷ παῖδα Ἀρκάδα θυομένῳ ἐπὶ τὸν βασιλέα, καὶ ἐπᾶραι αὐτὸν τοῖς ἱεροῖς τούτοις, πεπρᾶχθαι δὲ ταῦτα νύκτωρ φθίνοντος ἤδη τοῦ μηνός.

2   "Τοῦτο δὲ τὸ κατηγόρημα, ἐπειδὴ πολλῷ μεῖζον, μὴ ἕτερόν τι παρ' ἐκεῖνο ἡγώμεθα, ὁ γὰρ λαμβανόμενος τοῦ σχήματος καὶ τῆς διαίτης καὶ τοῦ προγιγνώσκειν ἐς τοῦτο δήπου ξυντείνει, καὶ ταῦτά γε καὶ τὴν παρανομίαν τὴν ἐς αὐτὸν[11] δοῦναί σοί φησι καὶ τὸ ἐς τὴν θυσίαν θάρσος. χρὴ οὖν παρεσκευάσθαι τὴν ὑπὲρ τούτων ἀπολογίαν, ἔστω δέ σοι ὁ λόγος μὴ ὑπερορῶν τοῦ βασιλέως."

3   Καὶ ὁ Ἀπολλώνιος "τοῦ μὲν μὴ ὑπερορᾶν ἔστω τεκμήριόν σοι τὸ ὑπὲρ ἀπολογίας ἀφῖχθαί με, εἰ δὲ καὶ θρασέως οὕτω τἀμὰ εἶχεν, ὡς ὑπὲρ τυραννίδος αἴρεσθαι, ἀλλὰ σοί γε ὑπέσχον ἐμαυτὸν τοιῷδε ὄντι καὶ ἀγαπῶντί με. τὸ μὲν γὰρ ἐχθρῷ πονηρὸν δόξαι δεινὸν οὔπω, οἱ γὰρ ἐχθροὶ μισοῦσιν οὐκ ἀφ' ὧν

___
[11] αὐτὸν Kay.: αὐτὰ

20. "The counts of the indictment," said Aelianus, "are varied and numerous. They criticize your clothing and general habits, with receiving obeisance from some people, and for making a prediction in Ephesus once about a plague,[36] and they say you spoke against the emperor both in private and in public, or as if with divine authorization. One allegation is the least plausible of all to me, since I know that you find even the blood of sacrificial animals intolerable, but it is the most plausible to the emperor. You are said to have gone to Nerva in the country, and butchered an Arcadian boy for him when he was sacrificing for the emperor's harm; by these rites you raised his hopes, and all this was done at night towards the end of the month.

"Since this charge is much the gravest, let us not consider any other one comparable with it. When he seizes on your clothes, your habits, and your foreknowledge, he is clearly leading up to this charge, and claiming that those things led to your crime against him, and to your daring to perform the sacrifice. You must, then, prepare to answer all these charges, while your language must not be disrespectful towards the emperor."

"I do not disrespect him," said Apollonius, "as I have proved to you by appearing in my defense. Even if my situation gave me the courage to look down on tyrants, I would still have submitted to you, a man of your worth and a friend. To be thought wicked by an enemy is nothing very terrible, since enemies hate you not for what is alleged

36 Cf. IV 10.

APOLLONIUS OF TYANA

δημοσίᾳ διαβέβληταί τις, ἀλλ᾽ ἀφ᾽ ὧν ἰδίᾳ προσ-
κέκρουκε, τὸ δὲ πρὸς ἀνδρὸς φίλου λαβεῖν αἰτίαν, ὡς
κακὸς φαίνοιτο, βαρύτερον τοῦτο ἢ τὰ ἐχθρῶν ὁμοῦ
πάντα, οὐ γὰρ ἂν διαφύγοι τὸ μὴ οὐ κἀκείνοις, δι᾽ ἃ
κακὸς ἦν, ἀπηχθῆσθαι."

4   Ἐδόκει τῷ Αἰλιανῷ εὖ λέγειν, καὶ παρακελευ-
σάμενος αὐτῷ θαρρεῖν ἑαυτοῦ ἐλάβετο ὡς μὴ ἂν
ἐκπλαγέντος τοῦ ἀνδρός, μηδ᾽ ἂν <εἰ>¹² Γοργείη κεφα-
λὴ ἐπ᾽ αὐτὸν αἴροιτο. καλέσας οὖν τοὺς προστεταγμέ-
νους τὰ τοιαῦτα "κελεύω" ἔφη "ξυνέχειν τοῦτον, ἔστ᾽
ἂν ὁ βασιλεὺς ἥκοντά τε αὐτὸν μάθῃ καὶ λέγοντα
ὁπόσα εἴρηκε," καὶ ἐῴκει τοῖς μάλα ὠργισμένοις.
παρελθὼν δὲ ἐς τὰ βασίλεια τὰ προσήκοντα τῇ ἀρχῇ
ἔπραττεν.

21. Ἐνταῦθα ὁ Δάμις ἀπομνημονεύει ἔργου ὁμοίου
τε καὶ ἀνομοίου τῷ ἐπ᾽ Ἀριστείδου ποτὲ Ἀθήνησιν.
ὀστράκῳ μὲν γὰρ τὸν Ἀριστείδην ἐλαύνειν ἐπ᾽ ἀρετῇ,
ἔξω δὲ τείχους ἤδη ὄντι προσελθόντα τῶν ἀγροίκων
τινὰ δεῖσθαι αὐτοῦ γράφειν τι αὐτῷ ἐπ᾽ Ἀριστείδην
ὄστρακον. ἐκεῖνος μὲν οὔτε τὸν ἄνδρα εἰδὼς οὔτ᾽ αὐτὸ
τὸ γράφειν, ἀλλὰ μόνον τὸν ὑπὲρ τοῦ δικαίου φθόνον,
χιλίαρχος δὲ τῶν σφόδρα γιγνωσκόντων τὸν Ἀπολλώνιον προσειπὼν αὐτὸν ἤρετο κατὰ ὕβριν, ὑπὲρ ὅτου
κινδυνεύοι, τοῦ δὲ οὐκ εἰδέναι φήσαντος "ἀλλ᾽ ἐγὼ"
ἔφη "οἶδα· τὸ γὰρ προσκυνεῖσθαί σε ὑπὸ τῶν ἀνθρώπων διαβέβληκεν ὡς ἴσων ἀξιούμενον τοῖς θεοῖς."
"καὶ τίς" εἶπεν "ὁ προσκυνήσας ἐμέ;" "ἐγὼ" ἔφη "ἐν

against you in public, but from their private resentment. But to be accused by a true friend of showing yourself a coward is something more dreadful than all your enemies' deeds put together, since there is no escaping the condemnation of good men too for your cowardice."[37]

Aelianus thought these arguments good, and after 4 urging him to feel confidence, recovered his composure knowing that Apollonius would not be terrified even if threatened with the Gorgon's head. Summoning the men assigned to such duties, he said, "I order you to keep this man under guard until the emperor knows of his arrival and of the statements he has made." Putting on an appearance of great anger, he went to the palace and attended to the duties of his office.

21. Here Damis records an event both like and unlike what happened to Aristides at Athens. They were ostracising Aristides because of his virtue, and he was already outside the wall when a peasant came up to him, and asked him to inscribe a potsherd for him against Aristides. The man knew neither that excellent man nor how to write, but only that he was disliked for being just. [38] Apollonius, on the other hand, was addressed by a tribune who knew him very well, and asked him mockingly the cause of his danger. When he replied that he did not know, the other said, "Well, I do. The fact that you receive obeisance from human beings has exposed you to the charge of receiving equal honors with the gods." "Well, who has done obeisance to me?" asked Apollonius. "I did," he said,

[37] The Greek is uncertain.　　　[38] Cf. VI 21.4.

---

[12] ⟨εἰ⟩ Kay.

Ἐφέσῳ παῖς ἔτι ὤν, ὁπότε ἡμᾶς ἰάσω τοῦ λοιμοῦ."
"καλῶς ποιῶν," εἶπεν "αὐτός τε[13] σὺ καὶ ἡ σωθεῖσα
Ἔφεσος πόλις."

2   "Διὰ ταῦτ᾽ οὖν" ἔφη "καὶ ἀπολογίαν ὑπὲρ σοῦ
παρεσκεύακα, ἥ σε ἀπαλλάξει τῆς αἰτίας· ἴωμεν γὰρ
ἔξω τείχους, καὶ ἢν μὲν ἀποκόψω σου τὸν αὐχένα τῷ
ξίφει, διαβέβληται ἡ αἰτία καὶ ἀφεῖσαι, ἢν δὲ ἐκπλή-
ξῃς με καὶ μεθῶ τὸ ξίφος, θεῖόν τε ἀνάγκη νομίζεσθαί
σε καὶ ὡς ἐπ᾽ ἀληθέσι κρίνεσθαι." τοσῷδε μὲν δὴ
ἀγροικότερος οὗτος τοῦ τὸν Ἀριστείδην ἐλαύνοντος,
ἔλεγε δὲ ταῦτα μασώμενός τε καὶ ἐγγελῶν,[14] ὁ δ᾽ οὐκ
ἀκηκοότι ὅμοιος διελέγετο πρὸς τὸν Δάμιν ὑπὲρ τοῦ
Δέλτα, περὶ ᾧ φασι τὸν Νεῖλον σχίζεσθαι.

22. Ἐπεὶ δὲ καλέσας αὐτὸν ὁ Αἰλιανὸς ἐκέλευσε τὸ
ἐλευθέριον οἰκεῖν δεσμωτήριον "ἔστ᾽ ἂν γένηται σχο-
λή" ἔφη "τῷ βασιλεῖ, ξυγγενέσθαι γάρ σοι ἰδίᾳ
πρότερον βούλεται," ἀπῆλθε μὲν τοῦ δικαστηρίου καὶ
παρελθὼν ἐς τὸ δεσμωτήριον "διαλεγώμεθα," ἔφη
"Δάμι, τοῖς ἐνταῦθα· τί γὰρ ἂν ἄλλο πράττοι τις ⟨ἐς⟩[15]
τὸν χρόνον τοῦτον, ὃν διαλέξεταί μοι ὁ τύραννος ὑπὲρ
ὧν δεῖται;" "ἀδολέσχας" εἶπεν "ἡγήσονται ἡμᾶς, ἢν
ἐκκρούωμεν αὐτοὺς ὧν ἀπολογήσονται, καὶ ἄλλως
ἄτοπον περιπατεῖν ἐς ἀνθρώπους ἀθύμως ἔχοντας."
"καὶ μὴν τούτοις μάλιστα δεῖ" ἔφη "τοῦ διαλεξομένου
τε καὶ θεραπεύσοντος· εἰ γὰρ ἐνθυμηθείης τὰ τοῦ

---

[13] τε Cob.: γε   [14] ἐγγελῶν Cob.: ξυγγελῶν.
[15] ⟨ἐς⟩ Cob.

"when I was still a boy in Ephesus, when you cured us of the plague." "Then you acted rightly," said Apollonius, "both you and the city when it was saved."

"Well, because of that," said the man, "I have arranged 2 a defense that will get you acquitted from the charge. Let us go outside the wall, and if I cut off your head with my sword, that will refute the charge and you will be acquitted. But if you terrify me into dropping my sword, we will have to take you for someone superhuman, against whom the accusations are true." This shows how much more boorish this man was than the one who exiled Aristides, and he said all this while smirking and mocking. Apollonius, however, as if he had not heard him, talked with Damis about the Delta, around which they say the Nile divides.

22. Aelianus then summoned him, and ordered him to stay in the free prison[39] "until," he said, "the emperor is at leisure, since he wants to talk with you privately first." So after leaving the court and entering the prison, Apollonius said, "Let us converse with the people here, Damis. What else can one do until the time when the tyrant talks with me about his wishes?" "They will think us chatterboxes," said Damis, "if we distract them from preparing their defenses, and besides it is incongruous to argue with people who are depressed." "No," said Apollonius, "these people particularly need someone to converse with them, and to show them sympathy. You may remember the lines of

---

[39] That is, the part of the prison in which free persons were held.

Ὁμήρου ἔπη, ἐν οἷς Ὅμηρος τὴν Ἑλένην φησὶ τὰ ἐξ
Αἰγύπτου φάρμακα οἰνοχοεῖν ἐς τὸν κρατῆρα, ὡς τὰ
ἄχη τῆς ψυχῆς ἀποβρέχοιτο, δοκῶ μοι τὴν Ἑλένην
λόγους Αἰγυπτίους ἐκμαθοῦσαν ἐπᾴδειν τοῖς ἀθύμοις
ἐν τῷ κρατῆρι, ἰωμένην αὐτοὺς λόγῳ τε ἀναμὶξ καὶ
οἴνῳ."

2 "Καὶ εἰκὸς μέν," εἶπεν "εἴπερ ἐς Αἴγυπτόν τε ἦλθε
καὶ ὡμίλησε τῷ Πρωτεῖ, ἢ ὡς Ὁμήρῳ δοκεῖ, Πολυ-
δάμνῃ ξυνεγένετο τῇ τοῦ Θῶνος· νυνὶ δὲ ἀναβε-
βλήσθων οὗτοι, δέομαι γάρ τι ἐρέσθαι σε." "οἶδα,"
ἔφη "ὅ με ἐρήσῃ, τοὺς γάρ τοι λόγους, οἳ γεγόνασί
μοι πρὸς τὸν ἄνδρα, καὶ ἄττα εἶπε, καὶ εἰ φοβερὸς ἦν
ἢ πρᾶος, βούλει ἀκοῦσαί μου"· καὶ διῆλθε πάντας.
προσκυνήσας οὖν ὁ Δάμις "οὐκ ἀπιστῶ," ἔφη "καὶ τὴν
Λευκοθέαν ποτὲ κρήδεμνον τῷ Ὀδυσσεῖ δοῦναι μετὰ
τὴν ναῦν, ἧς ἐκπεσὼν ἀνεμέτρει ταῖς ἑαυτοῦ χερσὶ τὸ
πέλαγος· καὶ γὰρ ἡμῶν ἐς ἀμήχανά τε καὶ φοβερὰ
ἐμβεβηκότων θεῶν τις ὑπερέχει, οἶμαι, χεῖρα, ὡς μὴ
ἐκπέσοιμεν σωτηρίας πάσης."

3 Ἐπιπλήττων δ' ὁ Ἀπολλώνιος τῷ λόγῳ "ποῖ παρα-
τενεῖς," ἔφη "δεδιὼς ταῦτα καὶ μήπω γιγνώσκων, ὅτι
σοφία μὲν τὰ ξυνιέντα ἑαυτῆς ἐκπλήττει πάντα, αὐτὴ
δ' ὑπ' οὐδενὸς ἐκπλήττεται;" "ἀλλ' ἡμεῖς" εἶπε "παρὰ
ἀξύνετον ἥκομεν καὶ οὐ μόνον οὐκ ἐκπληττόμενον
ἡμᾶς, ἀλλ' οὐδὲ ἀξιοῦντα εἶναί τι, ὃ ἐκπλήξει αὐτόν."
"ξυνίης οὖν," ἔφη "ὦ Δάμι, ὅτι τετύφωται καὶ ἀνοήτως
ἔχει;" "ξυνίημι, τί δ' οὐ μέλλω;" εἶπε. "καὶ σοὶ δὴ" ἔφη

Homer in which he makes Helen pour Egyptian potions into the wine bowl to wash away the sorrows of the heart.[40] It seems to me that Helen had learned Egyptian doctrines, and charmed the despondent with them over her mixing bowl, relieving them with a blend of conversation and wine."

"Quite likely," said Damis, "since she had been to Egypt 2 and met Proteus, or in Homer's version became the friend of Polydamna, the wife of Thon.[41] However, let us postpone these topics, since I have a question for you." "I know what it will be," said Apollonius; "you want me to tell you the conversation I had with that good man, and all he said, and whether he was fierce or gentle," and he gave a full account. Damis bowed down before him, and said, "Now I believe that Leucothea once gave Odysseus her veil to use after he had lost his ship, and was crossing the open sea by swimming.[42] Though we too have fallen into a hopeless and dangerous situation, still some god is watching over us, I believe, so that we will not lose all chance of rescue."

Apollonius scolded him for these words. "How long will 3 you go on harboring such fears, and not realizing that wisdom scares all those who understand it, but itself is scared of nobody?" "But we," said Damis, "have come to somebody ignorant, who so far from being scared of us thinks that nothing should exist that scares him." "Well, Damis," said Apollonius, "you see him to be vain and foolish, do you not?" "I do," said Damis, "for how could I not?" "Then

40 *Odyssey* 4.220–30.
41 *Odyssey* 4.228.
42 *Odyssey* 5.333–53.

"καταφρονητέα τοῦ τυράννου τοσούτῳ μᾶλλον, ὅσῳ
καὶ γιγνώσκεις αὐτόν."

23. Διαλεγομένοις δ' αὐτοῖς ταῦτα προσελθών τις,
οἶμαι, Κίλιξ "ἐγώ," ἔφη "ἄνδρες, ὑπὲρ πλούτου κινδυνεύω." καὶ ὁ Ἀπολλώνιος "εἰ μὲν ἀφ' ὧν οὐ θεμιτόν"
ἔφη "πλουτῶν, οἷον λῃστείας ἢ φαρμάκων, ἃ δὴ
ἀνδροφόνα, ἢ τάφους κινήσας,[16] ὅσοι τῶν πάλαι βασιλέων εἰσίν, οἱ πολύχρυσοί τε καὶ θησαυρώδεις, οὐ
κρίνεσθαί σε χρὴ μόνον, ἀλλὰ καὶ ἀπολωλέναι, ταυτὶ
γὰρ πλοῦτος μέν, ἀλλ' ἐπίρρητός τε καὶ ὠμός, εἰ δὲ
κληρονομήσας ἢ διδούσης ἐμπορίας ἐλευθερίου τε καὶ
μὴ καπήλου, τίς οὕτω βαρύς, ὡς ἀφελέσθαι σε νόμου
σχήματι τὰ κτηθέντα σοι κατὰ νόμους;"

2   "Τὰ μὲν ὄντα μοι παρὰ πλειόνων" ἔφη "ξυγγενῶν
ἐστιν, ἐς μίαν δ' οἰκίαν τὴν ἐμὴν ἥκει, χρῶμαι δ'
αὐτοῖς οὔθ' ὡς ἑτέρων, ἐμὰ γάρ, οὔθ' ὡς ἐμοῖς, κοινὰ
γὰρ πρὸς τοὺς ἀγαθοὺς ἐστί μοι. διαβάλλουσι δ'
ἡμᾶς οἱ συκοφάνται μὴ ἐπ' ἀγαθῷ τῆς τυραννίδος
ἐκτῆσθαι τὸν πλοῦτον, ἐμοῦ τε γὰρ νεώτερα πει-
ρωμένου πράττειν ἐφόδιον ἂν γενέσθαι αὐτόν, ἑτέρῳ
τε, ὅτῳ προσθείμην, ῥοπὴν ἂν οὐ σμικρὰν τἀμὰ εἶναι.
μεμαντευμέναι δ' ἤδη καθ' ἡμῶν αἰτίαι, ὡς ὕβριν μὲν
τίκτει πᾶς ὁ ὑπὲρ τὸ μέτρον πλοῦτος, ὁ δ' ὑπὲρ τοὺς
πολλοὺς τὸν αὐχένα ἵστησι καὶ τὸ φρόνημα ἐγείρει,
νόμοις τε οὐκ ἐᾷ πείθεσθαι καὶ τοὺς ἄρχοντας, οἳ ἐς τὰ
ἔθνη φοιτῶσι, μόνον οὐκ ἐπὶ κόρρης παίει, δουλούμενος[17] τοῖς χρήμασιν ἢ ὑπερορῶν[18] αὐτῶν διὰ τὴν
ἰσχὺν τοῦ πλούτου.'

your contempt for the tyrant," said Apollonius, "should increase as you get to know him better."

23. While they were conversing in this way, someone came up (a Cilician, I think) and said, "I, gentlemen, am in danger because of my wealth." "If your wealth is from a forbidden source," said Apollonius, "from robbery for example, or some fatal of kind poison, or if you have plundered tombs that belonged to ancient kings, full of gold and treasure, then you should not only be tried but executed too. All those things are wealth, but of an abominable, savage kind. But if you have gained it by inheritance, or by trading in a respectable way and not a sordid one, who is so harsh as to deprive you in the name of law of what you have gained lawfully?"

"My fortune comes from several relatives," said the man, "and has devolved on my family alone. I do not treat it either as other people's, since it is mine, or as my own, since I share it with those who are good. But the informers allege that my acquiring this wealth is to the tyrant's disadvantage; if I attempted revolution, they say, it would give me the means, and anyone else I was to support would get no slight advantage from my estate. Enigmatic charges have already been laid against me, for example, 'All wealth above the average breeds arrogance, but wealth such as few have makes people stiff-necked, engenders pride, encourages lawlessness, and is virtually a slap in the face to the governors coming to the provinces, since either it enslaves them with bribes or despises them through the power of wealth.'

2

---

16 κινήσας Rsk.: ἐκίνησας   17 δουλούμενος Rsk.: δουλουμένους   18 ὑπερορῶν Rsk.: ὑπερορῶντας

APOLLONIUS OF TYANA

3 Ἐγὼ δὲ μειράκιον μὲν ὤν, πρὶν οὐσίαν ἑκατὸν
ταλάντων ἐκτῆσθαι, κατάγελων ἡγούμην πάντα καὶ
σμικρὰ ὑπὲρ τῶν ὄντων ἐδεδίειν, ἐπεὶ δὲ τάλαντά μοι
πεντακόσια ἐπὶ μιᾶς ἡμέρας ἐγένετο τελευτήσαντος
ἐπ' ἐμοὶ τοῦ πρὸς πατρὸς θείου, τοσοῦτον ἡ γνώμη
μετέβαλεν, ὅσον οἱ καταρτυθέντες[19] τῶν ἵππων καὶ
μεταβαλόντες[20] τοῦ ἀπαιδεύτου τε καὶ ἀκολάστου
ἤθους. ἐπιδιδόντος δέ μοι τοῦ πλούτου καὶ τὰ μὲν ἐκ
γῆς, τὰ δὲ ἐκ θαλάττης φέροντος, οὕτω τι ἐδουλώθην
ὑπὸ τοῦ περὶ αὐτὸν δέους, ὡς ἀπαντλεῖν τῆς οὐσίας τὸ
μὲν ἐς τοὺς συκοφάντας, οὓς ἔδει μειλίττεσθαι τῇ
ἀπομαγδαλιᾷ ταύτῃ, τὸ δὲ ἐς τοὺς ἄρχοντας, ὡς ἰσχὺς
πρὸς τοὺς ἐπιβουλεύοντας εἴη μοι, τὸ δὲ ἐς τοὺς
ξυγγενεῖς, ὡς μὴ φθονοῖεν τῷ πλούτῳ, τὸ δὲ ἐς
τοὺς δούλους, ὡς μὴ κακίους γίγνοιντο ἀμελεῖσθαι
φάσκοντες, ἐβουκολεῖτο δέ μοι καὶ ἀγέλη φίλων λαμ-
πρά· προορῶντες γὰρ οὗτοί μου τὰ μὲν αὐτοὶ ἔδρων,
τὰ δέ μοι προὔλεγον.

4 Ἀλλ' ὅμως οὕτω μὲν χαρακώσαντες τὸν πλοῦτον,
οὕτω δὲ ἀσφαλῶς τειχισάμενοι κινδυνεύομεν περὶ
αὐτῷ νῦν, καὶ οὔπω δῆλον οὐδ' εἰ τὸ σῶμα ἀθῷοι
μενοῦμεν." καὶ ὁ Ἀπολλώνιος, "θάρρει," ἔφη "τὸν γὰρ
πλοῦτον τοῦ σώματος ἐγγυητὴν ἔχεις· δέδεσαι μὲν
γὰρ δι' αὐτόν, ἀνήσει δέ σε ἀπολυόμενον οὐ μόνον τοῦ
δεσμωτηρίου τοῦδε, ἀλλὰ καὶ τοῦ θεραπεύειν τοὺς
συκοφάντας τε καὶ τοὺς δούλους, οἷς δι' αὐτὸν ὑπ-
έκεισο."

24. Ἑτέρου δ' αὖ φήσαντος γραφὴν φεύγειν,

268

"When I was young, before I had acquired an estate of a 3
hundred talents, I took nobody seriously, and had little
worry about my property. But then I came into five hundred talents in a single day when my paternal uncle left me
as his heir, and my way of thinking changed as much as that
of full-grown horses that give up their untamed, unbridled
ways. My wealth increased as it brought profit from both
land and sea, and I became such a slave to worrying about
it that I used up my fortune partly on informers, whom I
had to mollify by these tidbits, partly to governors, in order
to get support against conspirators, partly to relatives, so
that they would not envy my wealth, and partly to slaves, so
that they would not deteriorate because of my alleged neglect of them. I also found myself tending a fine flock of
friends, who watched out for me, sometimes acting themselves, and sometimes warning me about other people.

"Even so, after building this fence around our wealth 4
and fortifying it so strongly, we are now in danger because
of it, and are not sure even now of escaping bodily harm."
"Take courage," said Apollonius, "your wealth will go bail
for your person. It has caused you to be imprisoned, but
after your acquittal it will release you not only from this
prison, but from fawning on the informers and the slaves to
whom it subjected you."

24. Another man said that he was under indictment

---

19 καταρτυθέντες Valck.: καταρτύοντες
20 μεταβαλόντες Rsk.: μεταβάλλοντες

APOLLONIUS OF TYANA

ἐπειδὴ θύων ἐν Τάραντι, οὗ ἦρχε, μὴ προσέθηκε ταῖς
δημοσίαις εὐχαῖς, ὅτι Δομετιανὸς Ἀθηνᾶς εἴη παῖς
"σὺ μὲν ᾤήθης" ἔφη "μὴ ἂν τὴν Ἀθηνᾶν τεκεῖν παρ-
θένον οὖσαν τὸν ἀεὶ χρόνον, ἠγνόεις δ', οἶμαι, ὅτι ἡ
θεὸς αὕτη Ἀθηναίοις ποτὲ δράκοντα ἔτεκε."

25. Καθεῖρκτό τις καὶ ἐπὶ τοιᾷδε αἰτίᾳ· χωρίον ἐν
Ἀκαρνανίᾳ περὶ τὰς ἐκβολὰς τοῦ Ἀχελῴου ἔχων,
περιέπλει τὰς Ἐχινάδας ἐν ἀκατίῳ μικρῷ, διασκε-
ψάμενος δὲ αὐτῶν μίαν, ἢ ξυνῆπτεν ἤδη τῇ ἠπείρῳ,
δένδρεσί τε ὡραίοις διεφύτευσε καὶ ἀμπέλοις ἡδυοί-
νοις, δίαιτάν τε ἱκανὴν τῷ σώματι κατεσκευάσατο ἐν
αὐτῇ, καὶ γάρ τι καὶ ὕδωρ ἐκ τῆς ἠπείρου ἐσήγετο
ἀποχρῶν τῇ νήσῳ· ἐκ τούτου ἀνέφυ γραφή, μὴ καθαρὸς εἶναι ὁ Ἀκαρνὰν οὗτος, ἔργα δὲ αὐτῷ ξυνειδὼς οὐ
φορητὰ τῆς μὲν ἄλλης γῆς ἐξίστασθαί τε καὶ ἀπο-
φοιτᾶν ὡς μεμιασμένης ἑαυτῷ, τὴν δ' Ἀλκμαίωνος τοῦ
Ἀμφιάρεω λύσιν, δι' ἣν τὰς ἐκβολὰς τοῦ Ἀχελῴου
μετὰ τὴν μητέρα ᾤκησεν, ᾑρῆσθαι αὐτόν, εἰ μὴ καὶ
ἐφ' ὁμοίοις, ἀλλ' ἐπὶ σχετλίοις ἴσως καὶ οὐ πόρρω
ἐκείνων. ὁ δ' οὐ τοῦτ' ἔφασκεν, ἀλλὰ ἀπραγμοσύνης
ἐρῶν ἐκεῖ οἰκῆσαι, τὸ δὲ ἄρα ἐς δίκας αὐτῷ περι-
στῆναι, δι' ἃς καὶ εἴρχθαι αὐτόν.

26. Προσιόντων δὲ τῷ Ἀπολλωνίῳ πλειόνων ἔνδον

---

43 Domitian had a personal devotion to Athena, but is not
known to have thought himself her son. Athena did not give
birth to a snake, but she did set two snakes to guard the baby
Erechtheus, one of the Athenian heroes.

because when sacrificing in Tarentum, where he was a magistrate, he had not added to the public prayers the fact that Domitian was the son of Athena. "You," said Apollonius, "thought that Athena could not have children as a perpetual virgin, but you seem to have forgotten that this goddess once gave birth to a snake for the Athenians."[43]

25. Someone else was imprisoned on the following charge. He had an estate in Acarnania near the mouth of the Achelous, and used to sail round the Echinades in a small boat.[44] Noticing that one of them was now connected to the mainland, he planted it with fruit-bearing trees and vines that produce sweet wine, and built a retreat on it sufficient for his bodily needs, also bringing a water supply from the mainland that fed the whole island. Out of this there grew an indictment that this Acarnanian was polluted; because he had intolerable deeds on his conscience, he had retired and retreated from the rest of the world as if it were taboo to him; he had chosen the expiation that Amphiaraus's son Alcmaeon used after the death of his mother, if not for a similar crime, still for something wicked and perhaps not greatly different.[45] He however denied all this, saying that he had settled there from love of relaxation, and that this had brought the charges against him on which he was now imprisoned.

26. Many of those inside came to Apollonius with

[44] Acarnania: region of northwestern Greece, with the Achelous as its chief river. The Echinades islands are just off the coast.

[45] After killing his mother Eriphyle (cf. IV 38.3), Alcmaeon settled on one of the Echinades.

APOLLONIUS OF TYANA

καὶ ὀλοφυρομένων τοιαῦτα, πεντήκοντα γάρ που εἶναι
οἱ ἐν τῷ δεσμωτηρίῳ τούτῳ καὶ οἱ μὲν νοσεῖν αὐτῶν, οἱ
δὲ ἀθύμως παρεῖσθαι, οἱ δὲ ἐγκαρτερεῖν τὸν θάνατον,
οἱ δ᾽ ἐπιβοᾶσθαι τέκνα καὶ γονέας τοὺς αὐτῶν καὶ
γάμους, "ὦ Δάμι," ἔφη "δοκοῦσί μοι τοῦ φαρμάκου
δεῖσθαι οἱ ἄνδρες, οὓς κατάρχας ἐπεμνήσθην. εἴτ᾽ οὖν
Αἰγύπτιον τοῦτο, εἴτ᾽ ἐν πάσῃ τῇ γῇ φύεται ῥιζοτο-
μούσης αὐτὸ Σοφίας ἐκ τῶν ἑαυτῆς κήπων, προσδῶμεν αὐτοῦ τοῖς ἀθλίοις τούτοις, μὴ προανέλῃ σφᾶς ἡ
γνώμη." "προσδῶμεν," ἦ δ᾽ ὃς ὁ Δάμις "ἐοίκασι γὰρ
δεομένοις."

2   Ξυγκαλέσας οὖν αὐτοὺς ὁ Ἀπολλώνιος "ἄνδρες,"
εἶπεν "οἱ κοινωνοῦντες ἐμοὶ ταυτησὶ τῆς στέγης, ἐλεῶ
ὑμᾶς, ὡς ὑφ᾽ αὑτῶν ἀπόλλυσθε, οὔπω εἰδότες, εἰ ⟨ἡ⟩[21]
κατηγορία ἀπολεῖ ὑμᾶς· δοκεῖτε γάρ μοι προαποκτιν-
νύντες αὐτοὺς τοῦ καταψηφισθέντος ἂν ὑμῶν, ὡς
οἴεσθε, θανάτου, [καὶ][22] θαρρεῖν μὲν ἃ δέδιτε, δεδιέναι
δ᾽ ἃ θαρρεῖτε. οὐ μὴν προσήκει γε, ἀλλ᾽ ἐνθυμηθέντας
τὸν Ἀρχιλόχου τοῦ Παρίου λόγον, ὃς τὴν ἐπὶ τοῖς
λυπηροῖς καρτερίαν τλημοσύνην καλῶν θεῶν αὐτήν
φησιν εὕρημα οὖσαν, ἀναφέρειν τῶν σχετλίων τούτων, ὥσπερ οἱ τέχνῃ τοῦ ῥοθίου ὑπεραίροντες, ἐπειδὰν
τὸ κῦμα ὑπὲρ τὴν ναῦν ἱστῆται, μηδ᾽ ἡγεῖσθαι χαλεπὰ
ταῦτα, ἐφ᾽ ἃ ὑμεῖς μὲν ἄκοντες, ἐγὼ δὲ ἑκὼν ἥκω.

3   "Εἰ μὲν γὰρ ξυντίθεσθε ταῖς αἰτίαις, ὀλοφυρτέα ἡ
ἡμέρα μᾶλλον, ἐν ᾗ ὁ λογισμὸς ἐς ἄδικά τε καὶ ὠμὰ

---

[21] ⟨ἡ⟩ Rsk.   [22] [καὶ] secl. Cob.

272

similar sorrows, for there were about fifty people in this prison.[46] Some of them were ill, others were despondent and resigned, others faced death boldly, others groaned for their children, parents, and marriages. "Damis," said Apollonius, "these good people seem to me to need the remedy I mentioned earlier. Whether it is Egyptian or grows throughout the world, Wisdom culls it from her own garden, so let us share it with these poor souls so that their state of mind does not kill them too soon." "Yes, let us do so," said Damis, "as they look like people in need."

Apollonius therefore summoned them and said, "You 2 good men who are sharing this shelter with me, I pity you for doing away with yourselves before you know if an accusation will do so for you. In my opinion, you are committing suicide before the death to which you believe yourselves already condemned, so that you are confident about your fear, and fearful of your confidence. But that is not right. You should instead recall the words of Archilochus of Paros, who calls steadfastness in the face of misfortune 'fortitude' and an invention of the gods. [47] You should rise above these misfortunes, like those whose skill lets them ride the surge when a wave towers over their ship. You should not think our situation a hard one, when you fell into it against your will, but I by my own choice.

"If you agree with the charges, then you should mourn 3 instead for the day when your own judgment drove you into unlawful and cruel acts, and so brought you down.

46 I.e., the "free" prison, cf. 22.1.

47 Fragment 13 in D. Gerber, *Greek Iambic Poetry* (Loeb Classical Library).

ὁρμήσας ὑμᾶς ἔσφηλεν, εἰ δ᾽ οὔτε σὺ τὴν ἐν τῷ
Ἀχελῴῳ νῆσον ὑπὲρ ὧν ὁ κατήγορός φησιν ἐρεῖς
ᾠκηκέναι, οὔτε σὺ τὸν σεαυτοῦ πλοῦτον ἔφεδρόν ποτε
τῇ βασιλείᾳ στήσασθαι, οὔθ᾽ ἑκὼν σὺ τοῦ μὴ πρὸς
Ἀθηνᾶς δοκεῖν ἀφῃρῆσθαι τὸν ἄρχοντα, οὔθ᾽ ὑπὲρ ὧν
ἀφῖχθε κινδυνεύων ἕκαστος, ἀληθῆ ταῦτα εἶναι φή-
σει, τί βούλεταί" φησιν "ὁ ὑπὲρ τῶν οὐκ ὄντων θρῆνος
οὗτος; ὅσῳ γὰρ τοὺς οἰκειοτάτους ἐπιβοᾶσθε, τοσῷδε
χρὴ ἐρρῶσθαι μᾶλλον, ἆθλα γάρ που τῆς τλημοσύ-
νης ταύτης ἐκεῖνα.

4   "Ἦ τὸ καθεῖρχθαι δεῦρο δεινὸν εἶναί φατε, καὶ τὸ
ἐν τῷ δεσμωτηρίῳ ζῆν; ἢ ἀρχὴν ὧν πείσεσθε²³ ἡγεῖ-
σθε; ἢ καὶ καθ᾽ αὑτὸ τιμωρίαν, εἰ καὶ μηδὲν ἐπ᾽ αὐτῷ
πάθοιτε; ἀλλ᾽ ἔγωγε τὴν ἀνθρωπείαν εἰδὼς φύσιν
ἀναδιδάξω λόγον ὑμᾶς οὐδὲν ἐοικότα τοῖς τῶν ἰατρῶν
σιτίοις, καὶ γὰρ ἰσχὺν ἐνθήσει²⁴ καὶ ἀποθανεῖν οὐκ
ἐάσει. οἱ ἄνθρωποι ἐν δεσμωτηρίῳ ἐσμὲν τὸν χρόνον
τοῦτον, ὃς δὴ ὠνόμασται βίος· αὕτη γὰρ ἡ ψυχὴ
σώματι φθαρτῷ ἐνδεθεῖσα πολλὰ μὲν καρτερεῖ, δου-
λεύει δὲ πᾶσιν, ὁπόσα ἐπ᾽ ἄνθρωπον φοιτᾷ, οἰκία τε
οἷς ἐπενοήθη πρῶτον, ἀγνοῆσαί μοι δοκοῦσιν ἄλλο
δεσμωτήριον αὑτοῖς περιβάλλοντες, καὶ γὰρ δὴ καὶ
ὁπόσοι τὰ βασίλεια οἰκοῦσιν, ἀσφαλῶς ἐν αὑτοῖς
κατεσκευασμένοι, δεδέσθαι μᾶλλον τούτους ἡγώμεθα
ἢ οὓς αὐτοὶ δήσουσι.

5   "Πόλεις δ᾽ ἐνθυμουμένῳ μοι καὶ τείχη δοκεῖ ταῦτα
δεσμωτήρια εἶναι κοινά, ὡς δεδέσθαι μὲν ἀγοράζον-
τας, δεδέσθαι δὲ ἐκκλησιάζοντας καὶ θεωμένους αὖ

But suppose that *you* deny settling on the island in the Achelous for the reasons which your accuser alleges; *you* that you ever intended your wealth as a rival for the throne; *you* that you deliberately robbed the ruler of his alleged birth from Athena; suppose that none of you acknowledges the truth of the charges that endanger you and have brought you here, then what point is there in this crying over nothing? The more you grieve for your most loved ones, the more steadfast you should be, since they are the rewards of this courage of yours.

"But perhaps you consider it terrible to be pent up here   4
and to live in a prison? Is it that you think it a foretaste of your future sufferings, or a punishment in itself, even if you suffer nothing further? Now I know human nature, and will teach you a doctrine that is completely different from a doctor's prescription, since it will both give strength and save you from death. We mortals are in prison for the whole of the time named 'life.' This soul of ours is chained to a perishable body, has many sufferings, and is a slave to everything that befalls a human being. Whoever first had the idea of a house seems to me to have enclosed himself in a second prison without knowing it. Why, even those who live in palaces, safely ensconced within them, we may consider to be more confined than those whom *they* hope to confine.

"And when I consider cities and their walls, they seem   5
to me communal jails, so that people are imprisoned within them when trading, imprisoned when attending the assembly or the theater or when holding processions.

---

23 πείσεσθε Rsk.: πείσεσθαι
24 ἐνθήσει Cob.: ἐντίθησι

καὶ πομπὰς πέμποντας. καὶ Σκυθῶν ὁπόσοι ἁμαξεύου-
σιν, οὐ μεῖον ἡμῶν δέδενται, Ἴστροι τε γὰρ αὐτοὺς
ὁρίζουσι καὶ Θερμώδοντες καὶ Τανάιδες οὐ ῥᾴδιοι
ποταμοὶ ὑπερβῆναι, ἢν μὴ ὑπὸ τοῦ κρυμοῦ στῶσιν,
οἰκίας τε ἐπὶ τῶν ἁμαξῶν πέπανται καὶ φέρονται μέν,
ἀλλ᾽ ἐν αὐταῖς ἐπτηχότες. εἰ δὲ μὴ μειρακιώδης ὁ
λόγος, φασὶ καὶ τὸν Ὠκεανὸν δεσμοῦ ἕνεκα τῇ γῇ
περιβεβλῆσθαι.

6   "Ἴτε, ὦ ποιηταί, ταυτὶ γὰρ ὑμέτερα, καὶ ῥαψῳδεῖτε
πρὸς τούτους τοὺς ἀθύμους, ὡς Κρόνος μέν ποτε ἐδέθη
βουλαῖς τοῦ Διός, Ἄρης δὲ ὁ πολεμικώτατος ἐν οὐρανῷ μὲν ὑπὸ Ἡφαίστου πρότερον, ἐν γῇ δὲ ὑπὸ τῶν
τοῦ Ἀλωέως. ταῦτ᾽ ἐνθυμούμενοι καὶ πολλοὺς τῶν
σοφῶν τε καὶ μακαρίων ἀνδρῶν, οὓς δῆμοί τ᾽ ἀσελ-
γεῖς ἔδησαν, τυραννίδες δὲ προὐπηλάκισαν, δεχώ-
μεθα καὶ ταῦτα, ὡς μὴ τῶν δεξαμένων αὐτὰ λει-
ποίμεθα." οὕτω τοὺς ἐν τῷ δεσμωτηρίῳ τὰ ῥηθέντα
μετέβαλεν, ὡς σίτου τε οἱ πολλοὶ ἅψασθαι καὶ ἀπελθεῖν τῶν δακρύων βῆναί τε ἐπ᾽ ἐλπίδος μηδ᾽ ἂν παθεῖν
μηδὲν ἐκείνῳ ξυνόντες.

27. Τῆς δ᾽ ὑστεραίας διελέγετο μὲν ἐς τὸν αὐτὸν
νοῦν ξυντείνων, ἐσπέμπεται δέ τις ἀκροατὴς τῶν διαλέξεων ὑπὸ τοῦ Δομετιανοῦ καθειμένος, τὸ μὲν δὴ
σχῆμα αὐτοῦ, κατηφὴς ἐδόκει καὶ κινδυνεύειν τι, ὡς
ἔφασκε, μέγα, γλώττης δὲ[25] οὐκ ἀνεπιτηδεύτως εἶχεν,
οἷοι τῶν συκοφαντικῶν οἱ συνειλοχότες ὀκτὼ ῥήματα

────────

25 δὲ West.: τε

276

Even those Scythians who live on carts are imprisoned no less than we are, since they are confined by your Ister, Thermodon, or Tanais,[48] rivers not easy to cross unless they are frozen hard. They too possess houses built on carts, and carry them around, but do so crouching inside them. If the idea is not childish, it is said that the ocean surrounds the earth like fetters.

"Come, you poets, since this is your province, weave 6 songs for these despondent people about Cronos who was once imprisoned by the will of Zeus, and about the most warlike Ares, who was first bound by Hephaestus in heaven, and then by the sons of Aloeus on earth.[49] Think of all that, and of the many wise and blessed men whom a licentious citizenry imprisoned or a tyranny insulted, and let us too accept our lot, and not fail those who accepted theirs." These words so altered those in the prison that most of them took food and left off crying, and went in hope that they would not suffer any harm at all so long as he was with them.

27. The next day Apollonius was discoursing in the same vein when someone was admitted whom Domitian had suborned to overhear his discourses. In appearance the man seemed dejected, and claimed to be in great danger, and he was quite a skilled talker, as informers are when they have got up eight or ten phrases. Understanding his

48 Ister: the Danube. Thermodon: unidentified river of the Caucasus. Tanais: the Don.

49 Zeus and Cronos: Aeschylus, *Eumenides* 641, Plato, *Republic* 378 A, etc. Hephaestus and Ares : *Odyssey* 8.266–366. Ares and the sons of Aloeus, Otos, and Ephialtes: *Iliad* 5.385–391.

277

ἢ δέκα, ὁ δὲ Ἀπολλώνιος ξυνιεὶς τῆς τέχνης διελέγετο,
ἃ μὴ ἐκείνῳ προὔβαινε, ποταμῶν τε γὰρ πρὸς αὐτοὺς
ἐμέμνητο καὶ ὀρῶν καὶ θηρία διῄει καὶ δένδρα, ὑφ' ὧν
οἱ μὲν διήγοντο, ὁ δ' οὐδὲν ἐπέραινεν. ὡς δὲ καὶ
ἀπάγειν αὐτὸν ἐς λοιδορίας τοῦ τυράννου ἐπειρᾶτο "ὦ
τᾶν," ἔφη "σὺ μέν, ὅ τι βούλει, λέγε, οὐ γὰρ διαβε-
βλήσῃ γε ὑπ' ἐμοῦ, ἐγὼ δὲ ὁπόσα μέμφομαι τὸν
βασιλέα, πρὸς αὐτὸν λέξω."

28. Ἐγένετο καὶ ἕτερα ἐν τῷ δεσμωτηρίῳ τούτῳ
ἐπεισόδια, τὰ μὲν ἐπιβεβουλευμένα, τὰ δέ, ὡς ξυν-
έπεσεν, οὔπω μεγάλα, οὐδ' ἄξια ἐμοὶ σπουδάσαι,
Δάμις δέ, οἶμαι, ὑπὲρ τοῦ μὴ παραλελοιπέναι τι
αὐτῶν ἐπεμνήσθη, τὰ δὲ λόγου ἐχόμενα. ἑσπέρα μὲν
ἦν, καθεῖρκτο δὲ ἡμέραν ἤδη πέμπτην, παρελθὼν δέ
τις ἐς τὸ δεσμωτήριον Ἑλληνικὸς τὴν φωνὴν "ποῦ"
ἔφη "ὁ Τυανεύς;" καὶ ἀπολαβὼν αὐτὸν "αὔριον" ἔφη
"διαλέξεταί σοι ὁ βασιλεύς· Αἰλιανοῦ δὲ ταῦτα ἀκηκοέναι δόκει." "ξυνίημι" ἦ δ' ὃς "τοῦ ἀπορρήτου, μόνου
γὰρ δὴ ἐκείνου εἰδέναι αὐτό." "καὶ μὴν καὶ τῷ ἐπὶ τοῦ
δεσμωτηρίου προείρηται" ἔφη "πᾶν, εἴ τι βούλοιο,
ἐπιτηδείῳ σοι εἶναι."

2   "Καλῶς μὲν ποιοῦντες ὑμεῖς," εἶπεν "ἐγὼ δὲ καὶ τὸν
ἐνταῦθα βίον καὶ τὸν ἔξω ταὐτὸν πράττω, διαλέγομαι
μὲν γὰρ ὑπὲρ τῶν παραπιπτόντων, δέομαι δ' οὐδενός."
"οὐδὲ τοῦ ξυμβουλεύσοντος," ἔφη "Ἀπολλώνιε, ὡς
διαλέξῃ τῷ βασιλεῖ;" "νὴ Δί'" εἶπεν "εἰ μὴ κολακεύειν
πείθοι." "τί δ', εἰ μὴ ὑπερορᾶν," ἔφη, "μηδ' ὑπερ-
φρονεῖν αὐτοῦ;" "ἄριστα" εἶπε "ξυμβουλεύσει, καὶ ὡς

ruse, Apollonius conversed on subjects of no use to him, mentioning rivers and mountains to his audience and describing animals and trees, which entertained them but gave no help to the man. When he tried to induce Apollonius to abuse the emperor, Apollonius said, "My friend, you may say what you like, since you will not be accused by me. All my criticisms of the emperor I will make to his face."

28. There were other episodes in this prison, some of them contrived, others fortuitous, but they are not important or worth my describing, though Damis doubtless recorded them so as to leave nothing out. The following, however, are relevant. It was the evening of Apollonius's fifth day under guard, when someone who spoke Greek entered the prison and said, "Where is the man from Tyana?" Taking Apollonius aside, he said, "The emperor will talk with you tomorrow. Consider this a message from Aelianus." "I understand the secret," said Apollonius, "and that you have heard it from him alone." "Moreover," said the other, "the superintendent of the prison has been instructed to be at your service for anything you desire."

"It is kind of you all," replied Apollonius, "but I lead the same life here and outside. I talk on any subject that offers, and need nothing." "Not even an adviser, Apollonius," the man asked, "about addressing the emperor?" "I do indeed need that," replied Apollonius, "unless he urges me to use flattery." "Suppose he urges you not to show contempt or disrespect for him?" asked the man. "That will be excellent advice," answered Apollonius, "and what I had decided on

2

ἐμαυτὸν πέπεικα." "ὑπὲρ τούτων μὲν ἥκω" ἔφη "καὶ
χαίρω παρεσκευασμένον σε ὁρῶν ξυμμέτρως, δεῖ δὲ
καὶ πρὸς τὸ φθέγμα τοῦ βασιλέως παρεσκευάσθαι σε
καὶ πρὸς τὸ δύστροπον τοῦ προσώπου, φθέγγεται μὲν
γὰρ βαρύ, κἂν πράως διαλέγηται, ἡ δ' ὀφρὺς ἐπίκει-
ται τῷ τοῦ ὀφθαλμοῦ ἤθει, μεστὴ δ' ἡ παρειὰ χολῆς,
τουτὶ γὰρ μάλιστα ἐπιφαίνει. ταῦτα, ὦ Τυανεῦ, μὴ
ἐκπληττώμεθα, ἔστι γὰρ φύσεως μᾶλλον καὶ ἀεὶ
ὅμοια."

3   Καὶ ὁ Ἀπολλώνιος "Ὀδυσσεὺς μέντοι" ἔφη "παριὼν ἐς τὸ τοῦ Πολυφήμου ἄντρον, καὶ μηδ'[26] ὁπόσος
ἐστὶ προακηκοὼς πρότερον, μηδ' οἷα σιτεῖται, μηδ' ὡς
βροντᾷ ἡ φωνή, ἐθάρρησέ τε αὐτὸν καίτοι ἐν ἀρχῇ
δείσας καὶ ἀπῆλθε τοῦ ἄντρου ἀνὴρ δόξας, ἐμοὶ δὲ
ἐξελθεῖν αὔταρκες ἐμαυτόν τε σώσαντα καὶ τοὺς ἑταίρους, ὑπὲρ ὧν κινδυνεύω." τοιαῦτα διαλεχθεὶς πρὸς
τὸν ἥκοντα καὶ ἀπαγγείλας αὐτὰ πρὸς τὸν Δάμιν
ἐκάθευδεν.

29. Περὶ δὲ ὄρθρον γραμματεύς τις ἥκων τῶν
βασιλείων δικῶν "κελεύει σε ὁ βασιλεύς," ἔφη "ὦ
Ἀπολλώνιε, περὶ πλήθουσαν ἀγορὰν ἐς τὴν αὐλὴν
ἥκειν, οὔπω ἀπολογησόμενον, ἀλλ' ἰδεῖν τέ σε, ὅστις
ὢν τυγχάνεις, βούλεται καὶ ξυγγενέσθαι μόνῳ." "τί
οὖν" εἶπεν "ὑπὲρ τούτων ἐμοὶ διαλέγῃ;" "οὐ γὰρ σὺ"
ἔφη "Ἀπολλώνιος;" "νὴ Δί'," εἶπεν "ὁ Τυανεύς γε."
"πρὸς τίνα οὖν" ἔφη "ταῦτα εἴπω;" "πρὸς τοὺς ἄξοντάς
με," εἶπε "χρὴ γάρ που ὡς ἐκ δεσμωτηρίου φοιτᾶν."
"προστέτακται" ἔφη "προτέροις γε ἐκείνοις ταῦτα,

myself." "That is my mission," said the man, "and I am glad
to see you reasonably well prepared. But you also have to
be ready for the emperor's voice and his grim expression,
since he sounds harsh even when he is talking kindly, his
brow matches the expression of his eye, and his cheek is
flushed with anger (this feature is very conspicuous). We
must not be scared by these things, man of Tyana, since
they are part of his general nature and always the same."

"And yet," replied Apollonius, "Odysseus went into the 3
Cyclops's cave without any previous knowledge of the giant's size, or food, or thunderous voice, and still he faced
up to him, after his initial fear, and left the cave by proving
himself a man. For me it is enough to leave after saving myself and the friends for whose sake I am in jeopardy." After
this conversation with the visitor, which he reported to
Damis, he went to sleep.

29. At daybreak there arrived a secretary of the royal
tribunal who said, "Apollonius, the emperor orders you to
come to court at mid-morning, not yet to make your defense, but so that he can see what kind of person you may
be. He also wants to talk with you alone." "Why then," said
Apollonius, "are you talking with me about this?" "You are
Apollonius, are you not?" he asked. "Yes," he replied, "the
one from Tyana." "Then to whom should I say this?" "To
those who are going to escort me," said Apollonius, "because it is a prison that I have to come from." "They have
already received these orders," said the clerk, "and I too

---

²⁶ μηδ' Jon.: μήτε

κἀγὼ δὲ ἀφίξομαι τοῦ καιροῦ, νυνὶ δὲ παραγγελῶν[27]
ἦλθον, ταυτὶ γὰρ μάλα ἑσπέρας προστέτακται."

30. Ὁ μὲν δὴ ἀπῆλθεν, ὁ δ' Ἀπολλώνιος ἀνα-
παύσας ἑαυτὸν ἐπὶ τῆς κλίνης "ὕπνου" ἔφη "δέομαι,
Δάμι, χαλεπὴ γάρ μοι ἡ νὺξ γέγονεν, ἀναμνησθῆναι
βουλομένῳ ὧν Φραώτου ποτὲ ἤκουσα." "καὶ μὴν ἐγρηγορέναι τε" εἶπεν "ἐχρῆν μᾶλλον καὶ ξυντάττειν ἑαυτὸν ἐς τὸ παρηγγελμένον, μέγα οὕτως ὄν." "καὶ πῶς
ἂν ξυντατοίμην" ἔφη "μηδέ, τί ἐρήσεται, εἰδώς;"
"αὐτοσχεδιάσεις οὖν" εἶπεν "ὑπὲρ τοῦ βίου;" "νὴ Δί'"
ἔφη "ὦ Δάμι, αὐτοσχεδίῳ γὰρ αὐτῷ χρῶμαι.

2   "Ἀλλ' ὅ γε ἀνεμνήσθην τοῦ Φραώτου βούλομαι
διελθεῖν πρὸς σέ, χρηστὸν γὰρ ἐς τὰ παρόντα καὶ σοὶ
δόξει. τοὺς λέοντας, οὓς τιθασεύουσιν ἄνθρωποι, κελεύει Φραώτης μήτε παίειν, μνησικακεῖν γὰρ αὐτούς,
εἰ παίοιντο, μήτε θεραπεύειν, ἀγερώχους γὰρ ἐκ τούτου γίγνεσθαι, ξὺν ἀπειλῇ δὲ μᾶλλον καταψῶντας ἐς
εὐάγωγα ἤθη ἄγειν. τοῦτο δὲ οὐχ ὑπὲρ τῶν λεόντων
εἶπεν, οὐ γὰρ ὑπὲρ θηρίων ἀγωγῆς ἐσπουδάζομεν,
ἀλλ' ἡνίαν ἐπὶ τοὺς τυράννους διδούς, ᾗ χρωμένους
οὐκ ἂν ἐκπεσεῖν ἡγεῖτο τοῦ ξυμμέτρου."

3   "Ἄριστα μὲν" ἔφη "ὁ λόγος οὗτος ἐς τὰ τυράννων
ἤθη εἴρηται. ἀλλ' ἔστι τις καὶ παρὰ τῷ Αἰσώπῳ λέων
ὁ ἐν τῷ σπηλαίῳ, φησὶ δ' αὐτὸν ὁ Αἴσωπος οὐ νοσεῖν
μέν, δοκεῖν δέ, καὶ τῶν θηρίων, ἃ ἐφοίτα παρ' αὐτόν,
ἅπτεσθαι, τὴν δὲ ἀλώπεκα 'τί τούτῳ χρησόμεθα,'

---

[27] παραγγελῶν Rsk.: παραγγέλλων

will come in good time, but for now I have only come to re-lay the message, since the orders were given late yesterday evening."

30. The secretary then left, while Apollonius lay down on his bed and said, "I need sleep, Damis, since I have had a bad night trying to recall something I once heard from Phraotes." "But you ought to stay awake, rather," said Damis, "and prepare yourself for the appointment, since it is so important." "How could I prepare myself," asked Apollonius, "before knowing what he is going to ask?" "Will you improvise, then," asked Damis, "when your life is at stake?" "Yes indeed, Damis," he replied, "for my life is an improvisation.

"But I want to tell you the remark of Phraotes which I 2 recalled, because you will consider it useful in the circum-stances too. When people tame lions, so Phraotes advises, they should not strike them, since striking makes them vengeful, nor spoil them, because that makes them arro-gant. Instead, they should both threaten and stroke them to lead them into docile ways. He was not referring to lions, since our conversations were not about animal train-ing, but to give me reins to control tyrants. If I used them, he thought, I would not leave the path of reason."

"That observation," replied Damis, "is very apposite to 3 a tyrant's character, but in Aesop too there is the lion in the cave.[50] According to Aesop, it was not ill, but only pretend-ing, and seized any animals that visited it. But the vixen said, 'What am I to make of him? Nobody comes away from

[50] No. 142 Perry.

εἰπεῖν,[28] 'παρ' οὗ μηδὲ ἀναλύει τις, μηδὲ δείκνυταί τι τῶν ἐξιόντων ἴχνος;'" καὶ ὁ Ἀπολλώνιος "ἀλλ' ἐγὼ" ἔφη "σοφωτέραν τὴν ἀλώπεκα ἡγούμην ἄν, εἰ παρελθοῦσα ἔσω μὴ ἧλω, ἀλλ' ἐξῆλθε τοῦ σπηλαίου τὰ ἴχνη τὰ ἑαυτῆς δεικνῦσα."

31. Ταῦτα εἰπὼν ὕπνου ἔσπασε κομιδῇ βραχὺ καὶ ὅσον ἐπ' ὀφθαλμοὺς ἦλθεν, ἡμέρα δ' ὡς ἐγένετο, προσευξάμενος τῷ Ἡλίῳ, ὡς ἐν δεσμωτηρίῳ εἰκός, διελέγετο τοῖς προσιοῦσιν, ὁπόσα ἠρώτων, καὶ οὕτως ἀγορᾶς πληθούσης ἀφικνεῖται γραμματεὺς κελεύων ἐπὶ θύρας ἤδη εἶναι "μὴ καὶ θᾶττον" ἔφη "ἐσκληθῶμεν." ὁ δὲ εἰπὼν "ἴωμεν" ξὺν ὁρμῇ προῆλθε. πορευομένῳ δ' αὐτῷ δορυφόροι ἐπηκολούθουν τέτταρες πλέον ἀπέχοντες ἢ οἱ φυλακῆς ἕνεκα ὁμαρτοῦντες, ἐφείπετο δὲ καὶ ὁ Δάμις δεδιὼς μέν, ξυννοοῦντι δ' ὅμοιος. ἑώρων μὲν δὴ ἐς τὸν Ἀπολλώνιον ἅπαντες, αὐτοῦ τε γὰρ τοῦ σχήματος ἀπεβλέπετο καὶ θεία ἐδόκει ἡ περὶ τῷ εἴδει ἔκπληξις, καὶ αὐτὸ δὲ τὸ ἥκειν ὑπὲρ ἀνδρῶν κινδυνεύσοντα καὶ τοὺς βασκαίνοντας αὐτῷ πρότερον ἐπιτηδείους ἐποίει τότε.

2   Προσεστὼς δὲ τοῖς βασιλείοις καὶ τοὺς μὲν θεραπευομένους ὁρῶν, τοὺς δὲ θεραπεύοντας, ἐσιόντων τε καὶ ἐξιόντων κτύπον "δοκεῖ μοι," ἔφη "ὦ Δάμι, βαλανείῳ ταῦτα εἰκάσθαι, τοὺς μὲν γὰρ ἔξω ἔσω ὁρῶ σπεύδοντας, τοὺς δὲ ἔσω ἔξω, παραπλήσιοι δέ εἰσιν οἱ μὲν ἐκλελουμένοις, οἱ δ' ἀλούτοις." τὸν λόγον τοῦτον ἄσυλον κελεύω φυλάττειν καὶ μὴ τῷ δεῖνι ἢ τῷ δεῖνι προσγράφειν αὐτὸν οὕτω τι Ἀπολλωνίου ὄντα,

him, and no tracks are visible of those exiting.'" Apollonius replied, "For myself, I would have thought the vixen more clever if she had gone inside and not been caught, but had left the cave making her own tracks visible."

31. After saying this, he snatched a very short sleep, just as much as settled on his eyes, and at daybreak prayed to the Sun, so far as was possible in a prison, and conversed with those who came to him about their various problems. Eventually the secretary came at mid-morning and said that Apollonius should be at the doors at once, "in case we are summoned sooner." "Let us go," replied Apollonius, and started out eagerly. As he went, four armed men followed him, keeping a greater distance than those who follow in the manner of bodyguards, and Damis came along also, fearful but with a meditative expression. Everyone looked at Apollonius, since he drew attention by his appearance, there was an unearthly majesty in his expression, and the very fact that he had come to risk his life for honorable men now made even his previous detractors supportive of him.

Standing outside the palace, he saw some people receiving flattery and others paying it, and the hubbub of people going in and out, at which he said: "This place, Damis, seems to me like a bathhouse. I see those outside hurrying to get in and those inside hurrying to get out, and some look washed and others unwashed." (This remark, I give notice, is to be kept under copyright, and is not to be ascribed to this person or that. It is so much Apollonius's

2

---

28 εἰπεῖν Rsk.: εἶπε

ὡς καὶ ἐς ἐπιστολὴν αὐτῷ ἀναγεγράφθαι. ἰδὼν δέ τινα
μάλα πρεσβύτην ἐπιθυμοῦντα μὲν ἄρχειν, δι' αὐτὸ δὲ
τοῦτο ἀρχόμενον καὶ θεραπεύοντα τὸν βασιλέα "τοῦτον," ἔφη "ὦ Δάμι, οὐδὲ Σοφοκλῆς πω πέπεικε τὸν
λυττῶντά τε καὶ ἄγριον δεσπότην ἀποφυγεῖν." "ὃν
ἡμεῖς," εἶπεν "Ἀπολλώνιε, καὶ αὐτοὶ ἠρήμεθα· ταῦτά
τοι καὶ προσεστήκαμεν θύραις τοιαύταις."

3   "Δοκεῖς μοι" ἔφη "ὦ Δάμι, καὶ τὸν Αἰακόν, ὅσπερ
ἐν Ἅιδου λέγεται, φρουρὸν ἡγεῖσθαι τουτωνὶ τῶν
πυλῶν εἶναι, τεθνεῶτι γὰρ δὴ ἔοικας." "οὐ τεθνεῶτι,"
ἔφη "τεθνηξομένῳ δέ." καὶ ὁ Ἀπολλώνιος, "ἀφυής,"
εἶπεν "ὦ Δάμι, πρὸς τὸν θάνατον εἶναί μοι φαίνῃ,
καίτοι ξυνῶν μοι χρόνον, ἐκ μειρακίου φιλοσοφῶν,
ἐγὼ δὲ ᾤμην παρεσκευάσθαι τέ σε πρὸς αὐτὸν καὶ τὴν
ἐν ἐμοὶ τακτικὴν εἰδέναι πᾶσαν, ὥσπερ γὰρ τοῖς
μαχομένοις καὶ ὁπλιτεύουσιν οὐκ εὐψυχίας δεῖ μόνον,
ἀλλὰ καὶ τάξεως ἑρμηνευούσης τοὺς καιροὺς τῆς
μάχης, οὕτω καὶ τοῖς φιλοσοφοῦσιν ἐπιμελητέα τῶν
καιρῶν, ἐν οἷς ἀποθανοῦνται, ὡς μὴ ἄτακτοι, μηδὲ
θανατῶντες, ξὺν ἀρίστῃ δ' αἱρέσει ἐς αὐτοὺς φέροιντο.
ὅτι δὲ ἄριστά τε καὶ κατὰ τὸν προσήκοντα φιλοσοφίᾳ
καιρὸν εἱλόμην ἀποθνήσκειν, εἴ τις ἀποκτείνειν βού-
λοιτο, ἑτέροις τε ἀπολελόγημαι σοῦ παρόντος, αὐτόν
τε σὲ διδάσκων ἀπείρηκα."

32. Ἐπὶ τοσοῦτον μὲν δὴ ταῦτα, ἐπεὶ δὲ σχολὴ τῷ
βασιλεῖ ἐγένετο, τὰ ἐν ποσὶ διωσαμένῳ πάντα, ἐς
λόγους ἀφικέσθαι τῷ ἀνδρί, παρῆγον μὲν αὐτὸν ἐς τὰ
βασίλεια οἱ ἐπιμεληταὶ τῶν τοιούτων, οὐ ξυγχωρή-

own that he incorporated it in a letter.[51]) Seeing a very old man eager to be a governor and for that same reason acting like a subject and flattering the emperor, he said, "This man, Damis, has not yet even been persuaded by Sophocles to shun his raging, savage master."[52] "Yes, Apollonius," said Damis, "the very master that we have chosen too: that is why we are standing at such doors as these."

"You seem to me, Damis," replied Apollonius, "to suppose that the same Aeacus who is said to be in Hades also guards these gates, for you look like a dead man." "Not dead," replied Damis, "but on the point of death." Apollonius replied, "You appear to me, Damis, to be unready for death, even though you have been with me for a while, studying philosophy from your youth. I thought you were ready for it, and knew all the tactics I command. Just as fighters and heavy-armed soldiers need not only courage, but also the tactical skill that perceives the crisis of a battle, so also philosophers must watch for the crisis at which they will die, so that they may not advance towards it in a disorderly or suicidal manner, but with perfect judgment. I have chosen to die in the best way and at the moment suitable for a philosopher, if someone wishes to kill me. I have explained this to others in your presence, and am tired of teaching it to you in particular."

32. So much for this. The emperor having set aside all immediate business and being at leisure to talk with the Master, he was led into the palace by those assigned to such duties, who did not allow Damis to follow him. The

---

[51] This letter is not preserved.
[52] See on I 13.3.

σαντες τῷ Δάμιδι ἐπισπέσθαι οἱ. θαλλοῦ δὲ στέφανον
ἔχων ὁ βασιλεὺς ἄρτι μὲν τῇ Ἀθηνᾷ τεθυκὼς ἐτύγχανεν ἐν αὐλῇ Ἀδώνιδος, ἡ δὲ αὐλὴ ἀνθέων ἐτεθήλει
κήποις, οὓς Ἀδώνιδι Ἀσσύριοι ποιοῦνται ὑπὲρ ὀργίων, ὁμωροφίους αὐτοῖς²⁹ φυτεύοντες. πρὸς δὲ τοῖς
ἱεροῖς ὢν μετεστράφη καὶ ἐκπλαγεὶς ὑπὸ τοῦ εἴδους
τοῦ ἀνδρὸς "Αἰλιανέ," εἶπε "δαίμονά μοι ἐπεσήγαγες."

2   Ἀλλ' οὔτε ἐκπλαγεὶς ὁ Ἀπολλώνιος, καθαπτόμενός
τε ὢν ἤκουσεν, "ἐγὼ δὲ" ἔφη "τὴν Ἀθηνᾶν ᾤμην
ἐπιμεμελῆσθαί σου, βασιλεῦ, τρόπον, ὃν καὶ τοῦ Διομήδους ποτὲ ἐν Τροίᾳ, τὴν γάρ τοι ἀχλύν, ὑφ' ἧς οἱ
ἄνθρωποι χεῖρον βλέπουσιν, ἀφελοῦσα τῶν τοῦ Διομήδους ὀφθαλμῶν ἔδωκεν αὐτῷ θεούς τε διαγιγνώ-
σκειν καὶ ἄνδρας, σὲ δ' οὔπω ἡ θεὸς ἐκάθηρεν, ὦ
βασιλεῦ, τὴν κάθαρσιν ταύτην· ἦ μὴν ἔδει γε, ὡς
αὐτὴν τὴν Ἀθηνᾶν ὁρῴης ἄμεινον, τούς τε ἄνδρας μὴ
ἐς τὰ τῶν δαιμόνων εἴδη τάττοις." "σὺ δέ," εἶπεν "ὦ
φιλόσοφε, πότε τὴν ἀχλὺν ἐκαθήρω ταύτην;" "πάλαι"
ἔφη "κἀξ ὅτου φιλοσοφῶ."

3   "Πῶς οὖν" εἶπε "τοὺς ἐμοὶ πολεμιωτάτους ἄνδρας
θεοὺς ἐνόμισας;" "καὶ τίς" ἔφη "πρὸς Ἰάρχαν σοι
πόλεμος ἢ πρὸς Φραώτην τοὺς Ἰνδούς, οὓς ἐγὼ μό-
νους ἀνθρώπων θεούς τε ἡγοῦμαι καὶ ἀξίους τῆς
ἐπωνυμίας ταύτης;" "μὴ ἄπαγε ἐς Ἰνδούς," εἶπεν "ἀλλ'
ὑπὲρ τοῦ φιλτάτου σοι Νερούα καὶ τῶν κοινωνούντων
αὐτῷ τῆς αἰτίας λέγε." "ἀπολογῶμαι ὑπὲρ αὐτοῦ" ἔφη

²⁹ αὐτοῖς Rsk.: αὐτούς

emperor was wearing an olive crown, having just sacrificed to Athena in the court of Adonis, and this court was bright with the flowerpots that the Assyrians prepare for the rites of Adonis, planting them within their houses.[53] Intent on his sacrifice, the emperor turned around and, taken aback by the Master's appearance, said, "Aelianus, you have brought a demon before me."

Undismayed, and taking his cue from what he had just heard, Apollonius said, "I would have thought Athena had made the same provision for you, Majesty, that she once did for Diomedes in Troy. She took away from Diomedes's eyes the mist that prevents men from seeing fully, and gave him the power to distinguish gods and men.[54] But the goddess has not yet cleansed you in that way, Majesty. She really should have done so, in order that you could see Athena herself better, and not take men for demons in disguise." "And you, philosopher," said Domitian, "when were you cleansed of this mist?" "Long ago," said Apollonius, "ever since I became a philosopher."

"Then how is it," asked Domitian, "that you judged my worst enemies to be gods?" "What enmity," asked Apollonius, "is there between you and Iarchas or Phraotes, the Indians? They are the only humans whom I consider gods and worthy of being called so." "Do not wander off to India," said the emperor; "tell me about your beloved Nerva and his partners in crime." "Do you expect me to defend

2

3

---

[53] Devotees of Adonis grew flowers and other plants in small pots called "gardens." Nothing is known of this room in Domitian's palace.

[54] *Iliad* 5.127.

"ἢ τί;"³⁰ "μὴ ἀπολογοῦ" εἶπεν "ἀδικῶν γὰρ εἴληπται,
ἀλλ᾽ ὡς οὐκ³¹ αὐτὸς ἀδικεῖς ξυνειδὼς ἐκείνῳ τοιαῦτα,
τοῦτό με ἀναδίδασκε." "εἰ, ἃ ξύνοιδα," ἔφη "ἀκοῦσαι
βούλει, ἄκουε, τί γὰρ ἂν τἀληθῆ κρύπτοιμι;"

33. Ὁ μὲν δὴ βασιλεὺς ἀπορρήτων τε λαμπρῶν
ἀκροάσεσθαι ᾤετο, καὶ ἐς τὸ ξυντεῖνον τῆς ἀπωλείας
τῶν ἀνδρῶν ἥκειν πάντα, ὁ δ᾽ ὡς μετέωρον αὐτὸν ὑπὸ
τῆς δόξης ταύτης εἶδεν, "ἐγὼ" ἔφη "Νερούαν σωφρο-
νέστατον ἀνθρώπων οἶδα καὶ πρᾳότατον καὶ σοὶ ἐπι-
τηδειότατον καὶ ἄρχοντα μὲν ἀγαθόν, εὐλαβῆ δ᾽ οὕτω
πρὸς ὄγκον πραγμάτων, ὡς καὶ τὰς τιμὰς δεδιέναι, οἱ
δὲ ἀμφ᾽ αὐτόν, Ῥοῦφον γάρ που λέγεις καὶ Ὄρφιτον,
σώφρονες μὲν καὶ οἵδε οἱ ἄνδρες, ὁπόσα οἶδα, καὶ
διαβεβλημένοι πρὸς πλοῦτον, νωθροὶ δὲ πράττειν
ὁπόσα ἔξεστι, νεώτερα δὲ οὔτ᾽ ἂν αὐτοὶ ἐνθυμηθεῖεν
οὔτ᾽ ἂν ἑτέρῳ ἐνθυμηθέντι ξυνάραιντο."

2   Ἀνοιδήσας δ᾽ ὁ βασιλεὺς ὑφ᾽ ὧν ἤκουσε "συκο-
φάντην με οὖν" εἶπεν "ἐπ᾽ αὐτοῖς εἴληφας, ἵν᾽ οὓς ἐγὼ
μιαρωτάτους ἀνθρώπων καὶ τοῖς ἐμοῖς ἐπιπηδῶντας
εὗρον, σὺ δ᾽, ὡς χρηστοί τέ εἰσι λέγεις καὶ νωθροί; καὶ
γὰρ ἂν κἀκείνους ἡγοῦμαι ὑπὲρ σοῦ ἐρωτωμένους
μήθ᾽ ὡς γόης εἶ, φάναι, μήθ᾽ ὡς ἴτης, μήθ᾽ ὡς ἀλαζὼν,
μήθ᾽ ὡς φιλοχρήματος, μήθ᾽ ὡς φρονῶν ὑπὲρ τοὺς
νόμους. οὕτως, ὦ μιαραὶ κεφαλαί, κακῶς ξυντέταχθε.
ἐλέγξει δ᾽ ἡ κατηγορία πάντα· καὶ γὰρ ὁπόσα ὀμώ-
μοται ὑμῖν, καὶ ὑπὲρ ὧν καὶ ὁπότε καὶ τί θύσασιν,
οὐδὲν μεῖον οἶδα, ἢ εἰ παρετύγχανόν τε καὶ ἐκοι-
νώνουν."

him," asked Apollonius, "or what?" "Do not defend him," replied Domitian, "since he has been found guilty. Instead, prove to me that you yourself are not guilty as his fellow conspirator in all this." "If you want to know what I am conscious of, Majesty," replied Apollonius, "let me tell you, since why should I hide the truth?"

33. The emperor thought he was going to hear a splendid secret, and that everything was pointing towards the destruction of the three heroes. Seeing him overjoyed by this supposition, Apollonius said, "I know that Nerva is the most temperate and moderate of men, most loyal to you and a good governor, but so distrustful of official pomp that he shrinks from power. His associates, by whom you must mean Rufus and Orfitus, are also moderate men, so far as I know, and enemies of wealth, and too inactive to do all that they might. They could neither plot revolution themselves, nor join in if someone else was doing so."

Exploding at these words, the emperor said, "So you   2
take me to be accusing them falsely, do you, when I have found them to be utterly depraved and to be plotting against my position, and you call those same people good and 'inactive'? Yes, I suppose if I were to ask them about you, they would not confess that you were a sorcerer, a hothead, a braggart, a money-grubber, a person who looks down on the laws. That is your evil conspiracy, you pack of scoundrels. But the trial will bring everything out. I know all you swore to do, and why you made that sacrifice and when and what it was, just as if I had been there to join in."

---

30 ἢ τί Cob.: τι ἢ
31 ὡς οὐκ Cob.: οὐχ ὡς

3   Ὁ δὲ οὐδὲ ταῦτα ἐκπλαγεὶς "αἰσχρόν," ἔφη "βασιλεῦ, καὶ οὐκ ἐκ τῶν νόμων ἢ δικάζειν ὑπὲρ ὧν <μὴ>[32]
πέπεισαι, ἢ πεπεῖσθαι ὑπὲρ ὧν μὴ ἐδίκασας. εἰ δ'
οὕτως ἔχει, ξυγχώρησον ἐνθένδε μοι τῆς ἀπολογίας
ἄρξασθαι· κακῶς, ὦ βασιλεῦ, περὶ ἐμοῦ φρονεῖς, καὶ
πλείω με ἀδικεῖς ἢ ὁ συκοφάντης, ἃ γὰρ ἐκεῖνος
διδάξειν ἔφη, σὺ πρὶν ἀκοῦσαι πέπεισαι." "τῆς μὲν
ἀπολογίας" εἶπεν "ὁπόθεν βούλει, ἄρχου, ἐγὼ δὲ καὶ
ἐς ὅ τι παύσομαι οἶδα καὶ ὁπόθεν ἤδη προσήκει
ἄρξασθαι."

34. Ἄρχεται τὸ ἐνθένδε τῆς ἐς τὸν ἄνδρα ὕβρεως,
γενείων τε ἀποκείρας αὐτὸν καὶ χαίτης, ἔν τε τοῖς
κακουργοτάτοις δήσας, ὁ δ' ὑπὲρ μὲν τῆς κουρᾶς
"ἐλελήθειν, ὦ βασιλεῦ," ἔφη "περὶ ταῖς θριξὶ κινδυνεύων," ὑπὲρ δὲ τῶν δεσμῶν "εἰ μὲν γόητά με ἥγῃ,"
ἔφη "πῶς δήσεις; εἰ δὲ δήσεις, πῶς γόητα εἶναι
φήσεις;" "καὶ ἀνήσω γε οὐ πρότερον," εἶπεν "ἢ ὕδωρ
γενέσθαι σε ἤ τι θηρίον ἢ δένδρον." "ταυτὶ μὲν" ἔφη
"οὐδ' εἰ δυναίμην, γενοίμην ἄν, ὡς μὴ προδοίην ποτὲ
τοὺς οὐδεμιᾷ δίκῃ κινδυνεύοντας, ὢν δ', ὅσπερ εἰμί,
πᾶσιν ὑποθήσω ἐμαυτὸν οἷς ἂν περὶ τὸ σῶμα τουτὶ
πράττῃς, ἔστ' ἂν ὑπὲρ τῶν ἀνδρῶν ἀπολογήσωμαι."
"ὑπὲρ δὲ σοῦ" εἶπε "τίς ὁ ἀπολογησόμενος ἔσται;"
"χρόνος" ἔφη "καὶ θεῶν πνεῦμα καὶ Σοφίας ἔρως, ᾗ
ξύνειμι."

35. Τὸν μὲν δὴ προάγωνα τῆς ἀπολογίας, ὃς [δὴ][33]
ἐγένετο αὐτῷ πρὸς Δομετιανὸν ἰδίᾳ, τοιόνδε διαγράφει
ὁ Δάμις, οἱ δὲ βασκάνως ταῦτα ξυνθέντες ἀπολελο-

Not cowed by this either, Apollonius said, "It is a dis- 3
grace and a violation of the laws, Majesty, to decide a case
when you are not yet convinced, or to be convinced when
you have not yet decided. If you are so, let me begin my defense this way. You are ill disposed to me, Majesty, and you
wrong me more than my false accuser, since you believed
what he promised to tell you before you had heard it." "Begin your defense where you like," said the other, "but I
know both where it will end and how it ought to begin."

34. At this point he began his outrages against the Master, shearing off his beard and his hair, and shackling him in
the company of the most hardened criminals. Apollonius
said about his shearing, "I had not realized, Majesty, that
my hair had put me in the dock," and about being chained
up, "If you think me a sorcerer, how will you chain me?
And if you chain me, how will you say I am a sorcerer?"
"Yes," replied the other, "I will not set you free until you
turn into water, or some animal or tree." "I would not
turn into such things," replied Apollonius, "even if I could,
since I would never betray people who are in the dock for
no crime at all. In my own self I will submit to everything
you may do to this body of mine, until I have defended
those heroes." "Whom do you expect to defend *you*?"
asked the emperor. "Time," said Apollonius, "the Divine
Spirit, and the love of my companion, Wisdom."

35. The preliminaries to Apollonius's defense, occurring between him and Domitian alone, are thus described
by Damis. Malicious chroniclers of these events say that

----

32 ⟨μὴ⟩ Rsk.
33 [δὴ] secl. Kay.

γῆσθαι μὲν αὐτόν φασι πρότερον, δεδέσθαι δὲ μετὰ
ταῦτα, ὅτε δὴ κείρασθαι, καί τινα ἐπιστολὴν ἀνέπλα-
σαν ξυγκειμένην μὲν ἰωνικῶς, τὸ δὲ μῆκος ἄχαρι, ἐν ᾗ
βούλονται τὸν Ἀπολλώνιον ἱκέτην τοῦ Δομετιανοῦ
γίγνεσθαι παραιτούμενον ἑαυτὸν τῶν δεσμῶν. Ἀπολλώνιος δὲ τὰς μὲν διαθήκας τὰς ἑαυτοῦ τὸν Ἰώνιον
ἑρμηνεύει τρόπον, ἐπιστολῇ δὲ ἰαστὶ ξυγκειμένῃ οὔπω
Ἀπολλωνίου προσέτυχον, καίτοι ξυνειλοχὼς αὐτοῦ
πλείστας, οὐδὲ μακρηγορίαν πω τοῦ ἀνδρὸς ἐν ἐπιστολῇ εὗρον, βραχεῖαι γὰρ καὶ ἀπὸ σκυτάλης πᾶσαι.
καὶ μὴν καὶ νικῶν τὴν αἰτίαν ἀπῆλθε τοῦ δικαστηρίου,
καὶ πῶς ἄν ποτε ἐδέθη μετὰ τὴν ἀφεῖσαν ψῆφον;
ἀλλὰ μήπω τὰ ἐν τῷ δικαστηρίῳ, ἐπεὶ³⁴ καὶ τὰ ἐπὶ τῇ
κουρᾷ καὶ ἅττα διελέχθη λεγέσθω πρότερον, ἄξια γὰρ
σπουδάσαι.

36. Δυοῖν γὰρ ἡμέραιν δεδεμένου τοῦ ἀνδρός, ἀφ-
ικνεῖταί τις ἐς τὸ δεσμωτήριον τὸ προσελθεῖν αὐτῷ
ἐωνῆσθαι φάσκων, ξύμβουλος δὲ σωτηρίας ἥκειν. ἦν
μὲν δὴ Συρακούσιος οὗτος, Δομετιανοῦ δὲ νοῦς τε καὶ
γλῶττα, καθεῖτο δ᾿, ὥσπερ ὁ πρότερος, ἀλλ᾿ ὑπὲρ
πιθανωτέρων οὗτος. ὁ μὲν γὰρ πόρρωθεν, ὁ δ᾿ ἐκ τῶν
παρόντων ἑλὼν "ὦ θεοί," ἔφη "τίς ἂν ᾠήθη δεθῆναι
Ἀπολλώνιον;" "ὁ δήσας," εἶπεν "οὐ γὰρ ἄν, εἰ μὴ
ᾠήθη, ἔδησε." "τίς δ᾿ ἂν τὰς ἀμβροσίας ποτὲ ἀποτμη-
θῆναι χαίτας;" "ἐγὼ" εἶπεν "ὁ κομῶν." "φέρεις δὲ πῶς
ταῦτα;" "ὥς γε εἰκὸς" εἶπε "τὸν μήθ᾿ ἑκουσίως μήτ᾿
ἀκουσίως ἐς αὐτὰ ἥκοντα."

2   "Τὸ δὲ σκέλος πῶς" ἔφη "καρτερεῖ;" "οὐκ οἶδα,"

Apollonius defended himself first, and was only imprisoned later, at the same time as he was shorn. They have
fabricated a letter written in the Ionic dialect and of
tedious length, making out that Apollonius implored
Domitian and asked to be freed from his chains. Certainly
Apollonius wrote his own will in Ionic, but a letter of his in
that dialect I have never come across, though I have made
a large collection of them, and I never observed verbosity
in one of the Master's letters, since they are all brief and
telegraphic. Furthermore, he had won his case when he
left the court, and how could he have been jailed after a favorable verdict? But let us not come to the court yet, but
first mention the aftermath of his shearing and his various
discourses, for they deserve our attention.

36. The Master had been in prison for two days when a
man came there claiming that he had paid to get admittance to him, and had come with a plan to rescue him. This
man was from Syracuse, and was the mind and the tongue
of Domitian. He was an agent like the previous one, but
had a more plausible message in that the other reached
Apollonius in advance of events, but this one as they were
occurring. "Gods above," he said, "who would have expected Apollonius to be in jail?" "The man who put me
there," was the reply, "because he would not have put me
in chains if he had not expected it." "And who would have
expected that those heavenly locks would ever be cut off?"
"I, their owner," said Apollonius. "How are you taking all
this?" "As is natural," said Apollonius, "for someone who
faced it neither willingly nor unwillingly."

"How is your leg taking the pain?" the man asked. "I do   2

---

34 ἐπεὶ Jon.: ἔτι

εἶπεν "ὁ γὰρ νοῦς πρὸς ἑτέροις ἐστί." "καὶ μὴν πρὸς
τῷ ἀλγοῦντι"[35] ἔφη "ὁ νοῦς." "οὐ μὲν οὖν," εἶπε "νοῦς
μὲν γὰρ ὅ γ᾽ ἐν ἀνδρὶ τοιῷδε ἢ οὐκ ἀλγήσει ἢ τὸ
ἀλγοῦν παύσει." "τί δὲ δὴ ἐνθυμεῖται ὁ νοῦς;" "αὐτὸ"
εἶπε "τὸ μὴ ἐννοεῖν ταῦτα." πάλιν δ᾽ αὐτοῦ τὰς χαίτας
ἀνακαλοῦντος καὶ περιάγοντος ἐς αὐτὰς τὸν λόγον,
"ὤνησαι," ἔφη "νεανίσκε, μὴ τῶν ἐν Τροίᾳ ποτὲ Ἀχαι-
ῶν εἷς γενόμενος, ὡς σφόδρα ἄν μοι δοκεῖς τὰς Ἀχιλ-
λείους κόμας ὀλοφύρασθαι Πατρόκλῳ τμηθείσας, εἰ
δὴ ἐτμήθησαν, καὶ λιποθυμῆσαι δ᾽ ἂν ἐπ᾽ αὐταῖς· ὃς
γὰρ τὰς ἐμάς, ἐν αἷς πολιαί τε ἦσαν καὶ αὐχμός,
ἐλεεῖν φάσκεις, τί οὐκ ἂν πρὸς ἐκείνας ἔπαθες τὰς
ἠσκημένας τε καὶ ξανθάς;"

3   Τῷ δὲ ἄρα ξὺν ἐπιβουλῇ ταῦτα ἐλέγετο, ἵν᾽ ὑπὲρ ὧν
ἀλγεῖ μάθοι, καὶ νὴ Δία, εἰ λοιδορεῖται τῷ βασιλεῖ
ὑπὲρ ὧν πέπονθεν· ἀνακοπεὶς δ᾽ ὑφ᾽ ὧν ἤκουσε "δια-
βέβλησαι," ἔφη "πρὸς τὸν βασιλέα περὶ πλειόνων,
μάλιστα δ᾽ ὑπὲρ ὧν οἱ περὶ Νερούαν ὡς ἀδικοῦντες
φεύγουσιν, ἀφίκοντο μὲν γάρ τινες ἐς αὐτὸν διαβολαὶ
καὶ περὶ τῶν ἐν Ἰωνίᾳ λόγων, οὓς ἀντιξόως τε αὐτῷ
καὶ ἀπηχθημένως εἶπας, καταφρονεῖ δὲ τούτων, ὥς
φασιν, ἐπειδὴ πρὸς τὰ μείζω παρώξυνται, καίτοι τοῦ
κἀκεῖνα διαβάλλοντος ἀνδρὸς ὑψοῦ προήκοντος τῆς
δόξης." "οἷον" ἔφη "Ὀλυμπιονίκην εἴρηκας, εἰ δόξης
φησὶν ἅπτεσθαι διαβολαῖς ἰσχύων. ξυνίημι δ᾽ ὡς
ἔστιν Εὐφράτης, ὃν ἐγὼ οἶδα πάντ᾽ ἐπ᾽ ἐμὲ πράττοντα,

---

[35] τῷ ἀλγοῦντι Kay.: τὸ ἀλγοῦν

not know," replied Apollonius, "for my mind is on something else." "But your mind must be on your pain," said the other. "Not at all," replied Apollonius; "the mind of a man with my character will either feel no pain or end the pain." "What is your mind occupied with, then?" "Precisely with not thinking about my circumstances," said Apollonius. When the man kept recalling his hair and bringing the conversation back to it, Apollonius said, "It is lucky for you, young man, that you were not one of the Greeks at Troy. You would have grieved terribly for the hair of Achilles, I think, when he cut it for Patroclus,[55] if he really did, and you would have fainted over it. If you say you are sorry for my hair, which was squalid and turning gray, what would you have felt about his hair, which was groomed and blond?"

The man had really spoken with malicious intent to find 3 what would pain Apollonius, and better still to see if he would abuse the emperor because of his mistreatment. But foiled by what he heard, he said, "You have been denounced to the emperor on many grounds, above all the crimes for which Nerva and others are being charged. Certain denunciations have also come to him about speeches that you made in Ionia opposing and attacking him. He does not care about these, I am told, because his anger is concentrated on the graver charges, even though the person who made the other ones is a man enjoying a high reputation." "This must be some kind of Olympic victor you mean," said Apollonius, "if he says he enjoys reputation when his strength consists of malice. I perceive that he is Euphrates, whose only aim is to harm me, and indeed I

55 *Iliad* 23.141.

ἠδίκημαι δ᾿ ὑπ᾿ αὐτοῦ καὶ μείζω ἕτερα. αἰσθόμενος
γάρ ποτε φοιτήσειν μέλλοντα παρὰ τοὺς ἐν Αἰθιοπίᾳ
Γυμνούς, ἐς διαβολάς μου πρὸς αὐτοὺς κατέστη, καὶ
εἰ μὴ τῆς ἐπιβουλῆς ξυνῆκα, τάχ᾿ ἂν ἀπῆλθον μηδ᾿
ἰδὼν τοὺς ἄνδρας."

4   Θαυμάσας οὖν ὁ Συρακούσιος τὸν λόγον "εἶτ᾿" ἔφη
"τοῦ διαβληθῆναι βασιλεῖ μεῖζον ἡγῇ τὸ τοῖς Γυμνοῖς
μὴ χρηστὸς ἂν ἐξ ὧν Εὐφράτης καθίει δόξαι;" "νὴ
Δί᾿," εἶπεν "ἐκεῖ μὲν γὰρ μαθησόμενος ἦα, ἐνταῦθα δὲ
ὑπὲρ διδασκαλίας ἥκω." "τῆς τί" ἔφη "διδασκούσης;"
"τὸ εἶναί με" εἶπε "καλὸν κἀγαθόν, τουτὶ δὲ ὁ βασιλεὺς οὔπω οἶδεν." "ἀλλ᾿ ἔστιν" ἔφη "τὰ σεαυτοῦ εὖ
θέσθαι διδαξαμένῳ αὐτόν, ἃ καὶ πρὶν ἐνταῦθα ἥκειν
λέξας οὐδ᾿ ἂν ἐδέθης." ξυνιεὶς οὖν τοῦ Συρακουσίου
ξυνελαύνοντος αὐτὸν ἐς τὸν ὅμοιον τῷ βασιλεῖ λόγον,
οἰομένου τε ὡς ἀπαγορεύων πρὸς τὰ δεσμὰ ψεύσεταί
τι κατὰ τῶν ἀνδρῶν, "ὦ βέλτιστε," εἶπεν "εἰ τἀληθῆ
πρὸς Δομετιανὸν εἰπὼν ἐδέθην, τί πείσομαι μὴ ἀλη-
θεύσας; ἐκείνῳ μὲν γὰρ τἀληθὲς δοκεῖ δεσμῶν ἄξιον,
ἐμοὶ δὲ τὸ ψεῦδος."

37. Ὁ μὲν δὴ Συρακούσιος ἀγασθεὶς αὐτὸν ὡς
ὑπερφιλοσοφοῦντα, ταυτὶ γὰρ εἰπὼν ἀπῆλθεν, ἐχώρει
ἐκ τοῦ δεσμωτηρίου, ὁ δ᾿ Ἀπολλώνιος ἰδὼν ἐς τὸν
Δάμιν "ξυνίης" ἔφη "τοῦ Πύθωνος τούτου;" "ξυνίημι
μὲν" εἶπε "ὑποκαθημένου τε καὶ ὑπαγομένου σε, τί δ᾿ ὁ
Πύθων βούλεταί σοι καὶ τίς ὁ τοῦ ὀνόματος νοῦς, οὐκ
οἶδα." "ἐγένετο" ἔφη "Πύθων ὁ Βυζάντιος ἀγαθός,
φασί, ῥήτωρ τὰ[36] κακὰ πείθειν. οὗτος ὑπὲρ Φιλίππου

have already received greater injuries than this from him. Hearing that I planned to visit the Naked Ones in Ethiopia, he set about slandering me to them, and if I had not understood his design, I might perhaps have left without even seeing those gentlemen."

The Syracusan was amazed at his words, and said, "So you think it matters less if you are accused before the emperor than if the Naked Ones do not think you virtuous because of what Euphrates puts about?" "Of course," replied Apollonius, "for I went there to study, but I have come here to teach." "What is it you teach?" the man asked. "The fact that I am an honorable man, something that the emperor has yet to know." "You could," replied the other, "put yourself to rights by telling him certain things that would have saved you from prison, if you had said them before coming here." He realized that the man was pressing him to say something similar to what the emperor had said, and that he thought that the exhaustion of prison would make him lie about the three heroes. "My friend," he said, "if I am in chains for speaking the truth to Domitian, what will happen to me for not telling it? He thinks the truth deserves imprisonment, but I think falsehood does."

37. The man from Syracuse hailed him as the greatest of philosophers, for such were his words on departing, and left the prison. Apollonius looked at Damis and said, "Do you see through this Python?" "I see," said Damis, "that he was trying to trap and entice you, but what you mean by 'Python' and what the significance of the name is, I do not know." "There once was a Python of Byzantium," said Apollonius, "a speaker good at giving bad advice, they say.

4

---

³⁶ τὰ Cob.: τὸ.

τοῦ Ἀμύντου πρεσβεύων παρὰ τοὺς Ἕλληνας ὑπὲρ
τῆς δουλείας αὐτῶν, τοὺς μὲν ἄλλους εἴα, ἀλλ᾽ ἐν
Ἀθηναίοις γε αὐτοῖς, ὅτε δὴ μάλιστά γε ῥητορικῇ
ἔρρωντο, ἀδικεῖσθαί τε ὑπ᾽ αὐτῶν ἔφασκε τὸν Φίλιππον, καὶ δεινὰ πράττειν Ἀθηναίους τὸ Ἑλληνικὸν
ἐλευθεροῦντας. ὁ Πύθων ταῦτα ⟨πολὺς⟩[37] ῥέων, ὥς
φασιν, ἀλλὰ Δημοσθένης ὁ Παιανιεὺς ἀντειπὼν θρα-
συνομένῳ μόνος, τὸ ἀνασχεῖν αὐτὸν τάττει ἐν τοῖς
ἑαυτοῦ ἄθλοις.[38] ἐγὼ δὲ τὸ μὴ ὑπαχθῆναι ἐς ἃ ἐδόκει
τούτῳ οὐκ ἄν ποτε ἄθλον ἐμαυτοῦ φαίην, Πύθωνι
δ᾽ αὐτὸν ταὐτὸν πράττειν ἔφην, ἐπειδὴ τυράννου τε
μισθωτὸς ἀφίκετο καὶ ἀτόπων ξύμβουλος."

38. Διαλέγεσθαι μὲν δὴ τὸν Ἀπολλώνιον πλείω
τοιαῦτα, ἑαυτὸν δὲ ὁ Δάμις ἀπορεῖν μὲν ὑπὲρ τῶν
παρόντων φησί, λύσιν δὲ αὐτῶν ὁρᾶν οὐδεμίαν, πλὴν
ὅσαι παρὰ τῶν θεῶν εὐξαμένοις τισὶ κἀκ πολλῷ[39]
χαλεπωτέρων ἦλθον. ὀλίγον δὲ πρὸ μεσημβρίας "ὦ
Τυανεῦ," φάναι, σφόδρα γὰρ δὴ χαίρειν αὐτὸν τῇ
προσρήσει, "τί πεισόμεθα;" "ὅ γε ἐπάθομεν," ἔφη
"πέρα δ᾽ οὐδέν." "οὐδὲ ἀποκτενεῖ ἡμᾶς οὐδείς;" "καὶ
τίς" εἶπεν "οὕτως ἄτρωτος;" "λυθήσῃ δὲ πότε;" "τὸ μὲν
ἐπὶ τῷ δικάσαντι" ἔφη "τήμερον, τὸ δὲ ἐπ᾽ ἐμοὶ ἄρτι."[40]

2   Καὶ εἰπὼν ταῦτα ἐξήγαγε τὸ σκέλος τοῦ δεσμοῦ
καὶ πρὸς τὸν Δάμιν ἔφη "ἐπίδειξιν πεποίημαί σοι τῆς

37 ⟨πολὺς⟩ J. Taylor (Kay.)
38 ἄθλοις West.: λόγοις
39 πολλῷ Rsk.: πολλοῦ

He came sent by Philip, the son of Amyntas, to the Greeks in the hope of making them slaves. Most of them he ignored, but when addressing the Athenians in particular, at a time when they were unsurpassed in oratory, he said that they had wronged Philip, and it was outrageous of them to champion Greek freedom. Python said all this 'in a mighty flood,' so we hear, but only Demosthenes of Paeania replied to his insolence, and he counts his opposition to him among his crowning achievements.[56] I would never call it an achievement not to be induced to do what this man desires. I meant, however, that he was acting like Python because he came as a tyrant's hireling and with shocking advice."

38. Apollonius gave other discourses of the sort, according to Damis, though he himself was in despair at their predicament, and saw no way out of it, except the kind that the gods have granted to some people's prayers in much worse circumstances. Shortly before noon he said to him, "Man of Tyana" (since Apollonius liked very much to be addressed this way), "what will become of us?" "What has already," replied Apollonius, "and nothing more." "And no one will kill us?" "Who is so invulnerable as that?" was the reply. "And when will you be set free?" "As far as my judge is concerned, today," said Apollonius, "but as far as I am, immediately."

So saying, he took his leg out of its shackle and said 2 to Damis, "I have given you proof of my own freedom, so

---

[56] Philip of Macedon sent Python to negotiate with Athens in 343, but Demosthenes argued him down (*On the Crown* 136).

---

40 "ὦ̂ Τυανεῦ̂ . . . ἄρτι" distinxit Rsk.

APOLLONIUS OF TYANA

ἐλευθερίας τῆς ἐμαυτοῦ, καὶ θάρρει." τότε πρῶτον ὁ
Δάμις φησὶν ἀκριβῶς ξυνεῖναι τῆς Ἀπολλωνίου φύσεως, ὅτι θεία τε εἴη καὶ κρείττων ἀνθρώπου, μὴ γὰρ
θύσαντα, πῶς γὰρ ἐν δεσμωτηρίῳ; μηδ᾽ εὐξάμενόν τι,
μηδὲ εἰπόντα καταγελάσαι τοῦ δεσμοῦ καὶ ἐναρμό-
σαντα αὖ τὸ σκέλος τὰ τοῦ δεδεμένου πράττειν.

39. Οἱ δὲ εὐηθέστεροι τῶν ἀνθρώπων ἐς τοὺς γόητας ἀναφέρουσι ταῦτα, πεπόνθασι δ᾽ αὐτὸ ἐς πολλὰ
τῶν ἀνθρωπείων· δέονται μὲν γὰρ ⟨τῆς τέχνης⟩ ταύ-
της⁴¹ ἀθληταί, δέονται δὲ ἀγωνισταὶ πάντες διὰ τὸ
νικᾶν γλίχεσθαι, καὶ ξυλλαμβάνει μὲν αὐτοῖς ἐς τὴν
νίκην οὐδέν, ἃ δὲ ἀπὸ τύχης νικῶσι, ταῦθ᾽ οἱ κακοδαίμονες αὐτοὺς ἀφελόμενοι λογίζονται τῇ τέχνῃ ταύτῃ,
ἀπιστοῦσι δ᾽ αὐτῇ οὐδ᾽ οἱ ἡττώμενοι σφῶν, "εἰ" γὰρ
"τὸ δεῖνα ἔθυσα καὶ τὸ δεῖνα ἐθυμίασα, οὐκ ἂν δι-
έφυγέ με ἡ νίκη," τοιαῦτα λέγουσι καὶ τοιαῦτα οἴονται. φοιτᾷ δὲ καὶ ἐπὶ θύρας⁴² ἐμπόρων κατὰ ταὐτά, καὶ
γὰρ δὴ κἀκείνους εὕροιμεν ἂν τὰ μὲν χρηστὰ⁴³ τῆς
ἐμπορίας λογιζομένους τῷ γόητι, τὰ δὲ ἄτοπα τῇ
αὐτῶν φειδοῖ καὶ τῷ μὴ ὁπόσα ἔδει θῦσαι.

2   Ἀνῆπται δὲ ἡ τέχνη τοὺς ἐρῶντας μάλιστα, νοσοῦντες γὰρ εὐπαράγωγον οὕτω νόσον, ὡς καὶ γραι-
δίοις ὑπὲρ αὐτῆς διαλέγεσθαι, θαυμαστόν, οἶμαι, οὐδὲν πράττουσι προσιόντες τοῖς σοφισταῖς τούτοις καὶ
ἀκροώμενοι σφῶν τὰ τοιαῦτα, οἳ κεστόν τε αὐτοῖς
φέρειν διδοῦσι καὶ λίθους, τοὺς μὲν ἐκ τῶν τῆς γῆς
ἀπορρήτων, τοὺς δὲ ἐκ σελήνης τε καὶ ἀστέρων, ἀρώ-
ματά τε ὁπόσα ἡ Ἰνδικὴ κηπεύει, καὶ χρήματα μὲν

302

BOOK VII

take courage." That was the first time, says Damis, that he
clearly understood Apollonius's nature to be godlike and
more than human. Without sacrifice (for how could he sacrifice in jail?), or prayer, or a single word, he made light of
his chains, and then put his leg back into them and acted
like a prisoner.

39. Less intelligent folk put such acts down to magicians, a delusion they apply to many things that are purely
human. Athletes call on these people's profession, and so
do all competitors because of their greed for victory. It
contributes nothing to their victory, but if they happen to
win, the poor fools deprive themselves of the credit, and
assign it to this profession of magic. Even those who lose to
them do not lose faith in it; "If I had made this sacrifice and
burned that incense, victory would not have eluded me,"
so they say and believe. This profession visits the houses
of merchants similarly. Them too one may see ascribing
their successes in trade to the magician, but their reverses
to their own meanness and their failure to make all the
proper sacrifices.

However, this profession especially attracts lovers. So
easily misled is their disease that they talk to old hags about
it, and thus it is no wonder, I think, that they go to these
swindlers and take such advice from them. These people
give them a belt to wear, and stones that come from the recesses of the earth, or from the moon or the stars, as well as
every spice produced by India; and while they exact a

2

41 ⟨τῆς τέχνης⟩ ταύτης Jon. (αὐτῶν ⟨τῆς τέχνης⟩ Kay.):
αὐτῆς

42 θύρας Kay.: θύραις

43 χρηστὰ West.: χρήματα

αὐτοὺς λαμπρὰ ὑπὲρ τούτων πράττονται, ξυνδρῶσι δὲ
οὐδέν. ἢν μὲν γὰρ παθόντων τι τῶν παιδικῶν πρὸς
τοὺς ἐρῶντας ἢ δώροις ὑπαχθέντων προβαίνῃ τὰ ἐρωτικά, ὑμνεῖται ἡ τέχνη ὡς ἱκανὴ πάντα, εἰ δ᾽ ἀπο-
τυγχάνοι ἡ πεῖρα, ἐς τὸ ἐλλειφθὲν ἡ ἀναφορά, μὴ γὰρ
τὸ δεῖνα θυμιᾶσαι, μηδὲ θῦσαι ἢ τῆξαι, τουτὶ δὲ μέγα
εἶναι καὶ ἄπορον.

3   Οἱ μὲν οὖν τρόποι, καθ᾽ οὓς καὶ διοσημίας καὶ
ἕτερα πλείω τερατεύονται καὶ ἀναγεγράφαταί τισιν,
οἳ ἐγέλασαν πλατὺ ἐς τὴν τέχνην, ἐμοὶ δ᾽ ἀποπεφάνθω
μηδ᾽ ἐκείνοις ὁμιλεῖν τοὺς νέους, ἵνα μηδὲ παίζειν τὰ
τοιαῦτα ἐθίζοιντο. ἀποχρῶσα ἡ ἐκτροπὴ τοῦ λόγου· τί
γὰρ ἂν πλείω καθαπτοίμην τοῦ πράγματος, ὃ καὶ
φύσει διαβέβληται καὶ νόμῳ;

40. Ἐνδειξαμένου δὲ τοῦ Ἀπολλωνίου τῷ Δάμιδι
ἑαυτὸν καὶ πλείω διαλεχθέντος, ἐπέστη τις περὶ μεσημβρίαν σημαίνων ἀπὸ γλώττης τοσαῦτα· "ἀφίησί
σε ὁ βασιλεύς, Ἀπολλώνιε, τούτων τῶν δεσμῶν Αἰλιανοῦ ξυμβουλεύσαντος, τὸ δὲ ἐλευθέριον⁴⁴ δεσμωτήριον ξυγχωρεῖ οἰκεῖν, ἔστ᾽ ἂν ᾖ ἡ ἀπολογία, ἐς
ἡμέραν δὲ ἴσως ἀπολογήσῃ πέμπτην." "τίς οὖν" ἔφη
"ὁ μετασκευάσων με ἐνθένδε;" "ἐγώ," εἶπε "καὶ ἕπου."
καὶ ἰδόντες αὐτὸν οἱ ἐν τῷ ἐλευθερίῳ δεσμωτηρίῳ
περιέβαλλον πάντες, ὡς οὐδ᾽ οἰηθεῖσιν αὑτοῖς ἐπανή-
κοντα. ὃν γὰρ δὴ πόθον ἴσχουσι πατρὸς παῖδες ἐς
νουθετήσεις καθισταμένου σφίσιν ἡδείας τε καὶ ξυμμέτρους, ἢ τὰ ἐφ᾽ ἡλικίας ἀφερμηνεύοντος, τὸν αὐτὸν

fine fee from them for all this, they help them not at all. Suppose a boy shows some affection for his lover, or is swayed by presents, and the affair makes progress: the lover praises magic as capable of anything. But if the attempt fails, he blames some omission, there was this or that which he did not burn or sacrifice or melt, and this is something crucial but unobtainable.

The ways in which they manufacture signs from heaven 3 and many other such things have actually been described by certain people who have laughed out loud at the art. Let me simply advise young men to avoid these people's company too, so they may not grow casual about such matters. That is a long enough digression from my account. Why should I spend more time attacking a practice abhorrent both to nature and to law?

40. When Apollonius had revealed himself to Damis and spoken at length, a man came in about noon and delivered the following spoken message. "The king releases you from these chains immediately, Apollonius, on the advice of Aelianus, and permits you to stay in the free prison until your defense takes place. You may perhaps defend yourself in four days' time." "Who will conduct me from here?" asked Apollonius. "I will," said the man, "so follow me." When those in the free prison saw him, they all embraced him, never having thought that he would come back. Just as children love their father when he corrects them kindly and moderately, or narrates adventures of his youth, so

---

ἐλευθέριον Kay.: ἐλεύθερον

κἀκεῖνοι τοῦ Ἀπολλωνίου εἶχον καὶ ὡμολόγουν ταῦτα,
ὁ δ' οὐκ ἐπαύετο ἀεί τι ξυμβουλεύων.

41. Καλέσας δὲ τῆς ὑστεραίας τὸν Δάμιν "ἐμοὶ
μὲν" ἔφη "τὰ τῆς ἀπολογίας ἐς τὴν προειρημένην
ἡμέραν ἔσται, σὺ δὲ τὴν ἐπὶ Δικαιαρχίας βάδιζε,
λῷον γὰρ πεζῇ ἰέναι, κἂν προσείπῃς Δημήτριον,
στρέφου περὶ τὴν θάλατταν, ἐν ᾗ ἐστιν ἡ Καλυψοῦς
νῆσος, ἐπιφανέντα γάρ με ἐκεῖ ὄψει." "ζῶντα" ἔφη ὁ
Δάμις "ἢ τί;" γελάσας δὲ ὁ Ἀπολλώνιος "ὡς μὲν ἐγὼ
οἶμαι, ζῶντα," εἶπεν "ὡς δὲ σὺ οἴει, ἀναβεβιωκότα." ὁ
μὲν δὴ ἀπελθεῖν φησιν ἄκων καὶ μήτ' ἀπογιγνώσκων
ὡς ἀπολουμένου μήτ' εὔελπις ὡς οὐκ ἀπολεῖται. καὶ
τριταῖος μὲν ἐλθεῖν ἐς Δικαιαρχίαν, ἀκοῦσαι δὲ καὶ
περὶ τοῦ χειμῶνος, ὃς περὶ τὰς ἡμέρας ἐκείνας ἐγένετο, ὅτι πνεῦμα ὕπομβρον καταρραγὲν τῆς θαλάσ-
σης τὰς μὲν κατέδυσε τῶν νεῶν, αἳ ἐκεῖσε ἔπλεον, τὰς
δὲ ἐς Σικελίαν τε καὶ τὸν πορθμὸν ἀπεώσατο, καὶ
ξυνεῖναι τότε ὑπὲρ ὅτου ἐκέλευσεν αὐτὸν πεζῇ κομίζεσθαι.

42. Τὰ ἐπὶ τούτοις ἀναγράφει Δάμις ἐξ ὧν Ἀπολλωνίου φησὶν ἀκηκοέναι πρὸς Δημήτριόν τε καὶ πρὸς
αὑτὸν εἰπόντος. μειράκιον μὲν γὰρ ἐκ Μεσσήνης τῆς
ἐν Ἀρκαδίᾳ περίβλεπτον ὥρᾳ ἀφικέσθαι ἐς τὴν Ῥώμην, ἐρᾶν δ' αὐτοῦ πολλοὺς μέν, Δομετιανὸν δὲ παρὰ
πάντας, τοὺς δ' οὕτως ἐρᾶν, ὡς μηδὲ τὸ ἀντερᾶν ἐκείνῳ
δεδιέναι, ἀλλ' ἐσωφρόνει τὸ μειράκιον καὶ ἐφείδετο
τῆς ἑαυτοῦ ὥρας. εἰ μὲν δὴ χρυσοῦ κατεφρόνησεν
ἢ χρημάτων ἢ ἵππων ἢ τοιῶνδε δελεασμάτων, οἷς

these people loved Apollonius and admitted the fact, and he never failed to give them some advice.

41. The next day he called Damis and said, "I have to make my defense on the appointed day, but you must walk to Dicaearchia, because it is better to go on foot. If you talk to Demetrius, stroll by the sea where the isle of Calypso is, because you will see me appear there." "Alive," asked Damis, "or how?" Laughing, Apollonius said, "To my way of thinking, alive, but to yours, risen from the dead." Damis says he left reluctantly, neither despairing for him as already lost nor confident that he would not be. Reaching Dicaearchia two days later, he heard about the storm that had occurred during those days. A rainstorm had broken over the sea, and sunk some ships that were sailing in that direction, and carried others to Sicily and the Straits. Only then did he understand why Apollonius had told him to travel by land.

42. What follows Damis says he learned from what Apollonius told Demetrius and himself. A conspicuously good-looking youth from Messene in Arcadia came to Rome, and many fell in love with him, above all Domitian, though other men too were so much in love that they did not fear even him as a rival. The youth, however, was prudent and did not abuse his good looks. If he had merely despised gold, money, horses, or other kinds of enticement that people use to seduce their lovers, we should not praise

ὑπάγονται τὰ παιδικὰ ἔνιοι, μὴ ἐπαινῶμεν, χρὴ
γὰρ οὕτω παρεσκευάσθαι τὸν ἄνδρα, ὁ δὲ μειζόνων
ἀξιωθεὶς ἂν ἢ ὁμοῦ πάντες, οὓς ὀφθαλμοὶ βασιλέων
ἐσπάσαντο, οὐκ ἠξίου ἑαυτὸν ὧν ἠξιοῦτο.

2   Ἐδέθη τοίνυν, τουτὶ γὰρ τῷ ἐραστῇ ἔδοξε. καὶ
προσελθὼν τῷ Ἀπολλωνίῳ, βουλομένῳ μέν τι λέγειν
ἐῴκει, αἰδὼ δὲ ξύμβουλον σιωπῆς ἔχων οὔπω ἐθάρρει.
ξυνεὶς οὖν ὁ Ἀπολλώνιος "σὺ μὲν οὐδ' ἡλικίαν πω τοῦ
ἀδικεῖν ἄγων καθεῖρξαι," ἔφη "καθάπερ ἡμεῖς οἱ δει-
νοί." "καὶ ἀποθανοῦμαί γε," εἶπε "τὸ γὰρ σωφρονεῖν
θανάτου τιμῶνται οἱ ἐφ' ἡμῶν νόμοι." "καὶ οἱ ἐπὶ
Θησέως," εἶπε "τὸν γὰρ Ἱππόλυτον ἐπὶ σωφροσύνῃ
ἀπώλλυ ὁ πατὴρ αὐτός." "κἀμὲ" εἶπεν "ὁ πατὴρ ἀπολώλεκεν. ὄντα γάρ με Ἀρκάδα ἐκ Μεσσήνης οὐ τὰ
Ἑλλήνων ἐπαίδευσεν, ἀλλ' ἐνταῦθα ἔστειλε μαθησό-
μενον ἤθη νομικά, καί με ὑπὲρ τούτων ἥκοντα ὁ
βασιλεὺς κακῶς εἶδεν."

3   Ὁ δ' ὥσπερ οὐ ξυνιεὶς ὃ λέγει, "εἰπέ μοι," ἔφη
"μειράκιον, μὴ γλαυκὸν ἡγεῖταί σε ὁ βασιλεὺς καίτοι
μελανόφθαλμον, ὡς ὁρῶ, ὄντα, ἢ στρεβλὸν τὴν ῥῖνα,
καίτοι τετραγώνως ἔχοντα καθάπερ τῶν ἑρμῶν οἱ
γεγυμνασμένοι, ἢ τὴν κόμην ἕτερόν τι παρ' ὅ ἐστιν;
ἔστι δ', οἶμαι, ἡλιωσά τε καὶ ὑποφαίνουσα. καὶ μὴν
καὶ τὸ στόμα οὕτω ξύμμετρον, ὡς καὶ σιωπῇ πρέπειν
καὶ λόγῳ, δέρη τε ⟨ἐπὶ⟩[45] τούτοις ἐλευθέρα καὶ φρο-

45 ⟨ἐπὶ⟩ Rsk.

him, since a true man should be armed against such things. This youth, however, had a higher price set on him than all the youths together whom the eyes of monarchs ever tried to seduce, and yet he did not put the price on himself that others did.

After being jailed as his suitor wished, therefore, he 2 came up to Apollonius, looking as if he wanted to say something, but since his modesty counseled silence, he still lacked the courage. Apollonius understood, and said, "You are not yet of an age to commit crime, and yet you are in prison, as if you were a public menace like us." "Yes," said the youth, "and I am to die, because nowadays the laws make death the reward for modesty." "So did the laws in the time of Theseus," said Apollonius, "since Hippolytus's own father destroyed him because of his modesty."[57] "I too," replied the youth, "have been destroyed by my father. Although I was an Arcadian of Messene, he did not give me a Greek education, but sent me here to learn legal science. I came here for that, and I unluckily caught the emperor's eye."

As if not understanding, Apollonius said, "Tell me, 3 young man, does the emperor think you have gray eyes, though I see you have dark ones, or does he think you have a hooked nose when you have a foursquare one, like a finely carved herm, or that your hair is other than it is? It is radiant and shining, I think, your lips are so well formed as to suit both silence and speech, and in addition your neck

[57] Theseus, the husband of Phaedra, caused the death of his son Hippolytus when Phaedra falsely accused him of making advances to her (cf. VI 3.1).

νοῦσα. τί οὖν ἕτερον τούτων ὁ βασιλεὺς ἡγήσεταί σε,
ἐπειδὴ κακῶς ὑπ' αὐτοῦ λέγεις ὀφθῆναι;"

4   "Αὐτό με τοῦτο ἀπολώλεκεν, ὑπαχθεὶς γάρ μου
ἐρᾶν οὐ φείδεται ὧν ἐπαινεῖ, ἀλλ' αἰσχύνειν διανοεῖταί
με, ὥσπερ οἱ τῶν γυναικῶν ἐρῶντες." ἀγασθεὶς δ'
αὐτὸν ὁ Ἀπολλώνιος τὸ μὲν ξυγκαθεύδειν ὅ τι ἡγοῖτο
καὶ εἰ αἰσχρὸν τοῦτο ἢ μή, καὶ τὰ τοιαῦτα τῶν ἐρω-
τημάτων παρῆκεν, ἐπειδήπερ ἐρυθριῶντα ἑώρα τὸν
Ἀρκάδα καὶ κεκοσμημένως φθεγγόμενον. ἤρετο δ'
αὐτὸν ὧδε· "κέκτησαί τινας ἐν Ἀρκαδίᾳ δούλους;" "νὴ
Δί'," ἔφη "πολλούς γε." "τούτων οὖν" εἶπε "τίνα ἡγῇ
σεαυτόν;" "ὅν γε," ἔφη "οἱ νόμοι, δεσπότης γὰρ αὐτῶν
εἰμι." "δεσποτῶν δ'," εἶπεν "ὑπηκόους εἶναι δούλους
χρὴ ἢ ἀπαξιοῦν, ἃ δοκεῖ τοῖς τοῦ σώματος κυρίοις;"

5   Ὁ δ' ἐνθυμηθεὶς ἐς οἵαν ἀπόκρισιν περιάγοιτο "ἡ
μὲν τῶν τυράννων ἰσχὺς" ἔφη "ὡς ἄμαχός τε καὶ
χαλεπή, οἶδα, δι' αὐτὸ γάρ που[46] καὶ δεσπόζειν τῶν
ἐλευθέρων βούλονται, τοῦ δ' ἐμοῦ σώματος ἐγὼ
δεσπότης καὶ φυλάξω αὐτὸ ἄσυλον." "πῶς;" εἶπε
"πρὸς ἐραστὴν γὰρ ὁ λόγος κωμάζοντα μετὰ ξίφους
ἐπὶ τὴν σὴν ὥραν." "τὸν τράχηλον" ἔφη "ὑποσχὼν
μᾶλλον, ἐκείνου γὰρ δεῖ τῷ ξίφει." ἐπαινέσας δὲ αὐτὸν
ὁ Ἀπολλώνιος "Ἀρκάδα σε" ἔφη "ὁρῶ.

6   Καὶ μὴν τοῦ μειρακίου τούτου καὶ ἐν ἐπιστολῇ
μέμνηται, καὶ διαγράφει αὐτὸ πολλῷ ἥδιον ἢ ἐγὼ

46 που Kay.: πω

is free and proud. Which of these does the emperor think to be other than as they are, since you say that you caught the emperor's eye unluckily?"

"It is precisely this which has ruined me, for having 4 fallen in love with me, he will not spare the object of his admiration, but plans to dishonor me in the way lovers of women do." Full of admiration, Apollonius forbore to ask him what he thought of sleeping together and whether it was immoral or not, and similar questions, because he saw that the Arcadian blushed and spoke modestly. So he asked him, "Do you have some slaves in Arcadia?" "Why, many," was the reply. "What do you think your relation to them is?" asked Apollonius. "What the laws say:" he replied, "I am their master." "Should slaves be obedient to their masters," asked Apollonius, "or refuse the wishes of those who possess their bodies?"

Realizing what answer he was being led to, the youth 5 said, "I know that the power of tyrants is irresistible and harsh, because that is why they want to be the masters of the free, but I am the master of my own body, and I will keep it from being violated." "How?" asked Apollonius, "since you are dealing with a lover who lays siege to your beauty with a sword." "I will offer him my neck instead," said the youth, "since that is what he needs his sword for." Apollonius said approvingly, "A true Arcadian, I see."

Moreover, he mentions this youth in a letter, where he 6 describes him much more charmingly than I do here.[58] He

[58] This letter is not preserved.

ἐνταῦθα, σωφροσύνης τε ἐπαινῶν πρὸς ὃν γράφει
φησὶ τὸ μειράκιον τοῦτο μηδ' ἀποθανεῖν ὑπὸ τοῦ
τυράννου, θαυμασθὲν δὲ τῆς ῥώμης ἐπὶ Μαλέαν
πλεῦσαι, ζηλωτὸν τοῖς ἐν Ἀρκαδίᾳ μᾶλλον ἢ οἱ
τὰς τῶν μαστίγων καρτερήσεις παρὰ Λακεδαιμονίοις
νικῶντες.

praises him to his correspondent for his modesty, saying that he was not even killed by the tyrant, but admired by him for his firmness, and sailed back to Malea, more admired by the Arcadians than those who win the endurance contest of the whips at Sparta.

Η΄

1. Ἴωμεν ἐς τὸ δικαστήριον ἀκροασόμενοι τοῦ ἀνδρὸς ἀπολογουμένου ὑπὲρ τῆς αἰτίας, ἡλίου γὰρ ἐπιτολαὶ ἤδη καὶ ἀνεῖται τοῖς ἐλλογίμοις ἡ ἐς αὐτὸ πάροδος, τὸν βασιλέα τε οἱ ξυνδιαιτώμενοί φασι μηδὲ σίτου ἅψασθαι, διορῶντα, οἶμαι, τὰ ἐν τῇ δίκῃ· καὶ γάρ τι καὶ βιβλίον πρόχειρον ἔχειν αὐτὸν τὰ μὲν ξὺν ὀργῇ, τὰ δὲ ἧττον. ἀνατυποῦσθαι δὲ χρὴ οἷον ἀχθόμενον τοῖς νόμοις, ἐπειδὴ εὗρον δικαστήρια.

2. Ἐντευξόμεθα δὲ καὶ τῷ ἀνδρὶ διαλέξεσθαι ἡγουμένῳ μᾶλλον ἢ δραμεῖσθαί τινα ὑπὲρ τῆς ψυχῆς ἀγῶνα, τουτὶ δ᾽ ἂν τεκμηραίμεθα τοῖς γε πρὸ τοῦ δικαστηρίου· προϊὼν γὰρ ἤρετο τὸν γραμματέα, ὑφ᾽ οὗ ἤγετο, οἷ βαδίζοιεν, τοῦ δὲ ἐς τὸ δικαστήριον ἡγεῖσθαι αὐτῷ φήσαντος "δικάσομαι" ἔφη "πρὸς τίνα;" "πρός γε τὸν σεαυτοῦ" εἶπε "κατήγορον, δικάσει δὲ ὁ βασιλεύς." "ἐμοὶ δὲ" ἔφη "καὶ τῷ βασιλεῖ τίς ὁ δικάσων; δείξω γὰρ αὐτὸν φιλοσοφίαν ἀδικοῦντα." "καὶ τίς" εἶπε "βασιλεῖ φιλοσοφίας λόγος, κἂν ἀδικῶν ταύτην τύχῃ;" "ἀλλὰ φιλοσοφίᾳ πολὺς" ἔφη "βασιλέως, ἵν᾽ ἐπιτηδείως ἄρχῃ."

2   Ἐπαινέσας δὲ ὁ γραμματεύς, καὶ γὰρ δὴ καὶ

BOOK VIII

1. Let us go into the court to hear the Master defending himself against the charge, for it is already sunrise, and the courthouse is now open for the notables to enter. The emperor's intimates say that he has not even tasted food, I suppose because he is reading over the contents of the case. In fact, they say, he holds a document in his hand and is at one moment angry, at another less so. We must imagine him like one annoyed with the laws for devising trials.

2. We will also meet the Master expecting to have a discussion rather than to run a race for his life, as we can infer from what happened outside the courthouse. As he went along, he asked the clerk who was leading him where they were going. When the man said that he was leading him to the courthouse, he asked, "Against whom will I be on trial?" "Against your accuser," said the other, "and the emperor will be the judge." "But who," asked Apollonius, "will judge between me and the emperor? I will prove that he is doing an injustice to philosophy." "What concern," said the other, "does an emperor have about philosophy, even if he happens to do it an injustice?" "But philosophy," said Apollonius, "has much concern about an emperor, to ensure that he rules properly."

The clerk approved of this, for in fact he was fairly well   2

μετρίως διέκειτο πρὸς τὸν Ἀπολλώνιον, ὡς καὶ κατ᾽
ἀρχὰς ἐδείκνυ, "πόσῳ δὲ" εἶπε "τὸν λόγον διαμετρή-
σεις ὕδατι; τουτὶ γάρ με χρὴ πρὸ τῆς δίκης εἰδέναι."
"εἰ μὲν ὁπόσα" ἔφη "ἀπαιτεῖ ἡ δίκη ξυγχωρεῖ μοι
λέγειν, οὐκ ἂν φθάνοι διαμετρηθεὶς οὐδὲ ὁ Θύμβρις, εἰ
δὲ ὁπόσα ἐρήσεται, μέτρον τοῦ ἀποκρινομένου ὁ ἐρωτῶν." "ἐναντίας" εἶπεν "ἀρετὰς ἐπήσκησας, βραχυλο-
γεῖν τε καὶ μακρηγορεῖν ὑπὲρ τῶν αὐτῶν φάσκων."
"οὐκ ἐναντίας," ἔφη "ἀλλ᾽ ὁμοίας· ὁ γὰρ θάτερον
ἱκανὸς οὐδὲν ἂν θατέρου λείποιτο. καὶ ξυμμετρία δὲ
ἀμφοῖν ξυγκειμένη τρίτη μὲν οὐκ ἂν φαίνῃ, πρώτη δ᾽
ἂν εἴη ἀρετὴ λόγου, ἐγὼ δὲ καὶ τὸ σιωπᾶν ἐν δικαστηρίῳ τετάρτην ἀρετὴν οἶδα." "ἀνόνητόν γε" εἶπε "σεαυτῷ καὶ παντὶ τῷ κινδυνεύειν μέλλοντι." "καὶ μὴν καὶ
Σωκράτην" ἔφη "τὸν Ἀθηναῖον μέγα ὤνησεν, ὅτε
ἔφυγε τὴν γραφήν." "καὶ πῶς ὤνησεν" εἶπε "τόν,
ἐπειδὴ ἐσιώπα, ἀποθανόντα;" "οὐκ ἀπέθανεν," ἔφη
"Ἀθηναῖοι δὲ ᾤοντο."

3. Ὧδε μὲν παρεσκεύαστο πρὸς τὰ ἐκ τοῦ τυράννου
πάντα, προεστῶτι δ᾽ αὐτῷ τοῦ δικαστηρίου προσελθὼν ἕτερος γραμματεὺς "ὦ Τυανεῦ," ἔφη "γυμνὸς
ἔσελθε." "λουσόμεθα οὖν" εἶπεν "ἢ δικασόμεθα;" "οὐχ
ὑπὲρ ἐσθῆτος" ἔφη "ταῦτα προείρηται, ἀλλ᾽ ἀπαγο-
ρεύει σοι ὁ βασιλεὺς μήτε περίαπτον, μήτε βιβλίον,
μήτ᾽ ἄλλο γραμματεῖον ὅλως μηδὲν ἐσφέρειν ἐνταῦθα." "μηδὲ νάρθηκα" εἶπεν "ἐπὶ τοὺς ἀνοήτως αὐτὸν
ταῦτα πείθοντας;" ἀναβοήσας δὲ ὁ κατήγορος "ὦ
βασιλεῦ, πληγὰς" ἔφη "ἀπειλεῖ μοι ὁ γόης, ἐγὼ γάρ

316

disposed towards Apollonius, as he showed from the start. So he said, "How much water will you need to measure your speech?[1] I must know this before the trial." "If my judge allows me to say as much as the case demands," said Apollonius, "the Tiber itself would be measured out sooner, but if only as much as his questions require, then the interrogator will be the measure of my reply." "You have studied two opposing skills," said the other, "if you claim to be both brief and lengthy on the same subject." "Not opposing skills," said Apollonius, "but similar ones, for someone good at the one cannot fail in the other. And a balanced combination of the two would be, not a third skill in speaking, but the first. I also know that keeping silence in court is a fourth skill." "Yes," said the clerk, "but not a helpful one for you or for anyone entering danger." "Still," said Apollonius, "it greatly helped Socrates the Athenian when he defended his case." "How did it help him," asked the other, "since his silence led to his death?" "He did not die," replied Apollonius; "the Athenians only thought so."

3. In this way he was prepared for any action of the tyrant. As he stood outside the courthouse, another clerk came up and said, "Man of Tyana, remove everything before going in." "Is this a bath," said Apollonius, "or a trial?" "This warning does not concern clothes," said the other; "the emperor forbids you to bring any amulet, paper, or any other document at all into this place." "Not even a cane for those persons who gave him this stupid advice?" asked Apollonius. His accuser shouted out, "Majesty, the magician is threatening to beat me, because it was I who gave

---

[1] That is, for the water clock (*clepsydra*).

σε ταυτὶ πέπεικα." "οὐκοῦν" εἶπε "σὺ μᾶλλον γόης, ἃ
γὰρ μὴ ἐγὼ πέπεικά πω τὸν βασιλέα, ὡς οὐκ εἰμί, σὺ
φῂς αὐτὸν ὡς εἴην πεπεικέναι." παρῆν δὲ τῷ κατηγόρῳ
λοιδορουμένῳ ταῦτα καὶ τῶν Εὐφράτου τις ἀπελευθέρων, ὃν ἐλέγετο Εὐφράτης ἄγγελον τῶν ἐν Ἰωνίᾳ τοῦ
Ἀπολλωνίου διαλέξεων στεῖλαι ὁμοῦ χρήμασιν, ἃ τῷ
κατηγόρῳ ἐπεδόθη.

4. Τοιαῦτα ἠκροβολίσαντο πρὸ τῆς δίκης, τὰ δὲ ἐν
αὐτῇ· κεκόσμητο μὲν τὸ δικαστήριον ὥσπερ ἐπὶ ξυν-
ουσίᾳ πανηγυρικοῦ λόγου, μετεῖχον δὲ αὐτῆς οἱ ἐπί-
δηλοι πάντες, ἀγῶνα ποιουμένου τοῦ βασιλέως ὅτι ἐν
πλείστοις ἑλεῖν αὐτὸν ἐπὶ τῇ τῶν ἀνδρῶν αἰτίᾳ. ὁ δ'
οὕτω τι ὑπερεώρα τοῦ βασιλέως, ὡς μηδὲ ἐς αὐτὸν
βλέπειν, ἐπηρεάσαντος δὲ τοῦ κατηγόρου τὴν ὑπεροψίαν καὶ κελεύσαντος ὁρᾶν αὐτὸν ἐς τὸν ἁπάντων
ἀνθρώπων θεόν, ἀνέσχεν ὁ Ἀπολλώνιος τοὺς ὀφθαλμοὺς ἐς τὸν ὄροφον, ἐνδεικνύμενος μὲν τὸ ἐς τὸν Δία
ὁρᾶν, τὸν δὲ ἀσεβῶς κολακευθέντα κακίω τοῦ κολα-
κεύσαντος ἡγούμενος. ἐβόα καὶ τοιαῦτα ὁ κατήγορος
"ἤδη μέτρει, βασιλεῦ, ὕδωρ, εἰ γὰρ ξυγχωρήσεις αὐτῷ
μῆκος λόγων, ἀπάγξει ἡμᾶς. ἔστι δέ μοι καὶ βιβλίον
τοῦτο ξυγγεγραμμένον τὰς αἰτίας, ὑπὲρ ὧν χρὴ λέγειν αὐτόν, ἀπολογείσθω δὲ κατὰ μίαν."

5. Ὁ δ', ὡς ἄριστα ξυμβουλεύσαντος ἐπαινέσας
ἐκέλευσε τὸν ἄνδρα κατὰ τὴν τοῦ συκοφάντου ξυμ-
βουλίαν ἀπολογεῖσθαι, τὰς μὲν ἄλλας παρελθὼν αἰτίας, ὡς οὐκ ἀξίας καταστῆσαί τινα ἐς λόγον, ὑπὲρ
τεττάρων δέ, ἃς ἀπόρους τε καὶ δυσαποκρίτους ᾤετο,

318

you this advice." "Well then," said Apollonius, "you are the magician rather, not I, since I have yet to persuade the emperor that I am not what you claim to have persuaded him that I am." Standing beside the accuser, as he hurled this abuse, was a freedman of Euphrates, whom Euphrates had apparently sent to report Apollonius's discourses in Ionia, together with money that was given to the accuser in addition.

4. These were their skirmishes before the trial, and the course of it was as follows. The courthouse had been arranged as if to accommodate an audience for a rhetorical display. All the famous people were there, since the emperor was striving to convict Apollonius before as many people as possible in order to implicate the three heroes.[2] He however neglected the emperor so much as not even to look at him. His accuser attacked his neglect, and told him to keep his eyes "on the god of all mankind."[3] So Apollonius turned his eyes to the ceiling, showing that he had his eyes on Zeus, and considering the man who accepted this impious flattery worse than the flatterer. The accuser also shouted, "Measure out the water now, Majesty, since if you allow him a long speech, he will choke us. I also have a paper containing the charges to which he must speak, and let him do so one by one."

5. Thanking the man for this excellent advice, the emperor ordered the Master to make his defense as the informer advised. Most of the charges he passed over as not worth making anybody answer, but he questioned him as follows about four, which he thought difficult and

[2] I.e. Nerva, Orfitus, and Rufus, VII 8.1, etc.

[3] Domitian liked to be addressed as "master and god."

ὧδε ἐρωτήσας· "τί γὰρ μαθών," ἔφη "Ἀπολλώνιε, οὐ
τὴν αὐτὴν ἔχεις ἅπασι στολήν, ἀλλ᾽ ἰδίαν τε καὶ
ἐξαίρετον;" "ὅτι με" εἶπεν "ἡ τρέφουσα γῆ καὶ ἀμφι-
έννυσι, ζῷα δὲ ἄθλια οὐκ ἐνοχλῶ." πάλιν ἤρετο "τοῦ
χάριν οἱ ἄνθρωποι θεόν σε ὀνομάζουσιν;" "ὅτι πᾶς"
εἶπεν "ἄνθρωπος ἀγαθὸς νομιζόμενος θεοῦ ἐπωνυμίᾳ
τιμᾶται." ὁ λόγος οὗτος ὁπόθεν ἐφιλοσοφήθη τῷ
ἀνδρί, δεδήλωκα ἐν τοῖς Ἰνδῶν λόγοις. τρίτον ἤρετο
ὑπὲρ τοῦ ἐν Ἐφέσῳ λοιμοῦ "πόθεν γὰρ" ἔφη "ὁρμώ-
μενος ἢ τῷ ξυμβαλλόμενος προεῖπας τῇ Ἐφέσῳ
νοσήσειν αὐτούς;" "λεπτοτέρᾳ," εἶπεν "ὦ βασιλεῦ,
διαίτῃ χρώμενος πρῶτος τοῦ δεινοῦ ᾐσθόμην· εἰ δὲ
βούλει, λέγω καὶ λοιμῶν αἰτίας."

2   Ὁ δ᾽, οἶμαι, δείσας μὴ τὴν ἀδικίαν καὶ τοὺς μὴ
καθαροὺς γάμους καὶ ὁποῖα οὐκ εὐλόγως ἔπραττεν,
ἐπιγράψῃ ταῖς τοιαύταις νόσοις "οὐ δέομαι" ἔφη
"τοιᾶσδε ἀποκρίσεως." ἐπεὶ δὲ τὴν τετάρτην ἐρώτησιν
ἐπέφερεν ἐς τοὺς ἄνδρας, οὐκ εὐθὺς ὥρμησεν, ἀλλὰ
πολὺν μὲν χρόνον διαλιπών, πολλὰ δὲ ἐνθυμηθείς,
ἰλιγγιῶντι δὲ ὅμοιος ἠρώτησεν οὐ κατὰ τὴν ἁπάντων
δόξαν· οἱ μὲν γὰρ ᾤοντο αὐτὸν ἐκπηδήσαντα τοῦ
πλάσματος μήτε τῆς προσηγορίας ἀφέξεσθαι τῶν
ἀνδρῶν, σχέτλιά τε ὑπὲρ τῆς θυσίας βοήσεσθαι, ὁ δὲ
οὐχ ὧδε, ἀλλ᾽ ὑφέρπων τὴν ἐρώτησιν "εἰπέ μοι," ἔφη
"προελθὼν τῆς οἰκίας τῇ δεῖνι ἡμέρᾳ, καὶ ἐς ἀγρὸν
πορευθείς, τίνι ἐθύσω τὸν παῖδα;"

3   Καὶ ὁ Ἀπολλώνιος, ὥσπερ μειρακίῳ ἐπιπλήττων,
"εὐφήμει" ἔφη "εἰ μὲν γὰρ προῆλθον τῆς οἰκίας,

unanswerable. "What knowledge, Apollonius," he asked, "makes you wear clothing that is not the same as everyone else's, but peculiar and idiosyncratic?" "The knowledge that the earth that feeds me clothes me too," replied Apollonius, "and I leave poor animals undisturbed." Next he asked, "Why is it that men call you a god?" "Because every man who is considered good is honored with the title of 'god.'" (Where the Master got this philosophic idea I have shown in my account of the Indians.)[4] Third, he asked him about the plague at Ephesus. "On what basis, or on what evidence, did you predict to the Ephesians that they would have the plague?"[5] "I have a rather light diet, Majesty," said Apollonius, "and so was the first to sense the danger. But if you like, I will tell you what causes plagues."

Fearing, I suppose, that Apollonius would ascribe such diseases to his injustice, his incestuous marriage,[6] and his other ill famed acts, the emperor said, "I do not want an answer of that kind." When he began to aim his fourth question at Apollonius's heroic friends, he did not start in immediately, but waited for a long time deep in thought. Then, as if he were dizzy, he asked a question quite unlike what everyone expected. They thought he would throw aside the mask and not avoid naming the others, but shout his indignation about the sacrifice. He did not, however, but approached the question stealthily by saying, "Tell me, when you left the house on such and such a day and went to the country, on whose behalf did you sacrifice the boy?"

As if he were scolding a young man, Apollonius said, "Watch your language! If I left the house, I visited the

2

3

---

[4] III 18.   [5] IV 4, 10.
[6] See above, VII 7.

ἐγενόμην ἐν ἀγρῷ, εἰ δὲ τοῦτο, καὶ ἔθυσα, εἰ δὲ ἔθυσα,
καὶ ἔφαγον. λεγόντων δὲ αὐτὰ οἱ πίστεως ἄξιοι."
τοιαῦτα τοῦ ἀνδρὸς εἰπόντος καὶ ἐπαίνου ἀρθέντος
μείζονος ἢ βασίλειον ξυγχωρεῖ δικαστήριον, ξυμμαρ-
τυρεῖν αὐτῷ νομίσας ὁ βασιλεὺς τοὺς παρόντας καὶ
παθών τι πρὸς τὰς ἀποκρίσεις, ἐπειδὴ ἔρρωντό τε καὶ
νοῦν εἶχον "ἀφίημί σε" εἶπε "τῶν ἐγκλημάτων, περι-
μενεῖς δέ, ἔστ' ἂν ἰδίᾳ ξυγγενώμεθα." ὁ δὲ ἐπιρρώσας
ἑαυτὸν "σοὶ μὲν χάρις, ὦ βασιλεῦ," ἔφη "διὰ δὲ τοὺς
ἀλιτηρίους τούτους ἀπολώλασι μὲν αἱ πόλεις, πλήρεις
δ' αἱ νῆσοι φυγάδων, ἡ δὲ ἤπειρος οἰμωγῆς, τὰ δὲ
στρατεύματα δειλίας, ἡ δὲ ξύγκλητος ὑπονοίας. δός,
εἰ βούλοιο, κἀμοὶ τόπον, εἰ δὲ μή, πέμπε τὸν ληψό-
μενόν μου τὸ σῶμα, τὴν γὰρ ψυχὴν ἀδύνατον. μᾶλλον
δὲ οὐδ' ἂν τὸ σῶμα τοὐμὸν λάβοις, 'οὐ γάρ με κτενέεις, ἐπεὶ οὔτοι μόρσιμός εἰμι.'"

4   Καὶ εἰπὼν ταῦτα ἠφανίσθη τοῦ δικαστηρίου, τόν τε
παρόντα καιρὸν εὖ τιθέμενος ὑπὲρ ὧν οὐδ' ἁπλῶς ὁ
τύραννος, ἀλλὰ καὶ ἐκ περιουσίας ἐρωτήσων δῆλος ἦν
(ἐμεγαλοφρονεῖτο γάρ που τῷ μὴ ἀπεκτονέναι αὐτὸν)
τοῦ τε μὴ ἐς τὰ τοιαῦτα ὑπαχθῆναι προορῶν. τυχεῖν δ'
αὖ τούτου ἄριστα ἡγεῖτο, εἰ μὴ ἀγνοοῖτο τῆς φύσεως,
ἀλλὰ γιγνώσκοιτο, ὡς ἔχοι τοῦ μὴ ἄν ποτε ἁλῶναι
ἄκων. καὶ γὰρ τὸ δέος τὸ περὶ τοῖς ἀνδράσιν εὖ ἤδη
αὐτῷ εἶχεν, ὑπὲρ ὧν γὰρ μηδὲ ἐρέσθαι τι ὁ τύραννος
ὥρμησε, πῶς ἂν τούτους ἐς τὸ πιθανὸν ἀπέκτεινεν ἐπὶ
ταῖς οὐκ ἐν δικαστηρίῳ πεπιστευμέναις αἰτίαις; τοιάδε
2   εὗρον τὰ ἐν τῇ δίκῃ.

country; and if I did that, I sacrificed; and if I did that, I ate. But make sure that your witnesses are people deserving of credit." When the Master said this, greater applause broke out than the emperor's court allows, and the emperor, thinking that those present were testifying on Apollonius's behalf, and somewhat affected by his replies, which were firm and sensible, said, "I acquit you of the charges, but you will remain until we converse in private." Apollonius, however, summoned up his courage and said, "Thank you, Majesty, but because of these accursed men the cities are ruined, the islands are full of fugitives, the mainland of groaning, the armies of cowardice, and the senate of suspicion. Assign me a place too, if that be your wish, but if not, send someone to seize my body, because you cannot seize my soul, or rather, you can never even seize my body; 'you will not kill me, since I am not mortal.'"[7]

So saying he disappeared from the court, taking good advantage of the situation. The tyrant was evidently planning not to question him sincerely, but from a position of advantage, no doubt being proud of not having executed him. Anticipating a way not to be put into such a situation, Apollonius thought he could achieve this best by not concealing his nature, but making clear that he could never be caught against his will. Moreover, his fears for his friends had now been allayed, since the tyrant had never even ventured to question him about them, and how could he plausibly put them to death on charges that he had not believed in court? So much for what I have found about the trial.

4

[7] *Iliad* 22.13.

APOLLONIUS OF TYANA

6. Ἐπεὶ δὲ καὶ λόγος μὲν αὐτῷ ξυνεγράφη τις ὡς πρὸς ὕδωρ ἐς τὴν ἀπολογίαν ἀφήσοντι, ξυνεῖλε δὲ αὐτὸν ὁ τύραννος ἐς ἃς εἴρηκα ἐρωτήσεις, ἀναγεγράφθω καὶ ὁ λόγος. οὐκ ἀγνοῶ μὲν γάρ, ὅτι διαβαλοῦσιν[1] αὐτὸν οἱ τὰς βωμολόχους ἰδέας ἐπαινοῦντες, ὡς ἧττον μέν ἢ αὐτοί φασι δεῖν κεκολασμένον, ὑπεραίροντα δὲ τοῖς τε ὀνόμασι καὶ ταῖς γνώμαις, τὸν δὲ ἄνδρα ἐνθυμουμένῳ οὔ μοι δοκεῖ ὁ σοφὸς ὑγιῶς ἂν ὑποκρίνεσθαι τὸ ἑαυτοῦ ἦθος πάρισα ἐπιτηδεύων καὶ ἀντίθετα, καὶ κροτάλου δίκην κτυπῶν τῇ γλώττῃ, ῥητορικοῖς μὲν γὰρ πρὸς τρόπου ταῦτα καὶ οὐδὲ ἐκείνοις δεῖ· δεινότης γὰρ ἐν δικαστηρίοις ἡ μὲν φανερὰ κἂν διαβάλοι τινὰ ὡς ἐπιβουλεύοντα τοῖς ψηφιουμένοις, ἡ δ' ἀφανὴς κἂν ἀπέλθοι κρατοῦσα, τὸ γὰρ λαθεῖν τοὺς δικάζοντας, ὡς δεινός ἐστιν, ἀληθεστέρα δεινότης.

2 Σοφῷ δὲ ἀνδρὶ ἀπολογουμένῳ (οὐ γὰρ κατηγορήσει γε ὁ σοφός, ἃ ἐπιτιμᾶν ἔρρωται) ἤθους τε δεῖ ἑτέρου παρὰ τοὺς δικανικοὺς ἄνδρας, λόγου τε κατεσκευασμένου μέν, μὴ δοκοῦντος δέ, καὶ ὑπόσεμνος ἔστω καὶ μὴ πολὺ ἀποδέων τοῦ ὑπερόπτης εἶναι, ἔλεός τε ἀπέστω λέγοντος· ὁ γὰρ μὴ ἀντιβολῆσαι ξυγχωρῶν τί ἂν οὗτος ἐπὶ ἐλέῳ εἴποι; τοιόσδε ὁ λόγος δόξει τοῖς γε μὴ μαλακῶς ἀκροασομένοις ἐμοῦ τε καὶ τοῦ ἀνδρός· ξυνετέθη γὰρ αὐτῷ ὧδε·

7. Ὁ μὲν ἀγὼν ὑπὲρ μεγάλων σοί τε, ὦ βασιλεῦ, κἀμοί· σύ τε γὰρ κινδυνεύεις ὑπὲρ ὧν μήποτε αὐτοκράτωρ, εἰ πρὸς φιλοσοφίαν οὐδεμιᾷ δίκῃ διαβεβλῆ-

6. He also composed a speech to recite in his defense during his allotted time; but since the tyrant confined him to the questions I have mentioned, let me write out his speech. I am aware that admirers of a vulgar style will criticize it as lacking the finish which they consider necessary, and as overdone in its vocabulary and ideas. But when I consider the Master, I do not think a wise man would truthfully represent his own character by cultivating balanced phrases or antitheses, and making his tongue clack like a rattle, for these things are characteristic of practiced speakers. Even they do not need them, for obvious craftiness in court will give a bad impression, as if the speaker were plotting against the jurors,[1] while concealed craftiness will emerge the victor, since not letting your judges see that you are crafty is craft of the truer kind.

When a wise man defends himself, however (a wise 2
man will not use accusation in matters that he has the power to rebuke), he needs a manner different from those of men trained in law—a style that is practiced without appearing to be. He must be rather grave and little short of haughty, and his speech should avoid raising pity, since how could one who does not stoop to entreaty aim at pity when he speaks? That is how this speech will strike anyone who listens to me and the Master in a virile way, and here is the text.

7. "You and I, Majesty, are playing for high stakes. You are running a risk that no emperor ever did before, that of appearing an enemy of philosophy with no justification. I

---

1 διαβαλοῦσιν Kay.: διαβάλλουσιν

APOLLONIUS OF TYANA

σθαι δόξεις, ἐγώ τε ὑπὲρ ὧν μηδὲ Σωκράτης ποτὲ
Ἀθήνησιν, ὃν οἱ γραψάμενοι τὴν γραφὴν καινοῦν² μὲν
τὰ δαιμόνια ἡγοῦντο, δαίμονα δὲ οὔτε ἐκάλουν οὔτε
ᾤοντο. κινδύνου δὲ ἐφ᾿ ἑκάτερον ἡμῶν οὕτω χαλεποῦ
ἥκοντος οὐκ ὀκνήσω καὶ σοὶ ξυμβουλεύειν, ὁπόσα
ἐμαυτὸν πέπεικα. ἐπειδὴ γὰρ κατέστησεν ἡμᾶς ὁ κατήγορος ἐς τουτονὶ τὸν ἀγῶνα, ἐσῆλθε τοὺς πολλοὺς
οὐκ ἀληθὴς περὶ ἐμοῦ τε καὶ σοῦ δόξα· σὲ μὲν γὰρ
ᾤοντο ξυμβούλῳ τῆς ἀκροάσεως ὀργῇ χρήσεσθαι, δι᾿
ἣν κἂν ἀποκτεῖναί με, ὅ τι ποτέ ἐστι τὸ ἀποκτεῖναι,
ἐμὲ δ᾿ ἐκποιήσειν ἐμαυτὸν τοῦ δικαστηρίου τρόποις,
ὁπόσοι τοῦ ἀποδρᾶναί εἰσιν, ἦσαν δ᾿, ὦ βασιλεῦ,
μυρίοι.

2   "Καὶ τούτων ἀκούων οὐκ ἐς τὸ προκαταγιγνώσκειν
ἦλθον, οὐδὲ κατεψηφισάμην τῆς σῆς ἀκροάσεως ὡς
μὴ τὸ εὐθὺ ἐχούσης, ἀλλὰ ξυνθέμενος τοῖς νόμοις
ἔστηκα ὑπὸ τῷ λόγῳ. τούτου ξύμβουλος καὶ σοὶ
γίγνομαι· δίκαιον γὰρ τὸ μὴ προκαταγιγνώσκειν, μηδὲ καθῆσθαι πεπεισμένον, ὡς ἐγώ τί σε κακὸν εἴργασμαι, μηδ᾿ ὑπὲρ μὲν τοῦ Ἀρμενίου τε καὶ Βαβυλω-
νίου καὶ ὅσοι τῶν ἐκείνῃ ἄρχουσιν, οἷς ἵππος τε
παμπόλλη ἐστὶ καὶ τοξεία πᾶσα καὶ χρυσῆ γῆ καὶ
ἀνδρῶν ὄχλος, ὡς³ ἐγὼ οἶδα, ἀκούειν ξὺν γέλωτι τὸ
πείσεσθαί τι ὑπ᾿ αὐτῶν, ὅ σε καὶ τὴν ἀρχὴν ταύτην
ἀφαιρήσεται, κατ᾿ ἀνδρὸς δὲ σοφοῦ καὶ γυμνοῦ πι-
στεύειν, ὥς ἐστι τούτῳ ὅπλον ἐπὶ τὸν Ῥωμαίων αὐτοκράτορα, καὶ προσδέχεσθαι ταῦτα Αἰγυπτίου συκο-

am running one that not even Socrates did at Athens, since those who indicted him thought him a spiritual innovator, but neither called nor thought him a spirit. Since both of us are exposed to so great a risk, I will not hesitate to give you advice in a matter about which I am certain. Since the accuser brought us to this trial, most people have formed an incorrect opinion about you and me. They presumed that you were going to let your anger determine how you listened to me, and that you might kill me in your anger, whatever killing is. I, so they thought, would extricate myself from the court by one of the various ways of escape, and such ways, Majesty, were countless.

"Hearing this, I was not led to be prejudiced against you, or to condemn your judgment as other than upright. I submitted to the laws, and am standing trial. This is also what I want to advise you. It is not fair to be prejudiced, or to sit in judgment already convinced that I have done you some wrong. It is unfair that, though the Armenians, the Babylonians, and all those who rule in that region have abundant cavalry, every kind of artillery, gold-bearing lands, and a host of brave men, as I well know, you would laugh to be told that you might suffer some injury from them so great as to lose your throne, and yet you believe of one unarmed philosopher that he has a weapon against the emperor of Rome, and accept such a story from the lips of an Egyptian informer. You have never heard

---

2 καινοῦν Rsk.: καινὸν
3 ὡς Rsk.: ὃν

φάντου λέγοντος, ἃ μηδὲ τῆς Ἀθηνᾶς ποτε ἤκουσας,
ἣν σεαυτοῦ προορᾶν φῄς,

3   "Εἰ μή, νὴ Δία, ἡ κολακευτικὴ καὶ τὸ συκοφαντεῖν
οὕτω τι νῦν τοῖς ἀλιτηρίοις τούτοις ἐπιδέδωκεν, ὡς
τοὺς θεοὺς ὑπὲρ μὲν τῶν σμικρῶν καὶ ὁπόσα ὀφθαλ-
μίαι τέ εἰσι καὶ τὸ μὴ πυρέξαι, μηδ᾽ ἀνοιδῆσαί τι
τῶν σπλάγχνων, ἐπιτηδείους εἶναί σοι ξυμβούλους
φάσκειν, ἰατρῶν δίκην ἐφαπτομένους καὶ θεραπεύοντας, ὅτου αὐτῶν πονήρως ἔχοις, περὶ δὲ τῇ ἀρχῇ καὶ
τῷ σώματι κινδυνεύοντί σοι μηθ᾽ οὓς φυλάττεσθαι
χρὴ ξυμβουλεύειν μήθ᾽ ὅ τι ἔσται σοι πρὸς αὐτοὺς
ὅπλον διδάσκειν ἥκοντας, ἀλλ᾽ εἶναί σοι τοὺς συκοφάντας αἰγίδα Ἀθηνᾶς καὶ Διὸς χεῖρα, εἰδέναι μὲν
ὑπὲρ σοῦ φάσκοντας, ἃ μηδ᾽ οἱ θεοί, προεγρηγορότας
δέ σου καὶ προκαθεύδοντας, εἰ δὴ καθεύδουσιν οὗτοι,
κακοῖς, φασιν, ἐπαντλοῦντες κακὰ καὶ τὰς Ἰλιάδας
ταύτας ἀεὶ ξυντιθέντες.

4   "Καὶ τὸ μὲν ἱπποτροφεῖν αὐτούς, κἀπὶ ζευγῶν ἐς
τὴν ἀγορὰν ἐκκυκλεῖσθαι λευκῶν, καὶ ἡ ἐν ἀργύρῳ καὶ
χρυσῷ ὀψοφαγία, καὶ γάμοι <καὶ>[4] μυριάδων δύο καὶ
τριῶν ἐωνημένα παιδικά, καὶ τὸ μοιχεύειν μέν, ὃν
λανθάνουσι χρόνον, γαμεῖν δέ, ἃς ἐμοίχευσαν, ὅταν
ἐπ᾽ αὐταῖς ληφθῶσι, καὶ οἱ κροτοῦντες αὐτοὺς ἐπὶ ταῖς
καλαῖς νίκαις, ἐπειδὰν φιλόσοφός τις ἢ ὕπατος ἀδικῶν οὐδὲν ἁλῷ μὲν ὑπὸ τούτων, ἀπόληται δὲ ὑπὸ σοῦ,
δεδόσθω τῇ τῶν καταράτων τρυφῇ, καὶ τῷ μήτε νόμων
αὐτοῖς ἔτι μήτ᾽ ὀφθαλμῶν εἶναι φόβον,

5   "Τὸ δ᾽ οὕτω τι ὑπὲρ τοὺς ἀνθρώπους φρονεῖν, ὡς

such a thing from Athena, the goddess whom you call your protector.

"Perhaps, however, flattery and false accusation have now have been carried so far by these pests that you consider the gods competent advisers merely on minor matters such as inflammation of the eyes or how to avoid fever or swelling of the intestines, like doctors touching and soothing whichever of those parts ails you. But when you are in danger to your power or your person, you think them unable to come and advise you whom to take precautions against, or tell you what weapon you have against such people. Informers, you think, are now the aegis of Athena and the hand of Zeus to you, pretending to know things for your safety which not even the gods know, and waking and sleeping for your welfare, if indeed they ever sleep, as they pile 'evil upon evil,' as the saying is, and constantly compose these catalogs of crime. 3

"They may own stables, wheel into the forum drawn by teams of white horses, dine off silver and gold, and marry. They may buy boys for twenty or thirty thousand drachmas. They may be seducers as long as they avoid notice, and marry the women they have seduced if they are caught in the act. People may applaud them for their fine victories when a philosopher or consular, innocent of crime, is ruined by them and executed by you. Let us grant all that to the insolence of these scoundrels, and to their fearlessness before the laws and before the public gaze. 4

"But when their pride rises so far above humanity that 5

---

^{4} ⟨καὶ⟩ Rsk.

προγιγνώσκειν βούλεσθαι τῶν θεῶν, ἐγὼ μὲν οὔτ᾽
ἐπαινῶ καὶ ἀκούων δέδια, σὺ δ᾽ εἰ προσδέξοιο,
γράψονται καὶ σὲ ἴσως ὡς διαβάλλοντα τὴν περὶ τοῦ
θείου δόξαν, ἐλπὶς γὰρ καὶ κατὰ σοῦ ξυγκείσεσθαι
τοιαύτας γραφάς, ἐπειδὰν μηδεὶς τοῖς συκοφάνταις
λοιπὸς ᾖ. καὶ ξυνίημι μὲν ἐπιτιμῶν μᾶλλον ἢ ἀπολο-
γούμενος, εἰρήσθω δέ μοι ταῦθ᾽ ὑπὲρ τῶν νόμων, οὓς
εἰ μὴ ἄρχοντας ἡγοῖο, οὐκ ἄρξεις. τίς οὖν ξυνήγορος
ἔσται μοι ἀπολογουμένῳ; εἰ γὰρ καλέσαιμι τὸν Δία,
ὑφ᾽ ᾧ βεβιωκὼς οἶδα, γοητεύειν με φήσουσι καὶ τὸν
οὐρανὸν ἐς τὴν γῆν ἄγειν. διαλεγώμεθα οὖν περὶ
τούτου ἀνδρί, ὃν τεθνάναι μὲν οἱ πολλοί φασιν, ἐγὼ δὲ
οὔ φημι· ἔστι δὲ οὗτος ὁ πατὴρ ὁ σός, ᾧ ἐγὼ τοσούτου
ἄξιος, ὅσουπερ ἐκεῖνος σοί· σὲ μὲν γὰρ ἐποίησεν, ὑπ᾽
ἐμοῦ δὲ ἐγένετο. οὗτος, ὦ βασιλεῦ, ξυλλήπτωρ ἔσται
μοι τῆς ἀπολογίας πολλῷ τἀμὰ βέλτιον ἢ σὺ γιγνώσκων.

6   Ἀφίκετο μὲν γὰρ ἐς Αἴγυπτον οὔπω αὐτοκράτωρ,
θεοῖς τε τοῖς ἐν Αἰγύπτῳ θύσων κἀμοὶ ὑπὲρ τῆς ἀρχῆς
διαλεξόμενος. ἐντυχὼν δέ μοι κομῶντί τε καὶ ὧδε
ἐσταλμένῳ, οὐδὲ ἤρετο οὐδὲ ἓν περὶ τοῦ σχήματος,
ἡγούμενος τὸ ἐν ἐμοὶ πᾶν εὖ ἔχειν, ἐμοῦ δ᾽ ἕνεχ᾽ ἥκειν
ὁμολογήσας, ἀπῆλθεν ἐπαινέσας καὶ εἰπὼν μὲν ἃ μὴ
πρὸς ἄλλον, ἀκούσας δ᾽ ἃ μὴ παρ᾽ ἄλλου. ἥ τε
διάνοια, ᾗ ἐς τὸ ἄρχειν ἐχρῆτο, ἐρρώσθη αὐτῷ παρ᾽
ἐμοῦ μάλιστα, μεθεστηκυῖα ἤδη ὑφ᾽ ἑτέρων, οὐκ ἀν-

they claim to have more prescience than the gods, that is something that I do not praise, and tremble to hear. If you were to believe it, they may perhaps indict yourself for impugning religious beliefs, since there is a chance that such charges will be laid against you when the informers have no one else left. I know well that I am rebuking you rather than defending myself, so let that be enough about the laws. If you do not think them your governors, you too will not govern. Who then will support me in my defense? If I were to invoke the Zeus under whom I know I have lived, they will say I am a sorcerer and am bringing the sky down to the earth. So let us discuss this matter with a man whom most people think to be dead, though not I: your father.[8] I was as valuable to him as he was to you, because he made you, but I made him. He, Majesty, will be my supporter in my defense, and indeed knows me much better than you do.

"He came to Egypt before he was emperor in order to   6 sacrifice to the gods of Egypt and to discuss his position with me. Although he found me with my hair long and my present clothing, he never put any question to me about my appearance, because he thought well of everything about me. Admitting that he had come to see me, he thanked me when he left, after speaking to me as to none other, and hearing from me what none other told him. His determination to take power was strengthened by me more than anyone, when previously others had shaken it.

[8] I.e. Vespasian. For Apollonius's meeting with him in Alexandria, V 27–28.

ἐπιτηδείων[5] μέν, οὐ μὴν σοί γε δόξαι, οἱ γὰρ μὴ
ἄρχειν αὐτὸν πείθοντες καὶ σὲ δήπου αὐτὸ ἀφῃροῦντο
τὸ μετ' ἐκεῖνον ταῦτ'[6] ἔχειν, ἐμοῦ δὲ ξυμβουλεύοντος
ἑαυτόν τε μὴ ἀπαξιοῦν ἀρχῆς ἐπὶ θύρας αὐτῷ φοι-
τώσης, ὑμᾶς τε κληρονόμους αὐτῆς ποιεῖσθαι, εὖ
ἔχειν τὴν γνώμην φήσας αὐτός τε μέγας ἤρθη καὶ
ὑμᾶς ἦρεν.

7   "Εἰ δὲ γόητά με ᾤετο, οὐδ' ἂν ξυνῆψέ μοι κοινωνίαν
φροντίδων, οὐδὲ γὰρ τοιαῦτα ἥκων διελέγετο, οἷον·
'ἀνάγκασον τὰς Μοίρας' ἢ 'τὸν Δία τύραννον ἀπο-
φῆναί με' ἢ 'ψεῦσαι[7] διοσημίας ὑπὲρ ἐμοῦ, δείξας τὸν
ἥλιον ἀνίσχοντα μὲν ἀπὸ τῆς ἑσπέρας, δυόμενον δέ,
ὅθεν ἄρχεται.' οὐ γὰρ ἄν μοι ἐπιτήδειος ἄρχειν ἔδοξεν
ἢ ἐμὲ ἡγούμενος ἱκανὸν ταῦτα, ἢ σοφίσμασι θηρεύων
ἀρχήν, ἣν ἀρεταῖς ἔδει κατακτᾶσθαι. καὶ μὴν καὶ
δημοσίᾳ διελέχθην ἐν ἱερῷ, γοήτων δὲ ξυνουσίαι
φεύγουσι μὲν ἱερὰ θεῶν, ἐχθρὰ γὰρ τοῖς περὶ τὴν
τέχνην, νύκτα δὲ καὶ πᾶν, ὅ τι ἀφεγγές, αὐτῶν
προβαλλόμενοι οὐ ξυγχωροῦσι τοῖς ἀνοήτοις οὐδὲ
ὀφθαλμοὺς ἔχειν οὔτε ὦτα. διελέχθη μοι καὶ ἰδίᾳ μέν,
παρετύγχανον δὲ ὅμως Εὐφράτης καὶ Δίων, ὁ μὲν
πολεμιώτατά μοι ἔχων, ὁ δ' οἰκειότατα, Δίωνα γὰρ μὴ
παυσαίμην γράφων ἐν φίλοις. τίς ἂν οὖν ἐπ' ἀνδρῶν
σοφῶν ἢ μεταποιουμένων γε σοφίας ἐς γόητας ἔλθοι
λόγους; τίς δ' οὐκ ἂν παραπλησίως φυλάξαιτο καὶ ἐν
φίλοις καὶ ἐν ἐχθροῖς κακὸς φαίνεσθαι;

5 ἀνεπιτηδείων Kay.: ἐπιτηδείων

They were not ill disposed, though you might disagree, since those who urged him against taking power were in effect cheating you of holding the same position after him. However, I advised him not to think himself unworthy of power when it had come knocking on his door, and to take the two of you as his heirs.[9] Admitting that the advice was good, he rose to greatness himself, and raised you both to it too.

"Had he thought me a sorcerer, he would not have dis- 7 cussed his concerns with me. He did not come and say such things as 'Force the Fates or Zeus to make me tyrant' or 'Produce a false weather sign for me by showing the sun rising in the west and setting where it rises.' I would not have thought him fit to rule if he had ascribed such powers to me, or had used tricks to capture a position that he had to acquire by virtue. Besides, I talked to him publicly in a sanctuary, whereas sorcerers avoid divine sanctuaries for their meetings as unpropitious for their trade. They screen themselves in night or in any ill lit place, and do not allow fools to have either eyes or ears. He also talked with me privately, though with Euphrates and Dio present, of whom the former is very hostile to me, the latter is very close, and may I never cease counting Dio among my friends. Who then would talk of magic before wise men, or at any rate pretenders to wisdom? Would not anybody avoid appearing evil as much before enemies as before friends?

[9] I.e. his sons Titus and Domitian.

---

6 ταὐτ᾽ (i.e. τὰ αὐτὰ) Jon.: ταῦτ᾽
7 ψεῦσαι Rsk.: ψεύσασθαι

8   "Καὶ οἱ λόγοι ἦσαν ἐναντιούμενοι τοῖς γόησι· σὺ
μὲν γὰρ ἴσως τὸν πατέρα ἡγῇ τὸν σεαυτοῦ βασιλείας
ἐρῶντα γόησι μᾶλλον ἢ ἑαυτῷ πιστεῦσαι καὶ ἀνάγκην
ἐπὶ τοὺς θεούς, ἵνα τούτου τύχοι, παρ' ἐμοῦ εὑρέσθαι,
ὁ δὲ τοῦτο μὲν καὶ πρὶν ἐς Αἴγυπτον ἥκειν ἔχειν ᾤετο,
μετὰ ταῦτα δ' ὑπὲρ μειζόνων ἐμοὶ διελέγετο, ὑπὲρ
νόμων καὶ ὑπὲρ πλούτου δικαίου, θεοί τε ὡς θεραπευ-
τέοι, καὶ ὁπόσα παρ' αὐτῶν ἀγαθὰ τοῖς κατὰ τοὺς
νόμους ἄρχουσι, μαθεῖν ᾔρα. οἷς πᾶσιν ἐναντίον χρῆμα οἱ γόητες, εἰ γὰρ ἰσχύοι ταῦτα, οὐκ ἔσται ἡ τέχνη.

9   "Προσήκει δέ, ὦ βασιλεῦ, κἀκεῖνα ἐπεσκέφθαι·
τέχναι ὁπόσαι κατ' ἀνθρώπους εἰσί, πράττουσι μὲν
ἄλλο ἄλλη, πᾶσαι δ' ὑπὲρ χρημάτων, αἱ μὲν σμικρῶν,
αἱ δ' αὖ μεγάλων, αἱ δ' ἀφ' ὧν θρέψονται, καὶ οὐχ αἱ
βάναυσοι μόνον, ἀλλὰ καὶ τῶν ἄλλων τεχνῶν, σοφαί
τε ὁμοίως καὶ ὑπόσοφοι πλὴν ἀληθοῦς φιλοσοφίας.
καλῶ δὲ σοφὰς μὲν ποιητικήν, μουσικήν, ἀστρονο-
μίαν, σοφιστὰς καὶ τῶν ῥητόρων τοὺς μὴ ἀγοραίους,
ὑποσόφους δὲ ζωγραφίαν, πλαστικήν, ἀγαλματοποι-
ούς, κυβερνήτας, γεωργούς, ἢν ταῖς ὥραις ἔπωνται,
καὶ γὰρ αἵδε αἱ τέχναι σοφίας οὐ πολὺ λείπονται.

10   "Ἔστι τι, ὦ βασιλεῦ, ψευδόσοφοί τε καὶ ἀγείροντες,
ὃ μὴ μαντικὴν ὑπολάβῃς, πολλοῦ μὲν γὰρ ἀξία, ἢν
ἀληθεύῃ, εἰ δ' ἐστὶ τέχνη, οὔπω οἶδα, ἀλλὰ τοὺς
γόητας ψευδοσόφους φημί· τὰ γὰρ οὐκ ὄντα εἶναι καὶ
τὰ ὄντα ἀπιστεῖσθαι, πάντα ταῦτα προστίθημι τῇ τῶν
ἐξαπατωμένων δόξῃ, τὸ γὰρ σοφὸν τῆς τέχνης ἐπὶ τῇ
τῶν ἐξαπατωμένων τε καὶ θεωμένων ἀνοίᾳ κεῖται, ἡ δὲ

334

"Our discussions, too, were completely opposite to 8
those of sorcerers. You may think that your own father in
his eagerness for the throne trusted sorcerers rather than
himself, and acquired from me a spell over the gods in
order to obtain it. In fact, even before reaching Egypt he
already thought himself to have power, and thereafter he
talked with me on higher subjects—laws, and the just use
of wealth. He wanted to hear how to worship the gods and
what blessings they gave to law-abiding rulers. All these
things are the very opposite of sorcery, because if they
prevail magic will no longer exist.

"The following too, Majesty, deserves consideration. 9
All the arts that exist among mankind have different
spheres of action, but all aim at money, whether little
or much, or simply enough to subsist on. This includes
not only menial arts, but all the others too, the learned
ones and the semi-learned ones alike, except for that
of true wisdom. By 'learned' arts I mean those of poetry,
music, astronomy, oratory, and public speaking except of
the forensic kind, and by 'semi-learned' those of painting,
sculpture, of statue makers, of pilots, of farmers as long as
they follow the seasons, since these arts too are not far
removed from learning.

"But there is also, Majesty, a kind of sham learning and 10
hucksterism that you should not equate with prophecy, because prophecy is very valuable if it tells the truth, though
I am not sure it is an art. By 'sham learning' I refer to
sorcerers, because to make the nonexistent exist, and the
existent to be doubted, all this I ascribe to the beliefs of
those they dupe. Whatever learning there is in magic
lies in the stupidity of those that are tricked as spectators.

335

τέχνῃ φιλοχρήματοι πάντες, ἃ γὰρ κομψεύονται,
ταῦθ᾽ ὑπὲρ μισθοῦ σφισιν εὕρηται, μαστεύουσι δ᾽
ὑπερβολὰς χρημάτων ὑπαγόμενοι τοὺς ὁτουδὴ ἐρῶντας ὡς ἱκανοὶ πάντα.

11   "Τίνα οὖν, ὦ βασιλεῦ, πλοῦτον περὶ ἡμᾶς ἰδὼν
ψευδοσοφίαν ἐπιτηδεύειν με οἴει, καὶ ταῦτα τοῦ σοῦ
πατρὸς κρείττω με ἡγουμένου χρημάτων; ὅτι δ᾽ ἀληθῆ
λέγω, ποῦ μοι ἡ ἐπιστολὴ τοῦ γενναίου τε καὶ θείου
ἀνδρός; ὅς με ἐν αὐτῇ ᾄδει τά τε ἄλλα καὶ τὸ πένε-
σθαι. ʽΑὐτοκράτωρ Οὐεσπασιανὸς Ἀπολλωνίῳ φιλοσόφῳ χαίρειν. εἰ πάντες, Ἀπολλώνιε, κατὰ ταὐτά σοι
φιλοσοφεῖν ἤθελον, σφόδρα ἂν εὐδαιμόνως ἔπραττε
φιλοσοφία τε καὶ πενία· φιλοσοφία μὲν ἀδεκάστως
ἔχουσα, πενία δὲ αὐθαιρέτως. ἔρρωσο.᾽ ταῦθ᾽ ὁ πατὴρ
ὁ σὸς ὑπὲρ ἐμοῦ ἀπολογείσθω, φιλοσοφίας μὲν τὸ
ἀδέκαστον, πενίας δὲ τὸ αὐθαίρετον ἐμοὶ ὁριζόμενος,
ἐμέμνητο γάρ που καὶ τῶν κατὰ τὴν Αἴγυπτον, ὅτ᾽
Εὐφράτης μὲν καὶ πολλοὶ τῶν προσποιουμένων φιλοσοφεῖν προσιόντες αὐτῷ χρήματα οὐδ᾽ ἀφανῶς ᾔτουν,
ἐγὼ δ᾽ οὐ μόνον οὐ προσῄειν ὑπὲρ χρημάτων, ἀλλὰ
κἀκείνους ἐώθουν ὡς οὐχ ὑγιαίνοντας.

12   "Διεβεβλήμην δὲ πρὸς χρήματα μειράκιον ὢν ἔτι·
τὰ γοῦν πατρῷα, λαμπρὰ δ᾽ ἦν οὐσία ταῦτα, μιᾶς
μόνης ἰδὼν ἡμέρας ἀδελφοῖς τε τοῖς ἐμαυτοῦ ἀφῆκα,
καὶ φίλοις, καὶ τῶν ξυγγενῶν τοῖς πένησι, μελετῶν
που ἀφ᾽ ἑστίας τὸ μηδενὸς δεῖσθαι, ἐάσθω δὲ Βαβυ-
λὼν καὶ Ἰνδῶν τὰ ὑπὲρ Καύκασόν τε καὶ ποταμὸν
Ὕφασιν, δι᾽ ὧν ἐπορευόμην ἐμαυτῷ ὅμοιος· ἀλλὰ τῶν

The trade consists entirely of money-grubbers. All their boasted devices they have invented for the sake of gain, and they hunt piles of money by inducing others, whatever they desire, to think them omnipotent.

"What wealth do you see in me that makes you think I 11 practice false learning, especially when your own father thought me superior to money? To prove that what I say is true, where is the letter from that excellent and inspired man? He extols me in it for poverty among other things. 'The emperor Vespasian greets the philosopher Apollonius. If everyone were willing to be a philosopher of your kind, Apollonius, it would be well both for philosophy and for poverty, since philosophy would be incorruptible and poverty voluntary. Goodbye.'[10] Let that be how your father defended me, equating my philosophy with incorruptibility and my poverty with volition. No doubt he remembered events in Egypt, when Euphrates and many self-styled philosophers came to him with unconcealed requests for money, whereas I not only did not come to him for money, but tried to banish them for their diseased minds.

"I was averse to money even as a young man. My ances- 12 tral property consisted of a wealthy estate, and yet after looking on it for only a day I gave it to my brothers, my friends, and the poorer of my relatives, clearly making self-sufficiency begin at home. Let me not talk of Babylon, and India that lies beyond the Caucasus and the river Hyphasis, across all of which I traveled and remained true

[10] This also survives as Letter 77f.

γε ἐνταῦθα, καὶ τοῦ μὴ πρὸς ἀργύριον βλέπειν, ποιοῦμαι μάρτυρα τὸν Αἰγύπτιον τοῦτον. δεινὰ γὰρ πε-
πρᾶχθαί τε μοι καὶ βεβουλεῦσθαι φήσας οὔθ᾽ ὁπόσων
χρημάτων ἐπανουργουν ταῦτα, εἴρηκεν, οὔθ᾽ ὅ τι ἐνθυμηθεὶς κέρδος, ἀλλ᾽ οὕτως ἀνόητος αὐτῷ δοκῶ τις, ὡς
γοητεύειν μέν, ἃ δ᾽ ὑπὲρ πολλῶν ἕτεροι χρημάτων,
αὐτὸς ἀδικεῖν οὐδ᾽ ἐπὶ χρήμασιν, ἀγοράν, οἶμαι, προ-
κηρύττων τοιαύτην· ἴτε, ὦ ἀνόητοι, γοητεύω γὰρ, καὶ
οὐδ᾽ ὑπὲρ χρημάτων, ἀλλὰ προῖκα, κερδανεῖτε δὲ
ὑμεῖς μὲν τὸ ἀπελθεῖν ἕκαστος ἔχων, ὅτου ἐρᾷ, ἐγὼ δὲ
κινδύνους καὶ γραφάς.᾽

13   "Ἀλλ᾽ ἵνα μὴ ἐς ἀνοήτους ἴωμεν λόγους, ἐρώμεθα
τὸν κατήγορον, ὑπὲρ ὅτου χρὴ λέγειν πρῶτον. καίτοι
τί χρὴ ἐρωτᾶν; διῆλθε γὰρ ὑπὲρ τῆς στολῆς κατ᾽
ἀρχὰς[8] τοῦ λόγου, καί, νὴ Δί᾽, ὧν σιτοῦμαί τε καὶ οὐ
σιτοῦμαι. ἀπολογοῦ δὴ ὑπὲρ τούτων, θεῖε Πυθαγόρα,
κρινόμεθα γὰρ ὑπὲρ ὧν σὺ μὲν εὗρες, ἐγὼ δὲ ἐπαινῶ.
ἀνθρώποις ἡ Γῆ φύει, βασιλεῦ, πάντα, καὶ σπονδὰς
ἄγειν πρὸς τὰ ζῷα βουλομένοις δεῖ οὐδενός, τὰ μὲν
γὰρ δρέπονται αὐτῆς, τὰ δ᾽ ἀροῦνται κουροτροφού-
σης, ὡς ταῖς ὥραις ἔοικεν, οἱ δ᾽ ὥσπερ ἀνήκοοι τῆς
Γῆς μάχαιραν ἐπ᾽ αὐτὰ ἔθηξαν ὑπὲρ ἐσθῆτός τε καὶ
βρώσεως.

14   "Ἰνδοὶ τοίνυν Βραχμᾶνες αὐτοί τε οὐκ ἐπήνουν
ταῦτα, καὶ τοὺς Γυμνοὺς Αἰγυπτίων ἐδίδασκον μὴ
ἐπαινεῖν αὐτά. ἔνθεν Πυθαγόρας ἑλών, Ἑλλήνων δὲ
πρῶτος ἐπέμιξεν Αἰγυπτίοις, τὰ μὲν ἔμψυχα τῇ Γῇ
ἀνῆκεν, ἃ δ᾽ αὐτὴ φύει, ἀκήρατα εἶναι φάσκων ἐσι-

to myself. As for my conduct here and my indifference to profit, I call this Egyptian to witness. He says I have done and planned wicked things, but he has neither said for how much money I committed these crimes, nor what profit I had in mind. He thinks me such as fool as to be a sorcerer, and yet that I charge nothing to commit crimes for which others charge a fortune. No doubt I advertise as follows: 'Roll up, you fools, I practice sorcery, and not for money but free of charge. Your profit will be to leave each with his desires satisfied, and my profit will be risks and indictments.'

"However, so as not to wander into foolish topics, let me   13
ask my accuser what I should speak about first. And yet why should I ask? He devoted the beginning of his speech to my clothing and to what I eat and do not eat, for heaven's sake. Defend yourself on this charge, then, inspired Pythagoras, since we are on trial for customs that you invented and I approve. Everything Earth produces is for humanity's sake, Majesty, and those who are willing to live at peace with animals have need of nothing. They can gather or reap, as the seasons dictate, from the nourishing earth. But some people, as if deaf to the earth, sharpen knives against animals for the sake of clothing and food.

"The Indian Brahmans themselves abhorred such prac-   14
tices, and taught the Naked Ones of Egypt to abhor them too. It was from there that Pythagoras, who was the first Greek to associate with Egyptians, derived the principle. Animals he regarded as sacred to Earth, but things that

---

8 κατ' ἀρχὰς Rsk.: τὰς ἀρχὰς

APOLLONIUS OF TYANA

τεῖτο, ἐπιτήδεια γὰρ σῶμα καὶ νοῦν τρέφειν, ἐσθῆτά
τε, ἣν ἀπὸ θνησειδίων οἱ πολλοὶ φοροῦσιν, οὐ καθα-
ρὰν εἶναι φήσας λίνον ἠμπίσχετο, καὶ τὸ ὑπόδημα
κατὰ τὸν αὐτὸν λόγον βύβλου ἐπλέξατο. ἀπέλαυσέ τε
τοῦ καθαρὸς εἶναι πολλὰ μέν, πρῶτον δὲ τὸ τῆς
ἑαυτοῦ ψυχῆς αἰσθέσθαι· γενόμενος γὰρ κατὰ τοὺς
χρόνους, οὓς ὑπὲρ τῆς Ἑλένης ἡ Τροία ἐμάχετο, καὶ
τῶν τοῦ Πάνθου παίδων κάλλιστος ὢν καὶ κάλλιστα
ἐσταλμένος ἀπέθανε μὲν οὕτω νέος, ὡς καὶ Ὁμήρῳ
παρασχεῖν θρῆνον, παρελθὼν δ᾽ ἐς πλείω σώματα
κατὰ τὸν Ἀδραστείας θεσμόν, ὃν ψυχὴ ἐναλλάττει,
πάλιν ἐπανῆλθεν ἐς ἀνθρώπου εἶδος καὶ Μνησαρχίδῃ
ἐτέχθη τῷ Σαμίῳ, σοφὸς ἐκ βαρβάρου καὶ Ἴων ἐκ
Τρωὸς καὶ οὕτω τι ἀθάνατος, ὡς μηδ᾽ ὅτι Εὔφορβος
ἦν ἐκλελῆσθαι. τὸν μὲν δὴ πρόγονον τῆς ἐμαυτοῦ
σοφίας εἴρηκα καὶ τὸ μὴ αὐτὸς εὑρών, κληρονομήσας
δὲ ἑτέρου ταῦτ᾽ ἔχειν.

15   "Κἀγὼ μὲν οὐ κρίνω τοὺς τρυφῶντας ὑπὲρ τοῦ
φοινικίου ὄρνιθος, οὐδ᾽ ὑπὲρ τοῦ ἐκ Φάσιδος ἢ Παι-
όνων, οὓς πιαίνουσιν ἐς τὰς αὑτῶν δαῖτας οἱ τῇ
γαστρὶ χαριζόμενοι πάντα, οὐδ᾽ ἐγραψάμην πω
οὐδένα ὑπὲρ τῶν ἰχθύων, οὓς ὠνοῦνται πλείονος ἢ
τοὺς κοππατίας ποτὲ οἱ λαμπροί, οὐδ᾽ ἀλουργίδος
ἐβάσκηνα οὐδενί, οὐδὲ Παμφύλου τινὸς ἢ μαλακῆς
ἐσθῆτος, ἀσφοδέλου δέ, ὦ θεοί, καὶ τραγημάτων καὶ

---

11 I.e., Euphorbus, cf. I 1.1.   12 Lament: *Iliad* 17.51–60.
Adrasteia: alternative name of goddess Nemesis.

grow from Earth, he said, were pure, and so were fitted to
nourish body and soul. Clothing made from dead creatures, which most people wear, he considered unclean,
and hence he dressed in linen and made his shoes out of
papyrus bark for the same reason. He derived many advantages from his purity, above all that of recognizing his own
soul. He had been born in the time when the Trojans were
fighting on behalf of Helen, and he was the handsomest of
the sons of Panthus and the most handsomely equipped.[11]
He died so young as to give Homer a subject for a lament, and passed through several bodies in obedience
to Adrasteia's law about the migration of souls.[12] Finally
he returned to human form, and was born the son of
Mnesarchides of Samos, a wise man instead of a barbarian,
an Ionian instead of a Trojan, and so exempt from death
that he did not even forget having been Euphorbus. I have
told you who originated my philosophy and how it is not
my invention, but an heirloom handed down from someone else.

"For myself, I do not condemn those who dine off the   15
flamingo, or off the bird from the Phasis or Paeonia,[13] even
though those who indulge their stomach's every wish fatten them up for their own dinners. I have never indicted
anybody because of the fish for which people pay more
than aristocrats once paid for Corinthian steeds, nor have I
envied anyone his purple or his soft Pamphylian clothing.[14]
I myself am indicted, gods above, because of asphodel,[15]

[13] The first bird is the pheasant, but the second cannot be
identified.

[14] A highly valued kind of wool.

[15] A plant eaten by the poor.

καθαρᾶς ὀψοφαγίας γραφὴν φεύγω, καὶ οὐδὲ ἡ ἐσθὴς
ἄσυλος, ἀλλὰ κἀκείνην λωποδυτεῖ με ὁ κατήγορος ὡς
πολλοῦ ἀξίαν τοῖς γόησι.

16   "Καίτοι ἀφελόντι τὸν ὑπὲρ ἐμψύχων τε καὶ ἀψύχων
λόγον, δι᾽ ὧν καθαρός τις ἢ μὴ δοκεῖ, τί βελτίων ἡ
ὀθόνη τοῦ ἐρίου; τὸ μέν γε πραοτάτου ζῴου ἐπέχθη
καὶ σπουδαζομένου θεοῖς, οἳ μὴ ἀπαξιοῦσι τὸ ποι-
μαίνειν καί, νὴ Δί᾽, ἠξίωσάν ποτε αὐτὸ καὶ χρυσοῦ
εἴδους ἢ θεοὶ ἢ λόγοι. λίνον δὲ σπείρεται μέν, ὡς
ἔτυχε, χρυσοῦ δὲ οὐδεὶς ἐπ᾽ αὐτῷ λόγος, ἀλλ᾽ ὅμως,
ἐπειδὴ μὴ ἀπ᾽ ἐμψύχου ἐδρέφθη, καθαρὸν μὲν Ἰνδοῖς
δοκεῖ, καθαρὸν δὲ Αἰγυπτίοις, ἐμοὶ δὲ καὶ Πυθαγόρᾳ
διὰ τοῦτο σχῆμα γέγονε διαλεγομένοις, εὐχομένοις,
θύουσι. καθαρὸν δὲ καὶ τὸ ἐννυχεύειν ὑπ᾽ αὐτῷ, καὶ
γὰρ τὰ ὀνείρατα τοῖς, ὡς ἐγώ, διαιτωμένοις ἐτυμωτέ-
ρας τὰς αὐτῶν φήμας ἄγει.

17   "Ἀπολογώμεθα καὶ ὑπὲρ τῆς οὔσης ποτέ ἡμῖν
κόμης, ἐπειδή τις γραφὴ καὶ αὐχμοῦ εὕρηται, κρινέτω
δὲ μὴ ὁ Αἰγύπτιος, ἀλλὰ τὰ ξανθὰ καὶ διεκτενισμένα
μειράκια, τοὺς ἐραστὰς ἐξαψάμενα καὶ τὰς ἑταίρας,
ἐφ᾽ ἃς κωμάζει, καὶ ἑαυτὰ μὲν εὐδαίμονα ἡγείσθω καὶ
ζηλωτὰ τῆς κόμης καὶ τοῦ λειβομένου ἀπ᾽ αὐτῆς
μύρου, ἐμὲ δὲ ἀναφροδισίαν πᾶσαν καὶ ἐραστὴν τοῦ
μὴ ἐρᾶν. εἰρήσεται γὰρ πρὸς αὐτά· ὦ κακοδαίμονες,
μὴ συκοφαντεῖτε τὸ Δωριέων εὕρεμα, τὸ γὰρ κομᾶν ἐκ
Λακεδαιμονίων ἥκει κατὰ ⟨τοὺς⟩[9] χρόνους ἐπιτηδευ-

    [9] ⟨τοὺς⟩ Cob.

dried fruits, and pure delicacies. Not even my clothing is sacrosanct, but my accuser is filching that from me too, as if it were much prized by sorcerers.

"But leaving aside discussion of things animate and in-   16
animate, which cause a person to appear pure or otherwise, in what way is linen better than wool? Wool was shorn
from the gentlest of animals, one dear to the gods, who do
not disdain to be shepherds.[16] By heaven, the gods or
storytellers once thought wool worthy to resemble gold.[17]
Linen, on the other hand, is sown casually, and no myth
ever made it into gold, and yet because it is not harvested
from a living creature, the Indians think it pure, as do the
Egyptians, and it has become the material which I and
Pythagoras wear as we converse, pray, and sacrifice. It is a
pure coverlet under which to sleep, too, since the dreams
of those who live my kind of life bring them truer predictions.

"Let me defend next the hair I once had, since being   17
unkempt has now become an indictable offense. Let my
accuser no longer be the Egyptian, but those blond, care-
fully groomed youths with their strings of lovers and mis-
tresses whom they go reveling after. They may consider
themselves lucky and enviable for their hair and the perfume that drips from it, and consider me ugliness personi-
fied, and a lover of abstention from love. I will say this to
them: 'You miserable creatures, do not impugn the institu-
tion of the Dorians. Wearing long hair comes from the

16 Apollo once herded sheep for the Thessalian king Admetus.
17 Allusion to the ram with a golden fleece that carried the
hero Phrixus to Colchis.

θὲν αὐτοῖς, [ἐς]¹⁰ οὓς μαχιμώτατα αὐτῶν εἶχον, καὶ
βασιλεὺς τῆς Σπάρτης Λεωνίδας ἐγένετο κομῶν ὑπὲρ
ἀνδρείας καὶ τοῦ σεμνὸς μὲν φίλοις, φοβερὸς δὲ
ἐχθροῖς φαίνεσθαι· ταῦτά τοι καὶ ἡ Σπάρτη ἐπ᾽ αὐτῷ
κομᾷ μεῖον οὐδὲν ἢ ἐπὶ Λυκούργῳ τε καὶ Ἰφίτῳ.’

18   "Σοφοῦ δὲ ἀνδρὸς κόμης φειδέσθω σίδηρος, οὐ γὰρ
θεμιτὸν ἐπάγειν αὐτόν, οὗ πᾶσαι μὲν αἰσθητηρίων
πηγαί, πᾶσαι δ᾽ ὀμφαί, ὅθεν εὐχαί τε ἀναφαίνονται
καὶ σοφίας ἑρμηνεὺς λόγος. Ἐμπεδοκλῆς μὲν γὰρ καὶ
στρόφιον τῶν ἁλουργοτάτων περὶ αὐτὴν ἁρμόσας
ἐσόβει περὶ τὰς τῶν Ἑλλήνων ἀγυιὰς ὕμνους ξυντιθείς, ὡς θεὸς ἐξ ἀνθρώπου ἔσοιτο, ἐγὼ δὲ ἠμελημένῃ
κόμῃ χρώμενος καὶ οὔπω τοιῶνδε ὕμνων ἐπ᾽ αὐτῇ
δεηθεὶς ἐς γραφὰς ἄγομαι καὶ δικαστήρια. καὶ τί φῶ
τὸν Ἐμπεδοκλέα; πότερ᾽ ἑαυτὸν ἢ τὴν τῶν ἐπ᾽ αὐτοῦ
ἀνθρώπων εὐδαιμονίαν ᾄδειν, παρ᾽ οἷς οὐκ ἐσυκοφαν-
τεῖτο ταῦτα;

19   "Μὴ πλείω διαλεγώμεθα ὑπὲρ τῆς κόμης, ἐτμήθη
γὰρ καὶ προὔλαβε τὴν κατηγορίαν ὁ φθόνος, δι᾽ ὃν
ὑπὲρ τῆς ἑτέρας αἰτίας χρὴ ἀπολογεῖσθαι χαλεπῆς
οὔσης, καὶ οἵας, ὦ βασιλεῦ, μὴ σοὶ μόνον, ἀλλὰ καὶ
τῷ Διὶ παρασχεῖν φόβον· φησὶ γὰρ τοὺς ἀνθρώπους
θεὸν ἡγεῖσθαί με καὶ δημοσίᾳ τοῦτ᾽ ἐκφέρειν ἐμβε-
βροντημένους ὑπ᾽ ἐμοῦ. καίτοι καὶ πρὸ τῆς αἰτίας
ἐκεῖνα διδάσκειν ἔδει, τί διαλεχθεὶς ἐγώ, τί δ᾽ οὕτω
θαυμάσιον εἰπὼν ἢ πράξας ὑπηγαγόμην τοὺς ἀνθρώ-

¹⁰ [ἐς] secl. Cob.

Spartans, and they practiced it when they were at their most warlike, and when the king of Sparta was Leonidas,[18] who grew his hair to show his courage, and to inspire respect in his friends and terror in his enemies. That is why the Spartans grow their hair in his honor no less than for Lycurgus or Iphitus.'[19]

"Iron should spare a wise man's hair, because it is impi-   18
ous to apply it to the place that contains all the sources of his perception, all his utterances, from which all his prayers proceed, as does the discourse that conveys his wisdom. Empedocles actually tied a ribbon of the purest purple around his hair, and strutted around the streets of Greece, composing hymns to the effect that he would pass from mortal to god.[20] I kept my hair neglected and never needed such hymns about it, and yet I am exposed to indictments and law courts. And yet what should I say about Empedocles? That he celebrated himself, or rather that humanity was lucky in his day, since such things were not attacked then?

"Let us no longer dwell on my hair, because it has   19
been cut off and malice has forestalled the accusation. But malice forces me to defend myself on another charge, a severe one and such as to inspire terror not only in you, Majesty, but in Zeus himself. The man here says that people consider me a god, and have been entranced by me into proclaiming as much publicly. But before making that accusation, he should have shown by what conversation of mine, or by what amazing speech or act, I induced human

---

[18] King of Sparta at the time of the battle of Thermopylae, 480 BCE.   [19] Lycurgus (see VI 21.6) together with Iphitus of Elis refounded the Olympic games.   [20] See I 1.3.

πους προσεύχεσθαί μοι. οὔτε γάρ, ἐς ὅ τι ἢ ἐξ ὅτου
μετέβαλεν[11] ἢ μεταβαλεῖ μοι ἡ ψυχή, διελέχθην ἐν
Ἕλλησι, καίτοι γιγνώσκων, οὔτε δόξας περὶ ἐμαυτοῦ
τοιαύτας ἀπέστειλα, οὔτ᾽ ἐς λόγια καὶ χρησμῶν ᾠδὰς
ἐξῆλθον, οἷα τῶν θεοκλυτούντων φορά, οὐδ᾽ οἶδα
πόλιν οὐδεμίαν, ἐν ᾗ ἔδοξε ξυνιόντας Ἀπολλωνίῳ
θύειν. καίτοι πολλοῦ ἄξιος ἑκάστοις ἐγενόμην, ὁπόσα
ἐδέοντό μου, ἐδέοντο δὲ τοιαῦτα· μὴ νοσεῖν οἱ νοσοῦντες, ὁσιώτεροι μύειν, ὁσιώτεροι θύειν, ὕβριν ἐκτετμῆσθαι, νόμους ἐρρῶσθαι.

20   "Μισθὸς δ᾽ ἐμοὶ μὲν τούτων ὑπῆρχε τὸ βελτίους
αὐτοὺς αὑτῶν φαίνεσθαι, σοὶ δὲ ἐχαριζόμην ταῦτα.
ὥσπερ γὰρ οἱ τῶν βοῶν ἐπιστάται τὸ μὴ ἀτακτεῖν
αὐτὰς χαρίζονται τοῖς κεκτημένοις τὰς βοῦς, καὶ οἱ
τῶν ποιμνίων ἐπιμεληταὶ πιαίνουσιν αὐτὰ ἐς τὸ τῶν
πεπαμένων κέρδος, νόσους τε ἀφαιροῦσι μελιττῶν οἱ
νομεῖς αὐτῶν, ὡς μὴ ἀπόλοιτο τῷ δεσπότῃ τὸ σμῆνος,
οὕτω που καὶ ἐγὼ τὰ πολιτικὰ παύων ἐλαττώματα σοὶ
διωρθούμην τὰς πόλεις, ὥστ᾽ εἰ καὶ θεὸν ἡγοῦντό με,
σοὶ κέρδος ἡ ἀπάτη εἶχε, ξὺν προθυμίᾳ γάρ που
ἠκροῶντό μου, δεδιότες πράττειν, ἃ μὴ δοκεῖ θεῷ. ἀλλ᾽
οὐχὶ τοῦτο ᾤοντο, ὅτι δ᾽ ἐστί τις ἀνθρώπῳ πρὸς θεὸν
ξυγγένεια, δι᾽ ἣν μόνον ζῴων θεοὺς οἶδε, φιλοσοφεῖ δὲ
καὶ ὑπὲρ τῆς ἑαυτοῦ φύσεως καὶ ὅπῃ μετέχει τοῦ
θείου.

21   "Φησὶ μὲν οὖν καὶ τὸ εἶδος αὐτὸ θεῷ ἐοικέναι, ὡς
ἀγαλματοποιία ἑρμηνεύει καὶ χρώματα, τάς τε ἀρετὰς
θεόθεν ἥκειν ἐπ᾽ αὐτὸν πέπεισται, καὶ τοὺς μετέχοντας

beings to pray to me. For what my soul had changed into or
from, or will change into hereafter, this I did not discuss
with the Greeks, though I knew it. Nor did I ever spread
such ideas about myself, or resort to predictions or to
versified oracles as the tribe of diviners do. Nor do I know
of a city in which it was ever decided to assemble and sacrifice to Apollonius. And yet I have been of great value to
everyone in whatever they asked of me, and they asked for
such things as this: that their sick should not be sick, that
they should be more pure in their initiations, more pure in
their sacrifices, that violence should be uprooted and the
laws strengthened.

"My reward for all this was to see them grow in virtue,   20
and in this I benefited you. Herdsmen make a present of
their herds' good behavior to the owners of the herds;
those who tend sheep fatten them to profit the possessors,
and beekeepers remove diseases from the bees so that the
master does not lose his hive. So also when I put an end to
civic misconduct, I corrected the cities on your behalf.
Had they thought me a god, you would have benefited
from the illusion, since they would no doubt have obeyed
me with alacrity from fear of doing what displeases a god.
They did not believe that, however, but rather that mankind has a sort of kinship with God, and hence he is the
only animal who knows the gods, and speculates about his
own nature and in what way he partakes of divinity.

"A human being claims to be like God in shape too, as   21
the arts of sculpture and painting make clear, and holds
that the virtues come to him from God, and that those who

---

11 μετέβαλεν Cob.: μετέβαλον

αὐτῶν ἀγχιθέους τε εἶναι καὶ θείους. διδασκάλους δὲ
τῆς διανοίας ταύτης μὴ Ἀθηναίους καλῶμεν, ἐπειδὴ
τοὺς δικαίους καὶ τοὺς Ὀλυμπίους καὶ τὰς τοιάσδε
ἐπωνυμίας πρῶτοι ἔθεντο, θειοτέρας, ὡς τὸ εἰκός,
οὔσας ἢ ἐπ᾽ ἀνθρώπῳ κεῖσθαι, ἀλλὰ τὸν Ἀπόλλω τὸν
ἐν τῇ Πυθοῖ· ἀφίκετο μὲν γὰρ ἐς τὸ ἱερὸν αὐτοῦ
Λυκοῦργος ὁ ἐκ τῆς Σπάρτης, ἄρτι γεγραμμένων αὐτῷ
τῶν νόμων, οἷς ἡ Λακεδαίμων τέτακται, προσειπὼν δ᾽
αὐτὸν ὁ Ἀπόλλων βασανίζει τὴν περὶ αὐτοῦ δόξαν, ἐν
ἀρχῇ τοῦ χρησμοῦ φάσκων ἀπορεῖν, πότερα χρὴ θεὸν
ἢ ἄνθρωπον καλεῖν, προϊὼν δὲ ἀποφαίνεται καὶ ψηφί-
ζεται τὴν ἐπωνυμίαν ταύτην, ὡς ἀνδρὶ ἀγαθῷ. καὶ
οὐδεὶς ἐπὶ τὸν Λυκοῦργον ἀγὼν ἢ κίνδυνος ἐκ τούτων
παρὰ Λακεδαιμονίοις, ὡς ἀθανατίζοντα, ἐπεὶ μὴ ἐπέ-
πληξε τῷ Πυθίῳ προσρηθεὶς τούτοις, ἀλλὰ ξυνετί-
θεντο τῷ μαντείῳ, πεπεισμένοι δήπου καὶ πρὸ τοῦ
χρησμοῦ ταῦτα.

22   "Τὰ δὲ Ἰνδῶν καὶ Αἰγυπτίων ταῦτα. Ἰνδοὺς Αἰγύπτιοι τὰ μὲν ἄλλα συκοφαντοῦσι καὶ διαβάλλουσιν
αὐτῶν τὰς ἐπὶ τοῖς πράγμασι δόξας, τὸν δὲ λόγον, ὃς
ἐς τὸν δημιουργὸν τῶν ὅλων εἴρηται, οὕτω τι ἐπαινοῦ-
σιν, ὡς καὶ ἑτέρους διδάξασθαι Ἰνδῶν ὄντα. ὁ λόγος
δὲ τῆς μὲν τῶν ὅλων γενέσεώς τε καὶ οὐσίας θεὸν
δημιουργὸν οἶδε, τοῦ δὲ ἐνθυμηθῆναι ταῦτα αἴτιον τὸ
ἀγαθὸν εἶναι αὐτόν. ἐπεὶ τοίνυν ξυγγενῆ ταῦτα, ἔχο-
μαι τοῦ λόγου, καὶ φημὶ τοὺς ἀγαθοὺς τῶν ἀνθρώπων
θεοῦ τι ἔχειν. κόσμος δὲ ὁ μὲν ἐπὶ θεῷ δημιουργῷ
κείμενος τὰ ἐν οὐρανῷ νομιζέσθω καὶ τὰ ἐν θαλάττῃ

share in them are close to the gods and holy. Let us not call
the Athenians the originators of this doctrine, just because
they were the first to assign such titles as 'the Just' and 'the
Olympian,' which are perhaps titles too godlike to be applied to humans. Let us rather name Apollo of Delphi.
Once there came to his sanctuary Lycurgus of Sparta, just
after he had drawn up the laws that regulate Sparta. When
addressing him, Apollo weighs his own belief about him,
saying at the opening of the oracle that he doubts whether
to call him a god or a man, but as he proceeds he assigns
and awards that title to him, as a man of virtue.[21] Yet
Lycurgus was never in any danger or put on trial at Sparta
for having divine ambitions, just because he did not re-
prove the Pythian god for this form of address. The Spartans concurred with the shrine, having no doubt had that
belief even before the oracle.

"As for the Indians and Egyptians, the Egyptians criti-   22
cize the Indians on many grounds, and speak ill of their
beliefs about the conduct of affairs, but so highly do they
approve the doctrine that the Indians preach about the
creator of the universe that they impart it to others, even
though it is Indian. This doctrine recognizes God as the
creator of the universe in its origin and in its essence, and
his goodness as the motive that give him the idea of this
plan. Since these qualities are related, I accept the doctrine, and believe that men who are good have some part in
God. We must understand the order that is dependent on
God's creation to be everything in heaven, sea and earth, in

[21] Herodotus 1.65.

καὶ γῇ πάντα, ὧν μετουσία ἴση ἀνθρώποις, πλὴν
τύχης. ἔστι δέ τις καὶ ἐπ' ἀνδρὶ ἀγαθῷ κόσμος, οὐχ
ὑπερβάλλων τὰ σοφίας μέτρα, ὅν που καὶ αὐτός, ὦ
βασιλεῦ, φήσεις ἀνδρὸς δεῖσθαι θεῷ εἰκασμένου.

23   "Καὶ τί τὸ σχῆμα τοῦ κόσμου τοῦδε; αἱ ψυχαὶ
ἀτακτοῦσαι μανικώτερον ἅπτονται παντὸς σχήματος,
καὶ ἔωλοι μὲν αὐταῖς νόμοι, σωφροσύνη δ' οὐδαμοῦ,
θεῶν δὲ τιμαὶ ἄτιμοι, λαλιᾶς δ' ἐρῶσι καὶ τρυφῆς, ἐξ
ὧν ἀργία φύεται πονηρὰ ξύμβουλος ἔργου παντός. αἱ
δὲ μεθύουσαι ψυχαὶ πηδῶσι μὲν ἐπὶ πολλά, τὸ δὲ
σκίρτημα τοῦτο ἴσχει οὐδέν, οὐδ' εἰ πάντα πίνοιεν,
ὁπόσα, ὥσπερ ὁ μανδραγόρας, ὑπνηλὰ ἐνομίσθη.
ἀλλὰ δεῖ ἀνδρὸς ὃς ἐπιμελήσεται τοῦ περὶ αὐτὰς
κόσμου, θεὸς ὑπὸ σοφίας ἥκων. οὑτοσὶ γὰρ ἀπόχρη
αὐτὰς ἐρώτων τε ἀπάγειν, ἐφ' οὓς ἀγριώτερον τῆς
ξυνήθους ὁμιλίας ἐκφέρονται, καὶ φιλοχρηματίας, δι'
ἣν οὔπω πᾶν ἔχειν φασίν, ἐπεὶ μὴ καὶ τὸ στόμα
ὑπέχουσιν ἐπιρρέοντι τῷ πλούτῳ. φόνων γὰρ ἀνασχεῖν μὲν αὐτὰς μὴ προσάπτεσθαι οὐκ ἀδύνατον
ἴσως ἀνδρὶ τοιούτῳ, ἀπονίψαι δὲ οὔτε ἐμοὶ δυνατὸν
οὔτε τῷ πάντων δημιουργῷ θεῷ.

24   "'Έστω, βασιλεῦ, κατηγορία καὶ ὑπὲρ τῆς Ἐφέσου, ἐπειδὴ ἐσώθη, καὶ κρινέτω με ὁ Αἰγύπτιος, ὡς
ἔστι πρόσφορον τῇ γραφῇ. ἔστι γὰρ δήπου ἡ κατηγορία τοιαύτη· περὶ Σκύθας ἢ Κελτούς, οἳ ποταμὸν
Ἴστρον ἢ Ῥῆνον οἰκοῦσι, πόλις ᾤκισται μείων οὐδὲν
Ἐφέσου τῆς ἐν Ἰωνίᾳ. ταύτην ὁρμητήριον βαρβάρων
οὖσαν, οἳ μὴ ἀκροῶνταί σου, λοιμὸς μέν τις ἀπολεῖν

all of which humans have an equal share, except by misfortune. But there is also a kind of order dependent on a good man, which does not transgress the bounds set by wisdom; and you yourself, Majesty, will admit that this needs a true man who resembles God.

"What form, then, does this order take? Souls that are 23 disordered madly attack every dignity, and for them the laws are obsolete, temperance is of no account, the honors due to the gods are no honors. They adore gossip and extravagance, from which issues the wicked indolence that prompts their every course. Souls that are drunken leap in many directions, and nothing restrains ther skittishness, not even if they drank every soporific that was ever imagined, such as mandrake. A true man is needed to see to the ordering of these souls, a God sent by wisdom. Only he has the power to divert them, first from passions to which they are swept with a frenzy too great for normal society, and second from avarice, in which they say they always lack something until they put their lips to a stream of wealth. As for restraining souls from attempting murder, that is perhaps not impossible for such a man, but to absolve them from it is what neither I nor the God who made the world can do.

"Let me also, Majesty, be accused in the matter of 24 Ephesus, because I saved it, and let the Egyptian indict me as the charge requires. The indictment must be as follows. 'Among the Scythians or the Celts, who live on the Danube or the Rhine, there is a city not inferior to Ephesus in Ionia. This is a base for barbarians who are not obedient to you, but Apollonius cured it when a plague was about to

ἔμελλεν, Ἀπολλώνιος δὲ ἰάσατο.ʼ ἔστι μὲν γάρ τις καὶ
πρὸς ταῦτα ἀπολογία σοφῷ ἀνδρί, ἣν ὁ βασιλεὺς τὸ
ἀντίξοον ὅπλοις, ἀλλὰ μὴ νόσοις αἱρεῖν βούληται, μὴ
γὰρ ἐξαλειφθείη πόλις μηδεμία, μήτε σοί, βασιλεῦ,
μήτε ἐμοί, μήτε ἴδοιμι πρὸς ἱεροῖς νόσον, διʼ ἣν οἱ
νοσοῦντες ἐν αὐτοῖς κεῖσονται.

25   "Ἀλλὰ μὴ ἔστω ἐν σπουδῇ τὰ βαρβάρων, μηδὲ
τάττωμεν αὐτοὺς ἐς τὸ ὑγιαῖνον, πολεμιωτάτους ὄντας
καὶ οὐκ ἐνσπόνδους τῷ περὶ ἡμᾶς γένει. τὴν δὲ Ἔφεσον τίς ἀφαιρήσεται τὸ[12] σώζεσθαι, βεβλημένην μὲν
τὰς ἀρχὰς τοῦ γένους ἐκ τῆς καθαρωτάτης Ἀτθίδος,
ἐπιδεδωκυῖαν δὲ παρὰ πάσας, ὁπόσαι Ἰωνικαί τε καὶ
Λύδιοι, προβεβηκυῖαν δὲ ἐπὶ τὴν θάλατταν διὰ τὸ
ὑπερήκειν τῆς γῆς, ἐφʼ ἧς ᾠκίσθη, μεστὴν δὲ φρον-
τισμάτων οὖσαν φιλοσόφων τε καὶ ῥητορικῶν, ὑφʼ ὧν
ἡ πόλις οὐχ ἵππῳ, μυριάσι δὲ ἀνθρώπων ἰσχύει,
σοφίαν ἐπαινοῦσα; τίς δʼ ἂν σοφὸς ἐκλιπεῖν σοι δοκεῖ
τὸν ὑπὲρ πόλεως τοιαύτης ἀγῶνα, ἐνθυμηθεὶς μὲν
Δημόκριτον ἐλευθερώσαντα λοιμοῦ ποτε Ἀβδηρίτας,
ἐννοήσας δὲ Σοφοκλέα τὸν Ἀθηναῖον, ὃς λέγεται καὶ
ἀνέμους θέλξαι τῆς ὥρας ὑπερπνεύσαντας, ἀκηκοὼς
δὲ τὰ Ἐμπεδοκλέους, ὃς νεφέλης ἀνέσχε φορὰν ἐπʼ
Ἀκραγαντίνους ῥαγείσης;

26   "Ἐπικόπτει με ὁ κατήγορος· ἀκούεις γάρ που καὶ
σύ, ὦ βασιλεῦ, καί φησιν, οὐκ ἐπειδὴ σωτηρίας αἴτιος
Ἐφεσίοις ἐγενόμην, γράφεσθαί με, ἀλλʼ ἐπειδὴ προ-
εῖπον ἐμπεσεῖσθαί σφισι τὴν νόσον, τουτὶ γὰρ ὑπὲρ
σοφίαν εἶναι καὶ τερατῶδες, τῆς δʼ ἐπὶ τοσόνδε ἀλη-

destroy it.' Even against this charge a wise man has a kind of defense, if the emperor is willing to defeat his opponents with arms and not with germs. I pray that no city, Majesty, ever be obliterated either by you, Majesty, or by me, and that I may never see disease in holy places and the sick lying in them.

"But let us not feel concern for the affairs of barbarians   25
seriously, or think them to be in their right mind, since they are bitterly hostile and inveterate enemies of our nation. But who will rob Ephesus of its preservation? It is a city founded at the very origin of our race from the most sacred land of Attica. It has surpassed all the cities of Ionia and Lydia; it has spread to the sea, after outgrowing the land on which it was founded. It is packed with philosophical and rhetorical studies, and those make the city strong not in cavalry but in tens of thousands of inhabitants, as a place that honors wisdom. What wise man do you think would hesitate to fight on behalf of such a city, when he remembered Democritus, who once freed Abdera from plague, or when he considered Sophocles the Athenian, who is said to have calmed the winds when they blew too fierce for summer, or when he had heard of Empedocles's deed, who checked the onset of a storm that broke over Acragas?

"My accuser breaks in, as no doubt you too can hear,   26
Majesty, and says that the charge against me is not that I was the savior of the Ephesians, but that I predicted the onset of the plague to them. This, he says, is more than wisdom, it is uncanny, and I would not have hit the truth so

---

12 τὸ Kay.: τοῦ

θείας οὐκ ἂν ἐφικέσθαι με, εἰ μὴ γόης τε ἦν καὶ
ἀπόρρητος. τί οὖν ἐνταῦθα ἐρεῖ Σωκράτης ὑπὲρ ὧν
ἔφασκε τοῦ δαιμονίου μανθάνειν; τί δὲ Θαλῆς τε καὶ
Ἀναξαγόρας, τὼ Ἴωνε, ὁ μὲν τὴν εὐφορίαν τὴν τῶν
ἐλαιῶν, ὁ δὲ πολλὰ τῶν οὐρανίων παθῶν προειπόντε; ἢ
γοητεύοντε προειπεῖν ταῦτα; καὶ μὴν καὶ ὑπήχθησαν
οὗτοι δικαστηρίοις ἐφ᾿ ἑτέραις αἰτίαις, καὶ οὐδαμοῦ
τῶν αἰτιῶν εἴρηται γόητας εἶναι σφᾶς, ἐπειδὴ προ-
γιγνώσκουσι. καταγέλαστον γὰρ τοῦτο ἐδόκει καὶ
οὐδ᾿ ἐν Θετταλίᾳ πιθανὸν κατ᾿ ἀνδρῶν λέγεσθαι σοφῶν, οὗ τὰ γύναια κακῶς ἤκουεν[13] ἐπὶ τῇ τῆς σελήνης
ἕλξει.

27   "Πόθεν οὖν τοῦ περὶ τὴν Ἔφεσον πάθους ᾐσθόμην;
ἤκουσας μὲν καὶ τοῦ κατηγόρου εἰπόντος, ὅτι μὴ κατὰ
τοὺς ἄλλους διαιτῶμαι, κἀμοὶ δὲ ὑπὲρ τῶν ἐμαυτοῦ
σιτίων, ὡς λεπτὰ καὶ ἡδίω τῆς ἑτέρων συβάριδος, ἐν
ἀρχῇ εἴρηται· τοῦτό μοι, ὦ βασιλεῦ, τὰς αἰσθήσεις ἐν
αἰθρίᾳ τινὶ ἀπορρήτῳ φυλάττει κοὐκ ἐᾷ θολερὸν περὶ
αὐτὰς οὐδὲν εἶναι, διορᾶν τε, ὥσπερ ἐν κατόπτρου
αὐγῇ, πάντα γιγνόμενά τε καὶ ἐσόμενα. οὐ γὰρ περι-
μενεῖ γε ὁ σοφὸς τὴν γῆν ἀναθυμιῶσαν ἢ τὸν ἀέρα
διεφθορότα, ἢν τὸ δεινὸν ἄνωθεν ῥέῃ, ἀλλὰ ξυνήσει
αὐτῶν καὶ ἐπὶ θύραις ὄντων ὕστερον μὲν ἢ οἱ θεοί,
θᾶττον δὲ ἢ οἱ πολλοί, θεοὶ μὲν γὰρ μελλόντων,
ἄνθρωποι δὲ γιγνομένων, σοφοὶ δὲ προσιόντων αἰ-
σθάνονται. λοιμῶν δ᾿ αἰτίας ἰδίᾳ, βασιλεῦ, ἐρώτα,
σοφώτεραι γὰρ ἢ ἐς τοὺς πολλοὺς λέγεσθαι.

28   "Ἆρ᾿ οὖν τὸ οὕτως διαιτᾶσθαι λεπτότητα μόνον

354

exactly unless I were a sorcerer with mysterious powers. What then will Socrates say to this in defense of what he claimed to have heard from his guardian spirit? Or Thales and Anaxagoras, the Ionians, of whom one predicted a heavy crop of olives and the other predicted many celestial events? Will they say that they predicted all this because they were sorcerers? Indeed, they were brought to court on other charges, but nowhere among these charges is it specified that they were sorcerers just because they knew the future. That would have seemed ridiculous, and even in Thessaly would not have been a plausible charge against those men of wisdom, even though women there had a bad name for bringing down the moon.

"How, then, did I sense the disaster at Ephesus? You 27 have heard even my accuser saying that my way of life differs from other people's, and I too said when I began that my food is light and tastier than other people's delicacies. This, Majesty, keeps my senses in a kind of mysterious atmosphere, and prevents any kind of cloudiness from affecting them. It lets me discern everything that is and will be, like a reflection in a mirror. A wise man will not wait for the earth to give off a miasma, or for the air to be corrupted if the misfortune falls from above. He will perceive these events when they are at hand, later than the gods but sooner than the majority, since the gods sense the future, humans the present, and wise men what is imminent. But the causes of disease you should ask me about privately, Majesty, because they are too lofty to be expounded to the multitude.

"Well then, does this kind of diet merely induce a re- 28

---

13 ἤκουεν Cob.: ἤκουσεν

ἐργάζεται τῶν αἰσθήσεων ἢ ἰσχὺν ἐπὶ τὰ μέγιστά τε
καὶ θαυμασιώτατα; θεωρεῖν δ' ἔξεστιν ὃ λέγω καὶ ἀπ'
ἄλλων μέν, οὐχ ἥκιστα δὲ κἀκ τῶν ἐν Ἐφέσῳ περὶ τὴν
νόσον ἐκείνην πραχθέντων· τὸ γὰρ τοῦ λοιμοῦ εἶδος,
πτωχῷ δὲ γέροντι εἴκαστο, καὶ εἶδον καὶ ἰδὼν εἷλον,
οὐ παύσας νόσον, ἀλλ' ἐξελών, ὅτῳ δ' εὐξάμενος,
δηλοῖ τὸ ἱερόν, ὃ ἐν Ἐφέσῳ ὑπὲρ τούτου ἱδρυσάμην,
Ἡρακλέους μὲν γὰρ Ἀποτροπαίου ἐστί, ξυνεργὸν
δ' αὐτὸν εἱλόμην, ἐπειδὴ σοφός τε καὶ ἀνδρεῖος ὢν
ἐκάθηρέ ποτε λοιμοῦ τὴν Ἦλιν, τὰς ἀναθυμιάσεις
ἀποκλύσας, ἃς παρεῖχεν ἡ γῆ κατ' Αὐγέαν τυραν-
νεύοντα.

29   "Τίς ἂν οὖν σοι, βασιλεῦ, δοκεῖ φιλοτιμούμενος
γόης φαίνεσθαι θεῷ ἀναθεῖναι, ὃ αὐτὸς εἴργαστο;
τίνας δ' ἂν κτήσασθαι θαυμαστὰς τῆς τέχνης θεῷ
παρεὶς τὸ θαυμάζεσθαι; τίς δ' ἂν Ἡρακλεῖ εὔξασθαι
γόης ὤν; τὰ γὰρ τοιαῦτα οἱ κακοδαίμονες βόθροις
ἀνατιθέασι καὶ χθονίοις θεοῖς, ὧν τὸν Ἡρακλέα ἀπο-
τακτέον, καθαρὸς γὰρ καὶ τοῖς ἀνθρώποις εὔνους.
ηὐξάμην αὐτῷ καὶ ἐν Πελοποννήσῳ ποτέ, λαμίας γάρ
τι φάσμα κἀκεῖ περὶ τὴν Κόρινθον ἤλυε σιτούμενον
τῶν νέων τοὺς καλούς, καὶ ξυνήρατό μοι τοῦ ἀγῶνος
οὐ θαυμασίων δεηθεὶς δώρων, ἀλλὰ μελιττούτης καὶ
λιβανωτοῦ καὶ τοῦ ὑπὲρ σωτηρίας τι ἀνθρώπων ἐρ-
γάσασθαι, τουτὶ γὰρ καὶ κατὰ τὸν Εὐρυσθέα μισθὸν
τῶν ἄθλων ἡγεῖτο. μὴ ἄχθου, βασιλεῦ, τὰ Ἡρακλέους
ἀκούων· ἔμελε γὰρ αὐτοῦ τῇ Ἀθηνᾷ, ἐπειδὴ χρηστὸς
καὶ σωτήριος τοῖς ἀνθρώποις.

finement of the senses, or a power over very great and formidable forces? You may judge my meaning from many
things, but not least from what occurred at Ephesus during
that epidemic. When the disease took the form of an old
beggar, I recognized it, and having done so I caught it out. I
did not check the disease but eradicated it, and the god to
whom I prayed is shown by the cult image that I set up in
gratitude. It is that of Heracles the Averter. I made him my
helper because, clever and brave as he is, he once purged
Elis of a plague, and washed away the exhalations that the
earth sent up in the tyranny of Augeas.

"Do you think that someone ambitious to be consid-   29
ered a sorcerer, Majesty, would ascribe to a god what he
had achieved himself? What admirers for his craft would
he win if he yielded the admiration to a god? And what
sorcerer would pray to Heracles? Those scoundrels ascribe such acts to trenches and to the infernal gods, among
whom we must not reckon Heracles, for he is pure and
friendly to humanity. I also prayed to him once in the
Peloponnese, since there was a ghostly vampire there too,
haunting the region of Corinth, and feeding off handsome
youths.[22] Though he helped me in my struggle, he did not
ask for any amazing reward, but only for honey cake, frank-
incense, and the chance to do something to preserve the
human race, which he also considered the fee for his labors
in the time of Eurystheus. Do not take umbrage, Majesty,
at hearing about Heracles, since Athena supported him as
a virtuous person and a savior of humanity.[23]

22 See IV 25.
23 Cf. VII 24.

30   "Άλλ' ἐπεὶ κελεύεις με ὑπὲρ τῆς θυσίας ἀπολογεῖσθαι, τουτὶ γὰρ καὶ τῇ χειρὶ ἐνδείκνυσαι, ἄκουε
ἀπολογίας ἀληθοῦς. ἐγὼ γὰρ πάνθ' ὑπὲρ σωτηρίας
τῶν ἀνθρώπων πράττων οὔπω ὑπὲρ αὐτῶν ἔθυσα, οὐδ'
ἂν θύσαιμι οὐδέν, οὐδ' ἂν θίγοιμι ἱερῶν, ἐν οἷς αἷμα,
οὐδ' ἂν εὐξαίμην ἐς μάχαιραν βλέπων ἢ θυσίαν, ἥν
φησιν. οὐ Σκύθην με, ὦ βασιλεῦ, ἥρηκας, οὐδ' ἐκ
γῆς[14] ἀμίκτου ποθέν, οὐδ' ἐπέμιξά πω Μασσαγέταις ἢ
Ταύροις, ὡς κἀκείνους ἂν τοῦ τῆς θυσίας ἔθους μετ-
έβαλον· ἀνοίας δ' ἂν ποῖ ἤλαυνον, ἵνα πλεῖστα μὲν
ὑπὲρ μαντικῆς διαλεγόμενος καὶ ὅπη ἔρρωται ἢ μή,
ἄριστα δ' ἀνθρώπων ᾐσθημένος, ὅτι τὰς αὐτῶν βου-
λὰς οἱ θεοὶ τοῖς ὁσίοις τε καὶ σοφοῖς ἀνδράσι καὶ
μὴ μαντευομένοις φαίνουσι, μιαιφονίας ἅπτωμαι καὶ
σπλάγχνων ἀθύτων ἐμοὶ καὶ ἀκαλλιερήτων; ἐφ' οἷς
ἀπέλιπεν ἄν με καὶ ἡ τοῦ δαιμονίου ὀμφὴ μὴ καθαρὸν
ὄντα. καὶ μὴν εἴ τις ἀφελὼν τὸ τῆς θυσίας μύσος
ἐξετάζοι τὸν κατήγορον πρὸς ἃ μικρῷ πρόσθεν εἴρηκεν, ἀπαλλάττει με τῆς αἰτίας αὐτός, ὃν γάρ φησι
προειπεῖν Ἐφεσίοις τὴν νόσον θυσίας οὐδεμιᾶς δεη-
θέντα, τί σφαγίων ἐδεήθην ἐφ' ἃ καὶ μὴ θυσαμένῳ
παρῆν εἰδέναι; μαντικῆς δὲ τί ἐδεόμην ὑπὲρ ὧν αὐτός
τε ἐπεπείσμην καὶ ἕτερος;

31   "Εἰ γὰρ ὑπὲρ Νερούα καὶ τῶν ἀμφ' αὐτὸν κρίνομαι,
λέξω πάλιν, ἃ καὶ πρώην εἶπον, ἡνίκα ᾐτιῶ ταῦτα·
Νερούαν γὰρ ἄξιον μὲν ἀρχῆς ἡγοῦμαι πάσης καὶ

---

[14] γῆς Rsk.: τῆς

"Since you want me to defend myself in the matter of 30
the sacrifice, as you signify by your gesture, hear a truthful
defense. I would do anything to save human beings, but
never sacrificed for their sake, nor would I ever do so. I
would never touch offerings in which there was blood, or
pray with my eyes fastened on a knife or on the kind of sacrifice that they allege. I am not a Scythian captive or yours,
Majesty, or from some inhospitable land, I have never
visited the Massagetae or the Tauri,[24] and I would have
converted even them too from their manner of sacrifice.
What a level of folly I would have reached if, after my many
discussions of prophecy, of what it can and cannot do, and
when I know better than anyone that the gods reveal their
intentions to holy and wise men without their using prophecy, I were then to set my hand to slaughter, or to entrails
that I regard as unfit for sacrifice and abominable. After
such a deed, the voice of my guardian spirit would have deserted me as unclean. But, leaving aside the pollution of
the sacrifice, if one were to interrogate my accuser in the
light of what he said just now, he himself acquits me of
guilt. He says that I predicted the plague to the Ephesians
without needing any sacrifice, and how then could I need
victims to learn what I could know without sacrificing?
Why did I need divination for something of which I and
someone else were convinced?

"If I am on trial because of Nerva and his associates, I 31
will repeat what I said the other day, when you charged me
with this. I think Nerva suited to any kind of office, and to

24 Barbarian tribes reputed to practice human sacrifice.

APOLLONIUS OF TYANA

λόγου παντὸς ἐπ᾽ εὐφημίαν ἥκοντος, ἀγωνιστὴν δὲ
φροντίδων οὐ χρηστόν, καταλέλυται γὰρ τὸ σῶμα
ὑπὸ τῆς νόσου, δι᾽ ἣν καὶ ἡ γνώμη μεστὴ ἄσης καὶ
οὐδὲ τὰ οἴκοι ἱκανή. σὲ γοῦν ἐπαινεῖ μὲν σώματος,
ἐπαινεῖ δὲ γνώμης, εἰκὸς μὲν οἶμαί τι πράττων, προ-
θυμοτέρα γὰρ ὄντως ἡ ἀνθρωπεία φύσις ἐπαινεῖν, ἃ
μὴ αὐτὴ ἔρρωται. πέπονθε δέ τι καὶ πρὸς ἐμὲ χρηστὸν
Νερούας, καὶ οὔτε γελάσαντά πω αὐτὸν ἐπ᾽ ἐμοῦ οἶδα,
οὔτε εὐηθισάμενόν τι τῶν εἰωθότων ἐν φίλοις, ἀλλ᾽
ὥσπερ τὰ μειράκια πρὸς τοὺς πατέρας τε καὶ διδασκάλους τοὺς αὑτῶν, εὐλαβῶς μὲν φθέγγεται τὸ ἐπ᾽
ἐμοῦ πᾶν, ἐρυθριᾷ δὲ ἔτι, εἰδὼς δὲ τὸ ἐπιεικὲς ἐπαι-
νοῦντά με οὕτω τι ἄγαν ἐπιτηδεύει αὐτό, ὡς κἀμοὶ
ταπεινότερος τοῦ μετρίου φαίνεσθαι.

32   "Πῶς οὖν πιθανὸν ἡγήσαιτο ἄν τις ἀρχῆς ἐπιθυ-
μῆσαι Νερούαν, ἀγαπῶντα εἰ τῆς ἑαυτοῦ οἰκίας ἄρξοι;
ἢ ὑπὲρ μεγάλων διαλέγεσθαί μοι τὸν μηδ᾽ ὑπὲρ μικρῶν τεθαρρηκότα; ἢ ξυνάπτειν ἐμοὶ γνώμην ὑπὲρ ὧν
μηδ᾽ ἂν πρὸς ἄλλον, εἰ τοὐμὸν ἐνεθυμήθη, ξυνῆψεν;
ἢ πῶς ἔτ᾽ ἐγὼ σοφὸς γνώμην ἑρμηνεύειν τἀνδρὸς[15]
μαντικῇ μὲν πιστεύων, ἀπιστῶν δὲ σοφίᾳ; τὸν δὲ
Ὄρφιτον καὶ τὸν Ῥοῦφον, τοὺς δικαίους μὲν καὶ
σώφρονας, νωθροὺς δὲ ἄνδρας, ὡς εὖ οἶδα, εἰ μὲν
ὡς τυραννησείοντας[16] διαβεβλῆσθαί φασιν, οὐκ οἶδ᾽
εἴτε τούτων πλέον διαμαρτάνουσιν, εἴτε Νερούα, εἰ δ᾽
ὡς ξυμβούλω γεγονότε, πιθανώτερος ἀρχῇ ἐπιθέσθαι

360

all the praise that accompanies good repute, but he is not a proper person to contend with responsibilities. His body has been weakened by disease, which has also made his mind full of vexation and inadequate even for his own affairs. He admires you for your strength and your intellect, and in my opinion he is right to do so, since human nature is truly more inclined to praise things for which it lacks strength itself. Nerva also has kind feelings towards me. I have never known him to laugh in my presence, or joke as people often do among friends, but instead, like young men with their own fathers or teachers, he invariably minds his language in my presence, and moreover he blushes. Knowing that I preach moderation, he practices it to such an extent that even I think him more humble than is proper.

"How then could anyone plausibly think that Nerva desires office, when he is satisfied to manage his own household? Or that he could talk with me on important matters when he has not summoned the courage to do so even on trivial ones? Or that he would impart such a plan to me that if he had any consideration for me he could not concoct even with someone else? How could I still be wise enough to discern the man's intention, if I trusted in divination and mistrusted wisdom? As for Orfitus and Rufus, who are just and prudent men, but unambitious, as I know well, if anybody says they are charged with aiming at tyranny, I do not know whom he mistakes more, them or Nerva. But if the two of them are rumored to be his associates, is it more

32

---

15 τἀνδρὸς (i.e. τοῦ ἀνδρὸς) Jon.: ἀνδρὸς
16 τυραννησείοντας Abresch (Kay.): τυραννεύσαντας

Νερούας, ἢ οἴδε ξυμβουλεῦσαι;

33 "Ἀλλὰ μὴν τόν γε ὑπὲρ τούτων κρίνοντα κἀκεῖνα
εἰκὸς ἦν ἐνθυμεῖσθαι, τί ἐβούλετό μοι τὸ ξυλλαμ-
βάνειν τοῖς ἐπὶ νεώτερα ἥκουσι· χρήματα μὲν γὰρ οὔ
φησι παρ' αὐτῶν γεγενῆσθαί μοι, οὐδὲ δώροις ἐπ-
αρθέντα με ταῦτα εἰργάσθαι. σκεψώμεθα δέ, μὴ μεγάλων δεόμενος ἀνεβαλόμην τὰς παρ' αὐτῶν εὐεργεσίας
ἐς ὃν ᾤοντο ἄρξειν χρόνον, ἐν ᾧ μεγάλα μὲν ἂν αἰτεῖν
ὑπῆρξε, μειζόνων δ' ἀξιοῦσθαι· πῶς οὖν ταῦτα ἔσται
δῆλα; ἐνθυμήθητι, βασιλεῦ, σεαυτὸν καὶ τοὺς ἔτι πρὸ
σοῦ ἄρχοντας, ἀδελφὸν δήπου τὸν σεαυτοῦ καὶ πατέρα Νέρωνά τε, ἐφ' ὧν ἦρξαν, κατὰ τούτους γὰρ μάλιστα τοὺς βασιλέας βεβίωταί μοι ἐς τὸ φανερόν, τὸν
ἄλλον χρόνον Ἰνδοῖς φοιτῶντι. τούτων δὴ τῶν ὀκτὼ
καὶ τριάκοντα ἐτῶν, τοσοῦτον γὰρ τὸ ἐς σὲ μῆκος,
οὔτε ἐπὶ θύρας βασιλείους ἐφοίτησα πλὴν ἐν Αἰγύπτῳ
τοῦ σοῦ πατρός, ἐπεὶ μήτε βασιλεύς πω ἐτύγχανεν
ὢν ὡμολόγει τε δι' ἐμὲ ἥκειν, οὔτε ἀνελεύθερόν τι
διελέχθην βασιλεῦσιν ἢ ὑπὲρ βασιλέων δήμοις, οὔτ'
ἐπιστολαῖς ἐλαμπρυνάμην ἢ γραφόντων ἐμοὶ βασιλέων ἢ αὐτὸς ἐνδεικνύμενος γρά- φειν, οὔθ' ὑπὲρ
δωρεῶν κολακεύων βασιλέας ἐμαυτοῦ ἀπηνέχθην.

34 "Εἰ γοῦν ἔροιό με πλουσίους ἐνθυμηθεὶς καὶ πέ-
νητας, ποτέρου τῶν ἐθνῶν τούτων ἐμαυτὸν γράφω, τῶν
πλουσιωτάτων φήσω, τὸ γὰρ δεῖσθαι μηδενὸς ἐμοὶ
Λυδία καὶ τὸ Πακτωλοῦ πᾶν. πῶς οὖν ἢ τὰς παρὰ τῶν
οὔπω βασιλέων δωρεὰς ἀνεβαλλόμην ἐς ὃν ἄρξειν

likely that Nerva is aiming at power, or that they are abetting him?

"Indeed, someone accusing me because of these men   33
should also ask another question, what motive I could have had to collaborate with usurpers. He does not allege that I took money from them, or that I was induced by presents to take these actions. Let us speculate that I perhaps wanted a great reward, but deferred any favors from them until such time as they expected to be in power, and I could ask for much and be granted even more. How then might this be proved? Consider yourself, Majesty, and those who preceded you in power, your own brother, and father, and Nero, and how long these have ruled, since it has been mainly under these emperors that I have lived in the public eye, having previously been on a voyage to India. Now in all those thirty-eight years, since it is that length of time down to your day, I have never gone to the doors of emperors except to your father's in Egypt, though he was not in fact yet emperor, and admitted that he had come to see me. I have never made servile speeches to emperors or about emperors to cities. I have never boasted about letters that emperors sent to me, or that I was proud of writing to them. I have never fawned on emperors for gifts and betrayed myself.

"If someone were to consider the rich and the poor, and   34
to ask me in which of these classes I include myself, I would say the very rich, since having no needs is for me the equivalent of Lydia and everything in the Pactolus.[25] How therefore could I have postponed gifts from men who were

---

[25] Referring to the legendary wealth derived from the gold-bearing Pactolus River by Croesus, king of Lydia.

APOLLONIUS OF TYANA

αὐτοὺς ᾤμην χρόνον ὁ μηδὲ τὰς παρ᾽ ὑμῶν ἑλόμενος,
οἷς βέβαιον ἡγούμην τὸ ἄρχειν; ἢ βασιλειῶν μετα-
βολὰς ἐπενόουν μηδὲ ταῖς καθεστηκυίαις ἐς τὸ τιμᾶσθαι χρώμενος; καὶ μὴν ὁπόσα γίγνεται φιλοσόφῳ
ἀνδρὶ κολακεύοντι τοὺς δυνατούς, δηλοῖ τὰ Εὐφράτου.
τούτῳ γὰρ ἐντεῦθεν τί λέγω χρήματα; πηγαὶ μὲν οὖν
εἰσι πλούτου, κἀπὶ τῶν τραπεζῶν ἤδη διαλέγεται
κάπηλος, ὑποκάπηλος, τελώνης, ὀβολοστάτης, πάντα
γιγνόμενος τὰ πωλούμενά τε καὶ πωλοῦντα, ἐντετύ-
πωται δ᾽ ἀεὶ ταῖς τῶν δυνατῶν θύραις, καὶ προσ-
έστηκεν αὐταῖς πλείω καιρὸν ἢ οἱ θυρωροί, ἀπελήφθη
δὲ καὶ ὑπὸ θυρωρῶν πολλάκις, ὥσπερ τῶν κυνῶν οἱ
λίχνοι, δραχμὴν δὲ οὐδὲ φιλοσόφῳ ἀνδρὶ προέμενός
ποτε ἐπιτειχίζει τὸν ἑαυτοῦ πλοῦτον ἑτέροις, τὸν Αἰγύπτιον τουτονὶ βόσκων χρήμασι καὶ ὀξύνων ἐπ᾽ ἐμὲ
γλῶτταν ἀξίαν ἐκτετμῆσθαι.

35   Εὐφράτην μὲν δὴ καταλείπω σοί, σὺ γάρ, ἢν μὴ
κόλακας ἐπαινῇς, εὑρήσεις τὸν ἄνθρωπον κακίω ὧν
ἑρμηνεύω, τῆς δὲ λοιπῆς ἀπολογίας ἀκροῶ· τίς οὖν
αὕτη καὶ ὑπὲρ τίνων; ᾔδετό τις, ὦ βασιλεῦ, παιδὸς
Ἀρκάδος ἐν τῇ κατηγορίᾳ θρῆνος, τετμῆσθαι μὲν
αὐτὸν ὑπ᾽ ἐμοῦ νύκτωρ, εἰ δ᾽ ὄναρ φησίν, οὔπω οἶδα,
εἶναι δὲ πατέρων τε ἀγαθῶν ὁ παῖς οὗτος, καὶ τὸ εἶδος
οἷοι Ἀρκάδων οἱ ἐν αὐχμῷ καλοί. τοῦτόν φασιν ἱκε-
τεύοντά τε καὶ ὀλοφυρόμενον ἀπεσφάχθαι, κἀμὲ τὰς
χεῖρας ἐς τὸ τοῦ παιδὸς αἷμα βάψαντα θεοῖς ὑπὲρ
ἀληθείας εὔχεσθαι. μέχρι τούτων ἐμὲ κρίνουσιν, ὁ δὲ
ἐφεξῆς λόγος τῶν θεῶν ἅπτεται, φασὶ γὰρ τοὺς θεοὺς

364

not yet emperors to the time when I thought they would be in power, considering that I have never accepted gifts from you, whose power I thought secure? How could I have plotted to overthrow regimes when I have never used the established ones for my own honor? The career of Euphrates shows all that a champion of philosophy can earn by fawning on the powerful. From that source he has got, I will not say money, but streams of wealth, and nowadays he gives his lectures at the bank, making himself into a tradesman, a tradesman's assistant, a taxman, a moneychanger, everything that is sold or sells. He is always glued to the doors of the powerful, and stands at them longer than the doorkeepers do. Often he has actually been barred by the doorkeepers, like a greedy dog. While he has never spared a penny for a true philosopher, he uses his wealth to undermine others, and is supplying this Egyptian here with money and sharpening his tongue against me, though it deserves to be cut out.

"However, I leave Euphrates to you, for unless you approve of flatterers, you will find the man even worse than I describe him. Now hear the rest of my defense. What is it, and what is it about? They chanted a dirge, Majesty, for an Arcadian boy, saying that I butchered him at night, or perhaps they mean in a dream. They say this boy was of good parentage and in looks a typical Arcadian, unkempt yet handsome. They say that he was slaughtered despite his entreaties and sobs, and that with my hands dipped in the boy's blood I prayed the gods for a revelation. Thus far I am the accused, but the next allegation impugns the gods, 35

ἀκοῦσαι μὲν ὧδέ μου εὐξαμένου, δοῦναι δὲ ἱερὰ εὔ-
σημα καὶ μὴ ἀποκτεῖναι ἀσεβοῦντα.

36   "Τὴν μὲν οὖν ἀκρόασιν, ὡς οὐ καθαρά, τί ἄν, ὦ
βασιλεῦ, λέγοιμι; ἀλλ᾽ ὑπὲρ ὧν γέ μοι ἀπολογητέα,
τίς ὁ Ἀρκὰς οὗτος; εἰ γὰρ μὴ ἀνώνυμος τὰ πατέρων,
μηδ᾽ ἀνδραποδώδης τὸ εἶδος, ὥρα σοι ἐρωτᾶν, τί μὲν
ὄνομα τοῖς γειναμένοις αὐτόν, τίνος δὲ οἰκίας οὗτος,
τίς δ᾽ ἐθρέψατο αὐτὸν ἐν Ἀρκαδίᾳ πόλις, τίνων δὲ
βωμῶν ἀπαχθεὶς ἐνταῦθα ἐθύετο. οὐ λέγει ταῦτα καίτοι δεινὸς ὢν μὴ ἀληθεύειν. οὐκοῦν ὑπὲρ ἀνδραπόδου
κρίνει με. ᾧ γὰρ μήτ᾽ αὐτῷ ὄνομα μήθ᾽ ὧν ἔφυ, μὴ
πόλις, μὴ κλῆρός ἐστιν, οὐχί, ὦ θεοί, τοῦτον ἐν ἀνδρα-
πόδοις χρὴ τάττειν; ἀνώνυμα γὰρ πάντα.

37   "Τίς οὖν ὁ κάπηλος τοῦ ἀνδραπόδου; τίς ὁ πρι-
άμενος αὐτὸ ἐξ Ἀρκάδων; εἰ γὰρ τὸ γένος τούτων
ἐπιτήδειον τῇ σφαττούσῃ μαντικῇ, πολλῶν μὲν χρημάτων εἰκὸς ἐωνῆσθαι τὸν παῖδα, πεπλευκέναι δέ τινα
ἐς Πελοπόννησον, ἵν᾽ ἐνθένδε ἡμῖν ἀναχθείη ὁ Ἀρκάς,
ἀνδράποδα μὲν γὰρ Ποντικὰ ἢ Λύδια ἢ ἐκ Φρυγῶν
πρίαιτ᾽ ἂν κἀνταῦθά τις, ὧν γε καὶ ἀγέλαις ἐντυχεῖν
ἔστιν ἅμα φοιτώσαις δεῦρο, ταυτὶ γὰρ τὰ ἔθνη καὶ
ὁπόσα βαρβάρων, πάντα τὸν χρόνον ἑτέρων ἀκροώμενοι οὔπω τὸ δουλεύειν αἰσχρὸν ἡγοῦνται· Φρυξὶ
γοῦν ἐπιχώριον καὶ ἀποδίδοσθαι τοὺς αὑτῶν καὶ ἀν-
δραποδισθέντων μὴ ἐπιστρέφεσθαι,

38   "Ἕλληνες δὲ ἐλευθερίας ἐρασταὶ ἔτι καὶ οὐδὲ δοῦ-
λον ἀνὴρ Ἕλλην πέρα ὅρων ἀποδώσεται, ὅθεν οὐδὲ
ἀνδραποδισταῖς οὔτε ἀνδραπόδων καπήλοις ἐς αὐτοὺς

because they say that the gods heard this prayer of mine, and gave me favorable signs rather than killing me for my impiety.

"This very narrative is unholy, as I do not need to say, 36 Majesty, but as to the points on which I must defend myself, who is this Arcadian? Unless he was of unknown parentage, or of servile appearance, it is high time that you asked what name his parents had, what family he belonged to, what city of Arcadia brought him up, what altars he was torn from to be sacrificed here. All this my accuser does not say, despite being a practiced liar, so he must be indicting me because of a slave. If neither the boy nor his parents had a name, if he has neither city nor estate, must we not, for heaven's sake, class him as a slave, since the whole story is anonymous?

"Well then, what merchant sold me the slave? Who 37 purchased him from Arcadia? If that race is suitable for divination that uses butchery, doubtless the boy was purchased at a high price, and somebody sailed to the Peloponnese to bring the Arcadian to us here. Slaves from Pontus, Lydia, or Phrygia one can buy here, and you may meet droves of them all coming in this direction. Those races, like every race of barbarians, are always subject to others, and do not consider slavery a disgrace. The Phrygians in fact have the custom of selling even their own kin, and forgetting them once they have been enslaved.

"But the Greeks are still lovers of freedom, and a true 38 Greek will not even sell a slave across his borders. Hence no slaver or slave merchant may visit them, and still less

APOLLONIUS OF TYANA

παριτητέα, ἐς δὲ Ἀρκαδίαν καὶ μᾶλλον, πρὸς γὰρ
τῷ παρὰ πάντας ἐλευθεριάζειν Ἕλληνας δέονται καὶ
ὄχλου δούλων. ἔστι δὲ πολλὴ ἡ Ἀρκαδία καὶ ὑλώδης
οὐ τὰ μετέωρα μόνον, ἀλλὰ καὶ τὰ ἐν ποσὶ πάντα. δεῖ
δὴ αὐτοῖς πολλῶν μὲν γεωργῶν, πολλῶν δὲ αἰπόλων
συφορβῶν τε καὶ ποιμένων καὶ βουκόλων τῶν μὲν ἐπὶ
βουσί, τῶν δ' ἐφ' ἵπποις, δρυτόμων τε δεῖται πολλῶν ἡ
χώρα καὶ τοῦτο ἐκ παίδων γυμνάζονται. εἰ δὲ καὶ μὴ
τοιάδε ἦν τὰ τῶν Ἀρκάδων, ἀλλ' εἶχον, ὥσπερ ἕτεροι,
προσαποδίδοσθαι τοὺς αὑτῶν δούλους, τί τῇ θρυλου-
μένῃ σοφίᾳ ξυνεβάλλετο τὸ ἐξ Ἀρκαδίας εἶναι τὸν
σφαττόμενον; οὐδὲ γὰρ σοφώτατοι τῶν Ἑλλήνων Ἀρ-
κάδες, ἵν' ἑτέρου τι ἀνθρώπου πλέον περὶ τὰ λογικὰ
τῶν σπλάγχνων φαίνωσιν, ἀλλὰ ἀγροικότατοι ἀνθρώπων εἰσὶ καὶ συώδεις τά τε ἄλλα καὶ τὸ γαστρί-
ζεθαι τῶν δρυῶν.

39   Ῥητορικώτερον ἴσως ἀπολελόγημαι τοὐμοῦ τρόπου, τὰ τῶν Ἀρκάδων ἀφερμηνεύων ἤθη καὶ παριὼν ἐς
Πελοπόννησον τῷ λόγῳ. ἡ γὰρ ἐμοὶ προσήκουσα
ἀπολογία τίς; οὐκ ἔθυσα, οὐ θύω, οὐ θιγγάνω αἵματος, οὐδ' εἰ βώμιον αὐτὸ εἴη, Πυθαγόρας τε γὰρ ὧδε
ἐγίγνωσκεν οἵ τε ἀπ' αὐτοῦ παραπλησίως, καὶ κατ'
Αἴγυπτον δὲ οἱ Γυμνοὶ καὶ Ἰνδῶν οἱ σοφοί, παρ' ὧν
καὶ τοῖς ἀμφὶ Πυθαγόραν αἱ τῆς σοφίας ἀρχαὶ ἐφοί-
τησαν, κατὰ ταὐτὰ[17] θύοντες οὐ δοκοῦσιν ἀδικεῖν τοῖς
θεοῖς, ἀλλὰ γηράσκειν τε αὐτοῖς ξυγχωροῦσιν ἀρτίοις
τὰ σώματα καὶ ἀνόσοις, καὶ σοφωτέροις ἀεὶ δοκεῖν,
μὴ τυραννεύεσθαι, μηδενὸς δεῖσθαι. καὶ οὐκ ἀπεικός,

the Arcadians, because these are not only the most free-dom-loving of all Greeks, but also need a mass of slaves. Arcadia is large and heavily wooded, not only in its upland parts but in all the accessible ones too. It needs many farm-ers, many goatherds, swineherds, shepherds, and cattle-men for their cattle and their horses, and the land needs many woodcutters, who are trained from boyhood. Even supposing that Arcadia was not like this, and that they were able to sell their surplus slaves as other peoples are, how did it aid my celebrated wisdom that the sacrificial victim was an Arcadian? The Arcadians are not the wisest of the Greeks, so that they reveal something more than other people through the eloquence of their intestines. No, they are completely rustic folks, and swinish not least in that they stuff themselves with acorns.

"Perhaps I have defended myself with more rhetoric 39 than is my way, describing the customs of the Arcadians and wandering off to the Peloponnese in my discourse. Yet what kind of defense would be suitable? I did not sacrifice, nor do I. I do not touch blood, even if it is on the altar. That was the rule of Pythagoras and of his followers after him. The Naked Ones of Egypt and the Wise Men of India, to whom the school of Pythagoras traces the sources of its wisdom, sacrifice in the same way, and yet the gods do not think them sinful, but permit them to grow old, sound and healthy in body, to grow in wisdom, to be free of tyranny, and to have no needs. It is not implausible, I think, that the

---

¹⁷ ταὐτὰ Radermacher: ταῦτα

οἶμαι, ἀγαθῶν δεῖσθαι σφᾶς ὑπὲρ καθαρῶν θυμάτων. δοκῶ γάρ μοι καὶ τοὺς θεοὺς τὸν αὐτὸν ἐμοὶ νοῦν ὑπὲρ θυσιῶν ἔχοντας τὰ λιβανοφόρα τῆς γῆς ἐν καθαρῷ τῆς οἰκουμένης ἐκφυτεύειν, ἵν᾿ ἀπ᾿ αὐτῶν θύοιμεν μὴ σιδηροφοροῦντες ἐν ἱεροῖς, μηδ᾿ αἷμα ἐς βωμοὺς ῥαίνοντες. ἐγὼ δ᾿, ὡς ἔοικεν, ἐμαυτοῦ καὶ τῶν θεῶν ἐκλαθόμενος ἔθυον τρόπον, ὃν μήτ᾿ αὐτὸς εἴωθα μήτε τις ἀνθρώπων θύοι.

40 "Ἀπαλλαττέτω με τῆς αἰτίας καὶ ὁ καιρός, ὃν εἴρηκεν ὁ κατήγορος· τὴν γὰρ ἡμέραν ἐκείνην, ἐν ᾗ ταῦτα εἰργάσθαι μοί φησιν, εἰ μὲν ἐγενόμην ἐν ἀγρῷ, ἔθυσα, εἰ δὲ ἔθυσα, καὶ ἔφαγον. εἶτά με, ὦ βασιλεῦ, θαμινὰ ἐρωτᾷς, εἰ μὴ ἐπεχωρίαζον τῇ Ῥώμῃ τότε; καὶ σύ, βέλτιστε βασιλέων, ἐπεχωρίαζες, ἀλλ᾿ οὐκ ἂν εἴποις θῦσαι τοιαῦτα, καὶ ὁ συκοφάντης, ἀλλ᾿ οὐχ ὁμολογήσει τὰ τῶν ἀνδροφόνων πράττειν, εἰ κατὰ τὴν Ῥώμην διηγᾶτο, καὶ μυριάδες ἀνθρώπων, ἃς βέλτιον ξενηλατεῖν ἢ ὑπάγειν γραφαῖς, ἐν αἷς τεκμήριον ἀδικημάτων ἔσται τὸ ἐνταῦθα εἶναι. καίτοι τὸ ἐς τὴν Ῥώμην ἥκειν καὶ παραιτεῖται τάχα τῆς τοῦ νεώτερα πράττειν δοκεῖν αἰτίας, τὸ γὰρ ἐν πόλει ζῆν, ἐν ᾗ πάντες μὲν ὀφθαλμοί, πᾶσα δὲ ἀκρόασις ὄντων τε καὶ οὐκ ὄντων, οὐ ξυγχωρεῖ νεωτέρων ἅπτεσθαι τοῖς γε μὴ λίαν θανατῶσι, τοὺς δ᾿ εὐλαβεστέρους τε καὶ σώφρονας βραδέως ἄγει καὶ ἐφ᾿ ἃ ἔξεστι.

41 "Τί οὖν, ὦ συκοφάντα, κατὰ τὴν νύκτα ἐκείνην ἔπραττον; εἰ μὲν <ἐμὲ>[18] ὡς σεαυτὸν ἐρωτᾷς, ἐπειδὴ καὶ σὺ ἐρωτᾶν ἥκεις, ἀγῶνας ἡτοίμαζον καὶ κατηγο-

gods need virtuous men in order to receive pure offerings.
It is my belief that the gods share my opinion about sacrifices, and hence have planted the incense-bearing regions
in an unpolluted part of the world, so that we can sacrifice
with products from there, and not bring iron into holy
places or spray blood on altars. Yet I, it is alleged, forgot
myself and the gods, and sacrificed in a way not customary
for myself, and such as I pray that no human being may
follow.

"The time mentioned by my accuser may also acquit   40
me of the charge. On the day when he says I performed
these deeds, if I was in the country, I sacrificed, and if I sacrificed, I ate. And yet, Majesty, do you keep asking me
whether I was not in Rome at the time? You were too, most
excellent Majesty, but you would not say that you made
such a sacrifice. So was that informer, but he will not admit
to be acting like a murderer, just because he was living in
Rome. So too were tens of thousands of people, whom it
would be better to expel than to expose to indictments that
make presence here evidence of criminality. Yet my coming to Rome may perhaps acquit me of the charge that I appeared to plot revolution. To live in a city where there are
eyes and ears everywhere both for the true and the false
prevents you from attempting revolution, unless you are
very fond of death, while it makes more cautious and dis-
creet people hesitate even when their business is proper.

"What then was I doing that night, you slanderer? If   41
you ask me as someone like yourself, since you take the
liberty of asking, I was preparing trials and accusations

---

18 ⟨ἐμὲ⟩ Rsk.

ρίας ἐπ' ἄνδρας χρηστούς, καὶ ἀπολέσαι[19] τοὺς οὐκ
ἀδικοῦντας, καὶ πεῖσαι τὸν βασιλέα μὴ ἀληθῆ λέγων,
ἵν' ἐγὼ μὲν εὐδοκιμοίην, μιαίνοιτο δὲ οὗτος, εἰ δ' ὡς
φιλοσόφου πυνθάνῃ, τὸν Δημοκρίτου ἐπῄνουν γέλω-
τα, ὃν ἐς πάντα τὰ τῶν ἀνθρώπων γελᾷ, εἰ δ' ὡς ἐμοῦ,
Φιλίσκος ὁ Μηλιεὺς ἐτῶν ξυμφιλοσοφήσας ἐμοὶ τεττάρων ἐνόσει τότε, καὶ παρ' αὐτῷ ἀπεκάθευδον οὕτω
διακειμένῳ χαλεπῶς, ὡς καὶ ἀποθανεῖν ὑπὸ τῆς νόσου. καίτοι πολλὰς ἂν ηὐξάμην ἴυγγας ὑπὲρ τῆς
ἐκείνου ψυχῆς γενέσθαι μοι, καί, νὴ Δί', εἴ τινες
Ὀρφέως εἰσὶν ὑπὲρ τῶν ἀποθανόντων μελῳδίαι, μηδ'
ἐκείνας ἀγνοῆσαι, καὶ γὰρ ἄν μοι δοκῶ καὶ ὑπὸ τὴν
γῆν πορευθῆναι δι' αὐτόν, εἰ ἐφικτὰ ἦν ταῦτα· οὕτω με
ἀνήρτητο πᾶσιν οἷς φιλοσόφως τε καὶ κατὰ τὸν ἐμὸν
νοῦν ἔπραττε.

42   "Ταῦτ' ἔστι μέν σοι, βασιλεῦ, καὶ Τελεσίνου ἀκοῦσαι τοῦ ὑπάτου, παρῆν γὰρ κἀκεῖνος τῷ Μηλιεῖ,
θεραπεύων αὐτὸν νύκτωρ, ὁπόσα ἐγώ. εἰ δὲ Τελεσίνῳ
ἀπιστεῖς, ἐπειδὴ τῶν φιλοσοφούντων ἐστί, καλῶ τοὺς
ἰατροὺς μάρτυρας, εἰσὶ δ' οὗτοι Σέλευκός τε ὁ ἐκ
Κυζίκου καὶ Στρατοκλῆς ὁ Σιδώνιος. τούτους ἐρώτα, εἰ
ἀληθῆ λέγω. καὶ μαθηταὶ δ' αὐτοῖς ὑπὲρ τοὺς τριάκοντα εἵποντο, τῶν αὐτῶν δήπου μάρτυρες, τὸ γὰρ
προκαλεῖσθαι δεῦρο τοὺς τῷ Φιλίσκῳ προσήκοντας
ἀναβολὰς ἴσως ἡγήσῃ τῆς δίκης, ἐπειδὴ αὐτίκα τῆς
Ῥώμης ἀπῆραν ἐς τὰ Μηλιέων ἤθη κατὰ ὁσίαν τοῦ
νεκροῦ. ἴτε, ὦ μάρτυρες, καὶ γὰρ δὴ καὶ παρήγγελται
ὑμῖν ὑπὲρ τούτου. ΜΑΡΤΥΡΕΣ. παρ' ὅσον μὲν τοίνυν

against men of virtue, to ruin the innocent and convince the emperor with falsehoods for the purpose of glorifying myself and besmirching him. If however you ask me as a philosopher, I was praising the laughter that Democritus laughs at all human affairs. But if you ask me as myself, Philiscus of Melos, who had studied with me for four years, was ill at the time, and I was sleeping over at his house; he was in such a bad way that he later died of the disease. And yet I could have prayed to have many spells to save his life, and, by Zeus, also to learn any melodies that Orpheus might have had for restoring the dead. Indeed I believe I would have traveled to the underworld for Philiscus's sake if such deeds were possible, so greatly had he won me over by all he did as a philosopher after my own heart.

"All this, Majesty, you may hear from Telesinus the consular,[26] since he too attended the man from Melos, looking after him at night just as I did. If you do not believe Telesinus because he is a student of philosophy, I call the doctors as witnesses, namely Seleucus of Cyzicus and Stratocles of Sidon,[27] and you may ask them if I am telling the truth. They came followed by more than thirty pupils, who no doubt will testify to the same effect. To summon the relatives of Philiscus you may perhaps think would delay the case, since they left Rome immediately for their native Melos to give the body the last rites. Step up, witnesses, since you must have been summoned for this purpose. (The witnesses testify.) How far this fabricated   42

---

[26] See IV 40.1.   [27] Otherwise unknown.

---

[19] ἀπολέσαι Kay.: ἀπολεῖσθαι

τῆς ἀληθείας ἡ γραφὴ ξυνετέθη, δηλοῖ σαφῶς ἡ
μαρτυρία τῶν ἀνδρῶν, οὐ γὰρ ἐν προαστείοις, ἀλλ' ἐν
ἄστει, οὐκ ἔξω τείχους, ἀλλ' ἐπ' οἰκίας, οὐδὲ παρὰ
Νερούᾳ, παρὰ Φιλίσκῳ δέ, οὐδὲ ἀποσφάττων, ἀλλ'
ὑπὲρ ψυχῆς εὐχόμενος, οὐδ' ὑπὲρ βασιλείας, ἀλλ'
ὑπὲρ φιλοσοφίας, οὐδ' ἀντὶ σοῦ χειροτονῶν νεώτερον,
ἀλλ' ἄνδρα σώζων ἐμαυτῷ ὅμοιον.

43   "Τί οὖν ὁ Ἀρκὰς ἐνταῦθα; τί δ' οἱ τῶν σφαγίων
μῦθοι; τί δὲ τὸ τὰ τοιαῦτα πείθειν; ἔσται γάρ ποτε καὶ
ὃ μὴ γέγονεν, ἂν ὡς γεγονὸς κριθῇ· τὸ δ' ἀπίθανον
τῆς θυσίας, ὦ βασιλεῦ, ποῖ τάξεις; ἐγένοντο μὲν γὰρ
καὶ πρότερον σφαγίων μάντεις ἀγαθοὶ τὴν τέχνην καὶ
οἷοι ὀνομάσαι, Μεγιστίας ἐξ Ἀκαρνανίας, Ἀρίσταν-
δρος ἐκ Λυκίας, Ἀμπρακία δὲ Σιλανὸν ἤνεγκε, καὶ
ἐθύοντο ὁ μὲν Ἀκαρνὰν Λεωνίδᾳ βασιλεῖ Σπάρτης, ὁ
δὲ Λύκιος Ἀλεξάνδρῳ τῷ Μακεδόνι, Σιλανὸς δὲ Κύρῳ
βασιλείας ἐρῶντι, καὶ εἴ τι ἐν ἀνθρώπου σπλάγχνοις
ἢ σαφέστερον ἢ σοφώτερον ἢ ἐτυμώτερον ἀπέκειτο,
οὐκ ἄπορος ἦν ἡ θυσία, βασιλέων γε προϊσταμένων[20]
αὐτῆς, οἷς πολλοὶ μὲν ἦσαν οἰνοχόοι, πολλὰ δ' αἰ-
χμάλωτα, παρανομίαι δ' ἀκίνδυνοι καὶ φόβος οὐδεὶς
κατηγορίας, εἴ τι ἔσφαττον. ἀλλ', οἶμαι, παρίστατο
τοῖς ἀνδράσιν, ὃ κἀμοὶ νῦν κινδυνεύοντι ὑπὲρ τοιούτων, ὅτι τὰ μὲν ἄλογα τῶν ζῴων εἰκός, ἐπειδὴ ἐν
ἀγνοίᾳ τοῦ θανάτου σφάττεται, μὴ θολοῦσθαί τι τῶν
σπλάγχνων ὑπὸ ἀξυνεσίας ὧν πείσονται· ἄνθρωπον
δὲ ἀεί τι ἐν τῇ ψυχῇ ἔχοντα θανάτου καὶ μήπω

indictment is from the truth these gentlemen's evidence clearly shows. I was not in a suburb but in the city, not outside the wall but in a house, not with Nerva but Philiscus, not committing butchery but praying for a man's life, not concerning myself with the throne but with philosophy, not replacing you with someone else, but preserving a man of my own kind.

"Where is the Arcadian in all this? Or in these tall stories about slaughter? Or in the attempt to prove such things? What has never happened will one day be a fact, if it is judged as fact. How will you measure the implausibility of the sacrifice, Majesty? For there have been seers in former times too who were skilled in the art of interpreting sacrifices, and left a name: Megistias of Acarnania, Aristander from Lycia, Silanus who came from Ambracia. The Acarnanian sacrificed for Leonidas king of Sparta, the Lycian for Alexander of Macedon, and Silanus for Cyrus when he coveted the throne. If there had been something especially indicative, revealing, or reliable hidden in human entrails, a sacrifice would not have been difficult for them, since it was promoted by kings who had many stewards and many captives, freedom to commit crime with impunity, and no fear of accusation for any act of butchery. I suppose, however, that those diviners had the same thought as I now have when facing trial on these charges, that is, that unreasoning animals, when they are slaughtered without knowing what death is, probably suffer no disturbance in their entrails, lacking comprehension of their fate. A human, however, always carries the fear of death in his mind even when it is not imminent, so that

43

---

20 προϊσταμένων Kay.: παρισταμένων

ἐφεστηκότος δεῖμα πῶς εἰκός, παρόντος ἤδη καὶ ἐν
ὀφθαλμοῖς ὄντος, δεῖξαί τι ἐπὶ τῶν σπλάγχνων μαντικὸν ἢ ὅλως εὔθυτον;

44   "Ὅτι δὲ ὀρθῶς τε καὶ κατὰ φύσιν στοχάζομαι
τούτων, σκόπει, βασιλεῦ, ὧδε. τὸ ἧπαρ, ἐν ᾧ φασι τὸν
τῆς αὐτῶν μαντικῆς εἶναι τρίποδα οἱ δεινοὶ ταῦτα,
ξύγκειται μὲν οὐ καθαροῦ αἵματος, πᾶν γάρ, ὅ τι
ἀκραιφνές, καρδία ἴσχει δι᾽ αἱματηρῶν φλεβῶν ἀπο-
χετεύουσα ἐς πᾶν τὸ σῶμα, χολὴν δ᾽ ἐπὶ ἥπατι κει-
μένην ὀργὴ μὲν ἀνίστησι, φόβοι δὲ ὑπάγουσιν ἐς τὰ
κοῖλα τοῦ ἥπατος. ὑπὸ μὲν δὴ τῶν παροξυνόντων
ζέουσα καὶ μηδὲ τῷ ἑαυτῆς ἀγγείῳ φορητὸς οὖσα
ὑπτίῳ ἐπιχεῖται τῷ ἥπατι, καθ᾽ ὃ ἐπέχει χολὴ πᾶσα τὰ
λεῖά τε καὶ μαντικὰ τοῦ σπλάγχνου, ὑπὸ δὲ τῶν
δειματούντων ξυνιζάνουσα ξυνεπισπᾶται καὶ τὸ ἐν
τοῖς λείοις φῶς, ὑπονοστεῖ γὰρ τότε καὶ τὸ καθαρὸν
τοῦ αἵματος, ὑφ᾽ οὗ σπληνοῦται τὸ ἧπαρ, ὑποτρέχον-
τος φύσει τὸν περὶ αὐτὸ ὑμένα καὶ τῷ πηλώδει ἐπιπο-
λάζοντος.

45   "Τί οὖν, ὦ βασιλεῦ, τῆς μιαιφονίας ἔργον, εἰ ἄσημα τὰ ἱερὰ ἔσται; ἄσημα δ᾽ αὐτὰ ἡ ἀνθρωπεία φύσις
ἐργάζεται ξυνιεῖσα τοῦ θανάτου καὶ αὐτοὶ οἱ ἀποθνήσκοντες, οἱ μὲν γὰρ εὔψυχοι ξὺν ὀργῇ τελευτῶσιν,
οἱ δ᾽ ἀθυμότεροι ξὺν δέει. ἔνθεν ἡ τέχνη παρὰ τοῖς οὐκ
ἀνεπιστήμοσι βαρβάροις χιμαίρας μὲν καὶ ἄρνας
ἐπαινεῖ σφάττειν, ἐπειδὴ εὐήθη τὰ ζῷα καὶ οὐ πόρρω
ἀναισθήτων, ἀλεκτρυόνας δὲ καὶ σῦς καὶ ταύρους,
ἐπειδὴ θυμοειδῆ ταῦτα, οὐκ ἀξιοῖ τῶν ἑαυτῆς ἀπορρή-

when it is at last present before his eyes, how can he reveal something by means of his entrails that is prophetic or in any way acceptable?

"That my theory about this matter is correct and in ac-   44
cordance with nature you can gather from the following, Majesty. The liver contains the seat of their divination, so say the experts in such things. This is not composed of pure blood, since the heart contains all the unmixed blood, and channels it through the whole body by means of the arteries. The bile which lies above the liver is stimulated by anger, but contracted by fear into the recesses of the liver. If then it seethes under the influence of irritation, and can no longer be contained by its own vessel, it spills onto the liver below, and then all the bile covers the soft and prophetic part of the stomach. If however, it contracts under the influence of fear, it absorbs all the luminosity of the soft parts, since at the same time there is a withdrawal of the pure blood, and this distends the liver by naturally filling the membrane around it, and floating above the part that is obscured.

"What then, Majesty, does butchery achieve if the rites   45
are meaningless? They are made meaningless by human nature, which is aware of death, and by the dying themselves, for the courageous feel anger when they die, and the timid fear. Hence when this art is practiced by the more intelligent of the barbarians, it favors the slaying of she goats and lambs, since these animals are stupid and practically insensible, but cocks, pigs, and bulls it does not

APOLLONIUS OF TYANA

των. ξυνίημι, ὦ βασιλεῦ, παροξύνων τὸν κατήγορον,
ἐπειδὴ σοφώτερόν σε ἀκροατὴν εἴργασμαι, καί μοι
δοκεῖς καὶ προσέχειν τῷ λόγῳ· εἰ δὲ μὴ σαφῶς τι
αὐτοῦ φράζοιμι, ξυγχωρῶ σοι ἐρωτᾶν με.

46   "Εἴρηταί μοι τὰ πρὸς τὴν τοῦ Αἰγυπτίου γραφήν.
ἐπεὶ δ', οἶμαι, χρὴ μηδὲ τὰς Εὐφράτου διαβολὰς
ὑπερορᾶσθαι, σύ, ὦ βασιλεῦ, δικάζοις, ὁπότερος
ἡμῶν φιλοσοφεῖ μᾶλλον· οὐκοῦν ὁ μὲν ἀγωνίζεται μὴ
τἀληθῆ περὶ ἐμοῦ λέγειν, ἐγὼ δ' οὐκ ἀξιῶ, καὶ ὁ μέν
σε ἡγεῖται δεσπότην, ἐγὼ δ' ἄρχοντα, καὶ ὁ μὲν ξίφος
ἐπ' ἐμέ σοι δίδωσιν, ἐγὼ δὲ λόγον.²¹

47   "'Αλλ' ὑπὲρ ὧν γε διαβέβληκεν, οἱ λόγοι εἰσίν, οὓς
ἐν 'Ιωνίᾳ εἶπον, φησὶ δ' αὐτοὺς οὐκ ἐς τὸ σοὶ ξυμφέρον ὑπ' ἐμοῦ εἰρῆσθαι. καίτοι τὰ μὲν λεχθέντα ἦν
ὑπὲρ Μοιρῶν καὶ ἀνάγκης, παράδειγμα δ' ἐγίγνετό
μοι τοῦ λόγου τὰ τῶν βασιλέων πράγματα, ἐπειδὴ
μέγιστα τῶν ἀνθρωπείων δοκεῖ τὰ ὑμέτερα, Μοιρῶν τε
ἰσχὺν ἐφιλοσόφουν καὶ τὸ οὕτως ἄτρεπτα εἶναι, ἃ
κλώθουσιν, ὡς, εἰ καὶ βασιλείαν τῳ ψηφίσαιντο ἑτέρῳ
δὴ ὑπάρχουσαν, ὁ δ' ἀποκτείνειε τοῦτον, ὡς μὴ ἀφαι-
ρεθείη ποτὲ ὑπ' αὐτοῦ τὸ ἄρχειν, κἂν ἀναβιοίη ὁ
ἀποθανὼν ὑπὲρ τῶν δοξάντων ταῖς Μοίραις. τὰς γὰρ
ὑπερβολὰς τῶν λόγων ἐσαγόμεθα διὰ τοὺς τοῖς πιθα-
νοῖς ἀπειθοῦντας, ὥσπερ ἂν εἰ καὶ τοιόνδε ἔλεγον·
'ὅτῳ πέπρωται γενέσθαι τεκτονικῷ, οὗτος, κἂν ἀπο-
κοπῇ τὼ χεῖρε, τεκτονικὸς ἔσται, καὶ ὅτῳ νίκην ἐν
'Ολυμπίᾳ δρόμου ἄρασθαι, οὗτος, οὐδ' εἰ πηρωθείη τὸ
σκέλος, ἁμαρτήσεται τῆς νίκης, καὶ ὅτῳ ἔνευσαν

378

consider right for its mysteries. I am aware, Majesty, that I
annoy my accuser by making you a more knowledgeable
listener, and because you seem to me to be interested in
my discourse, and if any of it is not clear, I permit you to
question me.

"I have answered the Egyptian's indictment. Since, 46
however, I do not think I should disregard the slanders of
Euphrates either, Majesty, you must judge which of us is
the truer philosopher. His ambition is always to tell lies
about me, whereas I refuse to do the same about him. In
his eyes you are a despot, but in mine a ruler. He gives you
a sword to use with me, but I give you rational argument.

"The main topic of his slanders is the speeches that I 47
gave in Ionia, for he says I gave them in opposition to your
interests. Yet my topics were the Fates and Necessity, and I
illustrated my discourse from the fortunes of kings, because yours is thought the highest of all human estates.
Lecturing on the power of the Fates, I said this: so inexora-
ble are the threads they spin that if they were to assign to
someone a throne belonging to another, and the incum-
bent were to kill his rival in order never to be deposed by
him, even so the dead man would come to life again so the
decisions of the Fates might be fulfilled. For we employ
exaggerated language because of those who disbelieve the
believable, as if I were to say the following: 'If a man is
fated to be a carpenter, even though his hands are cut off
he will still be a carpenter. If he is destined to win in the
footrace at Olympia and his leg is injured, he will still not

---

21 λόγον Kay.: μὲν οὖν

Μοῖραι τὸ ἐν τοξείᾳ κράτος, οὗτος οὐδ᾿ εἰ ἀποβάλοι
τὰς ὄψεις, ἐκπεσεῖται τοῦ σκοποῦ.᾿ τὰ δὲ τῶν βασιλέων ἔλεγον ἐς τοὺς Ἀκρισίους δήπου ὁρῶν καὶ τοὺς
Λαίους, Ἀστυάγη τε τὸν Μῆδον, καὶ πολλοὺς ἑτέρους
εὖ τίθεσθαι τὰ τοιαῦτα²² ἐν ἀρχῇ δόξαντας, ὧν οἱ μὲν
παῖδας, οἱ δὲ ἐκγόνους ἀποκτείνειν οἰηθέντες ἀφῃρέ-
θησαν ὑπ᾿ αὐτῶν τὸ βασιλεύειν, ἀναφύντων ἐξ ἀφα-
νοῦς ξὺν τῷ πεπρωμένῳ.

48   "Καὶ εἰ μὲν ἠγάπων κολακευτικήν, εἶπον ἂν καὶ τὰ
σὰ ἐντεθυμῆσθαι, ὅτε ἀπείληψο μὲν ὑπὸ Βιτελίου
ἐνταῦθα, κατεπίμπρατο δὲ ὁ νεὼς τοῦ Διὸς περὶ τὰς
ὀφρῦς τοῦ ἄστεος, ὁ δ᾿ εὖ κείσεσθαι τὸ ἑαυτοῦ ἔφασκεν, εἰ μὴ διαφύγοις αὐτόν (καίτοι μειράκιον ἱκανῶς
ἦσθα καὶ οὔπω οὗτος), ἀλλ᾿ ὅμως, ἐπειδὴ Μοίραις
ἐδόκει ἕτερα, ὁ μὲν ἀπώλετο αὐταῖς βουλαῖς, σὺ δὲ
τἀκείνου νῦν ἔχεις. ἐπεὶ δ᾿ ἁρμονίᾳ κολακευτικῇ ἄχθο-
μαι, δοκεῖ γάρ μοι τῶν ἐκρύθμων τε καὶ οὐκ εὐφθόγ-
γων εἶναι, τεμνέσθω μοι ἥδε ἡ νευρὰ καὶ μηδὲν ἡγοῦ
τῶν σῶν ἐντεθυμῆσθαί με, ἀλλὰ διειλέχθαι μόνα τὰ
ὑπὲρ Μοιρῶν καὶ ἀνάγκης, ταυτὶ γάρ φησιν εἰρῆσθαί
μοι ἐπὶ σέ. καίτοι τὸν λόγον τοῦτον ἀνέχονται μὲν καὶ
οἱ πολλοὶ τῶν θεῶν, οὐκ ἄχθεται δὲ οὐδὲ ὁ Ζεὺς
ἀκούων καὶ ταῦτα τῶν ποιητῶν ἐν τοῖς Λυκίοις λόγοις
'ὤμοι ἐγών, ὅτε μοι Σαρπηδόνα᾿ καὶ τοιαῦτ᾿ ἐς αὐτὸν

²² τοιαῦτα Euseb.: αὐτῶν τοιαῦτα

fail to win. If the Fates have allotted him skill at archery, even supposing he loses his eyesight he will still not miss the target.' But I referred to the fortunes of kings thinking of such as Acrisius, of course, or Laius, Astyages the Mede, and many others. These at first thought they had settled such problems, believing they had killed their sons or grandsons, and yet they lost their thrones to them when Fate produced them from obscurity.[28]

"If I were given to flattery, I would claim to have been 48 thinking of your history, and how you were cut off by Vitellius here, and the temple of Zeus caught fire at the summit of the city. He said that his own situation would be secure if you did not escape him, though you were only a youth, and not yet as great as you now are. Nonetheless the Fates decreed otherwise, he perished and his plans with him, and you now have his position. But I dislike the music of flattery, because I think it of the ill timed and ill tuned kind, so I will snap this string, and you may suppose that I did not have your affairs in mind at all, but spoke only about the Fates and Necessity. He says that I spoke as I did in opposition to you, and yet even the majority of the gods tolerate this doctrine. Zeus himself takes no offense even when he hears the poets in their tales of Lycia reciting 'Alas for me, when Sarpedon...' and so on, though in the epi-

---

[28] Acrisius, king of Argos, was forewarned that his daughter's son would kill him, and Laius, king of Thebes, that his own son would kill him; similarly Astyages, king of Media, was forewarned that his daughter's son would rule his empire. All three tried, and failed, to do away with their prospective enemies while still infants, respectively Perseus, Oedipus, and Cyrus the Great.

ᾀδόντων, ἐν οἷς τοῦ υἱέος ἐξίστασθαί φησι ταῖς
Μοίραις, λεγόντων τε αὖ ἐν ψυχοστασίᾳ, ὅτι Μίνω
τὸν ἀδελφὸν τοῦ Σαρπηδόνος ἀποθανόντα χρυσῷ μὲν
σκήπτρῳ ἐτίμησε, καὶ δικάζειν ἔταξεν ἐν τῇ τοῦ Αἰ-
δωνέως ἀγορᾷ, Μοιρῶν δ' οὐ παρῃτήσατο.

49   "Σὺ δ', ὦ βασιλεῦ, τοῦ χάριν ἄχθῃ τῷ λόγῳ, θεῶν
καρτερούντων αὐτόν, οἷς πέπηγεν ἀεὶ τὰ πράγματα,
καὶ μὴ ἀποκτεινόντων τοὺς ποιητὰς ἐπ' αὐτῷ; προσήκει γὰρ ταῖς Μοίραις ἕπεσθαι καὶ πρὸς τὰς μετα-
βολὰς τῶν πραγμάτων μὴ χαλεποὺς εἶναι, Σοφοκλεῖ
τε μὴ ἀπιστεῖν ᾽μόνοις οὐ γίγνεται θεοῖσι γῆρας, οὐδὲ
μὴν θανεῖν ποτε, τὰ δ' ἄλλα συγχεῖ πάνθ' ὁ παγκρα-
τὴς χρόνος,᾽ ἄριστα δὴ ἀνθρώπων λέγοντι.

50   "Ἐγκύκλιοι γὰρ αἱ κατ' ἀνθρώπους εὐπραγίαι καὶ
ἐφήμερον, ὦ βασιλεῦ, τὸ τοῦ ὄλβου μῆκος. τἀμὰ
οὗτος καὶ τὰ τούτου ἕτερος καὶ ὁ δεῖνα τὰ τοῦ δεῖνος
ἔχων οὐκ ἔχει. ταῦτ' ἐννοῶν, ὦ βασιλεῦ, παῦε μὲν
φυγάς, παῦε δ' αἷμα, καὶ φιλοσοφίᾳ μὲν ὅ τι βούλει
χρῶ, ἀπαθὴς γὰρ ἥ γε ἀληθής, δάκρυα δὲ ἀνθρώπων
ἀφαίρει. ὡς νῦν γε ἠχὼ μυρία μὲν ἐκ θαλάττης, πολλῷ
δὲ πλείων ἐξ ἠπείρων φοιτᾷ θρηνούντων, ὅ τι ἑκάστῳ
θρήνου ἄξιον. τὰ δὲ ἐντεῦθεν φυόμενα, πλείω ὄντα ἢ
ἀριθμεῖσθαι, ταῖς τῶν συκοφαντῶν γλώτταις ἀνῆπται
διαβαλλόντων σοί τε πάντας[23] καὶ σέ, ὦ βασιλεῦ,
πᾶσιν."

8. Ὧδε μὲν δὴ τῷ ἀνδρὶ τὰ ἐκ παρασκευῆς εἶχεν,

[23] πάντας Bentl.: πάντα

sode he says he yields his son to the Fates, [29] or when he hears them tell in the *Weighing of Souls* how he granted Minos, the brother of Sarpedon, a golden scepter after his death, appointed him judge in the court of Aidoneus, and did not beg him back from the Fates.[30]

"But you, Majesty, why should you take offense at the 49 doctrine when the gods, whose estate is established for ever, bear with it, and do not make it a reason to kill the poets? It is right to obey the Fates and not resent changes of fortune, or disbelieve Sophocles when he makes that superlative statement,

> For gods alone
> There is no age, nor ever do they die;
> All other things all-conquering time confounds.[31]

"Human prosperity is cyclical, and pomp, Majesty, has 50 only a brief span. This man has what was mine, another what was his, so-and-so has so-and-so's, and yet does not have it. Think of that, my Majesty, put an end to exile and an end to bloodshed, treat philosophy as you please, because true philosophy cannot suffer, but wipe away the tears of humankind. At present an endless sound arises from the sea, but a much louder one arises from the land, as each person grieves over his own reason for grief. As for the sorrows that breed here, too numerous to be counted, they depend on the tongues of informers who slander all to you and you, Majesty, to all."

8. This then was the Master's prepared speech, and at

29 *Iliad* 16.433–38.
30 *Odyssey* 11.568–571.
31 *Oedipus at Colonus* 607–09.

ἐπὶ τελευτῇ δ' εὗρον τοῦ λόγου τὰ τελευταῖα τοῦ
προτέρου τὸ "οὐ γάρ με κτενέεις, ἐπεὶ οὔτοι μόρσιμός
εἰμι," καὶ τὰ πρὸ τούτου ἔτι, ἀφ' ὧν τοῦτο. ἐπεὶ δὲ
ἀπῆλθε τοῦ δικαστηρίου δαιμόνιόν τε καὶ οὐ ῥᾴδιον
εἰπεῖν τρόπον, οὐκ ἔπαθεν ὁ τύραννος, ὅπερ οἱ πολλοὶ
ᾤοντο· οἱ μὲν γὰρ ᾤοντο αὐτὸν σχέτλια ὑπὲρ τούτου
βοήσεσθαι καὶ δίωξιν ποιήσεσθαι τοῦ ἀνδρὸς κηρύ-
ξειν τε ἐς τὴν αὐτοῦ πᾶσαν, μηδαμοῦ παριτητέα εἶναί
οἱ, ὁ δ' οὐδὲν τούτων, [ἀλλ']²⁴ ὥσπερ ἀγωνιζόμενος
πρὸς τὴν τῶν πολλῶν δόξαν ἢ ξυνιεὶς λοιπόν, ὅτι
μηδὲν ἐπὶ τὸν ἄνδρα οἱ αὔταρκες. εἰ δ' ὑπερεώρα,
ξυμβαλώμεθα τοῖς ἐφεξῆς, φανείη γὰρ ἂν ξυντα-
ραχθεὶς μᾶλλον ἢ καταφρονήσας.

9. Ἠκροᾶτο μὲν γὰρ ἑτέρας ἐπ' ἐκείνῃ δίκης, πόλις
δ' ἦν ἀγωνιζομένη πρὸς ἄνδρα ὑπὲρ διαθηκῶν, οἶμαι,
διέφευγον δ' αὐτὸν οὐ μόνον τὰ τῶν δικαζομένων
ὀνόματα, ἀλλὰ καὶ ὁ νοῦς τῆς δίκης, ἀνόητοι μὲν γὰρ
αἱ ἐρωτήσεις ἦσαν, αἱ δ' ἀποκρίσεις οὐδ' ὑπὲρ ὧν ἡ
κρίσις· ἃ σφόδρα ἤλεγχε τὸν τύραννον, ὡς ἐξεπέ-
πληκτό τε καὶ ἠπόρει δι' αὐτὸ μάλιστα τὸ πεπεῖσθαι
πρὸς τῶν κολακευόντων, ὅτι μηδὲν ἂν διαφύγοι αὐτόν.

10. Οὕτω τὸν τύραννον διαθεὶς καὶ παίγνιον τῆς
ἑαυτοῦ φιλοσοφίας ἀποφήνας τὸν Ἕλλησί τε καὶ
βαρβάροις φοβερὸν πᾶσι, πρὸ μεσημβρίας μὲν ἀπῆλθε τοῦ δικαστηρίου, περὶ δείλην δ' ἐν Δικαιαρχίᾳ
ἐφάνη Δημητρίῳ τε καὶ Δάμιδι, καὶ τοῦτ' ἄρ' ἦν τὸ
παρακελεύσασθαι αὐτὸν τῷ Δάμιδι μὴ περιμείναντι
τὴν ἀπολογίαν πεζεῦσαι²⁵ ἐς Δικαιαρχίαν· τὰ μὲν γὰρ

the end of it I found the end of the previous one, "You will
not kill me, since I am not mortal," and also what precedes
this quotation. When he had left the court in some super-
natural way not easy to describe, the tyrant did not react as
most people expected, since they thought this would make
him roar with indignation, start a hunt for the Master, and
have it announced throughout the realm that Apollonius
was to be forbidden admittance everywhere. He did none
of this, as if counteracting the general belief, or finally realizing that he was powerless against the Master. Whether he
thought him insignificant we may infer from the sequel, in
which he will show consternation rather than contempt.

9. For he began to hear another case after that one, in-
volving a city contesting a will against an individual, I
think, and he forgot not only the names of the parties but
even the point of the dispute. His questions were silly and
his answers not even relevant to the hearing, all of which
clearly proved that the tyrant was befuddled and confused
precisely because his flatterers had convinced him that
nothing could escape him.

10. After producing this effect on the tyrant, and proving that the man whom all Greeks and barbarians feared
was a mere plaything of his own wisdom, Apollonius left
the court before noon, and about evening he appeared to
Demetrius and Damis in Dicaearchia. This was why he
had urged Damis not to wait for his defense, but to walk to

---

24 [ἀλλ'] secl. Kay.
25 πεζεῦσαι Valck.: πλεῦσαι

APOLLONIUS OF TYANA

βεβουλευμένα οὐ προὔλεγε, τὸν δ᾽ ἑαυτῷ ἐπιτηδειότα-
τον ἐκέλευε πράττειν, ἃ τοῖς βεβουλευμένοις εἵπετο.

11. Ἐτύγχανε μὲν δὴ ὁ Δάμις τῆς προτεραίας
ἀφιγμένος καὶ τῷ Δημητρίῳ ξυγγεγονὼς ὑπὲρ τῶν
πρὸ τῆς δίκης, ὁ δ᾽ εὐλαβέστερον ἢ τὸν ὑπὲρ Ἀπολλωνίου ἀκροώμενον εἰκὸς ἦν διατεθεὶς²⁶ ὑφ᾽ ὧν
ἤκουσε, καὶ πάλιν τῆς ὑστεραίας ὑπὲρ τῶν αὐτῶν
ἠρώτα, ξυναλύων αὐτῷ παρὰ τὴν θάλατταν, ἐν ᾗ τὰ
περὶ τὴν Καλυψὼ μυθεύματα. ἀπεγίγνωσκον μὲν γὰρ
ὡς οὐχ ἥξοντος, ἐπειδὴ τὰ τῆς τυραννίδος χαλεπὰ ἦν
πᾶσι, τὰ δ᾽ ὑπ᾽ αὐτοῦ προσταττόμενα ἐτίμων διὰ τὴν
φύσιν τοῦ ἀνδρός. ἀπειπόντες οὖν ἐκάθηντο ἐς τὸ
νύμφαιον, ἐν ᾧ ὁ πίθος, λευκοῦ δ᾽ οὗτός ἐστι λίθου
ξυνέχων πηγὴν ὕδατος οὔθ᾽ ὑπερβάλλουσαν τοῦ στο-
μίου οὔτ᾽, εἴ τις ἀπαντλοίη, ὑποδιδοῦσαν. διαλεχθέντες δ᾽ ὑπὲρ τῆς φύσεως τοῦ ὕδατος οὐ μάλα ἐσπουδα-
κότως διὰ τὴν ἐπὶ τῷ ἀνδρὶ ἀθυμίαν ἐπανῆγον τὸν
λόγον ἐς τὰ πρὸ τῆς δίκης.

12. Ἀνολοφυραμένου δὲ τοῦ Δάμιδος καί τι καὶ
τοιοῦτον εἰπόντος "ἆρ᾽ ὀψόμεθά ποτε, ὦ θεοί, τὸν
καλόν τε καὶ ἀγαθὸν ἑταῖρον;" ἀκούσας ὁ Ἀπολλώνιος, καὶ γὰρ δὴ καὶ ἐφεστὼς ἤδη τῷ νυμφαίῳ
ἐτύγχανεν, "ὄψεσθε," εἶπε "μᾶλλον δὲ ἑωράκατε."
"ζῶντα;" ἔφη ὁ Δημήτριος "εἰ δὲ τεθνεῶτα, οὔπω
πεπαύμεθα ἐπὶ σοὶ κλάοντες." προτείνας οὖν ὁ Ἀπολλώνιος τὴν χεῖρα "λαβοῦ μου," ἔφη "κἂν μὲν διαφύγω
σε, εἴδωλόν εἰμί σοι ἐκ Φερσεφάττης ἧκον, οἷα φαί-

Dicaearchia, not announcing his plans in advance, but telling his closest friend to do something that accorded with those plans.

11. It happened that Damis had arrived the day before, and had discussed the preliminaries of the trial with Demetrius. Hearing this made Demetrius more concerned than was natural considering that Apollonius was in question, and the next day he was interrogating Damis again on the same subject as they loitered beside the sea in which the tales about Calypso are set.[32] They had despaired of his ever coming back, since the tyrant's ways were harsh to everyone, but they honored his instructions because of the Master's nature. They were sitting dejectedly in the sanctuary of the Nymphs that contains the jar (this is of white stone and holds a spring of water, which neither overflows over the edge nor goes down when you draw from it). They were discussing the explanation of the water, but only desultorily because of their despondency over the Master, and were bringing the subject back to the preliminaries of the trial.

12. With a loud groan, Damis said something like, "Gods above, will we ever see our good, noble comrade?" This Apollonius heard, since he was now standing at the entrance to the grotto. "You will," he said, "or rather you already have." "Alive?" asked Demetrius. "But if dead, we have never stopped weeping for you." Stretching out his hand, Apollonius said, "Take hold of me, and if I elude you, I am a ghost come back from Persephone's domain, like

[32] Cf. VII 10.2.

26 ἦν διατεθεὶς Rsk.: διατεθεὶς ἦν

νουσιν οἱ χθόνιοι θεοὶ τοῖς ἀθυμοτέροις τὰ πένθη, εἰ
δὲ ὑπομείναιμι ἁπτόμενον, πεῖθε καὶ Δάμιν ζῆν τέ με
καὶ μὴ ἀποβεβληκέναι τὸ σῶμα."

2   Οὐκέθ᾽ οἷοι ἀπιστεῖν ἦσαν, ἀλλ᾽ ἀναστάντες ἐξ-
εκρέμαντο τοῦ ἀνδρὸς καὶ ἠσπάζοντο ὑπέρ τε τῆς
ἀπολογίας ἠρώτων· ὁ μὲν γὰρ Δημήτριος οὐδ᾽ ἀπολελογῆσθαι αὐτόν, ἀπολέσθαι γὰρ ἂν καὶ μὴ ἀδικοῦντα, Δάμις δ᾽ ἀπολελογῆσθαι μέν, θᾶττον δ᾽ ἴσως,
οὐ γὰρ ἐπ᾽ ἐκείνης γε τῆς ἡμέρας ᾤετο. ὁ δ᾽ Ἀπολλώνιος "ἀπολελόγημαι," ἔφη "ὦ ἄνδρες, καὶ νικῶμεν,
γέγονε δέ μοι τὰ τῆς ἀπολογίας τήμερον οὐ πρὸ
πολλοῦ τῆς ἡμέρας, προῄει γὰρ ἤδη ἐς μεσημβρίαν."
"πῶς οὖν" ἔφη ὁ Δημήτριος "τοσήνδε ὁδὸν ἐν σμικρῷ
τῆς ἡμέρας ἤνυσας;" καὶ ὁ Ἀπολλώνιος "πλὴν κριοῦ"
ἔφη "καὶ πτερῶν κηροῦ ξυγκειμένων πάντα οἴου, θεὸν
ἐπιγράφων τῇ πομπῇ ταύτῃ."

3   "Πανταχοῦ μὲν" ἦ δ᾽ ὁ Δημήτριος "τῶν σῶν ἔργων
τε καὶ λόγων θεὸν ἀεί τινα προορᾶν ἡγοῦμαι, παρ᾽ οὗ
τὰ σὰ οὕτως ἔχει, τὴν δ᾽ ἀπολογίαν, ἥ τις γέγονε καὶ
ἅττα ἡ κατηγορία εἶχε, καὶ τὸ τοῦ δικάζοντος ἦθος καὶ
ὅ τι ἤρετο καὶ ὅτῳ ξυγκατέθετο ἢ ὅτῳ μή, λέγε ὁμοῦ
πάντα, ἵνα καὶ Τελεσίνῳ ἕκαστα φράζοιμι, οὐ γὰρ
ἀνήσει ἐρωτῶν τὰ σά, ὅς γε καὶ πρὸ πεντεκαίδεκα
ἴσως ἡμερῶν ἐμοὶ ξυμπίνων ἐν Ἀνθίῳ κατέδαρθε μὲν
ἐπὶ τῆς τραπέζης, μεσούσης δ᾽ αὐτῷ τῆς κύλικος
ἔδοξεν ὄναρ πῦρ ἐν τῇ γῇ πελαγίσαν τοὺς μὲν ἀπο-
λαμβάνειν τῶν ἀνθρώπων, τοὺς δὲ φθάνειν ὑποφεύ-
γοντας, καὶ γὰρ δὴ καὶ ῥεῖν αὐτὸ παραπλησίως τῷ

the ghosts that the infernal gods reveal to men when they are overly despondent with grief. But if I remain when grasped, persuade Damis too that I am alive and have not lost my body."

Unable to disbelieve any longer, they stood up, hugged 2 the Master, welcomed him, and questioned him about his defense. Demetrius thought that he had not even made one, but would have been put to death even when innocent, while Damis thought he had made one, but perhaps earlier and not that very day. But Apollonius said, "I have given my defense and won, and my defense took place today fairly early in the day, when it was getting towards noon." "How then," asked Demetrius, "have you come such a distance in so short a part of the day?" "Other than a ram or wings made with wax,"[33] said Apollonius, "you may imagine anything, but ascribe my safe conduct to a god."

"Everywhere," said Demetrius, "a god always watches 3 over your actions and words, I believe, and is responsible for your present fortune. But tell us all about your defense, how it went, what the charges were, how your judge behaved, what he asked, where he agreed with you and where not. Then I can tell the details to Telesinus, who will never stop asking how you fared. About fifteen days ago, when he was dining with me at Antium,[34] he fell asleep at the table, and when his cup was half-full he dreamed that a wave of fire swept the earth, cutting some people off and overtaking others in their escape, since it ran as fast as

[33] Allusion to the wings of Icarus and the winged ram that carried Phrixus.

[34] Modern Anzio.

ὕδατι, σὲ δ' οὐχ ὅπερ οἱ πολλοὶ παθεῖν, ἀλλὰ δια-
νεῦσαι αὐτοῦ σχισθέντος. ἐπὶ δὲ τῷ ἐνυπνίῳ τούτῳ
θεοῖς εὐξυμβόλοις ἔσπεισεν ἐμοί τε παρεκελεύσατο
ὑπὲρ σοῦ θαρρεῖν."

4   Καὶ ὁ Ἀπολλώνιος "οὐ θαυμάζω Τελεσῖνον" εἶπεν
"ὑπερκαθεύδοντα, καὶ γὰρ δὴ καὶ ὑπερεγρήγορέ μου
πάλαι, τὰ δ' ὑπὲρ τῆς δίκης πεύσεσθε μέν, οὐ μὴν
ἐνταῦθα, δείλη τε γὰρ ἱκανῶς ἤδη καὶ βαδίζειν ὥρα ἐς
ἄστυ, ἡδίους δ' οἱ καθ' ὁδὸν λόγοι παραπέμψαι βαδί-
ζοντας. ἴωμεν οὖν διαλαλοῦντες ὑπὲρ ὧν ἐρωτᾶτε,
λέξω δὲ τὰ τήμερον δήπου ἐν τῷ δικαστηρίῳ πρα-
χθέντα. τὰ γὰρ πρὸ τῆς κρίσεως ἄμφω ἴστε, σὺ μὲν
παρατυχών, σὺ δ' ἠκροαμένος, οἶμαι, τούτου, μὰ Δία,
οὐχ ἅπαξ, ἀλλὰ καὶ πάλιν, εἰ μὴ ἐκλέλησμαι Δημητρίου, ἃ δ' οὔπω ἴστε, δίειμι, διείρων ἀπὸ τῆς
προρρήσεως καὶ τοῦ γυμνοῦ ἐσελθεῖν."²⁷ διῄει δὲ καὶ
τοὺς ἑαυτοῦ λόγους καὶ ἐπὶ πᾶσι τὸ "οὐ γάρ με
κτενέεις" καὶ τὸ ἀπελθεῖν τῆς κρίσεως, ὡς ἀπῆλθε.

13. Τότε ἀναβοήσας Δημήτριος "ἐγὼ μὲν ᾤμην
σεσωσμένον ἀφῖχθαί σε, σοὶ δ' ἀρχὴ κινδύνων ταῦτα,
ξυλλήψεται γάρ σε καταγγελλόμενον καὶ πάσης ἀποστροφῆς εἰργόμενον." ὁ δ' ἐρρῶσθαι τῷ Δημητρίου
δέει φράζων "εἰ γὰρ καὶ ὑμεῖς" εἶπεν "ὧδε αὐτῷ
εὐάλωτοι ἦτε· ἀλλ' ὅπως μὲν τἀκείνου νῦν ἔχει, ἐγὼ
οἶδα· κολακευόντων γὰρ ἀεὶ λόγων ἀκροατὴς γιγνόμενος, νῦν ἐπιπληττόντων ἠκρόαται, ῥήγνυνται δ' ὑπὸ
τῶν τοιούτων αἱ τύραννοι φύσεις καὶ περὶ ταῦτα χο-

water, but you were not affected the way most people were, since it parted for you to swim through it. After this dream he made a libation to the gods of good omen, and urged me to have hopes for you."

"I am not surprised that Telesinus slept for me," said Apollonius, "since long ago he stayed awake for me. You will hear all about the trial, though not here, since it is now well into the evening and time to walk into the town, and conversations along the way make pleasant companions for walkers. Let us go, then, chatting about any questions you may have, and I will tell you what must have happened in court today. The preliminaries of the trial are known to you both, one of you because you were there, and the other because I think you have heard about it, heaven knows, not once but many times, unless I have forgotten my Demetrius. I will narrate what you do not yet know, beginning from the summons and my disrobing before entering." So he recounted his own remarks, closing with "You shall not kill me," and his leaving the trial in the way he did.

13. Thereupon Demetrius shouted out, "I thought you were safe when you arrived, but this is only the beginning of your dangers. He will catch you by denouncing you and banning you from any shelter." Dismissing Demetrius's fears, Apollonius replied, "If only you were as easy for him to catch! But I know the state he is now in. Having always listened to words of flattery, he has now listened to ones of rebuke, and such things infuriate tyrannical natures and

4

---

27 ἐσελθεῖν Cob.: ἐπελθεῖν

λῶσιν. ἐμοὶ δὲ ἀναπαύλης δεῖ γόνυ οὔπω κάμψαντι ἐκ
τοῦ ἄθλου."

2   Καὶ ὁ Δάμις "ἐγώ, Δημήτριε, διεκείμην μὲν οὕτως"
ἔφη "πρὸς τὰ τοῦδε τοῦ ἀνδρὸς πράγματα, ὡς καὶ τῆς
ὁδοῦ ταύτης ἀπάγειν αὐτόν, ἐφ' ἧς ἥκει, ξυνεβούλευες
δέ που καὶ σὺ ταῦτα, ὡς μὴ ἐς κινδύνους ἑκουσίους τε
καὶ χαλεποὺς ἴοι, ἐπεὶ δ' ἐτύγχανε μὲν δεδεμένος, ὡς
ἐμοὶ ἐφαίνετο, ἄπορα δ' ἡγουμένῳ τὰ περὶ αὐτόν, ἐφ'
ἑαυτῷ ἔφη τὸ λελύσθαι εἶναι, καὶ τὸ σκέλος ἐλευθε-
ρώσας τοῦ δεσμοῦ ἔδειξε, τότε πρῶτον κατενόησα τοῦ
ἀνδρός, θεσπέσιόν τε εἶναι αὐτὸν καὶ κρείσσω τῆς
ἡμεδαπῆς σοφίας· ὅθεν, εἰ καὶ χαλεπωτέροις τούτων
ἐντύχοιμι, οὐδὲν ἂν δείσαιμι ὑπὸ τούτῳ καὶ κινδυνεύων. ἀλλ' ἐπειδὴ πλησίον ἑσπέρα, βαδίζωμεν ἐς τὴν
καταγωγὴν ἐπιμέλειαν ποιησόμενοι τοῦ ἀνδρός." καὶ
ὁ Ἀπολλώνιος "ὕπνου" ἔφη "δέομαι μόνον, τὰ δ' ἄλλα
ἐν ἴσῳ τίθεμαι λόγῳ, κἂν παρῇ τι αὐτῶν, κἂν ἀπῇ."
μετὰ ταῦτα εὐξάμενος Ἀπόλλωνι καὶ ἔτι τῷ Ἡλίῳ
παρῆλθεν ἐς τὴν οἰκίαν, ἣν ᾤκει ὁ Δημήτριος, καὶ τὼ
πόδε ἀπονιψάμενος, παρακελευσάμενός τε τοῖς ἀμφὶ
τὸν Δάμιν δειπνεῖν, ἐπειδὴ ἄσιτοι αὐτῷ ἐφαίνοντο,
ἔρριψεν ἐς τὴν κλίνην ἑαυτὸν καὶ ἐφυμνήσας τῷ ὕπνῳ
τὸ Ὁμήρου ἔπος ἐκάθευδεν, ὡς οὐκ ἐπ' ἀξίοις φρον-
τίσαι τοῖς παροῦσιν.

14. Περὶ δὲ ὄρθρον ἐρομένου αὐτὸν τοῦ Δημητρίου,
ποῖ τῆς γῆς τρέψοιτο, καὶ κτυπεῖσθαι δοκοῦντος τὰ
ὦτα ὑπὸ ἐννοίας ἱππέων, οὓς ᾤετο ἐπικεῖσθαι ἤδη τῷ
Ἀπολλωνίῳ διὰ τὴν ὀργὴν τοῦ τυράννου "διώξεται

make them angry. But I need to rest, not having relaxed my limbs after the struggle."

"As for me, Demetrius," said Damis, "my feelings   2 about the Master's plight were such that I tried to advise him against the journey that he has now taken. You surely would have given him the same advice, not to walk into grave dangers of his own free will. But at the time when he was in chains, or so I thought, and I considered his position hopeless, he said his liberation depended on himself, and freeing his leg from its chain he showed it to me. That was the first time I comprehended the Master as someone god-like and above ordinary wisdom. So, even if I run into something worse, I will never feel fear when endangered in his company. But since the evening is near, let us go to our lodging to attend to the Master." "I only need sleep," said Apollonius, "everything else is indifferent to me, whether present or absent." Then after praying to Apollo and also to the Sun, he entered the house in which Demetrius was staying. There he washed his feet, and urged Damis and the others to dine, since he thought them in need of food. Then he threw himself down on his bed and fell asleep, after first singing the line of Homer in praise of sleep,[35] as if the situation were not worth worrying about.

14. At about daybreak Demetrius asked him what place on earth he would turn to. His ears already seemed to be ringing from the idea of horsemen, since he thought they were already pursuing Apollonius because of the tyrant's

---

[35] Probably *Iliad* 14.233, "Sleep, lord of all gods and of all humankind."

μέν" ἔφη "με οὐδὲ αὐτός, οὐδὲ ἕτερος, ἐμοὶ δὲ ἐς τὴν
Ἑλλάδα ὁ πλοῦς ἔσται." "σφαλερός γε," εἶπε "τὸ γὰρ
χωρίον φανερώτατον· ὃν δὲ μηδ' ἂν ἐν τῷ ἀφανεῖ
διαφύγοις, πῶς ἂν ἐν τῷ φανερῷ λάθοις;" "οὐ δέομαι"
ἔφη "λανθάνειν, εἰ γάρ, ὡς σὺ οἴει, τοῦ τυράννου ἡ γῆ
πᾶσα, βελτίους οἱ ἐν τῷ φανερῷ ἀποθνήσκοντες τῶν
ἐν τῷ ἀφανεῖ ζώντων." καὶ πρὸς τὸν Δάμιν "αἰσθάνῃ"
ἔφη "νεὼς ἀφιείσης ἐς Σικελίαν;" "αἰσθάνομαι," εἶπε
"καὶ γὰρ ἐπὶ θαλάττῃ καταλύομεν καὶ ὁ κηρύττων
ἀγχοῦ θυρῶν, στέλλεταί τε ἡ ναῦς ἤδη· ξυμβάλλομαι
δ' αὐτὸ τῇ τῶν ἐμπλεόντων βοῇ καὶ οἷς περὶ τὴν
ἀναίρεσιν τῶν ἀγκυρῶν πράττουσιν." "ἐπιβῶμεν" εἶπε
"τῆς νεὼς ταύτης, ὦ Δάμι, πλευσούμενοι νῦν μὲν ἐς
Σικελίαν, ἐκεῖθεν δ' ἐς Πελοπόννησον." "ξυνδοκεῖ μοι,"
ἔφη "καὶ πλέωμεν."

15. Καὶ προσειπόντες τὸν Δημήτριον ἀθύμως ἐπ'
αὐτοῖς ἔχοντα, θαρρεῖν τε πείσαντες ὡς ἄνδρα ὑπὲρ
ἀνδρῶν, ἔπλευσαν ἐπὶ Σικελίας ἀνέμῳ ἐπιτηδείῳ,
Μεσσήνην τε παραπλεύσαντες ἐγένοντο ἐν Ταυρομε-
νίῳ τριταῖοι. μετὰ ταῦτ' ἐπὶ Συρακουσῶν κομισθέντες
ἀνήγοντο ἐς Πελοπόννησον περὶ μετοπώρου ἀρχάς,
ὑπεράραντες δὲ τοῦ πελάγους ἀφίκοντο δι' ἡμέρας
ἕκτης ἐπὶ τὰς τοῦ Ἀλφειοῦ ἐκβολάς, ἀφ' ὧν ὁ ποταμὸς
οὗτος Ἀδρίᾳ καὶ Σικελικῷ πελάγει ἐπιχεῖται πότιμος.
ἀποβάντες οὖν τῆς νεὼς καὶ πολλοῦ ἄξιον ἡγούμενοι
τὸ ἐς Ὀλυμπίαν ἥκειν διῃτῶντο ἐν τῷ ἱερῷ τοῦ Διός,
οὐδαμοῦ ὑπὲρ Σκιλλοῦντα ἀποφοιτῶντες,

fury. "Neither he," said Apollonius, "nor anyone else will pursue me, and my course is for Greece." "A dangerous one," said Demetrius, "since it is a very open place. You could not escape him in hiding, and how will you elude him in the open?" "I do not need to," replied Apollonius, "since if the whole earth belongs to the tyrant, as you suppose, those who die in the open are better off than those who live in obscurity." Then he said to Damis, "Do you know of a ship sailing for Sicily?" "I do," he replied, "as our lodging is near the sea, the crier is at the door, and the ship is already setting sail. I can tell this from the crew's shouts and their preparations for weighing anchor." "Let us take this ship, Damis," said Apollonius, "and sail to Sicily now, and from there to Greece." "That suits me," said Damis, "so let us go aboard."

15. After saying goodbye to Demetrius, who was despondent for their sake, and persuading him to be cheerful for them as a true man like themselves, they sailed for Sicily with a favorable wind, and after passing Messina reached Tauromenium in two days. Next they put in at Syracuse, and then sailed for the Peloponnese about the beginning of autumn. After crossing the open sea, they arrived after five days at the mouth of the Alpheus, at the point where the river enters the Adriatic and Sicilian seas,[36] still fresh. Disembarking from the ships and thinking it very important to reach Olympia, they stayed in the sanctuary of Zeus, never going away further than Scillous.[37]

---

[36] That is, the Ionian sea lying between Greece and Sicily. The term "Adriatic" was sometimes used of this sea as well as for the modern Adriatic. [37] Town south of Olympia.

2   Φήμης δ' ἀθρόας τε καὶ ξυντόνου κατασχούσης τὸ
Ἑλληνικὸν ζῆν τὸν ἄνδρα καὶ ἀφῖχθαι ἐς Ὀλυμπίαν,
κατ' ἀρχὰς μὲν ἐδόκει μὴ ἐρρῶσθαι ὁ λόγος, πρὸς
γὰρ τῷ μὴ ἐλπίδος τι ἀνθρωπείας ἐπ' αὐτῷ ἔχειν,
ἐπειδὴ δεδέσθαι αὐτὸν ἤκουσαν, οὐδὲ ἐκείνων ἀνήκοοι
ἦσαν ἀποθανεῖν καταφλεχθέντα, οἱ δ' ἑλχθῆναι ζῶντα
καταπαγέντων ἐς τὰς κλεῖδας αὐτοῦ ἀγκίστρων, οἱ δ'
ἐῶσθαι ἐς βάραθρον, οἱ δ' ἐς βυθόν, ἐπειδὴ δὲ ἥκειν
ἐπιστεύθη, οὐδ' ἐπ' Ὀλυμπιάδα οὐδεμίαν μετέωρος
οὕτω ξυνῄει ἡ Ἑλλάς, ὡς ἐπ' ἐκεῖνον τότε, Ἤλις
μὲν καὶ Σπάρτη αὐτόθεν, Κόρινθος δὲ ἀπὸ τῶν τοῦ
Ἰσθμοῦ ὁρίων, Ἀθηναῖοι δέ, εἰ καὶ Πελοποννήσου
ἔξω, ἀλλ' οὐκ ἐλείποντο τῶν πόλεων, αἳ ἐπὶ θύραις
εἰσὶ τῆς Πίσης, αὐτοὶ μάλιστα οἱ ἐπικυδέστατοι Ἀθηναίων ἐς τὸ ἱερὸν στείχοντες καὶ νεότης ἡ ἐξ ἁπάσης
τῆς γῆς Ἀθήναζε φοιτῶσα. καὶ μὴν καὶ Μεγαρόθεν
τινὲς ἐπεχωρίασαν τῇ Ὀλυμπίᾳ τότε, κἀκ Βοιωτῶν
πολλοὶ κἀργόθεν, Φωκέων τε καὶ Θετταλῶν ὅ τι εὐδό-
κιμον, οἱ μὲν ξυγγεγονότες ἤδη τῷ Ἀπολλωνίῳ ἀνα-
κτησόμενοι σοφίαν, ἐπειδὴ πλειόνων τε καὶ θαυμα-
σιωτέρων ἀκροάσασθαι ᾤοντο, οἱ δ' ἄπειροι αὐτοῦ
δεινὸν ἡγούμενοι τοιοῦδε ἀνδρὸς ἀνήκοοι φαίνεσθαι.

3   Πρὸς μὲν δὴ τοὺς ἐρωτῶντας, ὅτῳ τρόπῳ διαφύγοι
τὸν τύραννον, οὐδὲν ᾤετο δεῖν φορτικὸν φράζειν, ἀλλ'
ἀπολελογῆσθαί τε ἔφασκε καὶ σεσῶσθαι, πολλῶν δ'
ἐξ Ἰταλίας ἡκόντων, οἳ ἐκήρυττον τὰ ἐν τῷ δικαστηρίῳ, διέκειτο μὲν ἡ Ἑλλὰς οὐ πόρρω τοῦ προσκυνεῖν

The Greek world buzzed with a general and persistent   2
rumor that the Master was alive and had come to Olympia.
At first the story was thought to be unfounded, since not
only did they have no earthly hope for him, once they had
heard he was in prison, but they had also heard other
things: that he had been burnt to death, or had been
dragged still living with hooks fastened in his collarbones,
or had been thrown down a crevasse or into the deep. But
when they were sure he had come, the Greeks assembled
in such excitement for his sake as they had never for
any Olympics.[38] The Eleans and the Spartans came from
near by, the Corinthians from the borders of the Isthmus.
The Athenians too, though from outside the Peloponnese,
were as numerous as those from the cities on the very
threshold of Pisa, so that the most distinguished of the
Athenians came to the sanctuary, as well as the youths
that come to Athens from the whole world. Some visited
Olympia from Megara on that occasion, as did many from
Boeotia and Argos, and all the leading lights of Phocis and
Thessaly. Some had previously studied with Apollonius,
and wanted to increase their wisdom, since they hoped to
learn even more marvelous lessons. Others who did not
know him were ashamed to be thought not to have heard
so great a man.

When he was asked how on earth he had escaped the   3
tyrant, he did not see fit to say anything pompous, but re-
peated that he had made his defense and survived. But
many visitors from Italy gave the news of what had happened in court, until the Greeks could barely keep from

[38] Apollonius's visit took place when the Olympics were not
being held.

αὐτόν, θεῖον ἡγούμενοι ἄνδρα δι᾿ αὐτὸ μάλιστα τὸ μηδ᾿ ἐς κόμπον μηδένα ὑπὲρ αὐτῶν καθίστασθαι.

16. Νεανίσκου δὲ τῶν ἡκόντων Ἀθήνηθεν μάλα εὔνουν τὴν Ἀθηνᾶν εἶναι τῷ βασιλεῖ φήσαντος, "πέπαυσο" εἶπεν "Ὀλυμπίασιν ὑπὲρ τούτων κροτῶν²⁸ καὶ διαβάλλων τὴν θεὸν τῷ πατρί." ἐπιδιδόντος δὲ τοῦ νεανίσκου τῇ ἀχθηδόνι καὶ δίκαια πράττειν τὴν θεὸν φήσαντος, ἐπειδὴ καὶ ὁ βασιλεὺς τὴν ἐπώνυμον Ἀθηναίοις ἦρξεν "εἴθε" ἔφη "καὶ ἐν Παναθηναίοις" ἐπιστομίζων αὐτὸν τῇ μὲν προτέρᾳ τῶν ἀποκρίσεων, ὡς κακῶς εἰδότα περὶ τῶν θεῶν, εἰ τυράννοις αὐτοὺς εὔνους ἡγοῖτο, τῇ δὲ ἐφεξῆς, ὡς οὐκ ἀκόλουθα τοῖς ἐφ᾿ Ἁρμοδίῳ καὶ Ἀριστογείτονι ψηφιζομένων Ἀθηναίων, εἰ τοὺς ἄνδρας ἐκείνους τιμᾶν ἐπ᾿ ἀγορᾶς νομίζοντες ὑπὲρ ὧν ἐν Παναθηναίοις ἔδρασαν, τυράννοις λοιπὸν χαρίζονται τὸ κεχειροτονημένους αὐτῶν ἄρχειν.

17. Ξυμβουλεύοντος δ᾿ αὐτῷ τοῦ Δάμιδος ὑπὲρ χρημάτων, ἐπειδὴ τῶν ἐφοδίων σφίσι πάνυ σμικρὰ ἐλείπετο "αὔριον" ἔφη "τούτου ἐπιμελήσομαι." καὶ παρελθὼν τῇ ὑστεραίᾳ ἐς τὸ ἱερὸν "δός," εἶπεν, "ὦ ἱερεῦ, χιλίας μοι δραχμὰς ἀπὸ τῶν τοῦ Διὸς χρημάτων, εἰ μὴ σφόδρα οἴει χαλεπανεῖν αὐτόν." καὶ ὁ ἱερεὺς "οὐχ ὑπὲρ τούτων" ἔφη "χαλεπανεῖ, ἀλλὰ μᾶλλον, εἰ μὴ πλείω λήψῃ."

18. Θετταλοῦ δὲ ἀνδρός, ᾧ ὄνομα Ἰσαγόρας, ξυνόντος αὐτῷ ἐν Ὀλυμπίᾳ "εἰπέ μοι" ἔφη "ὦ Ἰσαγόρα, ἔστι τι πανήγυρις;" "νὴ Δί᾿," εἶπε "τό γε ἥδιστον καὶ θεοφιλέστατον τῶν κατ᾿ ἀνθρώπους." "τίς δὲ δὴ ὕλη

doing obeisance to him. They thought the Master to be superhuman precisely because he never made any parade about his record.

16. But among the visitors from Athens was a young man claiming that Athena was very favorable to the emperor. "Stop babbling about such matters at Olympia," said Apollonius, "and slandering the goddess to her father." When the youth persisted in this annoying behavior, and said that the goddess was only doing right, since the emperor too had been eponymous magistrate at Athens, Apollonius said, "If only it had been at the Panathenaea." By his first answer he silenced the youth for the false supposition that the gods favored tyrants, and by his second he showed the Athenians to have cast a vote inconsistent with their honors for Harmodius and Aristogeiton. They thought they were honoring those heroes in the marketplace for what they had done at the Panathenaea, and then they granted a tyrant the position of their own elected magistrate.

17. When Damis advised him about their finances, saying that they had very few traveling funds left, Apollonius said, "I will correct that tomorrow." Entering the sanctuary the next day, "Priest," he said, "give me a thousand drachmas from Zeus's funds, unless you think he will be very annoyed." "He will not be annoyed by that," said the priest, "but rather because you will not take more."

18. To a Thessalian gentleman named Isagoras who joined him in Olympia, Apollonius said, "Tell me, Isagoras, is there such a thing as a festival?" "Certainly," he replied, "the most delightful and blessed thing on earth." "What

---

28 κροτῶν Kay.: ἐρωτῶν

τούτου; ὥσπερ ἂν εἰ ἐγὼ μὲν ἠρόμην ὑπὲρ ὕλης τοῦδε
τοῦ ἀγάλματος, σὺ δ᾽ ἀπεκρίνου χρυσοῦ καὶ ἐλέφαντος ξυντεθῆναι αὐτό." "καὶ τίς" ἔφη "ὕλη, Ἀπολλώνιε, τοῦ γε ἀσωμάτου;" "μεγίστη" εἶπε "καὶ ποι-
κιλωτάτη, τεμένη τε γὰρ ἐν αὐτῇ, καὶ ἱερά, καὶ δρόμοι,
καὶ σκηνὴ δήπου, ἔθνη τε ἀνθρώπων τὰ μὲν ἐκ τῆς
ὁμόρου, τὰ δὲ ἐκ τῶν ὑπερορίων τε καὶ ὑπὲρ θάλατταν." καὶ μὴν καὶ τεχνῶν πλείστων αὐτὴν ξυγκεῖσθαι,
καὶ σοφισμάτων σοφίας τε ἀληθινῆς, καὶ ποιητῶν,
καὶ ξυμβουλιῶν, καὶ διαλέξεων, γυμνῆς τε ἀγωνίας
καὶ μουσικῆς, ὡς Πυθοῖ πάτριον. "ἔοικεν," ἔφη
"Ἀπολλώνιε, οὐ μόνον σωματοειδὲς εἶναι ἡ πανήγυρις, ἀλλὰ καὶ θαυμασιωτέρας ὕλης ἢ αἱ πόλεις, τὰ
γὰρ τῶν σπουδαίων σπουδαιότατα καὶ τὰ τῶν ἐλλο-
γίμων ἐλλογιμώτατα ξυγκαλεῖ καὶ ξυνοικίζει."

2   "Ἆρ᾽ οὖν," εἶπεν "ὦ Ἰσαγόρα, καθάπερ ἔνιοι τείχη
καὶ ναῦς ἡγοῦνται, τοὺς ἄνδρας ἡγησόμεθα, ἢ ἑτέρας
ἐπ᾽ αὐτῆς²⁹ δέῃ δόξης;" "τελεία," ἔφη "ὦ Τυανεῦ, ἥδε ἡ
δόξα, καὶ δίκαιον ἕπεσθαι αὐτῇ." "καὶ μὴν ἀτελὴς"
εἶπεν "ἐνθυμουμένῳ περὶ αὐτῆς ὃν ἐγὼ τρόπον· δο-
κοῦσι γάρ μοι καὶ νῆες ἀνδρῶν δεῖσθαι καὶ ἄνδρες
νηῶν καὶ μηδ᾽ ἂν ἐνθυμηθῆναί ποτε ἀνθρώπους τὴν
θάλατταν, εἰ μὴ ναῦς ἦν, σώζειν τε ἄνδρας μὲν τείχη,
τείχη δὲ ἄνδρας, πανήγυρις δὲ κατὰ τὸν αὐτὸν λόγον
εἶναι μὲν καὶ ἡ τῶν ἀνδρῶν ξύνοδος, εἶναι δὲ καὶ αὐτὸ
τὸ χωρίον, ἐς ὃ χρὴ ξυνιέναι, καὶ τοσούτῳ μᾶλλον,

²⁹ αὐτῆς Valck.: αὐτῇ

does it consist of? For example, if I were to ask you what this image consists of, you would say that it was a combination of gold and ivory."[39] "What can be the substance of something abstract, Apollonius?" said the other. "The most precious and heterogeneous substance," he replied, "since a festival incorporates sacred enclosures, sanctuaries, walkways, a stage, and every race of humanity, some from nearby, others from abroad and across the sea." In addition, he said, it consisted of many arts and sciences, of true wisdom, poetry, sermons, lectures, gymnastic competitions and musical ones, as was traditional at Delphi.[40] "It would seem, Apollonius," said Isagoras, "that a festival is not merely something corporeal, but has a substance more miraculous than cities do, since it attracts and assembles the most virtuous of the virtuous and the most famous of the famous."

"Well, then, Isagoras," said Apollonius, "are we to consider the attendees at a festival in the way that some consider city walls and ships, or will we need a different conception of it?" "This one is sufficient, man of Tyana," said the other, "and we are right to accept it." "And yet it is insufficient," said Apollonius, "when you think about a festival as I do. Ships seem to me to need men and men ships, since men would never have thought about the sea if there had been no ships, and men protect walls and walls men. But a festival is at one and the same time both a gathering of men, and also the place where they have to gather, 2

[39] The chryselephantine (gold and ivory) statue of Zeus.
[40] The Olympics did not include musical events.

ὅσῳ τείχη μὲν καὶ νῆες οὐδ' ἂν ἐγένοντο, εἰ μὴ δι'
ἀνθρώπων χεῖρας, τὰ δὲ χωρία ταῦτα ὑπὸ χειρῶν μὲν
ἀνθρωπείων ἐφθάρη τὸ αὐτοσχέδια μὴ εἶναι ἀφαιρε-
θέντα, φύσεως δ' εὖ ἥκοντα ἐπάξια τοῦ ξυμφοιτᾶν ἐς
αὐτὰ ἐνομίσθη,

3   "Γυμνάσια μὲν γὰρ καὶ στοαὶ, καὶ κρῆναι, καὶ
οἶκοι, τέχνῃ ταῦτα ἀνθρωπείᾳ εἰργάσθη, καθάπερ τὰ
τείχη καὶ αἱ νῆες, Ἀλφειὸς δὲ οὗτος καὶ ἱππόδρομος
καὶ στάδιον καὶ ἄλση πρὸ ἀνθρώπων δήπου ἐγένετο, ὁ
μὲν ἀποχρῶν ποτὸν εἶναι καὶ λουτρόν, ὁ δ' εὐρὺ
πεδίον ἐναγωνίσασθαι τοῖς ἵπποις, τὸ δ' ἐγκονίσα-
σθαι καὶ διαδραμεῖν ἀθληταῖς διὰ τὸ παρέχεσθαί
τινα ὅρον, αὐλῶνα σταδίου μῆκος, τὰ δὲ ἄλση στεφα-
νῶσαι τοὺς νικῶντας καὶ τοὺς δρομικοὺς τῶν ἀθλητῶν
γυμνάσαι. ταῦτα γάρ που καὶ Ἡρακλεῖ ἐνθυμηθέντι
καὶ τὸ αὐτοφυὲς τῆς Ὀλυμπίας ἀγασθέντι ἐπάξιος
ἐφάνη ὁ χῶρος τῶν ἔτι νῦν σπουδαζομένων ἐνταῦθα."

19. Ἡμερῶν δὲ τετταράκοντα διαλεχθεὶς ἐν Ὀλυμπίᾳ καὶ πλεῖστα σπουδάσας "καὶ κατὰ πόλεις μὲν"
ἔφη "διαλέξομαι ὑμῖν, ἄνδρες Ἕλληνες, ἐν πανηγύρε-
σιν, ἐν πομπαῖς, ἐν μυστηρίοις, ἐν θυσίαις, ἐν σπον-
δαῖς, ἀστείου δὲ ἀνδρὸς δέονται· νῦν δὲ ἐς Λεβάδειαν
χρὴ καταβῆναί με, ἐπεὶ τῷ Τροφωνίῳ μήπω ξυγγέ-
γονα καίτοι ἐπιφοιτήσας ποτὲ τῷ ἱερῷ." καὶ εἰπὼν
ταῦτα ἐχώρει δὴ ἐπὶ Βοιωτίας,[30] οὐδενὸς λειπομένου
τῶν θαυμαζόντων αὐτόν. τὸ δ' ἐν Λεβαδείᾳ στόμιον
ἀνάκειται μὲν Τροφωνίῳ τῷ Ἀπόλλωνος, ἐσβατὸν

indeed all the more so in that ships and walls would not have come about except by human hand, whereas human hand has ruined these places by taking away their natural state. Being well endowed by nature, they seemed worth making into meeting places.

"Gymnasia, colonnades, fountains, rooms, all these 3 were made by human skill, as are walls and ships. But the Alpheus here, the racecourse, the stadium, and the groves doubtless existed before humans did. The first was enough to provide drinking and bath water, the second a broad space for horses to compete in, the third a place for athletes to dust themselves down and run, since it provided a sort of boundary in the form of a valley one stade long, and the groves yielded crowns for the victors and exercised those athletes who ran. All this Hercules had in mind, no doubt, when he admired the natural advantages of Olympia, and deemed it a worthy setting for those who compete here even now."

19. After he had held discussions in Olympia for forty days, and covered many subjects, he said, "City by city, men of Greece, I will converse with you, at your festivals, your processions, your mysteries, your sacrifices, and your libations, because these matters require a man of virtue. But for the present I must go down to Lebadea, since I have never met Trophonius, though I once visited his sanctuary."[41] With these words he was on his way to Boeotia, leaving none of his admirers behind. The cave mouth at Lebadea is dedicated to Trophonius the son of Apollo, and

[41] See IV 24.1.

---

30 ἐπὶ Βοιωτίας Jac.: ἐπ᾽ Ἀρκαδίας

μόνον τοῖς ὑπὲρ χρησμῶν φοιτῶσιν, ὁρᾶται δ᾽ οὐκ ἐν
τῷ ἱερῷ, μικρὸν δ᾽ ἄνω τοῦ ἱεροῦ ἐν γηλόφῳ, ξυγκλεί-
ουσι δ᾽ αὐτὸ σιδήρεοι ὀβελίσκοι κύκλῳ περιβάλλοντες, ἡ δὲ κάθοδος οἷα ἱζήσαντα ἐπισπάσασθαι. λευκῇ
δ᾽ ἐσθῆτι ἐσταλμένοι πέμπονται, μελιτούττας ἀπάγοντες ἐν ταῖν χεροῖν μειλίγματα ἑρπετῶν, ἃ τοῖς κατιοῦ-
σιν ἐγχρίπτει. ἀναδίδωσι δ᾽ ἡ γῆ τοὺς μὲν οὐ πόρρω,
τοὺς δὲ πορρωτάτω, καὶ γὰρ ὑπὲρ Λοκροὺς ἀναπέμ-
πονται καὶ ὑπὲρ Φωκέας, οἱ δὲ πλεῖστοι περὶ τὰ
Βοιωτῶν ὅρια.

2   Παρελθὼν οὖν ἐς τὸ ἱερὸν "βούλομαι" ἔφη "κατα-
βῆναι ὑπὲρ φιλοσοφίας." ἀντιλεγόντων δὲ τῶν ἱερέων
καὶ πρὸς μὲν τοὺς πολλοὺς λεγόντων, μὴ ἄν ποτε
γόητι ἀνθρώπῳ παρασχεῖν ἔλεγχον τοῦ ἱεροῦ, πρὸς δὲ
τὸν ἄνδρα πλαττομένων ἀποφράδας καὶ οὐ καθαρὰς
χρῆσαι, τὴν μὲν ἡμέραν ἐκείνην διελέχθη περὶ τὰς
πηγὰς τῆς Ἑρκύνης ὑπὲρ αἰτίας τοῦ μαντείου καὶ
τρόπου, μόνον γὰρ ἐκεῖνο δι᾽ αὐτοῦ χρᾷ τοῦ χρω-
μένου, ἑσπέρα δ᾽ ὡς ἐγένετο, ἐλθὼν ἐπὶ τὸ στόμιον
μετὰ τῶν ξυνακολουθούντων νέων καὶ τέτταρας τῶν
ὀβελίσκων ἀνασπάσας, οἳ ξυνέχουσι τὰς τῆς παρόδου κλεῖδας, ἐχώρει ὑποχθόνιος αὐτῷ τρίβωνι,
καθάπερ ἐς διάλεξιν ἑαυτὸν στείλας, οὕτω τι τῷ θεῷ
φίλα πράττων, ὡς ἐπιστάντα τοῖς ἱερεῦσι τὸν Τρο-
φώνιον ἐς ἐπίπληξίν τε αὐτοῖς καταστῆναι ὑπὲρ τοῦ
ἀνδρός, ἐς Αὐλίδα τε ἕπεσθαι κελεῦσαι πάντας, ὡς
ἐκεῖ ἀναδυσομένου θαυμασιώτατα ἀνθρώπων. ἀνέσχε
γὰρ δι᾽ ἡμερῶν ἑπτά, ὅσων μήπω τις τῶν ὑπελθόντων

may only be entered by those who come to receive an oracle. It is to be seen not in the sanctuary but a little way
above it on a hill, enclosed by a circular palisade of iron
stakes, and you enter as it were by sitting down and being
drawn in. People go in processions dressed in white clothing and carrying honey cakes in their hands to mollify the
serpents that bite people as they descend. The consultants
emerge from the earth, some not far away, some very far
away, as when they are carried beyond Locris and Phocis,
but most of them emerge on the borders of Boeotia.

On entering the sanctuary, Apollonius said, "I want to   2
go down with a question about philosophy." The priests
opposed him, telling most people that they would never let
some sorcerer-type test the oracle, though to the Master
they alleged unpropitious days on which it was taboo to
consult the oracle. So for that day he held a discussion at
the source of the Hercyna[42] on the origin of the sanctuary
and its procedure, since it is the only one to give its re-
sponses through the medium of the consultant. When evening came, he proceeded to the cave mouth with his young
disciples, pulled up four of the stakes that form bars before
the entrance, and proceeded below ground dressed only in
his cloak, just as if prepared for a discussion. In all this he
pleased the god so much that Trophonius appeared to his
priests, rebuked them for their treatment of the Master,
and told them all to follow him to Aulis,[43] where he was to
make the most miraculous emergence of all time. And indeed he emerged after seven days, longer than any who

[42] The river of Lebadea.

[43] Port city on the Euboean Strait, famous as the departure
point for the Greek expedition against Troy.

405

τὸ μαντεῖον, φέρων βιβλίον προσφορώτατον τῇ ἐρω
τήσει. ὁ μὲν γὰρ κατῆλθεν εἰπὼν "τίνα, ὦ Τροφώνιε,
καὶ σὺ τὴν ἀρτιωτάτην καὶ καθαρωτάτην φιλοσοφίαν
ἡγῇ;" τὸ δὲ βιβλίον τὰς Πυθαγόρου εἶχε δόξας, ὡς
καὶ τοῦ μαντείου τῇ σοφίᾳ ταύτῃ ξυντιθεμένου.

20. Ἀνάκειται τὸ βιβλίον τοῦτο ἐν Ἀνθίῳ καὶ
σπουδάζεται διὰ τὴν αἰτίαν (τὸ δὲ Ἄνθιον Ἰταλῶν τῶν
ἐπὶ θαλάττῃ). ταῦτα μὲν δὴ καὶ τῶν Λεβάδειαν οἰκούν
των ξυγχωρῶ ἀκροᾶσθαι, περὶ δὲ τοῦ βιβλίου τούτου
γνώμη ἀποπεφάνθω μοι, διακομισθῆναι μὲν αὐτὸ βα
σιλεῖ Ἀδριανῷ ὕστερον, ὅτε δὴ καί τινας τῶν τοῦ
Ἀπολλωνίου ἐπιστολῶν, οὐ γὰρ δὴ πάσας γε, κατα
μεῖναι δὲ ἐς τὰ βασίλεια τὰ ἐν τῷ Ἀνθίῳ, οἷς μάλιστα
δὴ τῶν περὶ τὴν Ἰταλίαν βασιλείων ἔχαιρεν.

21. Ἀφίκοντο δ' αὐτῷ κἀξ Ἰωνίας οἱ ὁμιληταὶ
πάντες, οὓς ὠνόμαζεν Ἀπολλωνιείους ἡ Ἑλλάς, καὶ
ξυμμιχθέντες τοῖς αὐτόθεν νεότης ἐγένοντο θαυμάσαι
ἄξιοι τοῦ πλήθους καὶ τῆς ἐς τὸ φιλοσοφεῖν ὁρμῆς.
ῥητορικὴ μὲν γὰρ ἀπέκειτο ἀμελουμένη, καὶ σμικρὰ
προσεῖχον τοῖς τὴν τέχνην ξυγκροτοῦσιν, ὡς μόνης
διδασκάλου τῆς γλώττης, ὠθίζοντο δὲ ἐπὶ τὴν ἐκείνου
φιλοσοφίαν πάντες. ὁ δ', ὥσπερ τοὺς Γύγας φασὶ καὶ
τοὺς Κροίσους ἀκλείστους παρέχειν τὰς τῶν θησαυ
ρῶν θύρας, ἵν' ἀπαντλεῖν εἴη τοῖς δεομένοις, οὕτω
παρεῖχε τὴν ἑαυτοῦ σοφίαν τοῖς ἐρῶσι, περὶ παντὸς
ἐρωτᾶν ξυγχωρῶν.

22. Διαβαλλόντων δ' αὐτὸν ἐνίων, ὅτι τὰς τῶν
ἡγεμόνων ἐπιδημίας ἐκτρέποιτο καὶ ἀπάγοι τοὺς

had descended to the oracle before, and was carrying a book very germane to his question. On going down he had said, "Which of the philosophies, Trophonius, do you consider the best and the purest?" The book contained the doctrines of Pythagoras, showing that the oracle too agreed with this philosophy.

20. This book is dedicated at Antium, and is highly regarded because of its history. (Antium is a town on the coast of Italy.) All this I must admit to having heard from the inhabitants of Lebadea, but let me give my belief about the book. This is that it came into the hands of emperor Hadrian later, at the same time as certain of Apollonius's letters, though not all, and that it remained in the residence at Antium, which he loved most among his residences in Italy.

21. There also came to see him all his disciples from Ionia, whom the Greeks dubbed "Apollonians," and they combined with those in Greece to form a young band, remarkable for its numbers and its zeal for philosophy. Public speaking was left in neglect and little attention was paid to purveyors of that art, as one that taught only the tongue, while all flocked to Apollonius's brand of philosophy. As is said of men like Gyges and Croesus, who kept the doors of their treasuries unlocked in order to give lavishly to those in need, he made his wisdom available to its admirers, letting them question him on any subject.

22. Some people criticized him for avoiding the visits of the governors, and instead taking his listeners towards

ἀκροατὰς ἐς τὰς ἡσυχίας μᾶλλον, καί τινος ἀποσκώ-
ψαντος μετελαύνειν αὐτὸν τὰ πρόβατα, ἐπειδὰν τοὺς
ἀγοραίους προσιόντας μάθῃ, "νὴ Δί'," εἶπεν "ἵνα μὴ
ἐμπίπτωσι τῇ ποίμνῃ οἱ λύκοι." τί δ' ἐβούλετο αὐτῷ
τοῦτο; τοὺς ἀγοραίους ὁρῶν ἀποβλεπομένους ὑπὸ τῶν
πολλῶν, καὶ προϊόντας ἐκ πενίας ἐς πλοῦτον, ἀπ-
εχθείας τε οὕτως ἀσπαζομένους ὡς αὐτὸ τὸ ἀπέχθε-
σθαι πωλεῖν, ἀπῆγε τοὺς νέους τοῦ ξυνεῖναί σφισι καὶ
τοὺς ξυγγενομένους αὐτοῖς ἐνουθέτει πικρότερον, οἷον
ἀποπλύνων βαφῆς ἀτόπου. διεβέβλητο μὲν γὰρ πρὸς
αὐτοὺς καὶ τὸν ἄλλον χρόνον, ὑπὸ δὲ τῶν ἐν τῇ Ῥώμῃ
δεσμωτηρίων καὶ τῶν δεδεμένων τε καὶ ἀπολλυμένων
οὕτω διετέθη πρὸς τὴν τέχνην, ὡς πάντα ταῦτα τῶν
συκοφαντούντων καὶ τῶν δεινότητι ἐπηρμένων ἡγεῖσθαι μᾶλλον ἢ τοῦ τυράννου.

23. Περὶ δὲ τὸν χρόνον, ὃν τῇ Ἑλλάδι ἐνεσπού-
δαζεν, ἐπεῖχε τὸν οὐρανὸν διοσημία τοιαύτη· τὸν τοῦ
ἡλίου κύκλον περιελθὼν στέφανος ἐοικὼς ἴριδι τὴν
ἀκτῖνα ἠμαύρου. ὅτι μὲν δὴ ἐς νεώτερα ἡ διοσημία
ἔφερε, δῆλα ἦν πᾶσιν, ὁ δ' ἄρχων τῆς Ἑλλάδος
καλέσας αὐτὸν ἐξ Ἀθηνῶν ἐς Βοιωτίαν "ἀκούω σε,"
εἶπεν "Ἀπολλώνιε, σοφὸν εἶναι τὰ δαιμόνια." "εἴ γε"
ἔφη "ἀκούεις, ὅτι καὶ τὰ ἀνθρώπεια." "ἀκούω" εἶπε
"καὶ ξύμφημι." "ἐπεὶ τοίνυν" ἔφη "ξυνομολογεῖς, μὴ
πολυπραγμόνει θεῶν βουλάς, τουτὶ γὰρ ἡ τῶν ἀνθρώπων σοφία ἐπαινεῖ." ἐπεὶ δὲ ἐλιπάρει τὸν Ἀπολλώνιον
εἰπεῖν, ὅπῃ διανοεῖται, δεδιέναι γὰρ μὴ ἐς νύκτα

quiet places. When someone joked that he led his flock
elsewhere when he heard lawyers coming, he replied, "I
do, by heaven, so that wolves do not attack the fold." What
was the meaning of this? Lawyers, he saw, had the admiration of the vulgar, rose from poverty to wealth, and
welcomed feuds so much as to put them on sale. He therefore dissuaded the young from their company, and rather
sharply rebuked those who associated with them, as if
washing some ugly dye out of them. He had had a low opinion of this class even before, but the Roman jails, with their
prisoners and their dying, had given him such a view of the
profession that he blamed all these things more on the
informers and on those who owed their rise to cunning
than on the tyrant.

23. About the time when he was lecturing in Greece,
the following portent appeared in the sky. A halo[44] like a
rainbow encircled the sun's disc, dimming its rays, and all
could see that the portent signified change. The governor
of Greece summoned Apollonius from Athens to Boeotia
and said, "I hear that you are wise in heavenly matters,
Apollonius." "Yes," he said, "if you hear the same about
human ones." "I do," he replied, "and I agree." "Well, if
you assent to that," said Apollonius, "do not meddle with
the decisions of heaven, since that is what human wisdom
recommends." The man begged Apollonius to give his interpretation, being afraid that all the world would pass into

[44] Literally a "crown" (*stephanos*), alluding to Stephanus,
Domitian's assassin (cf. 25.1).

μεταστῇ πάντα, "θάρρει," ἔφη "ἔσται γάρ τι ἐκ τῆς
νυκτὸς ταύτης φῶς."

24. Μετὰ ταῦθ' ὁ μέν, ἐπειδὴ τῶν κατὰ τὴν Ἑλλάδα
ἱκανῶς εἶχε δυοῖν ἐνδιατρίψας ἐτοῖν, ἔπλει ἐς Ἰωνίαν
ξυνεπομένης αὐτῷ τῆς ἑταιρείας, καὶ τὸν μὲν πλείω
χρόνον ἐφιλοσόφει περὶ τὴν Σμύρναν τε καὶ τὴν
Ἔφεσον, ἐπιὼν καὶ τὰς ἄλλας καὶ ἐν οὐδεμιᾷ τῶν
πόλεων ἀηδὴς εἶναι δοκῶν, ἀλλὰ καὶ ποθεῖσθαι ἄξιος
καὶ κέρδος μέγα τοῖς δεξιοῖς.

25. Ἐώθουν δὲ οἱ θεοὶ Δομετιανὸν ἤδη τῆς τῶν
ἀνθρώπων προεδρίας. ἔτυχε μὲν γὰρ Κλήμεντα ἀπεκτονὼς ἄνδρα ὕπατον, ᾧ τὴν ἀδελφὴν τὴν ἑαυτοῦ
ἐδεδώκει, πρόσταγμα δ' ἐπεποίητο περὶ τὴν τρίτην
ἢ τετάρτην ἡμέραν τοῦ φόνου κἀκείνην ἐς ἀνδρὸς
φοιτᾶν. Στέφανος τοίνυν ἀπελεύθερος τῆς γυναικός,
ὃν ἐδήλου τὸ τῆς διοσημίας σχῆμα, εἴτε τὸν τεθνεῶτα
ἐνθυμηθείς, εἴτε πάντας, ὥρμησε μὲν ἴσα τοῖς ἐλευ-
θερωτάτοις Ἀθηναίοις ἐπὶ τὸν τύραννον, ξίφος δ'
ὑφείρας τῷ τῆς ἀριστερᾶς πήχει καὶ τὴν χεῖρα ἐπι-
δέσμοις ἀναλαβὼν οἷον κατεαγυῖαν, ἀπιόντι τοῦ
δικαστηρίου προσελθὼν "δέομαί σου," ἔφη "βασιλεῦ,
μόνου, μεγάλα γάρ, ὑπὲρ ὧν ἀκούσῃ." οὐκ ἀπαξιώ-
σαντος δὲ τοῦ τυράννου τὴν ἀκρόασιν ἀπολαβὼν
αὐτὸν ἐς τὸν ἀνδρῶνα, οὗ τὰ βασίλεια, "οὐ τέθνηκεν"
εἶπεν "ὁ πολεμιώτατός σοι Κλήμης, ὡς σὺ οἴει, ἀλλ'
ἔστιν οὗ ἐγὼ οἶδα, καὶ ξυντάττει ἑαυτὸν ἐπὶ σέ."

2   Μέγα δ' αὐτοῦ βοήσαντος περὶ ὧν ἤκουσε, τετα-
ραγμένῳ προσπεσὼν ὁ Στέφανος καὶ τὸ ξίφος τῆς

perpetual darkness, but Apollonius said, "Never fear, for out of this darkness will come a kind of light."

24. After this, when he had been in Greece long enough, since he had spent two years there, he sailed to Ionia followed by his disciples. Most of the time he spent practicing philosophy in Smyrna and Ephesus, though he also visited the other cities, and in none of them did he seem unwelcome, but rather someone to be desired and a great benefit to the intelligent.

25. The gods had at last begun to remove Domitian from his supremacy over mankind. He had just executed Clemens, a man of consular rank, to whom he had given his sister's hand, and about two or three days after the murder had issued an order that she was to follow her husband.[45] So Stephanus, the woman's freedman, who was indicated by the form of the portent, out of sympathy for the dead man, or for all the dead, plotted against the tyrant in a way worthy of the most freedom-loving Athenians. Tying a knife under his left forearm, and supporting his arm in a sling as if it were broken, he approached Domitian as he was leaving his court and said, "I must speak to you alone, Majesty. It is something important you are going to hear about." Domitian thought the matter worth his attention, and so Stephanus led him off to the men's quarters, where the royal chambers were, and said, "He is not dead as you suppose, your mortal enemy Clemens, but I know his whereabouts, and he is arming himself against you."

The emperor gave a great shout at the news, and Stephanus, attacking him off guard, drew the knife from

---

[45] Flavius Clemens and Flavia Domitilla.

ἐσκευασμένης χειρὸς ἀνασπάσας, διῆκε τοῦ μηροῦ
πρὸς μὲν τὸν αὐτίκα θάνατον οὐ καιρίαν, πρὸς δὲ τὸν
μετὰ ταῦτα οὐκ ἄκαιρον. ὁ δ' ἐρρωμένος μὲν καὶ
ἄλλως τὸ σῶμα, γεγονὼς δὲ περὶ τὰ πέντε καὶ τετταράκοντα ἔτη ξυνεπλάκη τρωθείς, καὶ καταβαλὼν
τὸν Στέφανον ἐπέκειτο τοὺς ὀφθαλμοὺς ὀρύττων καὶ
τὰς παρειὰς ξυντρίβων πυθμένι χρυσῆς κύλικος, αὐτοῦ κειμένης περὶ τὰ ἱερά, ἐκάλει δὲ καὶ τὴν Ἀθηνᾶν
ἀρωγόν. συνέντες οὖν οἱ δορυφόροι κακῶς πράττοντος
ἐσῆλθον ἀθρόοι καὶ τὸν τύραννον ἀπέκτειναν λιποθυ-
μοῦντα ἤδη.

26. Ταῦτ' ἐπράττετο μὲν κατὰ τὴν Ῥώμην, ἑωρᾶτο
δ' Ἀπολλωνίῳ κατὰ τὴν Ἔφεσον. διαλεγόμενος γὰρ
περὶ τὰ τῶν ξυστῶν ἄλση κατὰ μεσημβρίαν, ὅτε δὴ
καὶ τὰ ἐν τοῖς βασιλείοις ἐγίγνετο, πρῶτον μὲν ὑφῆκε
τῆς φωνῆς, οἷον δείσας, εἶτ' ἐλλιπέστερον ἢ κατὰ τὴν
ἑαυτοῦ δύναμιν ἡρμήνευσεν ἴσα τοῖς μεταξὺ λόγων
διορῶσί τι ἕτερον, εἶτα ἐσιώπησεν, ὥσπερ οἱ τῶν
λόγων ἐκπεσόντες, βλέψας τε δεινὸν ἐς τὴν γῆν καὶ
προβὰς τρία ἢ τέτταρα τῶν βημάτων "παῖε τὸν τύραννον, παῖε" ἐβόα, οὐχ ὥσπερ ἐκ κατόπτρου τινὸς
εἴδωλον ἀληθείας ἕλκων, ἀλλ' αὐτὰ ὁρῶν καὶ ξυλ-
λαμβάνειν δοκῶν τὰ δρώμενα.

2   Ἐκπεπληγμένης δὲ τῆς Ἐφέσου, παρῆν γὰρ διαλεγομένῳ πᾶσα, ἐπισχὼν ὅσον οἱ διορῶντες, ἔστ' ἂν
γένηταί τι τῶν ἀμφιβόλων τέλος "θαρρεῖτε," εἶπεν "ὦ
ἄνδρες, ὁ γὰρ τύραννος ἀπέσφακται τήμερον. τί λέγω

its hiding in his arm and drove it through Domitian's thigh, giving him a blow not immediately fatal, but destined to be fatal thereafter. Domitian was of generally strong physique, being about forty-five years old, and grappled with Stephanus despite his wound, knocked him down and pinned him, gouging his eyes and hitting his face with the stem of a golden cup that was standing there for use in ritual. At the same time he called on Athena for help. Realizing he was in distress, the bodyguards all burst in and killed the tyrant when he was already losing consciousness.

26. All this happened in Rome, but Apollonius observed it in Ephesus. He was holding a discussion among the trees of the park about noon, the very time when the events in the palace took place. First he dropped his voice, as if afraid, and then began to express himself with less than his usual power, as people do who observe something different in the middle of a speech, and then fell silent, as people do when breaking their speech off. He stared hard at the ground, stepped three or four paces forward, and shouted, "Strike the tyrant! Strike!" not as if he was drawing some reflection of reality from a mirror, but seeing the actual thing and seeming to take part in the action.[46]

All the Ephesians were present at the lecture, and were astounded until Apollonius, after waiting as people do to watch the outcome of a close contest, said, "Have no fear, gentlemen, since the tyrant was slaughtered today. Why do

2

[46] Cassius Dio (67.18) gives a similar account.

τήμερον; ἄρτι, νὴ τὴν Ἀθηνᾶν, ἄρτι, περὶ τὸν καιρὸν τῶν ῥημάτων, οἷς ἐπεσιώπησα." μανίαν δὲ ταῦθ᾽ ἡγουμένων τῶν κατὰ τὴν Ἔφεσον, καὶ βουλομένων ἀληθεύειν αὐτὸν, δεδιότων δὲ τὸν τῆς ἀκροάσεως κίνδυνον, "οὐ θαυμάζω" ἔφη "τῶν μήπω προσδεχομένων τὸν λόγον, ὃν μηδ᾽ ἡ Ῥώμη γιγνώσκει πᾶσα· ἀλλ᾽ ἰδοὺ γιγνώσκει, διαφοιτᾷ γάρ, καὶ πιστεύουσι μὲν ἤδη μύριοι, πηδῶσι δ᾽ ὑφ᾽ ἡδονῆς δὶς τόσοι καὶ διπλάσιοι τούτων καὶ τετραπλάσιοι καὶ πάντες οἱ ἐκείνῃ δῆμοι. ἀφίξεται τουτὶ τὸ ῥῆμα καὶ δεῦρο, καὶ τὸ μὲν θύειν ὑμᾶς ἐπ᾽ αὐτοῖς ἀναβεβλήσθω ἐς καιρόν, ὃν ἀπαγγελθήσεται ταῦτα, ἐγὼ δὲ εἶμι προσευξόμενος τοῖς θεοῖς ὑπὲρ ὧν εἶδον."

27. Ἔτ᾽ ἀπιστουμένων τούτων ἦλθον οἱ τῶν εὐαγγελίων δρόμοι μάρτυρες τῆς σοφίας τοῦ ἀνδρός, καὶ γὰρ ἡ τοῦ τυράννου σφαγὴ καὶ ἡ τοῦτο ἐνεγκοῦσα ἡμέρα καὶ ἡ μεσημβρία καὶ οἱ κτείνοντες, πρὸς οὓς ἡ παρακέλευσις, οὕτως εἶχεν, ὡς οἱ θεοὶ τούτων ἕκαστα διαλεγομένῳ τῷ ἀνδρὶ ἀνέφαινον. τριάκοντα δ᾽ ἡμέραις μετὰ ταῦτα ἐπιστείλαντος αὐτῷ τοῦ Νερούα τὴν μὲν ἀρχὴν ἤδη τῶν Ῥωμαίων ἔχειν θεῶν τε βουλαῖς κἀκείνου, κατασχεῖν δ᾽ ἂν αὐτὴν ῥᾷον, εἰ ξύμβουλος αὐτῷ ἔλθοι, τὸ μὲν αὐτίκα ἐκεῖνο γράφει πρὸς αὐτὸν αἴνιγμα· "ξυνεσόμεθα, ὦ βασιλεῦ, χρόνον ἀλλήλοις πλεῖστον, ὃν μήτε ἡμεῖς ἑτέρου, μήτ᾽ ἄλλος ἡμῶν ἄρξει," συνιεὶς ἴσως ἑαυτοῦ τε, ὡς μετ᾽ οὐ πολὺ μεταστησομένου ἀνθρώπων, Νερούα τε, ὡς χρόνον βρα-

I say today? Just now, I swear by Athena, just now, about the moment when I fell silent in my talk." Those in Ephesus thought this was madness, and although they wanted him to be right, were afraid of the danger if they listened. "I am not surprised," said Apollonius, "at those who do not yet accept the report, when not even all of Rome knows. But look, Rome is learning now, the rumor is spreading, now ten thousand believe it, now twice as many are jumping for joy, now twice that number, now four times, now all the cities there. This message will arrive here too, and you may postpone sacrificing for the event until the moment of its announcement, but I am going to thank the gods for what I have seen."

27. The story had still not gained credence when messengers came with the good tidings and confirmed the Master's wisdom. The killing of the tyrant, the day that had brought it about, the noon hour, the assassins whom Apollonius had cheered on, all these details proved exactly as the gods had revealed to the Master during his lecture. Thirty days later Nerva wrote to him saying that he now held power in Rome, by the gods' will and that of Apollonius, but he would retain it more easily if Apollonius came as his adviser. For the moment, Apollonius wrote an enigmatic reply as follows, "We will be together a very long time, Majesty, when we are nobody's rulers, and nobody is ours." Perhaps he realized that he himself was to leave this world not long after, and that Nerva was to rule only briefly,

χὺν ἄρξοντος, ἐς ἐνιαυτὸν γὰρ καὶ μῆνας τέτταρας τὰ τῆς βασιλείας αὐτῷ προὔβη σωφρονεστάτῳ δόξαντι.

28. Ἵνα δὲ μὴ ἀμελῶν φαίνοιτο φίλου τε ἀγαθοῦ καὶ ἄρχοντος, ξυνέθηκε μετὰ ταῦτα πρὸς αὐτὸν ἐπιστολὴν ξύμβουλον τῶν ἀρχικῶν καὶ καλέσας τὸν Δάμιν "σοῦ" ἔφη "δεῖται ταῦτα, τὰ γὰρ ἀπόρρητα τῆς ἐπιστολῆς γέγραπται μὲν πρὸς τὸν βασιλέα, ἔστι δ᾽ οἷα ἢ ὑπ᾽ ἐμοῦ λέγεσθαι ἢ διὰ σοῦ." καὶ ὀψὲ ὁ Δάμις ξυνεῖναί φησι τῆς τέχνης, τὴν μὲν γὰρ ἐπιστολὴν ἄριστά τε αὐτῷ καὶ ὑπὲρ μεγάλων ξυγγεγράφθαι, πεμφθῆναι δ᾽ ἂν καὶ δι᾽ ἑτέρου. τίς οὖν ἡ τέχνη τοῦ ἀνδρός; πάντα τὸν χρόνον, ὃν ἐβίω, λέγεται θαμὰ ἐπιφθέγγεσθαι "λάθε βιώσας, εἰ δὲ μὴ δύναιο, λάθε ἀποβιώσας"· ἀπάγων οὖν ἑαυτοῦ τὸν Δάμιν, ἵνα μὴ ὑπὸ μάρτυσι καταλύοι, τὴν ἐπιστολὴν ἐσκήψατο καὶ τὸ ἀναφοιτῆσαι αὐτὸν ἐς τὴν Ῥώμην. αὐτὸς μὲν δὴ παθεῖν τι ἀπιὼν αὐτοῦ φησιν οὐδὲ εἰδὼς τὰ μέλλοντα, τὸν δ᾽ εὖ εἰδότα μηδὲν μέν οἱ εἰπεῖν, ὥσπερ εἰώθασιν οἱ μηκέτ᾽ ἀλλήλους ὀψόμενοι, τοσοῦτον αὐτῷ περιεῖναι τοῦ πεπεῖσθαι, ὅτι ἀεὶ ἔσται, παρεγγυῆσαι δὲ ὧδε· "ὦ Δάμι, κἂν ἐπὶ σεαυτοῦ φιλοσοφῇς, ἐμὲ ὅρα."

29. Τὰ μὲν δὴ ἐς Ἀπολλώνιον τὸν Τυανέα Δάμιδι τῷ Ἀσσυρίῳ ἀναγεγραμμένα ἐς τόνδε τὸν λόγον τελευτᾷ, περὶ γὰρ τρόπου, καθ᾽ ὃν ἐτελεύτα, εἴγε ἐτελεύτα, πλείους μὲν λόγοι, Δάμιδι δὲ οὐδεὶς εἴρηται, ἐμοὶ δὲ οὐδὲ τοῦτο χρὴ παραλελεῖφθαι, δεῖ γάρ που τὸν λόγον ἔχειν τὸ ἑαυτοῦ πέρας. οὐδ᾽ ὑπὲρ ἡλικίας τοῦ ἀνδρὸς εἴρηται οὐδὲν τῷ Δάμιδι, ἀλλὰ τοῖς μὲν ὀγδο-

since his reign lasted for a year and four months, and he
showed great moderation.

28. Not however wanting to seem to slight a good friend
and a good ruler, Apollonius later composed a letter to him
with advice about kingship. Summoning Damis, he said,
"You are needed for this mission, since the confidential
parts of the letter are written for the emperor, but there
are matters such as only I or you can say to him." Damis
says he only understood Apollonius's stratagem later, for
although the letter was excellently written and concerned
weighty matters, it might have had another carrier. And
what was the Master's stratagem? Throughout his life, they
say, Apollonius often made this pronouncement: "Live unobserved, but if you cannot, leave this life unobserved."
In order therefore to make Damis leave him and to have
no witness to his own end, he thought up the letter and
Damis's mission to Rome. Damis says that he was rather
moved on leaving, though he did not know the future,
while Apollonius who knew it well said to him nothing
such as people say who are never to see each other again,
so fully was he certain of everlasting life. Instead he gave
him this injunction: "Even when you seek wisdom by yourself, Damis, observe me."

29. The account of Apollonius of Tyana given by Damis
the Assyrian ends with these words. As for the manner of
his death, if he did die, there are many versions, though
none given by Damis. I, however, must not leave this item
out, for my account surely must have its proper ending.
Damis has not said anything about the Master's age either,

ἥκοντα, τοῖς δ' ὑπὲρ τὰ ἐνενήκοντα, τοῖς δὲ καὶ πρόσω
τῶν ἑκατὸν ἐλθεῖν ἡβάσκων³¹ πᾶν τὸ σῶμα καὶ ἄρ-
τιος, νεότητος δὲ ἡδίων. ἔστι γάρ τις ὥρα καὶ περὶ
ῥυτίσιν, ἣ μάλιστα περὶ ἐκεῖνον ἤνθησεν, ὡς εἰκόνες
τε δηλοῦσι τἀνδρὸς ἐν τῷ Τυανάδε ἱερῷ καὶ λόγοι
μᾶλλον ὑμνοῦντες τὸ Ἀπολλωνίου γῆρας ἢ τὴν Ἀλκι-
βιάδου ποτὲ νεότητα.

30. Τελευτῆσαι δ' αὐτὸν οἱ μὲν ἐν Ἐφέσῳ θεραπευ-
όμενον ὑπὸ δυοῖν δμωαῖν, τεθνάναι γὰρ ἤδη οἱ ἀπ-
ελεύθεροι, περὶ ὧν κατ' ἀρχὰς εἶπον, ἐλευθερώσαντα
δὲ τὴν ἑτέραν αἰτίαν πρὸς τῆς ἑτέρας ἔχειν, ἐπεὶ μὴ
τῶν αὐτῶν ἠξίωτο, τὸν δ' Ἀπολλώνιον "καὶ δουλεῦσαι"
φάναι "προσήκει σὲ αὐτῇ, τουτὶ γάρ σοι ἀγαθοῦ
ἄρξει." τελευτήσαντος οὖν ἡ μὲν δουλεύειν ἐκείνη, ἡ δ'
ἐκ μικρᾶς αἰτίας ἀποδόσθαι αὐτὴν καπήλῳ, παρ' οὗ
πρίασθαί τις οὐδ' εὐπρεπῆ οὖσαν, ἀλλ' ἐρῶν οὗτος καὶ
χρηματιστὴς ἱκανὸς ὢν γυναῖκά τε ἀνειπεῖν καὶ παῖδας ἐξ αὐτῆς ἐγγράψαι.

2   Οἱ δ' ἐν Λίνδῳ τελευτῆσαι αὐτὸν παρελθόντα ἐς τὸ
ἱερὸν τῆς Ἀθηνᾶς καὶ ἔσω ἀφανισθέντα, οἱ δ' ἐν
Κρήτῃ φασὶ θαυμασιώτερον ἢ οἱ ἐν Λίνδῳ· διατρίβειν
μὲν γὰρ ἐν τῇ Κρήτῃ τὸν Ἀπολλώνιον μᾶλλον ἢ πρὸ
τούτου θαυμαζόμενον, ἀφικέσθαι δ' ἐς τὸ ἱερὸν τῆς
Δικτύννης ἀωρί, φυλακῇ δὲ τῷ ἱερῷ κυνῶν ἐπιτέτακται
φρουροὶ τοῦ ἐν αὐτῷ πλούτου, καὶ ἀξιοῦσιν αὐτοὺς οἱ
Κρῆτες μήτε τῶν ἄρκτων μήτε τῶν ὧδε ἀγρίων λεί-

³¹ ἡβάσκων Jon. (ἀνηβάσκων West.): γηράσκων

though some say it was eighty, some over ninety, and some
that he passed a hundred, youthful and sound in all his
body, and handsomer than a young man. Even wrinkles
have a kind of bloom, and in him it was especially evident,
as can be seen from the Master's statues in the sanctuary
at Tyana[47] and by descriptions that celebrate Apollonius's
old age more than they once celebrated the youth of
Alcibiades.

30. Some say he died in Ephesus in the care of two maid
servants, for the freedmen whom I mentioned at the beginning were now dead. When he set one of these women
free, and he was reproached by the other for not doing the
same favor to her, he said, "You should even be her slave,
since that will bring you luck." So at his death the one became the other's slave, until her mistress for some petty
reason sold her to a trader, and someone bought her from
him, though she was no beauty. Even so, this man fell in
love with her, and being a smart businessman made her his
wife and acknowledged his children by her.

Others say that he died in Lindos after passing into the　2
sanctuary of Athena and vanishing inside. Another version
is that he died in Crete even more miraculously than is related at Lindos. Apollonius was staying in Crete, admired
even more than before, when he visited the sanctuary of
Dictynna at dead of night. Protection of the sanctuary is
entrusted to dogs that guard its treasures, and the Cretans
consider them nothing short of bears or other animals
equally savage. But they did not even bark when Apollo-

---

[47] See 31.3.

πεσθαι, οἱ δ᾽ οὔθ᾽ ὑλακτεῖν ἥκοντα σαίνειν τε αὐτὸν
προσιόντες, ὡς μηδὲ τοὺς ἄγαν ἐθάδας.

3   Οἱ μὲν δὴ τοῦ ἱεροῦ προϊστάμενοι ξυλλαβόντες
αὐτὸν ὡς γόητα καὶ λῃστὴν δῆσαι, μείλιγμα τοῖς κυσὶ
προβεβλῆσθαί τι ὑπ᾽ αὐτοῦ φάσκοντες. ὁ δ᾽ ἀμφὶ
μέσας νύκτας ἑαυτὸν λῦσαι, καλέσας δὲ τοὺς δήσαν-
τας, ὡς μὴ λάθοι, δραμεῖν ἐπὶ τὰς τοῦ ἱεροῦ θύρας, αἱ
δ᾽ ἀνεπετάσθησαν, παρελθόντος δὲ ἔσω τὰς μὲν θύρας
ξυνελθεῖν, ὥσπερ ἐκέκλειντο, βοὴν δὲ ᾀδουσῶν παρ-
θένων ἐκπεσεῖν. τὸ δὲ ᾆσμα ἦν· "στεῖχε γᾶς, στεῖχε ἐς
οὐρανόν, στεῖχε." οἷον· ἴθι ἐκ τῆς γῆς ἄνω.

31. Περὶ ψυχῆς δέ, ὡς ἀθάνατος εἴη, ἐφιλοσόφει
ἔτι, διδάσκων μέν, ὅτι ἀληθὴς ὁ ὑπὲρ αὐτῆς λόγος,
πολυπραγμονεῖν δὲ μὴ ξυγχωρῶν τὰ ὧδε μεγάλα.
ἀφίκετο μὲν γὰρ ἐς τὰ Τύανα μειράκιον θρασὺ περὶ
τὰς ἔριδας καὶ μὴ ξυντιθέμενον ἀληθεῖ λόγῳ, τοῦ δὲ
Ἀπολλωνίου ἐξ ἀνθρώπων μὲν ἤδη ὄντος, θαυμα-
ζομένου δ᾽ ἐπὶ τῇ μεταβολῇ καὶ μηδ᾽ ἀντιλέξαι θαρ-
ροῦντος μηδενός, ὡς οὐκ ἀθάνατος εἴη, λόγοι μὲν οἱ
πλείους ὑπὲρ ψυχῆς ἐγίγνοντο, καὶ γὰρ νεότης τις ἦν
αὐτόθι σοφίας ἐρῶντες, τὸ δὲ μειράκιον οὐδαμῶς τῇ
τῆς ψυχῆς ἀθανασίᾳ ξυντιθέμενον "ἐγώ," ἔφη "ὦ παρ-
όντες, τουτονὶ μῆνα δέκατον Ἀπολλωνίῳ διατελῶ εὐχόμενος ἀναφῆναί μοι τὸν ὑπὲρ ψυχῆς λόγον, ὁ δ᾽
οὕτω τέθηκεν, ὡς μηδ᾽ ἐφίστασθαι δεομένῳ, μηδ᾽, ὡς
ἀθάνατος εἴη, πείθειν."

2   Τοιαῦτα μὲν τὸ μειράκιον τότε, πέμπτῃ δὲ ἀπ᾽
ἐκείνης ἡμέρᾳ περὶ τῶν αὐτῶν σπουδάσαν κατέδαρθε

nius arrived, but ran up and greeted him even more than
they did those they were fully accustomed to.

The officials of the sanctuary put him in chains as a sor-   3
cerer and a robber, claiming that he had thrown something
to the dogs to pacify them. But at about midnight he set
himself free, and after calling his jailers so that they would
notice, he ran to the doors of the sanctuary, which flew
open. As he entered, the doors returned to their original
position, and there emerged the sound of girls singing, and
their song went, "Proceed from earth! Proceed to heaven!
Proceed!" In other words, "Ascend from earth."

31. The immortality of the soul continued to be his
doctrine, and he taught that the account of it is correct,
but discouraged curiosity about such weighty matters. A
young man arrived in Tyana who was eager for disputes,
and did not accept the true doctrine. Apollonius had then
departed from humanity, but his transfiguration caused
amazement and nobody ventured to deny that he was immortal. Most of their discussions concerned the soul, since
there was a group of young men devoted to wisdom. The
young man, who in no way accepted the immortality of
the soul, said "I, my friends, have continually prayed to
Apollonius for nine months now to reveal the doctrine of
the soul. But he is so truly dead that he has not even appeared as I asked, or persuaded me of his immortality."

That was what the young man said then, but four days   2
later he was discussing the same subject when he fell

μὲν οὗ διελέγετο, τῶν δὲ ξυσπουδαζόντων νέων οἱ μὲν
πρὸς βιβλίοις ἦσαν, οἱ δ᾽ ἐσπούδαζον γεωμετρικοὺς
ἐπιχαράττοντες τύπους τῇ γῇ, τὸ δ᾽, ὥσπερ ἐμμανές,
ἀναπηδῆσαν ὡμόυπνον ἱδρῶτί τε πολλῷ ἐρρεῖτο καὶ
ἐβόα "πείθομαί σοι." ἐρομένων δ᾽ αὐτὸ τῶν παρόντων,
ὅ τι πέπονθεν, "οὐχ ὁρᾶτε" ἔφη "ὑμεῖς Ἀπολλώνιον
τὸν σοφόν, ὡς παρατυγχάνει τε ἡμῖν ἐπακροώμενος
τοῦ λόγου καὶ περὶ ψυχῆς ῥαψῳδεῖ θαυμάσια;" "ποῦ δ᾽
οὗτος;" ἔφασαν "ὡς ἡμῖν γε οὐδαμοῦ φαίνεται, καίτοι
βουλομένοις ἂν τοῦτο μᾶλλον ἢ τὰ πάντων ἀνθρώπων
ἀγαθὰ ἔχειν."

3   Καὶ τὸ μειράκιον "ἔοικεν ἐμοὶ μόνῳ διαλεξόμενος
ἥκειν ὑπὲρ ὧν μὴ ἐπίστευον· ἀκούετ᾽ οὖν, οἷα τῷ λόγῳ
ἐπιθειάζει·

ἀθάνατος ψυχὴ κοὐ χρῆμα σόν, ἀλλὰ προνοίης,
ἣ μετὰ σῶμα μαρανθέν, ἅτ᾽ ἐκ δεσμῶν θοὸς
       ἵππος,
ῥῃδίως προθοροῦσα κεράννυται ἠέρι κούφῳ,
δεινὴν καὶ πολύτλητον ἀποστέρξασα λατρείην.
σοὶ δὲ τί τῶνδ᾽ ὄφελος, ὅ ποτ᾽ οὐκέτ᾽ ἐὼν τότε
       δόξεις;
ἢ τί μετὰ ζῳοῖσιν ἐὼν περὶ τῶνδε ματεύεις;"

καὶ σαφὴς οὗτος Ἀπολλωνίου τρίπους ἕστηκεν ὑπὲρ
τῶν τῆς ψυχῆς ἀπορρήτων, ἵν᾽ εὔθυμοί τε καὶ τὴν
αὑτῶν φύσιν εἰδότες, οἳ τάττουσι Μοῖραι, πορευοί-
μεθα. τάφῳ μὲν οὖν ἢ ψευδοταφίῳ τοῦ ἀνδρὸς οὐδαμοῦ προστυχὼν οἶδα, καίτοι τῆς γῆς, ὁπόση ἐστίν,

asleep on the spot where he had been talking, while his young fellow students concentrated on their books, or busied themselves with drawing geometrical figures on the ground. But he, as if he were mad, jumped up out of a deep sleep sweating profusely, and shouted, "I believe you." When those present asked what had happened, he said, "Don't you see the wise Apollonius? He is with us listening to our conversation, and rhapsodizing marvelously about the soul." "Where is he?" they asked; "We cannot see him anywhere, though we would prefer that to all the riches in the world."

The youth said, "It seems that he has come to talk to me   3
alone about the things I failed to believe, so let me tell you how he immortalizes the doctrine:

Immortal is the soul, and is not yours
But Providence's. When the body wastes,
The soul starts like a racehorse from the gate,
And nimbly leaping mingles with light air,
Hating its fearful, heavy servitude.
For you, what use is this? When you're no more
You will believe it: why then while alive
Pry uselessly into such hidden things?"

This is Apollonius's clear pronouncement on the mysteries of the soul, enabling us with courage and knowledge of our own natures to journey to the place where the Fates station us. As for a tomb or cenotaph of the Master, I do not remember ever having met with one anywhere, although I have crossed most of the present world, but I have met

APOLLONIUS OF TYANA

ἐπελθὼν πλείστην, λόγοις δὲ πανταχοῦ δαιμονίοις,
καὶ ἱερὰ Τύανάδε βασιλείοις ἐκπεποιημένα τέλεσιν·
οὐδὲ γὰρ βασιλεῖς ἀπηξίουν αὐτὸν ὧν αὐτοὶ ἠξιοῦντο.

with unearthly accounts of him everywhere. There is also a sanctuary to him at Tyana, built at imperial expense,[48] since emperors have not denied to him what has been conferred on themselves.

[48] Caracalla dedicated a sanctuary to Apollonius at Tyana, cf. Cassius Dio 78.18.4.

INDEX

Abae: 4.24.1

Abaris: 7.10.1

Abdera: 8.7.25

Abinna: 5.1

Acarnania: 7.25

Acesines: 2.17.1

Achaea, Achaeans: 3.19.1, 4.13.2–3, 4.16.4, 5.26.1, 6.35.1, 7.10.1

Acharnae: 4.21.2

Achelous: 7.25

Achilles: as depicted by Homer, 2.22.5, 3.19.2, 3.20.3, 7.36.2; appears to A., 4.11–12, 4.13.2, 4.15.2–16.2, 4.16.4, 4.23

Acragas: 8.7.25

Acrisius: 8.7.47

Acropolis, Athenian: 3.13

Adonis: 7.32.1

Adrasteia: 1.25.3, 8.7.14

Adriatic Sea: 4.24.2, 5.11, 8.15.1

Aeacus: 5.26.1, 7.31.3

Aegaeon, title of Poseidon: 4.6

Aegeae: 1.7.2, 1.8.2, 1.12.1, 1.13.1, 2.14.4, 3.16.3

Aegean Sea: 1.24.2, 4.24.2

Aegina: 4.24.3

Aegospotami: 1.2.2

Aelianus (Casperius): 7.16–20, 7.22.1, 7.28.1, 7.32.1, 7.40

Aeolus: 3.14.2, 7.14.8

Aeschines, Athenian orator: 1.35.1

Aeschylus: 4.39.2, 6.11.10

Aesop: 5.14–16.1, 7.30.3

Africa, Africans: 2.13.1, 4.34.3, 5.1, 5.3, 5.11, 6.1.1

Aianteion: 4.13.1

Aidoneus: 8.7.48

Ajax: 2.22.5, 3.19.2

Alcestis: 4.45.1

Alcibiades: 8.29

Alcinous: 4.20.1

Alcmaeon, son of Amphiaraos: 4.38.4, 7.25

Alexander, of Macedon: 1.35.3, 7.2.3, 8.7.43; in India, 2.9.3, 2.12.2, 2.20.2–3, 2.21.2, 2.24, 2.33.1, 2.42, 3.53

Alexandria, Alexandrians: 5.24.1, 5.26.1, 5.43.1

Aloeus: 7.26.6

Alpheus: 8.15.1, 8.18.3

Amasis: 5.42.1–2

Ammon: 2.43

Amoebeus: 5.7.2

Amphiaraus: 2.37.2, 4.24.1

INDEX

Amphictyony: 4.23
Amphilochia: 6.43.1
Amymone: 1.25.2
Anaxagoras, of Clazomenae:
  1.2.2, 1.13.2, 2.5.3, 8.7.26
Anchises: 6.40.2
Andromache: 2.14.4
Andromeda: 1.25.2
Anthesterion: 4.21.1
Antioch, in Syria: 1.16.1,
  1.16.4–18, 1.31, 3.58, 6.38
Antiochus (I?): 1.38.1
Antisthenes, of Paros: 4.12,
  4.25.1
Antium: 8.12.3, 8.20
Anytos: 7.11.2, 7.13.2
Aornos: 2.10
Aphrodite: 3.58, 6.3.5, 6.40.1;
  her statue on Cnidus, 6.19.1
Apollo: 1.1.2, 1.16.1–2, 3.14.3,
  3.44, 4.14, 5.15.2, 8.13.2; of
  Delphi, 2.9.1, 2.43, 3.42.1,
  6.10.4, 7.14.9, 8.7.21. *See also*
  Delphi
"Apollonians": 8.21
Arabia, Arabs: 1.20.2–3, 3.57.2,
  4.38.3
Arcadia, Arcadians: 1.16.1–2,
  5.35.2; site of Olympic
  Games, 1.35.3, 4.28.1, 5.8,
  5.35.2; A. and Arcadian boy,
  7.20.1, 7.42.2, 7.42.4–5,
  8.7.35–38
Archelaus, last king of
  Cappadocia: 1.12.2
Archilochus, of Paros: 2.7.2,
  7.26.2
Archytas: 6.31.1
Arcturus: 5.18

Ares: 6.11.18, 7.12.4, 7.26.6
Arginusae: 4.32.1
Argos, Argives: 3.25.3, 3.31.3,
  8.15.2
Aricia: 4.36.1, 5.43.1
Aristander, of Lycia: 8.7.43
Aristides, son of Lysimachus:
  6.21.4–6, 7.21.1–2
Aristippus of Cyrene: 1.35.1
Aristotle: 5.36.2
Armenia, Armenians: 1.19.1,
  1.20.2, 2.2.1
Arsaces: 2.2.2
Artaphernes: 1.25.2
Artaxerxes: (I), 1.29; (II), 1.28.2
Artemis: 1.30, 6.20.2
Artemisia: 4.21.2
Asbamaean fountain: 1.6
Asclepiads (doctors), 3.44,
  6.35.2
Asclepius: 3.17.2, 3.44, 4.11.1,
  4.18.1, 4.34.3; cult at Aegeae,
  1.7.2, 1.8.2–9.1, 1.10.2,
  1.11.2–12.1
Asia: 7.5, 7.10.1
Aspendus: 1.15.2–3
Asses, wild: 3.2.1
Assyria, Assyrians: 2.9.2, 7.32.1
Astyages, the Mede: 8.7.47
Athena: 2.43, 3.14.3, 7.6, 8.30.2;
  Athena and Domitian, 7.24,
  7.26.3, 7.32.1–2, 8.7.2–3,
  8.7.29, 8.16, 8.25.2
Athens: 2.10, 2.23, 3.17.2,
  5.19.1, 6.6.1, 6.20.4, 6.21.4,
  8.25.1; in Persian Wars,
  1.25.2, 3.31.1–3; A. in, 4.17–
  18.1, 4.19, 4.22.1, 5.20.2,
  8.23; notable citizens of, 5.4,

428

INDEX

6.11.8, 6.11.10–11, 7.3.2,
7.21.1, 8.2.2, 8.7.1, 8.15.2,
8.16, 8.7.21
Athos: 1.25.2, 2.5.3, 4.40.4
Atlas: 2.13.1
Atreus: 5.26.1
Attica: 5.6, 8.7.25
Augustus: 5.7.2
Aulis: 1.22.2, 3.6.2, 8.19.2

Babylon: A. in, 1.18, 1.21.1,
1.21.3, 1.24.1, 1.25.1, 1.27;
king of, 2.27.1, 2.40.1–2,
3.58. *See also* Vardanes
Bacchus: 3.15.3, 6.10.2, 6.11.18
Bactria: 5.33.4
Baetica: 5.6, 5.9.1, 5.10.1
Baetis River: 5.6
Balara: 3.56
Bassus, of Corinth: 4.26
Bears: 2.14.2
Biblus: 3.53
Boeotia: 8.15.2, 8.19.1, 8.23
Boreas: 4.21.3
Brahmans: 1.2.1, 1.18, 3.15.1–2,
8.7.14

Cabiri of Samothrace: 2.43
Cadusians: 1.19.1
Calchas: 1.22.2
Callicratidas: 4.32.1
Callisthenes, of Olynthus: 7.2.2,
7.3.2
Calpis: 5.1
Calypso: 7.10.2, 7.41, 8.11
Cannibals: 6.25
Canus: 5.21.2, 5.21.4
Caphereus: 1.24.2
Capitol: 5.30.2

Cappadocia: 1.4, 1.12.2
Caria, Carians: 2.2.1, 3.25.1,
3.55, 4.21.2
Carmani: 3.55
Carthage: 4.32.1
Cassander: 1.35.1
Castalia: 6.10.4
Castration: 1.34.1
Catania: 5.14.1
Cataracts: 3.20.1, 6.25, 6.26.2–
27.1
Caucasus: 1.41.2, 2.2.1, 2.5.1,
2.9.2, 2.18.1, 3.4.1
Cephisus: 6.10.4
Celts: 5.2–3, 8.7.24
Chaeronea: 7.2.3, 7.3.2
Chaldaea, Chaldaeans: 6.41
Charybdis: 1.35.1, 5.11
Chios: 4.6, 5.21.1
Chrysippus: 1.7.2
Cicero: 7.11.1
Cilicia, Cilicians: 1.8.2, 1.10.1,
1.12.1, 1.15.1, 2.2.1, 6.35.1,
7.23.1
Cissia: 1.23.1–24.1
Cithaeron: 4.22.2
Clairvoyance: *see* Prescience
Claros: 4.14
Claudius, emperor: 5.27.1,
5.29.2, 5.32.2
Clemens: 8.25.1
Clytias: 5.25.2
Cnidos: 6.40.1
Cnossus: 4.34.2
Colonus: 4.21.2
Colophon: 4.1.1
Color: 2.19.2, 2.22.1, 2.22.4
Colossus: 5.21.1
Conscience: 7.14.10–11

429

INDEX

Cophen River: 2.8, 2.9.2

Corcyra: 4.20.1

Corinth, Corinthians: 4.25.6, 4.31.1, 7.10.1, 8.7.29, 8.15.2

Corinthian Games: 5.43.2

Cotton: 2.20.1, 3.15.4

Cotys, of Thrace: 7.2.2, 7.3.1

Crates, of Thebes: 1.13.2, 7.2.3, 7.3.2

Creon: 5.7.2

Cresphontes: 5.7.2

Crete, Cretans: 4.34.1–4, 8.30.2

Croesus: 6.37, 8.21

Cronos: 7.26.6

Croton, Crotoniates: 4.28.2

Ctesiphon: 1.21.1

Cures: 3.39, 3.44

Cyclops: 4.36.3, 6.11.18, 7.28.3

Cycnus, hero: 4.11.3

Cydnus: 1.7.1, 6.43.2

Cydonia: 4.34.2, 4.34.4

Cyllene: 6.20.6

Cynics: 4.25.1, 6.31.2

Cypress: 1.16.1

Cyprus: 3.58, 7.12.5

Cyrus (the Younger): 1.28.2, 8.7.43

Daedalus: 6.4.2

Damophyle: 1.30

Danaids: 7.7

Dancing: 4.21.1

Danube River: 3.1.1, 8.7.24

Daphne: 1.16.1

Daridaeus: 1.24.2

Darius: 1.23.2, 1.24.2, 1.28.2, 2.42

Datis: 1.25.2, 1.36

Delphi: 4.24.1, 5.7.3, 5.43.2,

6.10.2, 6.11.15, 8.18.1. *See also* Apollo

Demeter: 5.20.3

Demetrius, Cynic philosopher: as follower of A., 4.25.1, 6.31.1–2, 6.33, 7.10.2–11.2, 7.13.1, 7.16.2, 8.12.2–15.1; denounces Nero, 4.42.1–2, 5.19.1–2

Democritus: 1.2.1, 8.7.25, 8.7.41

Demons: 3.38.1–3, 3.56, 4.10.2–3, 4.20.1–2, 4.44.2–3, 7.32.1

Dicaearchia: 7.10.1, 7.16.1, 7.41, 8.10

Dictynna: 8.30.2

Didyma: 4.1.1

Dio, of Prusa: appears before Vespasian, 5.27.1–3, 5.28.2, 5.31–32.1, 5.34.1, 5.35.4, 5.37.2, 5.38.2; his speaking style, 8.7.7

Diogenes, of Sinope: 7.2.3, 7.3.2

Diomedes: 5.5.1, 7.32.2

Dion, of Syracuse: 7.2.1

Dionysia: 4.21.1, 6.11.11–12, 6.20.6

Dionysius: 1.35.1, 7.2.2, 7.3.1

Dionysus: in India, 2.2.2, 2.7.2, 2.8–9.2, 2.9.1, 2.33.2, 3.13; cult at Athens, 3.14.3, 4.22.2

Dioscorides, of Egypt: 4.11.2, 4.38.1, 5.43.1

Dirce in Boeotia: 3.17.1

Discord, civic: 4.8–9

Dodona: 3.43, 4.24.1

Domitian, emperor: A. before, 3.18, 4.44.2, 7.27, 8.1–14; tyr-

430

anny of, 6.32.2, 6.42, 7.4.1, 7.4.3, 7.6, 7.11.2, 7.24, 7.42.1; assassination of, 7.9.1–2, 8.25.1–2. *See also* Athena

Dorians: 8.7.17

Dreams: 1.23.1

Eagles: 2.3

Earth: 6.39.1–2, 6.41

Earthquakes: 4.16.2, 6.38, 6.41

Ecbatana: 1.24.2, 1.39.1

Echinades: 7.25

Eclipse: 4.43.1–2

Edonians: 6.11.18

Egypt, Egyptians: 5.43.4, 7.22.1–2, 8.7.22; geography of, 1.20.2, 6.1.1, 6.2.1; connections with India, 3.19.1, 3.25.1, 3.30.3, 3.32.1–2, 3.35.1, 6.11.13, 6.16.3, 8.7.16; lore and wisdom of, 3.49, 4.24.3, 6.19.3, 6.41, 7.22.1–2. *See also* Naked Ones, Proteus, Vespasian

Elephants: 2.6, 2.11.1–14.1, 2.15.1, 2.16, 6.25

Eleusis, Eleusinian Mysteries: 4.18.1, 6.20.6

Elis, Eleans: 3.30.3, 4.29, 5.43.2, 6.6.2, 8.7.28, 8.15.2. *See also* Olympia, Olympic Games

Empedocles, of Acragas: 1.1.3, 1.2.1, 6.5.3, 8.7.18, 8.7.25

Enceladus: 5.16.1

Enodia: 4.13.3

Ephesus: A. in, 1.16.4, 4.1.1, 4.2, 7.5, 7.7, 8.24, 8.26, 8.30.1; A. cures plague in,

4.4, 4.10.1–2, 7.20.1, 7.21.1, 8.5.1, 8.7.24–28, 8.7.30

Epicurus: 1.7.2

Epidauria: 4.18.1

Epidaurus: 4.18.1

Eretria, Eretrians: 1.23.2–24.3, 1.25.2, 1.36

Erytheia: 5.4

Erythras: 3.35.1, 3.50.2

Ethiopia, Ethiopians: geography and customs of, 2.18.2, 3.20.1, 6.1.1–2.1, 6.22.1, 6.25; A. in, 5.37.3, 5.43.1, 6.4.1. *See also* Naked Ones, Thespesion

Etna, Mount: 5.14.1, 5.16.1–2

Etruria: 3.50.2, 5.11

Euboea: 1.23.2, 1.24.2–3, 4.15.1

Eudoxus of Cnidus: 1.35.1

Eumenides: 7.14.10

Eunuchs: 1.33.2–34.1, 1.36–37.1

Euphorbus, son of Panthus: 1.1.1, 3.19.1–2, 8.7.14

Euphranor: 2.20.2

Euphrates, of Tyre: avarice, 1.13.3, 5.38.3, 8.7.11, 8.7.34; his disputes with A., 2.26.2, 5.39, 6.28, 7.9.2, 8.3, 8.7.46; speaks before Vespasian, 5.27.1–2, 5.28.2, 5.31, 5.33.1, 5.34.1, 5.35.4, 5.37.1–2, 5.38.1, 8.7.7; slanders A. to Naked Ones, 6.7, 6.9.1, 6.13.1, 6.13, 7.14.7, 7.36.3–4

Euphrates River: 1.20.2, 1.25.1, 1.38.2, 1.39.1, 3.58

Euripides: 2.14.4, 2.32.1,

2.33.1, 4.21.2, 5.14.3, 7.5,
7.14.10
Europe: 5.1
Eurymedon: 1.15.2
Eurystheus: 8.7.29
Euterpe: 5.21.4
Euthydemus of Phoenicia: 1.7.1
Euxenus, from Heracleia on the
Pontus: 1.7.2–8.1, 1.14.1

Falls: 6.1.1, 6.17, 6.23
Fates: 5.5.2, 5.12, 7.8.2–9.1,
7.12.2, 8.7.7, 8.7.47–48,
8.31.3
Favorinus: 4.25.1
Fish-eaters: 3.55
Flogging, Laconian: 6.20.1–3

Gadeira: 2.33.2, 4.47, 5.1–4,
5.8, 5.10.1
Gaetuli: 5.1
Gaius: 5.32.2
Galba: 5.11, 5.13.2, 5.32.2
Ganges, king: 3.20.1–2, 3.21
Ganges River: 2.9.2, 2.21.1,
2.33.1, 3.5.1, 3.50.2
Ganymede: 3.27.2
Gaul: 5.13.2
Geryon: 5.4–5.1, 6.10.6
Gladiators: 4.22.1
Glaucus, metal-worker: 6.11.15
Gods, unknown: 6.3.5
Gold vessels: 1.10.1
Gortyn: 4.34.2
Greek language: 1.7.1, 1.31–32,
3.12, 3.36, 6.36.1
Griffins: 3.48
Gryneion: 4.14
Gulf-dwellers: 6.16.4

Gyara: 7.16.2
Gyges: 3.8.2, 8.21

Hades: 3.25.2, 7.31.3
Hadrian: 8.20
Hair: 1.32.2, 7.36.1–2, 8.7.17–19
Harmodius and Aristogeiton:
5.34.3, 7.4.3, 8.16
Hector: 4.11.3–12
Helen: 3.20.3, 4.16.5, 7.22.1,
8.7.14
Heliad Poplar: 5.5.1
Helicon, from Cyzicus: 1.35.1
Helicon, Mount: 4.24.1
Helios: 2.12.2
Hellespont: 3.31.2, 6.41
Hephaestus: 2.22.5, 5.16.2,
6.11.18, 7.26.6
Hera: 4.28.2
Heracles: in India, 2.3, 2.33.2,
2.43, 3.13; the Averter,
4.10.1–3, 8.7.28; exploits of,
4.45.1, 4.46.2, 5.1, 5.7.1, 5.23,
7.2.3, 8.7.29, 8.18.3; Egyptian
and Theban, 5.4, 5.5.1;
Choice of, 6.10.5–6, 6.11.2
Heraclides, of Aenos: 7.2.2
Heraclitus: 1.9.2
Hercyna: 8.19.2
Hermes: 5.15.1–2
Herodes (Atticus): 3.11
Hierophant: 4.18.1–19, 5.19.1
Hippolytus: 6.3.5, 7.42.2
Hispola: 5.9.1–2
Hollows of Euboea: 3.23.2
Homer: on Euphorbus 1.1.1,
8.7.14; *Odyssey* cited, 1.4,
6.11.18, 6.31.2, 7.22.1; *Iliad*
cited, 1.22.2, 2.14.3, 3.6.2,

3.19.2, 4.7.2, 4.15.1, 4.16.5–6, 4.38.5, 7.14.11, 8.13.2; on Achilles, 3.20.3, 4.16.1–2. *See also Odysseus, Palamedes*
Hyacinthia: 6.20.1
Hydra: 6.10.6
Hydraotes: 2.9.2, 2.17.3, 2.32.1, 2.43
Hyphasis River: 2.21.1, 2.30.1, 2.31.1, 2.33.1, 2.43, 3.1.1, 3.50.2, 3.52, 8.7.12
Hyrcania, Hyrcanians: 1.18, 5.20.2

Iamos: 5.25.2
Iarchas, chief Indian philosopher: 2.40.3–41, 3.16–30, 3.31.2, 3.34–37, 3.51, 6.3.3
Ida, Mount: 4.34.2
Ilium: *see* Troy
Imitation: 2.22.1–5
Inachus: 1.19.1
India: features of, 1.11.2, 2.18.1–2, 4.16.1, 5.37.3, 6.1.1, 8.7.16, A. in, 2.1–3.51, 8.5.1; philosophers compared to Naked Ones of Egypt, 6.6.1, 6.10.6, 6.11.9–14, 6.11.20, 6.12.1–2, 6.14–15, 6.16.3, 6.21.1–2, 8.7.22.
Indus River: 2.4, 2.9.2, 2.11.1, 2.12.1, 2.14.1, 2.17.1, 2.40.2, 3.53, 6.1.1
Intoxication: *see* Wine
Ionia: 5.20.1, A. in, 3.58, 4.1.1–11.1, 6.35.1, 7.5–9, 7.36.3, 8.3, 8.7.47, 8.24–26; Panionian festival, 4.6; Ionic dialect, 7.35

Iphitus, of Elis: 4.32.3, 8.7.17
Isagoras, of Thessaly: 8.18.1
Islands of the Blessed: 5.3
Issus: 2.42
Ister: 7.26.5
Isthmian Games: 5.43.2
Isthmus: 3.31.3, 4.24.2, 5.7.4, 5.19.2
Italy: 4.34.1, 6.35.1, 7.10.1–2
Ithaca: 7.10.2
Ixion: 2.35.2, 6.40.2, 7.12.2

Jerusalem: 5.27.3, 6.29.1–2, 6.34.2
Jews: 5.33.4, 5.34.1
Juba: 2.13.1, 2.16
Judges of the Hellenes: 3.30.3, 6.10.1
Julia (daughter of Titus): 1.3.1, 7.7
Julius Caesar: 5.7.2
Justice: 1.39.2, 2.39.1–3, 3.24.3–25.1

"King's Ears": 1.28.1
"King's Eye": 1.21.1

Ladon: 1.16.1–2
Laius: 8.7.47
Lamia: 4.25.2–6
Lasthenes, of Apamea: 5.38.2
Lebadea: 8.19.1, 8.20
Leben: 4.34.3
Lechaeum: 4.24.2–3
Lemnos: 6.27.4
Leonidas, of Sparta: 4.23, 8.7.17, 8.7.43
Leontopolis: 5.42.2
Leopards: 2.2.1–2, 2.14.2

Lesbos: 4.13.2, 4.14, 4.16.6

Letters, of Apollonius: 7.31.2, 7.35, 8.20

Leucas: 5.18

Leucothea: 7.22.2

Levitation: 3.15.1, 3.17.2

Libations: 4.20.1

Libya: 2.12.1

Lilybaeum: 5.11

Lindos: 8.30.2

Linen: 1.8.2, 1.32.2, 2.40.3, 8.7.14, 8.7.16

Lions: 2.14.2

Locris: 8.19.1

Lotus-eaters: 1.40

Lycia: 8.7.48

Lycurgus, Spartan lawgiver: 4.31.2, 4.32.3, 6.20.1, 6.20.3, 6.21.6, 8.7.17, 8.7.21

Lydia, Lydians: 2.10, 4.27.1; wealth and luxury of, 4.27.1, 6.11.15, 8.7.34

Macedonia, Macedonians: 1.35.1, 1.35.3, 7.2.2

Maeonia: 3.5.2

Magi: 1.18, 1.25.3–26, 1.29, 1.32.1, 1.41

Magic, magicians: A. not a sorcerer (*goēs*), 1.2.1, 5.12, 7.17.1, 7.34, 8.3, 8.7.12, 8.7.26; magic an imposture, 7.39, 8.7.10, 8.7.29

Malea: 3.23.2, 4.24.2, 4.34.1–2, 7.42.6

Massagetae: 8.7.30

Maximus, of Aegeae: 1.3.2, 1.12.2

Media, Medes: 1.19.1, 1.24.1

Megabates: 1.31

Megara: 8.15.2

Megistias, of Acarnania: 4.23, 8.7.43

Melampus, seer: 5.25.2

Meles: 7.8.2

Meletos, accuser of Socrates: 7.11.2, 7.13.2

Melicertes: 3.31.3

Melos, Melians: 3.15.4

Memnon, favorite of Herodes Atticu: 3.11

Memnon, son of Dawa: 4.11.3, 6.3.1, 6.4.1

Memory: 1.14.1, 3.16.4, 3.43

Memphis, Memphites: 6.3.1, 6.5.1–2

Menestheus: 5.4

Menippus, of Lycia: affair with vampire in Corinth, 4.25, 4.38.1, 8.7.29; in company of A., 4.39.2, 4.44.1, 5.7.1–2, 5.14–15; answers Euphrates, 5.43.1, 6.28

Meroe: 3.20.1, 6.1.1

Meros: 2.9.2

Mesopotamia: 1.20.1–2

Messene, youth from, 7.42

Messina: 5.11, 8.15.1

Metapontum: 4.10.1

Metempsychosis: 3.22–23.1, 5.42.1, 6.5.2, 6.43.2; of Pythagoras, 1.1.1, 3.19.1–2

Methymna: 4.13.2, 4.16.6

Midas: 6.27.2

Miletus: 4.6

Milo: 4.28.1–2

Mimas: 2.5.3

Minos: 3.25.2, 4.34.2, 8.7.48

Minotaur: 4.34.2

Miracles: 4.45.1, 6.10.3, 7.38

Mnesarchides, of Samos: 8.7.14

Moeragenes: 1.3.2, 3.41.1

Mountains of the Cataracts: 2.18.2

Muses: 1.1.2, 4.16.4, 4.24.1, 4.38.6, 4.39.2, 7.11.1

Musonius (Rufus): 4.35, 4.46.1–5, 5.19.2, 7.16.2

Mycale: 2.2.1, 2.5.3

Mysteries: 4.17–18.1, 5.6

"Naked Games" at Sparta: 6.20.1

Naked Ones of Egypt (Ethiopia): 1.2.1, 5.37.3, 5.43.1, 6.4.3–23, 7.36.3–4, 8.7.14, 8.7.39

Nasamones: 6.25

Naucratis: 6.3.1, 6.8

Naxos: 1.25.2

Nearchus, admiral of Alexander: 2.17.1, 3.53, 7.2.1

Necessity: 7.8.2–9.1, 7.12.2, 8.7.47

Nemea, Nemean games: 1.35.3, 3.6.2

Nereids: 4.16.4

Nero, emperor: 4.33, 5.10–11, 5.29.2–3, 5.41, 6.32.2; persecutes philosophy, 4.35–36.3, 4.37.2–38.6, 4.46–47, 7.16.2; musical pretensions, 4.39.2, 4.42.1, 4.44, 5.7.1–9.1, 5.19.1–2, 5.28.1, 5.32.2, 5.33.5, 7.4.1, 7.12.3

Nerva: suspected by Domitian, 7.8.1, 7.11.2, 7.20.1, 7.32.3–33.1, 7.36.3, 8.7.31–32; becomes emperor, 7.9.1, 8.27

Nessus: 6.10.6

Nestor: 4.11.2

Nile River: features and lore of, 1.20.2, 2.18.1, 2.19.1, 5.26.2, 6.1.1, 6.11.9, 6.6.2, 7.21.2; explored by A., 5.37.3, 6.17, 6.22.1, 6.23, 6.26

Nilus, Egyptian follower of A.: 6.10.1, 6.12.1, 6.14, 6.18, 6.22.2, 6.26.2, 6.28

Ninos: 1.3.1, 1.19.1, 2.20.2, 3.58

Nireus: 3.19.2

Numbers: 3.30.2–3

Nymphs: 6.27.3, 8.11

Nysa: 2.2.2, 2.7.2, 2.8, 2.9.2–3

Ocean: 2.33.2, 4.47, 5.1–2, 5.5.2–6, 6.1.1

Odysseus: and Palamedes, 3.22.2, 4.16.6; and Achilles, 4.11.2; exploits of, 4.16.1, 4.20.1, 4.36.3, 6.32.2, 7.14.8, 7.22.2, 7.28.3. See also Calypso, Homer, Palamedes

Oedipus: 5.7.2

Oenomaus: 5.7.2

Oeta, Mount: 4.23

Olympia: 1.1.3, 1.2.2; site of Olympic Games, 1.35.2–3, 3.29, 5.7.2, 5.26.2, 5.35.2; visited by A., 4.27.1–31.1, 6.10.2, 8.15–18. See also Olympic Games, Phidias, Zeus

Olympic Games: 4.24.1–2, 4.29, 4.34.1, 5.7.1, 5.8, 5.43.2, 7.36.3

Olympus, Mount: 2.5.3, 4.23, 4.40.4
Olynthus: 1.35.3
Oreitae: 3.54
Oreithyia: 4.21.3
Orestes: 4.38.4, 7.14.10
Orfitus (Salvidienus): 7.8.1, 7.33.1, 8.7.32
Orpheus: 1.25.2, 4.14, 4.21.1, 8.7.41
Orthagoras, historian: 2.17.1, 3.53
Ostracism: 7.21.1
Otho, emperor: 5.11, 5.13.2, 5.32.2
Oxydrakae: 2.33.1

Pactolus: 6.37, 8.7.34
Pagala: 3.54
Painting: 2.22
Palaemon: 3.31.3
Palamedes: 3.22.2, 4.13.2–3, 4.16.6, 4.33, 6.21.4. *See also* Homer
Pamphylia: 1.15.1–2, 2.2.1–2
Panathenaea: 4.22.2, 7.4.3, 8.16
Pandora: 6.39.2
Pangaeus, Mount: 2.5.3
Pans: 3.13
Pantomime: 4.2
Paphos: 3.58
Paraka: 3.9
Paris: 4.16.5
Parnassus: 6.10.4
Paros: 4.16.6
Parthenon: 2.10
Patala: 3.53
Patroclus: 4.16.4, 7.36.2
Peacock fish: 3.1.2

Pearl-fishing: 3.57.1–2
Peleus: 3.19.2, 6.40.2
Peloponnese: 5.36.5, 8.7.29, 8.15.1–2
Pelops: 3.27.2, 3.31.3
Peppers: 3.4.2–3
Pergamum: 4.1.1, 4.11.1, 4.34.3
Peripatos: 1.7.2
Persephone: 8.12.1
Persia, Persians: 1.19.1, 1.33.1
Phaeacia: 4.20.1
Phaedimus, pupil of A.: 4.11.2
Phaedra: 6.3.1
Phaestus: 4.34.3
Phalerum: 4.17
Pharion: 5.24.2
Pharos: 3.24.1
Phidias: 4.7.2, 6.19.2–3
Philiscus, of Melos: 6.5.2, 8.7.41–42
Philip, of Macedon: 1.35.3, 7.2.3, 7.3.2
Philolaus, of Citium: 4.36.1, 4.37.1–2
Phocis: 8.15.2, 8.19.1
Phoenicia, Phoenicians: 3.24.1, 4.25.2, 6.35.1, 7.12.5
Phoenix, exotic bird: 3.49
Phoenix, companion of Achilles: 4.11.2
Phraotes, Indian king: 6.21.3, A.'s conversations with, 2.26–40, 3.18, 5.37.3, 7.14.8, 7.30.1–2; and Wise Men of India, 2.41, 3.17.2, 3.26.1, 3.28.1–2, 3.50.1
Phrygia: 2.10, 8.7.37
Phyle: 7.4.3
Phyton, of Aenos: 7.2.2

INDEX

Phyton, of Rhegium: 1.35.1,
    7.2.2, 7.3.1
Pillars of Hercules: 4.47, 5.1, 5.3
Pindar: 6.26.2, 7.12.4
Piraeus: 4.17, 5.20.1
Pirates: 2.29.2, 3.24.1–3
Pisa: 8.15.2
Piso: 5.32.2
Plague: *see* Ephesus
Planets: 3.41.2
Plato: 1.2.1, 1.7.2, 1.35.1, 4.36.2,
    6.11.8, 6.22.1, 7.2.1, 7.3.1
Polydamna, wife of Thon: 7.22.2
Polygnotus: 2.20.2, 6.11.15
Polyxena: 4.16.4
Pontus: 8.7.37
Portraiture: 2.22.4
Porus, Indian king: 2.12.2,
    2.20.2–21.2, 2.22.5, 2.24, 2.42
Poseidon: 4.9, 6.41
Praxiteles: 6.19.2
Prayer: A.'s doctrines about,
    1.11.1–12.1, 2.7.3, 4.19,
    4.40.2; his prayers: 1.33.2,
    1.36, 2.38, 4.16.1, 7.31.1,
    8.13.2
Prescience: A.'s prescience and
    predictions, 1.4, 3.33.2,
    4.18.2, 5.24.2, 5.42.1, 6.3.2,
    6.3.4, 6.5.2, 6.13.1, 6.32.2,
    6.39, 6.43.1, 7.10.1, 7.18.1;
    prescience of Iarchas, 3.16.1,
    3.21, 3.38.3; A.'s prescience
    divinely inspired, 4.44.3,
    5.12, due to his knowledge,
    7.14.2; due to his diet, 8.5.1.
    See also Prophecy, Telepathy
Priam: 4.11.2–12
Prodicus: 6.10.5, 6.11.2

Prometheus: 2.3
Prophecy: 1.2.2, 1.22.2, 1.40,
    2.37.1, 3.41–42.1, 3.44
Proteus: 1.4, 3.24.1, 4.16.5,
    7.22.2
Pygmalion: 5.5.1
Pygmies: 3.47, 6.1.2, 6.25
Pylaea: 4.23
Pythagoras, of Samos: 1.1–2.1,
    4.10.1, 6.20.6, 7.15.3, 8.19.2;
    A. a follower of, 1.7.2–3,
    1.13.3, 1.32.2, 3.12, 4.16.1,
    6.5.3, 6.11.3–7, 6.11.12–13,
    8.7.13–16, 8.7.39
Pythia, priestess: 6.11.17
Pythian Games: 1.35.1, 4.24.2,
    4.39.1, 5.9.1, 5.43.2

Red Sea: 2.2.2, 3.4.1, 3.8.3,
    3.20.2, 3.35.1, 3.50.2, 3.53,
    6.16.3–4
Rhea: 4.34.3
Rhegium: 1.35.1, 7.2.2
Rhine River: 8.7.24
Rhodes: 5.21.1–2, 5.22.1, 5.23
Rome: Roman Empire, 1.20.3,
    1.38.1–2, 3.25.1; A. in, 4.34.1,
    4.36–47, 7.17–8.8
Rubies: 3.46.1
Rufus (Verginius?): 7.8.1,
    7.33.1, 8.7.32

Sabinus (Flavius): 7.7
Sacrifice: 1.1, 6.39.1–2; A. con-
    demns blood sacrifice,
    1.10.1–11.1, 1.31; A. sacri-
    fices with incense, 1.31.2,
    5.25.1–2; his teachings about,
    4.16.3, 4.19, 4.40.1; sacrifice

437

of horses, 1.31.2, 2.19.2; of
humans, 6.20.3, 6.20.5,
7.11.3, 7.20.1, 8.5.2, 8.7.30,
8.7.35–45
Salamis: 4.21.1
Salex: 5.1
Samos: 4.6
Samothrace: 6.20.6
Sappho: 1.30
Sardinia: 1.11.2, 7.12.5
Sardis: 6.37
Sarpedon: 8.7.48
Satyrs: 6.27.1–4
Scillous: 8.15.1
Scopelian, sophist of
Clazomenae: 1.23.3, 1.24.3
Scythia, Scythians: 1.13.3,
5.20.2, 6.20.3, 6.20.5, 7.26.5
Selera: 3.56
Seleuceia (Pieria): 3.58
Seleucus (I?): 1.38.1
Seleucus of Cyzicus, doctor:
8.7.42
Semele: 2.9.1
Sexual desire: A.'s mastery of,
1.13.3, 2.2.2; felt by eunuchs,
1.34.1
Shadowfeet: 6.25
Sicily: 4.32.1, A. in, 5.11–18,
8.14–15.1
Silanus, of Ambracia: 8.7.43
Silence: 1.1.3, 1.14.1–15.1,
1.15.3, 1.16.2
Simonides: 1.14.1
Skylax: 3.47
Slaves: 3.25.1–2, 3.31.2
Sleep: 8.13.2
Smyrna, Smyrnaeans: 4.1.2,
4.5–7.1, 4.10.1, 7.8.2, 8.24

Snakes: 3.6–9
Socrates: 1.2.2, 4.25.1, 4.46.4–5,
6.19.5, 6.21.4, 7.11.2, 8.2.2,
8.7.1, 8.7.26
Solon: 6.21.6
Sophists: 7.16.2, 7.17.2
Sophocles: 1.13.3, 3.17.2,
7.31.2, 8.7.25, 8.7.49; plays
of, 4.38.6, 4.39.2, 7.4.2
Sorcery: see Magic
Soul: 1.38.3, 8.31.1–3
Sounion: 3.23.2
Sparta: A. and, 4.8.3, 4.27,
4.31–33, 7.42.6; Spartan prac-
tices, 1.39.1, 3.15.4, 4.8.3,
6.20, 7.42.6, 8.7.17
Spercheios, river: 4.16.2
Speusippus of Athens: 1.35.1
Spirits: 6.27.1, 8.7.26, 8.7.30
Stephanus: 8.25.1–2
Stesichorus: 6.11.14
Stobera: 3.55
Stones, precious: 2.40.3, 3.8.2,
3.45.2–46.2
Stratocles of Pharos, visitor to
Ethiopia: 6.10.2
Stratocles of Sidon, doctor:
8.7.42
Sun: 2.24, 3.15.1–2; A.'s rever-
ence for, 1.16.3, 1.31.2, 2.38,
7.6, 7.10.1, 7.31.1, 8.13.2;
Sun god: 3.28.2, 3.48,
6.11.20
Susa: 1.18, 5.33.4
Swimming: 2.27.2
Sycamore: 6.2.1
Syracuse: 5.13.1, 5.18, 7.36–37,
8.15.1. See also Sicily
Syria: 1.38.1, 6.38

Tanais: 7.26.5

Tantalus: 3.25.2–3, 3.32.2, 3.51, 4.25.4, 7.14.8

Tarentum: 7.8.1, 7.24

Tarsus: 1.7.1, 1.12.1, 6.30.1, 6.34.1, 6.43.1

Tauri: 8.7.30

Tauromenium: 8.15.1

Taurus, Taurians: 1.20.2, 2.2.1, 6.20.5

Taxila: 2.12.2, 2.20.1–2, 2.42

Taygetus: 4.31.2

Telemachus: 6.31.2

Telepathy, of A.: 5.30.1, 8.26

Telephus: 6.43.2

Telesinus (Luccius): 4.40.1–3, 4.43.1, 5.7.1, 7.11.3–4, 8.7.42, 8.12.3–4

Tellias: 5.25.2

Terpnus, musician: 5.7.2

Teucer, Telamonian: 5.5.2

Thales, of Miletus: 2.5.3, 8.7.26

Thamus: 6.5.2

Thebes, Thebans: 2.37.2, 5.11, 5.13.2, 7.3.2

Themistocles: 1.29, 5.4

Thera: 4.34.4

Thermodon: 7.26.5

Thermopylae: 1.25.2

Theseus: 4.46.2, 7.42.2

Thespesion, leader of Naked Ones: 7.14.6–7; dispute with A., 6.10–22

Thessaly, Thessalians: 3.25.3, 4.12, 4.16.2–3, 4.23, 8.7.26, 8.15.2

Thetis: 3.19.2

Thrace: 4.14

Thrasybulus, of Naucratis: 6.7, 6.9.1–3, 6.13.1

Thurii, Thurians: 3.15.4, 4.10.1

Tiber River: 7.16.1, 8.2.2

Tiberius: 1.15.2, 5.32.2, 7.14.4

Tigellinus: 4.42.2, 4.43.2–44.3, 5.35.5

Tigers: 3.45.1

Tigris River: 1.20.2, 1.21.3

Timasion, Egyptian youth: 6.3, 6.5.1–2, 6.9, 6.22.2, 6.26.2

Timomachus of Byzantium, painter: 2.22.5

Tingae: 5.1

Tiresias: 7.4.2

Titus, emperor: 6.29.1–30.2, 6.32.1–34.2, 7.7, 7.8.1, 8.7.33

Tmolos, mountain in Lydia: 2.8, 6.23, 6.37

Transmigration of souls: *see* Metempsychosis

Trophonius: 4.24.1, 8.19.1–2

Troy, Trojans: capture of 1.22.2, 3.19.1, 5.26.1; heroes of Trojan War, 2.21.2, 3.22.2, 6.4.1, 7.32.2, 7.36.2, 8.7.14; visited by A., 4.11–13, 4.16

Tusks: 2.12.2–13.3

Tyana: 1.4, 1.6, 1.13.1, 1.33.1, 8.29, 8.31.3

Typho: 5.13.1, 5.14.1, 5.16.1

Tyrants, Tyranny: 7.1, 7.13.2, 7.14.4, 7.30.2. *See also* Domitian, Nero

Tyrrhenian Sea: 5.11

Universe: 3.34.2–3, 3.35.2

Urns, magical, 3.27.2

Vampires: 2.4, 4.25.4–5, 8.7.29
Vardanes, Babylonian king:
    1.21.1–2, 1.29, 1.31, 2.17.2–3,
    2.40.1–2, 3.58, 7.14.6
Vegetarianism: practiced by A.,
    1.8.1, 1.21.3, 1.36.2, 6.15,
    8.7.15; by Iarchas, 2.26.3; by
    Indian Wise Men, 3.26.2,
    3.27.2; by Pythagoras, 6.11.3,
    8.7.14
Vespasian, emperor: 6.30.1–
    31.1; in Egypt, 5.27–38,
    7.18.1, 8.7.6–8, 8.7.33; corre-
    spondence with A., 5.41,
    8.7.11, 8.7.33
Vestal Virgins: 7.6
Vindex (Julius): 5.10–11,
    5.33.4–5
Vitellius, emperor: 5.11, 5.13.2,
    5.29.3, 5.30.2, 5.32.2, 5.33.2,
    5.33.5, 5.34.2–3, 8.7.48

Wealth: 5.36.2, 7.23.1–4, 8.7.12
Wine: renounced by A., 1.8.1,
    1.21.3, 2.6–7, 2.35.1, 6.11.5,
    6.42, 8.7.15; harmful effects
    of, 1.9.1, 2.37.2–37.3, 3.40
Wolves: 2.14.2
Wool: 8.7.16

Xerxes: 1.24.2, 1.25.2, 3.31.1–2,
    4.21.2, 5.7.3–4, 5.41.2

Zeno, of Elea: 7.2.1, 7.3.1
Zeugma: 1.20.1, 1.38.1
Zeus: 1.1.3, 1.6, 2.7.1, 2.7.3,
    2.9.1–2, 4.30.1, 4.34.1, 7.26.6,
    8.7.5; cult at Olympia, 1.15.2,
    2.43, 4.7.2, 4.28.1, 5.7.2,
    6.19.1, 8.15.1, 8.17. See also
    Olympia, Phidias
Zeuxis, painter: 2.20.2